SECOND EDITION

TCP/IP
running a successful network

Data Communications and Networks Series

Consulting Editor: Dr C. Smythe, University of Sheffield

Selected titles in the series

SECOND EDITION

TCP/IP

running a successful network

Kevin Washburn

Integralis Ltd, Reading

Jim Evans

Eclectic Systems, Chelford

Addison-Wesley

Harlow, England • Reading, Massachusetts • Menlo Park, California
New York • Don Mills, Ontario • Amsterdam • Bonn • Sydney • Singapore
Tokyo • Madrid • San Juan • Milan • Mexico City • Seoul • Taipei

© Addison Wesley Longman 1996

Addison Wesley Longman Ltd
Edinburgh Gate
Harlow
Essex
CM20 2JE
England

Cover designed by op den Brouw, Design & Illustration, Reading.
Printed and bound in United States of America.
Typeset by Meridian Colour Repro, Pangbourne in 10/12pt New Century Schoolbook, Futura and Melior.
Printed and bound in Great Britain by T.J. Press (Padstow) Ltd, Padstow, Cornwall.

First edition published 1993. Reprinted 1993, 1994 and 1995 (twice).
Second edition printed 1996. Reprinted 1997.

ISBN 0-201-87711-2

British Library Cataloguing in Publication Data

A catalogue record for this book is available from the British Library

Library of Congress Cataloging in Publication Data applied for.

To Penny and Stella

Preface

Society, its government and commerce depend on accurate, reliable and convenient ways of exchanging information between individuals, organizations and across national boundaries. In the late 1980s, the success of computers and their interconnecting networks (particularly the 'personal computer' and the 'local area network') completely changed the speed, accuracy and convenience of all manner of information transfer. The standards collectively known as TCP/IP, first developed to allow exchange of information between computers in the US government, defence and university research communities, appeared in attractive, useful and widely available products for general commercial computing. With the increasing interest in the use of TCP/IP for general commercial applications, there is a need to know what TCP/IP provides, how to exploit its functionality, and what management and technical difficulties will be encountered.

This book is about the practical problems of installing, configuring and maintaining information systems based on the TCP/IP set of standards, from initial installation to on-going maintenance.

For a system to be successful and to retain that success over a long time, requires frequent revision of initial assumptions; system designers must take account not only of technical, but also of social and organizational problems they will encounter. Successful systems grow and develop; they are used in ways and for purposes that the initial design probably did not predict. Once convenient and reliable operation is achieved, the users abandon and then lose the older, less convenient alternatives. The new system becomes part of the corporate infrastructure and day-to-day life, its value increases and any change in performance and availability can dramatically affect prosperity and well-being.

The planners and operators of any technology have responsibilities for its care and maintenance, if long-term viability is to be assured. In this book, we pass on our experience of designing, planning, installing and running large computer communications networks using TCP/IP, taking into account many of the factors that we have discovered can influence the short- and long-term success of computer networks.

When the first edition of this book was published in March 1993, it was hard to imagine the effect TCP/IP would have on the whole world in such a short space of time. Following the success of TCP/IP in the defence and research Internet, corporate organizations finally found a technology which would allow them to realize a dream many of them had been chasing for well over 20 years, the ability to communicate data globally and economically – and between different makes of computer. The Internet was reborn, now as a next generation commercial network connecting business and homes together, producing a new information age. Never has technology developed as fast as it is now within the Internet sphere.

Leading corporations have moved rapidly from simple file transfer and terminal access to multimedia communications. The technology which enables this rapid change is TCP/IP, a technology which has proved easy to understand. This has allowed organizations to concern themselves more with what to do with information than the technology of communications. Internet-based systems and application tools have become a standard mechanism for accessing and displaying information. The next phase in the development of information technology is becoming evident, a global, very high performance, fibre-based network carrying TCP/IP protocols. The high performance infrastructure is now being knitted into place, so it is time to start thinking about what you want to do with it, and how you will achieve the same high performance in your TCP/IP access network.

Choosing equipment

In a description of the practical issues, we will frequently point out that standards developers have included many features and facilities in the standards which are not generally implemented in available equipment. Equally, there are facilities in products which are not included in the standards. It is up to equipment users to recognize any gap between the potential of systems such as TCP/IP and the functionality of current products. In examining how improved systems would benefit their use of the technology, those with purchasing power can drive technology forward so that suppliers produce more advanced systems sooner. We will frequently emphasize the difference between the potential of the standards and recent practice.

Since the first edition of this book there have been many changes to TCP/IP. A lot of the advances in the technology, which remained unimplemented by some, have become the norm. Other important parts of the standards have been completely ignored and will only now appear in the new IPv6 standards which are beginning to emerge as products.

TCP/IP stacks have become an integral part of operating systems. However, what we said in 1993 still stands: differences in functionality between different products can be significant, only now these incompatibilities exist at the higher levels of the technology and continue to move upward.

How to use this book

The book is divided into three parts.

Part I describes the options and features of TCP/IP without discussing technology in detail. In particular, Part I is about the choices and decisions that must be made as any computer products which use TCP/IP for communications are introduced. It highlights key decisions which must be made early in the adoption of TCP/IP systems, if major upheaval and expense is to be avoided later. It shows how to make those decisions, and discusses the essential practical steps to producing reliable and flexible systems that are convenient both for commercial users and for system and network managers. We follow the development, expansion and day-to-day operations of the system, and outline how to maintain the performance of a TCP/IP system as it grows and is integrated into a corporation's infrastructure.

Part I is about 'what and how' not 'why'. It is for those who are content (for the moment at least) to work on the premise, 'if I don't need to change it and it is unlikely to cause trouble later, I don't need a detailed technological understanding'. For those configuring and managing small, unchanging TCP/IP networks, this information may be sufficient.

Part II describes the detailed technical standards behind TCP/IP systems, particularly where such technical detail leads to further choices which will influence the success of an installed system. Part II is about 'what else, why, what if, and what next'. It is intended for those who need to understand the detail of a protocol, the bits and bytes, in order to better manage and maintain large and complex computer networks. These are the people who may wish to take advantage of the most sophisticated features, who have a need to understand the 'why'. Equally, it is for those who seek knowledge out of technical interest.

Large networks often display problems and issues peculiar to their environment and configuration. Part II allows the more technical reader to determine the underlying limits of TCP/IP systems and to take action to ensure that systems, in particular, large systems, remain stable. It is concerned with tuning performance, achieving reliability, stability and cost effectiveness through a detailed technical understanding which allows optimizing the foundations laid in Part I.

Part III is a collection of reference material and tables extracted from TCP/IP and local area network standards which can greatly simplify the configuration and management of TCP/IP systems.

Parts I and II can be read in isolation, or in either order, according to interest and immediate need. Part III can be used as reference at any time. Part I will stand alone as a planning and implementation guide.

Acknowledgements

Many of the concepts, guidelines and drawings presented in this book were developed by the authors as part of their practical-based training activities and consultancy work performed on behalf of Integralis Ltd, Theale, Reading, RG7 5AH, England. With the permission of the directors of Integralis, material has been included from the following Integralis training courses:

- Introduction to data communications technology
- Introduction to local area networks
- Practical TCP/IP
- Internetworking with bridges and routers

The authors wish to thank the directors of Integralis Ltd for their permission to include the material, for their support in its development and for their encouragement during the writing of this book.

That this book could be written in the first place is due to the foundations laid by V.A. Thomson and J.A. Robinson, who showed us the way.

We must also express our thanks to the following people: to all researchers in the USA and worldwide who wrote informative and amusing, readable RFCs and showed that standardization does not have to read like OSI; to Penny Lyon for proofreading the first edition and to Sheila Chatten and Annette Abel for finding many idiosyncrasies in the second; to Margaret Davies for her typing of the early drafts of the first edition and preparation of the index; to Carol Turega for her sterling work in updating appendices and RFC lists and for making the index for the second edition match what is on paper.

And to the UNIX expert who on reviewing the first edition commented that TCP/IP networks are not planned, they just grow, we replied: exactly. That was the problem. In this one phrase, he justified our efforts to document a different approach.

Kevin Washburn
Jim Evans

Theale, England
June 1996

Contents

PART I

The key implementation decisions

1

Introducing TCP/IP

In this introductory chapter we discuss what TCP/IP is and its background, and examine the need for such a protocol suite and its applications. Many of the basic concepts introduced here will be developed in later chapters.

The subjects covered are:

- The need for internetworking
- OSI and TCP/IP initiatives
- TCP/IP as a communications architecture
- TCP/IP functionality
- Management choices
- The need for control
- The functions to be managed
- How organizational structure affects technology

The need for internetworking

It is some 13 years since the authors first began to work together on communications networks in a large commercial environment. In that early part of our careers, which of course predated readily available sophisticated systems like TCP/IP, we were first involved in the design and implementation of a large corporate terminal-based information network. The aims of our corporate network manager were expressed in three memorable phrases that appeared in many management presentations of the time:

- A single terminal on a desk
- One terminal per seated employee
- Total logical interconnectivity

The requirements were simple, if somewhat shrouded in the jargon of the day: employees should be able to access any information or system in the corporation (for which they had authority) from a single terminal on their own desk – they would not see the structure of the underlying communications medium; the terminal should become as important and widespread and as easy to use as the telephone; and the communications system that supported the terminals should be as reliable and responsive as our private telephone network.

Immediately, we were able to make some decisions based on the communications flows within the corporation rather than on the limitations of the technology. We needed any-to-any communications to move information reliably, we needed switching and we needed conversion systems that would allow access to different computers by any terminal type. As the number of terminals increased, it was also clear that we required a structured cabling system which would give an independent connection for each terminal, but which would greatly simplify installations and changes (Figure 1.1). The communications industry coined the terms 'local area network' and 'wide area network' to describe different aspects of this technology, but our organization had already seen the requirement for full interconnection of these two technologies as one integrated system. Certainly our data network users were not interested in the details of the technology as long as it delivered the data.

We thought of these requirements as just 'networking'. Since then, this level of integration has become known as 'internetworking'. In the late 1970s this was truly visionary for most commercial corporate environments.

The continued endurance of these statements is interesting. Despite the many advances of the 1980s, managers in Information Technology (IT) or of Management Information Systems (MIS) still have the same goals. But now the tool is the personal computer or workstation rather than a 'dumb terminal'. Data rates in common use in the 1990s were, in 1979, available only in research labs.

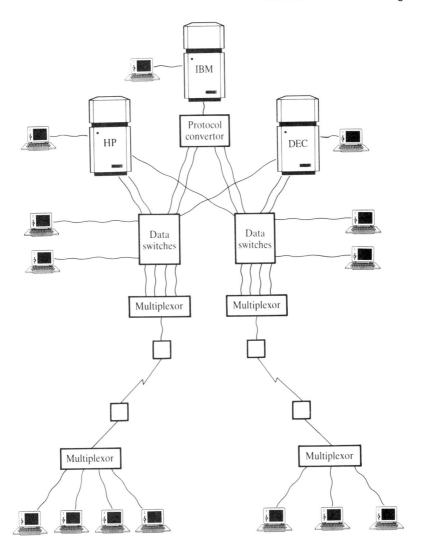

Figure 1.1 Terminal switching network.

Achieving the goals

If the goals described are to be achieved, three separate functions are required:

(1) The ability to move data anywhere in an organization with chosen reliability, security and performance.

(2) The correct interpretation of that data in a manner appropriate to the receiving equipment.

Figure 1.2 Communications transparency.

(3) Display of the interpreted information in an acceptable form for user consumption.

The requirement for communications transparency is often expressed by showing the communications network as a cloud (Figure 1.2). Network users are not interested in the technology that makes up the cloud, or indeed, where their communicating partner is located, only that the data is delivered reliably, in good time, and at acceptable cost. The network cloud can be surrounded by a second cloud which similarly disguises the technology and 'architecture' of the communicating machines. The two clouds represent the two key components of internetworking – intercommunication and interoperation. When these issues are solved, computer users can focus on using technology to further their businesses, rather than on the details of the machines, their locations or the way they are connected. If these technical details do become visible, system managers have perhaps failed the users. Creating the standards for these two clouds has, since 1977, been an aim of the International Organization for Standardization (ISO) with their Open Systems Interconnection (ISO OSI) initiative.

The third requirement, that of displaying data, is up to individual manufacturers and is one way they differentiate their products. In the early 1980s, OSI activity was perhaps strongest outside the USA. While ISO committees were developing the OSI protocols, the USA was developing in parallel, but with an interchange of ideas, an alternative set of techniques which became known as TCP/IP. These protocols became a US Department of Defense standard in 1983.

The popularity of TCP/IP

In recent years, knowledge of the capabilities of Transmission Control Protocol/Internet Protocol (TCP/IP) has spread far beyond the USA. IT managers in all types of organizations have begun to research its suitability as an internetworking technology. TCP/IP seems to be a ready-made solution to the commercial information systems requirements of intercommunication and interoperation.

Many in the US government and research communities and many UNIX aficionados are already well versed in the vocabulary and configuration issues of this set of protocols as UNIX system administrators. But for the newcomer to TCP/IP, there is less information about the practical problems of implementing TCP/IP from scratch, in, for example, a commercial rather than a technical or research environment; here the skills and constraints may be very different.

The first part of this book explains the commercial, organizational and technical issues that implementing TCP/IP raises. For the newcomer to TCP/IP, we present solutions where they exist. Where they are incomplete or do not exist, we try to offer alternatives or to highlight the limitations; it is to be hoped that equipment purchasers will explain their needs to suppliers in the manner that will best achieve the development of better products! The second part of this book develops the detailed technical aspects of the protocols, showing the implications of the bits, bytes and fields for the technical planners and implementors who must track down the difficult problems of interoperation and compatibility between different implementations.

TCP/IP emerges

When Berkeley Software Distribution released Berkeley UNIX 4.2BSD in September 1983, a comprehensive set of 'ready-made' communications protocols called TCP/IP became much more widely available and well-known than it had been before. This was not a coincidence; its inclusion in this release was funded by the US government. TCP/IP protocols are based on standards originally developed for the US government and US research community. With the release of UNIX 4.2BSD, these communications standards emerged from the confines of the US Department of Defense and the US university and research networks; TCP/IP became *the way* to interconnect UNIX systems. Berkeley UNIX 4.2BSD and subsequent releases spread quickly throughout the US university and commercial communities. As UNIX has achieved wide popularity as an 'open system', so the fame of TCP/IP has continued to spread. But TCP/IP is not, and never has been, narrowly confined to UNIX; it was developed to allow free interchange of data among all machines, independent of type, manufacturer, hardware or operating system.

In the late 1980s, TCP/IP received a further boost to its fortunes, when Sun Microsystems published the specification for Open Network Computing (ONC), often called the Network File System (NFS). NFS adds important functions to TCP/IP and is now very widely available and regarded as an integral part of the TCP/IP protocol suite. It is particularly valuable for the commercial implementor because of the simple user interfaces that it provides.

Cost-effective implementations of TCP/IP are now available for all types and sizes of machines from the largest mainframe to personal computers and workstations. This has brought TCP/IP and its capabilities to the attention of a very wide audience far beyond the initial US interest. Computer managers and users in commercial organizations throughout the world have begun to implement TCP/IP as a way of solving the problems of interworking between machines of different manufacture.

TCP/IP provides all the facilities for two computer systems to exchange information (intercommunication), interpret it properly, and present it in a format which can be understood by the local machine and its users (interoperation). NFS gives a simple and locally-familiar representation of a set of remote and possibly unfamiliar computer filing systems; like the original components of the TCP/IP suite, NFS is now available for many different computers.

In the mid-1990s, the explosion in commercial interest in the Internet gives a new market for TCP/IP products.

OSI and TCP/IP initiatives

In 1977, ISO began to develop a communications architecture which would become an international standard, a set of communications protocols known as **open systems interconnection** (OSI). This initiative had the same general aims as TCP/IP – intercommunication and interoperation across different manufacturers' computing architectures – but unlike TCP/IP, in a way that met a published set of 'open' international standards. OSI now comprises many hundreds of standards, each of which has taken years to develop, agree and publish in its final ISO form. Regrettably, the best known aspect of OSI is still the OSI reference model and its seven layers (Figure 1.3); the model itself is only a development aid to allow standards developers to produce the detailed communications standards within a consistent architectural framework.

In the standard which describes the reference model, OSI standards developers state that they will exclude any details which would be implementation dependent; the result is that while the standards have been kept 'pure', many details which would aid development of viable OSI products are excluded from the standards themselves. While some would argue that OSI is more rigorous in its standardization than TCP/IP, the OSI development process seems to have become enmeshed in procedures, weighed down by the difficulties of obtaining consensus in large committees and dogged by supplier politics. By confining OSI standards to abstract definitions in a complex vocabulary defined just for the purpose and then charging considerable sums for copies of those standards, ISO committees have undoubtedly, if unintentionally, slowed the OSI development process and the delivery of useful conforming products.

| Application |
| Presentation |
| Session |
| Transport |
| Network |
| Datalink |
| Physical |

Figure 1.3 ISO OSI reference model.

With a more restricted geographic and technical scope, TCP/IP developers adopted a pragmatic approach. TCP/IP standardization was based on the Request for Comments (RFC), a flexible and fast standardization process using electronic mail to publish and exchange comments and ideas, and to update drafts. Developers often outlined parts of a standard in a familiar computer language, usually 'C' which, while not intended to be implemented directly, gave a very good starting point for an initial implementation.

TCP/IP standards are freely available on-line from a number of computer systems, originally without full drawings or graphics, but today with all the quality of a laser-printed, desktop-published document as PostScript files. If you must resort to paper and the postal service, the charge in the recent past has been a minimal $10 per copy. For manufacturers of communications and computing products, the contrast with OSI could not be more stark; it is just so much easier to obtain TCP/IP information than OSI. Standards were produced more quickly and they are written in a readable and comprehensible form by developers for developers.

The US government demanded TCP/IP for all systems, thereby ensuring every US government computer supplier provided it. They also funded universities to implement the standards. In the USA, such publicly funded work enters the public domain, and, if not of a military nature, is freely available to all citizens. While it may not be used directly for commercial purposes, having a working example in 'C' source code certainly assists future developments by commercial suppliers!

Neither OSI nor TCP/IP has been developed in isolation. There has been a considerable interchange of ideas and techniques, particularly evident in the changes in OSI since the mid-1980s with the development of the connectionless OSI suite. Nor have the OSI standards been ignored by suppliers. As with TCP/IP in the USA, universities have been busy developing OSI implementations and governments have, since the mid-1980s, required OSI-conforming products (particularly European governments through the European Commission directives). But this activity did not create a general market demand and fully developed OSI computing products, except perhaps with the notable exception of X.25 network equipment X.400 Mail and X.500 Directory Services.

The 'pump priming' of TCP/IP has been more successful and has ensured that it has moved ahead much faster than OSI. Governments and commercial organizations worldwide have waited patiently for OSI to become available and to reap the benefits of the promised flexibility of an international standard for computer communications and inter-operation. Suffice it to say that the development of OSI has lagged considerably behind TCP/IP, despite support from a number of governments (including since 1985, the US government and Department of Defense).

When it comes to breaking down communications barriers between different computer suppliers, information systems managers in commercial companies now see TCP/IP as the only fully functional, proven and available option.

TCP/IP as a communications architecture

As with much of the specialist vocabulary which surrounds computers and telecommunications networks, the term TCP/IP will conjure up different concepts to different readers. TCP/IP is used as shorthand for a large set of standards with many different features and functions. The letters 'TCP/IP' stand for two communications protocols, Transmission Control Protocol (TCP) and Internet Protocol (IP). These were developed during the late 1970s and early 1980s as the key communications protocols for the 'Internet', the collected set of interconnected communications networks of the US government, the Department of Defense, the US military, and university, education, research and commercial organizations throughout the world.

The two protocols, TCP and IP, are but two of the building blocks required for a complete communications 'architecture', but the term 'TCP/IP' is most often used as a **shorthand** term for the whole communications 'architecture' specified originally by the US Department of Defense. This architecture is a much bigger set of standards than just TCP and IP and is more properly referred to as the Internet Protocol Suite (IPS) (Figure 1.4). We shall carry on the tradition and use 'TCP/IP' to mean the complete architecture, except where this will cause confusion.

Communications architectures have been developed by computer manufacturers since the mid-1970s. An architecture describes three facets of communications in an abstract way which is independent of particular hardware or technology. The three aspects are

(1) Data exchange (intercommunications)
(2) Data interpretation (interoperation)
(3) System management

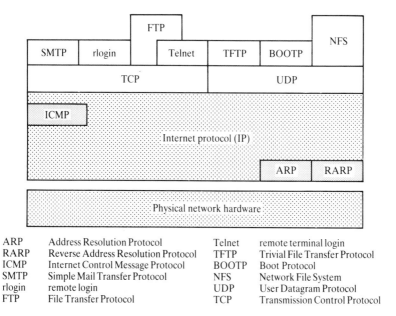

ARP	Address Resolution Protocol	Telnet	remote terminal login
RARP	Reverse Address Resolution Protocol	TFTP	Trivial File Transfer Protocol
ICMP	Internet Control Message Protocol	BOOTP	Boot Protocol
SMTP	Simple Mail Transfer Protocol	NFS	Network File System
rlogin	remote login	UDP	User Datagram Protocol
FTP	File Transfer Protocol	TCP	Transmission Control Protocol

Figure 1.4   TCP/IP architecture.

Like the OSI reference model, communications architectures are described in layers, each layer providing its own functions but using the functions of the layer below. This layering decouples the functions of one layer from another so that layered architectures are flexible; their designers can respond to changes in technology and in application software without a major upheaval for existing users. The implementation and existing installations can be extended, hopefully indefinitely as new, often faster techniques and technologies become available. It is important to realize that the standards do not specify the interfaces seen by computer users. Though suppliers often base their implementations on a competitor's successful product, you must expect that user interfaces will differ in major or minor ways from supplier to supplier.

For TCP/IP, the architectural standards are controlled by the Internet Architecture Board (IAB). The IAB devolves its responsibilities for development, operations and management to a number of subcommittees and working groups which it controls and to other commercial companies specializing in communications and computing research and consultancy.

TCP/IP – the complete suite

The two protocols, TCP and IP, describe only the communication aspects, the movement of data across a set of interconnected physical networks.

The complete architecture must include standard mechanisms for interpreting and converting data for the common tasks that users of computers have come to expect. As these tasks sit on top of and depend on the communications protocols, they are sometimes called the Upper Layer Protocols (ULPs).

Historically, computer users have needed three major functions:

- File transfer (including some simple file management)
- Terminal access (virtual terminal protocols)
- Mail preparation and transfer

But in today's commercial environments other tasks have become equally important

- Resource sharing (files, printers, plotters)
- Diskless workstations
- Computer conferencing
- Transaction processing
- Management
- Directory services
- Security
- Multimedia access

Those familiar with the resource-sharing Local Area Network (LAN) (such as Microsoft LAN Manager and Novell NetWare) will have seen the power of remote or distributed file and disk sharing and of peripheral sharing; for some companies, diskless workstations have a number of advantages.

In a complete, modern architecture, standard protocols are required for all these new distributed systems as well as for the proven minicomputer and mainframe-based architectures.

The TCP/IP protocol suite addresses these issues comprehensively. The standards are not static but are being added to at a steady rate. Recent activities relate to new facilities in information retrieval and display, and in directory services at the application layer and improvements to routing and addressing mechanisms at the lower layers.

Upper layer protocols

Beginning with the well-known application layer protocols, File Transfer Protocol (FTP), Telnet (TCP/IP's virtual terminal protocol), and Simple Mail Transfer Protocol (SMTP), NFS adds a disk/file system resource-sharing capability, LPR deals with printing, the BOOT Protocol, (BOOTP) provides the basis for diskless workstation operation, and

Simple Network Management Protocol (SNMP) is the Internet standard for management. As Figure 1.4 shows, TCP is complemented by the User Datagram Protocol (UDP). The differences between these are discussed in Chapter 11.

The explosion of information sources on the Internet has led to new ways of searching that information with Archie, Gopher, WAIS and the World Wide Web.

Lower layer protocols

IP is not the lowest level of the layered architecture. TCP/IP does not describe new standards for low-level communications but TCP/IP standards include descriptions of how IP operates over the commonly available long-distance and local physical (or link level) communications networks. These descriptions include many proprietary networks as well as ITU-T (formerly CCITT) and other international standard transmission mechanisms.

For long-distance operation over public telecommunications circuits, the standards include point-to-point leased and dial-up, synchronous and asynchronous links, and X.25 connections. For local communications, Ethernet Version 2 (as specified by DEC, Intel and Xerox) is by far the most widely used. ISO/IEEE networks (ISO 8802.3, 8802.4 8802.5) and FDDI (ISO 9314) are also specified as are proprietary networks such as ARCNET. Recent technologies like ISDN frame relay and Asynchronous Transfer Mode (ATM) are supported.

Management issues and responsibilities

The information systems manager in a commercial organization must take a highly technical product like TCP/IP and turn it into a success for the company's commercial activities, so that the investment in equipment, software and training speeds up, improves accuracy and reduces the costs of business processes. This can be a long road to travel.

Adopting and using any new system presents managers with new issues and 'opportunities' (problems!). These centre on the technology, its standards, the supplier and the organization. Many questions must be asked about the capabilities of the basic technology itself, the capabilities of the supplier and about the organization that will use that technology. Managers attempt to map the features that are available onto the day-to-day operations of the company. Only when they achieve a good fit between the facilities and features of the basic system, the capabilities and support of suppliers and the requirements and practices of the company will the system add the highest value to the business.

In some business sectors, the application of new information technology is so revolutionary that rather than merely applying it to existing organizational structures, procedures and practices, those structures, procedures and practices are revised and simplified by it in a fundamental way.

Whatever the magnitude of the effect, there are two keys to success:

(1) Making the right choices – technological and organizational.

(2) Providing the correct training for technologists *and* for commercial users.

Choices

Many standards for TCP/IP specify only the facilities that should be available between two communicating machines. They do not specify (in general) how those facilities are delivered to the screens, keyboards, printers and disk systems of end users. There will often be one *de facto* way of supporting some features, but the details of that support will differ (in what can be annoying ways). It is this variety that allows suppliers to differentiate their products and attract particular market sectors to their interpretation of the 'best' user interface for a given purpose.

The early 1990s saw a departure from some of the traditional command-line, text-based TCP/IP implementations of UNIX, towards assistance for less computer-literate users through window-based 'point and click' interfaces.

The selection of products involves choosing:

- A product with the best user interfaces for our needs.

- The features of the product to use in practice (not all facilities will be appropriate).

- How to implement and control the user features.

- How to implement and control the internal technical features.

Flexibility and control

Suppliers sell features and flexibility. Many organizations adopt TCP/IP precisely because it covers such a broad range of function and options. But flexibility is a two-edged sword: it demands a degree of imposed control otherwise freedom becomes licence, flexibility becomes a snare.

Introducing the full functionality of a system as complex as TCP/IP over a short period of time to a large user population would be likely to fail, even if it were physically possible! Dividing up the problems and phasing the introduction across a number of departments is essential. Fortunately, the model presented by Figure 1.4 is in itself the guide to how to divide the problems into manageable pieces. It is this subdivision and structured approach to problem solving that guarantees success, particularly in a large organization where there may be hundreds, or even thousands of computers, each using TCP/IP.

Separating the management functions

The layering of TCP/IP as a communications architecture allows us to separate different functions, to consider them individually, and to simplify the management of the complex whole. This approach is valid whether we merely wish to describe the tasks to be carried out by one person for a small network or to divide up the management of a large, geographically diverse, corporate network for management by many different departments and individuals. In the latter complex case, we must ensure that *all aspects* of the technology are addressed, otherwise what should appear as one 'seamless' cooperating system will expose the managerial divisions to the users.

As we have seen, TCP/IP provides two complementary functions: *interoperation* in applications processors through the use of the upper layer protocols (FTP, Telnet, SMTP, NFS) and *intercommunication*, through the use of the IP protocol operating over a collection of physical communications networks (LANs and point-to-point links). These two functions provide one possible division of responsibility: upper layer protocols operate only in personal workstations and shared mini- and mainframe computers; the internetworking protocols operate in all of these and in the routers/gateways that form the communications network. In a small implementation, one or two people are responsible for all aspects. In the larger network, the communications aspects are often implemented and managed by communications specialists. The applications are implemented and managed by business, computer system and programming specialists.

But this simple division of responsibility is a dangerous illusion. The application requires certain facilities and performance from the underlying communications networks. The communications networks must be planned with the application in mind; they must evolve with the changing use of applications and the demand that they impose. Consider two simple examples:

- The simplest change in the configuration files of a personal computer can have an unexpected impact on network load in resource-sharing systems such as NFS. An incorrect setting on 200 computers can make the difference between a system which performs well and one which is totally unsatisfactory.

- Application programmers today develop the applications to a standard network interface in the belief that the network will deliver everything in a short time. They often test the application on a lightly loaded, small, local area network and have no concept of how that application will perform in a more general environment. A simple change in the structure of a program can alter its loading on the network by a factor of 10 to 100.

Dividing communications architectures into layers has been very successful for the development of new low-level communications media and systems; it has been too successful at isolating the applications developers from the realities of available networks and the impact that their actions have upon them.

The upper layers of TCP/IP, the applications and their environment, must be managed and controlled not just from their interface to the user, but from their impact on communications. Unfortunately, this impact is often not well understood. When it is, we find that the controls and adjustments that are available require more intervention than is desirable and are not as obvious or instinctive as they should be.

A common aim of systems and network managers is to reduce costs while delivering good service; merely optimizing and reducing the costs of their own components is not likely to provide optimum performance of the whole system. Indeed, as expressed in Figure 1.5, squeezing costs in one area can have unexpected effects in other areas. Each group must have an understanding of how the actions that they take in pursuit of reduced costs impacts on the performance and spending of the other group. Communications and systems managers need to cooperate very closely to achieve an overall successful IT service.

In large installations the problem is even more complex, for the communications and applications management is subdivided further. Management of computer applications is usually divided in one (or more) of four ways:

- by department (a functional subdivision)
- by site (geographic subdivision)
- by manufacturer of computer system (technical subdivision)
- by computing function (FTP, SMTP, Telnet)

Figure 1.5 Squeezing costs in one area.

Communications functions are often split horizontally and vertically along the TCP/IP architectural model, by function and by technology into:

- Physical layer – building cabling
- Link layer – Ethernet, Token Ring, wide area circuits
- Network layer – Internet protocol (IP)

To this list should be added the transport layer; in TCP/IP the transport layer is TCP and UDP. Immediately there is a conflict of interest, for while these are quite definitely communications protocols and have the major impact on communications performance, they are only present in the host systems of TCP/IP, not in the traditional network components. If TCP/IP systems are to be successful, overcoming this territorial and organizational issue is key.

The design authority

Whatever the size of the organization and its networks, TCP/IP only operates correctly if the same high standards of configuration are used in every operational attached piece of equipment. This is easiest if the major design decisions are imposed by or agreed with a single (central) design authority which is educated to make the correct managerial and technical choices and then ensures their observance throughout the interconnected system. TCP/IP grew from a free culture of cooperating organizations and individuals with a collegiate and research ethos; overall standards and control came from the Internet Architecture Board. The same degree of cooperation and control must be present in an operational commercial TCP/IP network. The control will normally come from somebody with the necessary technical and organizational authority.

Technical decisions

What technical decisions must be made? The complexity of the management problem depends on the anticipated size and growth rate of the overall system. Size, growth rate and corporate organization and culture must all be considered when the technical (and organizational) choices are taken during the planning and implementation processes. These choices may be conveniently considered in the layered way that the TCP/IP architecture suggests to us. The important technical decisions to be made centre around the following topics:

- The size of the problem
- Reliability
- Availability

- Budget and costs
- Local and wide area networks to support TCP/IP
- Network addressing scheme (IP address space)
- Use of subnetwork addresses
- Router network and its routing protocols
- Domain name service
- Application layers, including their communications effects
- Overall system management and record keeping

These subjects are interdependent. The structure and geography of the organization determines the underlying communication requirements. This interacts with the layout of LANs. That layout predetermines the flexibility of network addressing, subnetwork addressing and the placement of routers.

Certain combinations of technology can at first sight appear to be compatible; the problems only become evident much later (Figure 1.6).

Subsequent chapters of Part I discuss each of the above as organizational, managerial and user issues without detailed technical description of the bits and bytes involved. Those discussions are deferred to Part II.

Choosing equipment

In a description of practical issues we frequently find that the standards include many features and facilities which are not generally implemented in available equipment.

Many descriptions of TCP/IP concentrate on the facilities that are available within the protocol and not on the features that can really be exploited by today's equipment. We have frequently found that TCP/IP was implemented for facilities which in practice it cannot provide. Once network managers have determined what facilities they require they should produce a requirements specification for their suppliers, so they can determine what facilities are supported and the level

Figure 1.6 Choosing the wrong combinations of technology.

of that support. Throughout the book we will give an indication of what is generally available, but that can be expected to change quite quickly. Readers must treat such statements as a trigger to ask the right questions of their suppliers to obtain the latest state of play.

Summary

In this chapter, we have introduced the components of TCP/IP which support interconnectivity and interoperability. We have discussed how technology affects and is affected by the size, growth rate, existing structures, culture and geography of the organization that deploys it.

The layered structure of the TCP/IP protocol suite suggests how we might divide up the management responsibilities, but it must be remembered that the technology must be treated as one integrated system if it is to operate successfully. Changes in one area cannot be made without considering the consequences for performance and costs in another.

Subsequent chapters in Part I discuss the parameters for success and the key managerial decisions that must be made on specific technical parameters if long-term success and stability is to be achieved with minimum effort.

2

Establishing the network foundation

The functions of an organization and the way in which it is structured directly affect its information flows and communications requirements. In this chapter we discuss the issues that must be considered when planning the networks that support TCP/IP.

The topics covered are:

- Structures of the organization and its networks
- Features of the corporate network
- Laying out the local and wide area networks
- Estimating the network size
- Management choices
- LAN cabling
- Bridging and routing

Any distributed computer system is composed of two major components: the processors, which provide applications services to computer users; the physical local and wide area networks and cable systems, which carry information between the sources of data (such as file servers) and the users of that data at workstations or personal computers. We shall discuss application questions later. First, we examine the local and wide area network implications of TCP/IP. This discussion cannot be completely divorced from a consideration of network addressing and of routing, for the three topics are interdependent. The structure of Local Area Network (LAN) and Wide Area Network (WAN) cables and the presence of bridges and routers change the TCP/IP addressing scheme. Computer systems on the same bridged LAN must be within the same address range. On either side of a router they are in different address ranges. Setting the right standards for the underlying LAN structure allows the design of TCP/IP to be right first time. It should be no surprise that addressing and routing are topics for the next chapters.

For reliable and efficient operation, TCP/IP must operate over a stable platform of LAN cabling and components and wide area circuits. In this chapter, we consider how to design and implement that low-level infrastructure.

Planning the supporting network

The aim of TCP/IP network planning and design is to provide a communications infrastructure that meets the requirements of the organization with readily available equipment and skills. It must provide the correct level of performance for different functions within the organization, at different places, and at acceptable costs. In setting up a local and wide area structure for TCP/IP, the first task of the designer is to consider what each of these terms means for that situation. Each case is unique but the overall size of the organization and its network requirements will determine the complexity of the problems to be solved.

Size and growth rate

Whatever aspect of human communications you consider, it could be said that a measurement of success is often that the size and usage grows rapidly. As a result of experience in road network planning, this has become known as the 'motorway (or highway) effect'. If a system is useful, people change their travel habits and use the system in new ways that the planners never envisaged (Figure 2.1). Traffic grows to fill the space available. In our organization the network grew at a rate which was totally unexpected and expanded rapidly to cover the company.

Figure 2.1   The motorway effect.

When planning a TCP/IP installation it is advisable to consider the initial size of the network and have some indication of maximum size and growth rate. This measure of size has two dimensions:

- The total number of attached ports, that is, computer and router connections to the network

- The geographic coverage

It is also important to consider in what ways the network could grow – by addition of devices on the same network or by connection to other TCP/IP installations, for example by mergers and acquisitions. In the first case, all the issues are under the control of one organization; in the second, they may not be. The problems to be solved will be different in each case. Today's computer applications and systems are distributed on work-stations and PCs throughout the sites and buildings where the computer users sit. Some types of change cannot be centrally managed and must be carried out at each machine. These changes are always difficult and labour-intensive, and hence costly. As far as possible, they must be pre-dicted and eliminated.

These considerations can affect the detailed planning process of the LAN and WAN links, the planning of the address space and of the bridges and routers which interconnect LANs and sites. Planners will wish to determine solutions to the following questions. How many cable systems will there be? How can they be interconnected successfully? Will bridges suffice or are routers required? How should the address plan for the network evolve? Is there a requirement for the Domain Name Service? Is responsibility split or with one person or body? If it is split, is the division by function, by location, or by technology? Is there a need to split application management from communications management? Is there a need (in a large corporation) to split communications management into more than one subfunction?

Existing standards

In an attempt to avoid duplication of effort and perhaps more importantly to avoid choosing incompatible solutions to the same TCP/IP options and problems, it is quite important to determine if there are any other existing TCP/IP implementations in the organization. Some systems may hide their use of TCP/IP; the Banyan VINES resource-sharing LAN or any communications management system which uses the simple network management protocol are current examples. If other examples do exist and will share the same cables or TCP/IP equipment at any time, the developments must be coordinated.

In some situations there may already be a central authority for TCP/IP implementation which has set local standards for the use of TCP/IP. These standards should relate to:

- Addressing conventions
- Host-naming conventions and domain name system
- Local area network
- Choice of equipment
- Choice of network software
- Configuration and management of the network
- Configuration and management of the applications
- Connection to the Internet
- Security

It is much easier if these standards can be used rather than starting from scratch.

Traffic flows and capacity

In planning the network layout and capacity it is important to know the volume of information that will be carried. At the simplest level, high-performance routes in the network must follow the high traffic flows in the organization. Faults on those major arterial routes will affect more users, so they may need to be protected against failure.

Judging future traffic flows is always one of the most difficult estimates in installing new TCP/IP systems. One of the great successes of modern software development techniques is to provide an effective barrier between the application developer and the underlying network. But it leaves the network planners with a major problem. Few people can relate the use of an application to the traffic it will generate.

Given the continued growth in workstation performance, existing LAN implementations already seem slow. For many commercial environments, a single physical LAN can support only 20 to 50 workstations and one or two file servers before the network must be partitioned with bridges or routers. The need for switching hubs, 'private' LANs and 100 Mbps Fibre Distributed Data Interface (FDDI) or even higher network speeds (110 Gbps) is evident, particularly for backbone networks and image systems, but the costs of such a system are not yet within the budgets of many network operators.

In the absence of such speeds, planners must ration the limited resource of normal speed LANs. They must understand how particular applications use the network and what the traffic flows between different user groups and applications processors are at different times of the day and business year. Key questions are:

- What will be the total volume of data on different parts of the network at the busiest time of the day? Is this traffic seasonal?

- How will the traffic grow with time, taking into account the changing and improving user perception of the network services and the increase in number of attached devices and a move towards more demanding applications?

- How is the traffic distributed among adjacent machines and to more remote machines?

Often the only way of obtaining such information is to measure the operation of real applications and extrapolate the results using spreadsheet or other modelling systems. Armed with the traffic information, and its growth, it is time to consider the network structure.

Network decisions

In a small, compact implementation of a few PCs and file servers in one building, the main issues and decisions centre on the choice of addresses (see Chapter 3) and on configuration and management of the computers. The network will be a few lengths of Unshielded Twisted Pair (UTP) cable or a simple Token Ring installation with, at most, one or two bridges to increase the total traffic capacity of the system. There are unlikely to be any routers. Implementation of the network is usually straightforward. In these small networks, one or two people make most of the decisions; they may also be responsible for carrying out the implementation and configuration.

Larger corporate networks often cover many sites and require long-distance PTT-provided (Telco-provided) circuits to interconnect those sites. Rentals for such circuits can form a major portion of the cost which may increase with time[†]. Complex configuration of remote bridges and

---

[†]In many countries the unit cost of intersite circuits has reduced considerably over the past 10 years, but the increase in capacity required for interconnected LANs has far outstripped the unit cost reductions.

Figure 2.2 Multiple protocols.

routers is required to ensure that these wide area circuits are used at optimum efficiency.

Networks are subject to hidden costs. Heavily loaded networks, where the traffic approaches the capacity of the cable, require more management time as systems are reconfigured and moved from cable to cable to reduce loading. Idiosyncrasies and limitations of the overall system and software faults always become apparent at high system loading. A heavily loaded network can also impose a load on application processors, reducing the amount of useful power available for end users.

Management decisions about networks centre on how to provide the right performance with chosen reliability to particular users and at acceptable cost. Options centre on the choice of technology for the cable, the interface cards and the bridges and routers that form the interconnection. These three components form the three lower layers of the OSI model. Cables are part of the OSI physical layer (layer 1); LAN bridges operate medium access control, a part of the OSI data link layer (layer 2); routers operate in the network layer (layer 3). TCP/IP performance is not affected by the choice of cable as long as that cable can support the LAN technology at the normal operating speed in an error-free way. We shall not therefore discuss the issues of cabling further.

Link layer options

LAN cables and wide area circuits may be a shared resource, carrying not only TCP/IP data, but data from other applications and systems as well (Novell NetWare, IBM SNA, DECnet to name but a few examples). Transporting multiple protocols on one infrastructure increases the organizational and technical complexity. In these networks it is certain that the management of network resources, the infrastructure which carries data between application processors, will present as many difficulties as the management of applications themselves. A detailed discussion of these issues is beyond the scope of this book, but for those contemplating using TCP/IP in a multiprotocol environment, it is much easier for protocols to coexist peacefully if the number of options is reduced (Figure 2.2).

The first decision is what option to use for carrying information across the LAN cable that everyone colloquially calls Ethernet. Ethernet (even Version 2 Ethernet) is a different standard from ISO 8802.3[†] (IEEE 802.3). While the hardware is compatible for both systems, the frame content[‡] is not. Furthermore, Ethernet V2 is a *de facto* standard; IEEE 802.3 is the Open Systems standard which was adopted as the international standard by ISO.

TCP/IP on LANs predates these international standards, so the most common implementation by far for TCP/IP is Ethernet V2; while most manufacturers of TCP/IP offer IEEE 802.3/802.2 with Sub Network Access Protocol (SNAP), the changeover to IEEE 802.3 encapsulation should not be undertaken lightly; the two standards can coexist on the same Ethernet cable, but they cannot directly interwork. Where both standards are in use, careful planning is required to be sure that all systems can see TCP/IP data in the form that they can recognize. Either the different systems must be segregated by frame type, or some device must selectively retransmit frames in the other format, effectively duplicating that traffic on the same cable and increasing the network loading. The technical aspects of IEEE 802.3 encapsulation are described in Chapter 10.

On Token Ring (IEEE 802.5) and FDDI (IS9314) networks there is less confusion; ISO standard frames are used exclusively with SNAP encapsulation carrying the Ethernet type field.

Structuring LAN interconnections

Directly attaching all computing resources to one extended 'local area' network of the highest possible speed without intervening bridges and routers gives the best possible performance.

Today's high performance file servers, personal computers and workstations can fill a single Ethernet (10 Mbps) or Token Ring (4 Mbps or 16 Mbps) segment. For satisfactory operation, the alternative to replacing the network with one of higher speeds is to partition the overall system into small groups with a common communications interest.

This subdivision was originally done with bridges or routers but increasingly 'switching hubs' are used to connect a user directly to a server for the duration of one LAN frame or message. With the proper structure, the LAN is no longer shared amongst many servers, but each server is effectively given its own high capacity 'pipe' to its groups of users.

[†]Rather than repeat the use of ISO and IEEE equivalent standards for LANs, we shall follow the practice of using the IEEE designations. These have been adopted verbatim for ISO OSI standards.

[‡]There are two standards for transmitting IP information on the cable that is commonly referred to as Ethernet. The first is accurately described as Ethernet Version 2; the second requires the lengthy description 'IEEE 802.3 + IEEE 802.2. + SNAP'. The detailed differences between these are left to Chapter 10.

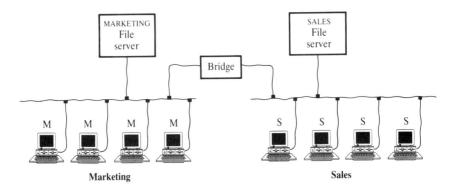

Figure 2.3 Location of servers.

Switching hubs are available in a wide variety of formats and sizes; within a building or local group of buildings (a campus), it is becoming common to use cut-through switching rather than bridges. Routers are then used between different technologies and across wide area links. As we shall see, this use of switching or high performance bridging rather than routing has a direct impact on the allocation of network addresses within TCP/IP systems.

Other than the implications for addresses, TCP/IP is transparent to the use of switching hubs, bridges or routers, or newer technologies such as Asynchronous Transfer Mode (ATM) in the LAN infrastructure.

Laying out LAN cables

Data flows tend to follow organization structure; a single department in an organization may not be located in one building or at one site. If everyone could share the same cable and there was still excess capacity, this would not be an issue. But where the cable is full and must be subdivided, how should we carry out that subdivision?

From some perspectives, LAN and WAN cables should be subdivided and labelled according to the departments that use them, not according to the locations they serve. Bridges and routers should provide the links for the infrequent traffic between departments, not for the bulk of traffic within a department. In organizations where recovery of network costs is important, such decisions are politically important. If one department takes a disproportionate share of the network capacity and drives it to the next phase of expansion, it is much simpler to allocate and justify costs if the network is structured by department rather than by site.

In practice, networks laid out on organizational needs, rather than geography, are not intuitive to manage; training of maintenance staff is more difficult and configuration mistakes are more likely. Most organizations take the intuitive approach and provide an infrastructure firstly for the building and secondly for sites (Figure 2.4a). As traffic grows to fill that structure, it may be necessary to restructure on an organizational basis. But the technical principle remains:

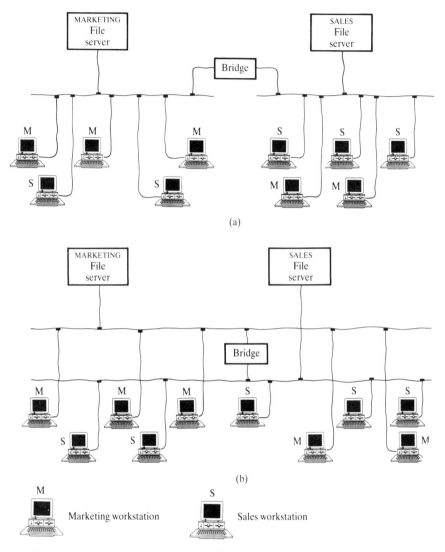

Figure 2.4 (a) Cabling organized by geography. (b) Cabling organized by department.

- If optimum throughput is the aim, then try to connect directly the various subsections of a department within and between sites, to reduce the number of bridges and routers, and not to minimize the quantity of fibre, copper cable, and separate intersite circuits (Figure 2.4b).
- If optimum reliability and simplified management is the aim, limit the geographic coverage of a single physical LAN and partition the users with bridges and routers to limit the propagation of faults (Figure 2.4a).

The LAN planner needs a flexible set of tools to choose the layout of cabling and which systems are to communicate directly. Developments in Ethernet and Token Ring Switching Hub technology allow the flexible creation of these groups of common interest within floor areas, between floors of a single building and across a single site using multiple copper or fibre optic backbones. It is worthwhile having a central point, a 'super hub' where the appropriate work areas can be joined into a single physical network with a common backbone fibre. Between geographically separated sites there is little option but to use remote bridges and routers. (Properly designed Token Ring and FDDI can have a degree of resilience to cable breaks.)

Splitting the network

Bridges and **routers** partition the network and improve performance for workstations on the same cable. The majority of network traffic should be local to the group of users and a small percentage (15–30%) should cross the bridges onto a backbone network which interconnects different user groups[†]. If this traffic split cannot be achieved, then the bridge is not used in the optimum way.

The prime purpose of a bridge in a LAN is to *prevent* traffic flowing where it does not need to, rather than to allow traffic to flow where it will. Bridges filter traffic (Figure 2.5). In many networks, it is only a secondary function of the bridge to provide communications where none existed by translating to a different type of cable and extending the cable length limits of the basic LAN specification.

In network partitioning, routers have some advantages and some disadvantages over bridges. They have a more positive role to play. Routers relay only what they are specifically told to relay. They are part of the IP protocol and are designed to interconnect network technologies of different performance. Routers are particularly useful at matching the high speeds of LANs to the much lower speeds of intersite (wide area) communications circuits that are now available. On the other hand they have a higher cost and lower performance and require more careful management than bridges. Such is the importance of the router that we devote the whole of Chapter 5 to routers and their management.

[†]Such 'rules of thumb' are not totally satisfactory, for the exact traffic distribution is dependent on the type of the application software and how it was designed to use communications facilities.

Figure 2.5 Bridges filter traffic.

Using bridges

Bridges filter traffic by Media Access Control (MAC) Address. They must examine each frame received on each port and build a table of frame source addresses with the port on which the frame was received. When the bridge learns that a source and destination are on the same port, it will not pass traffic for that destination to any other cable.

The important performance factors of bridges are:

- *Filtering rate* – the ability to examine frames for possible relaying.
- *Forwarding rate* – the ability to relay frames which have to be relayed.
- 'Routing' algorithm that allows bridges to be connected redundantly in parallel and in loops but prevents frames circulating round the loops.
- *Transit delay* – normally related to forwarding rate.
- Filter table size.
- Variations in performance with filter table occupancy.

Bridges now can filter at the theoretical maximum rate for Ethernet of 14 880 frames per second. Even in busy operational networks the offered traffic will not be this demanding, for this figure is based on all minimum-sized frames.

Broadcasts, broadcast storms and multicast frames

TCP/IP protocols use two techniques which impact on the performance of the network. They use **broadcast** and **multicast frames** for discovering the locations of resources and for communicating between systems which cooperate to provide a common service.

Multicast frames take capacity on the cable but are not processed by every station. They become a problem only on slower wide area bridged links. 'Slow' is a relative term; for today's LANs, 'slow' could be 256 kbps, 128 kbps or less.

Broadcast frames are much more detrimental to performance. They are generated by ARP, RARP, BOOTP, and RIP. Every system on an Ethernet or Token Ring network must process *every* broadcast frame. If the number of broadcast frames increases, the performance of every system will degrade noticeably. A frame takes some time to process, independent of its size. Each broadcast frame can reduce the performance of a PC by almost one normal data frame of 1000 to 1450 bytes. PCs slow down noticeably with 40 to 50 broadcast packets per second.

Bridges relay broadcast frames everywhere. To try to filter broadcasts is to destroy the possibility of any-to-any communication. So networks which are interlinked only with bridges reach a size where the percentage of broadcast traffic from all the devices is unacceptable. Unless the broadcast traffic can be reduced, it becomes impossible to manage the network or to grow it further successfully.

It has been known for in-house application programmers who do not appreciate the potential harmful effects to write applications using broadcasts. On more than one occasion, a complete LAN, including powerful minicomputers, has been brought to a standstill by a **broadcast storm** of about 100 packets per second. Broadcast storms are sometimes attributed to Ethernet design limitations; it is often not realized that the broadcast storm is usually caused by a combination of bad software design and a poor bridged network structure of any type of LAN and is not limited to Ethernet systems.

Bridging different technologies

Using bridges to convert from one cable type to another but within a single access control method introduces no new issues – that is all Token Ring or all CSMA/CD. Bridging between networks with different access control methods from Token Ring to CSMA/CD or to FDDI Token Ring

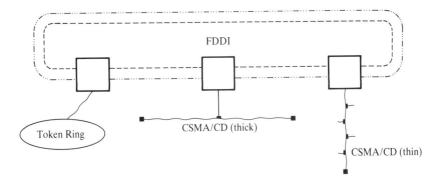

Figure 2.6 Bridging different technologies.

requires more careful planning, as the speeds of operation and hence the frame rate are different (Figure 2.6).

Contrary to popular belief, bridges between IEEE 802.5 Token Ring, IS9314 FDDI and IEEE 802.3 CSMA/CD networks are not transparent to protocol. Bridges must intercept the ARP/RARP protocols of TCP/IP and convert the MAC address representation. Depending on the bridge design this may affect delay and hence throughput. This conversion may limit the maximum number of frames which can be relayed. Do not assume that bridges will achieve the same performance when forwarding between two networks of different types as they do between networks of the same type.

Bridging to wide area links

Remote bridges operate in pairs to connect geographically separated sites over long-distance point-to-point links. The main issue is the large difference in speed between LAN technologies and the circuits which are generally available for this type of interconnection (Figure 2.7).

Circuit speeds

The cost of long-distance, high-speed digital services is still regarded by many as prohibitive. In large companies, with many computer users, the cost per user may be acceptable. Even so, few organizations can yet consider speeds above 2 Mbps. Outside the USA and UK many organizations find cost and availability of these circuits unacceptable and may be limited to 64 kbps or multiples of 64 kbps perhaps derived from the newer Integrated Services Digital Network (ISDN) services.

The time taken to send a typical TCP/IP datagram of 1024 bytes at 64 kbps is about 135 ms compared to 0.81 ms on a 10 Mbps network. Fortunately, TCP/IP Telnet and FTP were designed to be used in environments with long delays and have time-outs which can adjust to changes in network speed and loading. The performance of these slow

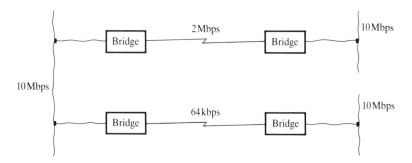

Figure 2.7 Remote bridge.

network links for file transfers and a system such as NFS, which was designed for the LAN environment, may not be acceptable.

'Routing' in bridges

In recent years, the use of the word 'routing' has been extended and applied to any mechanism which can determine and alter paths between end systems (hosts). Sophisticated filtering LAN bridges are often said to have routing features or routing capability. This type of routing does not use the network layer or IP address of TCP/IP, nor does it take account of the features of the 'best path' as requested by the communicating TCP/IP systems.

All IEEE LANs must ensure that all MAC frames arrive in the order they were transmitted and without duplication. Most systems therefore initially only allowed one path between source and destination. This precluded configurations with bridges in loops and in parallel. Such a limitation is unacceptable as a single failure can divide a network in two. The **spanning tree** and **source routing** algorithms incorporated in IEEE 802.1d overcome these limitations. For bridge routing, IEEE 802.1d has defined a mechanism called the transparent spanning tree algorithm which is particularly important for IEEE 802.3 (Ethernet) bridges.

Spanning tree is a disabling technique that suspends the activity of any bridge which provides a redundant path (Figure 2.8). Such bridges carry no traffic but come to life if the current active path fails. The switchover time is of the order of 15–30 seconds if the default configuration of bridges is not changed. This is slower than many computer users would wish but is faster than could be achieved by manual intervention. However, the technique is only fully satisfactory for on-site services. It is often not acceptable to have remote wide area links sitting idle. All the processing for the spanning tree algorithm is placed in the bridge and end

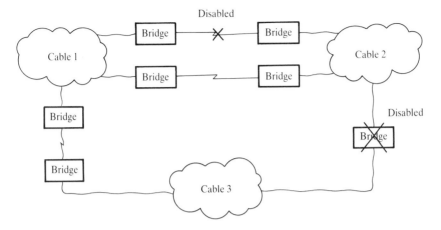

Figure 2.8 Spanning tree operation.

systems are unaware of the spanning tree operation. Spanning tree bridges are therefore called **transparent bridges**.

For Token Ring networks a different mechanism referred to as **source routing** was adopted by the IEEE 802.5 committee, though it is not widely used outside IBM equipment. End systems must be modified to take an active part in setting up a route across redundant source routing bridges. IEEE 802.1d later adopted source routing as part of the IEEE bridge routing standards, though the detail is different from source routing as used by IBM.

An advantage of source routing (Figure 2.9) is that it allows multiple active routes between the source and destination cable systems, although one conversation will follow one route for its duration. The main

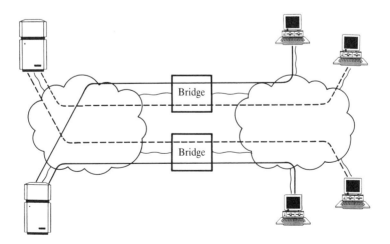

Figure 2.9 Source routing.

disadvantage is that LAN driver software must be modified to add and remove source routing fields from the data frames. Attached workstations begin by discovering possible routes between source and destination using either a single route explorer frame or an all routes explorer frame. Transmission of the single route frame relies on the fact that a single stable spanning tree route has been set up either manually by the network managers or automatically by a spanning tree algorithm. Having discovered all available routes, end stations insert a list of bridges which are to be used into each frame they transmit. If the link fails, then an alternate route may be selected instantly from a list maintained in the workstation.

Source routing is only likely to be found with TCP/IP end systems on Token Ring. It is not normally used on Ethernet.

Before choosing a bridge, managers should check that the implementation is fully IEEE 802.1d compliant, and that interoperation of that implementation of spanning tree has been checked with any other implementation that is used in the network. They should also be aware of how the spanning tree algorithm operates, and how bridges determine if they are to be in the active topology. For effective operation, the spanning tree algorithm must be managed. This means that network managers must change the default configuration of their bridges.

In networks which use bridges between Token Ring and Ethernet, the network designers must have a plan of how the conversion between source routing and spanning tree is to take place in a consistent manner.

The limits of bridging

While these algorithms can have a place in smaller networks, spanning tree in particular is often not satisfactory for the larger network with WAN interconnections, since spanning tree disables otherwise useful routes. This is one reason why bridged networks can only grow to a limited size (Figure 2.10). Another is that the standards allow for only seven bridges in series.

But there is another limitation which we have already hinted at. Bridged networks, even when well structured, can grow to the point where the volume of broadcast and multicast traffic degrades performance, where widely varying loads on intermediate (backbone) networks affect performance because of packet loss, where spanning tree and source routing algorithms provide less than optimum routing and where the problems of conversion between Token Ring and CSMA/CD technologies are all too evident. The performance of the network in such circumstances is at best poor. Network users may see wide variations in both reliability and response. Uncontrolled congestion prevents the successful transmission of data. For some applications, the network may become unstable and unreliable.

Various authorities have tried to put a figure to the size of network that can be successfully managed with bridges alone. It depends on many

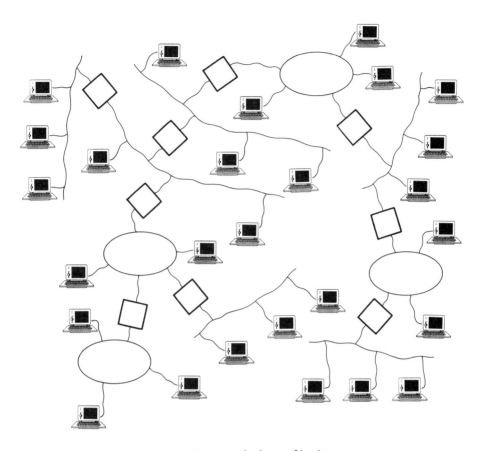

Figure 2.10 The limits of bridging.

factors other than technology. But many organizations find that when their network has a combination of many hundreds of interconnected devices, a few tens of servers and minicomputers, and ten to thirty bridges, the control of broadcast traffic can become impossible and the overall reliability and performance of the network decreases. The problems are made worse by having remote bridges with slow-speed links between sites.

In a poorly performing network, the network planner must carry out a more careful analysis of traffic volumes and flows and then take remedial action to alter network structure and the positioning of bridges to meet the corporate needs. If to these problems is added the possible inappropriate use of the network by badly designed software that propagates faults throughout the system, an alternative interconnection method that gives the network manager more control is required. Bridges do not normally limit the effects of excessive broadcast frames from poorly designed software. The router can provide the necessary control.

Using routers

In most communications architectures, routing is a network layer function, not the MAC or data link function performed by bridges. Network layer routing predates bridging; routers were in use in WANs before the link-level LAN bridge was introduced in the early 1980s by companies such as Sytek Inc. and by the Digital Equipment Corporation (which holds patents related to bridge algorithms).

During the mid and late 1980s, routing was eclipsed by an enthusiasm for bridging. It is only as the performance, stability and management limitations of large bridged networks using connectionless protocols have become apparent and the cost and performance of routers has improved, that routing has once again come to the fore in larger networks.

Routers do not represent a panacea for the problems of the network manager. They can usefully replace some bridges in a bridged internet which is already physically well structured; it is likely to be a waste of time and money to add them to a network which is not well structured, or where the traffic flows are not understood and well managed.

Routers only operate properly if the network addressing structure is correct. We therefore delay a full discussion of router technology until after we have described how to plan an IP network address structure.

Summary

In this chapter we have discussed the factors that allow the LANs and WANs which support TCP/IP to be planned successfully. The key points are:

- The planning process begins by understanding the size and structure of the problem to be solved.

- That will be determined by the organization, its size, structure and communications flows.

- New TCP/IP installations should follow existing internal standards for TCP/IP installations so that any requirement for interconnection is straightforward.

- On Ethernet there is more than one encapsulation method. TCP/IP systems predate OSI standards and use Ethernet encapsulation rather than full IEEE 802.3, IEEE 802.2 and SNAP.

- Bridges increase the capacity of a LAN by limiting traffic to cable segments where it needs to be.

- LANs interconnected with bridges must be carefully structured.

- Cut-through switching hubs can provide a high performance connection between workstations and a file server without the performance limitations of bridges or routers.

- Interconnecting LANs with wide area circuits requires careful consideration of intersite capacity. Today the interconnection speed is much less than the LAN speed and the data flows across those circuits must be adjusted accordingly.

- The bridge routing algorithms in bridged networks must be consistent.

- Broadcast frames limit the number of devices that can be connected together using bridges alone.

- Routers operating at the IP (network) layer of TCP/IP offer a solution to extending the LAN beyond the limits imposed by bridges and a more satisfactory method of interconnecting different local and wide area technologies.

3

Planning and managing IP addresses

Careful network planning is key to the long-term success of any networking technology, particularly for the larger installation. In the past, insufficient consideration has been given to planning the key parameter of IP addresses for TCP/IP. This leads to one of the commonest causes of escalating network support costs.

In this chapter we discuss the following topics related to IP addressing:

- Different ways of addressing computers in a TCP/IP system
- Functions of the IP address
- Format of the IP address
- The need for a unique IP address
- The need for IP address registration
- The need for autonomous system numbers and registration
- How to choose a nonregistered address
- Configuring IP addresses
- Organizational issues and IP address management
- The effects of moves and changes
- The need for record keeping

The focus of this chapter is how to plan and manage IP Version 4 addresses. Implementors of TCP/IP must select, configure and manage IP addresses correctly. Selecting an IP addressing scheme is the first major decision the TCP/IP implementor must make.

An IP address identifies the connection of a machine to an IP network uniquely, and in a way that is independent of the underlying network technology.

Since 1990, the IETF (Internet Engineering Task Force, a technical body under the IAB) has studied methods of overcoming some limitations in IP Version 4. The chosen solution is known as IP Next Generation (IPng) or IP Version 6 (IPv6).

IPv6 addressing is discussed at the end of this chapter, and in more detail in Chapter 11.

Identifying a network connection

Connections to a TCP/IP network are often known to each other and to users in three different ways, all of which identify the same connection to the network but at different levels of TCP/IP:

- As names: in the **fully qualified host** and **domain** name

    for example, www.integralis.co.uk

    Using the domain name scheme is often not considered early enough in the planning of commercial networks; users of larger networks will find it invaluable.

- As a group of four numbers separated by full stops (periods). This is the **IP** or **network address** used by the IP layer of TCP/IP

    for example, 193.128.143.1

- On a shared LAN by its network interface card address, the 48-bit **MAC address** (Medium Access Control address, often called the physical address)

    for example, 0060 8C 12 34 56

Why have three levels of address, since they all refer to the same connection to the TCP/IP Internet? The reason is that while at any one time these addresses identify the same location, over a period of time each may change for different reasons. The three types of address allow a degree of flexibility where none would exist if the functions were not separated:

- The host and domain name should remain unchanged for the longest time, for it is completely determined by the system designers and managers, though it will often change if there is a major change in machine location.

- The IP address may change due to network growth and reconfiguration, for example if a machine is moved from one location in a building to another.

- The MAC address may change for similar growth or performance reasons, or because the network card is replaced following a card failure. The shortest lived address is likely to be the MAC address.

The fully qualified domain name is for 'human consumption' and consists of a set of identifiers, separated by full stops, which describe a computer in a hierarchical relationship to all others. For example:

machine.department.site.organization.org_type.country

Introducing flexibility brings with it the possibility of error and communications failure if the flexible functions are not managed and controlled correctly. The domain name system is described in Chapter 14. This chapter describes the management of the IP address space. MAC addresses are not normally separately managed in TCP/IP systems.

Planning the IP address space

To plan an IP addressing scheme you must have or acquire the following information:

- The maximum number of host ports that your organization could ever wish to interconnect. The whole of your organization is not just your particular department, but the whole organizational structure, if necessary, worldwide, which may at any time be interconnected.

- An understanding of the numbers of devices at each location and in each building on each site. Think big. Assume one address per member of staff in those buildings and leave some 25% spare.

- An understanding of the different departments, their geographic locations, and the likelihood that they will need to communicate. An estimate of the amount of information that is exchanged is useful but it has a very short-lived value.

- A knowledge of any other current users of TCP/IP and any standardization decisions that have been taken already.

In a small organization of a few hundred people, getting this information is straightforward in comparison to a large corporation; but it is the large corporation that must have accurate figures and which must derive centralized standards that are adhered to everywhere.

Internet protocol

The Internet Protocol (IP) may be described as the network layer protocol of TCP/IP. IP is operated and interpreted by each intermediate relay in an interconnected set of LANs and WANs which is using the TCP/IP protocol suite to communicate. Such a collection is often called an **internetwork** and the intermediate relays are routers. IP provides a best efforts delivery service based on a technique called **datagram transmission**; 'best efforts' and 'datagram' because no attempt is made (by IP) to recover any errors which may occur in transmission.

IP supports routing and relaying of information between communicating hosts (end devices) according to the Type (or quality) Of Service (TOS) they require. IP allows routing errors to be trapped and reported and their effects on system performance to be minimized. IP does not make assumptions about the underlying network of physical cables, LAN hardware (Ethernet, Token Ring or FDDI) or the point-to-point wide area links (PTT circuits).

IP addressing

The IP address is one component in the Internet protocol. The IP address is a number that uniquely identifies the *connection* of a host computer (or end system as OSI would call it) to a physical network as it communicates with other computers (or end systems). Hosts with more than one connection have a different IP address for each one. IP routers also have their own IP addresses for they can be the source and destination of IP datagrams.

The purpose of the IP address is twofold: to identify each connection to the internetwork in a way that is independent of the underlying physical network (LAN or WAN) technology, and to collect a group of connections together to simplify routing. Internetwork routers use IP addresses to make routing decisions.

The need for address management

IP addresses must be unique in the communicating internetwork. If not, communications will fail erratically. It is up to network managers to configure and manage IP addresses correctly by traditional manual methods aided by database and network management technology or by using the Dynamic Host Configuration Protocol (DHCP), or BOOT Protocol (BOOTP), discussed later.

About MAC addresses

Where TCP/IP systems are connected to a shared cable such as an Ethernet or Token Ring LAN, communication between stations must take place using MAC addresses, normally built into the network adapter card. Since the IP address is configured independently of the MAC address, it remains unchanged even if the network card fails and is replaced.

Every Ethernet or Token Ring card comes with a preconfigured 48-bit MAC address, its universally managed address. LAN standards also allow locally managed addresses; network cards can be loaded with a 48-bit address chosen by the network manager. Locally managed addresses are not normally used in TCP/IP systems. As IP addresses in TCP/IP must be controlled and managed, there is little value in adding a second layer of management by also configuring and controlling MAC addresses.

But the issue of MAC address management does not disappear completely from the TCP/IP story; some of the facilities of TCP/IP (such as the Boot Protocol, BOOTP, and DHCP) use the MAC address as a fixed reference point for obtaining other information. If you wish to use these features, you must at least have a record of the MAC address of each computer for which the facility will be used. These addresses appear as a reference point in look-up tables in information servers. But, as described above, the MAC address can change if the network card is replaced. In a large network, keeping an up-to-date record of MAC addresses and ensuring that all servers have the correct record can be time-consuming.

Some UTP hubs have management facilities that can record the MAC address attached to each user drop cable (and can deny access if that LAN address changes to an unauthorized value). Such systems make it easier to record the location of particular MAC addresses.

Characteristics of the IP address

The IP address is a 32-bit number which must be unique in the internetwork. Devices which must have an IP address include every connection of each computer and of each network router. As mentioned previously, computers with more than one network connection have a different IP address for each connection (Figure 3.1). In TCP/IP literature, such computers are referred to as **multihomed**. These connections are usually on different networks. This is the reason for sizing the network-by-network connections rather than the number of computers, though these numbers will often be very similar.

Unlike some other network addressing schemes, the IP address does not necessarily convey any information about geographic location. Given an IP address you can only deduce a management authority; that authority could manage one corporate network which in itself has global coverage and meshes with many other global networks. This has interesting implications for routing between two worldwide networks. Put another way, the IP addressing scheme is *not hierarchical* (unlike the telephone or telex network or for that matter the CCITT X.121 addressing scheme for the X.25 interface to public packet switched networks).

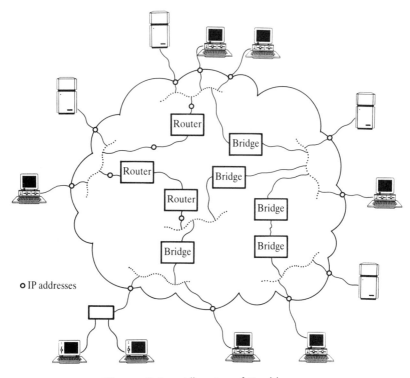

Figure 3.1 Allocation of IP addresses.

Network managers can choose to impose a geographic or organizational hierarchy on IP addresses (using subnet masks as described in Chapter 4) but this hierarchy is not a function of Internet standards.

IP address format and components

The 32-bit IP address has two components (Figure 3.2): a **network number** (or network identifier) and a **host number** or host identifier. Some 'class bits' can be extracted from the network number, but trying to examine these on their own can lead to confusion. It is safer always to think of the network number as containing the class bits.

It is the network number which identifies the controlling organization and the host number which identifies the particular connection within the authority of that organization. The term 'host number' is historic and this name could cause confusion for, as we have seen, a multihomed host has more than one IP address and hence more than one host number. For reasons that will become apparent later, it would be unusual for two ports on the same machine to have the same network number.

Class bits + Network number	Host number

Figure 3.2 Format of the IP address.

Table 3.1   The limitations of each class of IP address.

Network class	Max. number of network numbers	Max. number of hosts on each network number
A	126	16 777 214
B	16 382	65 534
C	2 097 150	254
D	Not applicable – reserved for multicast systems	
E	Reserved for IAB use	

The terms **net id** and **host id** are in common usage for network number and host number.

Classes of address

IP addresses are divided into five address classes (A to E). It is important to understand that these divisions were conceived to ease the management of addresses by the Internet Architecture Board (IAB); they have less immediate significance for the network manager.

The first three classes, A, B, C, are available for normal allocation and for host-to-host communications. Class D and class E addresses are not for general use; class D is reserved for special use by IAB designated protocols and class E is reserved for future use. One use of class D addresses is by routers, so network managers may encounter them while monitoring router protocols.

There are no practical distinctions in the way in which computer systems with class A, class B or class C addresses use those addresses. With some noted exceptions, which are discussed further below, any address from any class is equivalent for communications purposes. In principle, any host can communicate equally well using an address from any of these three classes. The distinguishing feature of each class of address is the number of network numbers and the number of host connections which each network number can support. The limitations of each class are shown in Table 3.1.

Most implementations give network managers full control over the IP addresses they allocate and configure into the equipment. It has been known for an implementation not to accept anything other than a class C address. There are situations where this could be unsatisfactory.

Network numbers and host numbers

The choice of network numbers is most important.

- Network connections with the same network number should communicate directly on the same physical LAN.

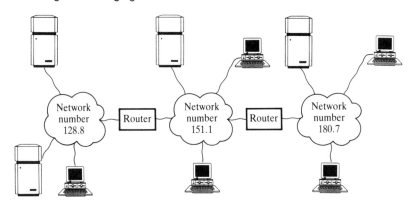

Figure 3.3 Choosing network numbers.

- Network connections with different network numbers do not communicate directly; they must use the services of a router. This router either is directly connected between the two LANs to which the hosts connect or it in turn knows of a router which can relay the message towards its ultimate destination (Figure 3.3). (The exact format of the IP address shown is explained in the next section.)

These factors determine the basic rules for choosing network numbers and host numbers. They may alternatively be stated as:

- Computers or workstations separated only by bridges or repeaters will have the same network number.

- Computers or workstations separated by routers have different network numbers.

For the network implementor, the most important factor is that the choice of IP address for a particular host is affected by the presence of routers. The positioning of routers is determined by the exact geography of the underlying physical networks which connect computers, floors, buildings, sites and countries into a complete internetwork. As we saw in Chapter 2, it is also heavily influenced by organizational needs, traffic flows and traffic volume. The layout will change as the network grows and matures. If a bridge is replaced by a router, the network number on one side of the new router must change.

When combined with the limitations of Table 3.1, the maximum number of network connections that are likely to communicate within one network[†] (or organization) is therefore a key to determining which address class should be selected.

[†]As we will see in the next chapter, there is a mechanism for dividing one network number into subnetworks. In practice, hosts on either side of a router must be in different subnetworks rather than within different network numbers. However, if they do have different network numbers, they must communicate via one or more routers.

Table 3.2   IP address representation.

Dotted decimal	Dotted hexadecimal	C-style hexadecimal	Binary
44.123.110.224	2C.7B.6E.E0	0x2c7b6ee0	00101100011110110110111011100000
129.6.48.100	81.06.30.64	0x81063064	10000001000001100011000001100100
128.240.1.109	80.F0.01.6D	0x80f0016d	10000000111100000000000101101101
192.33.33.109	C0.21.21.6D	0xc021216d	11000000001000010010000101101101

A TCP/IP addressing scheme evolves as the needs of users are better understood during the design process. Adding a TCP/IP addressing scheme to a LAN must take into account the existing layout of that LAN.

One factor is key. Network planners must attempt to design an addressing scheme that can remain substantially unchanged in a changing environment.

Writing down the address

The convention is that the address is written down, or described to software, in **dotted decimal notation**. Each eight bits of the address (each **octet**) is converted to a decimal number in the range 0 to 255, and separated by a dot (.).

While the US standards initially specified 'dotted decimal notation' some computer staff are more at home with hexadecimal notation. **Dotted hexadecimal**[†] (and UNIX or C-style hexadecimal) and **octal**[‡] notations are sometimes used and will be accepted by some (though by no means all) implementations. Occasionally it is useful, if somewhat long-winded, to represent these numbers in binary. Some valid addresses are shown in Table 3.2. Leading zeros in each octet, which have no significance, should not be included. 128.1.0.9 is valid and more usual than 128.001.000.009. However, 128.1.9 or 128...9 are not valid. (Some systems interpret numbers with leading zeros as 'octal' numbers.)

Distinguishing the class of address

The five classes of address have already been mentioned. The class of address is determined by certain bits in the first eight bits, that is, in the first decimal number of the four (Table 3.3). The magnitude of the first number that defines the class of the address is given in the table.

There are two important features of this system:

(1) The division between one class and the next is always at an octet boundary. This simplifies finding the boundaries between the classes of address, since each decimal number represents one octet.

[†]Counting in 16s, using the characters 0 to 9 and A to F.
[§]Counting in 8s, using the characters 0 to 7.

Table 3.3 Distinguishing the class of address.

Address class	Class bits	Number of network bits	First usable value	Last usable value	Comment
A	0	7	1	126	Values 0 and 127 are reserved
B	10	14	128.1	191.254	
C	110	21	192.0.1	223.255.254	
D	1110	–	224.0.0.0	239.255.255.255	Not available for general use
E	1111	–	240.0.0.0	255.255.255.254	Not available for general use

(2) When the network number is written down the 'class bits' are always included in the first octet, to ensure that the class of address and hence the true network number are unambiguous.

It is important that users of TCP/IP, planners and implementors should be fully familiar with the different classes of address and the limitations that they place on network growth. Many people new to the subject at first find the technique of dotted decimal notation a little eccentric. But it should become second nature to recognize the class of address, the network number, and the host id.

Compared with other network addressing schemes, the TCP/IP IPv4 addressing range is quite limited. IPv6 overcomes these limitations.

The IAB and network number registration

Since addresses in an internetwork must be unique, there has to be a registry which ensures that such a policy can be enforced.

TCP/IP was developed for use on the Internet. This collection of networks is managed by many different authorities, with the IAB as overall design authority. In this environment of devolved management, the network number has two functions. First, since each IP address on the whole set of interconnected networks must be unique, the network number is used to identify one addressing authority (often called an autonomous system) responsible for issuing unique connection ids in that part of the address space. The second function is to support routing.

The IAB ensures that IP addresses on the Internet are unique, by registering and issuing network numbers to organizations that have reasons to connect to the Internet. Such organizations *do not choose* their own network number[†], it is issued to them. They agree to undertake

---

[†]Those who have followed the text carefully may have noticed that an organization appears to require use of many network numbers if routers are to operate correctly. The IAB will issue at most a few different network numbers to one organization, which will not, on its own, apparently satisfy the requirements for a large router network. The alternative is subnetting of a single network number which is described fully in Chapter 4.

certain network management responsibilities when they request an official IAB address allocation. They must then issue host ids so that they are unique within their own network number address space. If they fail to issue unique host numbers, only the services of that organization will be affected.

The IAB has devolved the clerical task of registering and issuing IP network numbers to the Internet Registry, part of the Internet Assigned Numbers Authority (IANA). The Internet Registry is operated by the Department of Defense Network Network Information Center (DDN NIC), now located in Chantilly, Virginia. The NIC has devolved address management to RIPE (Réseaux IP Européens) in Europe, to APNIC (Asia–Pacific Network Information Center) for the Pacific region, and to Internet service providers.

To register or not to register

For any commercial organization, applying to a registration authority for a registered network number ensures that your IP addresses are unique in the whole world (of those who have similarly registered). But as Table 3.1 showed, the IP address space, other than class C addresses, is limited with only 16 408 'large' networks. Class C gives a further 2.1 million small networks. As worldwide interest in TCP/IP has grown, the address space is already under some pressure with much of the class B address space already allocated and all the class A address space issued or reserved. There has to be good reason for allocating one or more registered class A or class B addresses from this finite resource.

In early 1995, the total number of hosts accessible from the Internet through the name service was 4.852 million. As not all registered addresses are connected to the Internet community, this is a very conservative number. Growth is already onto the vertical portion of an exponential growth curve.

When should an organization apply for an IP address registration? At least one Request For Comment (RFC) recommends that all users of TCP/IP should register. We endorse that policy but the following gives guidance on which organizations *must* register, in decreasing order of importance:

- Any organization that connects to the worldwide Internet has no option; they must request a registered network number.

- Any organization that wishes to communicate with a parent organization which is itself connected to the Internet is advised to register. Accidental duplicate addresses advertised to the true Internet do not make the advertising organization popular with the Network Operations Center.

- Organizations that have subsidiaries or that acquire subsidiaries which connect to the Internet should consider registering.

- Large multinationals that wish to use TCP/IP for worldwide communications but which perhaps have limited control or knowledge of the activities of individual operating companies should consider registering.

For those who *do* register there are additional issues to resolve:

- Larger organizations, with many thousands of employees worldwide, will prefer a class B or class A address. All class A addresses are allocated or reserved; recent allocations have been to governments outside the USA. Class B addresses with 65 534 connections are difficult to obtain.

- As we analyse the use of these IP addresses in TCP/IP, you will discover that the address space is consumed more quickly than might be expected; in practical networks, it often is not possible to use the available space efficiently. Large organizations will then require more than one class B address to satisfy their requirements.

- Most organizations that register will be forced to use one or more class C addresses. Unfortunately, class C addresses cannot have more than 254 connections on one bridged or switched LAN. This is unacceptable for those organizations that wish to use large port switching LANs within one building.

Advantages and disadvantages of registering

The key advantage of registering is ensuring that as you use and extend TCP/IP to new applications, which may include communicating with external organizations using TCP/IP, your address and naming conventions are protected. If you are not registered and an address clash occurs in the future then the onus must be on the nonregistered organization to make changes.

Those wishing to pursue registration further should contact the Network Information Center (contact details are given in Appendix A), an Internet service provider or, in Europe, the IP Information Centre (RIPE).

How to choose your own network number

If you decide that registration is unnecessary, then *do* consider carefully which address you choose.

The maximum likely size of the network is the most important factor which will influence the choice of IP address class. Private self-contained networks may use any or many different network numbers, though there are good reasons to limit the range of network numbers used.

It is important to keep IP addresses unique in any internetwork of intercommunicating TCP/IP machines. As networks grow and develop and as TCP/IP is used to communicate with other external companies (for example for Electronic Data Interchange, EDI), this will become more difficult if the network number is not registered and a large number of network numbers are in use. An address is more likely to be unique if the network number is registered. If your organization does not fall into that group which should register, then to reduce the likelihood of an address duplication with another organization in the future you should:

- Avoid class A addresses, for they are all allocated to the largest networks to which everyone connects.

- Do not copy examples given in manufacturers' handbooks, text-books or sales literature.

- Avoid well-known addresses published in TCP/IP RFCs and other documentation.

- Do use one, or a limited number, of class B addresses which are registered to organizations you never want to communicate with.

- Do use a limited number of class C addresses chosen in a similar way.

- Do use one or more of the network addresses reserved for private networks by RFC 1597.

If at some point you wish to communicate with organizations with which your addresses clash, or with the Internet, then all is not lost. A 'gateway' that performs address translation between the two networks will map addresses from one network to the other in a static or dynamic fashion.

Autonomous systems

An **autonomous system** (AS) is a collection of LANs and WANs and the interconnecting routers which are under the control of one management authority for configuration, addressing, naming and routing decisions. Decisions made within such an authority should not be visible to the rest of the interconnected Internet. Ideally, one commercial organization should form one autonomous system. The IAB also registers AS numbers that uniquely identify an autonomous system.

The concept of autonomous systems is extended in the Internet to the Autonomous Confederation, a group of autonomous systems with a common interest which requires them to establish direct links to each other rather than route through the core Internet. The term autonomous confederation has a less clear value to commercial organizations unless they cannot achieve a single centralized control authority. This term seems to be falling into disuse with changes in Internet policy.

Autonomous system numbers

As well as registering a network number, commercial organizations should now register an AS number. The AS number is used by routers with the newer OSPF and BGP routing protocols to identify which AS is the source of routing information. This forms part of a low-level security facility.

Some organizations have registered more than one AS number. AS numbers can only distinguish 65535 different organizations so, in due course, this could become another scarce resource, with the rapid growth in interest in internetworking with TCP/IP.

Private network addresses

In March 1994, the IAB recognized the need for IP addresses for private networks, that is, for those networks not connected to the Internet. In an advisory document known as RFC 1597 (Address Allocation for Private Internets), they reserved three address ranges for use in private internets. They are:

10.0.0.0	– 10.255.255.255	1 Class A network
172.16.0.0	– 172.31.255.255	16 Class B networks
192.168.0.0	– 192.168.255.255	256 Class C networks

This RFC is an informational document only – it is not an accepted IAB standard.

Where companies that use these addresses become Internet connected, they must obtain one or more registered addresses and use address translation routers so that a registered address is seen on the Internet. Such techniques are now well proven and have considerable security advantages for commercial organizations where it may be undesirable that every workstation can be seen from the Internet.

RFC 1597 was not universally applauded; in July 1994, RFC 1627, [Network 10 Considered Harmful (Some Practices Shouldn't be Codified)] was issued. The authors of RFC 1627 argue that the deliberate duplication of addresses proposed in RFC 1597 is restrictive, reduces network reliability and security and will be costly in the long term. RFC 1627 argues that IP addresses can become embedded in software, and that changing IP addresses throughout an organization is costly; by adopting the address ranges of RFC 1597, an organization inevitably has an address clash in due course and must change addresses. It also argues that it is impossible to predict which machines must be visible from the Internet and hence the basis of using registered or unregistered addresses is unsatisfactory. It argues that the IAB should continue to promote only the use of registered addresses, even where those systems are not at first Internet connected.

Configuring the IP address

Every computer, workstation, personal computer, network router and network management station which 'speaks IP' must have a different IP address for each of its connections. The IP address is entered through the normal configuration management processes. IP addresses are usually represented and entered in dotted decimal notation; occasionally dotted hexadecimal notation is accepted. The address is usually stored in nonvolatile memory, either RAM or on a disk file when available.

Diskless workstations often have no nonvolatile storage. They obtain their IP address across the network at start-up time using BOOTP or RARP.

Visiting each device to change the IP address is time-consuming, particularly in dispersed networks. BOOTP and DHCP provide mechanisms for centralizing the distribution of IP addresses and other useful TCP/IP parameters, even for machines which do have storage. The key to distributing the correct IP address and other information via BOOTP/ DHCP is the MAC address of the interface card. It is then *essential* to record accurately the MAC address used by each machine on the network that uses the BOOTP service. This is excellent policy for fault diagnosis and security in any case, though it is often neglected.

BOOTP uses a static table to map MAC address to IP address. As its name suggests, DHCP can dynamically allocate IP addresses from an unused pool of IP addresses to new requesting workstations.

In an operational network, IP addresses become recorded in distributed tables and in software in machines. While this is bad practice, it is unavoidable. Frequent wholesale changes to IP addresses must not occur, so preplanning is essential. Such changes are labour-intensive because of the widespread distribution of addresses; the change introduces errors and has unpredictable consequences for the integrity of operational applications and for the time taken to restore any-to-any communications.

Reserved IP addresses

Certain IP network numbers and host numbers are reserved for the use of particular aspects of TCP/IP communication. If you configure a connection with a reserved IP address, the faults caused are likely to be obscure, apparently intermittent and difficult to isolate. Not all host software checks (or is even able to check under all circumstances) that the IP address it is requested to use is valid.

The following addresses are reserved:

- Network number 127.X.X.X, where X.X.X is any set of numbers. This is used for a local software loopback test.[†]

- A network number of all 0s is classless and means 'my current network which I do not know the number of' – sometimes referred to as 'this network'.

- A network number of all 1s with a particular class.

- Host number 0 is reserved to refer to a particular network number. For example, 192.0.1.1 is the first class C network address which could be allocated.

- Host number 'all 1s' is reserved to broadcast to all hosts on a specific network; it can only be used as a destination address.

- The full address 0.0.0.0 is reserved. It is used in two ways: as a source address when the host does not know its genuine address, for example during bootstrapping of a diskless workstation, and by routers in a list of addresses to advertise the default route, the route to all networks which are not explicitly listed. (It is not a source or destination address, merely an entry in a table.)

- The full address 255.255.255.255 is reserved as a destination address to mean 'broadcast to all hosts on my network'. 0.0.0.0 as a destination is an obsolete form of 255.255.255.255.

Further addresses become reserved when subnetworking is introduced. These are more difficult to recognize. Subnetworking is discussed in Chapter 4.

IP addresses with routers and dial-up devices

Some older router implementations require that a point-to-point wide-area PTT or dial-up link between two LANs should be identified with its own unique IP network number with only two connections attached. In the larger network this is wasteful of the limited resource of IP network numbers. Check with your router manufacturer that the most modern techniques, which conserve network and subnetwork numbers, are used in their implementation.

Common mistakes in choosing IP addresses

Common mistakes in choosing and managing IP addresses centre around the possibility of address duplication or using the wrong network number for the LAN to which the port is attached. This arises through the following:

[†]IAB standards say that any address beginning with 127. must not be transmitted across the physical interface and appear on the cable. Not all software implementations check and reject IP addresses beginning with 127 and some will transmit IP datagrams with that source or destination address. This has been known to cause networks to fail.

- Not controlling the issuing of addresses (and subaddresses) centrally, or at a sufficiently high point in the organizational tree.
- Using the example in the software manufacturer's literature.
- Giving a supplier the responsibility of choosing and configuring an IP addressing scheme without understanding the overall needs of the organization.
- Copying the addresses from another part of the organization.
- Duplicating the address from the machine next door.
- Choosing an address from a nearby machine and modifying it slightly.
- Not fully understanding the concept of network and host number.
- Misunderstanding that workstations on the same LAN must use the same network number.
- Misunderstanding that stations either side of a router must have different network numbers.
- Using a reserved network number or host number.
- Failing to anticipate how and why IP addresses may change at a later date and avoiding that change.

The organizational structure and the IP address

Allocating TCP/IP addresses in larger companies raises political and organizational issues. If no scheme for address allocation has been developed and agreed, the first people to introduce TCP/IP may find themselves attempting to take addressing decisions on behalf of the whole organization, but without the necessary authority and influence to carry their decisions through.

If you are in that position, you either take up the challenge of agreeing the address structure for the whole organization or you take the pragmatic approach to make a local decision and trust that it will not cause problems with address clashes or major updates later. Be assured that it will. In a changing environment, this pragmatic decision will eventually rebound in increased catchback costs, for, even if address clashes do not occur, the address will change as routers are introduced in the growing network.

The second organizational issue of IP addressing is that IP addresses are entered into the software of applications computers. Network routers also use IP addresses to communicate among themselves and with host computers. In large networks, network routers and application processors may be controlled by different managements. The addressing authority must issue IP addresses, but they may not be welcome if they attempt to configure them in the larger mini and mainframe application processors. The central authority described in Chapter 1 must be able to enforce IP address configuration and even reconfiguration decisions equally on the owners and operators of host processors and network routers. Fortunately, once addresses have been allocated they should not change frequently, if the network has been well designed. But over the life of even a well-designed network, it is to be expected that some address reconfiguration will be necessary because of activities in another department.

Moves and changes

It is a feature of life in many organizations that staff move office location regularly. If their PC or workstation at the new location is in a different network number or subnetwork number, the IP address must change. This may have a consequential impact on other levels of TCP/IP, the domain name service, mail, and on other parameters of the machine's software (default router, BOOTP server, domain name server). These issues are fully explained in Chapter 18.

Record keeping

If TCP/IP management is to be successful, there must be records of each IP address and where, how, and by whom it is used. Some features of TCP/IP require a record of the Ethernet or Token Ring MAC address associated with the IP address. BOOTP and DHCP supply the IP address for a specific MAC address; domain name service supplies an IP address given the host domain name, or, given an IP address, will supply the host domain name.

To keep these records up to date requires proper clerical procedures, training of clerical staff and the correct vetting of entries by software, so that the task becomes routine. The aim of system managers must be to reduce the amount of skilled time consumed by such clerical activities.

Subnetting

The network manager has an immediate need: to solve the issue of network numbering on either side of a router when only one network number can be used. The solution, introduced in 1985, is called **subnetwork addressing** and it is now standard on all TCP/IP equipment. This is such an important topic that the next chapter discusses it in detail.

IP Version 6 addresses

The IPv4 addressing scheme appears to give access to over 2 100 000 networks with a total of 3720 million hosts. This seems a large number even given the number of PCs in use. Not all of them are yet using TCP/IP. But because of the strict divisions between network numbers and host numbers, the address space is now under considerable pressure. For example, an organization may have a class B address for 10 000 hosts and the other 55 000 host addresses are effectively lost to the Internet community.

The advent of the personal computer running TCP/IP, with each requiring an individual IP address, coupled with the worldwide success of the IPS, has revealed the limitations of IPv4 addressing. For example, in the mid-1990s, allocations of registered addresses to large organizations have been of multiple class C networks because registered class B network addresses are now a scarce resource.

Starting in 1990, the IETF studied methods of overcoming these limitations. By late 1994, it had agreed the 'IP Next Generation' (known as IPng) for the long-term solution to addressing and other technical limitations of IPv4. This version is known as IP Version 6 (IPv6).

IPv6 uses 128-bit addresses. A design aim of IPng was that it should support at least 1000 million networks each of many addressable devices, an aim which is met in excess by 128-bit addressing. The concept of network number and host number remains for routing and for addressing of individual machines. However, there is much more structure in the way network numbers are used, leading to hierarchical routing and a significant improvement in the efficiency of the worldwide communications system that the IPS has become.

We consider three features of IPv6 to be particularly important:

(1) Workstations will be self-configuring, determining their own network number and unique host number. This reduces the costs of installation, moves and changes.

(2) Individual IPv6 systems can be installed, or IPv4 upgraded to IPv6, while continuing to interoperate with IPv4 systems. IPv6 will therefore support a phased implementation while coexisting with IPv4 systems.

(3) A single IPv6 network number can support an unlimited number of hosts. (The concept of Class has disappeared.) Large networks without routers are essential if the maximum benefit is to be gained from LAN switching hubs and Asynchronous Transfer Mode (ATM) transmission systems.

The 128-bit IPv6 address can contain an IPv4 32-bit address. By adding a unique registered address modifier to an unregistered IPv4 address, that unregistered address can be used on the Internet without other modification.

Other features allow for automatic configuration of mobile and portable systems which may be temporarily connected anywhere in the internetwork.

As requirements for these IPv6 systems emerge, a network manager must plan IPv6 addresses and upgrade routers in the network to support the two Network Layer Protocols simultaneously – IPv6 and IPv4. Routers can relay information between older systems which understand only IPv4 and newer systems which operate to either IPv6 or IPv4.

In time, though it may be a long time, IPv6 is likely to replace IPv4 as the single network layer protocol.

Summary

Choosing whether to register a network number, choosing a network number, and planning and then controlling the IP addressing scheme for a TCP/IP internetwork are the most important initial managerial tasks. In large, multisite networks the management problem must be subdivided using different network numbers for different sites, for different buildings or even different floors. Network managers must establish and enforce the responsibilities for managing the different parts of the address space. Subnetworking, described in the next chapter, gives the network manager more local control of his or her portion of the IP address space.

The important points about IP addressing are:

- An IP address uniquely identifies the connection of a computer or router to the network.
- The IP address space must be correctly managed.
- Some organizations should apply for and be issued with a registered address from the DDN NIC.
- Where addresses are not registered, the whole IP address space is available for 'private' use but you should not use addresses quoted in suppliers' literature or given as examples in TCP/IP documentation.
- The IP address has two parts, a network number and a 'host' or connection number. The address is not hierarchical.
- The network number identifies a controlling organization, not the location of the network.
- Hosts will have a different IP address for each connection on the Internet. It is connections which are identified, not hosts.
- The class of address determines the maximum number of hosts which can share a single network number.
- Addresses should be unique in the interconnected network at all times.
- Do not allocate network 0.0.0.0 or 127.X.X.X.
- Do not allocate host id 0 or host id all 1s on any network number.
- Do keep accurate records of the use of IP addresses by each machine on the network, its location, who uses it and who controls its configuration.

- Do keep a record of all Ethernet or Token Ring addresses and their associated IP addresses, if you wish to use some of the features of TCP/IP such as BOOTP/DHLP.

- Stations in a bridged LAN should have the same network number; stations on either side of a router should have different network numbers.

- IP addresses are stored on each workstation, computer or router in the network. They may also be used by software and stored in applications or in other parts of the TCP/IP protocol suite.

- Changes to the IP addressing scheme in the larger operational network could be difficult and expensive to implement.

- Moving a machine from one location (floor, building, site) to another may require a change in IP address.

- IPv6 addresses, which are 128 bits wide, will overcome the limitations of IPv4 32-bit addresses.

4

Subnetworks and supernetworks

With the increase in the use of information technology, and hence in the number of attached computers in a typical corporate network, the strict class A, B and C divisions of the IP addressing scheme, as described so far, are too limiting. The solution introduced in the mid-1980s was subnetwork addressing or 'subnets'. In this chapter, we discuss what subnetwork addressing is and how it can be used to give the TCP/IP network planner much more control over the allocation and sizing of network numbers and subnetwork numbers.

The topics considered are:

- The need for subnetwork addressing
- The structure and format of the subnetwork mask
- Managing subnetworks
- Supernetworks
- Configuring the subnetwork mask
- Creating hierarchical subnetwork address structures
- Using variable length subnetwork masks

The purpose of subnetting and the subnetwork mask is to allow network managers to allocate different subnetwork numbers to each port of a router using only one registered network number. If selecting an IP addressing scheme is the first major decision the TCP/IP implementor must make, the second parallel decision is how to subdivide an IP network number so that organizations can make efficient use of the available address space. It is often important to devolve management of IP addresses to local departments to give them more control of their own network implementation.

To optimize the allocation of a limited address space the IAB will issue an organization with the smallest number of class B or C network numbers for the total required hosts. But network managers must be able to control the allocation not only of host numbers but also of network numbers if the standard TCP/IP mechanisms for using routers are to operate. These require that two stations on the same bridged LAN share the same network number; on either side of a router stations must have different network numbers. How can this be achieved if an organization has only one or a few network numbers available? The solution to this problem is **subnetworks** or subnetworking through the use of the **subnetwork mask**.

Subnetworking and the subnetwork mask

Subnetworking or **subnetting** increases the network manager's control over the address space and provides a mechanism for using routers when only one or a small number of full network numbers is available. The mechanism for creating subnetworks is the subnetwork mask, another 32-bit number which is configured at the same time as the IP address.

Subnetworking divides the normal range of host ids (16 million for class A, 65 534 for class B and 254 for class C) into a number of subnetworks and a reduced number of hosts on each subnetwork. The product of these two numbers cannot exceed the original number of host ids. So, subnetting of class C addresses leads to a small number of networks with a very few host addresses on each. Some implementations may not allow subnetting of class C addresses, though it is sometimes used in research departments with high-performance RISC-based workstations where a few devices can saturate one LAN cable.

When should you use subnetting?

The simple answer is: 'Always plan for it even if you don't use it initially'. If an IP addressing scheme is planned without subnetwork addressing, then it is likely to be very labour-intensive to introduce it later, as a large percentage of addresses will change. Planning ahead is key. Most network implementors should plan their address space on the basis of subnetworks rather than multiple network numbers.

Small networks that will not use routers need not use subnetworking. Such networks are never likely to grow beyond a few physical LANs and up to 200 stations. Also, if you do not need to use a registered address and do not mind how many IP network numbers you use, then there is less impetus to use subnetwork addressing. However, careful use of subnetwork addressing, rather than multiple network numbers, can simplify future network growth and change, so it has advantages.

The subnetwork mask

All TCP/IP equipment which operates the network layer IP protocol, and hence has an IP address, must be capable of using subnetting and the subnetwork mask. The subnetwork mask is the 'number' under the network manager's control which determines how the subnetworks are structured. When two network numbers are compared to determine if a router must be used, they are compared after being 'filtered' by the subnetwork mask.

Inappropriate choice of the subnetwork mask can lead to great confusion when one tries to explain how routing will operate. The following description is a simple starting point. The interaction between routing and the subnetwork mask is discussed further in Chapters 5 and 16.

The subnetwork mask is a 32-bit number that allows a network manager to choose the number of subnets and hosts on each subnetwork. There are still certain strict limits imposed by the basic structure of class A, B and C addresses. There cannot be a greater number of connections than the basic address gives; in practice the total number of available connections is less due to inefficiencies in the way subnets can be allocated. What you gain is flexibility and control. By defining your own subnetworks you have some freedom to place routers for your own convenience without having to use different network numbers.

The rule, shown in Table 4.1, is simple:

- If there is a 1 in a bit position in the subnetwork mask, that bit forms part of the subnetwork number in this address space.

- If there is a 0 in a bit position in the subnetwork mask, that bit is part of the host (or connection) id.

Table 4.1 The subnetwork mask.

	Binary	*Dotted decimal*
IP address	10000001.10000010.01001111.01010101	129.130.79.85
Subnet mask	11111111.11111111.11111000.00000000	255.255.248.0
Network id	10000001.10000010.01001000.00000000	129.130.72.0
Host id	00000000.00000000.00000111.01010101	0.0.7.85

Table 4.2   The default subnet masks.

Address class	Default mask dotted decimal	Default mask dotted hex
Class A	255.0.0.0	FF.0.0.0
Class B	255.255.0.0	FF.FF.0.0
Class C	255.255.255.0	FF.FF.FF.0

Even if you do not choose to manage subnetwork addressing on your network, all equipment will still use the technique because it will generate default subnetwork masks that select the normal class A (8-bit), class B (16-bit) or class C (24-bit) network numbers. Once a piece of equipment is configured with its IP address it examines the 'class bits' to set the correct **default mask** automatically.

Subnetwork masks are represented in the same format as normal IP addresses: dotted decimal or hexadecimal. The three default subnet masks are shown in Table 4.2. The network manager takes control of the address space by changing 0s to 1s in the mask, which successively halves the number of hosts and doubles the number of subnets available. *It is strongly recommended that these 1s are added from the left of the address and that no intermediate 0 gaps remain.* This is sometimes referred to as a **mask of contiguous 1s**. Some software enforces this recommendation.

Subnetworks are used by routers. You may be able to work out how your routers will respond to a mask which is not contiguous, for example:

11111111.11111111.00011111.00000000

But have some thought for those who follow behind you, however. If you make a great success of this network, you will be promoted, but someone less able may be coming along behind! For the long-term viability of the network and the sanity of those who follow, do keep life as simple as possible!

The complete range of class B subnet options is shown in Appendix D. This shows the number of subnet bits, the resulting mask and the first and last usable host addresses on each subnetwork, together with the subnetwork broadcast address and the address that describes 'this subnetwork'.

Because the subnet bits are added from the left of a byte (the most significant bit) but are then represented in dotted decimal notation, the third octet has an unfamiliar pattern to it. These mystical numbers are formed as shown in Table 4.3. Only these eight different numbers should be used in a subnet mask. If a number in the mask is not 255. the numbers to the left of it must be 255.

Reserved subnet numbers

Subnetting is further complicated because a subnet of all 1s and a subnet of all 0s cannot be used. All 1s is a broadcast to all subnets in this overall network number. A host id of 'all 1s' remains the broadcast to all hosts,

Table 4.3 How a mask octet is calculated.

Value of 3rd octet	How 3rd octet is calculated	Binary 'mask'
0	0	00000000
128	128	10000000
192	128+64	11000000
224	128+64+32	11100000
240	128+64+32+16	11110000
248	128+64+32+16+8	11111000
252	128+64+32+16+8+4	11111100
254	128+64+32+16+8+4+2	11111110
255	128+64+32+16+8+4+2+1	11111111

either on a specific subnetwork or on all subnetworks in this network number. This makes the range of useful addresses (see Appendix D) more restricted than might have been thought. Because 'all 1s' is reserved, the first useful class B subnets are not 128.1.0.0 and 128.1.128.0 with a subnet mask of 255.255.128.0 or FF.FF.80.00 as might be expected. These addresses cannot be used, as 128.1.0.x refers to 'host x on this subnetwork' and 128.1.255.255 is 'broadcast to all subnetworks in the network 128.1.0.0'. 128.1.255.255 could also be 'broadcast to all hosts on the subnet 128.1.128.0'. The two conditions cannot be distinguished and therefore this subnet range is not used.

The first usable mask is the next mask of 255.255.192.0 or FF.FF.C0.0, giving four subnet values, but with only two usable subnetwork numbers of 128.1.64.0 and 128.1.128.0. While 128.1.192.0 at first seems usable, the address 128.1.255.255 again means 'broadcast to all hosts on all subnets in network number 128.1.0.0'. There is no separate way of defining a broadcast to all hosts on the single subnet 128.1.192.0. Any address 128.1.0.xxx refers to host xxx on 'this subnet' not on the specific subnet 128.1.0.0, so that subnet is also unusable. This is another reason why the IP address space is not, in practice, as large as might be thought.

Keeping it simple – one value of subnet mask

When represented in dotted decimal, it can be difficult to recognize the broadcast to a single subnet. Address management and routing is much simpler if the same subnet mask is configured on all IP equipment that has the same network number. If more than one network number is available, different masks can be used with each number.

Before using different subnet masks at connections with the same network number, there are a number of implications for routing that must be fully understood for the particular manufacturer's equipment you have chosen to use. The use of different masks is not fully defined by today's standards.

Choosing a subnet mask

Moving the subnet mask boundary exchanges host numbers for subnet numbers. Hosts on different subnetworks cannot communicate directly; they must have an intervening router. So changing the subnet mask may equally be thought of as exchanging bridges for routers. Before choosing the subnet boundary, you must know:

- What is the largest subnetwork that you can successfully manage when it is interconnected with bridges alone?

- What are the cost, performance and management implications of using routers rather than bridges?

The first question implies that, as a network grows, bridges will be replaced by routers at strategic points and hence either addresses will change or the subnet mask will change on all equipment on either side of the new router.

The answers to these questions determine the upper and lower bounds to the maximum size of a single subnetwork. These decisions are important for, in an internetwork with a single subnet mask, *all subnetworks will have the same maximum size*. For initial simplicity, we just recommended that a single network number should use one subnet mask throughout the internetwork. In normal corporate networks, it is probable that there will be a few large subnetworks and a larger number of small networks. To optimize the use of the address space around the larger number of smaller networks, the larger networks may have to be subdivided into small subnetworks and interconnected by routers rather than bridges. As the price and performance of routers continues to improve, the performance and cost disadvantages of routers decrease, though the relative performance of bridges may be expected to improve in the same way. It may be appropriate to use more than one network number with different subnet masks[†] to cater for different size and traffic requirements.

So, the power of subnetting is that it allows the network design authority a degree of flexibility in organizing the address space and in developing a router network to suit the organization. The issue is that this flexibility is not as great as managers of the larger corporate network would desire; they are restricted unless they can use multiple network numbers or different length subnet masks in different parts of the networks.

Subnetting a class B and class C address

Most larger commercial networks use one or more class B addresses. (The principles of subnetting apply also to class C addresses; only the scale is different.)

[†]We explain how to achieve subnetworks of different sizes below.

The limits of a single class B address space are from 2 subnetworks of 16 382 hosts to 16 382 subnetworks of 2 hosts. It is likely that most managements will choose one of the following subdivisions of a class B network:

- 254 subnets of 254 hosts (quite small subnets)
- 126 subnets of 510 hosts
- 62 subnets of 1022 hosts
- 30 subnets of 2046 hosts (large subnets)

These figures produce an acceptable balance between the use of bridges and routers. It has been found that it becomes increasingly difficult to manage a large network consisting only of bridges. A network based only on routers is manageable but can be expensive. Subnet addressing with a mask of 255.255.255.0, giving 254 subnets of 254 hosts, is easier to explain and manage.

There are only two practical options for class C subnets: 14 nets of 14 hosts with a mask of 255.255.255.240 and 6 nets of 30 hosts with a mask of 255.255.255.224.

Configuring subnet masks

Subnet masks are entered into each device at the same time that its IP address is configured and are stored along with that address. In a large network, making any change to the subnet mask may involve visiting the equipment and manually changing the mask. Obviously, this is to be avoided, particularly in large, geographically spread networks. The boot protocol, BOOTP, allows the subnet mask and the IP address to be obtained from a central server. In Chapter 13, we describe how to distribute subnet masks and IP addresses using BOOTP and DHCP.

If you do not provide a subnet mask, the installation software generates the default mask at the time you configure the IP address, by examining the class bits of the address you enter.

TCP/IP standards do not specify how particular parameters should be entered into machines, for they do not specify the user interface. Different TCP/IP implementations accept the subnet mask in different ways. These are:

- The full mask in dotted decimal (or hexadecimal) format,
- The number of bits or 'extension' bits in the mask.

A command of the form:

```
netmask = 255.255.224.0
```

allows you to enter the full subnet mask in dotted decimal format; such an entry may allow any dotted decimal number to be input, but remember it is incorrect to do other than extend the default subnet mask with contiguous 1s. For this reason an alternative (and preferred) representation is the 'number of 1s' in the mask, using a command like

```
subnetbits = 19
```

This example also produces a mask of 255.255.224.0 since the mask consists of $8 + 8 + 3$ ones. Yet another implementation expects the user to enter the *extra* number of bits added to the default mask. In such a case, for a class B address:

```
bits = 3
```

specifies the mask 255.255.224.0, since the default mask of 255.255.0.0 already has 16 ones.

Difficulties with a single mask

A single subnet mask and network number cannot satisfactorily span all the requirements of the larger corporation unless a class A address is used and the risk of an address clash is discounted. With a class B address, it is possible to have spare address capacity in some smaller subnetworks and to have exhausted address capacity in the large networks, but be unable to transfer the unused addresses. Without the flexibility of variable subnet masks, the network manager must either simply live with inefficient allocation of the address space or use more than one network number, possibly with a different subnet mask for each number. Using more than one network number has an impact on the operation of routers. This is discussed fully in Chapter 5.

Subnetworking with a single mask introduces a second level of hierarchy into IP address management. If available the use of variable subnet masks would allow a full hierarchical structure, doubling the number of subnets and halving the nodes for each bit added to the mask. Such a hierarchical structure is useful for a large corporate network, as illustrated in Table 4.4 for a nonregistered class A[†] address. The first level of division in IP addressing is the network number, the second level is the site or location and the third level is the area or subnetwork within that site. Each area has its contingent of attached hosts. A class A address gives the network planner 24 bits to divide into sites, areas and hosts with full flexibility as to where the boundaries should be, at least when the decision is made. Once deployed in equipment, the flexibility is reduced if not eliminated.

[†]The technique applies equally to registered class A addresses but they are unobtainable.

Table 4.4   Hierarchical subnetting of a (nonregistered) class A address.

Network number	Site or location	Subnetwork or area	Host id
8 bits fixed	Variable width	Variable width	Variable width

This technique can be used to overcome the problem of changing a bridge for a router, provided the addresses have been chosen correctly in the first instance. Using a router in the presence of subnets begins to bring local geography into play. If all addresses in one building are chosen from one of the subnet address ranges (see next section) and all those in another building are chosen from a second and correctly adjacent range then, merely by changing the subnet mask for the network, each area can be part of one or of two subnetworks, according to choice.

Consider the example of Figure 4.1. Two sites are initially connected by remote bridges using a 2 Mbps digital circuit. Two buildings on each site are connected by fibre optic links from the same bridge. All have the same network number, 191.250.0.0. But the distribution of addresses in the two sites and two buildings is such that by changing the subnet mask, the two sites and buildings within sites can become different subnetworks. At stage 1 the mask is the default of 255.255.0.0 and there is only one network, as required for a fully bridged LAN. In stage 2, by changing the mask to 255.255.240.0 no IP addresses need be altered when routers are introduced between the sites. A second change of the subnetwork mask to 255.255.252.0 places the buildings in different subnetworks (stage 3).

Grouping addresses together in this manner also assists with fault finding. When a fault is discovered, the IP address of the faulty equipment immediately identifies the location of that equipment. If a number of devices in the same area are found to be faulty at the same time, it gives a good indication of where to begin looking for the fault.

Should traffic become unmanageable in a bridged LAN, the changes required to incorporate routing are simplified by subnetting. This is only possible because the upgrade is predicted and the addressing scheme is preplanned. The alternative is labour-intensive, with major changes to the IP addressing scheme required possibly simultaneously at different parts of the network, and having to take place outside normal working hours to avoid disruption.

The practice is rather different, however. By default each IP address and its corresponding subnet mask is configured at each attached workstation. Unless addresses and subnet masks can be managed and changed centrally, it is just as labour-intensive to change one bit of a subnet mask on each machine as it is to change a complete IP address. There is increasing justification for managing and distributing IP addresses and subnet masks centrally through the BOOTP or DHCP.

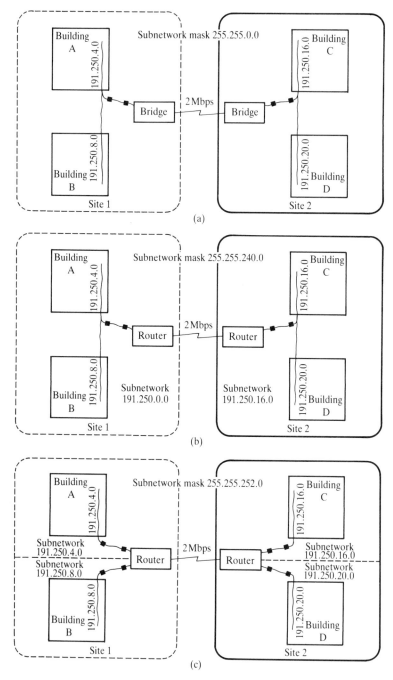

Figure 4.1 Planning routers using subnet addressing. (a) All one network.
(b) Two subnetworks. (c) Four subnetworks.

A class B hierarchical network

The network number in an IP address does not contain any concept of a geographic location, only of a controlling authority. The IP addressing scheme is not hierarchical. But since the subnet portion of the address is totally under the control of the autonomous system manager, he or she can introduce a geographic component into the address if there is value in so doing.

The following is an example of what can be achieved within a single class B address. IP addresses can be allocated to different geographic sites, in blocks which are on a high-numbered binary boundary. Buildings within a site can be allocated on binary boundaries lower down the hierarchy, according to the number of host addresses they require.

For example, suppose Integralis Ltd has been allocated the class B addresses 191.250.0.0. They wish to cover up to 16 sites with a maximum of 4000 devices on a site. There are up to four large buildings on each site. By using a subnet mask of six extra bits, that is, a mask of 255.255.252.0, there are 64 networks (of which 62 are usable) each with 1022 hosts. The result is shown in Table 4.5. The progression of addresses seems perhaps strange, because the boundaries are determined by binary bit patterns which are then expressed in decimal. It is important that those who configure TCP/IP equipment are fully familiar with the addressing scheme and the subnet addressing scheme. They should be able to spot instantly any peculiarities in a chosen address. It is worthwhile spending some time in studying the examples given.

Such a scheme is wasteful of address space where not all sites are of equal size. But it introduces a true, hierarchical address space where certain bits designate a site, certain bits designate a building and other bits can specify a floor. Some further flexibility can be achieved with the correct combination of bridges and routers.

Note also the scheme is based on geography which may not exactly correspond with an organizational structure. Individual groups in the organization must accept that they are allocated a specific address by a central authority. With care it is possible to allocate a block of addresses, but meeting the needs of groups of widely different sizes may mean that strict geographic boundaries are infringed. Each time such guidelines are infringed it will complicate future changes.

Using a subnet mask of 255.255.255.0 for a class B network simplifies management at the expense of more routers. The third octet will indicate the site or building number directly with no confusion to boundaries.

Using different subnet masks

Using a single subnet mask can lead to exhaustion of part of the address space, while other parts may have spare capacity which cannot be trans-

Table 4.5 A hierarchical class B network with a mask of 255.255.252.0.

Site	Building	Network number	First host	Last host	Comment
		191.250.0.0	191.250.1.1	191.250.3.254	Range not usable – seen as 'this subnetwork'
1	1		191.250.4.1	191.250.7.254	
	2		191.250.8.1	191.250.11.254	
	3		191.250.12.1	191.250.15.254	
2	1	191.250.16.0	191.250.16.1	191.250.19.254	
	2		191.250.20.1	191.250.23.254	
	3		191.250.24.1	191.250.27.254	
	4		191.250.28.1	191.250.31.254	
	⋮	⋮	⋮	⋮	
	⋮	⋮	⋮	⋮	
15	1	191.250.224.0	191.250.224.1	191.250.227.254	
	2		191.250.228.1	191.250.231.254	
	3		191.250.232.1	191.250.235.254	
	4		191.250.236.1	191.250.239.254	
16	1	191.250.240.0	191.250.240.1	191.250.243.254	
	2		191.250.244.1	191.250.247.254	
	3		191.250.248.1	191.250.251.254	
	–		191.250.252.1	191.250.254.254	Range not usable – seen as 'broadcast to all stations, this subnet'

ferred. In RFC 1219, P. Tsuchiya of Bellcore has suggested a technique which reduces these problems.

For this method to be successful, it requires an initial judgement of the maximum number of subnets and the maximum size of subnetworks. It also requires the use of **variable length subnet masks**[†] and of routers that understand, exchange and interpret variable length subnet masks. To date, the use of variable length subnet masks is still under discussion by the Internet Engineering Task Force[‡] (IETF); not all routers can be guaranteed to handle these in the same way.

The principles of the scheme are fairly simple, but the details could be difficult to implement in a real network with devolved management, unless there is close cooperation and a very good technical understanding of subnet masking.

[†]While the term 'variable length subnet masks' is frequently used, and we shall continue that use, the mask is always a fixed length of 32 bits – it is the number of contiguous 1s that varies.

[‡]The IETF is the committee of technical experts that has responsibility for the RFCs which are to become full IAB standards. They also vet all RFCs before general release.

The principle is that subnet numbers are allocated from the top of the mask boundary working downwards, while host ids are allocated from the bottom up. Some space is allocated between subnet bits and host bits for growth of either the number of subnetworks or the number of hosts. As the network develops this growth space can be allocated to hosts or to additional subnetworks as required. The procedure can become complex at the point an additional growth bit is allocated to either host or subnet; it requires a full understanding of the implications and careful coordination across different subnet addressing authorities in an organization. Those who require more detail should refer to RFC 1219.

Variable length subnet masks only work with routers that can exchange masks as part of their routing tables. This limits the choice of routing protocol and is discussed in Chapter 5. It may be impossible to broadcast throughout a number of subnets reliably if a variable length subnet mask is used.

Supernetworks, bridging and switching

As discussed in the next chapter, the standardized way to communicate between hosts which have IP addresses in different network numbers is via a router. Where an organization has been allocated a number of registered class C addresses, but has more than 254 hosts, there is apparently no option but to use routers to communicate between these different class C networks. Newer technologies such as high-speed switching hubs and 'cut-through' hubs operate at the medium access control layer (like bridges) and therefore cannot be used to the greatest effect if routers are present too.

Supernetworking is a technique which can overcome this limitation, if it is available in host and router software. Class C networks can then be aggregated together to form a smaller number of larger (bridged) networks, reducing the number of routers and making the optimum use of bridges and switches.

Supernetworking is achieved by using bits which belong to the *network address* as host bits. This is realized by altering the default class C subnet mask such that some of the bits which relate to the network address are set to 0 instead of 1s. This technique is not yet standardized; not all host software will allow a mask with fewer '1' bits than the default for a given class to be configured.

When the Network Information Center issues multiple class C addresses in one allocation to an organization with a requirement for more than 254 hosts, it will issue the addresses in multiples of 2, 4, 8, 16 or even 32 network numbers; those network numbers will be chosen so that they are on a 'binary boundary' – that is, some bits in the network address remain constant for that organization and that organization alone. For example, one organization requiring 1000 addresses might have four class C networks, 222.231.32.0, 222.231.33.0, 222.231.34.0,

222.231.35.0; another organization requiring 1000 addresses could have 222.231.36.0, 222.231.37.0, 222.231.38.0, 222.231.39.0. In this case, 32 and 36 in the third octet are both multiples of 4, the number of networks allocated.

Example

Using default class C mask and no supernetworking

With the default class C mask the following addresses are recognized as different, as the last two bits in the third octet (shown in italics) are different for each address, so software will request the services of a router. Software compares all bits under the '1' bits of the subnet mask to determine the effective network number.

```
11111111 11111111 111111 11  00000000 = mask 255.255.255.0
11010100 11011101 001000 00  00000000 = net 222.231.32.0
11010100 11011101 001000 01  00000000 = net 222.231.33.0
11010100 11011101 001000 10  00000000 = net 222.231.34.0
11010100 11011101 001000 11  00000000 = net 222.231.35.0
```

Modified class C mask giving supernetworking

If we modify the mask, setting some of the third octets bits to zero (shown in italics), a comparison of the address bits does not reveal a difference so software will not request the services of a router and will use ARP to acquire a direct connection to a node.

```
11111111 11111111 111111 00  00000000 = mask 255.255.252.0
11010100 11011101 001000 00  00000000 = net 222.231.32.0
11010100 11011101 001000 01  00000000 = net 222.231.33.0
11010100 11011101 001000 10  00000000 = net 222.231.34.0
11010100 11011101 001000 11  00000000 = net 222.231.35.0
```

This means that the address 222.231.32.0 with the mask 255.255.252.0 identifies all the networks of the first organization, and 222.231.36.0 with the same mask identifies the second organization. It also means that by using a mask of 255.255.252.0 these organizations can have a single bridged network of 1022 hosts, or with a mask of 255.255.254.0, they can have two bridged networks of 510 hosts.

This technique may not yet be widely available in host software and therefore should be approached with some caution. However, it does form the basis of Classless Inter-Domain Routing (CIDR) or route aggregation for routers. This is an important feature of the Internet and is particularly important to Internet service providers.

Discussion documents within the IETF suggest that host software may also be modified to allow classless networking.

Summary

Subnetting is an integral part of the IP addressing scheme. The two topics cannot be separated. In Chapter 3 we said that planning and then controlling the IP addressing scheme for a TCP/IP internetwork is the most important initial managerial task. In large multisite networks, the management problem must be further subdivided using either different network numbers or different subnet numbers for different sites, for different buildings or even different floors. The preferred mechanism for local management of the IP addressing scheme is subnetting with the subnet mask.

The important points about subnetwork addressing are:

- Subnetting allows the network manager to create different 'network numbers' (actually subnet numbers) from one IAB network number.

- Stations in a bridged LAN should have the same subnetwork number; stations on either side of a router should have different subnetwork numbers.

- Subnetworks should be planned from the outset as an integral part of the IP addressing scheme.

- Subnet masks should be generated from the default subnet mask for the address class in use by adding contiguous 1s starting from the most significant bits.

- Subnetwork 0 or subnetwork all 1s must not be allocated for the particular subnet mask in use.

- Host id 0 or host id all 1s must not be allocated on any network or subnetwork.

- The subnetwork mask should be added to the records of each machine on the network.

- Subnetting can produce a hierarchical or geographic-based address structure.

- Subnetting can protect the network from IP address changes as routers are introduced in the larger growing network.

- The choice of subnet mask affects the ratio of bridges and routers in a network.

- Until the implications of doing otherwise are fully understood, the same subnet mask should be used with a single network number.

- Like IP addresses, subnet masks are stored on each workstation, computer or router in the network.

- The subnetwork mask is today an integral part of the IP addressing scheme; any changes, particularly in the larger operational network, could be difficult and expensive to implement.

- Moving a machine from one location (floor, building, site) to another may result in a change in IP address and its associated subnet mask.
- Supernetworks.

5

Routing

Routing, the feature within the TCP/IP protocol suite which allows the 'best' path between two communicating systems to be chosen for a given application, depends on the correct choice of equipment and routing software. In this chapter we examine the choices available and the decisions to be taken.

The topics considered are:

- The need for routers
- What routing is
- Routers and IP
- Routing advantages
- Routers and the IP address
- Routing tables
- Choosing a routing protocol
- RIP, OSPF, integrated IS-IS, BGP, IGRP, Hello, EGP and GGP
- Configuring routers

The need for routers and their management

When designing and managing the IP internetwork, the router network is important to the overall stability and performance of any system based on TCP/IP. Particularly for larger networks of more than 250 devices, routers provide the network manager with more control over traffic flows and the containment of faults than does a network composed solely of bridges.

Routers (or **gateways** as they were originally called in TCP/IP literature) existed in TCP/IP networks before the simpler and lower cost bridge was introduced to LAN technology in the mid-1980s. In early commercial use of TCP/IP, UNIX systems were used as routers. UNIX systems are still delivered with routing software and any multihomed host can become a router. Indeed, if the default configuration of some UNIX implementations is not altered, any multihomed host will become a router!

Successful routing is complex and processor-intensive. Current recommendations are that routers should be computers reserved for that purpose and not shared as application servers. Not only does this leave computing power for delivering applications, but it clearly also separates the two different functions of communications management and applications management, a division which, if not enforced, can lead to conflicts of interest.

Routers are programmed to interpret Internet protocols. They take an active role in TCP/IP networks and must be managed as part of the IP addressing scheme.

What is routing?

Routing is the process by which two communicating stations 'find' and use the optimum (best) path across an internetwork of any complexity. The process has several components:

- Determining what paths are available.
- Selecting the 'best' path for a particular purpose.
- Using those paths to reach other systems.
- Adjusting the datagram formats to fit the underlying technology.

In routing, these decisions are made using the network number of the network layer address.

Routers and IP

The devices which perform routing based on IP addresses are (IP) routers. Historically, routers in TCP/IP have been called (IP) gateways, but since, in OSI, the terms 'router' and 'gateway' describe two different

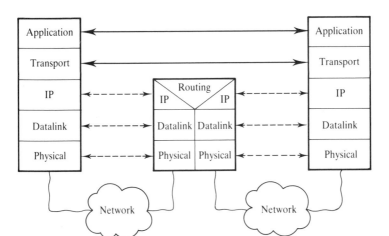

Figure 5.1   Routing with IP.

functions, we shall use the more modern term 'router' throughout, except
where quoting an RFC standard which uses the word 'gateway'. TCP/IP
literature has begun to use 'router' rather than 'gateway', but routing protocols are still referred to as gateway protocols in existing terms such as
GGP, IGP, IGRP, EGP and even in the recent BGP. (These terms will be
explained later.)

True network layer routing is performed in the IP layer of TCP/IP
and uses the network number or subnetwork portion of the IP address to
make routing decisions. The router relays IP datagrams between the IP
layers of end systems (Figure 5.1).

Features of IP also allow routing decisions to be made on type of
service, precedence, security and predefined routing options specified by
the communicating partners. These predefined fixed routing options are
called loose and strict source routing (see Chapter 11).

Routers must support **fragmentation**. This is the ability to
subdivide received information into smaller units where this is required
to match the underlying network technology. Fragmentation would occur
when a router relayed an 8000-octet datagram from a 16 Mbps Token
Ring to a 4 Mbps Token Ring which can only support 4472-octet frames.
If each of the fragments was subsequently relayed to an ISO 8802.3 network with SNAP encapsulation it might be further fragmented into two
1492-octet frames and one shorter frame. Each fragment must have its
own IP header, and after fragmentation the parts are treated as independent datagrams which can follow different paths. While fragmentation is
normally invisible to the application programmer and application user,
it can produce some bizarre effects for the network manager trying to
optimize the use of limited resources. In general, repeated fragmentation
in a network is undesirable because of the overhead of fragmentation in

routers, the extra headers and the processing power for reassembly. Where options are available[†] they should be set to avoid fragmentation.

This is a level of functionality not available in bridges.

Routing advantages

Why use IP routing rather than the much simpler and less costly bridges? The key points are:

- Better choice of routes,
- Matching different link-level technologies,
- Resilience and control,
- Error reporting.

While these are features of the IP standards, not all end systems and commercial routers support them.

Modern routers are designed so that the routing complexity is contained within a relatively small number of powerful multiprocessor machines specifically designed for the task. Hosts use simpler methods to discover and use their nearest and best router for the communications task in hand. This leaves all the processing power in the host and workstation end systems for the task that they should really be doing, processing the users' data, not expending effort trying to be a good communications processor. Applications processes should be performed in machines chosen for that specific task; likewise network relaying and communications should be devolved to specialist processors designed for that intensive process.

Better choice of route

Routers, using the best modern routing protocols, can have multiple parallel operational links, can find any available alternative route and will share traffic across those paths according to criteria established by the network manager and by software in the communicating hosts.

Matching different link-level technologies

Long-distance (wide area) point-to-point links and the variety of ISO/IEEE LAN standards have very different performance and data transmission characteristics. It is not possible to disguise the detail of the underlying technology from a bridge. A router is specifically designed to take account of the differences as it is made aware of maximum transmission units (related to frame data size) and can convert with fragmentation.

[†]To configure the maximum transmission unit, described below and in Chapter 11.

Resilience and control

Routers form an integral part of network layer protocols and network layer addressing. End systems (hosts) can choose one specific router to relay information. Routers will not relay MAC layer broadcast frames. They act as a barrier between network areas and prevent the propagation of certain types of faults (broadcast storms) from one area to another. Routers only act upon IP datagrams that are sent specifically to them.

Error reporting

Routers and hosts must use a protocol called the Internet Control Message Protocol (ICMP) to report and record error conditions and to try to control network congestion.

Routers and the link layer

While routers are network layer devices, they must encapsulate their network layer information in link layer frames. The issues of MAC layer encapsulation raised in Chapter 2 apply to routers. All manufacturers must support DIX Ethernet and SNAP encapsulation on ISO networks.

Routers and the IP address

Routers and end systems use the network number or subnetwork number to decide how to relay a particular IP packet (IP datagram). As described in Chapter 3, there is a very close correspondence between the network layout and structure (due to the geography of the organization) and the (subnetwork) address plan. Any change in the location of a host or workstation computer may mean that its IP address must change. (Its domain name may remain the same.)

A connection on a router is an IP connection on the network number or subnetwork number to which it attaches. Every router port can be the source or destination of IP datagrams. This is how a router knows which networks it is directly attached to. The router must be configured with IP addresses and subnet masks for each of its network connections. This is normally done through the hardware terminal port on the router chassis.

Workstations and dial-up TCP/IP

Workstations and PCs that dial in to a different TCP/IP network must have a valid IP address for the network they call into. There are three low-level protocols that support dial-in:

Table 5.1 Subnetting a class C address for point-to-point router connections.

Link no.	'A' end IP address	'B' end IP address	Comment
–	223.250.250.0		Not usable
1	223.250.250.1	223.250.250.2	
–	223.250.250.3		Not usable
2	223.250.250.5	223.250.250.6	
3	223.250.250.9	223.250.250.10	
4	223.250.250.13	223.250.250.14	
5	223.250.250.17	223.250.250.18	

- Serial Line Internet Protocol (SLIP)
- Compressed SLIP (CSLIP)
- Point-to-Point Protocol (PPP)

SLIP is a simple protocol which does not have the status of an IAB standard, though it is described in an RFC. SLIP does not allow the calling device to determine its IP address; it must be preconfigured. PPP is a more flexible protocol that has been accepted as a full IAB standard. Loosely based on ISO 7776 HDLC, PPP has a negotiation phase which allows a calling device to determine an acceptable IP address for that physical connection. The details of PPP are discussed in Chapter 10.

As these protocols can be used across slow-speed dial-up links, versions providing compression both for TCP and IP headers and for user data are available.

Routers with point-to-point wide area circuits

A router can be the source and destination of IP datagrams, so each of its connections must have an IP address with the appropriate network number. Where two routers connect two LANs over a point-to-point PTT-provided circuit, some router implementations require that this single intermediate circuit has its own unique network or subnetwork number. This is unsatisfactory. In a large network it will consume considerable numbers of network or subnetwork ids; more recent router implementations do not require point-to-point circuits to be explicitly labelled.

It may be appropriate to use a different network number and subnet mask for these point-to-point links. The subnet mask can be 255.255.255.252, which leaves two usable addresses for each end of the link; the addresses would progress ending in 1 and 2, 5 and 6, 9 and 10, 13 and 14, 17 and 18.... Addresses ending in 0 and 3, 4 and 7, 8 and 11... cannot be used as they are the 'this network' and 'broadcast' identifiers for the subnet. A single class C address could be partitioned into 64 subnets and thus support 64 point-to-point links. This is illustrated in Table 5.1.

When two routers from different manufacturers are connected together over point-to-point leased telephone company (PTT) circuits, there is no guarantee that they will work together unless both manufacturers have implemented the identical link-level protocols on the circuit. Even where two manufacturers claim to use the same protocol, the two routers may not interoperate when joined by a point-to-point link. If interoperability is important at this level, check with the manufacturers that it has been tested.

The accepted wide area protocol for routers is PPP. PPP is a low-level protocol that can be used by routers on point-to-point circuits; it is not a 'router protocol' or 'routing protocol'[†].

Routing tables

Every router contains a **routing table** of the network numbers (or sub-network numbers) that it knows about. The table records which router connection(s) can be used to reach a particular network and some indication of the performance or cost of using that connection to reach that network number. TCP/IP routing is based on a knowledge of only the 'next hop' in the path to the destination network number and host. To use an analogy from the road network, routers do not keep a 'road map' of the complete network, rather they have a set of 'signposts' with 'distances' or 'speed limits'. At each 'crossroads' (the next router), the next signpost is consulted to find the direction of the shortest or fastest path there. Like the road network, occasionally something turns a road sign around; traffic then takes a less than optimum route, or may even go round in circles.

In the simplest and older routing protocols the measure of performance of a particular link is the number of hops (routers) that have to be traversed to get to the destination network. Such a simple measure can lead to the use of totally anomalous routes.

One routing option is **static routing**. This may be appropriate where the network is small or because network managers wish to enforce a fixed routing policy for security or operational reasons. Static routing tables are generated manually by the network manager and loaded into the router either through the control port or across network links. Such a procedure is error-prone and cannot give the best response to network and wide area link failures. It becomes increasingly difficult to manage as the numbers of networks and routers increases, and only a limited number of routes and alternative routes can be devised and managed successfully by hand.

It is unusual in a closed corporate TCP/IP environment to implement static table-based routing. It is more usual to allow the routers to operate a routing protocol or interior gateway protocol (IGP) which will update routing tables dynamically. Routers exchange information about network numbers they are aware of and of the performance of the routes to those networks, on a regular basis, using the routing protocol. These

---

[†]A routing protocol allows routers to describe and exchange routing tables and updates.

exchanges provide routing table updates as conditions change. So 'routing protocols' are used not to perform routing but to exchange information about available routes and, in some cases, about their performance. The skill in designing routing protocols is to ensure that changing conditions and routes are tracked quickly throughout the internet without producing temporary routing anomalies or using up all available (wide area) capacity with routers exchanging routing information rather than useful user data.

Classless inter-domain routing (CIDR)

By default, a routing table will contain an entry for every network number or subnetwork number that exists. In an isolated corporate network these tables will, at most, be a few hundred entries. In the global Internet, there are potentially hundreds of thousands of operational networks, which would require an impossibly large table.

Such problems are solved in other network technologies by hierarchical routing: part of the address space is used to route to a continent, another part for routing to a country, yet another part for an area or organization within the country and finally to a site or building. This reduces the size of the table but can waste address space. Such a scheme is used in the addressing plan (numbering plan) of the international telephone network – country code, area code, exchange code, subscriber's line.

IP addressing and routing was not initially designed with hierarchical routing in mind. As the global Internet grew, the routing tables in the core of the internetwork also grew (to about 13 000 entries) and were reaching unworkable proportions. The number of entries has been reduced and the rate of growth brought almost to a standstill, by using Classless Inter-Domain Routing (CIDR).

In CIDR, groups of previously unused class C addresses were preallocated to three addressing authorities, one in the USA (NIC), one in Europe (RIPE) and one in Australasia–Pacific (APNIC). By using a single subnet mask which forms a large supernet (see Chapter 4) for these class C addresses, routers can hold a *single* route entry for the main trunks between these three continental areas, or between Internet service providers or into a single corporate network designated by multiple class C addresses. Since the concept of a class C address becomes meaningless on these routes between 'Domains', the technique is called 'Classless Inter-Domain Routing' or CIDR.

The default route

The routing table at a particular router can also be minimized by configuring a 'default route' and 'default router'. The default route is towards a router (the default router) which is assumed to know the routes to every network that is not explicity listed in this router's table. There must of course be a router that knows the routes to everywhere. This technique is particularly important in corporate networks which connect to the Internet – the router which provides access to the Internet is the ultimate default router for that organization.

Choosing a routing protocol

The first function of a **routing protocol** is to provide information from one router to another about the network numbers and the subnetwork numbers that are known to it, combined with some measure of performance such as distance, throughput, transit delay, error rate, and cost. These measurements are known as (routing) **metrics**. Today IP supports Delay, Throughput, Reliability and Cost (DTRC), where reliability indicates the desire for a low probability of datagram loss. (Remember that in datagram transmission there is no error correction.) Few routing protocols can support all metrics. Even fewer current computer applications indicate to IP the performance environment they wish to operate in. Much of the power in IPv4 is unused and yet to be fully exploited by applications.

Routers do not usually measure and update the DTRC metrics associated with a particular link or set of links; they are configured as static values by network managers. It has been found that dynamic load-measuring schemes can become unstable with traffic oscillating from one route to another and back again in response to rerouting from highly loaded links. TCP/IP documents discourage standards developers from devising dynamic load-balancing routing schemes.

Where variable length subnet masks are used, the routers must also exchange the network mask which they use to make a routing decision for a particular subnetwork. This itself depends on the choice of the routing protocol designed for the purpose. As described in Chapter 4, variable length subnetwork masks are important for hierarchical and efficient addressing in TCP/IP networks.

A routing protocol does not directly perform routing. It updates routing tables in routers so that they may perform routing. In the jargon of TCP/IP, a routing protocol 'advertises reachability information'. However, the performance information that is recorded in the routing table is dependent on the routing protocol for update; the basis of the router's choice of a particular route is completely determined by the ability of the routing protocol to convey that performance information.

Those implementing a TCP/IP-based internetwork have a wide choice of proven and newer routing protocols. Normally an Autonomous System (AS) manager will attempt to standardize on one routing protocol for use within the AS. This is referred to as the **Interior Gateway Protocol** (IGP) for that AS. So an IGP is a concept, not a single technical specification. In practice, many network managers find they must support several routing protocols simultaneously for reasons of flexibility and equipment compatibility.

Routing protocols are chosen on a number of criteria:

- Availability from suppliers;
- Speed to adapt and find alternate routes round network failures;
- Conveying best route information according to service needs or performance;
- Support for active alternate and parallel routes to a destination network;
- Speed to resolve routing anomalies such as routing loops and 'black holes';
- Load imposed on networks and internetwork links by the routing protocol itself;
- Load imposed on host systems by the presence of the routing protocol;
- Load imposed on the routing processors by calculating the 'best routes';
- Scalability – change in routing performance and routing traffic with the size of the network;
- Security;
- Support for 'policy-based routing';
- Legal requirements.

Some routing decisions that would be legal between organizations in one country may be against PTT and government policy in another. Restrictions are diminishing in many countries, but equally the regulations are often very different from the substantially deregulated nature of communications in the USA and the UK. The available protocols are not necessarily sophisticated enough for this type of routing decision (nor would governments allow control of routing to be within the authority of corporate network managers). Network managers working under such restrictions should be aware that inappropriate interconnection and configuration of their networks to their trading partners' networks could mean that they unwittingly act as a carrier for transit traffic between third parties.

The oldest routing protocols only convey the distance between networks as the number of hops – the number of routers that the information passes through to get to the destination from that router. This is a very limited and unsatisfactory measurement, for it takes no account of the performance and changing load of a route.

The routing protocols available for TCP/IP routers and end systems are:

- Routing Information Protocol (RIP)
- Open Shortest Path First (OSPF)
- Border Gateway Protocol (BGP)
- Interior Gateway Routing Protocol[†] (IGRP)
- Hello
- Exterior Gateway Protocol (EGP)
- Gateway to Gateway Protocol (GGP)

The protocol in most common use is RIP, because of its widespread availability. It has some limitations for internets with more than a few networks. OSPF is a recent full IAB standard. It has a number of advantages over RIP for the larger network.

Detailed discussion of these routing protocols can be found in Chapter 16 in the technical section of the book.

Configuring routers

Many modern routers are easily configured from a management terminal through simple menu-driven commands. The key parameters to configure for IP routing are, for each connection:

- IP address,
- Subnet mask,
- Routing protocols to be enabled,
- Maximum transmission unit of the interface,
- 'Cost' of using that interface.

Summary

Routers provide the network designer with options not available from bridges. Because they operate at the IP layer, they block link-layer broadcast and multicast traffic. They can also prevent the propagation of some faults which bridges would pass.

Routers are better adapted to connecting different network technologies than bridges: through fragmentation they can adjust (downwards) to the maximum frame size available.

[†]A Cisco proprietary protocol.

Routers base their routing decisions on the network portion of the IP address. Through sophisticated routing protocols, such as OSPF, routers exchange information about all possible paths. When a failure occurs they can quickly switch to a backup path. They can have multiple paths between any two networks and can use them simultaneously.

This is the functionality with which IP was designed and routers exploit the facilities.

6

TCP/IP upper layers, transport and application services

This chapter reviews, from a management perspective, the application level services that are usually supplied with the TCP/IP protocol suite. These services are discussed technically in Part II. To understand some of the management issues, it is also necessary to discuss the part played by the transport services that support these applications over the IP network which was described in Chapters 2 to 5.

In this chapter, we describe the management issues of:

- UDP
- TCP
- WINSOCK
- The X Window System
- Telnet
- FTP
- TFTP
- SMTP
- World Wide Web

The previous chapters highlighted the decisions to be made when choosing and setting up the equipment which forms the communications network of TCP/IP implementations. This chapter introduces the remaining components of the TCP/IP protocol suite: the transport layer, which interfaces to the underlying network, and the application layers, which support the services for the end users.

The TCP/IP standards leave each manufacturer considerable flexibility in how the standard upper layer communications services are presented to end users. The first products to the market provide basic functionality. As the market matures and feeds back ideas for improvements to developers, subsequent products will build more sophisticated user services onto the same basic standards. The size of the TCP/IP market expanded considerably in the early 1990s. The basic facilities have been overtaken by more highly integrated solutions, many based on graphical and Windows interfaces.

The transport layers

The **transport layers** of a protocol are the first layers in most communications systems that operate in the host end systems only and are not used by the intermediate network equipment. The transport layers allow multiple applications or users to share the same path between the same two machines; they provide a consistent interface to the applications and a mechanism for them to specify their communications requirements. As shown in Figure 6.1, the transport layer operates end to end whether the communication path is across a single network (interconnected with bridges) or across multiple networks interconnected with routers.

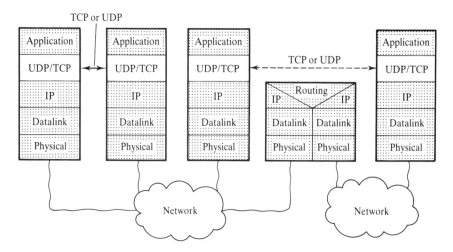

Figure 6.1 TCP/IP transport layers.

Today, most TCP/IP applications use one of two transport protocols, the **User Datagram Protocol** (UDP) and the **Transmission Control Protocol** (TCP). For applications which must operate over long-distance circuits, TCP is the protocol of choice, as it can be 'tuned' to provide better performance. This tuning process is described in Chapter 7. UDP has no alterable parameters.

UDP provides an unreliable service; there is no guarantee of message delivery. If the application requires absolute reliability, it must perform its own error checking and error correction. UDP is ideal for distribution of information which changes every few seconds – status reports for stock market screens or airport information systems for example. If one transmission is lost there will be another more up-to-date value transmitted in a few seconds. Unreliable datagram services can be 'broadcast' to many different destinations simultaneously, since the receiving systems can just listen, they do not need to reply.

On the other hand, TCP provides a reliable 'point-to-point' service and has facilities which improve performance over slower, wide area (PTT long-distance) circuits. TCP would be the choice for operating in a wide area environment. It was designed for point-to-point applications that must have reliability – file transfer, mail transfer and terminal access systems.

The transport protocol used by a particular application is usually fixed (at compile time) by the application developer. For the network operator, there is little opportunity to choose between UDP and TCP for a particular product. Further, because UDP involves less processing overhead and is perfectly adequate in a purely local LAN, many application programmers, who may not fully consider the implications for wide area telecommunications systems, choose UDP rather than the extra complexity (and hence larger processing overhead) of TCP. Alternatively, the application may be too restricted by a point-to-point connection for each conversation[†]. As a result, these applications have high throughput performance in a strictly local environment, but, as bridges, routers and slow-speed, long-distance circuits are introduced, the performance degrades quickly. If the path between two devices which use UDP includes multiple bridges, routers or multiple wide area links, the performance will be poor. We explore the reasons for this in Chapter 7. System planners may have to plan the location of network resources to avoid wide area links for certain applications that use UDP. Even though they may be able to justify and afford high-speed, multimegabit connections, the 'slow' speed of light and the delays in buffering of information will reduce the throughput of UDP.

[†]The Versatile Message Transport Protocol (VMTP) was developed for such applications. It provides the performance advantages of TCP for wide area operations, without imposing some of TCP's connection-oriented restrictions. VMTP is not widely used.

WINSOCK

Winsock (Windows Sockets) is an important Application Programming Interface (API) developed for and promoted by most TCP/IP software manufacturers. It allows application programs running under Microsoft Windows to access the TCP and UDP layers of a TCP/IP system. It has been instrumental in opening up the market for TCP/IP applications running on PCs with Windows. Any application written to the Winsock standard may be used with any TCP/IP communications software which provides a Winsock interface. Most Windows-based software uses the Winsock standard. The success of many of the Internet programs is in part due to the availability of Winsock.

In operation, the Windows application searches for a set of communications software routines in a file called WINSOCK.DLL. While the interface that this file provides to the application program is always the same, the way Winsock connects to a particular TCP/IP stack is different. In the unusual circumstances that there is more than one version of TCP/IP on a PC, it is important that an application finds the correct WINSOCK.DLL for the TCP/IP it is to use. This means that there should only be one WINSOCK.DLL accessible via the path statement or alternatively that the path to the required Winsock must be earlier in the path statement than any other copy of WINSOCK.DLL.

Open network computing or the network file system

The Network File System (NFS), as it is still commonly known, or Open Network Computing (ONC), as its creator Sun Microsystems Inc. now calls it, was developed for high performance UNIX workstations and later released to the 'public domain' as three RFCs which describe the major protocol components. Recognizing the importance of the IBM PC, Sun also developed NFS software for the IBM PC, the PC-NFS client. This allows PCs to use UNIX workstations as remote file and print servers. NFS client and server software is now available for most computer systems.

NFS provides user services familiar to any user of a proprietary resource-sharing LAN such as NetWare, LAN Manager or Banyan VINES. Files, directories and peripherals on a remote NFS server are mapped to 'virtual' drives, directories or peripherals on the local system. For most purposes, these virtual drives and printers are indistinguishable from, and are used identically to, local resources. This is illustrated in Figure 6.2.

On a UNIX system, each remote directory appears as an additional directory off the main local directory structure. For a PC, with PC-NFS,

Figure 6.2 NFS representation of resources.

the remote directories appear as additional disk drives. From the perspective of the commercial information systems manager, this is ideal, for unlike other TCP/IP applications described below, most business users require no new training to use NFS; they merely have access to more information with bigger disks and better printers.

But NFS can go beyond simple resource sharing. It provides the mechanism for true distributed computing, where processing power, not just data, is shared among networked machines.

NFS management

The major management issues of NFS can be hidden from the users. These issues centre on the security and mapping of user identifiers and access rights between different operating systems. NFS works in conjunction with the Network Information Services (NIS), a distributed database system for NFS security which provides for centralized management of a highly distributed system. Technically, the tools have been provided by Sun; the administration of a large user population still requires careful organization, with the correct clerical procedures in place to ensure that security meets the requirements of the organization. It must not be so lax as to compromise data integrity and not so tight that no one can get work done. The technicalities of setting access rights on different NFS systems are discussed in Chapter 15. The organizational issues depend on local circumstances.

As always in a network environment, security of access from a PC represents a problem. Unless PCs have nonstandard hardware, most security barriers can be overcome by a proficient and determined attacker. The NFS suite uses an authentication program for PCs, the PC-NFS Daemon, running on a server to validate user access to the filing system. This provides a basic level of security. Some operational environments require additional security features. 'Secure NFS' addresses these issues by using Data Encryption Standard (DES) authentication techniques.

NFS uses the UDP transport protocol. Remote disk data transfer rates can be reduced significantly by delay, particularly in wide area links. There are implementations providing NFS, over TCP transport. An alternative solution is to buy more servers and place them close to the users.

Where the main NFS activity is resource-sharing, poor configuration options in the workstations can have a dramatic effect on network traffic. The use of print spoolers, temporary files, backup files, PC batch files and the format of the 'path' statement can all influence the traffic a workstation generates on the network. These configuration issues are developed in the next chapter.

To make NFS completely invisible to end users, each workstation should have a script or batch file which executes the NFS 'mount' commands to make the remote resources locally available. The details of the command line can be totally hidden.

In the past, memory requirements for PC network software have left too little of the available 640k to run some of the more demanding PC applications. Some implementations of PC-NFS require in excess of 130 kbytes to load a LAN card driver, the TCP/IP core software and the NFS client application. By reducing the number of file systems which may be mounted and by tuning other parameters, this figure can be reduced by a few kilobytes. More advanced processors and more sophisticated operating systems than DOS are eliminating these concerns.

The X Window System

The **X Window System** was developed by Massachusetts Institute of Technology (MIT). It is a method of controlling an advanced graphical 'windowed' interface. From the perspective of TCP/IP, the X Window System is a message protocol between an X server and an X client (Figure 6.3).

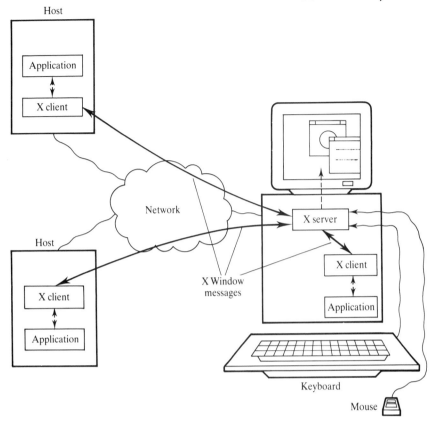

Figure 6.3 X Window protocol.

This protocol is described in RFC 1013. Copyright remains with MIT, though permission is given to distribute the RFC document as long as the copyright is acknowledged. Other aspects of the X Window System, although not published as RFCs, are described in standards available from the X Consortium at MIT.

With the X Window System, the boundary between user interface, which is not normally defined, and the communications protocol may seem to been breached, but in fact it is intact. RFC 1013 only describes the protocol between server and client. The style of the display is determined by other standards, typically the OSF/Motif display standard promoted by the Open Software Foundation Inc. (which includes DEC, Hewlett-Packard and Microsoft), Open Look from AT&T or Open Windows from Sun Microsystems Inc.

Unlike every other reference to client and server in TCP/IP, with X Window the server is normally at the user's workstation and the client, which generates the new drawing instructions, is at the application host.

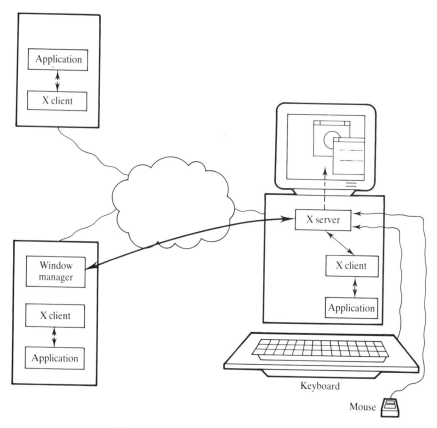

Figure 6.4   The X Window manager.

The X server operates the display terminal, drawing graphics objects and text in response to messages from the X client. The server must also report user actions such as keystrokes and mouse movements to any X clients that will be affected by them.

Since a window system may display output from many different applications and hosts simultaneously, each display should have a window manager, a special X client that supervises the construction of all the graphics objects on the screen (Figure 6.4). It is the window manager that implements the window style, or 'look and feel' as it has been called, of the display standard (OSF/Motif, Open Look or some other standard). More practically, it is the window manager that adds and controls the scroll bars, title line, move buttons, sizing, scaling and overlaying of windows in response to user actions. Any graphical interface with the modifications to provide the correct software interface to the X server can act as a window manager for an X Window server. Microsoft Windows has been adapted for this role.

The X terminal

The X terminal is an X Window display station that implements the X server. It runs no user applications (X clients) locally. All display requests are received on the network connection. Extensions to the X user interface can provide for colour, image support and Display PostScript among others.

Some X terminals have been adapted to operate over dial-up modem links (using either the SLIP or PPP protocols described in Chapter 10). Since modem links are limited to 14 400 bps or 28 800 bps before compression, many suppliers offer some form of data compression for this type of connection. The result is a usable, if somewhat sluggish, display system provided that the dial-up link is carrying data for a single X terminal user. Where possible, higher speed lines should be used for X terminals. The increasing availability worldwide of ISDN 64 kbps 'dial-up' circuits will alleviate these restrictions.

Managing the X Window System

Graphics applications, particularly when bit-mapped graphics is involved, are demanding both of processing power and of communications capacity. The communications requirements will increase if the X server and window manager are not on the same workstation. The earliest X Window terminals operated with a remote, host-based window manager; the standards specifically provided for it. In this case, every user action, from a key press to a pointer (mouse) movement generates network traffic, with a large movement of the pointer potentially generating a stream of X protocol messages.

The X Window protocol uses TCP reliable connections between a server and its clients. Each TCP data segment sent may be individually acknowledged, almost doubling the expected traffic. If the protocol is confined to a LAN segment reserved for the purpose, this traffic is unlikely to be an issue. Where X systems cross bridges or routers between LANs or more particularly cross wide area lines, the traffic generated by particular actions should be measured for every X implementation being considered. The network capacity and layout should then be planned carefully to carry the expected traffic. Some of the more recent X terminal implementations use a local window manager, which removes a high proportion of the traffic from the network.

Tuning TCP may not improve the performance of an interactive protocol like X Window as much as a bulk transfer protocol like FTP.

Telnet

Telnet is the virtual terminal protocol of TCP/IP. It operates over the TCP error-corrected transport layer. It provides the terminal service that was mentioned in the very first pages of this book – total terminal interconnectivity and interoperability.

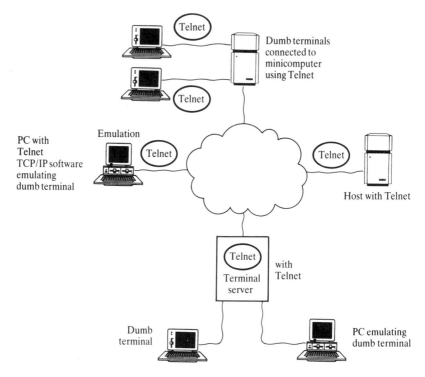

Figure 6.5 Telnet support for terminals.

Telnet gives terminal users the ability to log-on to many different 'Telnet hosts' from a single terminal on their desks. As shown in Figure 6.5, there are four ways of using Telnet. The terminal could be a simple 'dumb' terminal connected to a TCP/IP terminal server with a standard communications interface (V.24/V.28 or EIA232). Equally, that simple terminal could be a workstation or PC running a terminal emulator and connected to the same terminal server in the same way. A minicomputer can run Telnet software which provides the terminal server capability from within the minicomputer. Alternatively, a PC or other workstation could run a version of TCP/IP and a terminal emulator and connect directly to a LAN.

The Telnet service was one of the first to be provided in a standard way by the TCP/IP architecture. It delivers a similar service to that provided by the switching statistical multiplexers of the early to mid-1980s which provided many companies with their first example of flexible access to information.

The Telnet user interface

Telnet allows terminal or workstation users to gain access to a host system and to display host data on their screens. It is a remote terminal service; any terminal user must know how to operate the host system or host application from a terminal of that type. No attempt is made to map the user interface environments from one system to the other.

The Telnet service is most commonly used with ASCII asynchronous terminals such as the ANSI standard terminal or the DEC VT series. Most manufacturers of other terminal types have registered them with the Internet Assigned Numbers Authority (IANA) so that they can be identified to the Telnet protocol. That does not mean that a particular implementation of workstation Telnet will necessarily match the host software. Any-to-any protocol conversion is not necessarily a feature; systems which match must be carefully chosen.

The terminal server

The advantage of the Telnet terminal server is that it provides a low (capital) cost connection. But the interface often operates in asynchronous character-by-character mode; the terminal is strictly limited in its capabilities with little possibility of upgrading the service in the future.

Asynchronous interfaces can involve large management overheads. Cabling for the terminals may require only three wires, but for some terminal types and uses, it could be more. A structured cabling system with centrally located terminal servers can reduce management costs. At each interface, a number of parameters must be configured – speed, parity, flow control method and type of terminal (to ensure the correct control sequences are used). Unless a single standard for these parameters can be enforced throughout the organization, any apparent cost savings can be quickly swallowed up in increased management costs. This is particularly so in the larger installation, where the unit costs of supporting large numbers of terminal servers may not reduce with increasing size. Where terminal servers can be remotely configured from a central network management system, support costs may be more easily contained.

Configuring Telnet

One of the most difficult aspects of Telnet is ensuring that character and keyboard mappings are standardized across all systems. In a large organization, host configuration will be the responsibility of many different groups; the responsibility for terminal servers may also be devolved. But the workstation or terminal servers and hosts must be matched, particularly in their use of the backspace, delete and 'arrow' keys. A consistent policy is required across the organization. One of the responsibilities of technical management in an organization where many different systems run Telnet will be to standardize key mappings.

If every nationality used the same (US) keyboard with PCs, then there might be some possibility of consistency, but, when national keyboards and currency symbols are involved, that consistency may elude even the most vigorous attempts to introduce it. PC implementations of TCP/IP are famous for not being configured correctly. Trying to operate a remote system when keys marked '@' or '#' or ' | ' or '£' produce a different character on the screen can be quite demoralizing even for an experienced technical user. This situation is improving as US software developers recognize the international features of the IBM PC and include support for different national keyboards.

Many implementations of Telnet for workstations and PCs support IBM 3270 terminal operation intended for accessing IBM hosts (with an appropriate implementation of TCP/IP Telnet on the mainframe). Such a connection eliminates the need for IBM 317x cluster controllers. The support is likely to be limited to text only, but could include an emulation of 3278/9 colour terminals on PC colour screens with extended sizes of up to 32×80, 43×80 or 27×132 characters (model 3, 4 and 5). Where Telnet is used like this across different platforms, it may be impossible to map every key on one keyboard to a logical keystroke or combination on the other. At least one manufacturer includes the ASCII to EBCDIC translation table (PC to IBM character set translation) so that any modifications can be made by user management. As always, once a decision is made to change these defaults, continued local support will be essential throughout the life of the system. For keyboard mapping, the manufacturer's manuals should be kept to hand. 'Quick reference' keyboard templates permanently attached to each terminal may save a great deal of user frustration.

Most Telnet implementations allow the workstation user to open multiple connections simultaneously to different destination hosts. Terminal users may also 'escape' to the operating system (for example, a DOS shell) while still connected in Telnet. Depending on the operating system and program memory requirements, this allows other programs to be run. Some Telnet versions allow file transfer and Telnet to operate together. While this can provide a useful environment for computer development and maintenance staff, it is less useful as a general business tool, unless the mechanisms can be hidden from the commercial user by an in-house application.

Another feature of some PC Telnet implementations is the provision of a simple data transfer mechanism to which users can integrate their chosen terminal emulator package. (In a PC implementation, the software interface is often through software interrupt 14H.) The Telnet connection then replaces the PC's hardware communications port (COM1 for example). This means that any communications features of the emulator package can be used with Telnet. These could include support for nonstandard terminal types, graphics or colour support, and the use of a 'script' communications language to automate frequent communications tasks.

The place of Telnet in the 1990s

Even into the 1990s, a character mode terminal service can play an important role in commercial information systems, though it is beginning to look dated.

With the correct (text) menu-driven applications on the hosts, the data users can be protected from the command line of a particular operating system and can quickly navigate around complex commercial applications. Accessing text systems from one window in an X Window, Presentation Manager or Microsoft Windows environment with the ability to move data between applications easily, further enhances this traditional information systems environment. Delivering a text answer to an enquiry across a LAN in a fraction of a second, rather than in seconds across slow-speed links, brings a new perspective to such systems. Once the data is retrieved from the central resource, it can be massaged and presented in a graphical form at the workstation, if necessary.

But many factors dictate that for an increasing number of users, more transparent and sophisticated data retrieval and presentation are likely to be required.

File transfer protocol

The function of the **File Transfer Protocol** (FTP) is self-explanatory; it provides a means to move files from one computer system to another. So FTP usually only has a part to play on a workstation or host which has a local filing system, normally its own hard disk[†]. The FTP RFCs define the protocol which computers use to pass file transfer information between them, not how the user application or interface generates those commands.

As well as transferring files, FTP also provides facilities for managing files on remote systems; you can show or change the current disk directory, list the contents of that directory, delete files from the directory and rename files. While it is not part of the FTP standards, most systems also allow similar file management commands on the local system while connected to a remote computer. When FTP is running on a multitasking operating system, connections can be opened to different remote computers simultaneously; PC implementations often only allow a single remote connection.

FTP regards each file as a stream of bytes to be transferred. There is no concept of structured data or of opening a file to access individual records.

[†]There is no technical reason why this could not be a RAM drive or a floppy drive, though it is certainly less frequent in commercial operations.

The FTP user interface

The user interface to FTP is not defined by the RFC standards. The normal UNIX implementation is character based, and is similar to entering commands at a DOS or UNIX prompt. It was designed in the early 1980s for use by computer 'professionals'. While the interface looks similar, not all commands are implemented in the same way, or at all, in every implementation. The exact format may also be subtly different. Each command typed by the user translates into a sequence of FTP protocol commands on the network. Since some FTP commands are mandatory and others are optional, there may be a mismatch between workstations and host. These differences in user interface and host and workstation implementation can be a source of user frustration.

There are a number of FTP implementations that use Microsoft Windows or an X Window manager to present remote file systems and the FTP operations that are available in a familiar form of file and command selection boxes. This simplifies the interface to familiar mouse actions. This type of interface is provided by NetManage Chameleon as shown in Figure 6.6.

Like Telnet, FTP is not an application that should be delivered to the untrained or casual user whose main activity is commerce rather than computing. Some FTP versions allow a sequence of FTP commands to be taken from a local file. Some user tasks could be reduced to a single command which would log-on to the remote machine and manipulate and transfer files without intervention. But this command file is often not a true 'program'; it cannot change its actions because of user input and it cannot recover from changing conditions or errors encountered from one run to the next. Its use must be limited to simple recurrent tasks. An alternative but more costly option is to develop a custom application which uses FTP as its underlying file transfer mechanism. The FTP standards still limit the type of actions available.

Configuring FTP

There are few options with implementations of FTP. A common trap for new users is that FTP is aware of two types of files: text (or ASCII) files and binary (or image) files. If not told otherwise, FTP assumes that it is transferring text files. When files are stored in different environments (IBM, VAX, UNIX and PCs), this may corrupt any file which is not text and where the transfer is between different types of computer. Often the file transfer type must be changed manually once the workstation is logged-on to the remote host.

While almost any type of computer can act as a central file store for one other type of computer using FTP, file-naming conventions are a barrier to simple transfer among a range of different computer types. As an example, PCs use a name of eight characters with a three-character

Figure 6.6   NetManage Chameleon FTP interface.

extension; other systems use any length of name and file version numbers that cannot be represented in the PC environment. Some implementations attempt to translate long names to DOS names in a predictable way using 'globbing'.

FTP uses the TCP transport layer for reliability. Optimizing TCP (Chapter 7) improves the throughput of FTP over wide area links.

Trivial file transfer protocol

The **Trivial File Transfer Protocol** (TFTP) is a simple program with mimimal facilities, designed to be implemented in permanent memory (PROM), so that diskless computers may perform their initial loading of an operating system. It is often used in conjunction with the boot protocol. It is not usual for it to be used for other purposes.

TFTP lacks the security features of FTP and it is normal to disable the TFTP server on hosts which do not provide a BOOTP service.

Simple mail transfer protocol

The **Simple Mail Transfer Protocol** (SMTP) provides the mechanisms for TCP/IP users to exchange mail messages. SMTP with Multipurpose Internet Mail Extension (MIME) now supports binary file attachments or enclosures. Mail users are identified by their mail address, a combination of their name or nickname and the fully qualified domain name of a particular host computer which receives and stores their mail. Some possible mail addresses are:

```
catherinej@integv.integralis.co.uk
medavies@eclecticsys.co.uk
registrar@nic.ddn.mil
```

SMTP client software uses simple techniques to send text mail often directly from the source machine to a destination machine over a TCP (error-free) connection, using ASCII data streams and commands. Alternatively, the destination mail address can contain a list of machines that are to be used for forwarding mail to the ultimate destination. The sophistication in the mail protocol is that only a single copy of a mail item is sent to a group of users who are all on the same machine. The protocol between the machines can indicate a number of different user names at that machine and check that they are recognized at the destination. Where a user is not recognized, three different actions are possible:

(1) The receiving machine may refuse the mail.

(2) The receiving machine may, if it knows where that user is located, offer to forward the mail towards the user, in which case no further action is required by the sender.

(3) The receiving machine may refuse the mail and, again, knowing a possible address for that user, may suggest an alternative address.

Mail may also be sent to a distribution list retained at the receiving machine. Where implemented, the sender can request an expansion of the mail list into individual mail names.

For SMTP to operate, each sender must be able to convert the host and domain name into an IP address. The network must use the domain name system, or each host must have a list of destination hosts in a hosts file to map the domain name to an address. An alternative is to deliver all mail to a gateway computer which can use the domain name service.

The simplicity of SMTP and its ready availability mean that it is frequently used as the gateway protocol between other proprietary mail systems, though in some instances X.400 has assumed this role.

Managing SMTP

Some of the organizational issues of SMTP arise because of the association of a person with a particular computer. Those computers are the **mail servers** of SMTP and they must always be available to receive mail. An individual workstation or PC is unlikely to make a satisfactory mail server as its availability cannot be guaranteed. A mail server is more likely to be a part-time task carried out by another server machine.

Building on SMTP protocols, some manufacturers have introduced the **mail relay** or mail store, which receives and stores mail on behalf of workstation users until they access the store using an SMTP client on their workstation. A workstation can be a satisfactory generator of SMTP mail, but it is a poor and inattentive recipient.

Post Office Protocol (POP2 or POP3) is an extension to the SMTP mail protocols. It allows a mail user at a machine which is only occasionally used to interact with a mail storage system which is permanently available. This mail store will act as the permanently available destination for that user's mail. It may also act as an intermediate gateway for outgoing mail for that user.

Staff who travel must be able to access the mail system they are registered on, for that is where their mailbox resides. Alternatively, a method of mail forwarding can be devised, but such features are beyond SMTP itself and are implementation dependent.

If mail users change location permanently, their mail addresses may change. They will have to advise all their correspondents of that change. TCP/IP standards do not include a directory service to relate people to mail addresses (or for that matter to relate application servers to network addresses). Worldwide research into directory services has concentrated on perfecting and implementing the ITU-T X.500 recommendations which are accepted as part of OSI. Indeed, the Internet is said to be the biggest trial of X.500 directory services in the world. Several RFCs describe how X.500 is to be used on the Internet, and the adaption required to operate over TCP/IP protocols.

Another potential problem is that the name part of a mail address can in some implementations be case sensitive. The remainder of the domain name is not.

Internet applications – World Wide Web and News

The Internet is that worldwide collection of computer systems and physical networks which uses the Internet Protocol (IP) as its common communications standard. As the Internet has moved from research, more towards academic and commercial usage, a number of specific applications for information searching and retrieval have become widely used.

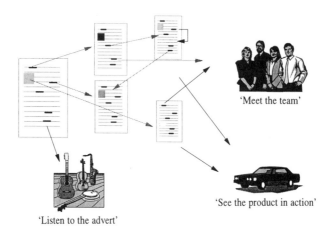

'Meet the team'

'See the product in action'

'Listen to the advert'

Figure 6.7 Hypertext links related topics – text, pictures, movies or sound.

These take advantage of the interconnectivity of computers provided by the Internet to present one 'integrated' information source.

A number of early systems, such as Archie and Gopher, are still in use. But the more widely used systems now are the World Wide Web (WWW or the Web) and News services. These applications are again based on a client/server architecture. With WWW, the client software, referred to as browser software, deals with the presentation of information to the user, and the server software manages the distribution of information to the browsers and the execution of special scripts (simple programs) designed to enhance the functionality of the basic text and graphics system.

The World Wide Web service is so called because of the logical connectivity it achieves between its servers; if you attempted to draw the connectivity across the Internet to these servers you would end up with a vast number of crossing lines which would resemble a spider's web spanning the globe. The web is an extremely powerful system for the distribution of information. Today's web browsers can present text, graphics, audio, animation and movies to the user. Through the use of underlined hypertext links, a user sees a linked set of related 'pages' or topics, each expanding on the information presented previously (Figure 6.7). The basic idea will be familiar to those who have used Help within Microsoft Windows.

The Web provides a completely new mechanism for business applications and the distribution of information relevant to internal corporate networks as well as external internets. In effect web technology is fast becoming a standard mechanism for accessing information and a completely new marketing, advertising and distribution medium.

A graphical web browser supports all the text entry fields, buttons and checkboxes of any graphical user interface. A WWW client can be used to build a database query or database update application with an

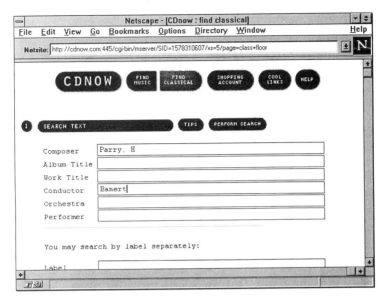

Figure 6.8   Database searching at CDNow with Netscape Navigator web browser.

input screen which is independent of the client hardware and operating system (Figure 6.8).

News systems allow common interest discussion groups to operate over the Internet. Those involved can air problems, concerns or just partake in inane banter. Such discussions pull on people's knowledge, ideas and interest from all around the world, a potentially powerful medium.

From the business perspective, the quality of information is variable. Any business use of public newsgroups should be approached with some caution. But the news application can be used totally internally to an organization for bulletin board discussions.

Internet application configuration

Internet applications require little configuration at the client end beyond choosing simple preferences.

For the web browsers, configurable options relate to the first page of information that will be retrieved on start-up (known as the default Home Page) and to storing the location of favourite places to go. These are all simple options to set. There are more sophisticated options for specialist situations such as interpreting sound and animation files.

For the news system users will 'subscribe' to the newsgroups they wish to be involved in. 'Subscribing' to a newsgroup involves no additional monetary outlay, merely a decision to retrieve messages from that group and perhaps a commitment of time (and sanity) to reading them.

Subscribing is done simply by point and click operations through the graphical user interface.

News server configuration

Configuration of a News server can be very complex. The server needs to know which machines in the Internet it retrieves articles from (the news feeds) and which ones it sends articles to ('posts' to). The newsgroups advertised by the server must also be configured. A server can be set only to acquire certain groups or it can be configured only to send certain groups, depending on where control is desired and bandwidth restrictions. There are also the issues of removing old messages in the group – there are a number of options on how this can be managed by the server – and the creation of new newsgroups. It is also possible to password protect groups, which requires registration of users and their passwords. To configure a News server requires knowledge of the specific News server being used and a clear understanding or policy on how the server is to be run.

Web server configuration

The configuration of a web server is an art, requiring not only technical knowledge but also artistic and graphic design skills to present information in the best possible way. Technical details of how this is done are covered in Chapter 19 which discusses the HyperText Mark-up Language (HTML). HTML defines the setup of web pages and the links between items on those pages and other pages in the Internet.

Summary

The TCP/IP protocol suite provides upper layer protocols that support the major computing requirements of most commercial users. As well as the communications environment NFS and X Window provide consistent user interfaces across different platforms, with NFS mapping disk and other peripheral resources and X Window complementing it for graphical displays. Because of the high network traffic these two applications can generate, they require more careful planning in a large installation.

The traditional applications of mail (SMTP), file transfer (FTP) and terminal access (Telnet) still have an important role in commercial systems. The text-based command line interfaces of the early 1980s have been improved with graphical 'front ends' that can isolate the inexperienced commercial user from the complexities of driving a system like FTP. Other in-house developments could provide further isolation, but any in-house development, other than simple configuration, is becoming unacceptable to many commercial IT managers.

7

System configuration and optimizing performance

This chapter is more technical than previous chapters, but continues to discuss the principle rather than the detail of any particular protocol: it considers technical aspects that can be skipped at first reading. In this chapter, we review the issues of configuration that affect system performance, both in the network and in the host end systems which provide user service.

The major topics of this chapter are:

- What is performance?
- Performance tuning and optimization
- Planning shared systems
- Measurement of network loading
- The effects of tuning
- Determining the changes required
- The effect of network buffers
- NFS retransmission timer
- Improving the bucket brigade delay
- Bridging Token Ring and Ethernet
- How applications load the network

This chapter is for those technical managers who wish to know how to get the most from their TCP/IP installation. It is about optimizing performance and identifying why systems do not deliver the expected performance. The discussion is more technical than in other chapters in Part I, but analogies are used extensively.

In modern resource-sharing systems or distributed computing systems, overall performance is dependent on network and host software and hardware configuration. The four components are interdependent in a complex way. Those managing the whole environment must cross traditional managerial boundaries to understand the complex inter-action between application and network. Many organizations are not yet structured correctly to foster the cooperation necessary for success.

This section considers both network and application issues.

What is performance?

The term 'performance' in general conjures up the idea of speed and power from its use by the motor industry to describe sports models. In computing and communications too, the same is true; speed and power are the terms that prevail. Undoubtedly a high-performance computer system can deliver more useful work to more users than a low-performance one. But the term needs closer analysis: does a 70-seat bus full of passengers have the same performance on a road as 35 two-seater sports cars? In the transport world, probably not; in the computing world, where one system is centralized and the other is distributed, more detailed analysis is necessary. The centralized system may still have an attraction for some managers.

However, without the concept of value for money, pure speed is a poor measure of performance in networks. Is a system that has 99% of its users content with the service 99% of the time, performing better than one that has 95% of users content only 95% of the time? Probably yes, until you learn that the first is three times over budget and the second is within budget.

Performance tuning and optimization

The question then arises as to what is to be done to satisfy more users for more of the time without increasing the budget. This is where **performance tuning** and **optimization** have a role to play. By under-standing the tuning parameters that are available in a particular system and managing them correctly, the performance can be improved and the life of a system extended, without incurring significant, if any, capital expenditure. Nothing is totally free however. Some of the expenditure will transfer from capital to revenue, as staff training and staff effort for system reconfiguration are now involved.

Tuning a network after installation is a long process because each alteration must be made at individual machines. A single change by itself may apparently have little effect. Taken together, a number of changes will lead to the required improvements. By understanding the tuning parameters at first installation, the system can be optimized at design time rather than involving a catchback, under pressure, when the user complaints reach an unacceptable level.

In general, however, performance and performance tuning involve designing and configuring a system to satisfy the computing and communications of the maximum number of users for a given amount of money. Where an existing installed base is involved, design options are restricted by that set of equipment.

Tuning can take two separate forms: changing soft parameters in communications and applications systems to alter throughput; and changing the location of network resources or altering the interconnection paths of resources to reduce the number of items between two communicating devices, so that traffic is localized and follows shorter, faster routes. The first is preferable, for it does not involve significant physical activity; in some TCP/IP systems only the second option is available for those applications that use UDP.

Planning shared systems

Communications systems should be planned with some service level in mind. The service level includes:

- The performance; that is, the time taken to deliver a certain quantity of data between two systems.
- The availability of the system; the time lost due to failures of the system, both planned and unplanned, due to faults. The frequency and duration of faults should be estimated.

As with any shared system, the performance varies depending on the activities of other users. Individual performance or service level can only be expressed as a statistical average based on **queuing theory**[†]. Given the average delay of a system, it is possible to estimate that 90% of transfers will be handled in less than a certain time based on the average, and similarly 95% of transfers will be completed in some higher figure. But all these measurements vary widely depending on how heavily loaded the system is.

[†]A detailed discussion is beyond the scope of this book.

As any system approaches 100% loading, over an extended period which is of interest to the users, and more particularly, a period which is of interest to the user protocols, then delays begin to vary dramatically and uncontrollably. Whether we are discussing the queues in a supermarket, the traffic on your favourite orbital motorway system[†], or indeed a local or wide area network cable, once the load reaches 70% of full capacity (or less in some circumstances) it is time to consider the effects on system users and whether there is a requirement to reconfigure or upgrade. At 70% loading, the delay is some three times what it is on an unloaded network.

Most shared communications systems are designed on the premise that one user can take only a small portion of the resource. Where the user is a Telnet session and the resource is a 10 Mbps CSMA/CD network, this may be a valid assumption. Where the users are two RISC-based UNIX workstations processing CAD/CAM images, further analysis is almost certainly required. Equally a relatively small number of Telnet users can fill a 64 kbps wide area circuit.

With RISC-based file transfer systems, simple queuing theory breaks down because one user can fill, that is they can load to 100%, a 10 Mbps LAN for an extended period. If two terminals try to use the resource together, they will share it equally between them. This doubles the time for each to complete the task. If that is a doubling from 0.1 to 0.2 seconds, it is unlikely to be a problem for human operators; where it is a doubling from 5 to 10 seconds, a service that was previously acceptable can become unacceptable. As more of these high-performance users are added to a network, the individual performance degrades rapidly for each user, precisely because each one really wants the whole network pipe for themselves.

Measurement of network loading

When deciding how heavily loaded a system is, the measurement time is important. As discussed in Part II, some applications which use UDP transport have a fixed time-out of 700 ms. If the application does not get a reply to a request in that time, it resends the request. These applications also use a maximum number of retransmissions after which an error is reported to the user. With a retransmission count of 5, an error occurs if the application cannot communicate reliably for 3.5 seconds and during that time it will have retransmitted information four times; it is operating at an efficiency of 20% and loading the network possibly at the worst time. For these protocols, the loading that matters is that measured over tens of seconds, not over minutes or hours. This is particularly important where slow-speed WAN links are involved.

[†]London's M25 or the Los Angeles freeway system.

The effects of tuning

System tuning involves the two processes of changing software parameters and hardware layout to optimize performance. These two cannot be totally separated; they interact in unpredictable ways. In some cases, tuning a system can cause it to cross that boundary between demanding a small or large percentage of the total capacity and hence between having little impact or a large impact on other users.

Correcting an anomaly in one area may reveal a bottleneck in another area. The bottleneck must be removed before the expected performance is achieved, but this in turn may reveal a third limitation. Complex systems often have a number of closely related limitations, with each one not evident until the previous one is removed. Put another way, the reason that 100 users can share one LAN may be that each workstation is badly tuned and sharing the same overloaded NFS file server. Tune the end systems and the file server or add a second file server and the LAN may become the bottleneck. The two bottlenecks may be so close together that it is not until both changes are made that any real benefit is evident. If your favourite firm of consultants recommended one change and then discovered after the event that a second change was necessary, it is a courageous, or at least knowledgeable, network manager who accepts the second recommendation.

Another disadvantage of tuning one host system to give the maximum throughput on an unloaded network is that when the network becomes loaded, the variation in response time is far greater and more obvious. If performance is poor on a lightly loaded LAN, the relative degradation on the loaded LAN will often be less and hence more acceptable. Computer users, like car users, are frequently more frustrated by wide variations in speed than by a low but consistent speed.

Determining the changes required

The starting point for a study of the likely effects and requirements for a network optimization and tuning exercise can be either with the network or with the hosts. A detailed knowledge of current network loading at every point in the path between two systems that are underperforming will show whether reconfiguring the hosts will help. If that loading is generally light, the bottleneck is either in the protocols or in the end system performance; it is less likely to be in network capacity if all links are loaded to less than 50% over approximately 30 seconds at a time when the response is unacceptable. In this case, the first consideration should be to change software parameters to allow the systems to exchange larger amounts of data in one transmission or to generate more transmissions per second. In either case this will immediately increase network loading!

If the network is already heavily loaded, the next question is whether the load is genuine user traffic or is due to retransmissions because of time-outs or errors. Here the statistics on application level (UDP) and TCP retransmissions collected by end systems are the starting point. Most modern TCP implementations have their own automatic time-out calculation which should not be altered. Lengthening the UDP time-outs may reduce the load on the network due to retransmissions[†] and produce a satisfactory service. This is likely to be a temporary respite except where the bottleneck is in a wide area link.

The technical argument is as follows. If 700 ms time-outs are occurring, then the systems are only exchanging one UDP datagram of up to 8 kbytes every 700 ms. In an NFS system, this amounts to 11.7 kbytes per second, low by today's standards. If frequent time-outs and hence retransmissions are occurring, it is more likely that an IP fragment of the UDP datagram is lost. If the reason for that loss cannot be corrected, assuming that it can easily be identified, then reducing the maximum size of the UDP datagram that the end systems can generate, from 8192 bytes to around 1400 bytes, may reduce the quantity of data retransmitted by a factor of 5. This will reduce the loading on the network and improve the throughput. Once the retransmission load is reduced, the network load is likely to remain high but it will all be useful activity!

If the high network load is not due to retransmissions, then altering end system speed and parameters will have a minimum effect on the end system performance. The only recourse is to increase the traffic capacity of the network by splitting the network with bridges and routers and reducing the number of devices on a shared cable. To return to the familiar analogy, a sports car on a heavily used motorway is limited by the performance of the vehicles in front. There is no point in increasing the engine size. More lanes are necessary[‡].

The effect of network buffers

Apart from LAN 'cut-through' switches, today's communications networks, including most of the link-layer protocols that support TCP/IP, work on the basis of buffering and relaying one complete frame of data. The unit of data transmission is the link-level frame. Each frame contains a frame check sequence to ensure that it has been transmitted correctly. To relay frames that are known to be in error is a waste of time, so only frames that are received correctly are relayed. This has the effect

---

[†]As discussed in Chapter 13, there are few technical reasons for decreasing default time-outs in systems. It is treating symptoms rather than the root cause and risks making the network unstable.

[‡]There is an alternative mechanism available in both transport systems. Charge more for using what has become a scarce and hence valuable resource. That is a political decision beyond the scope of this discussion.

Figure 7.1 Effects of network buffering.

of building up the network end-to-end delay quite quickly since the data cannot be sent on until it has been completely received. Figure 7.1 illustrates this as a sequence of buckets (the buffers) between a source and destination tank of liquid, the source and destination of data. The liquid cannot be poured out of one bucket into the next until it has all arrived from the previous bucket.

As long as the network buffering delay is much less than the transmission delay and processing time in an end system, the reduction in performance because of buffering is small. This small effect can be measured even on LAN systems where the path between systems contains only local bridges. For most medium-performance systems it causes a drop of between 4% and 30% but is unlikely to cause users any anxiety. It is most noticeable where there are multiple hops in a WAN across point-to-point links, across frame relay networks and X.25 systems. In some cases, the network planner has no control over the intermediate networks and cannot therefore commit to a definite performance. Protocols that use UDP are most affected; for those using TCP the system manager has the option to increase the window size.

NFS and the retransmission timer on wide area links

As NFS uses UDP transport and its applications are normally designed around high-speed LAN transfer, wide area circuits can have a major effect on performance. Even on a local circuit with minimum delay, the time to transmit a full Ethernet frame across a 64 kbps circuit is 190 ms. To send a full 8192-byte datagram in six frames takes over 1 s; immediately there is a configuration anomaly. The default timer for NFS retransmissions if no reply is received is 700 ms. As this default is less than 1 s, it ensures that when NFS data is sent across a 64 kbps wide area link, every 8192-byte datagram is always sent twice whether it is in error or not! Either the timer must be increased to around 2 seconds or the datagram size in the NFS end systems should be reduced to not greater than 3000 bytes. These figures assume that this system is the only user of the 64k bps link. Where there are other users, much higher timer figures or lower datagram sizes should be employed.

With the increased retry timer, this NFS system loads the 64 kbps link to about 97% or approaches 8000 bytes per second. If the datagram size is reduced to 1500 bytes, more requests are required and the throughput may drop to 88%.

The 'bucket brigade' effect of Figure 7.1 is most evident if a second remote link is added in series with the first. The time taken for the last of the 8192-byte datagram to arrive is increased by one maximum frame size or 190 ms. The throughput of the 64k link drops from 97% to 84%. If the frame size were only 1500 bytes to start with, each frame would be delayed by the same amount again for each bridge added; the throughput would drop to 50% for two bridges, 33% for three bridges and 25% for four bridges.

Where satellite circuits or intercontinental terrestrial circuits are used, the round trip delay due to the length of the path compared with the speed of light must be taken into account. As a satellite path has a round trip delay of over 0.5 s, it is unlikely to be satisfactory for UDP-based protocols.

Two facts are evident: too small a request size reduces efficiency, particularly in the wide area, but with too large a datagram size the probability of error increases to the point where retransmissions become too frequent – the network manager may have to tune each protocol for each possible route it could take. This is not satisfactory and in general it is not an option available in software. The latest version of NFS adjusts its time-out and data size dynamically to suit WAN delay characteristics.

Improving the bucket brigade delay

Remote bridges cannot improve the delay through the network as bridges must relay the received frame without modifying its size. On the other hand, routers have the ability to fragment. When a router fragments a low-level frame, the fragments travel more quickly across the network, as the buffers (the 'buckets') are smaller. Routers can improve the throughput across wide area links compared with remote bridges. More importantly, they adjust the fragment size automatically according to a configuration parameter, the Maximum Transmission Unit (MTU) with routers. The system manager does not have to adjust the end system configuration according to the path that will be used.

Bridging Token Ring and Ethernet – the MTU

Where bridges are used to link Token Ring to Ethernet, the larger maximum frame size of Token Ring cannot normally be used where hosts may wish to communicate with stations on the Ethernet. The frame size, or

MTU in TCP/IP terminology, is usually set and fixed for a particular interface. If it is set to the larger size for local communications within the Token Ring environment, any large frame which is sent across a bridge to the Ethernet will be discarded by the intervening bridge as being too large.

This can be an obscure fault to find as there are no error reports from bridges, though it may record some internal statistics. There are two solutions:

(1) Set the MTU for all Token Ring interfaces which could communicate with Ethernet to the Ethernet limit of 1500 octets.

(2) Use routers between the two environments.

There is a potential third solution; use source routing bridges on the Token Ring interfaces and appropriate bridges to convert between the two environments. Source routing can report the smallest MTU in a path between two systems, but it is not clear if IP software can make use of this information to vary the size of frame for each individual conversation. IP is normally given one fixed size of frame for an interface. Those using IP over Token Ring with source routing should ensure that the software can vary its frame size.

In due course, source routing drivers might become available for Ethernet systems, together with source routing bridges for Ethernet.

How applications load a network

In planning the larger TCP/IP networked systems, it is important to know what traffic is generated by each possible user transaction for typical commercial applications. Often this is dependent not on the TCP/IP standards, but on how the end user application uses the network. The only satisfactory method is to measure it for a particular set of user activities. Two different figures are required: frames per transaction and octets per transaction including all overhead. The first figure allows the loading on bridges and routers to be checked. The second allows the loading on LAN cables and WAN circuits to be estimated. Although no definitive figures can be given here, for they are implementation dependent, some guidelines are possible.

Telnet

The Telnet terminal service, described in Chapter 6 and with technical details in Chapter 12, provides a remote terminal service mostly for ANSI/VT-style terminal systems and their emulators. Originally, such terminals would have connected directly to minicomputers by V.24/EIA232 interfaces. Each character typed by the user is sent individually to the host computer and the identical character is echoed back (remote echo) or produces some other output action. For example a Tab character input is likely to produce a command to reposition the cursor to a particular screen position or to move to the start of the next unprotected field.

When Telnet was produced for TCP/IP terminal systems, remote echo was retained for these networked terminals. Each time a key is struck, it generates a single TCP segment containing that one user character. This is echoed by the remote host in a return segment containing one character. (See Chapter 12.) That echo normally carries an acknowledgement of the received character and the echo itself must be acknowledged by the originator. In the normal case, each character typed in a Telnet session generates three TCP segments of 40 or 41 octets of data in the data link frame. Where these are carried on Ethernet, they have a frame overhead of 18 octets and have 5 or 6 octets of padding to bring the frame to a minimum length of 64 octets. While this appears wasteful of Ethernet capacity, with 14 880 of these minimum-size frames available every second, there can be over 1000 two-fingered typists typing over a single cable before the cable reaches 70% loading. More important is the effect on a remote bridge or router.

Where Telnet is used over wide area circuits, the type of bridge used affects performance. Some remote bridges send the Ethernet frame unaltered including padding, some remove the padding and yet others compress either the TCP/IP headers or the whole frame. Compression increases the capacity of the wide area link. Compression algorithms can reduce the data transmitted by at least a factor of 2, doubling the capacity of a circuit. This can be most useful on long delay, high-cost international links.

If no compression is used, a 64 kbps remote bridged circuit is fully loaded by 90 typists typing at 2 characters per second. As a 64 kbps circuit is full duplex, half the typed traffic goes in one direction and the echo and acknowledge return in the other, as does any output from the host. The traffic flow is not symmetric. For text-based, full-screen data, a 64 kbps circuit can support about 480 kbytes per minute. Assuming a transaction or screenful of 1500 bytes, such a circuit will support 320 transactions per minute or between 50 and 100 active users depending on the type of application they are using.

Routers with compression, where available, are the most efficient method of remote interconnection for they will remove Ethernet padding.

Telnet uses TCP. The efficiency of transfer is improved in many implementations if the TCP window size is made large enough to allow one transaction to be sent without an intermediate acknowledgement. A window size of 2048 is more appropriate than 1024. There is no advantage in increasing beyond this for most text systems, though graphics output benefits from higher window sizes. This change does not produce an improvement noticeable by individual users at normal network loading.

At the limits, in the larger busy network, it reduces the network loading by reducing the number of acknowledgement segments.

Effects of host loading

We have on occasions observed that a host which is busy with application tasks is less efficient in its use of the network than the same host when normally loaded. For example, Telnet acknowledge segments are generated separately from the character echo. At the time when the host and the network are most heavily loaded, the host chooses to increase its load by 25%, taking four segments for each user character typed rather than three. The only solution here is to reduce the loading on the host, or to use a more efficient implementation of TCP/IP for that host.

Host buffering

Application hosts must devote sufficient buffers to handling network operations. In a UNIX environment, buffer performance is available through the *netstat -m* command. System managers should check that there are sufficient buffers of each size configured for reliable operation of the network software when the host is most heavily loaded.

In PC implementations, advanced configuration options allow the installer to choose between minimum memory (buffer) use, and maximum performance. PCs are often memory limited, but restricting the buffer available will reduce their performance and may impact traffic on the network. Where memory is available, it can usefully be given over to communications buffers.

File transfer protocol

FTP uses the TCP transport protocol. Since the highest performance file transfer must be able to stream data continuously, FTP operates most efficiently with the largest possible TCP window size. This is particularly true across wide area links where routers are not fragmenting the TCP segments generated by FTP. If the highest possible performance is required, then there is some advantage in setting the window size to release enough segments to fill all the buffers on the route. For example, if the standard MTU for the whole network is 1024 octets and there are three bridges in the path, a window size of 3072 should produce higher throughput than a window size of 1024, as three segments can then be in transit at the same time.

In general, the system manager does not know what the maximum number of bridges or routers will be. Also, it is the receiving workstation that controls the flow of data by advertising the size of buffers it is prepared to make available. When a user complains that the file transfer on a particular link is too low, it is their machine that should be reconfigured with more buffering to release data more quickly from the host.

Configuring NFS systems for performance

Because NFS presents an additional set of apparently local resources, it seems deceptively simple. Applications write to the normal interfaces for the disk or printer system locally and are redirected across the network to remote resources. Every access that should take place on the local resource is mapped into some network activity and duplicated at the remote resource.

The important management factors about resource-sharing systems using NFS from the system manager's point of view are:

- All processing and memory are local – disk and printers can be local or remote.

- Configuration choices apparently unconnected with networking can have a considerable effect on network load, for example, spool files and the program search 'path'.

- If resources are distributed around the network, data can transit the network several times between one buffering system and another before reaching its final destination.

- There is often inadequate or even no control over the size of frames used for particular purposes.

- It is often impossible to estimate the traffic that will be generated by a particular application except by measurement.

As an in-house application is developed, network planners should take measurements of the numbers of datagrams or segments and their sizes. Any anomalies should be fed back to developers for resolution. These figures can then be used to plan the network infrastructure that will be required to support a particular application.

These issues only arise when there is a resource limitation somewhere in the supporting network and the application does not perform as anticipated. It is then often found that applications are not using the network as expected or that a poorly designed application abuses local resources such as disks and printers. On a single user workstation, such abuse may go unnoticed as the application may just appear sluggish. Even in a shared minicomputer, such as a UNIX host, such abuse may never be fully uncovered, though it impacts more users. When the abuse is extended over the LAN, the effects on other systems are immediately noticed. Tracing the fault to a particular machine, application or even one user activity within an application can be much more difficult.

In what ways can an application 'abuse' the resources? This can arise because all remote resources appear to the operating system exactly as local resources. The network becomes an external extension of the computer's internal memory and peripheral buses. The following paragraphs give examples of how a resource-sharing network such as NFS is used.

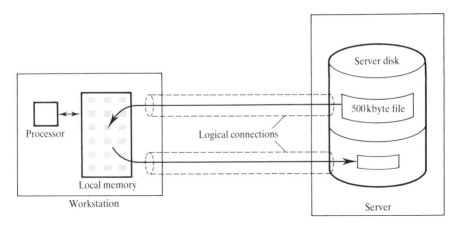

Figure 7.2   Copying a file.

Copying a file

Consider Figure 7.2 which shows a workstation copying 500 kbyte of data from one file to another on a remote file server. In a resource-sharing environment such as NFS, this generates in excess of 1 Mbyte of network traffic, a 500 k transfer between the file server and the workstation and a 500 k transfer from the workstation back to the file server. It occurs because the workstation treats the remote disk exactly as it would treat a local disk; each block of data to be copied is first loaded into the local memory and then written back to disk. This should not be regarded as abuse of the network, merely the normal operation of a resource-sharing system, but the traffic generated must be planned for. In a truly distributed computing system, the file server would copy the file locally – the network traffic would be minimal.

Printing and printer spool files

A major advantage of a system such as NFS is the ability to share a single high-performance, and hence costly, printer remotely across the network.

Remote printing can generate far greater network traffic than might at first be thought, particularly when the most modern printing methods are considered. It is likely that the shared printer is a laser printer. For the best results, print output is no longer purely text based. It may include graphics or bit-mapped images and it usually contains a number of different text fonts. Such sophisticated images are transmitted either in PostScript format, or as a bit-mapped image generated by the workstation.

Using PostScript as the printing mechanism increases the print data by a factor of 2 or more. For example, the RFC index of Appendix C was retrieved in both text and PostScript formats. The text file is 165 kbyte. The PostScript file is 303 kbyte.

When software-based fonts are used, a simple document of a few pages can turn into a print stream of several megabytes. This chapter of this book, prepared in Word for Windows is 41 k characters. When printed by Windows using TrueType fonts to a laser printer, the 'spool file' is 4.5 Mbytes. This file is printed at about 1 page per minute or 3.65 kbyte s^{-1}.

If colour is used files may increase in size by a factor of 4 to 8. Software fonts can be loaded to a printer. But to ensure that the correct set of fonts is in place on a shared printer, each application may by default load the fonts to the printer for every new task, whether it is a one page memo or a fifty page report. As more people change to using these sophisticated techniques and wish to access systems scattered throughout an organization, network planning becomes more difficult.

A remote shared printer collects files to be printed in a print queue called the print **spool file**. To ensure that pages from one task or job are not interleaved with pages from another, each print task will only start printing when the last page is delivered to the print queue and the file for that task is closed[†]. Depending on the speed of the processor creating the task, the speed of the network and the speed of the printer, this can double the time taken to print a task compared with sending it to a locally attached printer. There are few options other than to use a faster printer or a faster processor or both. As always it is important to determine what the bottleneck is by connecting the printer to the processor locally and comparing the time to print there with the time taken to print across a network. The time taken to print across a lightly loaded network could be compared with the normal network. Another possible option is to split each print task into smaller parts, with the attendant issue that they may be interleaved with output from other print users.

Microsoft Windows uses a print spooler, Print Manager, to buffer data to disk. Where a printer cannot keep up with the applications (common even with a laser printer when bit-mapped images or software fonts are involved) this can free up the application for more work more quickly than when Print Manager is not used. This print spool is in addition to that on the print queue. If both the printer and the Print Manager are remote resources, the print data may transit the network four times before it is printed. It should not normally be necessary to enable Print Manager with a remote spooled printer. For this reason, by default, Windows does not use Print Manager with a network printer.

If diskless workstations use Print Manager, the Print Manager spool files will be remote. The print data will transit the network twice even when printing locally.

[†]Ensuring that the file is properly closed is in itself an issue. This is discussed in Chapter 15.

While these figures may appear to generate high traffic, the load per printer is quite small. Except for very high performance printers using bit-mapped graphics, the load generated by one printer is likely to be insignificant. It is when a large number of systems share the same network and traffic must be reduced that consideration should be given to the load generated by printers, particularly if fonts are downloaded or software fonts are used.

The path statement

Operating systems maintain a list of disks and directories that are searched to find command files. In UNIX and MS-DOS this list is referred to as the **path**. If all disks are local, then users are unlikely to notice that the size and order of entries in the path command affect the performance of their application. When the resources are remote across a busy network and mapped to a number of different file servers, the length and order of entries in the path command may affect the performance of an application. More particularly, the order and length of items in the path command determine the number of network requests that are made by a workstation and hence the network load.

The network activity due to a path command can be reduced by ensuring that when an application is started, it is started from a batch command or script that sets the current directory to the main directory for the application, and that the path command is set up just for that application so that there are no redundant entries. The order of entries may make a difference; the most frequently used directories should come first. These will usually be the home directory and any data directories of the application. For a system using a remote copy of Word for Windows, a suitable path statement might be

```
G:\WINWORD;G:\WINDOWS;C:\MSDOS;C:\
```

The wrong way to set the path is to load one value that refers to every directory that the user of that workstation could ever wish to use. If the application is using a directory at the end of the list, it will search the complete path each time, generating many redundant datagrams. An unacceptable path for Word for Windows would be

```
E:\FRELANCE;F:\CAD;C:\MSDOS;C:\;G:\WINDOWS;G:\WINWORD
```

Backup files

Most workstation-based applications write timed backup files at intervals determined by a user-alterable parameter. For word processors and graphics packages, these files can amount to many hundreds of kilobytes where large documents are in preparation. The timed backup interval chosen is normally 5 or 10 minutes, though some users may reduce it. Where the default backup drive is a remote drive, these back-up files create additional network traffic of little value. Again, should the drive be over remote links the performance of all users could be compromised.

The time interval between backups should be extended where network loading is an issue. End users should be prevented from changing the configuration.

Temporary files

Workstation applications also produce temporary files (*.tmp files in some PC applications) for their own housekeeping requirements. This includes paging sections of memory to disk when system memory is a limitation. It is less clear when and how often these files will change. Most applications provide a degree of control by providing an option to set the drive and directory where the files are stored. Where possible, such files should be stored locally rather than generating network traffic.

These temporary files are frequently found on disks as the aftermath of a system crash.

Swap files

The operating system itself may page applications or sections of applications to disk when memory is limited. Again, allowances must be made for this traffic and the impact of any delays on system performance. Local disk, where available, has advantages for some purposes.

PC batch files

How the MS-DOS operating system interfaces batch files to the disk is not a concern when those files are local. When a batch file contains labels and GOTO statements the operating system closes and reopens the batch file whenever a label is discovered; it then rereads the batch file from the beginning in case the label was a 'jump back'. If the batch file is common to a number of users and is held on central remote storage, this additional traffic must be planned for.

Diskless workstations

For a diskless workstation, all disk resources are remote! While this is an obvious statement the effects on the network may be less clear. Having removed the disk, it is not reasonable to reduce the amount of memory. With increased memory, some can be allocated to a local disk cache to reduce network load. In a multitasking or task-switching environment increased memory will reduce the amount of paging of applications to disk and the creation of temporary files.

Summary

The parameters discussed in this chapter all affect the overall performance of a distributed system using TCP/IP. They cross the traditional boundaries between system design, application management and communications configuration. They interact in unexpected ways to impact on what is seen as the network service, though many of the adjustments are in end systems and in user applications. System and communications managers must cross the same boundaries to achieve the best performance for the integrated system.

For many of the effects discussed, the impact of a single occurrence or instance is small. Taken together in a complex internetwork of hundreds of workstations and servers, these minor changes can increase the system throughput considerably. Tuning these parameters can delay the need for costly hardware upgrades and system partitioning.

In many commercial applications, a 4 Mbps Token Ring or a 10 Mbps Ethernet appears to be an infinite resource. For other users, the loading factors from modern application systems are already a constraint and are forcing the consideration of faster systems not only for shared backbone systems but also right to the user's desk. Tuning gets the best from the installed base and can bridge the gap while other upgrades take place.

8

Request for comments

This chapter discusses the process by which TCP/IP has been standardized, the documents referred to as Request for Comments or RFC and
standard or STD. We describe what that process was and has become,
and the wealth of valuable information that is available through RFCs. You
will learn how to obtain RFCs – through the Internet, by electronic mail,
from bulletin boards and on paper from the Network Information Center.

Topics covered are:

- RFCs – what they are
- What information is available
- How you obtain RFCs

The Request for Comments (RFC) was the original mechanism through which all standards related to TCP/IP were agreed and produced. An RFC is often also the standards document that results from that standardization process. However, not all RFCs describe formal standards. RFCs can fall into a number of categories:

(1) Formal standards, which are accepted by the IAB as full standards that must be implemented by equipment which attaches to the Internet. These documents are indicated as an 'IAB standard' in the IAB official standards list, which is itself an RFC (see Appendix E).

(2) Proposed standards, formal standards which have not yet been fully evaluated and agreed.

(3) 'Informal' standards: techniques which were or are in common use but which, while solving a problem, are not considered the correct solution to be fully endorsed. (SLIP and RIP are two such protocols.)

(4) Documents that clarify the meaning of early standards which perhaps were less rigorously defined and where implementors have produced incompatible equipment.

(5) Information and education about the Internet, its services and protocols (For Your Information (FYI) documents).

(6) Managerial and organizational documents: descriptions of the composition and responsibilities of the various bodies which control and develop the Internet; descriptions of technical and managerial responsibilities for those sites attaching to the Internet.

(7) Discussion documents identifying and describing technical issues and limitations in the Internet architecture or in the existing protocols; issues which must be resolved if the latest networks and user applications are to be supported on the Internet.

It was this final category that gave the request for comments its apt name. RFCs are a rich source of education on how sophisticated computer systems are developed and on the present and past thinking about computer networks as seen by the developers in the US research communities and their colleagues worldwide.

Current RFCs

Appendix C contains an index of RFCs discussed in this book. These are listed in numerical order. At the end of each chapter in Part II is a list of the RFCs that are applicable to that chapter. In Appendix E, there is a list of the RFCs that are current IAB official protocol standards.

Numbering scheme

RFC documents are numbered RFC XXXX. At the time of writing, the latest RFCs issued have numbers in the high 1800s. There is no version number or issue number for the RFC itself. There may be a version number for the protocol or technique which is described, but if an update is required, a new RFC number is allocated. A reference in the RFC index indicates the RFC(s) which it replaces (obsoletes) or updates, or the RFC which has replaced it. In the RFC document itself, the heading gives the sequence of RFCs that refer to the standard, and the opening paragraphs give reasons for the replacement.

In March 1992 an additional reference, the STD, was introduced to identify the key protocol standards among the large number of RFCs which are purely informative. It was proposed that all IAB protocols which had reached the accepted status of IAB official standard should be identified with another designator, the STD. STD numbers will not change during the life-cycle of a protocol; however, the RFCs to which they refer will change as the protocol evolves and progresses following initial approval as an IAB official standard protocol. Some standard protocols require several RFCs to describe them fully.

The STD process is fully described in RFCs 1310 and 1311. When these RFCs were issued, there were 32 standard IAB protocols. Appendix E lists standards protocols from RFC 1311.

Style

For anyone who has tried to understand the functions of 'open' computer networks by studying ISO and ITU-T documents, RFCs are a welcome breath of fresh air in a muggy room. The style of writing is totally different from the dry, formal documents of international standards. An RFC is often more like a well-written research report.

RFC writers take time to explain, in detail, the nature of the problem to be solved, the options that were considered, their relative advantages, the solution chosen and the reasons for that choice. Where complex techniques are involved, the standard solution may be explained in terms of a concise piece of C or Pascal source code. While it is frequently emphasized that this does not imply anything about the implementation of products, when a standard is expressed in this form rather than in prose it certainly helps developers produce a consistent interpretation.

The changing RFC process

A request for comments was originally precisely that: an incomplete discussion document available throughout the research community, and to which objections and suggestions for improvement were required and expected. When a consensus was reached on the technical questions, the agreed solution would become a 'standard' for the Internet. Anyone with access to this discussion could contribute their ideas.

The discussion form of RFC does still exist; anyone may submit a document for publication as an RFC. It is vetted for content by the IAB and for technical content by the appropriate research or engineering task force. However, those RFCs which are to become IAB approved protocols now go through a rigorous vetting procedure, the 'standards track': maybe first as 'experimental', then as 'proposed standard', to 'draft standard', to 'standard'. For the most part, while comments are still invited, when RFCs become available to the public they are now much more mature, the result of considerable deliberation, and they are standards which could be implemented, not just first sketches. It is still possible for anyone to obtain the early working papers of the IETF, so this process is not carried out behind closed doors.

The standards track is not normally an issue for the commercial TCP/IP user. The details of an RFC will not usually be of interest until the standard is stable and is implemented in user equipment. However, in some circumstances, it may be important to know what work is in progress, for example to ensure that a supplier's development plans include the latest techniques.

RFC content

The process of moving towards a full protocol standard will result in multiple RFCs, having different numbers, with standard paragraphs that report the status of documentation, experience with implementations and work on standardizing the management of the equipment. It will include considerations like 'impact on the Internet' (traffic) and 'security architecture'.

Increased formality has arisen because of some equipment incompatibilities in the late 1980s and because of the considerable expansion in use of TCP/IP protocols. Unlike the current work in the OSI field, TCP/IP products have no formal conformance-testing procedures. Some products have failed to interwork immediately because their designers interpreted the standard differently. The more formal approach is intended to reduce the likelihood of a repetition of these problems.

This earlier lack of clarity was addressed in RFC 1122 and 1123. For Internet hosts, RFC 1122 describes the features of IP and TCP (the communications layers) that are mandatory or desirable and how specific events should be handled. RFC 1123 addresses the same issues for the application layers (Telnet, FTP, TFTP, SMTP, DNS and remote management). RFC 1009, Requirements for Internet Gateways, describes how routers should implement addressing, subnet addressing, some of the routing protocols and the ICMP error protocol. These documents represent the closest that TCP/IP has so far come to protocol implementation conformance requirements. They should ensure that all recent host and router implementations will interoperate correctly and to the highest level of compatibility. Equipment purchasers should ensure that their suppliers are aware of them.

The IAB standards track

As an example of the recent standards process, the IAB has defined how new gateway (router) protocols will be approved (RFC 1264). The standards must be written with sufficient clarity that the standard alone is sufficient for a successful implementation; a discussion with the authors should not be necessary to interpret exact meanings. At least two independent implementations of the standard must be produced. When the implementations are complete, interoperability tests are to be conducted among the different implementations. All major features of the standard must be tested for compatibility[†]. Any failure to interoperate in the expected manner must be highlighted, implementations corrected and the features retested. Where the failure to interoperate can be attributed to a lack of clarity in the standard, the text must be modified. Only when this process is complete can the RFC be adopted by the IAB as meeting the needs of the Internet community.

RFCs for the Open Shortest Path First (OSPF) routing protocol listed in the RFC index illustrate the above documentation procedures. The seven RFCs which refer to OSPF are listed in Table 8.1.

The initial published draft standard, RFC 1131, was used to produce three independent implementations and others derived from these. The implementors took part in three separate rounds of interoperability testing. No major problems were found with the standard, though one minor change was made and a number of clarifications were added. The version 2 protocol standard (RFC 1247) was published in July 1991. This replaced the earlier version. To meet the IAB requirements, further documents were also issued; RFC 1246 describes the results of the tests; RFC 1245 analyses the protocol, its implementation issues for hardware, memory in routers, scalability, and traffic on networks; RFC1248 introduces the Management Information Base (MIB) that is used with the Simple Network Management Protocol (SNMP). This was the first formal issue of an OSPF MIB and it appears to have elicited changes and extensions, for it was quickly replaced twice.

[†]This interoperability testing refers only to the interoperation of the protocol between like devices; a conformance test never implies any endorsement of the product by the tester or testing of the user or management interfaces or of the performance of an implementation.

Table 8.1 RFCs for OSPF

RFC	Subject	Date and size	Comment
1131	OSPF specification. Moy, J.	October, 1989; 107pp.	Obsoleted by RFC 1247
1245	OSPF protocol analysis Moy, J., ed.	July, 1991; 12pp.	
1246	Experience with the OSPF protocol. Moy, J., ed.	July, 1991; 31pp.	
1247	OSPF version 2. Moj, J.	July, 1991; 189pp.	Obsoletes RFC 1131
1248	OSPF version 2: Management Information Base. Baker, F.; Coltun, R.	July, 1991; 42pp.	Obsoleted by RFC 1252
1252	OSPF version 2: Management Information Base. Baker, F.; Coltun, R.	August, 1991; 42pp.	Obsoletes RFC 1248; obsoleted by RFC 1253
1253	OSPF version 2: Management Information Base. Baker, F.; Coltun, R.	August, 1991; 42pp.	

IAB official protocols

Periodically, the IAB updates the list of standard protocols and their status in an RFC entitled IAB Official Protocol Standards (for example, RFC 1280, March 1992). Protocols with the status of 'standard' are allocated an STD reference number.

Equivalent MIL-STDs

The US Department of Defense also uses the same protocol standards, and while its standards book has not been updated recently, the following MIL-STDs identify the key protocols. The text format is different, but the protocols are technically identical to the original RFCs:

Internet Protocol (IP)	MIL-STD-1777	RFC 791
Transmission Control Protocol (TCP)	MIL-STD-1778	RFC 793
File Transfer Protocol (FTP)	MIL-STD-1780	RFC 765
Simple Mail Transfer Protocol (SMTP)	MIL-STD-1781	RFC 821
Telnet Protocol and Options (TELNET)	MIL-STD-1782	RFC 854

The current RFC for FTP is RFC 959. This is a later version than MIL-STD-1780. The IAB clarified the requirements of hosts and gateways in later RFCs (1122, 1123 and 1009). These must be considered when consulting the MIL-STD documents which predate those RFCs.

All these MIL-STDs are available as The Department of Defense Network Protocol Handbook (1985).

Conformance to RFCs

Manufacturers will sometimes describe their products in terms of the RFCs they implement. It is important for a prospective buyer to have at least a list of the current RFCs in numerical order and categorized by function.

RFCs such as 1009, 1122, and 1123 are important when incompatibilities arise. It is important to confirm, before purchasing products, that the clarifications of these 'conformance' standards have been incorporated. In the limits, if products do not behave as expected, it may be necessary to prove which of two devices does not meet the standard as laid down. Fortunately, such problems are becoming increasingly rare.

Obtaining RFCs

Of all the standards in the communications and computing industry, RFCs are the most easily obtained and most widely available. These documents are generally in the public domain and may be freely copied and circulated; many contain the phrase 'distribution unlimited'. Furthermore, they are prepared and stored electronically on the Internet and are most often obtained and distributed by FTP, by electronic mail, and bulletin board systems[†]. Some systems keep RFCs in a compressed or archived format. The correct decompression program must be obtained, often from the same source as the RFC itself.

Early RFCs were prepared in ASCII text format. They are available on a number of different Internet-attached databases and mail systems worldwide. These text files may be downloaded across the Internet and reformatted with a word processor (see Appendix B). Some of the protocol descriptions in these early RFCs reproduce sketch drawings using ASCII mathematical symbols. While the effect is not totally aesthetic, it is quite satisfactory for many purposes.

Some of today's protocol specifications require more sophisticated drawings. Recent RFCs are also available as PostScript print files. These files, while large, give a quality equal to desktop publishing. The disadvantage to the user is that each file may be several megabytes long. They are also more expensive to transmit from mail systems over telephone or data networks, and mail system managers may object to megabyte files in someone's mailbox for any length of time. Mail and information system managers who might otherwise keep RFCs are

---

[†]In some organizations, obtaining any information from such sources is prohibited, as a virus might be unwittingly loaded. The RFC itself is not virus prone, since in the strictest sense this is not an executable program; however, where the RFC file is compressed it is important to check that the corresponding decompression program does not carry a virus.

likely to limit themselves to the text versions when disk space becomes a limitation. Even when storage compression techniques are used, RFCs can quickly consume disk space.

The following methods have been used by the authors to obtain copies of RFC documentation:

- Directly from a number of Internet information servers for those who can access the Internet directly.

- The Department of Defense Network Protocol Standards (1985) Book [MIL-STD] is obtainable from the Network Information Center at Government Systems, Inc. Full contact details are in Appendix A.

- Individual RFCs can be ordered from the Network Information Center. The cost of these RFCs has been particularly attractive; a copying charge of $10 is payable for any size of RFC.

For those not connected directly to the Internet, some Internet servers can still be accessed by electronic mail. Many commercial information systems provide mail access to the Internet. Two that the authors have used are CIX (Compulink Information Exchange) and CompuServe Information Service (CIS).

As well as information servers in the USA there are a number of mirror sites on research networks around the world. Whether access to these networks is available for commercial use may depend on local policy and regulations. A complete statement of how to obtain RFCs is itself available from the Internet. This lists all primary and secondary sites around the world which officially hold Internet information. See Appendix B for the appropriate mail mechanism. Appendix B also shows the content of a message to request a number of RFCs.

Mirror sites

A number of academic sites worldwide act as mirror sites for the storage of RFCs and other standards documents in the public domain. Some of these may be accessed for commercial purposes.

By this method, three RFCs with a total text content of 251 kbyte or some 160 pages were obtained and printed in around one hour.

Summary

Access to up-to-date information in the still evolving world of TCP/IP is most important for technical specialists, developers, consultants and trainers. But there are times when everyone operating and maintaining TCP/IP networks will wish to have access to definitive source documents.

The ability to retrieve this information on-line and at acceptable cost is a key difference between TCP/IP and other communications architectures. As storage techniques and printing technology improve along with the world's communications infrastructure, it will be the work of moments to produce a desktop-published, quality standards document anywhere in the world for discussion about TCP/IP.

PART II

Technology and standards

9

Introduction

Part II of this book is a detailed technical discussion of the components and protocols that make up a TCP/IP implementation. Before delving into the depths of the technology, this chapter discusses the growth of the successful network and offers some analogies to explain the performance problems that are likely to be encountered.

In this second part of the book, we consider the TCP/IP protocols and their configuration aspects in more detail. It is not always essential to understand the operation of a system in detail, but, if you do, you can get better performance, more efficiency and resolve problems more easily. We often compare a network to the motor car[†]. You can drive safely and quite adequately without knowing a thing about its workings, but when something goes wrong – it starts making an abnormal noise – a more detailed understanding of how the components operate allows you to judge how serious the problem is; whether to continue your journey, call out the rescue service or head for the nearest dealer to buy a new car.

Talking of cars brings to mind another analogy as to why we should understand a protocol in more depth. Suppose you stand on a motorway (freeway) bridge and watch vehicles passing below. You notice that the road is very busy; all lanes are full of fast-moving traffic. At first sight, you may believe this is all useful traffic and this transport system is working well. But you notice that occasionally traffic grinds to a halt and you might think, 'we need an extra lane on this stretch'. However, when you realize that there are many different types of vehicle and they each have different significance, you get another view; you start to understand what is really happening on your transport system.

How big are the lorries? Does the fact that there are only a few large lorries and many small vans indicate that whatever is being carried is being carried inefficiently? Could the goods being carried be handled more efficiently in larger lorries or some other transport system, by air, rail or canal? What does the presence of all the breakdown trucks indicate? They are adding to what initially seemed useful traffic, but they are probably towing away cars that had broken down. What about all these cars with just a driver? If this is a commuter route, can they be persuaded to form a car pool, or to use public transport? Would this save the need for that other lane, or at least postpone it? Adding an additional lane to an operational motorway is hugely expensive and, until the work is completed, tends to cause even more congestion. Planners sigh in disgust and say 'we told you so'.

Most of the above aspects apply to the life and operation of a network. Understanding the basic operation of a network protocol allows you to realize what is *really* happening on the transport system. We have seen a number of networks that *appeared* to have very high levels of traffic with users complaining about poor performance. Everyone was set to increase the capacity at great expense. On closer examination, the traffic was, in fact, generated by retransmissions due to high levels of errors. Correcting the problem on the network did not affect the level of traffic, but since it was now carrying useful data, not retransmissions, the

---

[†]There are a huge number of useful analogies, one of the most important of which is the traffic jam!

Figure 9.1 TCP/IP model.

effective throughput of the system increased significantly, and the cost and disruption of the upgrade was delayed. Of course, sometimes the planners just 'got it wrong' or it was never really planned in the first place or, returning to the analogy, some sharp salesman sold them the idea of motor transport and got them to build a country lane, when they really needed a four-lane highway. Alternatively, and more positively, perhaps no one really believed that the system would ever get that big!

So, in this part, we look in more depth at the workings of the TCP/IP protocol stack, starting at the lower physical layers and moving up to the application layer. We have also provided some of those useful bits of reference material that you often need, but can never find, when analysing TCP/IP systems.

Protocol layering

Communications protocols are described in layers. This divides up the huge problem of how to communicate data between two or more devices into smaller, manageable pieces which can be more easily understood. If the functionality of each layer can be described accurately, people can easily build systems that are totally compatible. The model resulting from combining the layers defined is often referred to as a **protocol stack**.

The TCP/IP protocol stack has been defined in this layered way and the definitions of how it should work are written down in RFCs. Each layer of the protocol stack has been carefully defined and developed over many years to provide a reliable and stable platform for implementation and for further development. In the following chapters, we will be considering the functions of each layer.

TCP/IP is a five-layered model (Figure 9.1), not seven-layered like the ISO OSI model. Figure 9.1 shows what the unit of information is at each layer; at layer 1 it is a **bit**, at layer 2 it is a **frame**, at layer 3 it is the **datagram**, at layer 4, it can be either a **segment** or a datagram, and at layer 5 a **message**.

Layers 1 and 2 of the model are not actually defined by the TCP/IP RFCs, as TCP/IP was designed to be independent of physical media. It can operate over any network that moves bits from one place to another with a reasonably low bit error rate[†]. However, when we come to install networks, we cannot ignore the foundations on which they are built just because they are not formally specified by the standards. We therefore discuss issues that relate to the physical medium in the next section.

Layer 3 is the Internet Protocol (IP) layer. This layer provides a basic datagram service, that is, IP moves data with its best effort but with no guarantee of delivery. A service called the Internet Control Message Protocol (ICMP) is normally provided within this layer. ICMP reports problems in the transmission of datagrams and allows systems to adapt to current conditions in a network. Also contained within the IP layer are the Address Resolution Protocol (ARP) and the Reverse Address Resolution Protocol (RARP). These are used for mapping IP addresses to MAC layer addresses.

At layer 4 there are two possible options, the User Datagram Protocol (UDP) and the Transmission Control Protocol (TCP):

- UDP just extends IP's connectionless datagram service to applications that do not require reliability – there are such things! UDP datagrams can be sent to a network without the overhead of creating and maintaining a connection. In some environments, this is more desirable.

- TCP provides a reliable service with error correction and flow control. The cost of providing a reliable service is more overhead in connection set-up and closedown, processing power for correcting errors and data transmission, but some applications need reliability irrespective of cost.

Connectionless protocols, like UDP, are used in a situation where a node wishes to send information quickly to a large number of destinations. This will often be a small amount of information and there will be a new better value coming along in a few seconds (for example, the time, users currently logged on, the stock market index). The most efficient way in a network that can support broadcasting to all nodes is to send one packet with a destination address which is recognized by all nodes, so they all receive it. If this were attempted with a reliable connection-based point-to-point service like TCP, broadcasting would not be possible and a large number of packets would be generated in building a connection, sending

---

[†]This should be as low as possible, but better than 1 in 5×10^5 (end to end) to give a block error rate of 10% for standard IP datagrams of 576 octets on a wide area link. Today, there is rarely any reason why this should not be improved upon by a factor of 10.

the message and closing the connection to each node. This would take time, processing power and large amounts of bandwidth, possibly just to repeat the process 10 seconds later, because the value sent is now out of date.

Layer 5 of TCP/IP is the application layer. This layer provides services suitable for the different types of application that might wish to use the network. It does not provide the application itself, although the two are closely related. Examples are terminal connections (Telnet), electronic mail, the Simple Mail Transfer Protocol (SMTP) and the File Transfer Protocol (FTP).

Achieving compatibility

When we consider the functionality required to connect computers and their users together across a network, there are two basic areas that must be addressed to perform some useful task: moving data and interpreting it. The lower layers of the model deal with getting data on and off the cabling systems, and moving it between cabling systems and into computers, reliably if required; the higher layer of the protocol stack deals with getting information into a form that each end can understand.

As network developers and managers, lower layer compatibility is an obvious requirement and hits you between the eyes. It is clear that we must use the same kind of medium and physical connector to attach two systems together in a compatible way; you would have difficulty attaching an optical-fibre-connected device to a radio-system-connected device without a conversion box. Similar problems arise at the higher layer with data compatibility, but the effects are often at first less striking. At the higher layers there is a difficulty because different computers and operating systems deal with data in different ways. It is up to the higher levels of the protocol stack to smooth out these differences, so that information sent from an application on one computer still has the same meaning when it arrives at another. It is not just a matter of transporting data transparently across a network.

For example, some operating systems store numeric values with their most significant byte first (68000 architectures) and others with least significant byte first (80x86). If we passed a value in one form to a machine that used the other form the actual value would be misread: see Figure 9.2. The value 480 (256 + 128 + 64 + 32) is shown represented in both ways. If the value 480 were sent from the machine that uses Most Significant Byte (MSB) first to the machine that is Least Significant Byte (LSB) first, the LSB machine would read the value as 57345. This is only a simple example to illustrate the point; the issue gets more complex as we look at more complex data structures.

The requirement for modern communication systems is to consider all levels of the problem – true internetworking.

LS byte representation of
480 (80x86 machines)
11100000 00000001

MS byte representation of
480 (680xx machines)
00000001 11100000

Figure 9.2 The representation of numbers.

'Packet' formation

The previous paragraphs highlighted differences in information within a machine. Across a network, the structure of data is under the control of the protocol designer. How is information structured as it travels across a network?

Figure 9.3 shows two TCP/IP protocol stacks in two separate nodes A and B. An application in node A wishes to send data to node B. The application calls the application layer communications service on A. The application layer takes this data and adds some information, the Application Header (AH), to that data, which tells the remote application layer on B what to do with the data. The application communications layer passes this complete data unit, AH and its data, to the transport layer and instructs it to send data to node B. Transport adds its own Transport Layer Header (TH) and passes the new longer data unit,

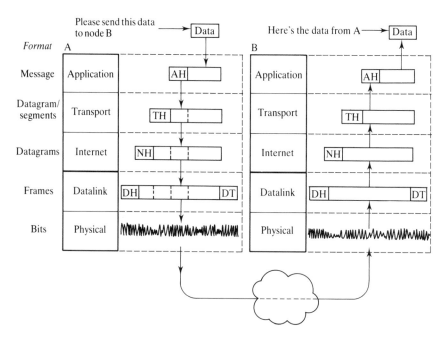

Figure 9.3 Building a frame.

a segment, to the network layer with instructions to pass it to node B. The network layer adds its own header, NH, and passes the new data unit[†], a datagram, all down to the datalink layer. The datalink layer adds its own header and often some form of checksum at the end to form a frame and passes it to the physical layer. The physical layer converts the bits of the data into relevant signals for this type of medium and sends it on to the interface cable.

When node B's physical layer receives the signals from the medium, it translates the electrical signals back into bits and into the octets[‡] of the frame sent by node A. It then passes it to the datalink layer which checks the checksum and then considers the information in the Datalink Header (DH) to ensure that this frame is for this node. If it is, then it removes the header and the trailer (DH and DT) and passes the information up to the network layer. The network layer considers NH to see what it needs to do with this datagram and, if destined for this machine, it passes it to the appropriate transport layer. The transport layer considers TH, removes it and passes the information to the application layer which again considers AH and passes the data to the correct application on node B.

In this way, data is sent between two computers. The headers added by each layer are messages between the equivalent layer in two machines (peer layers). We can consider each layer as sending information directly to its partner with instructions that relate to the information being carried. The layer is not concerned about how the information was carried, only that it is correct and what to do with it. Most of the header information is some form of addressing to ensure data reaches the correct computer and the relevant application in that computer.

TCP and OSI

In our training courses, we are often asked: how does TCP/IP relate to the OSI model? Or where does TCP/IP fit into the OSI model? First, let us look at the two models together (Figure 9.4). Quite clearly, OSI has more layers than TCP/IP, but if we consider the functionality of the layers, the bottom four layers are comparable. Up to layer 2, the models are compatible. OSI in layers 1 and 2 defines many different media systems that can be used, and TCP/IP was designed to be medium independent, so, in principle, TCP/IP *should* run on any OSI standard system. In general,

---

[†]As we shall see, the network layer may split the segment into several datagrams to fit the underlying network technology.

[‡]An ITU-T and OSI word meaning eight bits of information. Unlike a byte, there is no inference that these eight bits represent one character; they can be eight individual flags, or part of a 64-bit number or structure in between. We shall use the word octet rather than byte.

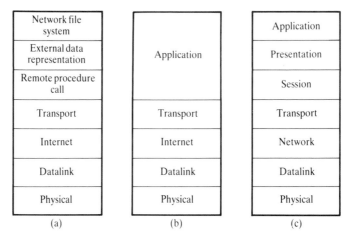

Figure 9.4 Comparing (a) NFS, (b) TCP/IP and (c) OSI.

and with some careful thought to configuration details, this is also true in practice. It allows us to operate both protocols on the same media.

When we consider layers 3 and 4, the Internet and transport of TCP/IP and network and transport of OSI, OSI has a number of different options that can be used at these layers. However, there is a set of options in OSI that produces almost identical functionality to TCP/IP, comparable but not compatible.

Major differences occur at the application layer of TCP/IP. At this level, the OSI model separates into three layers, adding, most importantly, the presentation layer. This is perhaps the most significant difference between the two protocol suites. The presentation layer of OSI deals with the problem mentioned above, that of unambiguously conveying and interpreting the full meaning of information between computers with very different architectures. In OSI, the power of these functions is far superior to traditional TCP/IP.

This level of functionality has been provided in TCP/IP through the Sun Microsystems Inc. Network File System (NFS), more correctly termed Open Network Computing (ONC). The architecture of this system added an extra three layers on top of the transport layer of TCP/IP, giving a seven-layered model. NFS adds powerful functions to the traditional TCP/IP application layer[†].

So how does TCP/IP fit into the OSI model? The strict answer is that it does not. TCP and OSI are similar in certain aspects with similar aims, but they are clearly different in the way they operate. At one low level, they should coexist, but they cannot interwork (without a gateway).

[†]While NFS is discussed in this book for completeness, a companion volume in this series, *TCP/IP and ONC/NFS: Internetworking in a UNIX Environment* 2nd edn by M. Santifaller, Addison-Wesley, 1995, covers NFS in more detail.

How does TCP/IP relate to OSI? There is a good match at layers 1 and 2, and a reasonable match at layers 3 and 4. At the higher layers, TCP/IP lacks a powerful presentation layer, making it more difficult to provide full transparency.

Summary

In this chapter, we introduced the layering of TCP/IP and compared it with OSI. We discussed why it is important to understand the detail of a protocol, for it allows us to ascertain exactly why a system is not performing as expected.

The rest of Part II considers each of the layers of TCP/IP in technical detail and points out the steps to take, the options to configure, and diagnostic techniques to use to optimize the performance of a TCP/IP installation.

10

The physical and datalink layers

The design of the TCP/IP protocol stack was intended to allow it to operate over any kind of communications system. To meet this requirement, features have been added to hide the various characteristics of these systems and allow the network layer (IP) to provide a unified view of all media to the transport layer[†]. We will explain some of the issues that relate to the most common medium types that TCP/IP uses.

In this chapter we will consider:

- Ethernet
- IEEE and ISO
- Token Ring
- FDDI
- SLIP
- PPP
- X.25
- ISDN
- Fast packet technology
- Bridging TCP/IP

[†] Normally the User Datagram Protocol (UDP) and the Transmission Control Protocol (TCP).

The TCP/IP model

Figure 10.1 shows the TCP/IP model. We can see that the Internet Protocol (IP) provides the network layer that operates over the two lower layers, the datalink and physical layers. In this chapter, we will consider the makeup of these lower layers and issues that relate to their use by IP.

The different types of media can all be used for end-node connections or for interconnection to other networks, but certain architectures are more suited to supporting one type of operation than another. Applications programs sitting on the transport layer above the IP layer must not be concerned with the underlying communications medium. Achieving this transparency begins with the IP layer.

The most significant differences between communications systems are their performances and the number of connections they can support. The most difficult characteristic to hide is performance; the different media successfully used by TCP/IP can vary in speed from 1200 bps (bits per second) through to 100 000 000 bps and beyond.

Ethernet

Probably the most common medium over which TCP/IP systems operate is **Ethernet**. Ethernet is a coaxial-based bus cabling system developed jointly by the Digital Equipment Corporation, Intel Corporation and Xerox Corporation often collectively referred to as DIX. Ethernet uses baseband transmission techniques to transport data, and is available on two sizes of coaxial cable known as **thick-wire Ethernet** and **thin-wire Ethernet**. These two types of cable are both widely used throughout the world.

Figure 10.1 TCP/IP model.

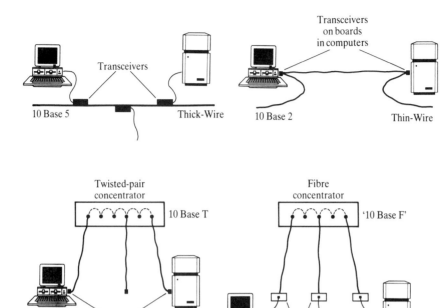

Figure 10.2   Ethernet topologies.

Ethernet topologies

Figure 10.2 shows the topologies available with Ethernet. Thick-wire Ethernet has better electrical characteristics than thin-wire, so longer lengths are possible before signal regeneration is necessary. Thick-wire Ethernet can support up to 100 connections over 500 metres of cable. Special devices called **transceivers** provide a standard interface to the cabling system for computer connections. This interface is usually referred to as the **Attachment Unit Interface** (AUI). An AUI or transceiver cable connects the network interface card (LAN card) in the computer to the transceiver.

Thin-wire coaxial systems are simpler and therefore cheaper; many LAN cards have transceivers suitable for thin wire built into them.

Ethernet's significant advantage in the early days of LANs was its speed. Operating at 10 Mbps, it provided extremely fast response to the interactive terminal systems then in use. As computers and their networking hardware have become faster and have begun to exchange larger amounts of data, this speed of the network is often a limiting factor.

				46–1500	
8 octets	6 octets	6 octets	2 octets	octets	4 octets
Preamble	Destination address	Source address	Type	Data	CRC

Figure 10.3   Ethernet frame.

The Ethernet frame

The Ethernet specification defines the physical aspects of layer 1 and the services of layer 2. It details the format of the packet, usually called a frame at the link layer. Figure 10.3 shows the format of an Ethernet frame. This frame encapsulates the TCP/IP protocol and is responsible for transporting it across the cabling system to layer 2 of the destination device, whether that device is a router, gateway or end node.

MAC addressing

The Ethernet frame uses addresses referred to as physical or **Medium Access Control** (MAC) **addresses**[†]. MAC addresses labelled 'destination' and 'source' identify the specific network cards the frame is travelling between. These MAC addresses are 48 bits long and are fixed. They are configured into the hardware of network cards at manufacture, normally on programmable read-only memory. It is possible with some systems to configure the card to use a local address defined by the user, rather than the address that is held in PROM. MAC addresses are supposed to be unique, so that every network card ever manufactured can be addressed explicitly. This address is often referred to as a **unicast** address, an address specifying a single LAN card.

Cards attached to a LAN cable decode all frames transmitted on that cable medium, but the hardware of the LAN card will only accept and fully process frames with three kinds of MAC address. This reduces the processing load on the LAN card's workstation. The first kind are those frames with a destination address corresponding to their unicast MAC address. The other two MAC addresses that are accepted are **broadcast** and **multicast**.

A broadcast MAC address, which must only be used as a destination address, has all 48 bits set to binary 1 (hexadecimal FF FF FF FF FF FF). A frame that has the broadcast address in its destination field will be fully processed by all LAN cards on the same network[‡] and may be passed by the card to the workstation software. This type of frame is used when the sender does not know the destination MAC address of the node with which it is trying to communicate.

[†]We will refer to layer 2 addresses as MAC addresses.
[‡]A network consists of cabling, repeaters and bridges. Routers separate networks.

Table 10.1 Ethernet type fields.

Type	Protocol
0x0800	IP
0x0806	ARP
0x8035	RARP

Multicast addresses refer to groups of LAN cards that are cooperating or are related in some way. The LAN cards have to be configured to know that they are members of a particular multicast group. An example of a MAC multicast is when a message is sent to all LAN cards of a particular make. This technique is used by some proprietary systems to address frames to all of their associated LAN cards.

The type field

The **type** field identifies different protocols. A computer running multiple protocols can easily differentiate between them and pass the contents of frames to the relevant network layer software.

TCP/IP systems generally use three Ethernet type values as listed in Table 10.1. We shall consider each of these protocols in detail later. Ethernet type numbers are registered with IEEE to ensure that the use of a particular number is unique.

The cyclic redundancy check

At the end of the frame is a **Cyclic Redundancy Check** (CRC). This is a 32-bit value that is calculated from all the bits of the Ethernet frame and its contents, but ignoring the preamble and the CRC itself. The CRC is passed with the frame to the remote node, which performs the same calculation. If none of the bits is corrupted, the destination node should produce the same result as the original node. If the frame has been corrupted, the value calculated will be different from that in the frame. The LAN card hardware will then not pass the frame to the network layer.

The service provided by Ethernet

Ethernet provides a shared medium access system that can be used by many different protocols. Hardware to support it is widely available and it is generally well known and understood. The most significant characteristics are its transmission speed, medium access mechanism and, as a transmission mechanism for TCP/IP, its frame sizes.

The medium access mechanism used by Ethernet is **Carrier Sense Multiple Access with Collision Detection** (CSMA/CD). This allows nodes on the network to manage shared access to the cable, but it restricts the length of the cabling system and also the number of nodes that use it. These restrictions are physical aspects of the network and do not affect the protocols, so they are not specific to TCP/IP, but network planners must ensure that the physical design constraints are adhered to otherwise the basis upon which TCP/IP operates will be unstable.

The minimum and maximum frame sizes of Ethernet are 64 and 1518 octets. This includes all of the frame, apart from the preamble.

The maximum size limits the amount of data that can be transferred in one frame. Because of the frame header fields, the CRC and then the overhead of the IP and TCP or UDP higher layer protocols, the amount left for useful application data is less than 1518. The actual value depends on a number of factors. To give an example, the Ethernet frame overhead consists of 18 octets and the higher layer protocols often need 40 octets. That leaves 1460 octets ($1518-40-18 = 1460$) for application data.

The minimum size of 64 octets increases the overhead for transmitting small IP datagrams. All frames must be padded out to 64 octets if the protocol carried produces a shorter frame. To transfer a single byte of application data in the TCP/IP environment requires a pad of an extra 5 octets. The minimum frame would typically consist of the Ethernet frame overhead of 18 octets, 40 octets for the higher layer protocols and 1 for the application data, a total of 59. This requires Ethernet to pad out the frame with an extra 5 octets to reach 64 octets.

In later chapters, we shall describe how these fields are used by the TCP/IP protocols to achieve effective communication across a cabling system.

Configuration and management

Configuration of TCP/IP to operate over Ethernet is limited to selecting the maximum frame size available to TCP/IP and the number of buffers available for receiving datagrams. The maximum size will normally default to 1500, the Ethernet maximum having removed its 18-byte overhead. Choosing alternative values is discussed in Chapter 18.

IEEE and ISO systems

By adopting the IEEE standards for LANs which are based upon the OSI reference model, the ISO has defined a collection of access control methods, cabling systems and cable types that are international standards. Figure 10.4 shows the most common systems used today. IEEE 802.3 uses the CSMA/CD[†] mechanism for medium access control. IEEE 802.4 uses a token-passing mechanism on a bus, whereas IEEE 802.5 and fibre distributed data interface (IS9314) use a token-passing mechanism on a ring.

[†]CSMA/CD is the same mechanism for accessing the medium as used by DIX Ethernet.

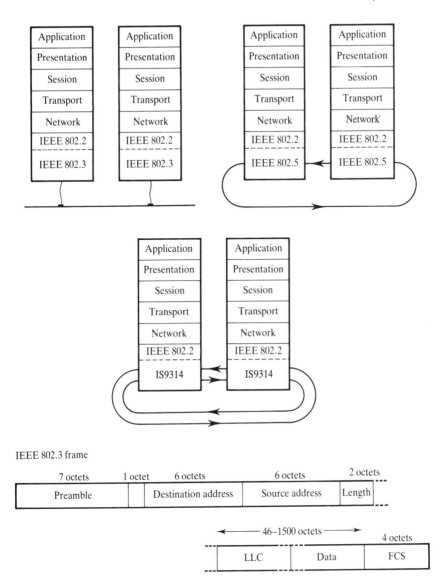

Figure 10.4 IEEE 802.3 frame and IEEE topology.

Apart from the topology and numbers of connections that can be made to the different OSI media, their major differences are their speeds of transmission and the maximum sizes of frame they support. Like DIX Ethernet, CSMA/CD systems usually operate at a speed of 10 Mbps, but token passing systems can be 4 Mbps, 16 Mbps or 100 Mbps. At present, 100 Mbps operation is available on fibre optic cable using the FDDI standard, but FDDI is expected to be augmented by the Copper Distributed Data Interface (CDDI), which allows the same speed of operation on copper wires.

For LANs, layer 2 of the OSI model is split into two sublayers. The lower sublayer is MAC and above it, **Logical Link Control** (LLC). LLC is a common sublayer which should always be used on top of any ISO/IEEE LAN implementation. It has its own standard number, IEEE 802.2.

As with Ethernet, MAC is the mechanism for sharing the cable. The two common techniques are CSMA/CD and token passing. The original intention was that the content of the frames would be similar, but there are some fundamental differences which reduce the options for network planners in mixing technologies from the different IEEE standards. After a preamble, which is dependent on the access method, all the basic frames contain the relevant 48-bit destination and source MAC addresses.

One of the major functions of LLC[†] is to differentiate between the different types of network layer protocols, in a similar way to the type field of Ethernet.

The IEEE 802.3 frame

The IEEE 802.3 frame has the same general format as the DIX Ethernet frame. Many discussions have not, in the past, distinguished these two technologies. However, the 16-bit field immediately following the source MAC address, which in Ethernet is the type field, is the **length** field in IEEE 802.3. The length field verifies the number of octets of protocol data between the end of the length field and the start of the **Frame Check Sequence** (FCS). The FCS is calculated in an identical way to Ethernet's CRC.

As there is no type field, it is not possible to detect which network layer protocol is carried at the MAC layer. The MAC frame consists of only addresses, length and FCS. It is the function of LLC to separate the different network layer protocols.

Coexistence with DIX Ethernet

The IEEE 802.3 standard was based on DIX Ethernet, so IEEE 802.3 cabling and components today only have minor differences, thus allowing the two types to be used together.

IEEE has standardized more cabling types than DIX Ethernet. As IEEE 802.3 transceivers also support the AUI interface to any of these cabling systems, a LAN card supporting AUI can connect indirectly to any of the different media. Some LAN cards have the transceiver circuitry fabricated into their hardware so the cabling system can connect directly to them.

[†]LLC has three variants called LLC1 to LLC3. Only LLC1 is likely to be used with TCP/IP.

One cabling system can support both IEEE 802.3 and DIX Ethernet transmission simultaneously, though the two systems cannot interwork. A station receiving a valid frame examines the 16 bits following the source MAC address. If this value is less than 1501 (hex 0x05DD), the frame must be an IEEE 802.3 frame as that is the maximum allowed length; if this field is greater than 1500, these 16 bits are an Ethernet type field and the frame is processed accordingly. For this to work, there are no commonly used Ethernet types of less than 0x600.

IEEE 802.3 cable types

The common IEEE 802.3 cabling types are:

- Thick-wire or 10Base5 using thick coaxial cable in a bus topology up to 500 metres per segment (often referred to as thick Ethernet).

- Thin-wire or 10Base2 using thin RG58 coaxial cable in a bus or star topology up to 185 metres per segment (often referred to as thin-wire Ethernet).

- Twisted pair or 10BaseT using unshielded twisted pair cable (UTP or telephone cable) in a star topology up to 100 metres radius from a wiring concentrator or hub.

The IEEE 802.5 frame

With IEEE 802.5 a simple frame, called the **token**, is passed around the medium from node to node. If any node wishes to transmit, it can only do so when it 'holds the token', which means it has received the token and the token is flagged as being free. When a node receives the token it has a specified amount of time (token hold time) to transmit data.

Figure 10.5 shows the format of an IEEE 802.5 frame. A token consists of the **start delimiter**, **access control** and **end delimiter** fields. The functions of each field are:

- *Start delimiter* The start delimiter provides synchronization with the incoming data.

- *Access control* This field is used to manage token priority. Nodes on a Token Ring can operate at different priorities so certain nodes can be given higher priority to use the ring and hence get preferential treatment for throughput. A node can use reservation bits if it has lower priority than the token so that it may get a chance to transmit next time the token comes around.

   The access control field also contains the token bit (T) and the monitor bit (M). The token bit is 0 for a token and 1 for a data frame. When the node accepts the token to transmit a data frame, this field is changed from 0 to 1.

Figure 10.5 IEEE 802.5 frame.

A frame will rotate around the ring and back to the originator; the originator is responsible for removing its frame and releasing a free token. The M bit is used to ensure that frames are removed from the ring in the event that this sending node fails to remove the frame. One node on a Token Ring acts as a monitor to manage the protocol. As frames go through the monitor the M bit is set to 1. The frame should be removed by the sender; if not, it will return to the monitor with the M bit set at 1. In this case the monitor will remove the frame from the ring and pass on a free token.

- *Frame control*   This field has two subfields within it. One is used to distinguish between token management frames and those carrying data. The second is used for LLC service call priority.

- *Destination and source MAC addresses*   These are the MAC addresses as discussed for IEEE 802.3 and Ethernet.

- *Routing information*   Token Ring systems can use a mechanism called source routing for determining the path to take through a multiple path bridged network. The routing information field carries a path in each frame indicating the route to the relevant bridges and networks. This field can be from 0 octets, when not using source routing, to 30 octets long.

- *Information*   LLC and its data field.

- *Frame check sequence*   A 32-bit frame check sequence.

- *End delimiter*   A special non-data pattern to define the end of the frame.

Table 10.2 The longest 802.5 frame header.

Field	Octets
MAC header	15
Routing information	30
LLC[†]	4
SNAP[†]	5
MAC trailer	6
Total	60

[†]Covered later in this chapter.

- *Frame status* A special octet which is two identical nibbles (4-bit quantities) with two flags, A and C. Flag A is used by a receiver to indicate that it has recognized that the frame was for itself and the C flag is used by a receiver to indicate that it has copied the frame into memory.

  It is possible for a node that is short of resource to recognize a frame but not be able to copy it. In this case, A would be set but not C. The nibbles are duplicated as this field is not protected by the FCS and so is unreliable. This field is not used by the protocol, but is for management purposes, to build statistics of resource problems.

The most significant factor of IEEE 802.5 for TCP/IP systems is the maximum amount of data that can be transmitted in a frame. Unlike CSMA/CD, this is not fixed, as the Token Hold Timer (THT) is configurable and alters the size of the maximum frame. Normally the THT is around 8 ms, so for a 4 Mbps transmission rate it is possible to transmit a frame which is 36 000 bits or 4500 (36 000/8) octets.

As shown in Table 10.2, the longest header, including a full routing information field, will be 60 octets long. Subtracting these 60 octets from 4500 leaves 4440 octets for TCP/IP headers and data.

The IS9314 FDDI frame

FDDI is based on the token-passing standards used in IEEE 802.5, but with a few adaptations to suit fibre and to build a highly reliable dual ring mechanism.

Figure 10.6 shows the physical architecture of FDDI which consists of a dual ring system with class A devices that attach to both rings and class B systems that only connect to a single ring. If the ring fails between two class A systems, they are able to loop the working part of the ring back on itself, so the system turns into a single ring, and remains operable.

The major benefits of FDDI are the distances that it can cover and its high speed: nodes can be up to 2 km apart with a perimeter of 200 km;

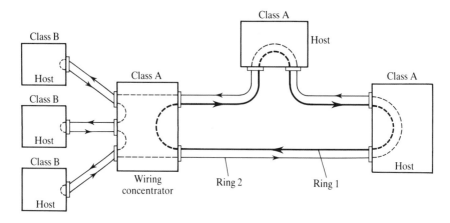

Figure 10.6 Topology of an FDDI ring.

it operates at 100 Mbps. FDDI makes an ideal backbone networking system because of its performance and the characteristics of fibre.

The maximum frame size of FDDI is 4500 octets and the normal FDDI header is shown in Table 10.3 with a size of 32 octets. It is recommended that 148 bytes are allocated for header fields to allow for future expansion, giving a recommended maximum IP frame of 4352 octets.

The FDDI frame is similar to the IEEE 802.5 frame but has a few differences to cater for the medium and its speed of operation. FDDI uses a special encoding mechanism called 4B/5B which encodes each 4 bits of data into a 5-bit 'symbol' for transmission. Not all combinations of five bits need be used; some are invalid and others are used to mark the beginning and end of a data frame. These symbols are transmitted at 125 Mbps so the 'normal' data rate is 100 Mbps. This makes it easy to recover the system clock and is more efficient than the encoding system used on Ethernet or Token Ring. Because of this mechanism, transmissions are considered in 4-bit quantities which make up each symbol.

The function of each field is as follows:

- *Preamble* This is a special sequence used to synchronize the incoming frame with the receiver clock – 16 symbols.

Table 10.3 Normal FDDI header.

Field	Octets
MAC header	16
LLC[†]	4
SNAP[†]	5
MAC trailer	7 (approx.)
Total	32

[†]Covered later in this chapter.

- *Start delimiter* The start delimiter indicates the beginning of the frame – 2 symbols.

- *Frame control* This field has a number of functions based on the flags used within it. It has the bit format CLFFZZZ, where C indicates whether the frame is synchronous or asynchronous (a basic priority scheme), L indicates whether 16- or 48-bit addresses[†] are used, FF is used to distinguish between MAC and LLC frames and ZZZ defines the type of MAC frame.

- *Destination and source MAC addresses* These are the MAC addresses as discussed for IEEE 802.3 and Ethernet.

- *Routing information* Token Ring systems can use a mechanism called source routing for determining the path to take through a multiple path bridged network. The routing information field carries a path indicating the route to the relevant bridges and networks in each frame. This field can be from 0 octets, when not using source routing, to 30 octets long.

- *Information* LLC and its data field.

- *Frame check sequence* A 32-bit frame check sequence – 8 symbols.

- *End delimiter* A special non-data transmission to define the end of the frame – can be 1 or 2 symbols.

- *Frame Status* A special field which is three or more symbols. The first three symbols are used to indicate the flags E, A and C respectively. Flag A is used by a receiver to indicate that it recognized that the frame was for itself and the C flag used by a receiver to indicate that it has copied the frame. E is used to flag a frame which was in error. It is possible for a node that is short of resource to recognize a frame is for itself, but not be able to copy it to memory, hence A would be set but not C. The symbols are duplicated as this field is not protected by the FCS and so is unreliable. This field is not used by the protocol but for management purposes, to build statistics of resource problems.

FDDI is included in OSI standards and is used with IEEE 802.2 LLC as described in the next section. A version of FDDI has been designed for use over copper cabling instead of fibre CDDI.

Logical link control, IEEE 802.2

The LLC layer provides a compatible interface, irrespective of the MAC layer used, so this interface remains consistent no matter what type of cabling system is used – Token Ring, FDDI or CSMA/CD.

[†]16-bit addresses were never widely used in IEEE LANs.

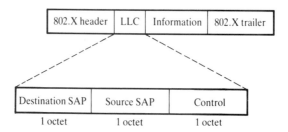

Figure 10.7 LLC in an IEEE frame.

LLC is responsible for passing incoming packets to the appropriate network layer protocol. Its variants are LLC1 to LLC3. LLC1 (logical link control, type 1, connectionless) is the only variant likely to be found with TCP/IP systems. Connectionless systems use datagrams – transmissions that are not acknowledged – so the sender does not know definitely whether the frame arrived or not. Error correction is the responsibility of a higher layer. This is the best match for TCP/IP's requirements.

LLC carries two more 8-bit addresses (Figure 10.7), the destination and source **Service Access Points** (SAPs). Since SAPs define a protocol, and protocols cannot talk to a protocol of a different type, these numbers are usually the same. To make sure systems do not interfere with each other, SAPs are registered with ISO. For example, there is a SAP defined for the ARPANET Internet Protocol (06). In principle, this would allow IP to operate over an OSI cabling system, but the recommended way of using TCP/IP protocols over OSI LLC is through use of the **SubNetwork Access Protocol** (SNAP). This uses the SAP 0xAA. SNAP is fully described later in this chapter.

While not necessary for supporting IP and ARP, all implementations of LLC are required to support IEEE 802.2 standard class 1 service. This requires support for Unnumbered Information (UI) commands, eXchange IDentification (XID) commands and responses, and TEST link (TEST) commands and responses. The third octet of LLC, the control field, is used to differentiate between these different types of frame.

The UI frame is key, for it carries data for the higher layer protocols. A UI frame has an LLC control field of 0x03 (3 decimal).

When either an XID or a TEST command is received, a response must be returned with the destination and source addresses, and the DSAP and SSAP swapped. The XID command or response has an LLC1 control field value of 0xAF (175 decimal) if poll is off or 0xBF (191 decimal) if poll is on. There is no significance to the poll or final bit in the LLC control field. In a UI frame it is always off or 0, but in XID and TEST it can be either on (1) or off (0).

A command frame is identified with the high-order bit of the SSAP address set to 0. Response frames have the high-order bit of the SSAP address set to 1.

The TEST command or response has an LLC control field value of 0xE3 (227 decimal) if poll is off or 0xF3 (243 decimal) if poll is on. TEST response frames should echo the information field received in the corresponding TEST command frame. TEST is used to perform loopback tests to check the path between two LLC entities.

XID response frames should include an 802.2 XID information field of 0x810100 indicating class 1 (connectionless) service (type 1). There is no specific usage of XID defined in the standards, merely suggestions.

The service provided by IEEE LANs

The service provided by IEEE 802.X/IEEE 802.2 is similar to that of Ethernet. They all provide a transparent network system for TCP/IP.

Token Ring systems, although quite different in their operation from CSMA/CD systems, show similar characteristics at the top of the LLC layer. The main differences are their speeds of operation and maximum and minimum frame sizes.

Token Ring operates at two different speeds, 4 Mbps and 16 Mbps. The maximum frame size on these systems can be altered but is normally 4000 octets on 4 Mbps Token Ring and 8000 octets on 16 Mbps Token Ring. Having such large maximum frame sizes makes them suitable for file transfer, as it reduces the number of frames required, therefore reducing the overhead and providing better performance.

FDDI operates at 100Mbps, much faster than other current systems. Its maximum frame size is still restricted to around 4000 octets. Because of its characteristics and cost it is generally used as a backbone technology.

Configuration and management issues

There are no specific configuration options for TCP/IP to operate successfully over these IEEE systems other than to consider the need for SNAP. All equipment should support SNAP encapsulation on CSMA/CD networks, sometimes referred to as 802.2 SNAP or wrongly as IEEE 802.3 framing.

When TCP/IP runs on CSMA/CD LANs which are bridged to token passing LANs, the bridge must carry out the correct conversions. This is discussed below.

SNAP

Initially, TCP/IP was used almost exclusively with DIX Ethernet LANs, but with the widespread availability of Token Ring and increasing use of FDDI, it is now a common requirement to use TCP/IP with IEEE-compliant cabling systems. IEEE networks must be able to support TCP/IP in a standard way.

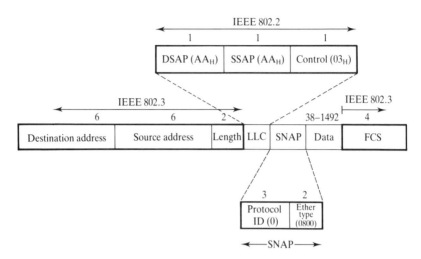

Figure 10.8   SNAP frame format.

As already described, IEEE/ISO LANs distinguish different network layer protocols by the SAP. SAP addresses are registered by ISO; half the space has been reserved for up to 63 ISO protocols and the other half for another 63 proprietary protocols from the rest of the world. This very limited address space is unsatisfactory. A SAP of 0x06 is registered for the IP but in practice TCP/IP implementations use the alternative SNAP.

SNAP is designed to allow any non-OSI protocol which has a type defined for DIX Ethernet to operate over an OSI datalink layer. So, SNAP overcomes the restricted number of SAPs available and allows any proprietary protocol to use IEEE LANs in a standard way. The SAP 0xAA has been allocated to SNAP. The format of SNAP is shown in Figure 10.8. The SNAP header immediately follows the LLC fields and is five octets long.

As well as the Ethernet type field, SNAP also provides a **Protocol ID**, which is important where different vendors' versions of a protocol are not compatible but use the same Ethernet type value. This is common with XNS systems, but not an issue with TCP/IP where the Protocol Id should be all zeros.

The example in Figure 10.9 shows a computer that can support OSI, XNS and TCP/IP stacks through the use of SNAP. This architecture can use a true OSI conformant medium, while allowing the use of non-OSI conformant protocols above it. The SNAP header of 5 octets further reduces the amount of higher level data that can be carried in an 802.3 frame to 1492 octets (1500 minus 3 for LLC minus 5 for SNAP).

SNAP is standard on Token Ring, FDDI and frame relay. SNAP encapsulation is available but rarely used on IEEE 802.3 CSMA/CD networks.

Figure 10.9   SNAP architecture.

Bridging TCP/IP

Bridging between IEEE LANs is often promoted as transparent to any protocol above the MAC layer, so one might expect no particular issues with TCP/IP. There are, however, four important differences that need consideration, especially if bridging bus[†] and ring[‡] architectures:

(1) The length field for the 802.3 bus

(2) The encapsulation on bus networks

(3) The maximum frame sizes

(4) The representation of MAC addresses

Length field

The IEEE 802.3 CSMA/CD network has a length field immediately before the LLC. Other IEEE networks do not. Bridging will at least involve changing the content of the frame and recalculating the FCS. This action will be totally transparent to the network planners; the other issues will not.

Encapsulation

The issue of encapsulation on bus networks (IEEE 802.3 + IEEE 802.2 + SNAP or DIX Ethernet) was covered above, but it too affects frame size.

[†]This could be Ethernet or IEEE 802.3 systems.
[‡]This could be Token Ring (IEEE 802.5) or FDDI (IS9314).

Frame size

A MAC layer bridge cannot change the higher level protocol content of a frame so it is unable to fragment (split) frames. If a frame that should be relayed is larger than the outgoing medium can support, the bridge must discard the frame. There is no mechanism within the protocol to notify the sender; the frame disappears almost without trace, except that a 'number of frames discarded counter' in the bridge will increment.

IEEE 802.3 is so closely modelled on DIX Ethernet that when bridging bus to bus one might expect there to be no particular problems. But if SNAP increases in popularity and a bridge is used to convert DIX Ethernet to SNAP protocol, then a maximum length Ethernet frame of 1500 octets of data cannot be converted; it must be discarded. The maximum data size in an IEEE 802.3 + 802.2 + SNAP frame is only 1492 octets. These two systems cannot communicate through a bridge unless the Ethernet station reduces its frame size.

The same type of problem will occur with ring-to-ring bridging, if the rings have different maximum frame sizes and spanning tree bridges are used. With ring-to-ring bridges using source routing instead of spanning tree, there is a mechanism for the end stations to detect the shortest allowed maximum frame size on any particular route. Hence the end stations should be able to adapt their transmissions to suit different connections.

For TCP/IP, the transmitted frame size is determined by the **Maximum Transmission Unit**[†] (MTU) set in the driver software for the LAN interface. It is possible on most TCP/IP implementations to modify the MTU to match the number of data octets carried by the link layer protocol. Setting the MTUs of each interface on a Token Ring to 1492 will prevent its frames from being too large for bridging to IEEE 802.3. However, this reduction will limit the efficiency of connections between nodes on Token Ring.

Representation of MAC addresses

The IEEE 802.1 committee defined how IEEE LANs should represent 48-bit MAC addresses as a bit stream on the cable, but IEEE 802.3 and 802.5 committees chose to represent these addresses in different ways higher up the protocol stack. IEEE 802.3 defines MAC addresses as having each octet LSbit first but IEEE 802.5 and FDDI represent MAC addresses MSbit first. This presents bridge manufacturers with one of their most difficult problems and it has a direct impact on bridging TCP/IP between CSMA/CD bus and Token Ring architectures.

Bridges connecting bus and ring architectures must reverse

[†]The concept of Maximum Transmission Unit is explained further in the next chapter.

the bits in each octet of a MAC address so that they are correctly represented to each network. This would be simpler if all information in the frame required reversal, but data octets go through unaltered[†]. Most bridges now deal with this issue quite adequately; it means they have to manipulate the frame and change the FCS. A bridge between a Token Ring and CSMA/CD is now complicated and, by strict definition, it is breaking the rules of bridging; a bridge is supposed to pass frame content through unaltered.

The real difficulty occurs when a MAC address has to be represented in the data field of a frame. This occurs in TCP/IP address look-up protocols such as ARP and RARP (see Chapter 11). When a sender uses ARP to request the MAC address of a node across a bridge, it will be given that MAC address in the format of the network the receiving node is located on. As the ARP response returns a MAC address in the data field of a LAN frame, if the two stations are on networks that use different MAC representations (one on a ring, the other on a bus), the address will be reversed, because data in the frame goes through unchanged. If the node requesting the ARP then attempts to use this MAC address, it will fail to get a response. (For a complete example see Chapter 11.)

To get around this problem, bridges connecting ring and bus architectures detect ARP (and RARP) packets and modify the MAC addresses in the ARP's data field so that they are correctly represented. The bridge is programmed to recognize the ARP protocol and to modify the MAC address in the data field. This is beyond the definition of a true IEEE 802.1 bridge.

The situation is further confused with FDDI. While this represents data and MAC addresses in the same way as IEEE 802.5, RFC 1188 proposes that TCP/IP nodes on FDDI should do the necessary conversion themselves, leaving the bridge transparent. For the unwary network developer, bridging TCP/IP from ring to bus architectures has some potential pitfalls, though many bridge manufacturers have now attempted to address the issue.

Where a ring or bus system is used solely as a backbone without any hosts on it and is connected to distribution areas of the opposite architecture through the same type of bridge, the problem will not occur. Here the MAC address reversal will occur an even number of times and hence cancel out. This issue will only cause difficulty if the originating and destination nodes are located on opposing cabling architectures, ring and bus.

This problem of MAC addresses only applies to **bridged** ring and bus networks. Where these are connected by a router, the significance of the MAC address is restricted to each side of the router independently so the problem does not occur.

[†]A hardware designer would complain that this description is inaccurate. It is how it appears to software.

Figure 10.10 (a) SLIP frame format. (b) Escape insertion where datagram has 0xC0 within.

Serial line Internet protocol

In some situations, it is advantageous to use asynchronous serial lines to carry TCP/IP protocols, either by dial-up modems, by modems on private wires, through an asynchronous network or by a direct-wired connection between two computers. The simple non-standard[†] **Serial Line Internet Protocol** (SLIP) defines how this can be done.

The service provided by SLIP

SLIP provides a point-to-point connection between two devices for the transmission of IP datagrams. The devices can be two computers or a computer and a router. It can be used to great advantage for remote access to a TCP/IP network or a simple connection between two machines.

    The name 'serial line IP' could be confusing in that it suggests the IP layer is different from normal IP, but this is not the case. The IP layer remains the same as for any other medium; SLIP defines a method of framing used to carry IP over asynchronous lines.

SLIP frame format

SLIP defines two special characters referred to as SLIP END and SLIP ESC (escape). SLIP END is a character of value 0xC0 and SLIP ESC is 0xDB. Datagrams sent using SLIP are framed by SLIP END characters as shown in Figure 10.10. If a data octet within a frame has the same value as SLIP END, a two-octet sequence of SLIP ESC and 0xDC is sent instead. If a data octet has the value of SLIP ESC, the two octets SLIP ESC and 0xDD are sent instead. The remote end then translates these two octet codes back to the original octet.

[†]SLIP is a *de facto* standard not an Internet standard, even though it is defined in RFC 1055.

Figure 10.11 SLIP functionality.

Figure 10.11 shows possible SLIP connections to a host using V.24 (RS232C). In this diagram PCs have been connected to the central host, but these could be any computer able to operate TCP/IP and SLIP. The host is also shown connected to a LAN, as it could be used as a router to allow the PCs to connect through to other services on that LAN.

Normal parameters for an asynchronous line apply to this protocol – speed in bits per second, parity and stop bits. As the data in the IP header could be of any octet value 0x00 to 0xFF, it would not be practical to use SLIP through buffered communications systems that use special characters for control purposes. A typical example would be the use of XON/XOFF (0x11, 0x13) for flow control. XON/XOFF is frequently enabled on terminal servers, PADs and multiplexor systems to control the flow of data and prevent data loss. SLIP requires a port configuration of 8 data bits, no parity, and EIA or hardware flow control, so that all 8 bits are available for the transmission of any octet value.

SLIP is a very simple protocol that does not provide any protection against line errors and frame corruption. It relies on the higher layer protocols for this. Some higher layer protocols which operate over UDP (such as NFS) normally rely on the datalink layer to detect errors, so the performance of these can be affected badly by corrupted frames. On error-prone communications lines, SLIP would not be satisfactory.

Configuration and management issues

SLIP connections need two IP addresses with the same network number at both ends of the link. A SLIP connection is treated as a network that has only two nodes.

SLIP is unable to determine its IP addresses dynamically unless ICMP information request is used; they must be loaded manually when the system is configured. This is seen as a significant limitation, particularly where a user is dialling into different networks using different routers. As each router would have a different IP network address, the computer must be configured with a different IP address each time.

In true TCP/IP fashion, the higher layer protocols will not recognize the difference between SLIP and other interfaces, apart from performance.

Point-to-point protocol

The **Point-to-Point Protocol** (PPP) is another datalink protocol that allows IP to be carried over serial lines. PPP overcomes a number of the limitations of SLIP. PPP has been designed to operate over both asynchronous (start/stop) connections and bit-oriented synchronous systems.

This protocol provides more than just a simple connection between hosts. It also defines several management and testing functions to deal with line quality, option negotiation and the setup of IP addresses. The standards suggest how data compression can be used to improve performance.

The service provided by PPP

PPP provides a point-to-point connection between two TCP/IP systems for the transfer of IP datagrams. These datagrams can carry any of the higher layer protocols (discussed later). PPP can operate over virtually any serial link interface. The only limitation is that it requires a full duplex connection. It does not need serial interface control signals, but the standard recommends that they can be used to help improve detection of physical layer problems. There is no restriction on the line speed used with PPP. RFC 1661 states that it is capable of operating over any Data Terminal Equipment (DTE)/Data Communications Equipment (DCE) interface, either asynchronous (character-based) or bit-oriented synchronous.

PPP is based on the HDLC standards of ISO, as adopted by the ITU-T for X.25 systems. This allows it to operate with standard bit-oriented hardware. It cannot connect to any other HDLC-based standard.

The PPP frame

The frame format is shown in Figure 10.12. The address field is all 1s and the control octet contains the value 0x03, the UI control field indicating a connectionless protocol.

The **protocol field** defines the protocol carried by this frame, which for TCP/IP systems would be:

Flag 01111110	Address 11111111	Control 00000011	Protocol 16 bits	Information	FCS 16 bits	Flag 01111110

Figure 10.12 PPP frame format.

Link Control Protocol	0xC021
Network Control Protocol	0x8021
Internet Protocol	0x0021

For IP, the Network Control Protocol is called the **Internet Protocol Control Protocol** (IPCP) with a protocol field of 0x8021. Other values assigned for the protocol field allow other protocols, including XNS, Novell's IPX, AppleTalk, and DECnet to share one PPP link.

Synchronous HDLC datalink protocols detect the end of a frame by recognizing the flag sequence 0x7E. Special techniques, often known as 'zero bit insertion' or 'bit stuffing', must be employed to prevent a data pattern that has the same bit pattern as the flag from being misintepreted as the end of the frame. It would be difficult to use the same techniques on asynchronous lines so an **octet insertion** principle is used instead.

The octet insertion principle is based on use of an escape character 0x7d. If a data octet has the same value as the flag 0x7E, or an octet containing a value of less than 0x20 is seen, 0x7d is placed in front of it and the original octet has its sixth bit complemented. At the receiver the 0x7d is removed and the sixth bit returned to normal. Figure 10.13 shows some examples.

Values of less than 0x20 represent ASCII control characters, so they are modified to prevent any misinterpretation by the communications link. Examples are flow control characters, XON and XOFF (0x11 and 0x13). If

Example 1 (data same as escape character)

Data	0x7D		0 1 1 1 1 1 0 1
Complement bit 6			0 1 0 1 1 1 0 1
Add escape	0x7D	0 1 1 1 1 1 0 1	0 1 0 1 1 1 0 1
Data transmitted	0x7D		0x5D

Example 2 (data is less than 0x20)

Data	0x01		0 0 0 0 0 0 0 1
Complement bit 6			0 0 1 0 0 0 0 1
Add escape	0x7D	0 1 1 1 1 1 0 1	0 0 1 0 0 0 0 1
Data transmitted	0x7D		0x21

Example 3 (data same as flag)

Data	0x7E		0 1 1 1 1 1 1 0
Complement bit 6			0 1 0 1 1 1 1 0
Add escape	0x7D	0 1 1 1 1 1 0 1	0 1 0 1 1 1 1 0
Data transmitted	0x7D		0x5E

Figure 10.13 Octet insertion with PPP on asynchronous lines.

these octets are transmitted into an asynchronous communications link they can disable or enable transmission at the wrong times, possibly causing loss of data and, at worst, total and irrevocable lockup of the link.

To initiate a connection, the Link Control Protocol (LCP) is used. It can test the quality of serial lines and then negotiate options for link establishment. The basic services provided by LCP are link establishment, link termination and link maintenance. It is intended that before a link is established the LCP will test its suitability for operation. However, a mechanism for performing this test is only hinted at and not explicitly defined. It is suggested that the LCP echo-request, echo-reply protocol is a method of testing a link.

After LCP establishes a connection through the use of the configure-request frame, IPCP comes into operation. It is responsible for handling the IP modules at each end of the serial link and will deal with negotiation of the IP addresses and the compression technique to be used. IP datagrams are carried in PPP frames with a protocol field of 0x0021. Once the connection is finished, LCP is used again to close the link with the terminate-link frame.

PPP can multiplex data from many sources, which makes it practical for high-speed connections between bridges or routers. RFC 1220 describes how PPP can be used for remote bridging. Because of the protocol field, it can be used to carry other protocols simultaneously with IP on the same point-to-point circuit.

One of PPP's strengths is its ability to configure a connection to a remote network dynamically. The LCP within PPP is responsible for selecting an appropriate IP address and testing that the link is usable.

Where PPP is used to interconnect bridges or routers from different manufacturers it is important to check the level of compatibility and interoperability. Careful testing is advised if mixing different vendors' equipment.

For the connection of a host to a remote network over a switched service, the major issue may be preventing unauthorized access. These issues are resolved by PPP Authentication Protocols.

PPP authentication protocols – PAP and CHAP

With the ever increasing demand for secure operation over the Internet, many new security protocols are being developed by the IETF. Where PPP is being used for dial-in operations to a router or terminal server, there are specific issues of user authentication due to the insecurities of dial-in systems. These issues have been addressed by two protocols; the Password Authentication Protocol (PAP) and the Challenge-Handshake Authentication Protocol (CHAP).

Type	Length	Authentication protocol

Figure 10.14 LCP configuration option frame.

Password authentication protocol (PAP)

PAP is a simple clear-text password protection method, that is, it is still possible to monitor the password being used if it is possible to monitor the link the PPP connection is made over. If stronger authentication is required, CHAP should be used.

After LCP has established the link, PAP is used to send an id/password pair, requesting authentication. A PAP frame is sent encapsulated in a configuration option frame, shown in Figure 10.14.

The type field is 3, the length is 4 and the authentication protocol value is 0xC023 for PAP. If this is accepted, the client host will send an authentication request. The service router (or terminal server) will either accept or decline the request. As requests and responses can be lost at this stage, a client will repeat requests which do not receive any response. The PAP frame is then sent in a PPP frame which has a protocol field of 0xC023. The format of PAP frames is as follows:

Code	Identifier	Length	Data

The code field is one octet long and identifies the type of PAP packet as follows:

(1) Authenticate request

(2) Authenticate acknowledge

(3) Authenticate non acknowledge

The identifier field is one octet long and used to identify requests and replies. The length field is two octets long. It measures the frame length from the code field through to the end of the data field.

The authentication request carries the ID and password of the client:

Code = 1	Identifier	Length	Peer-id length	Peer-id
Pwd length	Password			

Figure 10.15 CHAP challenge and response frame.

The peer-id length and pwd length fields are one octet long and indicate the length of their respective fields. The authentication acknowledge and non acknowledge have a message length and message field which can be used to return a readable response to be displayed to the user.

Challenge-handshake authentication protocol (CHAP)

CHAP provides a more secure system than PAP, as it is based on a 'one-way hash', one-time password mechanism. As the password is used once only, CHAP provides protection against playback or replay attacks, where an attacker obtains a valid password and then reuses it. CHAP relies on the client and a security server knowing a secret value which is used to generate the challenge and response values. This secret value must be sufficiently large to protect against exhaustive search attacks. The 'one-way hash' or trap-door algorithm is chosen such that it is not feasible to work backwards to the secret value by knowing the challenge and response values.

CHAP does not define the authentication mechanism used; it merely defines the challenge and response exchange mechanism.

Like PAP, CHAP is initiated through an LCP configuration option frame as shown previously in Figure 10.14, but with a length of 5, authentication protocol value of 0xC223 and an extra one-octet field indicating the 'one-way hash' algorithm to be used. Possible values are:

0–4   Unused (reserved)
5   MD5

The CHAP frames are carried in PPP frames with an authentication protocol value of 0xC223. They are similar in format to the PAP frames but having the following code values:

(1) Challenge
(2) Response
(3) Success
(4) Failure

A challenge is sent, by the access router, to initiate the authentication process. This can happen at the connection setup phase and it may be repeated throughout the connection period. The format of the CHAP challenge and response frames is shown in Figure 10.15.

The challenge or response is carried in the value field and the name field is used to identify the system transmitting the frames.

If a successful response is seen by the access router it will respond with a success message, otherwise it will send a failure message and the connection will be terminated.

PPP multilink protocol

The PPP Multilink Protocol (MP) provides a method for splitting, recombining and sequencing IP datagrams across multiple logical data links; it is designed to allow multiple parallel slow-speed links to be used together to give higher performance and greater resilience in the point-to-point transmission path between two systems. PPP multilink has similarities to the multilink protocol used with X.25 and X.75, and also for IBM transmission groups; however, the detail is different and potentially results in improved performance compared with those protocols. In particular, multilink PPP is recommended as the method to combine a number of 64 k ISDN link-layer channels into one group or 'bundle'. Other uses with X.25, frame relay and asynchronous communications paths are possible and are encouraged by the standard.

A major difference between PPP MP and these earlier protocols is that a single IP datagram may be split or 'fragmented' across multiple links and recombined at the receiving site. This reduces the 'latency' or delay of the transmission path compared with sending a complete datagram down one circuit. It also means that the traffic on all available circuits can be effectively balanced whatever the packet size and that the effective Maximum Transmission Unit (MTU) can be increased compared with that used for a single link.

The availability and use of PPP MP is negotiated by an extension to the link control protocol at the time the PPP link is established.

X.25

X.25 is a network interface defined for accessing packet switched public data networks. There are many national and international networks that provide this interface, making it a useful mechanism for interconnecting LANs. With this wide availability, it is not surprising that there is an RFC describing how IP datagrams should be carried over X.25 interfaces.

As shown in Figure 10.16, X.25 defines three layers: layer 1, physical (usually X.21 or X.21bis – V.24); layer 2, datalink (usually HDLC LAPB); and at layer 3, the network layer, the X.25 Packet Layer Protocol (X.25 PLP). Layer 1 deals with physical connections, bit representation, timing and control signals. Layer 2 provides the basic point-to-point connection between the terminal and the X.25 network. It defines the basic HDLC frame and how it provides reliability with error correction and

Figure 10.16 X.25 architecture.

flow control. Layer 3 gives X.25 its strength. It provides a switched service like the telephone network for multiplexing up to 4095 logical connections at a time over one link-level connection. In support of TCP/IP this allows a single X.25 interface to have connections to different destinations concurrently, that is, to appear as multiple point-to-point circuits.

The service provided by X.25

An X.25 network, a packet switched public data network using X.25 for example, provides switched virtual circuits – reliable, error-free, flow-controlled, point-to-point connections between two interfaces. Equipment with the appropriate X.25 interfaces can access remote networks transparently. With X.25's wide availability and coverage, it is common for it to be used to interconnect TCP/IP systems.

How TCP/IP uses X.25

The X.25 network provides a simple transport service for IP datagrams. When TCP/IP systems connect over X.25 they make no new assumptions about the underlying service; the fact that an X.25 connection is already error corrected is ignored. In fact, the IP layer is totally unaware that it is operating over X.25. It sees a single X.25 interface and the logical channels as it would multiple point-to-point links (Figure 10.17).

Because of the incompatibilities between the two systems, the equipment that connects a TCP/IP protocol stack with an X.25-based system is often referred to as a gateway. Gateways are normally regarded as protocol converters, but this gateway does not convert the protocol; it merely puts IP on top of X.25 and maps the IP network number to an X.25 destination address (NUA). The three layers of X.25 sit where the two layers of PPP (for example) would sit. An alternatively way of looking at this is that the network layer has two sublayers, X.25 PLP as the lower sublayer and IP as the upper sublayer (Table 10.4).

An IP gateway for X.25 should translate the destination IP address into a relevant X.25 **Network User Address** (NUA). If no connection exists to that destination, it must establish the connection to a remote gate-

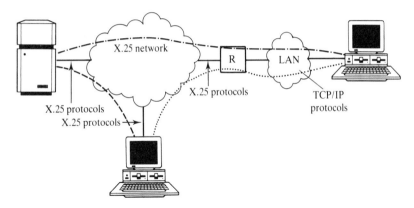

Figure 10.17   X.25 provides connections to hosts on different networks.

Table 10.4   IP and its use of X.25.

Layer	Protocol
Network b	IP
Network a	X.25 PLP
Link	HDLC
Physical	V.24

way. IP datagrams can then begin flowing between the two systems. Some gateways can open multiple **virtual circuits** between the same two interfaces to increase the traffic-carrying capacity (but this is only useful where capacity is limited by an X.25 packet level window size that cannot be increased). TCP/IP is ideally suited to using these multiple circuits, for it will reorder the IP datagrams which are received out of order.

IP X.25 gateways must be able to reject random incoming calls which are not carrying IP traffic. The convention in ITU-T is that a Network Layer Protocol Identifier (NLPID) is carried in the first octet of the Call User Data Field (CUD) of the call request packet. Using this technique, an X.25 virtual circuit may be dedicated to carrying one network protocol, or may multiplex several network protocols.

There are three recognized ways of identifying IP over X.25:

- A CUD NLPID of 0xCC (decimal 204) indicates that each X.25 packet sequence contains a single IP datagram. No other protocols are carried in the X.25 data packets on this virtual circuit and no other protocol identifier will be carried with the IP data. This is the normal method of carrying IP over X.25 and is that shown in Figure 10.18. The following two options are included for completeness.

- A CUD NLPID of 0x80 indicates there is also a SNAP header in the CUD. This SNAP header indicates the single protocol that

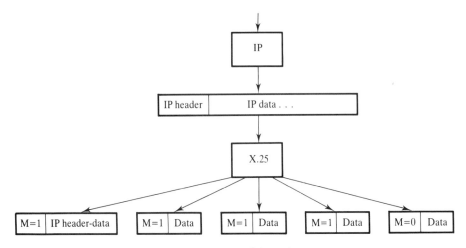

Figure 10.18 Use of the M-bit in X.25.

will be carried in subsequent X.25 data packets. The SNAP header is used exactly as it would be on a LAN or with frame relay (see below). X.25 packets do not contain any other protocol identification.

- A CUD NLPID of 0x00, the 'null' value, indicates that each X.25 packet sequence will contain its own NLPID, that is 0xCC for IP or 0x80 for SNAP. This allows many network layer protocols to be multiplexed over one virtual circuit. (Some older X.25 equipment does not adhere to this standard and will incorrectly interpret the null identifier as being from a Packet Assembler/Disassembler or PAD.)

All systems that carry IP over X.25 must accept the first format; they may accept other formats also. If a system cannot process the protocol indicated in the NLPID in the call request packet, it must not accept the incoming call.

Reducing X.25 public network charges

Public X.25 systems often charge by connection time and by the amount of data transmitted, measured in 'segments', where a segment may contain from 1 to 64 octets. If there is a connection time charge, the user pays for any idle periods. It is also more costly if packets are not filled to capacity. When choosing a gateway (or router) for X.25 it important that it closes idle connections after a time-out period which can be set by the network manager. It will re-establish them when IP data begins to flow again.

X.25 systems, by default, transfer data in 128-byte packets. Through configuration, or negotiation with the exchange equipment at call request time, this may be increased to 1024 or 4096 octets. IP, by convention, must support a minimum datagram size of 576 octets, that is, the MTU of all underlying networks should be at least 576 octets. If this cannot be achieved, there is a loss of efficiency as the 20-octet IP header must be copied into each smaller IP datagram. If no other action were taken, each 128-octet X.25 packet would contain a 20-octet IP header and only 108 octets of higher layer protocol data; hardly an efficient use of resources. The solution for IP is to use X.25's M-bit, the more data bit, and advertise the X.25 network as having an MTU of 576. If packet sizes larger than 512 can be negotiated, the MTU can be increased without the use of the M-bit.

In an X.25 packet, when the M-bit is one, it indicates that this packet is one of a sequence that are somehow related. The last packet in a sequence has the M-bit set to zero. IP X.25 gateways use the M-bit to relate 'fragments' of a 576-octet IP datagram. As shown in Figure 10.18, the first packet contains 20 octets of IP header and 108 octets of the datagram, the next three packets contain a full 128 octets from the datagram and the last contains 84 octets. More recent standards suggest that all systems should now carry an IP datagram of 1500 bytes rather than 576 bytes.

With the reduction in cost of router memory and with increased link speeds in wide area networks, a default MTU of 576 bytes is now considered undesirable. RFC 1356 suggests that the MTU of the interfaces should now be 1600 octets. This allows the transport of an Ethernet LAN frame without fragmentation in the IP layer. Such an IP datagram will still be fragmented into many 128-byte packets over X.25.

Configuration and management issues

The following parameters will need to be configured on X.25 gateways for IP or on routers that offer X.25 support for IP:

- Tables for mapping between X.121 addresses (X.25 NUAs) and IP network numbers or subnetwork numbers with subnetwork masks for each network;

- The time-out after which the X.25 call will be cleared if no traffic flows;

- Setting the MTU, enabling the use of the M-bit and negotiating packet sizes with the X.25 network where available;

- Ensuring that the protocol identifier of 204 is set in the call user data field.

Applications that generate UDP broadcasts between networks will prevent the idle timer from operating. Where connect time is charged, this is a costly item.

Traditionally, X.25 has been used for file transfer and terminal applications similar to TCP/IP's FTP and Telnet. Public network performance is often in the range from hundreds to thousands of bits per second. Tariffs are often set accordingly. Those intending to use public X.25 networks for general TCP/IP LAN interconnection should conduct careful pilot trials to check that this performance and the tariffs are acceptable.

Integrated Services Digital Network

The **Integrated Services Digital Network (ISDN)** comprises a number of different standards and facilities. Current ISDN services are available in two formats, basic rate and primary rate circuit switched services. In the future, high-speed broadband ISDN cell relay services will be offered. In this section we consider basic and primary rate ISDN. Later sections look at fast packet technologies – frame relay and the cell relay or Asynchronous Transfer Mode (ATM) of broadband ISDN.

Basic rate ISDN provides two independent 64 kbps data channels (B channels) and a 16 kbps signalling channel (D channel). Primary rate ISDN provides 30 B channels and a 64 kbps signalling D channel. The primary rate service is appropriate for large companies. B channels provide transparent 'bit-pipes' which are independent of link-layer protocols; all B channels may interoperate, that is a call may be established from a B channel on the basic rate service to a B channel on the primary rate service. Some authorities allow multiple B channels to be treated as one higher speed link at the bit level; for example the two B channels of a basic rate interface could form a single 128 kbps circuit. This facility is not necessarily available internationally and therefore cannot be recommended for carrying IP. A more acceptable technique is PPP multilink procedures, described previously.

The D channel uses a datalink protocol LAPD, with an HDLC frame format, for signalling to exchange equipment. LAPD is similar to the LAPB link-layer protocol of X.25. In some countries, the D channel may be available to the end user for data transmission in packet mode, but there is no guarantee of international service. Because of lack of standards and the relatively slow speed of the basic rate D channel service, the use of the D channel as an IP datalink is not encouraged.

Once a call is set up by using the signalling D channel, a B channel provides a 64 kbps point-to-point transparent bit stream between the local and remote interfaces. Two different and incompatible techniques have been documented for transferring IP data over this B channel circuit, one using the X.25 packet switching formats, the other using PPP, both of which were described above. So, to communicate successfully over ISDN, two systems must be configured to use the same bit representation, normally Non Return to Zero (NRZ), and the same frame formats, either synchronous PPP or X.25 packet mode, with the same method of identifying and carrying IP information. PPP has lower overhead and potentially higher throughput than X.25.

ITU-T ISDN standards also document a terminal adapter (V.120) which performs async to sync conversion to carry asynchronous data at standard speeds of 2400, 4800, 9600, 19 200, 38 400, and 57 600 bps over an ISDN 64 kbps link. Since PPP defines a method of carrying PPP frames in an asynchronous frame format, it is a simple process to carry PPP over V.120 over ISDN. Asynchronous operation has the advantage that all PCs can use it without additional hardware. However, this method is incompatible with those described above; the V.120 terminal adapter does not convert asynchronous framed PPP on the V.120 interface to synchronous framed PPP on the ISDN link. V.120 is to be avoided except perhaps as a short-term expedient within the confines of a private network, or where it is agreed and supported as an access method by an Internet service provider.

The fast connection setup time of ISDN makes it especially useful for routers. With this type of facility, routers can be designed to allocate bandwidth dynamically between remote sites. For example, a router detecting that its high-speed line is operating beyond some predefined high loading level could bring another connection into operation, effectively doubling the capacity between two LANs. This would allow the cost of intersite connections to be minimized, as they are only in place while they are needed, often for the busiest hour in the morning and afternoon. Such systems can 'peak-lop' transmission costs.

This feature of transmission on demand may also be used to back up failed leased point-to-point circuits. When a failure is detected the routers will re-establish the path via ISDN in a time scale which, for TCP/IP, will not lose any connections or user data. The users should experience only a few seconds' pause in activity while the failure is recognized and the alternative ISDN route is brought into operation.

The management of routers with ISDN connections is likely to be similar to X.25 connections so the following parameters must be configured on routers using ISDN to support IP:

- Tables for mapping between ISDN network numbers (telephone numbers) and IP network numbers or subnetwork numbers with subnetwork masks for each network;
- The time-out after which the ISDN call will be cleared if no IP traffic flows;
- Setting the MTU;
- Ensuring that the correct link-layer protocol is set once the connection is established.

Fast packet systems

Like X.25, the fast packet standards are interface standards for connection to public (or private) WANs. Interface standards do not describe how

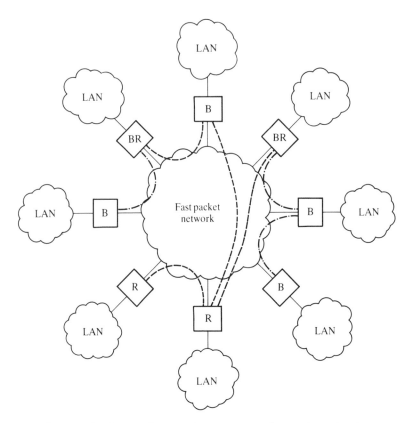

Figure 10.19 Bridging and routing using fast packet technology.

networks should operate internally, only how to connect to those networks.

Fast packet is a general term which is used to describe two very different technologies known as **frame relay** and **cell relay**. While they have some similarities, the performances that can be achieved, and the applications which they support, are different. For example, cell relay will support voice systems due to its more consistent delay characteristics, whereas frame relay is less suitable for voice as its delays are more variable.

For a single physical interface (connection), both systems provide multiple data streams to separate remote interfaces. As shown in Figure 10.19, a bridge or router with the correct hardware and link-level software need only have a single connection to a fast packet network to communicate with multiple destinations simultaneously through virtual circuits. If the intervening network is correctly designed, it creates an illusion of multiple point-to-point links directly from one bridge or router to another. A bridge or router with a single high-speed fast packet interface is similar to a multiport remote bridge or router.

The advantage of an underlying fast packet network is that it simplifies the structure of the bridge or router network that it supports. Each bridge or router can believe it has a direct connection to every other, rather than having to bridge or route through other LANs or WANs with the attendant delays. This simplification may be an illusion. The complexity (and delays) may still be there; they are transferred to the fast packet service supplier rather than within the TCP/IP LAN and its bridges and routers. More careful network design is required when using a fast packet network for data transmission than when using point-to-point links of the same speed. The design problem moves to another management area rather than being eliminated.

The chief advantage of fast packet is its potential to make available much higher speed public network connections at the same cost as slower speed point-to-point connections. The cost of the core high-speed public network is better shared among many subscribers each with different traffic requirements.

Frame relay

There are currently a number of proprietary standards for frame relay, although much of the work is based on standards from the ITU-T Q.922 recommendations and ANSI T1.618. RFC 1294 describes the use of frame relay networks for multiprotocol interconnection including IP interconnection with bridges and routers simultaneously.

Frame relay uses a variant of the HDLC frame, the link-layer protocol (ISO IS7776) used with X.25. Any equipment that can operate X.25 can, in principle, be reprogrammed to support frame relay instead. The same hardware can handle much more data with frame relay standards than it does with X.25, so frame relay techniques are rapidly gaining in popularity with suppliers of private and public network equipment.

Frame relay networks are so called because the network can carry the link-level protocol (frame) from any other type of LAN or WAN. The frame is carried transparently inside the modified HDLC frame of the frame relay network. Some frame relay networks send the frame exactly as received, others use their own form of fragmentation (see Chapter 11) to improve the 'bucket brigade' delay. For most implementations the header consists of two octets and contains the fields shown in Figure 10.20. Some networks allow a longer header of three or four octets. This allows more connections to be identified across the interface. We will confine this discussion to the two-octet header:

- *DLCI – 10 bits*   Datalink connection identifier, a 10-bit number uniquely identifying the virtual circuit (connection) to which this frame belongs.
- *C/R – 1 bit*   A command/response bit.

Flag				
DLCI (6)			C/R	EA
DLCI (4)	FECN	BECN	DE	EA
UI (03)				
Frame data				
FCS 1				
FCS 2				
Flag				

Figure 10.20 Frame relay header.

- *EA – 2 bits*   The extended address markers, 0 in the first octet and 1 in the second octet to indicate the end of the header.
- *FECN – 1 bit*   Forward explicit congestion notification.
- *BECN – 1 bit*   Backward explicit congestion notification.
- *DE – 1 bit*   Discard eligibility.

The FECN, BECN and DE flags are described below.

The frame begins and ends with a normal HDLC flag[†] with the end flag preceded by a 16-bit FCS used to detect frame transmission errors. Frames with an invalid FCS are discarded.

The DLCI identifies one of 1024 virtual circuits on an interface; it determines to which remote port and remote DLCI the frame will be delivered. The DLCI is used for routing within the frame relay network. The DLCI has a significance only at the local interface. As illustrated in Figure 10.21, the DLCIs are usually different at the two ends of the connection.

Frame relay networks do not today support broadcast or multicast. In the first releases of frame relay systems, the mapping between DLCIs and the remote nodes is agreed when you subscribe to a public service or when the network manager sets up the private frame relay network. Most current implementations do not include a mechanism for the DTE, the 'user equipment', to set up the connection dynamically. Frame relay

---

[†]HDLC flags delineate a frame by appearing at the beginning and end of a frame; the pattern of an HDLC flag is 0x7E.

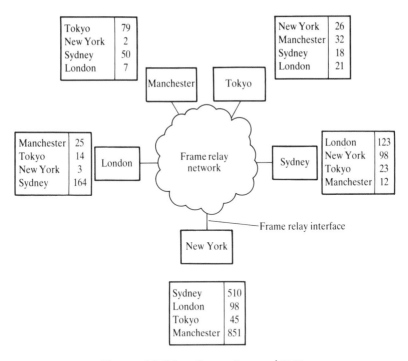

Figure 10.21   Connections and DLCIs.

systems today provide Permanent Virtual Circuits (PVCs), in imitation of point-to-point leased lines, not Switched Virtual Circuits as X.25.

The service provided by frame relay

Frame relay is so called because it relays the basic user frame as it is presented. If a 16 Mbps Token Ring network has an MTU of 8000 octets in a frame, the frame relay network will transmit frames of that size. (There is a maximum recommended frame for current frame relay implementations of 8192 octets but older systems used fragmentation and had a basic frame size of 262 octets.)

The frame relay service is sometimes referred to as connection oriented, for it supports virtual circuits, multiple data streams identified by the DLCI. These generally follow fixed routes and will not be delivered out of order or duplicated. However, unlike X.25, there is no error correction or reliable flow control in this network. Any frame with an FCS error will be discarded with no notification. If network congestion occurs, the network is entitled to discard frames. This is the same service that bridges and point-to-point links normally provide, so frame relay is a suitable mechanism for supporting TCP/IP transmission with bridges and routers, provided the intervening frame relay network is designed to have low rates of congestion and packet loss.

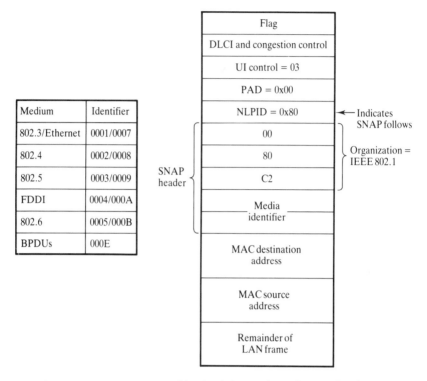

Figure 10.22 SNAP and bridged data within a frame relay frame.

In a private frame relay network, these design parameters are under the control of the one company using and providing the service, though the control may be under different management. With a public network, congestion control is outside the end user's authority, but in a properly configured large public network, where the shared resources are of higher overall capacity, congestion should be less likely to occur.

Frame formats for frame relay networks

Either bridges or routers may encapsulate their data in a **frame relay frame**. One interface may process both bridge and router frames simultaneously (a **router/bridge**).

The carrying of either router data (the network layer) or bridged data (the MAC layer) within a frame relay frame is identified by the **Network Layer Protocol IDentifier** (NLPID) which immediately follows the UI control field. The NLPID concept is described in an ISO Technical Report (ISO/IEC TR 9577) and NLPID values are registered with ISO. If the NLPID has a value 0x80, SNAP follows as shown in Figure 10.22. SNAP can be used with an NLPID as well as after a link layer protocol identifier such as SAP.

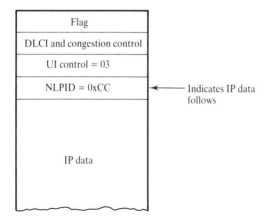

Figure 10.23   Router data within a frame relay frame.

When the frame relay frame carries bridge data, the SNAP header does not indicate an Ethernet type field. Instead, it contains an organization identifier for the IEEE 802.1 committee that standardized bridges and a two-octet code indicating which type of network or medium the frame came from (802.3, 802.4, 802.5, 802.6, FDDI or a spanning tree bridge).

When the frame relay frame carries IP (router data) the NLPID has a value of 0xCC, indicating that IP follows immediately (Figure 10.23). An alternative and incompatible way of carrying IP is to use SNAP – an NLPID of 0x80, followed by SNAP, followed by an Ethernet type of 0x800 and IP. This second method is discouraged as it has a higher overhead.

Since frame relay is a multiplexed protocol, routers (or hosts) using TCP/IP over frame relay interfaces must have a mechanism to determine the DLCI that should be used. A protocol called INverse ARP (INARP) has been developed for this.

Why is it 'fast'?

Frame relay technology is 'fast' in comparison with older X.25 public networks, but not necessarily fast in terms of the requirements of a LAN designer and implementor. The term 'fast' in fast packet can be justified by the higher interface speeds than normal X.25 packet networks and the reduction of switching time in each switching node.

Frame relay interface speeds range from 64 kbps to 2 Mbps, though special hardware will extend the upper range to 34 Mbps. These speeds begin where standard X.25 stops. Public telecommunications operators are introducing services with access speeds between 64 kbps and 1 Mbps. These speeds are likely to prove too low for the more demanding remote TCP/IP applications. Frame relay networks still introduce delay.

The processing power needed to switch a frame relay frame is small compared with standard X.25. Frame relay switching uses only the DLCI at link level, not a logical channel identifier at packet level. There is no lower level error correction or flow control. There is no packet level with its associated flow control for each virtual circuit. These features of X.25 allowed a public network operator to deliver a reliable error-free service over the error-prone analogue lines of the mid-1970s. In the 1990s, many public telecommunications systems are already installed on fibre optic systems where the interval between errors can be measured in days on the best routes. The overhead of X.25 error correction and flow control cannot be justified, hence the lightweight frame relay service.

Congestion control in frame relay networks

As mentioned, an overloaded frame relay network will discard frames (as will an overloaded bridged network). To reduce the rate of frame loss, the frame relay header format provides three bits for **congestion control:** Forward Explicit Congestion Notification (FECN), Backward Explicit Congestion Notification (BECN) and Discard Eligible (DE).

There is some discussion among standards makers as to how networks should use these flags; many current frame relay implementations ignore them. Using the DE bit, a DTE can indicate a preference that if frames are to be discarded, those with DE set should be dropped before those with DE clear, but it remains a preference. At the limits, the network may drop any frame.

RFC 1294 currently makes no recommendation of how these bits are to be used. In TCP/IP it would be appropriate to clear DE (that is, not to be discarded) for those IP frames with a high reliability TOS or a high precedence (see Chapter 11).

The FECN and BECN bits are set by the network to advise the receiving (forward) and sending (backward) nodes that the network is about to begin (or has begun) to discard frames on that connection. These bits correspond rather well with the ICMP source quench message. In future, routers with frame relay interfaces could be expected to interpret these bits in the same way as ICMP source quench messages, if necessary relaying a source quench message for a received FECN/BECN frame. Again, RFC 1294 does not suggest this.

The exact use of the congestion control mechanisms by public network operators and by attached equipment is still very much in the preliminary stages of standardization. Purchasers of frame relay equipment and services should ascertain exactly how these bits are used by each system. There are still some differences in the way they are used by different networks (switches) and terminal equipment (bridges and routers), if they are supported at all.

Delay in fast packet networks

When designing TCP/IP systems using fast packet frame relay, planners should focus on the word 'packet', not on the word 'fast'. The terminology can disguise the important fact that the delay across any packet network will never be less than twice the delay of a point-to-point leased circuit of the same speed as the access lines; it will often be more, perhaps considerably more. This delay is referred to as **network latency**. The reasons are exactly those highlighted in Chapter 7, where we discussed the bucket brigade delay effect. A switch should not decide where to send the information until it has examined the end of the frame (FCS) to be sure that the frame has been correctly received[†].

On a point-to-point leased circuit only the final destination must wait for the FCS; on a fast packet frame relay network each switch normally waits for the FCS, so the delay across the network increases for each network hop.

This network latency significantly affects the performance of internetworks using bridges or routers with frame relay interfaces.

Configuration and management issues

On a bridge or router, a frame relay interface replaces a number of individual interfaces each carrying point-to-point connections. For a connection of a given speed, the throughput of that frame relay interface will be less than a point-to-point circuit. The advantage comes from exchanging a number of heavily loaded point-to-point circuits, for example at 64 kbps, for one much higher speed frame relay access to a shared network with very high speed internal lines. Since not all traffic from all network users peaks at the same time, there are considerable benefits to the network supplier. It is the 'large pipe' – one user can only have a small impact on the overall service. The public network operator can then provide a high-speed connection at much lower cost than dedicated high-speed point-to-point connections. It is the responsibility of the network designer to ensure that they use higher speed connections to compensate for the greater delay (network latency) compared with point-to-point circuits. They themselves may benefit from aggregating several slow-speed lines into one high-speed interface. Where multiple 64 kbps are replaced, speeds between 128 kbps and 2 Mbps may be more appropriate. If 2 Mbps circuits are in use, careful traffic analysis is required to determine what should be provided.

[†]There is no apparent value in beginning to relay information that may be in error: if the error occurred in the DLCI, the information would be transmitted to the wrong destination; if the output line speed is higher than the input line speed, you could run out of input data and would then have to abort the frame and begin retransmitting. Some switches will take a risk on FCS and will check on speed mismatching to reduce network latency.

Fast packet interfaces are available for remote bridges or TCP/IP routers. The interface is multiplexed, so the access speed must be sufficient to process all anticipated traffic on all virtual circuits. If it is not, congestion will result and congestion control will operate if the equipment is programmed to use it.

A network which is operating without congestion control in its busiest periods is overconfigured and probably not operating at maximum efficiency. But once congestion begins, the service will deteriorate rapidly if traffic increases further. Congestion control in a growing network is a sign of the requirement for some rapid remedial action. Once congestion control leads on to frequent IP datagram loss in a fast packet network (or point-to-point router-based network), the service and performance levels seen by end users will degrade rapidly if the network is allowed to grow further.

Setting up frame relay bridges

In addition to the normal configuration of any LAN bridge, the network implementor must:

- Agree the allocation of DLCIs with the network supplier for the interface at each end of a virtual circuit.
- Configure the DLCIs into the bridge software so that only they are used to generate broadcasts and build filtering tables.
- Set the discard eligible operation for broadcast and multicast frames (if supported).

Setting up frame relay routers

Each virtual circuit is seen by the IP layer as a direct point-to-point link to a remote IP network number. Once the DLCIs are agreed, as for a bridge, the network manager must set up:

- The relationship between DLCI and network number. As with any other circuit, each DLCI will have its own subnet mask.
- The association of TOS and precedence bits with discard eligibility (where supported).
- The use of any FECN/BECN bits with ICMP, where supported.
- The use of any routing protocols across a particular interface.

Tariffs for frame relay services

Many network suppliers are introducing frame relay services specifically for remote LAN interconnection. The service can be offered potentially at a much lower initial cost than dedicated point-to-point links. A single high-speed connection to the network can support multiple remote destinations. The network user can choose the access speed, and hence cost, to meet the traffic needs of an individual site.

Most public network services are being introduced with a flat-rate fixed tariff dependent on access speed rather than the volume of data transmitted. This is perhaps fortunate. Estimating traffic volume requires the detailed knowledge of protocol operation; as discussed in Chapter 7, this can often only be determined by measuring and scaling the results. Few network planners have the time or the detailed knowledge to know what volume of traffic will be generated in what period of time by particular network implementations. While such information is very useful when designing and sizing a stable network, it is essential where public network tariffs and charges depend on traffic volume!

Asynchronous transfer mode or cell relay

Asynchronous Transfer Mode (ATM) was developed for very high speed operation on the wide area fibre communications infrastructures which will be commonplace in the late 1990s. ATM is part of the Broadband ISDN (B-ISDN) standards of the ITU-TS. B-ISDN systems operate over the Synchronous Digital Hierarchy (SDH) transmission systems of the ITU and the Synchronous Optical Network (SONET) transmission systems of ANSI. These two systems have compatible standards at the higher speeds of operation.

SDH and SONET replace the 64 kbps channel-based multiplexing systems that formed the backbone transmission systems of digital telephone networks from the late 1960s – for example, the Pleisochronous Digital Hierarchy, PDH, of the ITU. The standard multiplexing speeds of PDH are 64 kbps, 2 Mbps, 8 Mbps, 34 Mbps, 140 Mbps and 565 Mbps. The multiplexing speeds of SONET are 51 Mbps, 155 Mbps, 622 Mbps, 2.5 Gbps (2500 Mbps) and 10 Gbps. It is at these SONET speeds that ATM operates most efficiently and, at these speeds, it is ideal for combining data from voice systems, traditional LANs and multimedia applications.

Because PDH is based on fixed channels, the circuit capacity of 1980s telephone networks is used inefficiently. A major advantage of ATM is that it applies statistical multiplexing (packet switching) to the long-distance transmission networks in a way that will dramatically improve the efficiency of their use. This should make very high speed national (and international) operation possible, at much reduced costs.

Equipment manufacturers have recognized that these new standards are applicable not only to long-distance transmission at high speeds. They provide an alternative technology to existing LANs for connecting user workstations and servers together on copper cables. These manufacturers have produced ATM interface cards, operating at 25 Mbps and 51 Mbps, for the faster PC and workstation architectures. The

Figure 10.24 The ATM cell format.

25 Mbps cards utilize existing cable designed for 10 Mbps Ethernet/IEEE 802.3 or for 4 Mbps and 16 Mbps Token Ring 802.5 – 'Category 3 cable'. The 51 Mbps cards operate on 'Category 5 cable', installed for the 100 Mbps technologies that are available or are in development (CDDI/FDDI and Fast Ethernets).

While these ATM systems may appear slower than these other standards, the ATM sharing mechanism and switching system will ensure more predictable delays when compared with traditional LANs with large frame sizes.

Within the corporate network, ATM may therefore be used in three ways:

- As a replacement for existing WAN technologies for high-speed interconnection of local area networks. These interconnections may be part of a 'public' ATM service provided by a carrier or PTT, or provided in-house as part of a corporate ATM backbone.

- As a backbone ATM service, joining LANs together within one building or campus.

- As a LAN service replacing existing user segment LANs.

It is important that ATM can carry IP and other LAN protocols without changes to those protocols. This is achieved by ATM Adaptation Layers (AAL), in particular AAL5.

The ATM cell format

ATM, or cell relay, divides user data into fixed packets or cells each of 53 bytes, 5 bytes of control information and 48 bytes of data (Figure 10.24). As the cells are small and of identical size, hardware switches can switch many millions of cells per second. Furthermore the cells 'pack together' efficiently in one 'big pipe'. With the high data rates of SONET/SDH, this fixed small size and the use of hardware switching means that circuit capacity is used extremely efficiently for voice, data and image without an unacceptable increase in network delays as the network becomes heavily loaded. Also, the network is much less likely to reach saturation for extended periods when the core speeds are 622 Mbps, 2.5 Gbps or, in the future, 10 Gbps.

The fields of the 5-byte ATM header (Figure 10.24) have their direct counterparts in the frame relay header of Figure 10.20. A particular conversation or virtual connection between two devices is identified by the virtual path identifier and the virtual channel identifier which may be compared with the DLCI. Generic flow control may be compared with the FECN and BECN bits and cell loss priority with the discard eligible flag. There are more options for cell loss priority as ATM is designed to carry speech which is sensitive to data loss.

Frame formats for ATM networks (AAL5)

How is this small cell used to carry traditional LAN traffic? The frame format used by IP and other LAN-based protocols working over ATM is known as ATM Adaptation Layer type 5 (AAL5); a routed or bridged LAN frame is segmented into cells, padded out to an exact number of cells (less 8 bytes). The last cell of the sequence ends with an 8-byte trailer field which contains the actual 16-bit length of the LAN frame and a 32-bit FCS. (Two bytes are not used by IP over ATM.)

An ATM service must maintain the order of transmission of cells; however, the ATM service has no error correction so there is no guarantee of delivery of all cells forming one frame. Like a traditional LAN, it is the responsibility of higher layer protocols to provide error correction where required.

To carry the internet protocol across ATM, the problems to be solved are almost identical to X.25 or frame relay. A single virtual connection may be dedicated to IP or several protocols may be multiplexed over one VC.

- If a single virtual connection is dedicated to IP, the format is LLC plus SNAP, similar to that used with IEEE 802.5 and FDDI LANs with an Ethernet type of 0x0800 indicating IP.

- If IP is just one of a number of protocols on a single virtual circuit then the bridge formats of Figure 10.22 are used with an LLC and SNAP header indicating IEEE as the Organizationally Unique Identifier (OUI) and the medium type carried in the bridge format.

- The ATM equipment must relay multicast and broadcast frames on a number of virtual circuits where they may have a significance to the destination.

- AAL5 allows a single frame to be up to 65 527 bytes long; the MTU of the interface can support the maximum size of IP datagram without fragmentation at the IP layer.

ATM and routers

Initial implementations of IP with ATM use routers to interconnect LANs across an ATM network infrastructure, exactly as with frame relay and X.25. While this is a pragmatic approach, it is inefficient, for it involves reassembling and then segmenting the complete LAN frame at each router. As ATM becomes a generally available infrastructure, direct communications between hosts over ATM switches without intervening routers is possible, whether for local or long-distance communications. As we will discover in the next chapter, any-to-any communication over ATM without routers requires changes to the traditional method of operation of IP. Routers are therefore likely to remain as the key component in connecting to ATM for many years.

Segmenting and reassembling LAN frames into cells is best done with hardware. Some initial implementations were based on software in hosts and routers.

Like frame relay, ATM systems require a modified form of ARP, InATMARP, which is based on INARP for permanent virtual circuits and ATMARP for switched virtual circuits. Readers who require additional detail should consult the relevant RFCs quoted at the end of this chapter. (See also Appendix B.)

The opportunities offered by ATM

PTTs, Telcos and Internet Service Providers have installed 155 Mbps and 622 Mbps systems in the core of their networks. Higher speeds are on trial in experimental services. Major corporations are beginning to connect each site to that infrastructure at 51 or 155 Mbps. Governments have announced plans for information superhighways, or more correctly information infrastructures, for example the National Information Infrastructure in the USA and Information Society Projects in the European Union. These systems will require ATM speeds.

With ATM, and for the first time since LANs were developed, long-distance transmission systems will have the capacity and performance to interconnect LANs through a backbone which is potentially faster than the LAN itself. Because of the multiplexing efficiency, ATM can technically reduce the cost of long-distance communications to a fraction of that current in the mid-1990s. This is offset by the increasing demand for capacity to support multimedia applications. Networks based on ATM deserve the accolade of 'information superhighway' and we believe that they will replace other forms of long-distance communications. As with many other telecommunications developments, the users may be unaware of the change apart from the improved performance and reduced charges. The speed of this change to ATM will be determined by technical inertia and marketing and tariff issues; it will therefore take a decade or more for the ATM revolution to be completed.

Switched multimegabit data service and IEEE 802.6

The Switched Multimegabit Data Service (SMDS) is based on the IEEE 802.6 metropolitan area network Distributed Queue Dual Bus (DQDB) standard. IEEE 802.6 is the technological standard. SMDS is a public network service based on that standard. It is particularly advanced in the USA, but is now being piloted in a number of other countries.

SMDS provides a high-speed packet-switched connectionless datagram service on demand between geographically separated locations. Like a LAN, it has high throughput and low delay and supports individual and multicast addressing (although not broadcast as it is a public service!). The addressing allows the creation of closed user groups or a virtual private network over the service.

RFC 1209 describes how IP data is carried on this service for use by one organization in such a virtual private network for end systems and routers directly connected to the SMDS. It does not discuss how such a bearer service should be used by bridges. Neither does it discuss the issues of using the service for IP between different organizations.

The protocol layering with IEEE 802.6 and SMDS is exactly the same as the other IEEE networks: the IEEE 802.6 medium access control, 802.2 LLC type 1 with a DSAP and SSAP of 0xAA indicating SNAP. SNAP will have an organization code of 0x000000 indicating that the Ethernet type follows. The Ethernet type will distinguish the IP, ARP and RARP protocols. The format is as Figure 10.8, though the headers for the lowest layer, IEEE 802.6, are different.

An IEEE 802.6 frame has a maximum size of 9180 octets of IP data excluding the LLC and SNAP headers. It uses a 64-bit address field.

Because SMDS does not support broadcast, a multicast SMDS address allocated to the closed user group must be assigned to carry any broadcast traffic from the TCP/IP stack. A second address may be required for the multicast traffic of the TCP/IP stack. These assignments must be agreed with the network provider and configured into all the affected interfaces.

Relevant RFCs

894   Standard for the transmission of IP datagrams over Ethernet networks

895   Standard for the transmission of IP datagrams over experimental Ethernet networks

1042 Standard for the transmission of IP datagrams over IEEE 802 networks

1055 Non-standard for transmission of IP datagrams over serial lines: SLIP

1088   Standard for the transmission of IP datagrams over NetBIOS networks

1132   Standard for the transmission of 802.2 packets over IPX networks

1144   Compressing TCP/IP headers for low-speed serial links

1201   Transmitting IP traffic over ARCNET networks

1209   Transmission of IP datagrams over the SMDS service

1293   Inverse address resolution protocol

1332   The PPP Internet protocol control protocol (IPCP)

1333   PPP link quality monitoring

1334   PPP authentication protocols

1356   Multiprotocol interconnect on X.25 and ISDN in the packet mode

1374   IP and ARP on HIPPI

1377   The PPP OSI network layer control protocol (OSINLCP)

1378   The PPP AppleTalk control protocol (ATCP)

1390   Transmission of IP and ARP over FDDI networks

1469   IP multicast over Token Ring local area networks

1483   Multiprotocol encapsulation over ATM adaptation layer 5

1490   Multiprotocol interconnect over frame relay

1552   The PPP Internetwork packet exchange control protocol (IPXCP)

1570   PPP LCP extensions

1577   Classical IP and ARP over ATM

1618   PPP over ISDN

1619   PPP over SONET/SDH

1626   Default IP MTU for use over ATM AAL5

1638   Transmission of IP and ARP over FDDI networks

1661   The point-to-point protocol (PPP)

1662   PPP in HDLC-like framing

1663   PPP reliable tranmission

1717   The PPP multilink protocol (MP)

1735   NBMA address resolution protocol (NARP)

1755   ATM signalling support for IP over ATM

1762   The PPP DECnet phase IV control protocol (DNCP)

1763   The PPP Banyan Vines control protocol (BVCP)

1764   The PPP XNS IDP control protocol (XNSCP)

1841   PPP network control protocol for LAN extension

Summary

TCP/IP can run on many different types of media and little configuration is required to deal with them. MAC address connection can be dynamic on networks that support broadcast through use of the ARP protocol; on point-to-point networks end node addresses may need to be configured into the software.

The major factors to consider when operating TCP/IP on the different media systems are frame compatibility, throughput and frame sizes.

11

Internet protocol (IPv4 and IPv6)

This chapter studies the network layer of the TCP/IP protocol family, the Internet Protocol (IP). IP provides the basis for transporting all the higher layer TCP/IP protocols over all physical networks. Understanding the fields used in the IP header helps you to appreciate the facilities that IP supports and some of the configuration requirements for TCP/IP systems.

In this chapter you will learn:

- IP Version 4
- The format of the IP datagram
- The facilities provided by IP
- The Type of Service options used by IP
- About fragmentation and how it is performed
- The basis of IP routing
- The need for certain configuration options relating to IP
- IP multicasting and IGMP
- How the address resolution protocol works
- How the reverse address resolution protocol works
- ICMP and its use for network management
- IP Version 6
- ICMP Version 6

The Internet Protocol (IP) is the underpinning protocol for the TCP/IP stack. IP is the layer 3 or network component of the TCP/IP model, providing functions for transferring information between devices across any combination of underlying relay networks. The basic functions provided at the network layer deal with conveying data to the correct machine on the correct physical network; to put it another way, routing is performed in this layer.

IP is described as a 'connectionless datagram service'. Datagrams are packets of information that can be destined for one, many or all stations; they can have unique, multicast or broadcast destination addresses. There is no requirement for the intended recipient or recipients to acknowledge whether the datagram was received. No error correction takes place at this level and the reliability of the service is solely dependent on the basic error performance of the underlying networks. The service is connectionless because there is no call or virtual circuit set up before data transmission begins; each datagram contains all information needed to route it with the right performance.

In a connectionless datagram service each datagram is regarded as complete. There is no concept of a sequence of datagrams making up a message. The datagram service does not have to keep datagrams in the same order as they were sent. If important, a receiving station must allow for information arriving in the wrong order and for duplicate datagrams because they were retransmitted by the sender.

As IP is connectionless, no specific route is defined between two communicating nodes, so datagrams travelling between them can travel along different routes and possibly reach their destination in a different order than they were sent. But this is very flexible: because datagrams do not have to establish a connection along a fixed route they can easily be rerouted with little switching delay if there is a network failure.

One of the major functions of the IP layer is to make it unnecessary for higher layer protocols to understand anything about the physical capabilities of the media supporting them. IP provides a barrier between the physical layers discussed in the previous chapter and the next layer up, the transport protocols. This is important for application developers writing programs on top of the transport layer, as they need not produce variations to cater for different types of media.

The facilities of IP

For datagrams, the basic facilities of IP deal with **addressing, fragmentation** and obtaining a suitable **Type of Service**. There are some powerful network management and security options available, but today these are rarely used.

As was discussed in detail in Chapter 3, IP encodes the network number as part of the IP address; some protocols (XNS, IPX) have a

Figure 11.1 The IP architecture.

completely separate field for a network number which they call the network address. As mentioned in Chapters 3 and 5, the network number in IP addressing is used to determine how to route the datagram.

The IP address uniquely identifies an individual connection on a particular network number in a standard way which is completely independent of the technology of that network connection. The underlying datalink address could be the MAC address of a LAN card or an X.121 address on an X.25 network.

Often shown within the IP layer (Figure 11.1) are three other protocols that are needed with some types of media. They are:

(1) The Address Resolution Protocol (ARP)

(2) The Reverse Address Resolution Protocol (RARP)

(3) The Internet Control Message Protocol (ICMP)

All of these will be covered in detail in this chapter. ARP and RARP are shown at the bottom of the IP layer because they do not use IP and are recognized as separate protocols by the datalink layer supporting them. ICMP is shown at the top of the IP layer as it is transported across a network in IP datagrams. The IP layer recognizes ICMP datagrams by the protocol value of 1, which is also shown.

Encapsulation

Both the header and data field of the IP datagram become the data field of the datalink frame of whichever network they happen to be on. This is called **encapsulation** or, sometimes, **enveloping**. The IP datagram data field contains headers of the higher layer protocols and ultimately, end user information; IP itself encapsulates the higher layer protocols. An example is shown in Figure 11.2. This shows IP being encapsulated in both an Ethernet and an IEEE 802.3 frame.

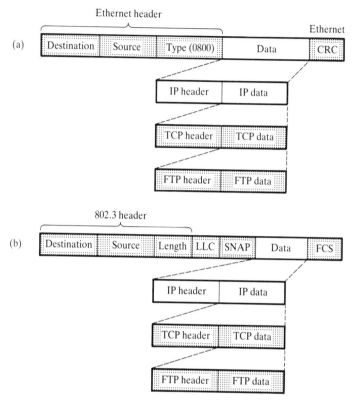

Figure 11.2   IP in: (a) Ethernet and (b) IEEE 802.3 frames.

Fragmentation, reassembly and the maximum transmission unit

One of the issues in hiding physical layer restrictions from the transport layer is to conceal the limited amount of data that can be sent in datalink frames. The IP layer has to give the impression of having no restriction on the amount of data that can be transmitted at one time. In principle, the higher layer protocols can send a datagram of whatever size they prefer. IP has to split datagrams that are larger than the medium can manage into fragments and reassemble them at the remote node as if they were a single datagram. The process is predictably called **fragmentation and reassembly**. For example, IEEE 802.3 and Ethernet systems have maximum data sizes of 1492 and 1500 octets respectively. The limit for IEEE 802.5 frames is not defined, but in practice it is usually no greater than 8192 octets. The packets used in an X.25 system are often no greater than 128 octets in size[†].

[†]Because of the way IP is carried within X.25, the 128-octet limit of X.25 may be invisible to IP as described in Chapter 10.

This size limit seen by IP is known as the **Maximum Transmission Unit** (MTU). In some, but not all, TCP/IP implementations, this value can be adjusted for each interface. It is not normally necessary to do so unless bridging different LAN technologies (ring and bus). To the higher layer protocols, this size limitation is invisible, as IP will take the data supplied to it and fragment it into smaller datagrams as necessary.

IP addressing

The mechanism for choosing an IP addressing scheme was thoroughly explored in Chapter 3. The fundamental purpose of the IP address is to provide an addressing scheme that is completely independent of physical network type. The same addressing structure is used independent of any medium, hardware and software used for layers 1 and 2. So from an application programmer's or user's perspective the addressing scheme is always the same.

As with telephone systems, even though some of them are electronic and others are electromechanical with completely different designs, the addressing scheme, the phone number, remains the same. We, as users, need not recognize that the destination is on a different type of system; it is not necessary to have different procedures for each system. Because the addressing scheme remains consistent and is part of an ITU-T 'international standard', the system type is transparent to users and application developers.

Normally, an IP address is allocated to a network connection when the TCP/IP software is installed. The address is configured to represent a particular network number and unique host connection on that network. If more than one connection is made to a computer, a different IP address is required for each one.

Type of service

In an attempt to provide a 'better' service, the IP header has a number of flags, the **Type of Service** (TOS) bits, that allow software to request different types of performance for a datagram: low delay, high throughput, high reliability and low cost (Figure 11.3). In this context, high reliability means that there should be a lower than normal probability that the datagram will be discarded because of either congestion or a transmission error.

When a higher layer protocol requests a particular TOS from IP, the relevant flags are set in the IP headers of the datagrams; routers that process these datagrams are expected to attempt to provide paths through the network that satisfy the options requested[†].

[†]Unfortunately, most routers ignore these bits.

Version	IHL	Type of service	Total length	
Identification			Flags	Fragment offset
Time to live		Protocol	Header checksum	
Source IP address				
Destination IP address				
Options				Padding
Data ⋮				

Figure 11.3   IPv4 datagram format.

It would be unusual for all three options to be valid and required at the same time. Their characteristics tend to be mutually exclusive. It is normal to set only one of these bits, but it is not unknown for a TCP/IP implementation to request all three services together – however, that is simply not playing fair. Protocols which support interactive traffic need low delay, as a user's performance is affected directly by long delays. Large data transfers that involve long blocks of information require high throughput. Higher layer protocols that provide datagram services should request high reliability. For standard TCP/IP applications, the recommended TOS for Telnet is low delay; for FTP it is low delay for the control connection and high throughput for the data connection (see Chapter 13).

A user or network manager does not normally have access to the TOS values; they are preset by developers when they build TCP/IP software. If you are developing your own application package it is possible to set your own values.

As more flexible implementations of TCP/IP become available, it may be worth checking to see which products support TOS, if this is seen as important for system performance. Remember, however, that it is only routers that can take decisions on these TOS bits. TOS is only important in internetworks which have routers and then only if those routers support TOS routing! Some diagnostic tools do allow TOS to be set for testing purposes, for example to verify that routers do make use of them.

The IPv4 datagram

The IPv4 datagram is shown in Figure 11.3 and, as is standard for TCP/IP systems, is shown as 32 bits wide. When transmitted to a network the transmission order is from top left to bottom right. This transmission order is called **network byte order** and applies to all TCP/IP-related diagrams. Since numbers are always represented with the most significant components on the left, all TCP/IP numbers are transmitted most significant octet first. This is most important when decoding any TCP/IP information on a protocol analyser.

We will now describe the fields in the header in order:

- *Version – 4 bits*   This field indicates the version of the IP protocol so incompatibility can be discovered. The current version is 4.

- *Internet header length – 4 bits*   This field indicates the length of the header in 32-bit words so the beginning of data can easily be found if any options are present. It is normally 5, which indicates no options are used.

- *Type of Service – 8 bits*   This field holds the flags used for TOS and precedence. The first three bits are used to indicate one of eight levels of precedence. This allows an IP node to designate certain datagrams as having higher priority than others. Some routers ignore these flags.

  The D-flag requests a low delay connection. If there is a path to a network that a router understands to be lower delay than others, it will be selected. Interactive traffic using remote echo could request this service.

  The T-bit signifies a requirement for high throughput. Again, a router should attempt to provide a route supplying this service.

  The R-bit requests high reliability, meaning there is a lower probability of the datagram being discarded. Some newer routing protocols are now setting the R-bit.

  A recent RFC adds the C-bit which requests a route with a lower cost.

  The last bit is unused.

- *Total length – 16 bits*   The total length of the IP datagram measured in octets including the header and data. The size of the data area is computed from the total length field and the IHL field.

  As this field is 16 bits, it means the maximum datagram size is 65 535 octets, which is very much larger than most physical networks support. (When a datagram is fragmented, this value indicates the new size of the fragment, not the size of the original datagram, so 16 bits is generous.)

- *Identification – 16 bits*   This is an integer value used to identify all fragments of a datagram. This field should be unique for each new datagram sent by a host and is often simply incremented.

  It is important not to think of this id as a sequence number. Since the IP service is connectionless, there is no concept of a sequence of datagrams, and since that IP service may be supporting several different transport layer 'conversations', there is not necessarily a correlation between the values of id and the order of datagrams sent over a particular conversation with another node. This concept will be developed more fully in the following section covering fragmentation.

- *Flags – 3 bits* The two low-order bits are used as flags to control fragmentation. The low-order bit, if zero, indicates the last fragment of a datagram, and hence is sometimes referred to as the more flag or MF bit. The middle bit is used to indicate that the datagram should not be fragmented, the **do not fragment flag** or DF bit. The high-order bit is unused. See the following section covering fragmentation for more details on usage of these bits.

- *Fragment offset – 13 bits* This field is used with fragmented datagrams to indicate the position that the data in this fragment occupies in the original message. It is measured in 8-octet units, so fragments must be built in 8-octet units; the minimum fragment size is 8 octets of data, not including the IP header (which is 20 octets without options), or the datalink header field. See the following section covering fragmentation for use of this field.

- *Time to live – 8 bits* The Time To Live (TTL) field is set by the datagram sender and is decremented by routers as the datagram passes through them. If this action reduces the TTL to 0 the datagram is discarded rather than relayed. This prevents datagrams that get routed in a loop from circulating forever. A router should never receive a datagram that has TTL set to 0.

  This TTL value may be configured in some implementations of TCP/IP software and its value can be important. If the value of this field is set too small, it is possible that datagrams may not reach the remotest parts of a large network; set too big and datagrams could travel unnecessarily in a routing loop creating unwanted traffic. The recommended value is 40 to 64, but it is not uncommon to find systems that are set to the maximum possible value of 255 or low values of 3 or 4.

- *Protocol – 8 bits* The protocol field indicates the transport layer protocol carried by this datagram. It tells the IP layer which transport layer to pass this datagram to. The normal values for this field are:

17	UDP
6	TCP
1	ICMP
8	EGP
89	OSPF

- *Header checksum – 16 bits* The IP header checksum is interesting in that the checksum only protects its header and thus does not protect the data it carries. The main reason for this is that the

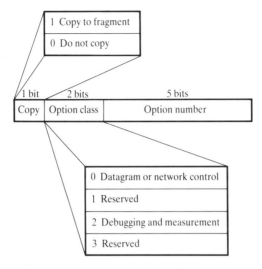

Figure 11.4   Measurement and security options.

checksum must be recalculated every time it passes through a router, for the value TTL, flags and fragment offset may change. If the data was also included in the checksum, it would take longer to calculate and hence delay the datagram further.

The checksum is a simple calculation. It is based upon taking the header as 16-bit integers, adding them together using 1s complement and taking the 1s complement of the result.

Some systems which work over error-detected networks do not set the header checksum. It is then all 0s.

- *Source IP address – 32 bits*   The source IP address.
- *Destination IP address – 32 bits*   The destination IP address.
- *Data – variable*   This includes the headers of higher layer proto-cols and sometimes user's data.
- *Padding – variable*   This field represents 0s used to pad the header out to a 32-bit word boundary so that the IHL can correctly point to the start of the data when the variable length options are present.
- *Options*   The options field supports debugging, measurement and security facilities. There can be multiple options in a single data-gram, each with the format shown in Figure 11.4. These options are normally used in diagnostic datagrams sent in such as a way as to be echoed back by the remote node, otherwise the sender cannot obtain the results!

In some TCP/IP implementations, the setting of these options is within a utility called **ping**, covered in more detail later. Other implementations give neither user nor network manager an interface to the options field.

The option fields are:

- *Copy (1 bit)*   Used to indicate whether this option has to be placed in all fragments. If set to zero (0) this option will only appear in the first fragment. The security options for example would need to be copied into all fragments.

- *Option class (2 bits)*   Used to specify the class of an option. The time stamp option has a class of 2, otherwise class is usually 0.

- *Option numbers (5 bits)*

    Security: option 2   The security options are assigned by the US Defense Intelligence Agency and define a datagram as ranging from unclassified to top secret. This allows a router to detect datagrams that are carrying sensitive information and prevent them from leaving a secure environment. These features have not had wide usage in commercial TCP/IP implementations.

    Time stamp – option 4   This option allows a datagram to be sent through the network and gather time stamps from each router it passes through. This can be used to assess delay and its variations within the router network. (The clocks in all routers must be synchronized, or time differentials used.)

    Loose source route: option 3   This is another management option that allows a datagram to be directed through a particular set of routers using a predefined list of IP addresses of routers which must be visited in sequence. A loose source route allows other routers to be used in between those defined in this list of routers.

    Record route: option 7   This datagram option causes each router to place its IP address in the datagram option field as the datagram travels through the network. This list is used to ascertain the path datagrams are using to reach a particular host or router. The datagram has to have enough space allocated in it to store the number of IP addresses it finds. This has to be allowed for by a developer when creating an application that uses this option.

    Strict source route: option 9   Similar to loose source route except that only the routers defined in the list can be used, no others. If the datagram cannot be routed, an ICMP error message should result (see below).

Fragmentation and reassembly

We have already used the term 'fragmentation' in explaining how IP is carried over X.25. Fragmentation has a strict meaning in TCP/IP. It is the process used by IP to reduce the size of datagrams that are too large

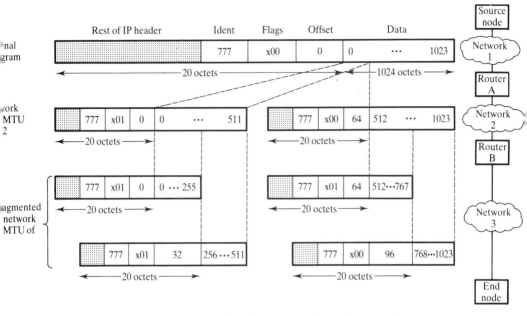

Figure 11.5 Fragmentation: the datagram has been fragmented twice.

to be transported over a specific medium. Fragments must not exceed the network interface MTU.

IP reduces the size of a large datagram by splitting the data field into suitably small parts. The IP header has to be transported with every fragment for them to be routed correctly, so the size of the datagram can only be changed by reducing the amount of data.

All fragments carry the 16-bit identification number of the original datagram. This is used to identify fragments of the original datagram when reassembling them at the receiving node. Once a datagram has been fragmented, it will not be reassembled until it reaches the final destination end node. Attempts to reassemble a datagram before the destination could be troubled by two problems. First, in a multiple path network, it is possible that fragments will take different paths; an intermediate node will not see all of them so it cannot reassemble the complete datagram. Secondly, to reassemble at an intermediate (router) node would require that node to collect all fragments before forwarding the whole datagram. This would cause unnecessary delay, just to find that the datagram has to be fragmented again further along the path.

Figure 11.5 shows an example of a datagram being fragmented. The IP header is shown shaded and in front of the identification, flags and fragment offset fields. This is not true in practice; it is only shown this way to ease the explanation. The figure also shows a network configuration that would require a datagram to be fragmented. Network 1 has an

MTU of 1200, network 2 has MTU of 532 and network 3 has MTU of 276. (These numbers are purely for illustration and are not representative of real networks.) Initially, the datagram has 1024 octets of data when transmitted onto network 1. For router A, the IP layer driving network 2 knows that network 2 has an MTU of only 532 and fragments the datagram into two datagrams each with 512 octets of data. The 20-octet IP header takes the maximum data at the datalink layer to 532 octets, the MTU for this system. (The frames on the networks will be larger as they include the datalink header but the MTU only refers to the amount of data a datalink can carry in one frame.) The fragment offset of the first fragment will be 0, indicating its position in the original datagram. The fragment offset in the second fragment will be 512/8, or 64, as the 13-bit fragment offset field indicates the position in units of 8 octets. The **more bit** in the first fragment will be 1 for there are more fragments to come; in the second it will be 0, as this is the last fragment.

When the fragments arrive at the next router they have to be fragmented again. As can be seen from Figure 11.5, the process is straightforward. The fragments are split again, with the **more flag** set to 1 in all but the current last fragment. The fragment offset indicates how the pieces fit together in the overall jigsaw which is the original datagram.

Using the fragment offset, the original datagram can be reassembled, even if the fragments arrive out of order. Fragments arriving out of order are impossible in the network shown, but in a large multi-path network it is quite conceivable. The end node starts a timer that is used to determine the maximum time the node will wait for all fragments to arrive, usually about 30 seconds. If any fragment fails to arrive within this fragment reassembly time-out, the complete datagram is discarded and since the service is connectionless no attempt is made by IP to recover the situation, though an ICMP error message may be generated.

Some systems do not have the power necessary to reassemble fragments. This, at one time, would have been the case with a diskless workstation that has a simple bootstrap program in PROM. Where this is known by an originator, although there is nothing in TCP/IP protocols that would allow a sender to determine this, the do not fragment (DF) bit in the fragmentation flags can be set to advise any intervening routers that this datagram must not undergo fragmentation. If fragmentation is required, the datagram will be discarded and an ICMP (discussed later) error message returned to the sender.

Management issues

From the above description, it might be thought that fragmentation is only an issue on networks with routers, particularly on WANs. But fragmentation can, and does, occur on LAN-only networks. Fragmentation can take place within the originating node before the datagram reaches the LAN. Then the loss of a single fragment which causes the complete datagram to be discarded can become a very serious problem, even on some LAN-only systems. For example, in many implementations, the NFS protocol attempts to send datagrams that are 8192 bytes long, (where the total transfer is more than 8192 bytes). Consider the impact of this on an Ethernet network that has an MTU of 1024 octets[†].

The IP layer in the source node will realize that the datagram is too large for a single frame and will fragment it into eight full datagrams plus one smaller datagram[‡]. If any one of these datagrams does not reach its destination, the complete 8192 bytes has to be transmitted again. The effect of this is to increase the load on the network for a given amount of data with a longer time to transfer it. This phenomenon can cause the performance of a network to degrade significantly and rapidly. In the worst case, it can cause a 'black hole' effect where network analysers show very high network activity but the users are not seeing much data delivered: all the activity is retransmissions. A runaway effect (a packet meltdown) has occurred at a high load where fragments are lost due to resource limitations, which causes them to be resent, which causes more fragments to be lost....

Why should frames be discarded on a LAN? The error rate on a LAN is supposed to be very low. This statement makes a number of assumptions:

- The LAN cabling system must be properly installed and within the cable design limits. Where unshielded twisted-pair cable is used, the electrical noise level must be low.

- There must be no frame loss due to resource limitations in LAN hardware and software.

These assumptions are often not met in practice.

A discussion of error rates on cabling systems is beyond the scope of this book, but resource limitations can occur in three ways:

(1) In receiving workstations, because they have a much lower performance than the file server which is feeding them;

(2) In networks with a high number of short broadcast frames which detract from the performance of receiving workstations;

(3) In bridges, which cannot forward frames, either because of insufficient forwarding rate or because of output congestion.

When a high-performance workstation sends a series of fragmented datagrams, it can stream them onto a quiet network at the maximum speed that the network specification allows. The receiving interface, in an end

---

[†]The MTU of Ethernet is normally 1500 and of IEEE 802.3, 1492.
[‡]The 20-octet IP header makes the total datagram size at the IP layer 8212 octets.

workstation, a bridge, or a router, must be able to receive all of these frames successfully. If it drops[†] any one frame, a fragment is lost and all are retransmitted, often only to be lost again, until other activity on the network splits up the fragments. We have observed this effect between a UNIX RISC-based NFS file server and a 286 PC with an 8-bit Ethernet card. As a connectionless system offers no flow control, it is important that two devices communicating on the same cable are reasonably well matched. The Ethernet card must have sufficient memory to take all frames which contain the fragments of one datagram.

As explained elsewhere, this problem is made worse by a high level of broadcast traffic on the medium, for every LAN card will process all broadcasts.

In Chapter 2, we emphasized the need for bridges with the highest possible filtering and forwarding rates and for a good network structure which maps the data flows within an organization. The reasons should now be clearer! Bridges can be real performance bottlenecks for TCP/IP systems if they lead to the loss of fragments.

Setting the MTU

Some systems have an option to set the MTU for a particular network interface. It will normally default to the recommended maximum for that network. IAB standards for TCP/IP recommend that all networks supporting TCP/IP have an MTU of at least 576 octets. This means they can forward a higher level data field of 512 octets and still have room for the transport and IP headers with some options. All common networks meet this requirement, including X.25 by using the M-bit as described in Chapter 10. Later work has suggested increasing the standard MTU from 576 bytes to 1500 bytes.

An MTU should be set for the maximum size possible on the local medium, unless for some reason another network is unable to support such large frames and the interconnection between the two networks cannot support fragmentation. An example is a bridge between Token Ring and CSMA/CD LANs. The Token Ring would normally operate with an MTU of 4000 octets, but if such a frame were to be sent across the bridge to a CSMA/CD system, that bridge would discard the datagram, as a bridge operating at the MAC layer cannot fragment. By reducing the MTU on the Token Ring to, say, 1024 or 1492, all frames will fit the Ethernet or IEEE 802.3 system. However, the MTU cannot be adjusted

---

[†]On CSMA/CD networks the sender has no notification that this has happened, though the receiving LAN card should record a receiver overrun. One advantage of Token Ring networks is that the sender does know there is a problem – the address-recognized bit at the end of the returned frame will be set but the frame-copied bit will be clear. Whether any use is made of this information is up to the protocol designer and the network manager. It is usually ignored!

for each path, so for reliable any-to-any operation, all nodes on the Token Ring would have to use the reduced MTU. Communications within the Token Ring then operate less efficiently, as all high-level datagrams would always fragment down to 1024 or 1492.

For these and other reasons it can be argued that it is better to use routers between Token Ring and CSMA/CD networks. The routers will automatically deal with fragmentation when it is necessary.

IP traces

The following shows actual traces of the IP protocol taken from an operational network. In this example we show an Ethernet frame in hexadecimal without the preamble or the CRC. The table beneath the frame shown in hexadecimal gives a breakdown of the fields in the frame and their values. For a further explanation of the format of these examples see Appendix F.

As IP is a datagram service there is no interplay between both ends at this level. IP is shown as the area which is unshaded. This example is part of a session between two hosts, IP address 30.0.0.1 and 30.0.0.99. The headers for Ethernet and TCP are shown in this example for completeness only. Later chapters in this book detail TCP operation.

Note that the IP headers for each node are independent. The values of ID increment with respect to each IP address, not each datagram.

Frame 1

```
0260  8C0A  C49D  AA00  0400  0104  0800  4508      .`..D.*.......E.
0028  0B6E  0000  3C06  36F7  1E00  0063  1E00      .(.n...6w...c..
0001  0014  0C17  180C  CD95  0000  0AA0  5010      .........M.... P.
0000  7704  0000  0000  0000  0000                  ..w.........
```

Datalink:	Dest MAC:	02608C 0AC49D	Source MAC:	AA0004 000104	Type(Length):	0800
IP:	Version:	4	IHL:	5	Type of service:	08 (Thruput)
	Length:	0028	ID:	0B6E	FLAGS:	0
	Offset:	0	Time to Live:	60	Protocol:	06
	Checksum:	36F7	Source IP:	30.0.0.99	Dest IP:	30.0.0.1
TCP:	Source Port:	FTP(0014)	Dest Port:	0C17	Sequence:	180CCD95
	Acknowledge:	00000AA0	Offset:	5	Code:	10(ACK)
	Window:	0	Checksum:	7704		

Frame 2

```
AA00  0400  0104  0260  8C0A  C49D  0800  4500      *......`..D...E.
003D  0097  0000  FF06  7EC0  1E00  0001  1E00      .=.......~@......
0063  1A57  0015  0000  17BA  1245  BC31  5018      .c.W.....:.EP.
0400  47C1  0000  504F  5254  2033  302C  302C      ..GA..PORT 30,0,
302C  312C  342C  3235  320D  0A                    0,1,4,252..
```

Translation:

Datalink:	Dest MAC:	AA0004 000104	Source MAC:	02608C 0AC49D	Type(Length):	0800
IP:	Version:	4	IHL:	5	Type of service:	00
	Length:	003D	ID:	0097	FLAGS:	0
	Offset:	0	Time to Live:	255	Protocol:	06
	Checksum:	7EC0	Source IP:	30.0.0.1	Dest IP:	30.0.0.99
TCP:	Source Port:	1A57	Dest Port:	FTP(0015)	Sequence:	000017BA
	Acknowledge:	1245BC31	Offset:	5	Code:	18(Push)
	Window:	0400	Checksum:	47C1		

Frame 3

```
0260  8C0A  C49D  AA00  0400  0104  0800  4500      .`..D.*.......E.
003B  0B6F  0000  3C06  36EB  1E00  0063  1E00      .;.o...6k...c..
0001  0015  1A57  1245  BC31  0000  17CF  5018      .....W.E...OP.
07C5  8931  0000  3230  3020  436F  6D6D  616E      .E.1..200Command
6420  6F6B  6179  2E0D  0A                          okay...
```

Translation:

Datalink:	Dest MAC:	02608C 0AC49D	Source MAC:	AA0004 000104	Type(Length):	0800
IP:	Version:	4	IHL:	5	Type of service:	00
	Length:	003B	ID:	0B6F	FLAGS:	0
	Offset:	0	Time to Live:	60	Protocol:	06
	Checksum:	36EB	Source IP:	30.0.0.99	Dest IP:	30.0.0.1
TCP:	Source Port:	FTP(0015)	Dest Port:	1A57	Sequence:	1245BC31
	Acknowledge:	000017CF	Offset:	5	Code:	18(Push)
	Window:	1989	Checksum:	8931		

Frame 4

```
AA00  0400  0104  0260  8C0A  C49D  0800  4500      *......`..D...E.
0028  0098  0000  FF06  7ED4  1E00  0001  1E00      .(.......~T......
0063  1A57  0015  0000  17CF  1245  BC44  5010      .c.W.....O.E.
0400  6EAC  0000  504F  5254  2033                  ..n,..PORT 3
```

Translation:

Datalink:	Dest MAC:	AA0004 000104	Source MAC:	02608C 0AC49D	Type(Length):	0800
IP:	Version:	4	IHL:	5	Type of service:	00
	Length:	0028	ID:	0098	FLAGS:	0
	Offset:	0	Time to Live:	255	Protocol:	06
	Checksum:	7ED4	Source IP:	30.0.0.1	Dest IP:	30.0.0.99
TCP:	Source Port:	1A57	Dest Port:	FTP(0015)	Sequence:	000017CF
	Acknowledge:	1245BC44	Offset:	5	Code:	18(Push)
	Window:	0400	Checksum:	6EAC		

IP multicasting and IGMP

IP multicasting is used by a group of hosts that have a common interest
in a higher layer protocol or application, such as a routing protocol or
'broadcasting' of text, sound or graphics to a group of displays. For example, IP multicasting is used for the router discovery protocol, for the OSPF
routing protocol and optionally for RIP V2 (all described later), and for
experimental audio distribution on the Internet over the multicast backbone (MBONE). IP multicasting is a recommended extension to normal IP
operation that may not be supported by all host software. The protocol

uses multicast addresses in the range 224.0.0.1 to 239.255.255.255 (previously referred to as class D) as the destination address in one IP datagram to send information simultaneously to a number of hosts in a group.

Multicast IP group addresses ideally are mapped to a LAN (IEEE 802.1) multicast MAC address. Hosts with modern Network Interface Cards (NICs) and drivers must program them to receive multicast MAC addresses that are of interest; other multicast MAC addresses are ignored by the NIC. Software could achieve the same effects by using LAN broadcasts but multicast operation reduces the load on host software; all broadcasts are processed by all stations on a LAN, even if bridging is used. Multicast is therefore used for all new IPS protocols.

RFC1112 standardizes how the multicast IP address is translated into a corresponding MAC address for Ethernet and IEEE 802.3 LANs. It is mapped to a multicast MAC address by placing the low-order 23 bits of the IP address into the low-order 23 bits of multicast MAC address 01-00-5E-00-00-00 (hex). As there are 28 significant bits in a group address, more than one host group address may map to the same MAC multicast address.

Many token ring cards do not support IEEE 802.1 multicast addresses though they do have 31 functional addresses which behave in a similar way. On Token Ring networks which do not support multicast, multicast IP addresses are mapped to the single functional address C0-00-00-04-00-00, by preference; alternatively, all multicast IP addresses may map to the LAN broadcast, FF-FF-FF-FF-FF-FF (with the disadvantages discussed above).

RFC 1112 describes two types of IP group addresses. Permanent addresses or permanent groups are assigned by the Internet community as part of Internet standards; transient addresses or groups use other nonassigned addresses from the IP multicast address range. To allow multicasting beyond the local network, multicast routers may route IP multicasts to other interfaces, if the TTL field is non-zero.

A host may send multicast packets without any additional protocols, but to be sure of receiving all relevant multicast IP datagrams, it must also inform multicast routers of its presence on a LAN by sending an Internet Group Management Protocol (IGMP) query. It must also join (or leave) a group by turning the reception of a particular multicast address on (or off). IGMP designates the permanent group address 224.0.0.1 as the all-IP-multicast-hosts group; multicast hosts will join this group when they start up.

About once a minute, multicast routers use IGMP to request that hosts visible on each interface identify which multicast addresses are of interest to them. The router relays multicast datagrams only to interfaces where they are required by one or more hosts (or other routers). To maintain the integrity of multicast protocols in a large routed network, multicast routing protocols will be required. These are subject to further development.

Address resolution protocol

As we have discussed in Chapter 10, LAN cards send and receive frames based on their MAC addresses. They can only respond to frames with broadcast, a recognized multicast or their own unicast address in the destination field.

TCP/IP uses IP addresses that are defined by the network manager at installation time; they are associated with the network layer of the protocol stack and have no direct relation to the MAC address.

All TCP/IP communications begin with the IP address. If we wish to connect to a remote computer we must know its IP address but we do not need to know its MAC address. End-to-end communication takes place with the IP address but hop-to-hop communication uses the MAC address. For efficient network operation, the MAC layer requires the unicast MAC address of the next MAC layer in the chain of hops between source IP address and destination IP address.

Early TCP/IP systems had to have a manually configured table which related MAC and IP address so that a frame could be unicast to the correct destination. Today, the **Address Resolution Protocol** (ARP) relates IP and MAC address but only on media that support broadcasts. Each node maintains a cache, called the **ARP cache**, of IP entries against their MAC addresses. When IP is requested to send a datagram to another IP address, it first looks in the ARP cache to find the corresponding MAC address that the datalink layer should use for the datagram. If there is no entry, it then attempts to find the MAC address from the IP address, using ARP.

To do this, ARP sends an **ARP request** datagram to all LAN cards, using the MAC broadcast address (0xFFFF_FFFF_FFFF). ARP uses its own Ethernet type 0x0806 for these requests, so they are passed to the ARP software in all nodes within a broadcast area. The ARP request carries the IP address corresponding to the required MAC address. All cards on a network read this request datagram and any that discover a match between their IP address and the requested IP address reply with an ARP response. If a response is received, the answer is entered in the ARP cache for future use; if none is received within a few seconds, the request is repeated. (The ARP might have been discarded due to a transmission error or bridge congestion.) To reduce the need for ARP broadcasts, a node responding to ARP requests will itself copy the IP and MAC address mapping of the source of the request in its own ARP cache. As the two systems are likely to communicate further, this removes the need for a second ARP in the reverse direction at some later time as it already knows the MAC address for that return IP address.

The ARP cache is often kept until the equipment is reset or powered off. With some TCP/IP implementations ARP cache entries have a

Frame header	ARP/RARP message

Hardware		Protocol
HLEN	PLEN	Operation
Sender HA (octets 0–3)		
Sender HA (octets 4–5)		Sender IA (octets 0–1)
Sender IA (octets 2–3)		Target HA (octets 0–1)
Target HA (octets 2–5)		
Target IA (octets 0–3)		

Figure 11.6 ARP datagram format.

time-out. If the entry is not used for a period, often of 15 minutes, that entry is deleted. Other systems provide an automatic refresh timer. An ARP is performed every 15 minutes to make sure the cache is up to date. Since MAC addresses usually only change when a piece of equipment is faulty or moved this seems of more limited value.

Some products allow you to view and alter the ARP cache and to change these timer values. This can be a useful diagnostic tool. It lists which hosts a node has communicated with. Where a system has failed, a card has been changed and the ARP cache contains an outdated value, the mapping can be altered. The MAC to IP address translation can be predefined for hosts that are not able to use ARP.

ARP datagrams are not passed through routers, as a router operates at the IP layer and will not relay MAC broadcast traffic; routers create a useful buffer between broadcast domains. This enables routers to prevent broadcast traffic from flooding all networks in a system.

ARP format

The format of the ARP datagram is shown in Figure 11.6. It is simple and was designed to be generic; it is not used purely for TCP/IP or for any one particular type of network. Its only restriction is that the medium must have the ability to send broadcast frames.

ARP operates directly over datalink and therefore is only encapsulated in the datalink frame. This requires it to have its own Ethernet type field of 0x0806 so that datalink can distinguish it from other incoming frames.

The fields of the ARP datagram are as follows:

- *Hardware*   This field indicates the type of network hardware this datagram was generated on. Valid types are:

Type	Description
1	Ethernet (10 Mbps)
2	Experimental Ethernet (3 Mbps)
3	Amateur radio AX.25[†]
4	Proteon ProNET Token Ring
5	Chaos
6	IEEE 802 networks
7	ARCNET
8	Hyperchannel
9	Lanstar
10	Autonet short address
11	LocalTalk
12	LocalNet (IBM PCNet or Sytek Inc. LocalNet)

- *Protocol* This field indicates which protocol requested this action. The values used in this field are the same as the Ethernet type field in the Ethernet frame. This is 0x0800 for IP.

- *HLEN* This indicates the length of the hardware addresses in octets. Normally a value of 6 for IEEE LAN MAC addresses.

- *PLEN* This indicates the length of network layer addresses in octets, normally a value of 4 for IP.

- *Operation* This field has a value 1 for an ARP request or 2 for an ARP response. This field is used by RARP with 3 for a RARP request and 4 for a RARP response (RARP is covered later in this chapter).

- *Addresses* Sender hardware address (the source MAC address); source IP address; target hardware address (the destination MAC address); destination IP address.

ARP in operation

Figure 11.7 shows an example of ARP in operation. The node with IP address 128.128.0.3 and with MAC address 0x02608121343 has been requested by its IP layer to find the MAC address of the node with IP address 128.128.0.1. First, 128.128.0.3 sends a broadcast ARP request which will be received by the ARP software on all nodes in that network. 128.128.0.1 will recognize its address in the request and return an ARP response but using the MAC address of the incoming ARP request. The ARP response will be processed and quickly discarded by the LAN cards of all other nodes on the network as it is a unicast frame with the wrong destination address.

ARP requesters trust the response they get. There is normally no check that a single MAC address is responding on behalf of many IP

[†]It may seem surprising to find amateur radio with its own reserved allocation. Radio amateurs have experimented with TCP/IP over the low speeds and poor error performance of packet radio links. In the best traditions of the hobby, a number of modifications to improve TCP/IP performance over these links have been adopted in mainstream TCP/IP standards.

Figure 11.7 The ARP process. (a) ARP request. (b) ARP response. Note the layers which are involved in each transaction.

addresses. This leaves the way open to some useful extensions to ARP, but also the way open for security abuses.

Fault management and ARP

ARP can produce some challenging faults for the network diagnostics teams. What happens when IP addresses are duplicated? How does ARP behave in a large bridged network, particularly one with remote bridges and relatively slow-speed links?

ARP with duplicated IP addresses

Of course, this will never happen in your network, because well-managed networks (like yours) do not have duplicated IP addresses. IP addresses must be unique, but what happens when they are not? It is useful to examine the operation of ARP when two nodes on the same bridged LAN have identical IP addresses, for example 142.1.32.99. We will refer to the two nodes as node A and node B.

Consider a scenario where two client systems connect to the same host. If they both connect to the same host, the effect they have on a host's ARP cache is the most significant issue; the resulting effect on the users of node A and node B is technically of great interest but frustrating and puzzling to the users and network troubleshooters alike!

First, node A connects to the host and performs an ARP request to exchange MAC addresses with it (Figure 11.8a). Both ends set up their ARP caches and the session starts as normal, until node B makes a connection to that same host. What happens then may be implementation dependent.

Secondly, node B attempts to connect. It also performs an ARP request to exchange MAC addresses with the host. Because node B has the same IP address as node A, and that IP address is already in the host's ARP cache, the host will normally change the entry for the duplicated IP address to the MAC address for node B (Figure 11.8b). Data for node A's connection will now find the wrong MAC address, node B, and all data for node A will go to node B in error. But node B is not expecting that data; it matches no higher layer protocol, so it either ignores it or gives an error message.

To the user's frustration, node A is meanwhile 'hung' and will eventually time out, as it is not receiving any response to its messages to the host. Node B's new connection will continue to operate normally until at some point the increasingly frustrated user at node A attempts to reconnect to the host, causing node B's connection to fail! If these users are at widely separated points in a large bridged network and rarely access the same host, the problem will be intermittent and extremely difficult to diagnose.

The second scenario for duplicate IP addresses is where a client system, such as a PC, is given the same address as a host system. This will manifest itself as some users not being able to access the host service on a permanent or intermittent basis. Whether this problem appears consistently or intermittently depends on the architecture of the network, whether routers and bridges are involved and the different types of computers and software in use, as timing of the ARP requests and responses could affect the results.

As with the previous scenario we will refer to the computers concerned as node A, node B and the host. In this case though, node B and the host have the same IP address, and node A is different. In this scenario, when node A attempts to connect to the host and performs an ARP request to obtain the MAC address of the host, it may obtain the MAC address of node B instead, as they will both reply. Which one is accepted depends on the implementation of the protocol stack involved. If node A accepts the MAC address for node B instead of that for the host, it will fail to connect, as node B is unlikely to have the appropriate servers running on it. On another attempt it may be possible that node A gets the

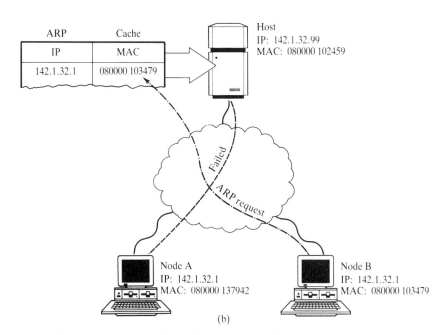

Figure 11.8   The effect of duplicate IP addresses on an ARP cache.

correct ARP from the host and hence connects. If node B is a PC, it is like-ly that it will be turned off when the user is not around, and therefore there will be times when this problem seems to go away. Whenever the PC is turned on the problem returns.

There is a third scenario. In this situation two host machines are given the same IP address. In this case, client machines can access dif-ferent machines on different occasions and either will not be able to log in or will not be able to find the applications or data they thought they had saved. This is less likely to happen as host machines are not normal-ly as abundant as client machines, and host addressing should be man-aged more carefully and be less likely to change.

With most client systems, it is quite possible for users to modify their IP addresses and cause the problems considered in these scenarios. The solution is simple. Do not allow IP addresses to be duplicated. This statement is more difficult to put into practice!

ARP after link failures

A problem can be caused by ARP when applications using a reliable ser-vice suffer a link failure. Most TCP/IP stacks will attempt to recover from the failure by retransmitting the lost datagrams a number of times and, where possible, expecting to be rerouted around the failure. Should all these attempts fail, the protocol stack will often revert to transmitting ARP broadcasts to see if the connection can be recovered from the lowest level (Figure 11.9).

This does not cause serious problems if there are only one or two devices that have lost a connection, but the flood of broadcasts can cause serious performance degradation to the whole network if many nodes start ARPing simultaneously. On systems that have a large number of networks connected by bridges, bridge failure, caused by line failure on a remote bridge or by failure of the bridge itself, can result in many con-nections failing at the same time. A large number of ARP broadcasts gen-erated simultaneously will pass throughout the complete bridged network; they will affect every host on every cabling system.

The effect of so many broadcasts, which may only be 40 to 80 broad-cast frames per second, can have an enormous impact on the performance of hosts. They will even affect applications that are not using the network, as some protocol stacks require a significant amount of processing power just to examine broadcasts. The simplest way to prevent this is to use routers instead of bridges. Care needs to be taken in large networks to prevent this type of issue affecting the complete network, causing it to fail or to reduce performance significantly because a single component has failed.

ARP traces

The following shows actual traces taken from an operational network of the ARP protocol. In this example we show Ethernet frames in hexadeci-

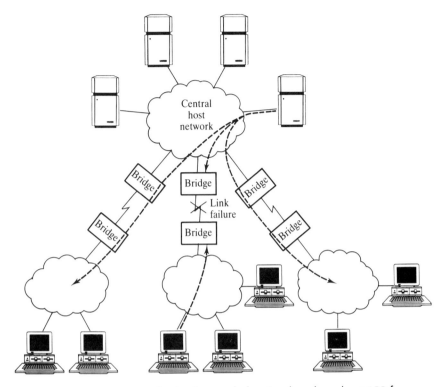

Figure 11.9 ARP on a bridged network showing the rebroadcast ARP frames for one connection.

mal without the preamble or the CRC. The table beneath the frame shown in hexadecimal gives a breakdown of the fields in the frame and their values. For a further explanation of the format of these examples see Appendix F.

In this example, we see IP node 30.0.0.1 starting a connection for the first time with IP address 30.0.0.99. Frame 1 shows the ARP broadcast from 30.0.0.1 with an ARP destination MAC set to all zeros which is responded to in frame 2 with an ARP response with all fields complete.

Frame 1

```
FFFF  FFFF  FFFF  0260  8C0A  C49D  0806  0001        ........`..D.....
0800  0604  0001  0260  8C0A  C49D  1E00  0001        ........`..D.....
0000  0000  0000  1E00  0063  0000  0000  0000        .........C......
0000  0000  0000  0000  0000  0000                    ............
```

Datalink:	Dest MAC:	FFFFFFFFFFFF	Source MAC:	02608C 0AC49D	Type(Length):	0806
ARP:	Hardware:	0001	Protocol:	0800	HLEN:	06
	PLEN:	04	Operation:	01	(ARP request)	
	Source IP:	30.0.0.1	Source MAC:	02608C 0AC49D		
	Dest IP:	30.0.0.99	Dest MAC:	000000000000		

Frame 2

```
0260  8C0A  C49D  AA00  0400  0104  0806  0001    .`..D.*.........
0800  0604  0002  AA00  0400  0104  1E00  0063    ......*........c
0260  8C0A  C49D  1E00  0001  0000  0000  0000    .`..D...........
0000  0000  0000  0000  0000  0000                ............
```

Datalink:	Dest MAC:	02608C 0AC49D	Source MAC:	AA0004 000104	Type(Length):	0806
ARP:	Hardware:	0001	Protocol:	0800	HLEN:	06
	PLEN:	04	Operation:	02	(ARP response)	
	Source IP:	30.0.0.99	Source MAC:	AA0004 000104		
	Dest IP:	30.0.0.1	Dest MAC:	02608C 0AC49D		

Reverse address resolution protocol

The **Reverse Address Resolution Protocol** (RARP) is intended for use with devices that cannot store their IP address, usually diskless workstations. Not surprisingly, RARP performs the reverse action to ARP: given the MAC address, what is the corresponding IP address? A requesting node supplies the MAC address in the RARP request.

RARP, like ARP, operates directly over the datalink layer and hence has an Ethernet type number of 0x8035 assigned to it so it can be distinguished from IP, ARP and any other protocols on a network. Nodes acting as RARP servers that find a match for the MAC address in their RARP tables will reply with the corresponding IP address in a RARP response. This system requires that at least one server is present and that the server has a table defining which IP addresses should be used by each MAC address.

The format of datagram is the same as ARP but in the operation field it uses 3 for a request and 4 for a response. When a RARP request is made, the originator only knows its own MAC address so that is the only field it can fill in. The response will normally have all fields filled in, defining the IP address the requester should use and often the IP and MAC address of the RARP server, although this is not necessary.

Although RARP fulfils its original intentions, it has several limitations in practice and has been largely superseded by the Boot Protocol (BOOTP). BOOTP is capable of operating through routers and provides more useful information than RARP when booting diskless workstations.

ARP and bridging

A bridge that connects the same type of cabling system together will transfer data transparently and hence gives no cause for concern. Problems occur when different types of media, such as IEEE 802.3 and

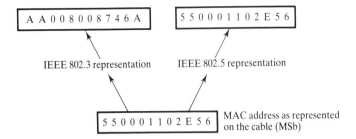

Figure 11.10 MAC addresses in different IEEE LANs.

IEEE 802.5, are bridged together. The issue is based upon the inconsistent standards of representation of MAC address for IEEE LANs (Figure 11.10).

The problem is that IEEE 802.3 (CSMA/CD) and IEEE 802.5 (Token Ring) or IS9314 (FDDI) media systems represent MAC addresses with different bit significance in each octet. The IEEE 802.1 standard which defines the address structure is the same for all, so the addresses in frames on the medium are identical, but when represented by the network hardware to the layers above they are different. This only causes problems when MAC addresses are passed between devices above the datalink layer, as with ARP. Figure 11.11 illustrates this problem. It shows a bus connected to a ring. To simplify the diagram, the MAC addresses used are only 8 bits long. In practice, they are 48 bits. 128.128.0.1 is connected to an IEEE 802.3 system and has a MAC address of 0xAA or 10101010 (in IEEE 802.3 representation). When the address is used on the 802.3 cable, the bits are swapped around by the hardware, so it appears as 01010101 or 0x55, so the lowest level hardware is looking for a bit stream that is 0x55.

The node on the ring network has a MAC address of 0x33 or 00110011, which is how it will appear on 802.5 and FDDI networks. 128.128.0.1 is about to attempt to connect to 128.128.0.3 for the first time and so will use ARP to obtain the MAC address of 128.128.0.3. 128.128.0.1 broadcasts an ARP searching for 128.128.0.3 which will be passed by the bridge to the ring. 128.128.0.3 will recognize its IP address. It replies to the ARP request with an ARP response, using the MAC address found in the hardware address field of the incoming request, giving its MAC address as 0x33 in the relevant field for its hardware address. From the ring, the response will return to a MAC address of 0xAA. 128.128.0.1 does not recognize itself as 0xAA but as 0x55, so the ARP response is ignored by the hardware in 128.128.0.1.

To get around this problem, bridges have to detect ARP frames and modify the addresses in the fields called hardware address of the request or response, so that they are appropriate for the destination network.

(a)

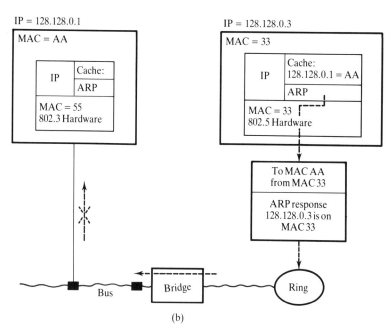

(b)

Figure 11.11 Bridging rings and buses. (a) ARP request for 128.128.0.3. (b) ARP response to the wrong MAC.

Proxy ARP

Proxy ARP is a technique used by some IP routers. It was developed early in the life of TCP/IP as one solution to the problem of inefficient use of the IP address space. Today, with the availability of bridges and the almost universal use of subnetwork addresses, its use is limited. But proxy ARP is still supported by many routers and it can, in some smaller installations, allow routers to be used without planning a full subnetwork addressing scheme.

As a network grows, a point is reached where no more nodes can be added to the existing medium because of physical limitations. To expand the network a separate physical cabling system has to be added. In the early days of IP, before bridges and subnetwork addressing, the only way that two cabling systems could be connected was with a router with a separate network number on either port, assuming repeaters were inadequate because traffic filtering was also required. This was wasteful if only a small number of IP addresses had been used from the original range[†].

As an example, assume a company has a class B registered address 130.1.0.0. They use Ethernet and wish to connect 2048 hosts using TCP/IP. The class B address provides them with 65 534 possible node addresses on their network. As their cabling system is Ethernet, they can only have 1024 nodes on a single cabling segment before they use a bridge or router (but bridges are not yet available). Since they need to support 2048 systems, it is necessary to install another cabling system and, because the expected traffic levels are high, to route between the two. For a conventional router to work, different network addresses are required on both interfaces of the router, but only 1024 out of 65 534 are being used, leaving 64 510 addresses wasted. To get the router to work, another class B address is required from which only 1024 will be used so another 64 510 addresses will be wasted. This approach is usually unacceptable in all but private networks without registered IP addresses.

IP uses ARP to get the MAC address of a unit if the network number in its own IP address is the same as that of the destination node; otherwise it communicates with a router or gateway. To reduce the wastage of addresses the same network number is required at either side of the relay connecting the networks together, which leaves the problem of how to decide which datagrams to direct to the other cabling system. Proxy ARP is one mechanism.

There are a number of ways that proxy ARP can be implemented, but the most effective way is based on the allocation of bits in the IP address to identify separate subnetworks of the original. Many ARP broadcasts can be blocked at the relay; only broadcasts for the other subnetworks need be passed. This can reduce the number of broadcasts throughout the network significantly.

[†]The solution today is subnetwork addressing, the subject of Chapter 4.

Figure 11.12 Proxy ARP.

The only devices that have to recognize which bits are used to identify separate networks are the proxy ARP units. Of course, the network manager has to ensure that the correct address range is allocated appropriately. For example, the first four bits of the host part of the IP address could be allocated to identify separate subnetworks[†]. In Figure 11.12 the first four bits of the host part of the network address are used to define subnetworks giving 14 usable subnetworks; subnet 0 and subnet 15 should not be used. When an ARP request is received on interface 1, the proxy ARP relay device examines the bits in the node address to see if those allocated to another subnetwork have been used. If so, the broadcast is relayed onto interface 2, but with the source MAC address of the proxy ARP unit on interface 2. When a reply is received, an ARP response is sent back to the originator on interface 1 giving the MAC address of the proxy ARP unit on interface 1, instead of that of the true MAC address destination node. The proxy ARP unit caches the MAC address of the ARP reply from the source and destination nodes together with the interface they are on.

[†]While this scheme seems very like the subnetwork addressing scheme discussed fully in Chapter 4, there is no subnetwork mask and the end nodes are not aware of any address structuring.

When the originator sends its next datagram on interface 1, it will contain the destination MAC address of the proxy ARP unit, so it will be accepted by the proxy ARP unit. The proxy ARP unit will then relay it to interface 2, substituting the true MAC address of the destination node from its ARP cache.

This works because the end nodes do not check the validity of the MAC address in an ARP response. It is possible to reply with any valid MAC address and act as a surrogate or proxy for another station. An examination of the ARP cache of an end node in a proxy ARP system will show the same MAC address (that of the proxy ARP relay) against many different IP addresses.

Proxy ARP allows two separate cabling systems with the same IP network number to be connected other than by a bridge. It regenerates frames from one network to another and filters traffic, as frames only pass through the proxy ARP unit if they are destined for the other cabling system.

Proxy ARP is especially useful if some nodes on a network cannot support Internet standard subnetting. The disadvantage is the management effort needed to ensure that the subnet addressing structure is enforced on the separate cabling systems.

Proxy ARP and routers

Some routers operate proxy ARP by default even if they are not aware of a subnetting scheme described above. If such a router intercepts an ARP request and recognizes that the destination requested is on a different network or subnetwork, it will reply to the ARP giving its own MAC address. It will then use its normal routing mechanisms to relay datagrams to that destination IP address.

This can only happen when a misconfigured workstation believes it is on the same network as another station, but the router sees the network addressing structure differently. In other words, there is an addressing fault as two devices have different views of the IP addressing scheme. The most likely cause is that the subnetwork masks are different in the end station and in the router. The router is aware of a network structure which is not apparent to the end system.

Internet subnets

Subnetting or subnetwork addressing today provides the standard mechanism for locally managing IP addresses efficiently. The structure of subnetworks is not understood from outside an autonomous system, where the whole address space appears as one IAB-defined class A, B, or C network.

The topic of subnetwork addressing, including its technical aspects, was fully explored in Chapter 4.

Internet control message protocol

Even though IP is a datagram service and there is no guarantee of information delivery, the **Internet Control Message Protocol** (ICMP), is provided within IP which generates error messages to help the IP layer give a better 'best efforts delivery service'. For the network manager, ICMP provides some useful diagnostics about network operation.

RFCs for IP say that ICMP must be supported, but the level of support varies, often limited to not generating an error when an ICMP datagram is received. Not all products support ICMP to the level required of a sophisticated TCP/IP implementation. ICMP requests may not be fully acted upon.

ICMP uses IP datagrams to carry its messages back and forth between relevant nodes. ICMP error messages are generated by a node recognizing there is a transmission problem and they are sent back to the originating address of the datagram that caused the problem. The originating address will usually be a host or end system. The generator of ICMP could be the ultimate destination node or an intermediate router. Routers and hosts can both be the source of ICMP datagrams.

Figure 11.13 shows the basic format of the ICMP message encapsulated in an IP datagram and the different messages possible. ICMP has its own IP protocol number (1) so the IP layer knows when it receives them. Even though ICMP uses the IP layer, it is considered as being

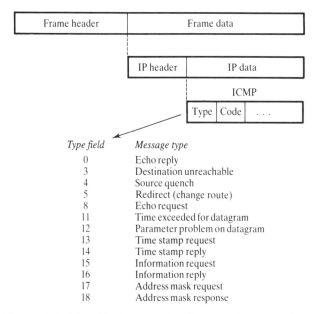

Type field	Message type
0	Echo reply
3	Destination unreachable
4	Source quench
5	Redirect (change route)
8	Echo request
11	Time exceeded for datagram
12	Parameter problem on datagram
13	Time stamp request
14	Time stamp reply
15	Information request
16	Information reply
17	Address mask request
18	Address mask response

Figure 11.13 ICMP encapsulated in IP and its type values.

Type	Code	Checksum
Context specific		
Context specific		
Context specific		

Figure 11.14 Basic ICMP header.

wholly within IP, because it does not necessarily provide any service to the layers above.

Since IP messages are carried in IP they may be discarded and fail to arrive for the same reasons as any IP datagram. It is worth noting that to maintain stability, ICMP messages are not generated about ICMP messages that themselves cause errors. Also, they are not generated about problems with IP fragments, unless it is the first one (fragment offset = 0).

The basic format of an ICMP datagram is shown in Figure 11.14, but the fields vary slightly depending on the type being used. The type field indicates the relevant ICMP message and the code field is used to provide more detailed information. The checksum, if used, is required because IP does not protect its data with a checksum. When operating over a physical network which has a frame check sequence the ICMP checksum may be 0, meaning 'not calculated'.

ICMP types 0 and 8 – echo

The most common ICMP messages when used for diagnostic purposes are type 0 and type 8. These are generated by the utility program widely known as 'ping'. Ping sends ICMP type 8 datagrams to a node and expects an ICMP type 0 reply, returning the data sent in the request (Figure 11.15).

The identifier and sequence numbers are used to identify these datagrams uniquely. If data is sent in the optional data field it must be returned in the reply. Varying data sizes on a ping are used to test for data transmission problems.

Earlier we said that ICMP is contained within IP and does not provide a service to layers above. How can ping generate ICMP echo requests if ICMP does not provide a service to the application ping? A ping implementation does not use ICMP to generate the request; it

Type	Code	Checksum
Identifier		Sequence number
Optional data		
⋯		

Figure 11.15 ICMP echo datagram format.

Type	Code	Checksum
Unused (must be 0)		
Internet header + 64 bits of datagram prefix		
. . .		

Code value	Meaning
0	Network unreachable
1	Host unreachable
2	Protocol unreachable
3	Port unreachable
4	Fragmentation needed and the do not fragment bit set
5	Source route failed
7	Destination host unknown
11	Network unreachablefor type of service
12	Host unreachable for type of service
13	Communication administratively prohibited e.g. firewall blocked
14	Host precedence violation
15	Precedence cut-off in effect

Figure 11.16   Code values for destination unreachable.

merely mimics what ICMP would do as a program that operates over the IP layer. Ping generates an IP datagram with a data field that equates to an ICMP echo request, that is, with a protocol number of 1 and the first octet of data being 8, an ICMP type of echo request. It then adds the rest of the fields including the data pattern that it expects to be echoed.

ICMP type 3 – destination unreachable

If a router is unable to deliver a datagram, it can return the destination unreachable ICMP datagram to indicate why. The code field is used to identify the cause of failure. The Internet header plus 64 bits of the datagram prefix are used to identify uniquely the datagram which caused the problem (Figure 11.16).

The values provided in the code field help pinpoint the reason the datagram failed to arrive at its destination. The circumstances under which they will occur need some clarification:

- *Network unreachable*   The network specified in the IP address cannot be found. The IP address used should be checked or there is a fault in the routing tables of the intervening routers.

    This error message is only generated by a router. The point at which the fault occurred can be ascertained from the source address in the IP header that carried the ICMP message. This is the router that identified the fault.

- *Host unreachable*   Unlike network unreachable, the datagram that caused the problem reached a router that is directly connected to the destination network, but, when the router tried to deliver the datagram, it could not communicate with the host.

Probably the ARP failed on the first datagram. The host is down, or otherwise unavailable, perhaps because that IP address does not exist.

This error message is only generated by a router. The point at which the fault occurred can again be ascertained from the source address in the IP header that carried the ICMP message. This is the router that identified the fault.

- *Protocol unreachable* In this case, the datagram reached the destination host, but the particular protocol carried in the IP datagram was not available. This would be rare, but is possible if the configuration of the remote machine is incorrect.

    The protocols normally carried by IP are mainly UDP, TCP, EGP or OSPF (see Figure 11.3 for more details). If one of these well-used protocols produces a protocol unreachable message for a particular host computer, the protocols which are operational should be checked. On UNIX systems, those protocols to be made operational on system start-up are normally defined in a configuration file called *protocols*. This should be checked.

- *Port unreachable* This message from a host indicates that the particular application layer service on the remote host to which a connection is being established is not available. On hosts, individual application services are enabled and disabled at start-up through a configuration file, usually called *inetd.conf*. This file should be checked to see if the service is available. Even if the name is present, be aware that a # in the left margin usually comments out the line and prevents that application from being automatically started.

- *Fragmentation needed and the do not fragment bit set* This message would normally come from a router, indicating that it needs to fragment the datagram, but is instructed not to by the do not fragment (DF) bit in the flags field of the IP header.

    This fault should be uncommon. DF is normally only used on diskless workstations booting via TFTP. TFTP only has 512 octets of user data. Why has this bit been set and why does the datagram need to be fragmented? Are the MTUs set correctly? All networks are supposed to be able to transport 576-octet datagrams without fragmentation.

    If there are no faults with the network configuration and if these datagrams do have to pass across a router, then it cannot be this one!

- *Source route failed* The management options in IP allow an IP datagram to carry a source route definition that identifies the complete path, based on the router addresses the IP datagram should take. This error message indicates that the datagram referred to failed to complete the route.

The point of failure will be the router that generated the ICMP message, again identified by the source IP address in the ICMP IP header. What was the next hop in the list of routers requested in the source route option? For some reason this router was not available from the router that detected the fault.

- *Destination host unknown* Generated only when a router can determine, from its link layer software, that the destination host does not exist.

- *Network unreachable for type of service* Generated by a router if a forwarding path (route) to the destination network with the requested or default TOS is not available.

- *Host unreachable for type of service* Generated if a router cannot foward a datagram because its routes to the destination do not match either the TOS requested or the default TOS.

- *Communication administratively prohibited* Generated if a router cannot forward a packet due to packet filtering, for example for security or local charging reasons.

- *Host precedence violation* Sent by the first hop router to a host to indicate that a requested precedence is not allowed for the combination of source/destination host or network, upper layer protocol, and source/destination port.

- *Precedence cut-off in effect* Indicates that the network manager has configured a minimum level of precedence that is required to use this route; the datagram was sent with a lower precedence than required.

ICMP type 4, code 0 – source quench

The format of the source quench datagram is the same as that for destination unreachable shown in Figure 11.16 but with a type of 4 and a code of 0. Source quench was intended to act as a method of flow control. A router which detected that its networks or processor were overloaded would send this ICMP message to a host (or hosts) that were the major cause of overload. The hosts would then reduce the rate at which they generated packets to the indicated destination

This presented router and host software developers with some interesting design problems! In practice, it was found that source quench did not improve the performance of a busy network and merely added to network congestion and communications processor loading. The router requirements RFC now states that routers must not generate source quench. Hosts must still accept the message but need take no action.

Even if source quench does not improve network performance, if source quench is generated by older routing software it is an indication that the router is overloaded and some redesign is required.

(a)

Type	Code	Checksum
Internet address of a more suitable router		
Internet header + 64 bits of datagram prefix		
• • •		

(b)

Code value	Meaning
0	Redirect datagrams to go to that network
1	Redirect datagrams to reach that host
2	Redirect datagrams for that network with that TOS
3	Redirect datagrams for that host with that TOS

Figure 11.17   (a) Format of the route change request message. (b) Code values used by route change request.

ICMP type 5 – route change request

The route change request is a function used only by routers. A router that knows that it is not the optimum router for a particular destination uses the relevant field of a route change request (Figure 11.17) to suggest a more suitable router to the originator, the source IP address of a datagram.

To ensure continuity of the data flow, the router also sends the datagram which caused the error message directly to the router that it believes has access to the better route.

Some host implementations of TCP/IP ignore the redirect messages. Because the router relays them to the start of the better path, overall the datagrams between this source and destination will follow a near optimum route, but the number of datagrams transmitted on the first cable system will double for this conversation, reducing throughput and increasing traffic.

The regular presence of ICMP route change request messages indicates that some optimization may be required on a system, or it could be that software needs upgrading. It could also be that the default gateway address configured into certain host systems is not targeting the most appropriate router (see Chapter 16).

ICMP router discovery protocol (types 9 and 10)

With older TCP/IP implementations, the only way a host system knows about the routers available to it, is either by manual configuration of the router addresses, or by listening to a routing protocol such as RIP. Introduced in 1991, ICMP router discovery is a dynamic protocol which allows systems to find all routers that are immediately available in a LAN environment. It eliminates manual configuration of router addresses and is independent of a particular routing protocol. ICMP router discovery is not a router-to-router protocol.

Type	Code	Checksum
Num addrs	Addr entry size	Lifetime
Router address [1]		
Preference level [1]		
Router address [2]		
Preference level [2]		
...		

Num addrs	The number of router addresses advertised in this message
Addr entry size	The number of 32-bit words of information per each router address (2, in the version shown here)
Lifetime	The maximum number of seconds that the router may be considered available (default 1800)
Router address [n][†]	The sending router's IP address(es) on the interface from which this message is sent
Preference level [n]*	The preferability of each router address [n]* as a default router address relative to other addresses on the same subnet. A signed, 2s-complement value; higher values mean more preferable

[†]n = 1 to (Num addrs)

Figure 11.18   ICMP router advertisement message.

ICMP type 9 – router advertisement

ICMP router advertisements (see Figure 11.18) allow routers to announce themselves to hosts on a network. Router adverts of this kind are sent at between 7 and 10 minute intervals or in response to a host 'router solicitation' (ICMP type 10). They should not be relied upon to indicate that a router has become unavailable if an advert is not seen within a given period.

By preference router advertisement messages are sent to the all-systems multicast address 224.0.0.1.

The router advertisement contains no information about the routes available to this router; if a host chooses an inappropriate first router for the ultimate destination, it will receive an ICMP route change request (type 5).

ICMP type 10 – router solicitation message

These messages can be sent by a host system, at any time, but certainly at start-up, to discover what routers are available on the local network. Routers respond with a router advertisement response. Thereafter, the host system will normally wait for unsolicited advertisements from the routers every 7 to 10 minutes. By preference router solicitation messages are sent to the all-routers multicast address 224.0.0.2. See Figure 11.19.

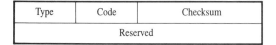

Type	Code	Checksum
Reserved		

Figure 11.19 ICMP router solicitation message.

ICMP type 11 – time exceeded for datagram

The format of this message is the same as destination unreachable. The time exceeded for datagram message is sent in one of two situations.

From routers, it is used to indicate that the Time To Live (TTL) value in the IP header has been decremented to 0. In this case it will have a code value of 0, so the datagram has been discarded before reaching its destination. This would most probably indicate that the original setting of TTL is not suitable for the number of routing hops this datagram needs to take or that there has been a failure in the network which is causing inordinate length routes to be used. Whichever it happens to be, it should be investigated to find out what is causing this message.

From an end node, the other use of this message, with a code value of 1, is to indicate that an attempt to re-create the original datagram by the reassembly of fragments failed. Time-out on reassembly should not be regarded as too serious unless it happens frequently, in which case investigation is needed to detect what is happening to the fragments: what routers and datalinks are involved? Are fragments delayed beyond the 30 second reassembly timer or are they corrupted? Is an underpowered bridge discarding them?

ICMP type 12 – parameter problem message

This message probably indicates that a wrong argument has been used with an option field in the IP header, but more seriously it could refer to an error in the implementation of IP. It indicates that there is a value in the header that cannot be understood. This message is not sent unless the datagram has been discarded. The pointer field indicates the position of the octet position of the suspect field, that is, 1 refers to the TOS field and 20 refers to the first option octet in the IP header (Figure 11.20).

ICMP types 13 and 14 – time stamp request and reply

This message is used to obtain the time from the clock in a distant machine. The requester sends message type 13 and the destination replies with message type 14. The originate time stamp is filled in immediately before the datagram is sent, the receive time stamp immediately on receipt of the request and the transmit time stamp immediately before the reply is sent back to the originator (Figure 11.21).

Type	Code	Checksum
Pointer	Unused (must be 0)	
Internet header + 64 bits of datagram prefix		
. . .		

Figure 11.20   Format of ICMP parameter problem message.

Type	Code	Checksum
Identifier		Sequence
Originate time stamp		
Receive time stamp		
Transmit time stamp		

Figure 11.21   Format of time stamp request/reply.

This message can be used to gather performance statistics of connections to a host or to synchronize clocks in hosts; it is rarely used today. Later RFCs suggest that ICMP should be used primarily to report network problems or routing changes and for ping.

ICMP types 15 and 16 – information request

This message is used to obtain the network number the requesting host is on if it is not known. The addresses used in the IP header will have a value of 0, often referred to as 'this network', which will be filled in correctly by the destination and returned (Figure 11.22).

This mechanism can be used with dial-in systems that use SLIP as a method of allocating appropriate network addresses for each end of the link.

ICMP types 17 and 18 – address mask request

This function can be used in conjunction with subnet addressing to allow a node to discover the subnet mask of the network it is connected to. The node can either send the request to a known address, probably a router, or broadcast the request to the network. The reply will be directed back, if the node knows its address, or broadcast if not.

Type	Code	Checksum
Identifier		Sequence

Figure 11.22   Format of ICMP information request message.

Type	Code	Checksum
Identifier		Sequence
Address mask		

Figure 11.23   Address mask request.

The subnet mask is entered in the address mask field of the reply (Figure 11.23).

Extensions to ICMP

Early 1990s versions of ICMP error messages contained a copy of the IP header and up to 64 bits (8 bytes) of the datagram that caused the problem. More recent work suggests that the ICMP message should contain as much as possible of the original datagram without exceeding 576 bytes. This aids identification and fault diagnosis.

Other extensions to ICMP have been proposed, one for translating IP addresses into domain names, another for estimating the smallest MTU that is used on the path between two communicating systems. The first is an experimental technique only. Path MTU discovery, though not widely implemented, is important for efficient use of router processing power in the Internet. It was issued with the status of draft standard.

Path MTU discovery

Fragmenting IP datagrams places a significant additional load on routers. In particular, efficiency of the Internet routers is improved if fragmentation is avoided. Fragmentation in routers occurs because the originating node has no knowledge of the Maximum Transmission Unit (MTU) of every link in every path. It is convention that each link will accept 576-byte datagrams without fragmentation, but smaller values are possible. If a host can discover the minimum MTU of a path being used, it can optimize its transmissions.

A host can easily estimate the smallest MTU by sending datagrams with the MTU of its own interface but setting the don't fragment (DF) bit in each datagram. If fragmentation *is* required at a link anywhere along the path the router attached to that link will return the 'Destination unreachable' message with code 4 – 'Fragmentation needed and the do not fragment bit set'. This informs the sending node that its datagram is too large for this path. What it does not tell the sending node is exactly what MTU the link can use.

RFC 1191 proposes a modification to the ICMP destination unreachable code 4 message. If the router places the exact MTU of the failing link in 16 currently unused bits of the header, it will allow the sending node to match the MTU exactly. It may be necessary to adjust the size more than once until the whole path is explored; since the path between source and destination is chosen for each IP datagram independently, the MTU may adjust downwards at any time. More detail on this topic is given in RFC 1191.

Where systems cannot update their software to accept or generate the enhanced ICMP message, it is still possible for a sending node to estimate the path MTU as the destination unreachable message carries details of which datagram failed, including the size of that datagram (in the IP header + 64 bits of original datagram). The host can make adjustments until the ICMP messages stop.

Management issues

In descriptions of TCP/IP, the power of ICMP is often ignored as it does not provide a direct service to the end user or the manager of a system. But ICMP messages provide an invaluable source of error reporting, performance information and diagnostic loopback tests for network planners and maintainers alike.

Unfortunately, the detail of the messages is not generally recorded in the equipment that receives them. Although these ICMP messages are sent across the network, they are rarely passed on to the system user who will be unaware that an ICMP message has been received. Most systems keep **statistics counters** of the number and types of each ICMP message received, but the source address and the other details of the IP header are not recorded. Loss of the source address reduces the value of the statistics considerably. These statistics are retrieved either by a console command (netstat -s in UNIX systems) or across the network by SNMP.

Some ICMP messages provide supplementary information in their code field that indicates in significant detail the reason a datagram failed to reach its destination. To an engineer analysing problems on a complex network, ICMP messages, once understood, will often explain the problem completely. In light of this, it is well worth understanding the use of ICMP messages. They can save hours searching for a solution to an obscure (or not so obscure!) problem, as ICMP can narrow down the search by pointing accurately to where to start.

Some TCP/IP applications allow ICMP messages to be viewed by operating in 'debug' mode. But by far the best way of reliably gathering this information is with a **network analyser**. This is an extremely useful tool for the maintainer of a larger network and while the more sophisticated ones are high cost, it may repay the investment quickly once the organization begins to depend on the network resource. Unfortunately, a network analyser cannot be used after the event or remotely. It must be attached to a point on the network where the ICMP message is passing. Infrequent but important events will require the dedication of an expensive unit permanently.

ICMP errors also raise organizational issues. Where data flows across organizational boundaries, an ICMP message may be generated by a piece of equipment under one management control, directed at an end system under a second management control and report a problem about resource availability in a third management area. It may be monitored on its path by any number of managements in between. Once management is aware of this it can set up the necessary procedures to resolve the problem. That is all part of the challenge of running a large internetwork.

ICMP traces

The following is a protocol trace of ping, the ICMP echo. In this example we show Ethernet frames in hexadecimal without the preamble or the CRC. The table beneath the frame gives a breakdown of the fields in the frame and their values. For a further explanation of the format of these examples see Appendix F.

This example shows IP node 30.0.0.1 pinging IP node 30.0.0.99. In this implementation of ping the data transmitted is an incremental count so is different in each frame sent.

Frame 1

```
AA00  0400  0104  0260  8C0A  C49D  0800  4500      *......`..D...E.
005C  0047  0000  FF01  7EF6  1E00  0001  1E00      .\.G....~v......
0063  0800  D7DE  0000  0001  0101  0101  0101      .c..W^..........
0101  0101  0101  0101  0101  0101  0101  0101      ................
0101  0101  0101  0101  0101  0101  0101  0101      ................
0101  0101  0101  0101  0101  0101  0101  0101      ................
0101  0101  0101  0101  0101                        ..........
```

Datalink:	Dest MAC:	AA0004 000104	Source MAC:	02608C 0AC49D	Type(Length):	0800
IP:	Version:	4	IHL:	5	Type of service:	00
	Length:	005C	ID:	0047	FLAGS:	0
	Offset:	00	Time to live:	FF	Protocol:	01
	Checksum:	7EF6	Source IP:	30.0.0.1	Dest IP:	30.0.0.99
ICMP:	Type:	08	Code:	0	Checksum:	D7DE
	Identifier:	0000	Sequence:	0001	Data:	0101......

Frame 2

```
0260  8C0A  C49D  AA00  0400  0104  0800  4500      .`..D.*.......E.
005C  0C00  0000  3C01  363E  1E00  0063  1E00      .\.....6...c..
0001  0000  DFDE  0000  0001  0101  0101  0101      ....._^..........
0101  0101  0101  0101  0101  0101  0101  0101      ................
0101  0101  0101  0101  0101  0101  0101  0101      ................
0101  0101  0101  0101  0101  0101  0101  0101      ................
0101  0101  0101  0101  0101                        ..........
```

Datalink:	Dest MAC:	02608C 0AC49D	Source MAC:	AA0004 000104	Type(Length):	0800
IP:	Version:	4	IHL:	5	Type of service:	00
	Length:	005C	ID:	0C00	FLAGS:	0
	Offset:	00	Time to live:	3C	Protocol:	01
	Checksum:	363E	Source IP:	30.0.0.1	Dest IP:	30.0.0.99
ICMP:	Type:	00	Code:	0	Checksum:	DFDE
	Identifier:	0000	Sequence:	0001	Data:	0101......

Frame 3

```
AA00  0400  0104  0260  8C0A  C49D  0800  4500      *......`..D...E.
005C  0048  0000  FF01  7EF5  1E00  0001  1E00      .\.H....~u......
0063  0800  B7BD  0000  0002  0202  0202  0202      .c..7=..........
0202  0202  0202  0202  0202  0202  0202  0202      ................
0202  0202  0202  0202  0202  0202  0202  0202      ................
0202  0202  0202  0202  0202  0202  0202  0202      ................
0202  0202  0202  0202  0202                         .........
```

Datalink:	Dest MAC:	AA0004 000104	Source MAC:	02608C 0AC49D	Type(Length):	0800
IP:	Version:	4	IHL:	5	Type of service:	00
	Length:	005C	ID:	0048	FLAGS:	0
	Offset:	00	Time to live:	FF	Protocol:	01
	Checksum:	7EF5	Source IP:	30.0.0.1	Dest IP:	30.0.0.99
ICMP:	Type:	08	Code:	0	Checksum:	B7BD
	Identifier:	0000	Sequence:	0002	Data:	0202......

Frame 4

```
0260  8C0A  C49D  AA00  0400  0104  0800  4500      .`..D.*.......E.
005C  0C01  0000  3C01  363D  1E00  0063  1E00      .\.....6=...c..
0001  0000  BFBD  0000  0002  0202  0202  0202      ....?=..........
0202  0202  0202  0202  0202  0202  0202  0202      ................
0202  0202  0202  0202  0202  0202  0202  0202      ................
0202  0202  0202  0202  0202  0202  0202  0202      ................
0202  0202  0202  0202  0202                         .........
```

Datalink:	Dest MAC:	02608C 0AC49D	Source MAC:	AA0004 000104	Type(Length):	0800
IP:	Version:	4	IHL:	5	Type of service:	00
	Length:	005C	ID:	0C01	FLAGS:	0
	Offset:	00	Time to live:	3C	Protocol:	01
	Checksum:	363D	Source IP:	30.0.0.1	Dest IP:	30.0.0.99
ICMP:	Type:	0	Code:	0	Checksum:	BFBD
	Identifier:	0000	Sequence:	0002	Data:	0202......

Trailer encapsulation

Some systems can be configured to allow Ethernet to carry IP and TCP data as **trailer encapsulation**. This mechanism was designed for 4.2BSD UNIX systems as a method of improving performance. Trailer encapsulation allowed the data to come before the headers in the datagrams. This mapped the data structures in UNIX memory that represented the data and so made it easier to manipulate the datagrams once

Format

Datalink header	Type	Data	Type	Length	IP header	TCP header	CRC

Example

Datalink header	1001	Data 512 octets	0800	Length	IP header	TCP header	CRC

Figure 11.24   Trailer encapsulation method.

they were loaded into receiving memory. This is because it is easier and more efficient in software to append headers to the end of data using pointer logic than to insert headers in front of the data which requires repeated buffer-to-buffer copying. This system has the opposite effect to that intended on a host which does not have the same architecture as the original UNIX 4.2BSD hosts; for example it may have different ways of storing numbers in memory. The performance of such a host will degrade when using trailer encapsulation.

Trailer encapsulation has two Ethernet type values allocated to it, 0x1001 and 0x1002. With trailer encapsulation the data is sent in 512-byte blocks. An Ethernet type of 0x1001 identifies one 512-byte block and 1002 identifies two 512-byte blocks. The format is shown in Figure 11.24.

For two nodes to communicate using trailer encapsulation they must both support it. This is normally activated on each network interface through use of the command that initializes that interface, such as *ifconfig* in UNIX.

IPng (IPv6)

Since late 1990 the Internet Engineering Task Force (IETF) have spent a significant amount of time defining a new version of IP generally called IP Next Generation or IPng during its development. The main reason for a new version is to overcome the limitations of the addressing structure of IP Version 4 (IPv4). It is also an opportunity to produce a much enhanced network layer protocol to carry the many new and fascinating systems which the Internet is now expected to support. These systems include mobile computing, video conferencing, audio distribution and remote device control. There is also a need for much improved security not available in IPv4 for commercial use of the Internet for shopping and electronic funds transfer.

Mobile computing is the ability to connect to your information sources as you travel the world, from wherever you happen to be. It presents major technical challenges and has implications for addressing, especially when you consider the number of people who could demand this level of flexibility and travel between service providers and across country borders.

The existing 32-bit IP addressing scheme can cater for 3.72 billion connections (hosts) on 2.11 million networks. However, it is not practical to make efficient use of this addressing space due to its structure. The remaining addresses are not sufficient to cater for a worldwide Internet of individually-addressed personal computers and workstations. As the addresses are being allocated so rapidly, the only class of registered address available is class C. Many organizations need more than one class C address. In 1991 it was noted that the size of routing tables in Internet backbone routers was growing faster than memory technology was growing to cater for it. For these reasons alone a new protocol is required.

To explore possible solutions, the IETF formed the ROuting and ADdressing (ROAD) group in November 1991. In March 1992, ROAD formally suggested CIDR (see Chapter 5) for reducing the rate of routing table growth; it recommended setting up other working groups to explore ways of achieving a bigger Internet address space.

In spring 1992, the IAB issued IPv7. This endorsed CIDR and recommended an immediate IETF study of the OSI Connnectionless Network Protocol (CLNP) as the basis for IPv7. This was quickly rejected by the IETF and a number of working groups were formed to investigate other ways of improving IPv4.

To predict how much time was available to develop the new standard, the Address Lifetime Expectations (ALE) group was set up. ALE produced a number of predictions saying that the Internet address space would run out between the years 2005 and 2011. However, these predictions have been criticized both as too optimistic and too pessimistic, and the mechanism they used to produce their figures was also called into question.

By the end of 1992 there were seven separate proposals for IPng: 'CNAT', 'IP Encaps', 'Nimrod', 'Simple CLNP', 'P Internet Protocol' (PIP), 'The Simple Internet Protocol' (SIP) and 'TP/IX'. 'Simple CLNP' evolved into 'TCP and UDP with Bigger Addresses (TUBA)' and 'IP Encaps' evolved into 'IP Address Encapsulation' (IPAE). The 'TP/IX' group changed its name to 'Common Architecture for the Internet (CATNIP)'. CATNIP considered how to integrate CLNP, IP and IPX (Internet Packet eXchange, Novell's standard NetWare network layer protocol) as well as producing technology which would scale to the size and performance requirements for a global Internet.

The TUBA specification also proposed replacing IPv4 with OSI CLNP network layer protocols. This would solve the addressing problem as OSI NSAP addresses were designed for a worldwide internetwork. TUBA had the flexibility to resolve most of the other issues. The IPAE working group was looking at ways to extend IP Version 4 to cater for a larger addressing structure. Later, SIP proposed a simplified IPv4 header with 64-bit addresses and options moved to separate extension headers. In parallel, Paul Francis founded a group to develop PIP, Paul's

Internet Protocol. This group took the opportunity to create a completely new IP protocol abandoning the IPv4 header. In time, SIP, the IPAE and PIP amalgamated and produced the Simple Internet Protocol Plus (SIPP). SIPP went on to be endorsed by the IETF in mid-1994 and became IPng, now know as IP Version 6 (IPv6).

So, SIPP has been adopted as the next version of IP, IPv6, but not before the addresses were increased to 16-byte (128-bit) fixed length addresses. This will be divided hierarchically to provide more flexible use of the address space, while providing efficient routing with a single route between large geographic areas. The new scheme will also allow reasonable compatibility with IPv4 addressing and autoconfiguration of workstations and hosts.

IPv6 supports 'unicast', 'multicast' and 'anycast' destination addresses. A new type of address, 'anycast', has been defined. The anycast address defines a topological region. Anycast is designed to reduce network traffic by using a destination address which identifies the 'nearest' of a group of machines. 'Nearest' is determined by the least cost routing path to the anycast region. A datagram sent to a unicast address goes to an individual device; to a multicast address it goes to a group of machines; to anycast it goes to the nearest of the 'anycast group'.

This 128-bit address space (2^{128}) provides a potential number of individual addresses of 340 282 366 920 938 000 000 000 000 000 000 000 000. This scheme provides more than enough addresses for every person in the world to own their own internet. It also supports a number of different formats, allows for redundancy and provides for future expansion.

Because of the large number of bits in the address, the way it is represented in text has been changed from the dotted decimal format used with IPv4. The first, and preferred, method is to show the address as eight hexadecimal values each representing 16 bits with the values separated by a colon, ':', resulting in a general form x:x:x:x:x:x:x:x, where 'x' is a 16-bit quantity expressed in hexadecimal. For example:

   4C54:356A:1245:B356:9371:1BAD:B00B:DAD2

   4123:0:0:0:0:24F3:46C1:936A

In cases where there are groups of zeros, compressing the zeros in the address is allowed using '::'. For example:

   FE89:0:0:0:0:0:0:53

can be represented as:

   FE89::53

If dealing with a mixed environment of IPv4 and IPv6 addresses it is allowable to use the form x:x:x:x:x:x:d.d.d.d, where the x's are hexadecimal values as used previously, and the d's are standard dotted decimal IPv4 representation. For example:

Table 11.1   IPv6 format prefix.

Allocation	Format prefix
Reserved / IPv4 compatibility	0000 0000
Unassigned	0000 0001
Reserved for NSAP allocation	0000 001
Reserved for IPX allocation	0000 010
Unassigned	0000 011
Unassigned	0000 1
Unassigned	0001
Unassigned	001
Provider-based unicast address	010
Unassigned	011
Reserved for geographic-based unicast	100
Unassigned	101
Unassigned	110
Unassigned	1110
Unassigned	1111 0
Unassigned	1111 10
Unassigned	1111 110
Unassigned	1111 1110 0
Link-local-use addresses	1111 1110 10
Site-local-use addresses	1111 1110 11
Multicast addresses	1111 1111

0:0:0:0:0:0:129.4.3.1

::FFFF:193.128.145.9

The format of IPv6 addresses is indicated by the leading bits (highest order) of the address as defined by Table 11.1. These bits are defined as the 'format prefix'. As can be seen from the table, apart from a multicast address, starting with 'FF', unicast addresses are:

- Global provider-based unicast
- Geographic-based unicast
- NSAP address
- IPX hierarchical address
- Site-local-use address
- Link-local-use address
- IPv4-capable host address

Other portions of the address space have been reserved for other possible address allocations in the future.

n bits	m bits	48 bits
Subscriber prefix	Subnet ID	IEEE 802 address

Figure 11.25 IPv6 address using 802.1 MAC address.

A number of recommendations have been made on how IPv6 addresses should be formatted; only time will tell exactly which way will become prevalent. The basic premise is that the address structure will be hierarchical. This also implies that the underlying router network must have a connectivity structure to match that of the addresses.

One address format likely to be popular is that which uses IEEE 802 MAC addresses as a unique interface identifier, that is the last 48 bits of the address are reserved for insertion of a MAC address and the rest of the address is divided into the subscriber prefix and subnet addressing, see Figure 11.25.

This use of MAC addresses allows a node to determine its own IPv6 address. The MAC address of every LAN network card should be unique. The node can then determine the rest of the address by listening for router advertisements.

An alternative scheme proposed is the 'provider-based global unicast address', see Figure 11.26. This scheme defines a hierarchical address structure; the first three bits (010) define this format of address, and are followed by a 'registry id'. The registry id authority will assign unique 'provider ids' to service providers. Providers will allocate 'subscriber ids' to organizations wishing to attach to the Internet. Those organizations will then divide the remaining bits into 'subnet' and 'interface' addresses. *At this stage, the size of each field has not been fixed.*

Two other formats allow for degrees of compatibility with IPv4 addressing. One is the 'IPv4-compatible IPv6 address', shown in Figure 11.27. This enables IPv4 routing systems to 'tunnel' IPv6 traffic from IPv6 nodes with these addresses during the transition between IPv4 and IPv6.

The second format is intended to allow nodes which support only IPv4 to communicate over an IPv6 routing system. This type of address is termed an 'IPv4-mapped IPv6 address' and is shown in Figure 11.28.

Table 11.1 also shows address structures which designate OSI Network Service Access Point (NSAP) addresses and Novell NetWare IPX protocol addresses.

3	n bits	m bits	o bits	p bits	128-m-n-o-p bits
010	Registry ID	Provider ID	Subscriber ID	Subnet ID	Intf ID

Figure 11.26 Provider-based global unicast address.

80 bits		16	32 bits
0000...	...0000	0000	IPv4 address

Figure 11.27 IPv4-compatible IPv6 address.

80 bits		16	32 bits
0000...	...0000	FFFF	IPv4 address

Figure 11.28 IPv4-mapped IPv6 address.

'Local-use' IPv6 unicast addresses are for networks that are not attached to the Internet and therefore do not require registered addresses (Table 11.1). There are two types, the link-local and site-local addresses. Link-local addresses are to be used on a single link for auto-address configuration, neighbour discovery or when no routers are present; site-local are used when a site does not wish to register for an official unique Internet address.

The IPv6 'anycast' address is a new concept. An anycast address is used by routers only and may not be used as a source address. The intended format for the anycast address is that the interface identifier is set to zero. One use is for a mobile host to communicate with any of the routers on its 'home' network.

IPv6 also defines two special individual addresses. One is the 'unspecified address', 0:0:0:0:0:0:0:0. This address must never be assigned to any node, but is used as the source address by a node when determining its own address at start-up. The other special address is the loopback address defined as 0:0:0:0:0:0:0:1. It is used by a node to send datagrams to itself. It should never be assigned to an interface or as a source address on the network. This address is available for diagnostic purposes within a protocol stack. Its use should be compared with address 127.0.0.1 in IPv4.

Multicast addresses have a more complex format than in IPv4 (Figure 11.29). Currently only one bit of the 4-bit flags (flgs) field is defined; this is the 'T' bit. If T is 0 the address is a non-permanent address; if 1, it is permanent as assigned by the Internet assigned numbers authority. The following four bits are known as the scope (scop) field as defined in Table 11.2.

8	4	4	112 bits
11111111	flgs	scop	group ID

Figure 11.29 Multicast address.

Table 11.2 Multicast scopfield.

0	Reserved
1	Node-local scope
2	Link-local scope
3	(Unassigned)
4	(Unassigned)
5	Site-local scope
6	(Unassigned)
7	(Unassigned)
8	Organization-local scope
9	(Unassigned)
A	(Unassigned)
B	(Unassigned)
C	(Unassigned)
D	(Unassigned)
E	Global scope
F	Reserved

IPv6 protocol

IPv6 is designed to overcome the limitations of IPv4. There are five areas where significant changes have been made. The first, and most important, is expanding the addressing capabilities. Next, the header has been simplified by moving all but essential features to options fields to reduce the bandwidth and processing requirements of the most common elements of the protocol. Options are encoded more efficiently, while allowing for flexible future expansion. A new function, 'flow labelling', has been added which identifies specific service or performance requirements of a transaction. Lastly, there are extensions to support authentication and data confidentiality.

Until IPv6 is fully implemented it is impossible to determine how effective these new features will be. However, significant thought and experience have been put into the design of this protocol. We believe it will provide significant improvements over IPv4 at a time when the use of the TCP/IP protocol suite is expanding at an unprecedented rate, and the Internet is required to support new, demanding, real-time and assured bandwidth services such as voice and video.

The simplest IPv6 header is shown in Figure 11.30. The minimum length of the header is 40 bytes when no options are required. When options are used they are placed in additional headers after the destination address, and are identified by the 'next header' field in the initial IPv6 header.

The *version field* is a 4-bit field containing the value 6. This will allow nodes which can support both IPv4 and IPv6 to differentiate between the two protocols. (It will also allow IPv4 nodes to discard IPv6 protocol without error).

Figure 11.30 The IPv6 header.

The *priority field* allows a sending node to prioritize traffic it sends. The intention is to allow traffic which is time critical to maintain service when network congestion is present. IPv6 documentation suggests what priority certain services should have. The priority field contains a value from 0 to 15; 0 to 7 is used for services that can tolerate congestion and 8 to 15 for those that cannot (Table 11.3). The lower values are used for those services most willing to allow traffic to be discarded.

The *flow label* is a new IP feature which is considered experimental. Its purpose is to allow routers to provide the required level of service to a 'flow' or collection of datagrams from a single host, without every datagram carrying the options headers which define that service. The flow label acts as a 'handle' or key to the performance requirements of that flow, extracted from one initial datagram and stored in each router in the path.

The *payload length* indicates the length (in octets) of the datagram following the header. If this is set to zero, it indicates that the payload length is carried in a hop-by-hop option defining a *jumbo payload*. The jumbo payload option allows datagrams greater than 65 535 octets to be transmitted.

The *next header field* is a way of building datagrams with variable length headers rather than a fixed number of header fields. Optional information can be added to the header only when required. With some additions, the next header field uses the same values, as the IPv4 *protocol* field. For example, for a basic IPv6 datagram, the next header field will specify UDP (17) or TCP (6).

The final field in the basic IPv6 header is the *hop limit*. This has the same function as the *time to live* field in IPv4. The value in this field is decremented by 1 by each router that forwards the datagram. If this value is decremented to 0 the datagram is discarded.

The hop limit field is followed by the source and destination IPv6 addresses, the 128-bit addresses discussed previously.

Options in IPv6

All other facilities of IPv6 are carried in additional extension headers identified by values of the next header field. Each extension header also contains its own next header field, which will allow almost unlimited extension of the protocol to support new facilities in the future.

Table 11.3 IPv6 priority field.

Type	Value	Suggested service
	0	Uncharacterized traffic
	1	'Filler' traffic (e.g. netnews)
	2	Unattended data transfer (e.g. email)
Congestion	3	(Reserved)
controlled traffic	4	Attended bulk transfers (e.g. FTP, NFS)
	5	(Reserved)
	6	Interactive traffic (e.g. Telnet, X)
	7	Internet control traffic (e.g. routing protocols, SNMP)
Non congestion	8	e.g. High fidelity video
controlled traffic	9	
	10	
	11	
	12	
	13	
	14	
	15	e.g. Low fidelity audio

For example, the basic IPv6 header format does not include facilities for fragmentation. If fragmentation is necessary, the next header field will indicate that the following header is a *fragment header* and not TCP or UDP. Then the fragment header is likely to say that the header following it is UDP or TCP, assuming no other headers are required (Figure 11.31).

There are also a small number of optional extension headers. They have a preferred order of inclusion within the datagram:

- IPv6 header
- Hop-by-hop option header
- Destination option header†
- Routing header
- Fragment header
- Authentication header
- Encapsulating security payload header
- Destination options header‡
- Upper-layer header

Two of the currently-defined extension headers, the hop-by-hop options header and the destination options header, have a variable number of Type-Length-Value (TLV) encoded options. The highest order two

†For options which need to be processed by the first and subsequent destination addresses in the routing header.

‡For options which need to be processed by the final destination of the datagram.

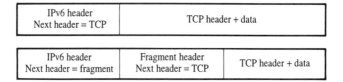

Figure 11.31 Next header examples.

Figure 11.32 Hop-by-hop options header.

bits of the option type field indicate actions that should be taken by the node processing the datagram if it does not recognize the option type. These are:

00 Skip over this option and continue processing the header
01 Discard the datagram
10 Discard the datagram and send an ICMP parameter problem, code 2, message
11 Discard the datagram and send an ICMP parameter problem message if the datagram's destination address is not a multicast

The next bit, the third highest order bit, is used to indicate whether the option can change *en route*. If the bit is zero (0) the option cannot change, if it is one (1), it can. The hop-by-hop options header is used to carry information which is to be examined at every hop, probably by a router. It is identified by the next header field in the IPv6 header set to 0 (Figure 11.32).

When options are used, the options header has to be padded out to a multiple of 8 octets. To do this, there are two padding options. Option 0 indicates a single octet of padding; this is known as the *pad1 option*. If more octets of padding are required, the Pad Option should be used. This is option 1 and is followed by a count of how many pad octets are inserted.

The other hop-by-hop option is the *jumbo payload option*. This is used to allow datagrams of over 65 535 octets to be transmitted over a suitable medium.

The *routing header option* is similar to IPv4 source route. It defines a path of router IPv6 addresses to be followed by the datagram. However, the routing header option is more flexible than IPv4 source route options. In IPv4 there are only two source route options, strict and loose, which apply to the whole path. In IPv6, a mask in the header, the *'strict/loose source route mask'*, indicates whether the next hop is strict or loose.[†]

[†]Strict and loose routing were discussed on page 208.

Figure 11.33   Routing header.

Apart from the strict/loose bit mask the functions of the fields in the routing header are straightforward (Figure 11.33). The *next header field* indicates what header follows this one; *routing type* is fixed at 0; *num addrs* indicates the number of router addresses in the routing header; *next addr* is incremented by each router to point to the next router to be visited. Addresses after the next addr pointer are still to be visited.

The *fragment header* is used for IPv6 to send payloads greater than the *minimum* MTU of the whole path datagrams are transmitted across. The important difference between operation of fragmentation in IPv6 and IPv4 is that IPv6 only performs fragmentation in source nodes, not in routers. This requires that the minimum MTU of a path is discovered before transmission commences, using the path MTU discovery protocol. The fragment header is identified by a next header value of 44 in the immediately preceding header. Otherwise fragmentation operates in a similar manner to fragmentation in IPv4 using a more fragments flag and a fragment offset field. Path MTU discovery eliminates the don't fragment flag.

The *authentication header* and the *encapsulating security payload header* will be used for the enhanced security features required of a worldwide Internet, designed to carry financial and critical business data.

The *destination options header* is designed to carry options only for the remote node. It is identified by a next header value of 60 in the immediately preceding header.

The *upper-layer header* is that of UDP or TCP and subsequent application layer header information and application data.

Neighbour discovery

While redesigning IP, it was also appropriate to consider how ARP could be improved upon. The result is the neighbour discovery protocol. This is a combination of ARP, ICMP router discovery and ICMP redirect.

Neighbour discovery uses ICMPv6 message types and multicast and unicast datagrams (instead of broadcast datagrams) for establishing the MAC address of hosts on the same network. This reduces the impact of finding local MAC addresses on all hosts.

Neighbour discovery uses five ICMPv6 message types: router solicitation, router advertisement, neighbour solicitation, neighbour advertisement, and redirect. These are covered in detail in the next section.

ICMPv6

ICMPv6 adds further functionality to ICMP and encompasses changes in IPv6. As with IPv4, ICMPv6 is considered an integral part of IPv6 and *must* always be implemented.

This new version has grouped ICMP messages into two classes: error messages and informational messages. The two groups are identified by the value of the high-order bit of the message type. Types in the decimal range 0 to 127 are used for error messages and 128 to 255 are used for informational messages. These messages are considered in detail below. ICMPv6 messages are carried by an IPv6 header with a next header value of 58. As with the latest recommendations for ICMPv4, an ICMP error message now returns a copy of as much of the original datagram that caused the problem as possible without exceeding 576 bytes.

Error messages

ICMPv6 type 1 – destination unreachable

If a router is unable to deliver a datagram, it can return a destination unreachable ICMP message to indicate why. The *code field* is used to identify the cause of the failure. As much as possible of the original datagram that generated the need for this response is put in the last field, while not exceeding a total datagram size of 576 octets. See Figure 11.34.

ICMPv6 type 2 – packet too big

This message must be sent by a router if it cannot forward a datagram because it is larger than the MTU of the next link (Figure 11.35).

ICMPv6 type 3 – time exceeded

If a router receives a datagram with a hop limit of zero or a router decrements a datagram's hop limit to zero, it discards the datagram and returns a time exceeded ICMP message as shown in Figure 11.36.

IPv6 systems are supposed to avoid fragmentation by using the path MTU discovery mechanism. However, end-to-end fragmentation is supported for backwards compatibility and therefore a time exceeded–fragment reassembly time exceeded is also supported.

Type = 1	Code	Checksum
Unused		

As much of the invoking packet as will fit
without the packet exceeding 576 octets

Code value	Meaning
0	No route to destination
1	Communications with destination administratively prohibited, for example, firewall filter
2	Not a neighbour
3	Address unreachable
4	Port unreachable
Unused	This field must be zero

Figure 11.34   Format and codes of ICMPv6 destination unreachable message.

Type = 2	Code	Checksum
MTU		

As much of the invoking packet as will fit
without the packet exceeding 576 octets

Code value	Always 0
MTU	The maximum transmission unit of the next-hop link

Figure 11.35   Format and codes of ICMPv6 packet too big message.

Type = 3	Code	Checksum
Unused		

As much of the invoking packet as will fit
without the packet exceeding 576 octets

Code value	Meaning
0	Hop limit exceeding in transit
1	Fragment reassembly time exceeded
Unused	This field must be zero

Figure 11.36   Format and codes of ICMPv6 time exceeded message.

ICMPv6 type 4 – parameter problem

If a device receives a datagram with a field it cannot process, it should discard the datagram and return a parameter problem with a pointer to the offending field. See Figure 11.37.

ICMPv6 type 5 – redirect

Sent to nodes by routers to indicate a better router to use to reach the intended destination network. See Figure 11.38.

Type = 4	Code	Checksum
Pointer		
As much of the invoking packet as will fit without the packet exceeding 576 octets		

Code value	Meaning
0	Erroneous header field encountered
1	Unrecognized next header type encountered
3	Unrecognized IPv6 option encountered
Pointer	This field identifies the offset to the octet octet which caused the problem within the invoking packet

Figure 11.37 Format and codes of ICMPv6 parameter problem message.

Type = 5	Code	Checksum
Reserved		
Target address		
Destination address		
Options ...		

Code	0
Reserved	Zero
Target address	An IP address of the node to which traffic should be sent
Destination address options	MAC layer address of the target, if known
	As much as possible of the IP packet header that triggered the sending of the redirect request

Figure 11.38 Format and codes of ICMPv6 redirect message.

Type = 128	Code	Checksum
Identifier		Sequence number
Data		
...		

Code value	Always 0
Identifier	An identifier to aid in matching echo replies to this echo request. May be zero
Sequence number	A sequence number to aid in matching echo replies to this echo request. May be zero
Data	Zero or more octets of arbitrary data

Figure 11.39 Format and codes of ICMPv6 echo request message.

ICMP informational messages

ICMPv6 type 128 – echo request

An echo request as in IPv4 and illustrated in Figure 11.39. This requests the ICMP layer of the receiving node to respond with an echo reply.

Type = 129	Code	Checksum
Identifier		Sequence number
Data …		

Code value | Always 0
Identifier | The identifier from the invoking echo request message
Sequence number | The sequence number from the invoking echo request message
Data | The data from the invoking echo request message

Figure 11.40 Format and codes of ICMPv6 echo reply message.

Type	Code	Checksum
Maximum response delay		Unused
Multicast address …		

Code value | Always 0

Maximum response delay | In a query message, the maximum time that the responding report messages may be delayed, in milliseconds
 | In report termination messages, this is set to zero
Unused | Zero
Multicast address | The address of the multicast group about which the message is being sent. If zero it is a query for all groups

Figure 11.41 Format and codes of ICMPv6 group membership messages.

ICMPv6 type 129 – echo reply

Sent in response to an echo request (Figure 11.40).

ICMPv6 types 130, 131, 132 – group membership messages

These consist of three messages, group membership query – type 130, group membership report – type 131 and group membership termination – type 132. They are used for communicating multicast group membership from a node to its neighbouring routers (Figure 11.41). These messages replace the IGMP protocol of IPv4.

ICMPv6 type 133 – router solicitation

This is a message sent to the all-routers multicast address (Figure 11.42). When a host interface becomes enabled, it can send a router solicitation, to which routers should reply with router advertisements. This provides the same function as ICMP router discovery in IPv4. Using router solicitations, a host can discover all the first hop routers that are available.

Type	Code	Checksum
Reserved		
Options ...		

Code	0
Reserved	Zero
Options	The MAC address of the sending device

Figure 11.42   Format and codes of ICMPv6 router solicitation message.

Type	Code		Checksum
Max hop limit	M	O	Reserved	Router lifetime
Reachable time			
Reachable retrans time			
Options ...			

Code	0
Max hop limit	A maximum hop limit that the router suggests should be used by hosts when sending IP datagrams
M	A 1-bit flag for managed address autoconfiguration
O	A 1-bit flag, the 'other configuration' flag used for autoconfiguration
Reserved	A 6-bit field must be zero
Router lifetime	The lifetime used for the default router in seconds
Reachable time	The time, in milliseconds, that a node considers a neighbour is reachable after receiving some reachability confirmation
Reachable retrans timer	The time, in milliseconds, between retransmitted neighbour solicitation requests to a neighbour that is not responding with neighbour advertisements
Options	The MAC address of the sending device. A router may omit this option to enable inbound load sharing across multiple MAC addresses

Figure 11.43   Format and codes of ICMPv6 router advertisement message.

ICMPv6 type 134 – router advertisement

Routers advertise their presence periodically, or as a response to a router solicitation message. These messages contain information for determining the address prefixes, maximum hop value and MTU values. See Figure 11.43.

On multicast networks, routers are allowed to send, as a multicast, router advertisements announcing their presence. This allows nodes to determine the complete list of routers available on their network. However, it is not a true routing protocol; it merely indicates the available first hop routers.

ICMPv6 type 135 – neighbour solicitation

Sent by a node to determine the MAC layer address of a neighbour and therefore replaces ARP in IPv4 (Figure 11.44). These messages are also

Type	Code	Checksum
Reserved		
Target address		
Options ...		

Code   0
Reserved   Zero
Target address The IP address of the target device
Options   The MAC address of the sending device

Figure 11.44 Format and codes of ICMPv6 neighbour solicitation message.

Type	Code	Checksum
R S Reserved		
Target address		
Options ...		

Code   0
R   A 1-bit flag. When set this flag indicates that the sender is a router
S   A 1-bit flag. When set indicates that the advertisement was sent in response
                to a neighbour solicitation
Reserved   A 30-bit field which should be zero
Target address The IP address of the target device
Options   The MAC address of the sending device

Figure 11.45 Format and codes of ICMPv6 neighbour advertisement message.

used to determine duplicate IP addresses on the network by sending a query for an address and observing if there is more than one reply.

ICMPv6 type 136 – neighbour advertisement

The response to a neighbour solicitation message. This message can also be sent to announce a MAC layer address change (Figure 11.45).

Transition from IPv4 to IPv6

As IPv6-based products become readily available, planning when and how to make the transition from IPv4 to IPv6 will become an important issue. The two protocols have different facilities and, more importantly, different address structures. Many network managers will need to plan a changeover carefully. Fortunately, IPv6 has been designed to coexist easily with IPv4 for a smooth transition.

The problems for Internet service providers are great indeed. They will have to support both protocols for a period of time, perhaps initially carrying IPv6 over IPv4, then moving to IPv4 over IPv6 and finally removing IPv4. Removing IPv4 completely is likely to take many years.

It is not practical for all but the smallest organizations to change all of their equipment from IPv4 to IPv6 in one operation. One option is to put both versions of the protocol on hosts and server systems; it is then possible to change client systems as and when convenient. Finally, when all client systems are changed, the IPv4 stacks can be removed from the host/server systems.

It will also be necessary to change routers and another option is to carry out that change early. Ideally, routers should be able to accept both versions of the protocol on any interface and convert IPv4 to IPv6 where necessary. If large numbers of hosts and servers are present, then a router that provides translation between the two protocols will maintain total connectivity, while individual hosts are changed, albeit with a doubling of traffic as it is translated from one format to the other. It is quite possible that some older systems may never support IPv6. The dual protocol router can maintain connectivity to those machines and will certainly ease the changeover of a large number of nodes, both server and client machines, in manageable stages.

Why change to IPv6

For those organizations with a successful installed base of IPv4 equipment, the question 'why change' has to be an important one. The key advantages of IPv6 are:

- A significantly larger registered address space,
- Significantly larger nonrouted networks (i.e. bridged or switched LANs),
- Simplification of addressing (no subnetwork mask),
- Self-configuration of workstations,
- Support for 'mobile' workstations,
- Better congestion management for busy networks ,
- Improved security features.

As described in Chapter 3, self-configuration is provided for IPv4, even if it was not widely implemented until the 1990s.

Flexibility of addressing is particularly important in a global internet in which every machine is uniquely identified and accessible, and requires connectivity to every other machine. It will be very important for academic and government organizations, for some international companies, and for those companies who communicate directly with many other external organizations.

For the smaller company, particularly aware of the need to cost justify spending on information technology, stronger arguments for changing to IPv6 may be necessary. For them, external connectivity to the Internet and to trading partners may be via a secure gateway. While this is a potential bottleneck, it is also a central place where IP address translation and IPv4 to IPv6 translation can be carried out.

The advantages for the organization depend on the existing company IT strategy. Until there is a good reason to change to IPv6, it will be an unnecessary overhead. The availability of stable and proven IPv6 software for the computer systems and routers used in the organization will be a key issue. We strongly recommend waiting a period of time after IPv6 becomes available. During that time one can perform evaluations of the new software, and wait for the software to mature. Before installing IPv6 software on a large scale, small pilot groups should be used. It is also an opportunity to train support staff in the new techniques.

The main advantage of IPv6 will be the ability to allocate addresses in a more manageable structure, to use autoconfiguration of workstations and hosts, and to provide better security and allow improved interconnectivity through the Internet. Most organizations will need the flexibility to change the protocol internally, use IPv4 to some external organizations, and IPv6 to others. This requires the relevant functionality in routers connecting to the outside world, and for the integration of IPv4 and IPv6 domain name servers. Indeed, there are significant issues for DNS during the transition period. The main issue is what address should be returned to the requester, an IPv4 or IPv6 address. Clearly this is dependent on the requester capabilities and the destination capabilities.

The evolution of the standards for IPv6 from 1990 to 1996 was slower than expected. If left to market forces alone, it may be some time before IPv6 becomes a corporate necessity; we expect IPv4 to be in use well past the year 2000.

Relevant RFCs

781   A specification for the Internet Protocol IP time stamp option
791   Internet Protocol (IP)
792   Internet Control Message Protocol
796   Address Resolution Protocol
815   IP datagram reassembly algorithms
893   Trailer encapsulation
894   A standard for the transmission of IP datagrams over Ethernet networks
903   A Reverse Address Resolution Protocol
1025   TCP and IP back off
1042   Standard for the transmission of IP datagrams over IEEE 802 networks

Summary

In this chapter, we have explored the facilities provided by IP, ARP, RARP and ICMP, all of which provide the ability to transport datagrams through a network and to report on their progress.

IP is the core protocol that allows TCP/IP systems to operate efficiently in local and wide area environments. IP itself is a datagram protocol; it is unreliable and no reliability is added at this level.

ICMP is provided to improve the probability that datagrams reach their destinations reliably by reducing the rate of discard through source quench and by changing routes dynamically if necessary through route change requests. As it is not connection-oriented, IP can easily redirect individual or whole groups of datagrams dynamically when network link failures or performance changes within the system require it, always assuming there are redundant paths. These changes are carried out in a manner that is transparent to higher layer protocols and more importantly, the user.

Through IP and its associated protocols, an interface is provided for higher layer protocols that is consistent, irrespective of the type of medium that is used below, be it a low-speed serial link or high-speed LAN. The only feature IP cannot hide is the performance of the underlying system; throughput will vary and therefore it cannot provide total transparency for the user application. It is up to the network manager to ensure that the facilities available to IP allow it to meet the application performance expectations of the user.

There is little to configure within IP, mainly the IP address itself and possibly a subnet mask or changes to the MTU. ICMP provides an invaluable source of diagnostic information to allow the network developer to plan network extensions and the maintainer to resolve the most complex problems.

12

Transport layer protocols

IP provides a transparent interface to media and an addressing mechanism to reach other nodes. These services need to be enhanced to enable datagrams to be directed to the appropriate application layer services and to provide reliable stream services for those applications that need it. The services are provided at this layer by the transport protocols, the User Datagram Protocol (UDP) and the Transmission Control Protocol (TCP).

In this chapter we will cover:

- The services provided by UDP
- The services provided by TCP
- How reliability is achieved
- Ports
- Sockets
- The relevant configuration options

So far we have considered the frames of the datalink layer and the datagrams of the IP layer. The IP data is encapsulated by the IP datagram, which is in turn encapsulated by the frame. At the transport layer, there are two separate options, UDP and TCP (Figure 12.1). Depending on what type of service is required by the user's application, one of these protocols is carried in the data field of the IP datagram.

Once information has been transferred to the correct machine by IP, it then has to be passed to the relevant application-level service on that machine. Multiplexing and demultiplexing data from many applications to and from the IP layer and directing data to the correct application is one of the responsibilities of the transport layer. Providing an error-free and flow-controlled (connection-oriented) datastream service or merely passing on the connectionless services of IP to the correct application are also dealt with at this layer.

The **User Datagram Protocol** (UDP) provides a connectionless unreliable service. It allows data to be transmitted to a machine or group of machines without the need to establish a connection. Single datagrams are sent to a remote node without any requirement for responses to indicate that the datagram has arrived. In certain environments this is the most efficient way to operate. Application services such as TFTP and NFS use this mode of transport. Where broadcast is required it may be the only option available.

The **Transmission Control Protocol** (TCP) provides a connection-oriented service. A connection is like a data pipe that runs between just two points. There is no broadcast or multicast facility with TCP. TCP has all the features necessary to provide a reliable service between two computers. In achieving reliability, it adds a significant amount of overhead to manage acknowledgements, flow control, timers and connection management facilities. It has more overhead than UDP in terms of both the processing power required and the size of the network headers it uses. Applications that require the services are Telnet and FTP.

Ports

Both UDP and TCP use port addressing to deliver information to the relevant application layer services. A port is a 16-bit address of which a number of well-known ports have been defined within a range of 0 to 255 (Figure 12.2). In other words, port numbers have been allocated for the most common application layer services, such as Telnet and FTP. If application developers create a program to work over UDP or TCP, they have to define which port they wish to use; to ensure that this number is unique on a particular machine it should at least be a value outside the reserved range of well-known ports.

There is a dynamic alternative to this fixed binding of ports. NFS uses a service known as the **portmapper**, which allows new ports to be

Figure 12.1 UDP and TCP.

defined and registered dynamically or the port used by a particular service to be discovered on request. We discuss the portmapper fully in Chapter 15.

For a full range of the well-known ports, see Appendix G.

Sockets

The term **socket** is frequently used in conjunction with TCP/IP. It is a fairly simple but important concept. The socket is a concatenation of the IP address and the port number. As the IP address is, in principle, unique to a node, assuming all nodes use registered IP addresses, and the port is unique on a node, the socket gives a unique identification of an application layer service. Because the socket reference is unique, both UDP and TCP include the IP address and port number in their checksum calculation. This is to ensure that a datagram arriving at the wrong host will not be accepted by the transport layer of that host even though that port, if it is well known, is likely to exist[†].

Most application layer services allow multiple sessions and thus need to be able to differentiate between these sessions to ensure that data is sent back to the appropriate computer. For example, a number of people are likely to be connected to the same host using Telnet (port 23), so all of them would be using the same Telnet port for access. One way to differentiate between different sessions might be to consider which IP address the datagrams came from, but it is possible that two users from the same host might be connected to one application. In this case, it would be extremely difficult to tell them apart.

To solve this problem, well-known port numbers are only used by server application layer services. Client programs select a unique port number that has not already been used on their machine. In this way, even if two sessions are set up to the same server host from the one client

---

[†]It is conceivable that an IP header could have its IP address corrupted and might therefore arrive at the wrong machine. If the IP checksum is ignored it will be passed to the transport layer where the port will be examined.

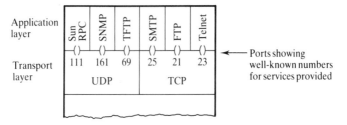

Figure 12.2 Ports used with UDP and TCP.

host, it is easy to use the source socket to differentiate between the two sessions, as they will always be unique. Application services transmit back to the source socket and this is one reason why both the source IP address and the source port are included in all communications between two machines.

A few services that operate on a peer-to-peer basis use the same port number for transmission and reception. These tend to be routing and management functions that have no need to differentiate between ports when returning messages.

User datagram protocol

UDP adds little to the underlying datagram service of IP, other than dealing with the problem of passing data to the correct application layer service. It does this by the source and destination port fields in its header. The block of data which UDP passes to IP, consisting of the UDP header and application layer data, is also referred to as a datagram. Figure 12.3 shows the fields added by UDP. They are:

- *Source port*   The port number of the application layer service the datagram came from.
- *Destination port*   The port number of the application layer service the datagram is intended for.
- *Length*   The length of the UDP datagram.
- *Checksum*   A checksum to protect the data carried by UDP.

Figure 12.3 UDP header fields.

Figure 12.4   The UDP checksum is based on the pseudo header as well as the UDP header.

The checksum is fairly basic. It is calculated from the 16-bit 1s complement of the 1s complement sum of all 16-bit words in the header and user data, like IP. What is unusual about this checksum is that not only does it consider the UDP fields, but it also includes what is referred to as a **pseudo header** based upon certain fields from the IP layer, to ensure that the calculation considers the socket and not just the port (Figure 12.4).

Some products allow the maximum size of a UDP datagram to be configured. This would be necessary if some component of the system were unable to receive large datagrams, but would be unusual. Reducing the **Maximum Datagram Size** (MDS) reduces the amount of memory required by UDP from the host but also reduces the performance of services using UDP. It is unusual to need to change this from default values.

Transmission control protocol

TCP adds reliability to IP and, like UDP, also provides application layer addressing through the use of ports. TCP is a connection-oriented protocol; not only is it reliable, but before transmission can commence from one machine to another, a connection must be opened. When transmission finishes, the connection is closed.

The block of data which TCP passes to IP, consisting of the TCP header and application layer data, is usually called a **segment**.

Adding reliability requires a number of facilities:

- Error detection and correction
- Flow control
- Resequencing
- Removing duplicate segments

Error detection and correction deals with the possibility of segments being corrupted by the medium or lower layers of software. Flow control

Source port			Destination port	
Sequence number				
Acknowledgement number				
Data offset	Reserved	Code	Window	
Checksum			Urgent pointer	
Options				Padding
Data				
⋮				

Figure 12.5 TCP header.

is used to prevent a transmitter overrunning a receiver owing to resource limitations. Resequencing is required because the underlying IP layer can deliver datagrams, carrying TCP segments, in any order; this happens when successive datagrams use different routes. Duplicate segments can occur because of the error-recovery mechanisms used by TCP.

TCP adds all these facilities by:

- Using sequence numbers to identify data;
- Positive acknowledgements of data received in the correct sequence;
- Retransmission of segments which have not been acknowledged within a (variable) time limit.

The exact mechanisms will be discussed in detail below.

The TCP header

To provide the functions outlined above, the TCP header (Figure 12.5) is a lot more complex, with more fields than UDP. Like UDP, and for the same reasons, the header includes the source and destination ports to identify the application. Most of the remaining fields add reliability and deal with connection control:

- *Sequence number – 32 bits* With most protocols that use sequence numbers for error control, the sequence numbers count segments[†] as they are transmitted and received. But with TCP, the sequence numbers count *octets* within the transmission stream. The sequence number in the header of a segment identifies the position in the overall data stream of the first data octet in that segment.

[†]Segment is a TCP term for the unit of transmission at this transport layer. The equivalent term in other protocols is often 'packet' or 'frame'.

On connection setup, new sequence numbers are agreed by both nodes and the connection starts. For system integrity after a machine crash, new sequence numbers do not start at zero.

If IP never delivered datagrams in a different order from that in which they were transmitted, data would always arrive in sequence and sequence numbers would increase smoothly. The sequence number allows TCP to slot a segment into the correct position in the data stream, even if IP delivers data out of order.

The sequence number is 32 bits, so that even on the fastest links the time taken for the same value of the counter to be valid again is very long[†]. This means that any segment received with the same sequence number as one already acknowledged can only be a duplicate, and due to the error correction process. Duplicates are allowed and are discarded without any action.

- *Acknowledgement number – 32 bits* The acknowledgement number acknowledges correct receipt of all octets up to the acknowledgement number –1. When a data sender receives a new value, it can dispose of data which was held for possible retransmission. The acknowledgement number is only valid if the ACK flag is set.

  Acknowledgement numbers are responses to the correct receipt of sequence numbers and in-sequence data from the remote end. An acknowledgement number contains the (sequence) number of the next octet in its received data stream that the sender will pass to its application (with the octet 'zero' numbered with the sequence numbers which were exchanged at connection setup). Thus, the acknowledgement number is one greater than the octet number of the last in-sequence octet received. It is therefore the same as the sequence number that will be in the next segment of immediately useful data.

  In TCP, it is possible to have sent a number of segments that have been received correctly but have not been acknowledged, because the critical segment, which is the next in sequence, has failed to arrive. Either it is delayed, because it was routed via a slow path, or it was discarded by IP. The acknowledgement number cannot advance until this missing piece of the jigsaw is provided through retransmission on the retransmission timer. This is discussed in the section on error correction and retransmission time-out later in this chapter.

- *Data offset* This measures the offset to the start of the application data field in 32-bit words. The normal value is 5 (20-octet header) when no options are used.

[†]For 2Mbps continuous transmission, it takes 9.5 hours to transmit 2^{32} octets!

- *Flags*   The flags are used to indicate the validity of other fields and for connection control. There are six separate flags:

  - *URG*   This indicates that the urgent pointer field is valid. This field points to an octet in the data field which is the end of urgent data. Urgent data is not considered as part of the normal data stream and should be processed before any other data. This operation is used in instances where a message has to be passed across the network to the application, even if some mechanism is preventing normal data from doing so. It can be used to interrupt programs.

  - *ACK*   This flag indicates that the acknowledge field is valid, which it is on most segments. The acknowledge field is normally only invalid on connection setup, before each node has been able to determine which sequence and acknowledge values to use. The value in the acknowledge field may not have changed between segments, so although the field is valid it may not acknowledge new data.

  - *PSH*   The push flag causes the remote TCP layer to pass this segment immediately to the application layer. TCP would normally hold on to the data from incoming segments and pass them to the application layer in larger buffers to reduce processing overheads, but in some situations, such as character-by-character terminal operation, this must not happen, even if only one octet of data has been received.

  - *RST*   The reset flag is used when all else fails. It indicates that an error has occurred and the connection should be forcibly closed (or, if sent as a reply to a connection open request, that the request is being rejected).

  - *SYN*   The synchronize flag is used at the beginning of connection setup between two nodes. At this stage neither end knows what acknowledge number to use. A connection setup consists of a two-way exchange of segments with the SYN flag set, each of which is acknowledged in a segment with the ACK flag set. Data transfer can then commence. This is covered in more detail later in this chapter.

  - *FIN*   The FIN flag is used to terminate connections. When one end of a connection has no more data to send, it sends a segment with the FIN flag set. When both ends of a connection have sent the FIN flag, the connection is closed.

- *Window – 16 bit*   The window advertises the amount of buffer space this node has allocated to this connection. The other node must not send more unacknowledged data than the buffer space indicated.

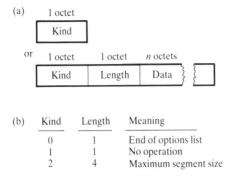

Figure 12.6 (a) Options format. (b) Options. (c) Example.

- *Checksum – 16 bit* The TCP checksum is a basic check on the header and data. It is calculated in the same fashion as that in UDP, from the 16-bit 1s complement of the 1s complement sum of all 16-bit words in the header and data.

- *Urgent pointer – 16 bit* The value in this field points to the end of data in the data field that is considered as urgent and requires immediate attention. This field is only valid if the URG flag is set.

- *Options – variable length* There is only one option normally used with TCP, which is **Maximum Segment Size** (MSS). It tells the destination TCP layer the maximum size of the segment (including the TCP header) which should be sent.

    The format of this option is shown in Figure 12.6. Kind 2 is the MSS option; kinds 0 and 1 are end-of-option list and no operation, respectively. The length field indicates the length in octets of the complete option, that is, it includes the kind and length fields.

- *Padding* If the options field is valid, padding ensures that the data starts on a 32-bit boundary, so that the data offset may correctly point to it.

In some implementations of TCP, MSS can be configured to set the maximum size of segment accepted by a node. This will normally be set to the maximum value possible to reduce the overhead of smaller segments. Some hardware may be restricted in the size of frames that it can receive and hence needs this value setting so that TCP will not allow the options parameters to exceed the abilities of the hardware.

The decision as to the size of MSS is quite complex. In a system which includes routers, they are required to support an MTU of at least 576 octets, allowing a maximum MSS of 556. (576 minus the minimum

IP header of 20 octets.) Smaller segments will give quicker response but create far greater overhead on the network, thereby decreasing efficiency, especially in routed connections. Large frames improve efficiency, but increase delay due to the time taken to fill each buffer. If a path in the network has a tendency to corrupt frames then the bigger they are, the more likely they are to be corrupted. So large frames increase the likelihood of larger retransmissions and of processing power in routers and hosts being taken up with fragmentation and reassembly.

With the improvements in WAN technology, error rates are significantly reduced, so the likelihood of lost or corrupt frames is also reduced significantly. This allows larger maximum-size segments to be configured. Only in extreme conditions should there be a need to alter these values from the maximum size possible.

TCP in action

To explain the operation of the features of TCP, we will consider the phases of a TCP connection. We will look at a connection setup between two nodes, 128.1.0.1 and 128.1.0.9, where 128.1.0.1 will establish a connection with 128.1.0.9.

The connection setup phase

The setup of a TCP connection is initiated through a request from the application layer of a node. In Figure 12.7, we consider node 128.1.0.1 requesting a connection to IP address 128.1.0.9. TCP then sends a segment to IP that has the SYN flag set, a value in the sequence number field (921) and the ACK flag not set, which denotes that this is the initial segment of a connection. At this stage, when the segment is passed to the IP layer, if the IP layer does not have an entry for IP address 128.1.0.9 in its ARP cache, it will submit an ARP request to obtain the MAC address of node 128.1.0.9. Once the MAC address has been acquired, the segment is transmitted as an IP datagram.

Node 128.1.0.9 will respond with a similar segment that has the SYN flag set, the ACK flag set and with its own sequence number (302). In the acknowledge field, there will be a value that is one greater than the sequence number sent by the node 128.1.0.1 (921 + 1 = 922).This segment is acknowledging that 128.1.0.9 received the sequence number from node 128.1.0.1 and is proposing its own sequence number.

Node 128.1.0.1 will acknowledge that it has received node 128.1.0.9's response by sending a second segment that only has the ACK flag set and with a value in the acknowledge field that is one greater than the sequence number sent by node 128.1.0.9 (302 + 1 = 303).

A TCP connection is now established; both ends have exchanged sequence numbers and are now ready to send data.

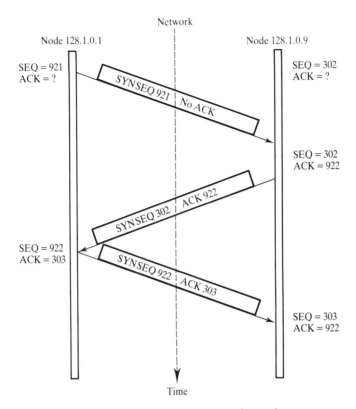

Figure 12.7   Connections setup phase of TCP.

The data phase

As node 128.1.0.1 sends data to node 128.1.0.9, the sequence number in the segment points to the first octet of data carried and the response from node 128.1.0.9 should have an acknowledge number that is one greater than the sequence number received plus the number of octets carried, that is, the acknowledge number indicates which octet 128.1.0.9 expects to see next.

If the application is a terminal emulation service that requires character echo from the application at the remote end (node 128.1.0.9), the segments will also have the PSH flag set. This will prevent the TCP layer in either node 128.1.0.1 or 128.1.0.9 from holding on to the data and will force them to pass it immediately across the network and to the application layer so that characters can be echoed as quickly as possible.

This continues until all data is sent. Acknowledgements are only returned if there was data in the last segment received, otherwise the protocol waits for the next data to be sent. **Keep-alive** segments sent to test that a connection is still in place were added to the TCP standard after its initial implementation. Often a TCP connection is totally idle when there is no application data to send. TCP keep-alive is discussed later.

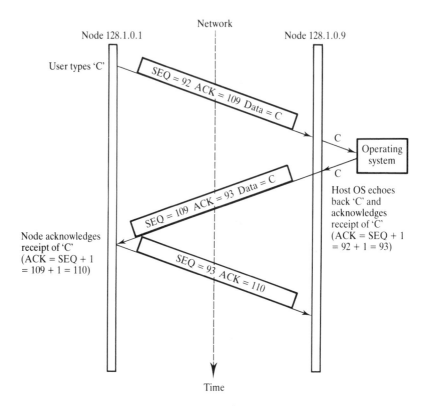

Figure 12.8 TCP acknowledgements for simple character echo with host.

As every segment has the same format, for either the transmission of data or control, TCP can acknowledge data from a remote node and carry outbound data in the same segment. TCP can be very efficient in the number of segments it uses. For a terminal connection using Telnet with character echo[†] from the remote host, TCP often requires just three segments for each character typed.

Figure 12.8 gives a simple example of TCP when a terminal connection such as Telnet is operating with a host in echo back mode. Characters typed by the user have to be passed to the computer and back to the screen to be displayed. They traverse the network twice between the user hitting the key and the character being displayed.

In this example the user has typed the character C, which is sent across the network with a sequence number of 92. The operating system echoes back the character and in the same frame the TCP protocol

---

[†]Character echo is used by most interactive systems. When a character is typed, it is not displayed on the local display until it has been sent back from the remote host. This gives the remote host the ability to decide what it wants to display in response to any character. In the early days of computing, it was used as an error-checking method.

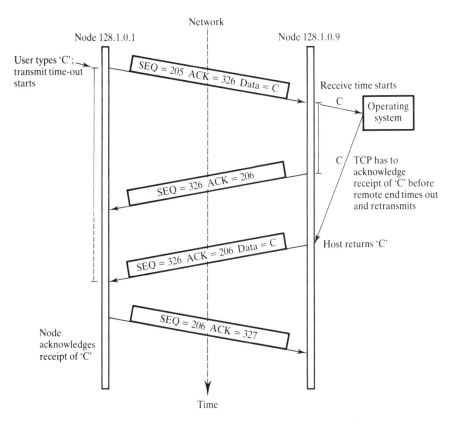

Figure 12.9 Four packets per character due to host delays.

acknowledges receipt of C from 128.1.0.1. Node 128.1.0.1 then has to acknowledge receipt of the character from 128.1.0.9, so an acknowledge segment is returned but with no data, the acknowledge field being set one beyond the sequence number received, as there is one character.

With systems that use remote echo, it is possible for more than three segments to be generated for each character typed, if the destination computer is under heavy load. This happens because each segment carrying a character must be acknowledged within a certain time, otherwise a retransmission will occur. If the application host is not ready to return its response within that time-out period it will generate a segment without the echoed character, but with an acknowledgement of the incoming segment. When the application is ready to echo the character back to the sender, it will send another segment and should receive an acknowledgement back from the terminal user's computer. In these circumstances, four segments are generated (Figure 12.9).

The impact of applications that use remote character echo in this way is worth careful consideration. Each segment has a TCP header, an

IP header and the single typed character, making 41 octets in all, and is carried in a datalink frame. On Ethernet, each frame must be a minimum size of 64 octets[†], which means that for the three or four segments sent for each character typed by a user, either 192 (64×3) or 256 (64×4) octets are transmitted between source and destination, depending on the load of the remote computer. So, when the application computer is put under load, it causes four packets per character typed and that puts a further load on the computer generating the extra acknowledgement. Network traffic for this application is increased by up to 33%, because the computer is loaded. The only way to reduce the overhead caused by this problem is to remove the resource bottleneck in the host computer, which may require a larger computer; it is likely that a computer causing this problem is slow performing its normal tasks as well.

A host which is under heavy load will often send responses in multiple segments, even though a single frame could support the amount of data to be carried. This happens because communications software usually runs at high priority and builds output frames on a timer. On a busy machine, the application is unable to assemble all the information required before the timer runs out.

While remote echo operation can be acceptable on purely local LANs with a capacity of 7000 to 14 000 frames per second, the traffic generated must be carefully considered when planning a WAN with remote bridges or routers. If each character typed generates three or four frames, this must be taken into account when sizing the speed of the intersite circuits. For example, the capacity of a 64 kbps circuit is about 120 minimum-size Ethernet frames per second (in each direction). If each user types two characters per second on average (20 words per minute – even today, computer users are often not trained typists), each may generate four frames in each direction. The line will be saturated in both directions by just 30 active users[‡]. This simplistic view does not take into account the purpose of all this typing, which is usually to request a computer-generated screen of information. Applications must be modelled individually and the traffic they generate considered at each point in the network. Traffic has two parameters: the number of bits per second required and the number of frames or packets per second. Bottlenecks are more likely in wide area links.

A spreadsheet model of the operation of a particular protocol is a very useful tool. While it cannot model the dynamics of user operation and the performance of the data sources, it can give a good indication of whether a particular design has any chance of working.

[†]As the Ethernet frame overhead is 18 octets, each frame carrying a single typed character will be padded by 5 octets ($18 + 41 + 5 = 64$). IEEE 802.3 frames will not require padding as LLC and SNAP add 8 octets, making a frame with a minimum TCP segment of 67 octets ($18 + 8 + 41 = 67$).

[‡]Bridges with a good data compression algorithm might help, but it must not extend the round trip delay to the point where users object to the delayed echo.

The amount of traffic than can be produced by TCP may appear high, but it can be less than other protocols.

The final phase

In the final phase, when one end has decided to close the connection, the FIN flag is used. For an interactive terminal connection, the user will most probably log out of their application and the application will tell the TCP layer to close the connection. This causes the application node to send a segment with the FIN flag set. The FIN flag tells the terminal node that there is no more data to send. The terminal node responds with a segment with ACK (to acknowledge the FIN) and its own FIN flag set. The connection is not regarded as closed completely until both ends have sent a segment with the FIN flags set and possibly acknowledged that the FIN segments were received. However, if segments are lost at this late stage, the connection will be regarded as closed after a short time-out. In practice, either end may initiate the graceful closing of a connection with FIN.

In Figure 12.10 the user has finished work so has typed 'logout' to close the connection. This message is sent to the operating system that releases the connection which needs to be closed. Note also that the data 'logout' is acknowledged as any other data. The host then closes the connection by indicating to the TCP stack that the connection is to be closed. That causes the TCP software to send a frame with the FIN code value set. If 128.1.0.1 decides it has also finished and it has no further data to send, it will return an acknowledge and a FIN which will instruct 128.1.0.9 that the connection is complete.

Error correction and retransmission time-out

TCP provides the error correction for those TCP/IP applications that require it. The TCP/IP architecture leaves error correction to this transport level because it wishes to make no assumptions about the error-correction capabilities of the underlying networks. Since it then has to do error correction for certain applications, why not just do it once in the end nodes at the transport layer? This means that all error correction in TCP/IP is assumed to be end-to-end[†] and not hop-to-hop, unlike some networks, such as implementations of X.25[‡].

There is an interesting management side-effect to this decision. While no assumption is made about the error performance of underlying

---

[†]If TCP operates over an error-corrected network like X.25, it just sees a system which is substantially error free and which has occasional sudden changes in delay as the error-correction mechanisms operate.

[‡]Unlike X.25 developers, TCP/IP developers were able to take a much higher level view of the application performance required, rather than just designing a data transmission network level service that had to deliver to the public certain guarantees of performance.

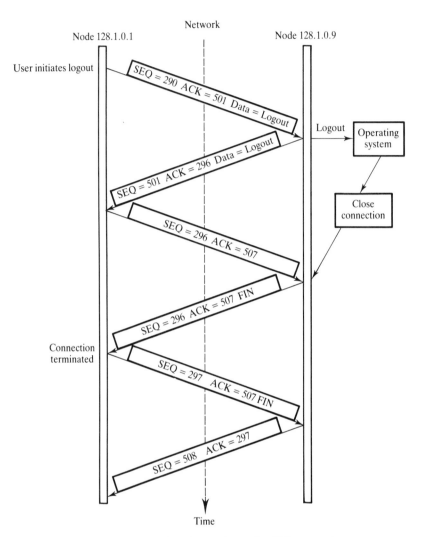

Figure 12.10 Closedown phase of a TCP connection.

networks, if that performance is not good, any single error will mean that a TCP segment is retransmitted end-to-end on every link. In an X.25 network, it would have been transmitted just on the one link in error. Indeed, the error-correction mechanism used by TCP works best when it is only occasionally required. Fortunately, the error rates on wide area circuits have improved considerably with the introduction of fibre optic transmission systems, so the decision by TCP/IP designers is justified.

TCP error correction uses one simple mechanism: if an acknowledgement has not been received for any particular segment sequence number within a certain time-out value, the segment is resent. This is the *only* mechanism for error recovery. Unlike some other error-correction methods, there is no way that a receiver can force the retransmission from a particular point, partly because there is no concept of retransmitting data when it is out of sequence. The receiver must await the expiry of the timer at the sender.

Because segments are only acknowledged when in sequence, it is probable that once the time-out operates, a series of segments (if the value of the window size and MSS allows more than one segment to be acknowledged) will be retransmitted. It is also possible in some implementations that resending a single segment will cause a number of outstanding segments to be acknowledged. The TCP standard can accommodate both mechanisms. What happens in practice depends on how adventurous the designer of the implementation has been.

In Figure 12.11, a number of TCP segments have been transmitted because the window size last advertised to 128.1.0.1 allowed that amount of data to be sent. The segment with sequence number 39 did not succeed in reaching the destination even though a later segment (sequence number 49) did. TCP does not acknowledge the segment with sequence number 49 as it has not yet received all intermediate data. This causes the retransmission timer started for the segment with sequence number 39 to mature, causing the segment to be retransmitted.

In Figure 12.12, the loss of an acknowledge segment does not require any further action, as the segment following the lost acknowledge got through, which implies that all data from sequence number 72 up to and including the data in the segment with sequence number 170 has arrived at 128.1.0.9.

The value of the retransmission time-out is critical. It depends on the round trip delay or Round Trip Time (RTT) on the path in use. LANs will acknowledge in 1–100 ms; wide area connections over slow-speed satellite circuits could take many seconds. It is difficult to know the delay characteristics of networks in advance, and they can vary by a factor of 10 during the life of a connection, depending on route and loading. This makes it almost impossible to decide on one time-out value for this retransmit timer. If the time-out is set too low, it will expire before the acknowledge returns, causing the segment to be sent again unnecessarily, and increasing the traffic. If the value is set too high, it causes long delays waiting for the time-out to mature before a retransmission can be sent, so the loss of one segment will significantly decrease throughput.

Modern implementations of TCP have a technique which can deal with this wide variation in possible RTTs. To solve the problem, all implementations of TCP are now supposed to use a mechanism that works out the average delay of a connection and adds a threshold above that delay to deal with variations. A dynamic time-out allows a connection to change its value to suit the immediate circumstances and helps build a robust

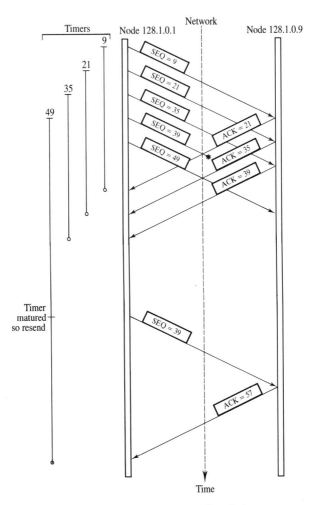

Figure 12.11 A segment carrying data failing to arrive.

protocol. It minimizes the number of unnecessary retransmissions while reducing the dead time when retransmission could have begun.

There are a number of issues about how this dynamic timer should be implemented. One of the most powerful techniques was developed for use on packet radio networks by Phil Karn, KA9Q. It accurately assesses the RTT regardless of lost segments. This mechanism has now been adopted by some commercial implementations of TCP/IP. Until this algorithm was introduced, it was found that some techniques would lock into a mode of reliably sending everything twice!

In TCP implementations a number of variants of the retransmission algorithm are used, so it is important to understand the basis of

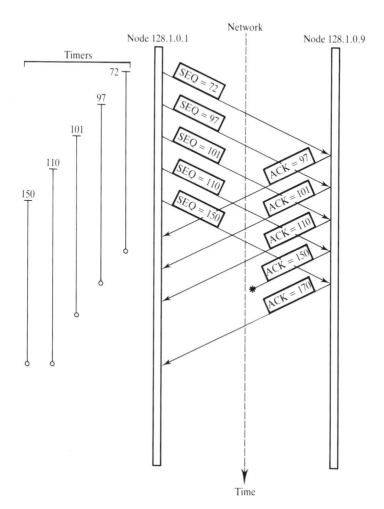

Figure 12.12 Acknowledge segment failing to arrive.

time-out algorithms and their stability under heavy load and high segment loss.

Even today, not all implementations of TCP/IP use dynamic time-out algorithms. Some have fixed timers and others have timers that can be configured. In some implementations different timer values can be set for each host in a table. None of these is as satisfactory as the dynamic timer unless the network topology is very simple.

Sliding windows, window advertisements and flow control

In networks that have long delays, positive acknowledge protocols can decrease throughput dramatically; each segment can be held up waiting for acknowledgements to travel through the system before the next segment can be sent. A medium or link can only be loaded to a fraction of its capacity, which decreases dramatically with increasing round trip delay. To improve on this, TCP employs a process known as **sliding windows**.

Sliding windows allows multiple segments to be transmitted without waiting for an acknowledgement for each individual segment. If multiple segments are received at a node before an acknowledgement is ready to be sent, it is possible to acknowledge just the last segment received, so reducing the need to acknowledge every segment. This allows higher throughput and more efficient use of the bandwidth.

Correct use of sliding windows is particularly important on paths through bridges and routers, especially where there are remote links. Even on a LAN which has only local bridges, delays will build up in the buffers of the bridges. Setting the correct window size will restore performance almost to that achievable on a direct cable connection. Sliding windows makes TCP (as opposed to UDP and other LAN protocols) particularly good at operating over long-distance WANs.

A receiver will have limited buffer space for each connection, so a limit has to be put on the amount of information that can be sent. This limit is the window size, which in TCP is measured in octets. There is a relationship between window size and the MSS. When a new window size is given, it is usually an integral multiple of the MSS (though that integer is often 1 in systems with restricted memory, PCs for example). The size of these windows is normally in the range of 1024 to 4096, which is only between one and four segments on an Ethernet with an MSS set to 1024 and an MTU of 1500.

A data receiver advertises a window size in each TCP segment it sends. When the unacknowledged data is the same as the advertised window size, no more information is sent until an acknowledgement is received which advertises a new window size of at least one maximum segment.

The window advertised in each segment is a useful monitor when performance difficulties are being encountered. If the window values are often low or reach zero in the middle of data transfer, a device does not have enough memory allocated to buffers. Performance is likely to be improved if the relevant buffers can be increased.

A receiver may validly reduce the window size to zero to stop the flow of data completely, that is, to invoke flow control. It is only permissible to reduce the window as it is used up by valid data on this connection. A receiver cannot reduce a previously advertised window which has not been filled with data.

Telnet uses flow control: when the keys <CTRL> and s are typed at the same time on a keyboard, it stops any further information from being displayed on the screen of that terminal. <CTRL> and s generate ASCII character DC3 or XOFF. In this event, a Telnet terminal server operating over TCP has to stop the remote host from transmitting to prevent the terminal server buffers overflowing, otherwise data will be lost. As data continues to be received and to fill the previously advertised window, TCP sends segments with reducing window sizes until the window size finally reaches zero. If the flow of data is re-enabled with <CTRL> and q together (ASCII character DC1 or XON), the data will start to flow to the terminal again, buffers will be released and segments to the remote host will indicate the increasing terminal server window size.

For efficiency, a newly advertised window must always be at least one maximum segment.

In Figure 12.13, the example shows a connection where the buffers are filling up on 128.1.0.9 so the window has shrunk to 200 octets and then to 0. When 128.1.0.9 has been able to deal with the data it received, effectively clearing its receive buffers, it re-advertises a window of 1024, so data starts to flow again.

TCP keep-alive

In the early versions of TCP implementation, if an application sent no data for an extended period, then no TCP or IP information was generated. With the use of PCs for TCP/IP applications, there is an increased possibility that the client machine will fail without closing TCP connections. For example, users often turn off the power on the PC without logging off. If the application is not written to check periodically for successful communication with the client machine, then this can leave open but 'hung' connections on the server which can only be cleared by manual intervention by the system manager.

The solution is for the server to operate TCP keep-alive. A TCP segment is sent periodically to elicit an acknowledge from the other machine. If no acknowledge is received after a number of retries, the TCP connection is reset. The keep-alive segment must not be passed to the application, so the mechanism which was adopted was to send a segment containing only the last byte of previously acknowledged data. All systems should ignore this retransmission, but repeat the acknowledge, confirming that they are still active.

TCP keep-alives should normally be enabled on hosts. The keep-alive interval time is often of the order of 90 seconds though much longer timers are also common. It may be configurable. Some protocol analysers wrongly show a keep-alive as a TCP retransmission. They are easily distinguished from normal retransmissions by the long delay, their regularity, and the presence of only one byte of data.

The TCP window and slow start

As we discussed above, TCP uses window advertisements to tell a remote node how much data it can receive without overflowing its buffers. This

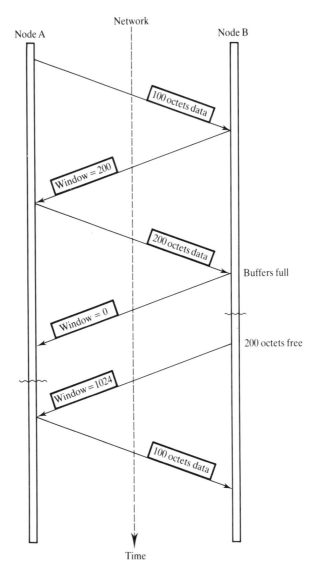

Figure 12.13 Window advertisements in TCP.

works well as a method of end-to-end flow control between the two nodes, but it does not provide for flow control within the network between them. The problem comes when the network between the nodes is congested. As the nodes have no knowledge of this, they will send the maximum amount of data allowed by the receiving node and in doing so, cause even more congestion.

To overcome this, a mechanism called 'slow start' is used. This keeps account of the unacknowledged segments in what is referred to as the 'congestion window'. At the start of a connection the value of the congestion window is one segment. If the first segment is acknowledged, the window is then increased in size; if retransmission occurs, the congestion window is decreased in size. So the congestion window keeps track of the state of the links between two nodes so as not to overload them.

This mechanism works well for an application protocol which establishes connections that last for a long period and sends many segments – protocols such as Telnet or FTP. However, it causes difficulty for protocols that use short-lived connections – the first version of HTTP (used with the World Wide Web) is an example. The reason is that throughput is initially throttled back by the slow start process, but improves with time and with the number of acknowledges received. If a connection doesn't last for much time, it will never reach optimum throughput.

TCP TIME_WAIT

When a connection is closed between a client and a server, the server remembers the connection for a significant period of time afterwards, usually in the region of 240 seconds. The reason for this is that a severely delayed segment could interfere with any subsequent sessions between the same client and server which use the same port numbers. To prevent this, servers go into a TIME_WAIT state. During the TIME_WAIT state, they remember the connection, refuse any new connections with those port numbers and reject any segments that arrive for the old connection.

The problem with this is that it holds resources on a server. During the TIME_WAIT state the pair of port numbers associated with the old connection cannot be reused. So a server which has a lot of activity, or connections that are short-lived, can run out of available port numbers and reject new connections until the TIME_WAIT state expires.

One would expect that this would not be a major problem as a subsequent connection between a client and server should use a different source port from the client and could therefore be differentiated from previous connections. But this does not always happen. Some protocols and some implementations of software use fixed client port numbers; some implementations of application software use a small subset of client port numbers, not picking a random value. This has some advantages for those who implement access controls based on port numbers, but the small range of usable port numbers must not recycle within the TIME_WAIT period of the destination host.

For a server that receives many short-lived connections this can become a significant problem. This feature of TCP/IP systems is also used by hackers to deny service at a particular host, by trying to push all available source port numbers into the TIME_WAIT state.

Configuration issues

There are not usually many parameters that can be modified at this level and there are none required for UDP at all, but some implementations allow certain TCP parameters to be set.

Connection time-out

This is the time to spend attempting to establish a connection with a computer. Changing this value affects the amount of time it will take to fail if the connection to a host is not possible.

Retransmission time-out

This is the time to wait between the retransmission of TCP segments. Modern implementations really should not leave this as a network manager's option!

This can be a difficult value to assess. One way is to use the ping utility, as it often displays the round trip delay to a host. If this utility is run for an extended time covering the busiest period on the system, the maximum delay seen could be taken as a reference and then used with some margin added. The margin would depend on the scatter in the values, but a factor of between 1.5 and 2 would be normal.

The maximum segment size

This is the maximum size of a TCP segment allowed. Probably the most sensible value for this field is the maximum size that prevents fragmentation from occurring across the most commonly used connection from that host. For operation in LAN-only environments, 1024 is a common figure.

Receive window

This is the maximum size of receive window that should be advertised. It should normally be a multiple of the MSS[†]. Where memory is a limitation, it will often be one or two maximum segments.

Setting a larger window size is the way to improve the performance of a TCP connection through bridges and routers. For example, in a route with two local bridges, maximum performance will be achieved when the receiver window is three times the MSS of the transmitter. As one segment is received by the end system, a second is being received by the second bridge. Just as the third segment, which exhausts the window, is

---

[†]MSS refers to transmission and window size refers to receiving. There is no real connection between them. If all systems are set with a similar MSS (1024) and a maximum window which is a small multiple (2,3,4) of that, they can all make efficient use of the network resources.

received by the first bridge, an acknowledge is generated, which releases the window for further transmission.

Different calculations apply where there is a mixture of high- and low-speed local and wide area facilities.

TCP keep-alive

Some systems allow TCP keep-alive parameters to be adjusted, and may include:

- Keep-alive enabled/disabled
- Delay between keep-alive segments
- Delay between retransmissions of keep-alive on no response
- Number of retransmissions before connection close/reset

Well-known ports used with TCP and UDP

Decimal	Keyword	Description
0	Reserved	
1	TCPMUX	TCP port service multiplexor
5	RJE	Remote job entry
7	ECHO	Echo
9	Discard	Discard
11	Users	Active users
13	Daytime	Daytime
17	Quote	Quote of the day
19	CHARGEN	Character generator
20	FTP-data	File transfer [default data]
21	FTP	File transfer [control]
23	Telnet	Telnet
25	SMTP	Simple mail transfer
247–255	Reserved	

For a complete list, see Appendix G.

TCP traces

The following shows actual traces taken from an operational network of the TCP protocol. In this example we show Ethernet frames in hexadecimal, without the preamble or the CRC. The table beneath the frame gives a breakdown of the fields in the frame and their values. For a further explanation of the format of these examples, see Appendix F. For completeness the datalink and IP information is shown shaded.

This example shows the initial three segments sent to initiate a TCP session. It shows the three segments required to synchronize the sequence and acknowledgement numbers.

Frame 1

```
AA00   0400   0104   0260   8C0A   C49D   0800   4500      *......`..D...E.
002C   0002   0000   FF06   7F66   1E00   0001   1E00      .,.......f......
0063   19CB   0017   0000   3E38   0000   0000   6002      .c.K....8....`.
0400   015D   0000   0204   0400   0000                    ...].........
```

Datalink:	Dest MAC:	AA0004 000104	Source MAC:	02608C 0AC49D	Type(Length):	0800
IP:	Version:	4	IHL:	5	Type of service:	00
	Length:	002C	ID:	0002	Flags:	0
	Offset:	0	Time to live:	255	Protocol:	06
	Checksum:	7F66	Source IP:	30.0.0.1	Dest IP:	30.0.0.99
TCP:	Source port:	19CB	Dest port:	Telnet(0017)	Sequence:	00003E38
	Acknowledge:	None	Offset:	6	Code:	02(Syn)
	Window:	0400	Checksum:	015D	TCP options:	Max Seg 1024

Frame 2

```
0260   8C0A   C49D   AA00   0400   0104   0800   4500      .`..D.*.......E.
002C   0B0B   0000   3C06   375E   1E00   0063   1E00      .,.....7^...c..
0001   0017   19CB   11E7   39AD   0000   3E39   6012      .....K.g9-..9`.
0400   B5B7   0000   0204   0400   0000                    ..57........
```

Datalink:	Dest MAC:	02608C 0AC49D	Source MAC:	AA0004 000104	Type(Length):	0800
IP:	Version:	4	IHL:	5	Type of service:	00
	Length:	002C	ID:	0B0B	Flags:	0
	Offset:	0	Time to live:	60	Protocol:	06
	Checksum:	375E	Source IP:	30.0.0.99	Dest IP:	30.0.0.1
TCP:	Source port:	Telnet(0017)	Dest port:	19CB	Sequence:	11E739AD
	Acknowledge:	00003E39	Offset:	6	Code:	12(Syn,Ack)
	Window:	0400	Checksum:	B5B7	TCP options:	Max Seg 1024

Frame 3

```
AA00   0400   0104   0260   8C0A   C49D   0800   4500      *......`..D...E.
0028   0003   0000   FF06   7F69   1E00   0001   1E00      .(.......i.....
0063   19CB   0017   0000   3E39   11E7   39AE   5018      .c.K....9.g9.P.
0400   CBB8   0000   0001   0800   0604                    ..K8........
```

Datalink:	Dest MAC:	AA0004 000104	Source MAC:	02608C 0AC49D	Type(Length):	0800
IP:	Version:	4	IHL:	5	Type of service:	00
	Length:	002C	ID:	0002	Flags:	0
	Offset:	0	Time to live:	255	Protocol:	06
	Checksum:	7F69	Source IP:	30.0.0.1	Dest IP:	30.0.0.99
TCP:	Source port:	19CB	Dest port:	Telnet(0017)	Sequence:	00003E39
	Acknowledge:	11E739AE	Offset:	5	Code:	18(Push/Ack)
	Window:	0400	Checksum:	CBB8	TCP options:	None

The following four frames ($n-3$ to n) signify the end of the session. The user types 'logout' to the host which signals the host to close the connection. This is initiated by the host sending a segment with the FIN flag set (frame $n-3$). The workstation acknowledges receipt of the FIN segment and then sends its own FIN segment (frame $n-1$) which is acknowledged by the host with segment n. The disconnection is complete. It is interesting to note that the workstation could have used a single frame instead of $n-2$ and $n-1$ to acknowledge the FIN and send its own FIN; for some reason this implementation of TCP/IP does not.

Frame n – 3

```
0260  8C0A  C49D  AA00  0400  0104  0800  4500      .`..D.*.......E.
0028  0B54  0000  3C06  3719  1E00  0063  1E00      .(.T...7....c..
0001  0017  19CB  11E7  4256  0000  3E62  5019      .....K.gBV..bP.
0001  C6E5  0000  0000  0000  0000                  ..Fe........
```

Datalink:	Dest MAC:	02608C 0AC49D	Source MAC:	AA0004 000104	Type(Length):	0800
IP:	Version:	4	IHL:	5	Type of service:	00
	Length:	0028	ID:	0B54	Flags:	0
	Offset:	0	Time to live:	60	Protocol:	06
	Checksum:	3719	Source IP:	30.0.0.99	Dest IP:	30.0.0.1
TCP:	Source port:	Telnet(0017)	Dest port:	19CB	Sequence:	11E74256
	Acknowledge:	00003E62	Offset:	5	Code:	19(Push,Fin)
	Window:	0001	Checksum:	C6E5	TCP options:	None

Frame n – 2

```
AA00  0400  0104  0260  8C0A  C49D  0800  4500      *......`..D...E.
0028  006D  0000  FF06  7EFF  1E00  0001  1E00      .(.m....~......
0063  19CB  0017  0000  3E62  11E7  4257  5010      .c.K....b.gBWP.
0400  C2EE  0000  0000  0000  0000                  ..............
```

Datalink:	Dest MAC:	AA0004 000104	Source MAC:	02608C 0AC49D	Type(Length):	0800
IP:	Version:	4	IHL:	5	Type of service:	00
	Length:	28	ID:	006D	Flags:	0
	Offset:	0	Time to live:	255	Protocol:	06
	Checksum:	7EFF	Source IP:	30.0.0.1	Dest IP:	30.0.0.99
TCP:	Source port:	19CB	Dest port:	Telnet(0017)	Sequence:	00003E62
	Acknowledge:	11E74257	Offset:	5	Code:	10(Ack)
	Window:	0400	Checksum:	C2EE	TCP options:	None

Frame n – 1

```
AA00  0400  0104  0260  8C0A  C49D  0800  4500      *......`..D...E.
0028  006E  0000  FF06  7EFE  1E00  0001  1E00      .(.n....~~......
0063  19CB  0017  0000  3E62  11E7  4257  5019      .c.K....b.gBWP.
0400  C2E5  0000  0000  0000  0000                  ...........
```

Datalink:	Dest MAC:	AA0004 000104	Source MAC:	02608C 0AC49D	Type(Length):	0800
IP:	Version:	4	IHL:	5	Type of service:	00
	Length:	0028	ID:	006E	Flags:	0
	Offset:	0	Time to live:	255	Protocol:	06
	Checksum:	7EFE	Source IP:	30.0.0.1	Dest IP:	30.0.0.99
TCP:	Source port:	19CB	Dest port:	Telnet(0017)	Sequence:	00003E62
	Acknowledge:	11E74257	Offset:	5	Code:	19(Push/Fin)
	Window:	0400	Checksum:	C2E5	TCP options:	None

Frame n

```
0260  8C0A  C49D  AA00  0400  0104  0800  4500      .`..D.*.......E.
0028  0B55  0000  3C06  3718  1E00  0063  1E00      .(.U...7....c..
0001  0017  19CB  11E7  4257  0000  3E63  5010      .....K.gBW..cP.
0000  C6ED  0000  0000  0000  0000                  ..Fm........
```

Datalink:	Dest MAC:	02608C 0AC49D	Source MAC:	AA0004 000104	Type(Length):	0800
IP:	Version:	4	IHL:	5	Type of service:	00
	Length:	0028	ID:	0B55	Flags:	0
	Offset:	0	Time to live:	60	Protocol:	06
	Checksum:	3718	Source IP:	30.0.0.99	Dest IP:	30.0.0.1
TCP:	Source port:	Telnet(0017)	Dest port:	19CB	Sequence:	11E74257
	Acknowledge:	00003E63	Offset:	5	Code:	12(Ack)
	Window:	0000	Checksum:	C6ED	TCP options:	Max Seg 1024

Relevant RFCs

675   Transmission control protocol [1]
700   A protocol experiment
721   Out-of-band control signals in a host-to-host protocol
761   Transmission control protocol [2]
768   User datagram protocol
793   Transmission control protocol [3]
794   Pre-emption
814   Name, address, ports and routes
816   Fault isolation and recovery
817   Modularity and efficiency in protocol implementation
872   TCP on a LAN
879   The TCP maximum segment size and related topics
889   Internet delay experiments
896   Congestion control in TCP/IP networks
964   Some problems with the specification of the military standard transmission control protocol
1006   ISO transport services on top of the TCP: Version 3
1072   TCP extensions for long-delay paths
1078   TCP port service multiplexer
1106   TCP big window option
1144   Compressing TCP/IP headers for low-speed serial links
1323   TCP extension for high performance
1692   Transport multiplexing protocol (TMux)

Summary

UDP and TCP provide the transport layer protocols of the TCP/IP protocol stack. UDP provides a datagram service adding only the necessary port addressing to define which application layer protocol data should be sent to. TCP, as well as providing application layer addressing, provides a reliable stream. Because TCP uses a windowing technique, it works efficiently on most media systems and it provides a flow control mechanism by way of its window advertising process.

Connections through the TCP/IP protocol stack are uniquely defined with sockets, which are a concatenation of the IP address and a port number. The more popular well-known applications, usually server software, use commonly defined well-known port numbers. Client software uses port numbers that are unique to their host and have not already been used by some other application on that host. This allows their connections to be described explicitly.

Setting the correct maximum segment size and maximum window size will dramatically improve TCP performance over buffered networks. For UDP it is possible to alter the maximum datagram size if necessary.

13

Application layer services

In the TCP/IP architecture, the application layer is responsible for interfacing between end-user applications and the transport layer services; the application service is *not* the end-user application, it merely interfaces that application to the communications network. There are several application layer services to suit the many different types of applications. There are also a few useful management utilities. For example, Telnet is a service to support terminal type activities, the File Transfer Protocol (FTP) suits file transfer type applications and the Simple Mail Transfer Protocol (SMTP) deals with mail applications. In this chapter we will look at the major services available and explain their operation.

Topics covered in this chapter are:

- Client/server
- Telnet
- FTP
- SMTP
- Post Office Protocol (POP3)
- R commands
- NetBIOS
- TFTP
- BOOTP
- DHCP
- WINSOCK interface
- The X Window System
- Line printer services

Client/server

TCP/IP application layer services are often referred to as having a **client/server** relationship (Figure 13.1). This means an application layer service consists of two complementary parts, one on each of the two nodes exchanging information. The originator of a connection is called the **client** and the receiver the **server**.

A server application layer service waits for incoming connections or **requests**. Client services make connections or requests to servers as required. Once the connection[†] is agreed and opened, clients make requests and servers give **responses** or replies to those requests. Servers do not initiate a transaction. Server software cannot communicate directly with server software and client software cannot communicate with client software. So, to establish connections and transfer information, there must be both client and server software operating at the application layer.

Since the application server is software, a computer with an operating system that supports multitasking (OS/2, UNIX or VMS for example) can have many different types of server and client software running at the same time. So, these multitasking computers can manage multiple connections into their services and make outgoing connections to other computer services in what appears externally to be a peer-to-peer fashion, but is based on a client/server architecture for each conversation.

Therefore two different pieces of software are required to enable communication. For example, if you were using a Telnet terminal, both the local computer you were using and the remote computer you were communicating with would require Telnet, but you require the Telnet client and the host end requires the Telnet server. This is true for FTP, TFTP and BOOTP; in fact most TCP/IP services operate this way.

Because of the close UNIX relationship with TCP/IP, the server software is usually referred to as a **daemon**, so the Telnet server is usually called **telnetd** (pronounced 'telnet-dee'), meaning the Telnet daemon, and the FTP server is called **ftpd** and so on. For a connection to work between two nodes, one must have Telnet and the other telnetd, or one must have FTP and the other ftpd. Table 13.1 lists client/server software modules.

Telnet

Before the PC became so common, users would connect to a computer using a dumb terminal. The terminal provided a keyboard and screen to display output from programs that ran on the computer – so-called inter-

---

[†]Connections need only be established in a connection-oriented environment. Connectionless systems just send requests and responses.

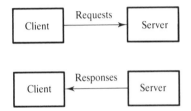

Figure 13.1 Client/server architecture.

active working. Computer data networks grew as users wished to access many computers without having a separate connection to each. Telnet was designed to provide this service, allowing users to access all computers that were connected to the 'network'. The remote host would appear to them, from their local host, as though they were attached directly to it. They would use standard commands on their local machine to access any type of computer.

Telnet is a terminal access application layer interface. It provides terminal access support for dumb terminals communicating with remote hosts. These terminals can connect in three ways:

(1)   Real terminals connected to TCP/IP Telnet 'terminal servers'

(2)   Real terminals directly connected to hosts running TCP/IP

(3)   PCs running both terminal emulation and TCP/IP software

The standard for the Telnet service does not provide terminal emulation in its own right. In practice, this is only apparent to programmers, as the command telnet for end users usually causes terminal emulation to be invoked on top of the standard client Telnet service.

The role of Telnet

The main functionality that Telnet aims to provide is compatibility between computer systems so that client-end applications can gain terminal access to a remote server-end host without having prior knowledge of how to support any particular terminal type. The specific use is

Table 13.1 The client/server software modules.

Client	Server	Port	Description
Telnet	telnetd	23	Terminal access services
FTP	ftpd	20/21	File transfer services
TFTP	tftpd	69	Remote boot services
LPR (721-731)	lpd	515	Remote print services
SMTP	smtpd	25	Electronic mail services
rlogin	rlogind	513	Remote login services

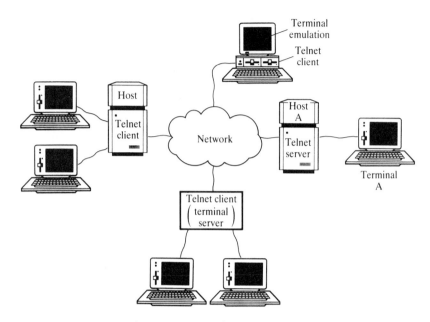

Figure 13.2 Telnet architecture.

to allow remote terminals to connect to an application server host, maybe through an intermediate computer, and appear as if they are terminals directly connected to that host.

The service the user sees is the terminal service of the remote host. Once connected, they are validated by userids and passwords and then are allowed access to authorized applications. The remote service is represented in the best possible fashion on their local terminal screen. They must know how to operate a terminal for the computer they access; no attempt is made to map two different computing command environments, only to translate the different keyboard and display mechanics to generate those commands and display the results.

The Telnet server has to make a connecting Telnet client appear like any other terminal user to its host operating system by activating all the necessary validation programs and creating an environment for each logical connection made to it. Once a user logs out from the Telnet server's host computer, it is also responsible for terminating the logical connection that was in place across the network.

In Figure 13.2, all users are able to access host A with the same functionality as if they were directly connected to the host as, for example, is terminal A. For such a connection to appear to the host as if it is a directly attached terminal, a reliable transport layer is required, so Telnet normally operates over TCP.

The environment of Telnet

Telnet was designed for an environment of many different terminal types, computer architectures and operating systems – a 'heterogeneous' environment. Many types of real terminal must be supported. No assumptions should be made about what type of terminal will wish to communicate with which type of host. Even though many terminals operate to the same basic character sets (ASCII), their enhanced features are incompatible.

Telnet attempts to match terminal and host systems. When a terminal first makes a connection, the protocols start by assuming that the terminal is the most basic type possible: a terminal that has a keyboard, produces line-by-line print output, uses local echo and uses the ASCII character set with a few simple control characters, such as carriage return, line feed, and form feed. This is a definition of the old TTY terminal (Teletype). This basic definition is referred to as the **Network Virtual Terminal** (NVT). Irrespective of how sophisticated the real terminal is, at initial connection time it is no grander than the NVT. As an NVT, all terminals can communicate with most types of host computer†; it is the basic level of compatibility between most terminals and computers.

Starting from this basic level of communication, Telnet provides a standard mechanism for agreeing the functionality of the real terminal and how it is to be used with this application. This process is referred to as **Telnet negotiation**. Before describing this in detail, we must know how Telnet distinguishes information that is flowing between the end users and their applications from control information that is to be interpreted by the client and server of Telnet itself.

Exchanging Telnet control information

In layered communications protocols, exchanging control information between peer layers at the two ends of a link would usually be by messages specifically reserved for the purpose and identified by a layer header, in this case the application layer header. Telnet does not have an application header as such. Rather, to communicate between the client and server, it uses special control commands that are inserted into the user data field of TCP and hence carried to the remote Telnet application layer service.

To explain how control information is carried, we can consider the handling of the < Break > key. Pressing the < Break > key is often used to interrupt processes on a computer by attracting the attention of the operating system. If we consider < Break > in the asynchronous ASCII

---

†Some computers assume a full-screen or forms-based system and cannot work well with TTYs. Many applications can only be successfully operated from a full-screen terminal.

V.24/EIA232 environment, it is not a character; it does not have an 8-bit code allocated to it. Hitting the <Break> key causes a binary 0 (high) signal to be placed on the transmit line of a terminal for at least 200 milliseconds. As a character on a line running at 9600 bits per second only lasts for around 1 millisecond, this is an abnormal signal state. It is not practical to use the same kind of approach to send a <Break> signal across shared media such as dedicated point-to-point lines or a LAN. The <Break> has to be encoded and transmitted in a standard message across the network. This is one of the functions of Telnet.

Telnet reserves a character which it inserts in the data stream when transmitting to the remote Telnet application layer to indicate that it is sending special control sequences. This character is decimal 255 or hexadecimal 0xFF. It is referred to as IAC meaning 'interpret as command'. Following IAC will be one of the commands shown in Table 13.2.

For example, if a user presses the <Break> key, the Telnet client will send IAC,BRK or 255,243 (decimal) in a TCP segment that will be received by the appropriate host. The Telnet server software, on receiving IAC,BRK, will translate it into an action that is allocated to <Break> in that operating system, for example to cause an interrupt to the relevant application program. Telnet only provides the mechanism to send the <Break>; what it means when it arrives at the server is outside the specification.

Having described the function of IAC, we can now look at how it is used in more detail.

Telnet negotiation

To take advantage of the more sophisticated features that the real terminal may have available and which the host may also be able to understand, Telnet performs negotiation, a process of building up terminal capability beyond the very basic NVT. It uses a special set of commands, IAC DO, IAC DON'T, IAC WILL, IAC WON'T (Table 13.2), as a conversational way of negotiating the facilities that both terminal and host can support. Some of these can be further modified by the options parameters listed in Table 13.3. This negotiation can be complex and arduous and may take many seconds. The frequently used shortcut is the special command IAC,DO,TERMINAL TYPE whereby one end of the connection suggests that a manufacturer's real terminal type is used.

If negotiation fails, the terminal can still interact with the remote host, but only enjoy the facilities of the NVT, which will only give line-by-line operation. The basis of negotiation is through the request for the remote end to use a feature, for example:

IAC, DO, ECHO

which is 'I want you to echo', to which the response could be,

IAC, WILL, ECHO

Table 13.2 Telnet commands.

Code	Decimal value	Explanation
SE	240	End of subnegotiation
NOP	241	No operation
DM	242	Data Mark
BRK	243	Break
IP	244	Interrupt Process; send an interrupt to the remote process
AO	245	Abort Output; clears all pending output until the next command prompt.
AYT	246	Are You There; requests the remote end to return some evidence that it is still there
EC	247	Erase Character; erase characters to the left
EL	248	Erase Line; erase the current line of data.
GA	249	Go Ahead; a half-duplex mode of operation required for terminals that can only transmit or receive at any one time
SB	250	Start subnegotiation
WILL	251	WILL negotiation command
WON'T	252	WON'T negotiation command
DO	253	DO negotiation command
DON'T	254	DON'T negotiation command
IAC	255	Interpret as command (the following)

which is 'I will echo' or,

IAC, WON'T, ECHO

'I won't echo'. If the request is negative the originator is now unable to change from local echo mode to remote echo mode. Once a feature has been refused, forcing the requester to take responsibility, it cannot be renegotiated.

The other way negotiation can go is with the 'I want to do' something or

IAC, WILL, ECHO

This is indicating 'I want to echo'. The response could be:

IAC, DO, ECHO

which is, 'OK go ahead and echo' or

IAC, DON'T, ECHO

which is 'Don't echo'.

Through these simple negotiation commands which are special character sequences placed in the data stream, Telnet is able to negotiate for a level of service, or maybe just control when echoing or some other feature is turned on or off. There are several other features for which Telnet has reserved command codes (Table 13.2).

Table 13.3 Telnet options.

Telnet options	Code	Explanation
Transmit binary	0	Ignore control codes in data
Echo	1	Character echoing
RCP	2	Reconnect option
Suppress-go-ahead	3	Suppress the half duplex go ahead function
NAMS	4	Negotiate Approximate Message Size
STATUS	5	View status of Telnet options
Timing-mark	6	Used to help on problems with type ahead
RCTE	7	Used with long echo delay circuits
NAOL	8	Negotiate output line width
NAOP	9	Negotiate page output size
NAOCRD	10	Used with NAOL and NAOP
NAOHTS	11	Negotiate horizontal tabstops
NAOHTD	12	Horizontal tabstop definition
NAOFFD	13	Form feed disposition option
NAOVTS	14	Vertical tabstop option
NAOVTD	15	Vertical tabstop disposition
NAOLFD	16	Linefeed disposition
EXTEND-ASCII	17	Extended ASCII option
LOGOUT	18	Logout option
BM	19	Byte Macro option
DET	20	Telnet Data Entry Terminal
SUPDUP	21	SUPDUP display controls
SUPDUP-OUTPUT	22	Used with SUPDUP
SEND-LOCATION	23	Send location id to Telnet server
TERMINAL-TYPE	24	Terminal type option
END-OF-RECORD	25	To alter the end of record character
TUID	26	User identification
OUTMRK	27	Output mark
EXOPL	255	To allow for more options...

Some options require further levels of negotiation or **subnegotiation**. Subnegotiation is required for a particular activity when parameters must be agreed, for example when screen sizes must be agreed. It is performed by the normal process of agreeing on an option through the DO or WILL command that is acknowledged with WILL or DO respectively. Then one end of the connection will send IAC,SB followed by the relevant parameters and then the SE command, such as

IAC, DO, STATUS
IAC, WILL, STATUS

⋮

some delay

⋮

One host may later ask for the current Telnet status of the other with:

IAC, SB, STATUS, SEND, IAC, SE

The other host replies 'My status is' as follows:

    IAC SB STATUS IS
    WILL ECHO
    DO SUPPRESS-GO-AHEAD
    WILL STATUS
    DO STATUS
    IAC SE

Negotiation happens mainly at the start of a connection, and in most cases is very rapid through the IAC,DO,TERMINAL TYPE, although further subnegotiation may occur at any time through the life of the connection. Apart from handling negotiation and these special characters, Telnet sends user data in both directions between workstation and host. This data is passed to the normal terminal operating system environment.

Telnet security

An important feature of Telnet is the level of security it provides. A user connecting to a host using Telnet will be vetted in the same way as any other interactive user. So logging in normally requires a user id and password.

One feature of operating systems is that, by default, users connecting across a network are prevented from logging in as a **privileged user**. Privileged use can be further restricted to a single directly attached console port. Often this means that somebody attempting to log in as a privileged user using Telnet will be disconnected immediately. This, of course, is a security feature to make it more difficult to gain illegal access to the operating system features of a host.

Telnet carries user information including login ids and passwords in TCP segments without encryption. Access to network cables and to monitoring equipment may be a security issue in some environments.

Telnet protocol traces

Appendix H shows actual traces taken from an operational network using the Telnet protocol. In that example, we show Ethernet frames in hexadecimal without the preamble or the CRC. The table beneath the frame gives a breakdown of the fields in the frame and their values. For a further explanation of the format of these examples, see Appendix F.

This example shows a user (system) logging in to a host. The frames are generated by the user typing their userid and the replies and acknowledgements to this. Notice the Telnet negotiation in certain frames and messages coming back from the host.

Table 13.4 Listing a directory.

Operating system	Directory command
VMS	dir
DOS	dir
Windows 3	(Click on folder)
UNIX	ls
Finder (Macintosh)	(Double click on folder)

File transfer protocol

It is common to wish to transfer files between different types of computers, but to do this a number of problems need to be dealt with. Moving the data is straightforward, but what happens when it arrives? The major problems are that computers store data in different formats, their operating systems use different commands for similar functions and they have different security restrictions to prevent unauthorized access to programs and data. These considerations apply to data files; they do not begin to address the differences between executable files in two environments (nor does FTP or any other file transfer system).

FTP was designed to provide a service for applications that want to move files between networked computers. It provides the basic application layer services needed to move files; it does *not* define the interface[†] to a user, so a true user application is required to provide the interface between the user and FTP. Although you invariably type 'FTP' to perform file transfer, you are invoking an interface program as well as the relevant FTP software.

Like a terminal service, a file transfer service must not introduce errors. FTP requires a reliable communications service, so it uses the TCP transport service.

The main function of FTP is to reduce or remove the incompatibilities between the handling of files in different operating systems. For example, if you connect to a remote computer, your first requirement might be to list all the files in a directory. The commands to do this differ for different operating systems (Table 13.4).

Listing a directory is part of file management. As well as file transfer, FTP must provide basic file management functions in a standard way. When a user on one computer operating system is communicating with a computer using a different operating system, the directory listing command requires translation. This is true for most other functions, such as change directory, login, create directory, delete file and so on.

A major facility of FTP is therefore to deal with the translation necessary to provide compatibility between different operating systems.

[†]Again, such is the relationship between UNIX and TCP/IP that the standard UNIX user interface for FTP has been copied to other environments.

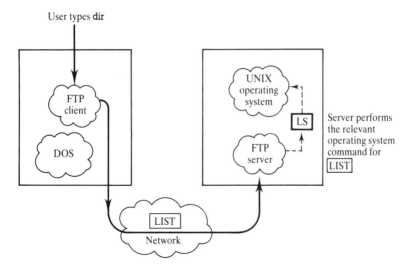

Figure 13.3 FTP command translation for a directory listing.

The way FTP does this is through a set of defined **network standard commands**. A standard list of common functions is defined for FTP to ensure that, irrespective of the operating system, the command passed across the network is always the same.

Figure 13.3 shows conceptually how FTP deals with this translation. In this example, an MS-DOS user is communicating with a UNIX operating system. The MS-DOS system user wishes to see a list of all files in the directory on the remote computer. On an MS-DOS-based PC, the user would instinctively use the dir command, the normal command to display a directory with MS-DOS. The FTP client converts this request into an FTP command which is LIST. LIST is the standard FTP command from an FTP client to an FTP server to request a directory listing. When the server software receives this command, it performs the necessary UNIX commands to get a directory listing and then returns the output to the client.

Table 13.5 shows a list of the standard FTP commands. These commands are the actual ASCII uppercase characters sent across the network in the data field of TCP segments. In practice, they can be seen in text with a network analyser as they are transmitted. This can be a powerful aid to resolving incompatibilities between implementations.

The list of commands in Table 13.5 is not complete, but these are the most common provided by most implementations. Knowing these commands is of no direct value to a user; they are only used by the FTP client and server software to communicate with each other. But these command names are sometimes visible to the user as FTP implementations will display them if tracing or debugging is switched on. Again, the value in knowing the commands comes in resolving system incompatibilities.

Table 13.5 FTP client/server commands.

Command	Description
USER (userid)<cr,lf>	User ID to be logged in
PASS (password)<cr,lf>	The user's password
ACCT<cr,lf>	Account information
CWD (directory)<cr,lf>	Change working directory
CDUP<cr,lf>	Change to parent directory
QUIT<cr,lf>	Logout
PORT(socket)<cr,lf>	Define the socket to be used
TYPE type<cr,lf>	Type definition
RETR(filename)<cr,lf>	Retrieve a file
STOR(filename)<cr,lf>	Send a file
DELE(filename)<cr,lf>	Delete the file
RMD(directory name)<cr,lf>	Delete the directory
MKD(directory name)<cr,lf>	Create the directory
LIST(directory name)<cr,lf>	A directory listing for users
NLST(directory name)<cr,lf>	A directory listing for programs
STAT<cr,lf>	Status
HELP<cr,lf>	List of these commands available on server

The FTP server has its own way of responding to these commands. Its responses come in two parts:

(Numeric value)(Response string)

For example:

230 User logged in, proceed

The FTP server sends these commands back to an FTP client. The number and the string always go together and mean the same thing. The numeric value is for use by the FTP client or by an application program controlling the client. The string can be displayed without further processing for human consumption. Common responses are:

220   Service ready
331   User name OK, need password
230   User logged in, proceed
150   File status OK, about to open data connection
226   Closing data connection
200   Command OK
550   Access denied

Figure 13.4 follows through a typical FTP transaction showing the prompt to the user, the commands the user types, the commands the FTP client sends to the FTP server and the responses back from the FTP server.

Notice that the dir command did not immediately produce a LIST command; first a PORT command was issued. This is because FTP uses

User prompts	User types	FTP client>	<FTP server
$	ftp oz		
			220 Service ready
Enter user name:	me	USER me	
			331 User name OK, need password
Enter password:	blob	PASS blob	
			230 User logged in, proceed
ftp>	dir	PORT (socket)	
			200 Command OK
		LIST	
			150 Opening data connection for (LIST) (socket)
<<<<Directory listing is transferred to the user over the new socket>>>>			
			226 Closing data connection
ftp>			

Figure 13.4 Typical set of FTP transactions.

separate logical connections, one for control and another for data. This is why FTP server has two well-known ports, 21 for control and 20 for data transfer. When any request is made to transfer information in either direction, a control message is sent to port 21 and a separate logical connection is built for data transfer to port 20. The response to a dir command returns data, so the client first has to tell the server to which socket to send the data response and it should not be the command port on the client. When a multiple file transfer is performed, a new logical data transfer connection using a new client port is created and closed for each file transferred.

Using FTP

The FTP definition details the commands used between the FTP client and FTP server software; it does not define the commands the users see. Although there is a general consensus of which FTP commands are used, there can be significant variations between different manufacturers' user interface presentations of FTP. Normally the commands given to the user are a combination of commands they would see on their local operating system and equivalent UNIX commands.

A common mistake by new users is to believe that the commands they use when in FTP are from the local operating system, indeed to believe that they are at the operating system prompt rather than within an application program called ftp. Though commands in the FTP client software look like commands to the operating system, quite often their syntax is just sufficiently different to cause annoyance when you are familiar with using a command in a certain way. For example, in DOS

Table 13.6 Typical FTP user commands.

Command	Usage
user	Login a new user
dir	Display a directory listing
ls	Display a directory listing
pwd	Display which directory we are looking at
cd	Change directory
get	Get or receive a file
put	Send a file
mget	Get multiple files
mput	Put multiple files
send	Send a file
receive	Get or receive a file
binary	Switch to binary
text	Switch to text
?	Help
!	Switch to local operating system without closing FTP
rmdir	Delete directory
open	Make a connection
quit	Close the connection
status	Show the status of the connection
remotehelp	Show the FTP commands implemented on the server

```
cd\tcpbk\msword
```

(without spaces) is valid. While the same command is used in ftp, in some implementations a space must be included:

```
cd \tcpbk\msword
```

Common FTP commands

Looking at the commands in Table 13.6, you will notice several commands have the same function, for example, get and receive. It is common for a number of the commands to be represented in the form they would be for different operating systems (ls, dir). This makes it easier to use any implementation of ftp without completely relearning the commands. But once again differences in exact syntax cause frustration.

Unlike a normal OS command line, in FTP multiple operations with **wildcards** (use of * to mean 'any') have their own commands. When trying to transfer all files ending with the extension .doc, the normal reaction is to try

```
get *.doc
```

This will fail because the get command does not support wildcards. The commands to use for multiple actions are those beginning with m, which stands for multiple, for example mget, mdelete.

The FTP network standard commands do not directly support multiple file operations. The m user commands have to take special action to provide it. Normally, an m command will perform a directory listing, unbeknown to the user, to get a list of files. Then it builds up the whole task with individual specific file actions on that list. These m commands often refuse to treat the * in the way your favourite operating system does. Files with extensions may be ignored with a single *; files without extensions may be ignored when using *.*; the * may not be accepted when you expect it to be.

The remotehelp command is another good command for causing confusion. One might expect it to provide help with accessing the remote system. In practice, it provides a list of the FTP network standard commands that are available on the FTP server (STOR, RETR, USER) and of course the end user has no interest in these! They are important for checking compatibility between different manufacturers' FTP implementations.

FTP file conversions

The commonest mistake newcomers to FTP make is with its file conversion capabilities. By default, FTP assumes you are transferring text files between computers. Text files are represented in a standard format during transmission and are converted to and from this format by the sending and receiving hosts. One conversion function ensures that the file has the correct end-of-line sequences, so it remains revisable as it is transferred from one operating system to another, as shown in Figure 13.5. FTP on an IBM host will also convert between ASCII and EBCDIC, if required.

This is fine so long as the file you are moving is text and not a binary data file or an executable file (sometimes also called an image file in FTP). FTP cannot tell the difference between different types of files, so unless the user tells FTP to operate in binary mode, it will transfer a binary file and do its best to translate it as it would a text file suitable for editing and displaying on the destination host. It adds end-of-line characters, carriage return and line feed (or just newline), in what it thinks are suitable places. This normally has the effect of making binary files unusable! If the file transferred is executable and has been put through this treatment, it will most likely cause a computer to hang or give unusual error messages when run!

If a binary file is to be transferred using FTP, the FTP user command binary should be issued before the put or get commands are used. Of course, binary mode can be used to transfer text files, but if this is done and the destination operating system is different from the source operating system, it is most likely that the files will no longer be in revisable form on the destination system or the text formatting will be unusual.

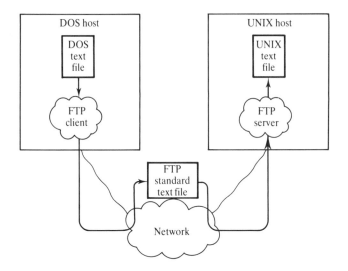

Figure 13.5 Text conversion in an FTP system.

Improving FTP

For the interface as just described, the FTP user must learn relatively obscure commands. It is a text-based interface from the early 1980s similar to the native interface to DOS or UNIX. It is a difficult interface for those who are not computer specialists, and even for those who are, it can be awkward due to the subtle differences in syntax of some commands and the differences between FTP implementations. For the average commercial user, this form of FTP is too cumbersome and one would expect it to be hidden by a front-end application program that interfaces to the file transfer facilities of the FTP application layer services.

With the growing use of graphical interfaces, as on the Apple Macintosh and with Windows or Presentation Manager for the PC, some recent TCP implementations are becoming easier to work with, as the syntactical issues which cause most user difficulty are hidden effectively.

FTP traces

Appendix I shows actual traces taken from an operational network using FTP. In that example, we show Ethernet frames in hexadecimal without the preamble or the CRC. The table beneath the frame gives a breakdown of the fields in the frame and their values. For a further explanation of the format of these examples, see Appendix F.

That example shows a user (system) logging in to a host. The frames are FTP requesting and transferring the user id and password, conducting port negotiation and preparing to transfer a directory listing.

Simple mail transfer protocol

For many years, the desire to use electronic mail has been strong. It can provide a quicker turn around than traditional mail and it can be used on most computer systems. Mail systems can be augmented to provide friendly services such as sending mail to groups of users, allowing word processors to transmit their files automatically, sending documents with the mail as attachments or handling registered mail so it is possible to know if and when the recipient has read an item.

The mail application layer in TCP/IP has undoubtedly helped in the development of the TCP/IP system itself by allowing information and ideas to be transferred freely throughout the Internet as draft RFCs.

SMTP is a service to allow mail packages to communicate with one another between different computers. As the name implies, it is a simple protocol. It operates in a similar way to FTP. The client sends ASCII-based commands to the server and the server responds with numeric and text responses as shown in Figure 13.6. Remember, such commands are intended for use between the SMTP client and server, not for end users.

As a moment's thought will show, mail has to be reliable, so SMTP uses TCP as its transport using well-known port 25.

The requests and responses shown in Figure 13.6 are carried in the data field of TCP, in ASCII, so a LAN analyser is able to display these transactions quite easily. Most mail systems have a debug option to help analyse problems. It allows the transactions to be viewed as they transfer between client and server.

Figure 13.7 shows a typical SMTP transaction. Notice that SMTP uses domain names (see Chapter 14) to identify hosts, and simply adds a

Client commands (minimum implementation)

Command	*Explanation*
HELO<Training>	A connection request from system training
MAIL FROM:<JIM@Training.edu>	From Jim on system training
RCPT TO:<Kevin@Sales.com>	Send to Kevin on system sales
DATA	The text DATA follows terminated by <cr,lf>.<cr.lf>
QUIT	Terminate this connection
RSET	Abort the connection
NOOP	No operation

Server responses (subset)

250 OK
251 User not local; will forward to <wherever>
550 Requested action not taken: mailbox unavailable
354 Start mail input; end with <cr,lf>. <cr.lf>
500 Syntax Error

Figure 13.6 SMTP commands and responses.

From client	From server
	220 Training.edu service Ready
MAIL FROM:<JIM@Training.edu>	
	250 OK
RCPT TO:<Kevin@Sales>	
	250 OK
DATA	
	354 Start mail input; end with <cr,lf>. <cr.lf>
This is the actual data that will be transmitted from JIM on the training system to Kevin on the sales systems.	
	250 OK
QUIT	
	250 OK

Figure 13.7 Typical SMTP transaction.

user's name from the domain name of the host using the @ symbol. So Maggie@Training.edu is Maggie on host training.edu. It is also possible to use IP addresses instead of domain names if necessary. SMTP has to get the IP address of the remote host (from the domain name system or a hosts file) so it can deliver the mail.

Using SMTP

A user will not normally see the commands just considered. The user will be operating behind a manufacturer's user interface program, designed to make the service easier to use. Behind the scenes, the user interface program will be generating client commands and handling responses from the server.

Mail servers do not instantly attempt to deliver mail messages but check to see if there are any available at regular intervals, typically about 30 minutes. At this time a mail system will check its mail directories to see if there is outgoing information to send or received information to deliver to individual users. It will then perform the actions necessary to deliver it. Figure 13.8 shows an example of a front end used with SMTP.

At first sight, these actions might seem similar to the International Standard X.400 (Plattner *et al.*, 1991) or MOTIS mail system. But there are some very important differences. X.400 distributes mail across a network of store and forward message switches. The unit of transmission between switches is the complete mail message. Although SMTP can use store and forward gateways, it normally delivers mail directly from originator user host to each recipient user host across a reliable TCP/IP connection. The unit of transmission is the TCP segment, not the message. For a single large message, SMTP should deliver faster. On the other hand, in X.400 the network of mail switches can expand and optimize the distribution list; the source need deliver the message to the network only once. With SMTP the source mail system must deliver the message to

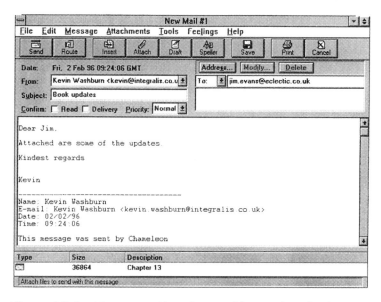

Figure 13.8 Netmanage Chameleon Mail front-end used with SMTP.

each receiving host across a separate TCP connection. The receiving host will create multiple copies for all recipients on its machine (on receipt of multiple RCPT commands).

It is possible to drive SMTP manually through a terminal connection as it accepts straight ASCII-based commands as shown above. This is not a recommendation, but an indication of how simple it is to communicate with the SMTP server protocol. It might have a diagnostic use for those perverse enough to try it.

SMTP and the domain name system

SMTP mail relies on the domain name system for correct operation. But this use of DNS also allows an organization to issue mail addresses that show only a company domain, for example

```
webmaster@integralis.co.uk
```

This mail address is independent of particular machine names in the company; it means Integralis can have more than one mail server, for reliability or for load sharing. Those mail servers will act as POP servers (see below) for company mail users, or they will forward incoming mail to the correct machine for that user. External correspondents do not need to know the internal routing details.

This flexibility is provided by Mail Exchange (MX) records in the DNS (Chapter 14). When an SMTP system attempts to deliver mail, it asks the DNS for all MX records for that domain. For example, integralis.co.uk returns:

```
integralis.co.uk    MX    5    mimesweeper.integralis.co.uk
integralis.co.uk    MX   10    mailhub0.integralis.co.uk
integralis.co.uk    MX   50    eros.britain.eu.net
integralis.co.uk    MX   70    ben.britain.eu.net
```

The number after the MX record indicates the order of preference, with a lower number indicating higher preference. So, by preference, all Integralis mail is delivered to `mimesweeper.integralis.co.uk`. If that machine is out of order, the sender will try other Integralis machines; if the line between `eu.net` and `integralis.co.uk` is faulty, the two `britain.eu.net` machines will be tried. When the line becomes operational, they are programmed to forward all waiting mail to the `integralis.co.uk` domain.

Post Office Protocol (POP)

The SMTP mail system was designed in an environment of mini- and mainframe computers where users' mailboxes were accessible most of the time. SMTP sends mail to port 25 on a mail server expecting it to be available; users cannot request mail from a mail server using SMTP. In a PC environment, when mailboxes on PCs are not available for significant lengths of time, it is better to have a store and forward mail service where users can collect mail from a mail store. This is what the Post Office Protocol was designed to provide. POP is a protocol which can connect to a mailbox system, validate the user and retrieve incoming messages which have been posted there. Outgoing mail is still posted from the users' system using SMTP; mail is sent using SMTP and retrieved using POP.

POP is a simple application protocol based on a command and reply, client/server relationship. Since its introduction (as POP), POP has been revised to POP version 2 (POP2) and later to POP version 3 (POP3).

The POP3 commands sent by a POP3 client to a POP3 server are as follows:

Mandatory POP3 commands

USER *name*	This is used to introduce the user 'name'
PASS *string*	The user's password for validation
QUIT	Delete any messages marked for deletion and close the connection
STAT	This command is used to gather information which can be implementation dependent but as a minimum it should give the number of messages in the mailbox and the total size of those messages
LIST [msg]	This commands calls for a list of the messages waiting at the POP3 server indicating the size of each. Again detail of the information returned can be implementation dependent. Example:

Client> LIST
Server< +OK 2 messages (320 octets)
Server< 1 120
Server< 2 200

RETR msg   This command retrieves messages from the server. Example:

Client> RETR 1
Server< +OK 120 octets
Server< the POP3 server sends the entire message here>
Server<.

Note that the end of the message is defined by a period '.' as the first character on a blank line

DELE msg   Marks messages for deletion. The message defined in the 'msg' parameter is marked

NOOP   No operation

LAST   Returns the number of the last message in the mailbox

RSET   Unmarks messages marked for deletion

Optional POP3 commands

RPOP user   Can be used instead of the password command to allow a user access to a POP3 server based on the address of the client s/he connects from (i.e. as with .rhosts on Berkeley UNIX systems)

TOP msg n   Asks the server to send the heading of the message 'msg' and 'n' lines of the message body

POP3 server replies

+OK   Command accepted

-ERR   Command failed

Example POP3 session

This example shows the client and server responses for a simple transaction where two messages are on the server with a total size of 320 octets. Each message is read and then deleted from the server.

Server< <waiting for connection on TCP port 110>
    ...
Client><open connection>
Server< +OK Integralis POP3 server ready (Comments to: PostMaster@integralis.co.uk)
Client> USER penny
Server< +OK Hello there penny
Client> PASS secret
Server< +OK penny's maildrop has 2 messages (320 octets)

```
Client>  STAT
Server<  +OK 2 320
Client>  LIST
Server<  +OK 2 messages (320 octets)
Server<  1 120
Server<  2 200
Server<  .
Client>  RETR 1
Server<  +OK 120 octets
Server<  <the POP3 server sends message 1>
Server<  .
Client>  DELE 1
Server<  +OK message 1 deleted
Client>  RETR 2
Server<  +OK 200 octets
Server<  <the POP3 server sends message 2>
Server<  .
Client>  DELE 2
Server<  +OK message 2 deleted
Client>  QUIT
```

R commands

The r commands (remote) are commonly supplied with TCP/IP implementations. These commands were intended as a simple mechanism for establishing connections between computers of the same type (UNIX), and were on a network where users were trusted. The security, or more accurately, potential lack of security, is a key concern with these commands. When they were developed, it was assumed that any user with access to them would already have passed some security check on another host. Since the environment was one of trust, the user could then be granted equivalent access rights on remote machines using the r commands. With TCP/IP readily available on PCs these assumptions are far from true. A DOS PC does no authorization check and is difficult to protect fully from unauthorized use by a knowledgeable person.

r commands do not have the negotiation facilities of Telnet, so the remote host has to know, or be configured to accept, the terminal type used. The common r commands are:

rlogin	Like Telnet, it allows connection to a remote computer
rsh	Allows a command to be executed on a remote computer
rexec	Allows a command to be executed on a remote computer

rcp Allows files to be copied between remote computers

`rlogin` provides a terminal connection service similar to Telnet. On PCs, it therefore requires terminal emulation software to communicate with the remote host. In a situation where a terminal is connected directly to one host and its users connect to a remote host, the remote host must support that type of terminal for successful operation, as no negotiation is performed.

Compared with Telnet or FTP services, user validation on r commands is minimal. Furthermore, it is impossible to be definite about the way validation works with r commands. To access a host using the r commands normally only requires an IP address and user name to be in one of two files on the remote host, either in .rhosts or in rhosts.equiv. This varies between implementations, so you have to study the manufacturer's literature to be sure. Often you find that these commands are not protected at all or are almost impossible to get to work.

So, `rlogin` allows a user to access information on a remote machine. When connecting to a remote machine as the `rlogin` client, the client will issue the user's name and IP address or node name to the `rlogin` server when the connection is attempted. The `rlogin` server checks the supplied information against the entries in the .rhosts and rhosts.equiv file for that user. If there is a match, then access is allowed, if not, then access is denied. On PC implementations one of the options is to include the user id in a configuration file. This saves the user from typing it each time they log in. It also effectively dispenses with one small security feature.

Using r commands

In a trusted environment, the user can simply make a connection to a remote host by typing `rlogin hostname`. There is no need for logging in, and where the terminal type is the same there is no need to configure terminal types, so connection is rapid and users can quickly switch between systems at will. It is ideal for a development or maintenance environment where resources are on many machines. But there are few large commercial networks which can afford to be so open. Usually, security is important and terminal types vary, so the security and negotiation functions of Telnet become essential.

None the less, these command can be useful for system managers and other trustworthy system maintainers: rsh allows them to initiate commands on a remote computer without having to log in. rexec and rcp operate in the same fashion. rcp copies files between two machines. The initiator may be at a third machine that is neither the source nor destination of the transfer.

The issue is that putting any IP addresses and user names into the two key files lowers the defences against anyone with the knowledge to load r commands onto a PC and to configure it with a correct user id. Some PC implementations ask the user for a password locally before running an r command, but of course this password is contained in a file on the local PC and therefore will not defeat the knowledgeable attacker. Many suppliers' manuals recommend that PC IP addresses are not put in the key security files and that r commands are not available to PC users.

The latest versions of UNIX have new security features which prevent activities by networked users. It is possible to indicate a degree of trust of a particular user id and IP address. This will help reduce some of the problems with r commands. But in the end it depends not on the availability of advanced security features, but on understanding and applying the features to your environment through careful planning and system configuration.

Trivial file transfer protocol

The **Trivial File Transfer Protocol** (TFTP), as its name suggests, is a basic protocol. It was designed to be a small, easy-to-implement program. Because of this it lacks most of the features found in FTP and normally operates over UDP, the unreliable service. It must therefore carry out its own error correction. TFTP is seldom used directly by users as a service, but is more often used by machines for downloading programs and files. It cannot list directories and rarely has any provision for effective user authentication.

Authentication is usually performed through files on the destination host which normally need have only the IP address of the client machine and perhaps a user id. These files are usually .rhosts or rhosts.equiv, the same as used for the r commands but this is implementation dependent.

As TFTP does not use TCP, it has to manage its own error correction. For this, it uses a simple positive acknowledge protocol with time-out. If a datagram gets lost, the sender will time-out and try again. Normally datagrams contain exactly 512 octets. If the data is less than 512 octets, it is considered to be the last datagram for that file and so indicates that the transmission of the file is complete. The protocol uses its own block numbering scheme at the application layer above UDP. A block number starting at 1 is incremented for each block transmitted to identify if any are dropped. Major errors will cause TFTP connections to fail. An error is reported through the transmission of an error message. There are five types of TFTP message, shown in Table 13.7.

The initial request is made to the well-known port 69 for TFTP, but the server will return a new port which subsequent transactions will use. Figure 13.9 shows an example of a TFTP transaction and the error message. The format of the read and write request are the same and the mode field is used to distinguish between the different types of file that can be

Table 13.7 Types of TFTP message.

Opcode	Command
1	Read request (RRQ)
2	Write request (WRQ)
3	Acknowledgement (ACK)
4	Data (DATA)
5	Error (ERROR)

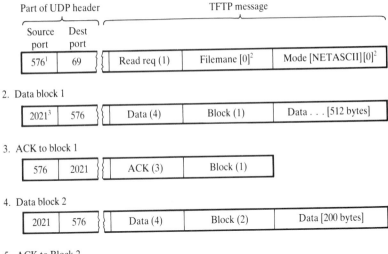

(a)

1. Read request

2. Data block 1

3. ACK to block 1

4. Data block 2

5. ACK to Block 2

(b) Error message

Possible error codes
0 Not defined
1 File not found
2 Access violation
3 Disk full
4 Illegal operation
5 Unknown transfer ID

Notes
[1] 576 is a randomly chosen port number not already in use by this host.
[2] Strings are terminated by null octets, shown as [0].
[3] 2021 is a randomly chosen port number not already used.

Figure 13.9 TFTP transactions, also showing the port numbers used in the UDP header.

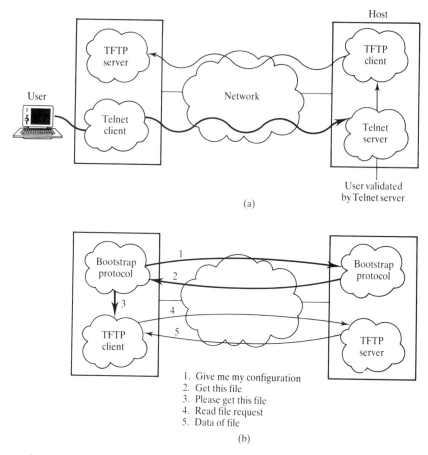

Figure 13.10 (a) Recommended usage of TFTP for improved security, and (b) TFTP with a bootstrap protocol.

transferred. The options this field can take are NETASCII, BINARY or MAIL. These options are transferred as words in ASCII terminated by a null.

Using TFTP

TFTP is not normally used for user-oriented file transfer as its facilities are too basic and its authentication mechanisms are, at best, suspect. It is often recommended that if TFTP is the only way, the user first accesses the remote host using Telnet. Once the access is approved by Telnet security, the user then uses the TFTP client on that remote system to connect back to their own originating host, before transferring files. This eliminates the need for a TFTP server on the remote host (Figure 13.10a). Unless automated behind some sort of front end, this type of convoluted communications activity is incomprehensible to the casual commercial computer user.

The major use for TFTP is as a bootstrap protocol. As it has small memory requirements and works with UDP, it can easily be configured into PROMs and installed on LAN cards. When a node is powered on or initialized the TFTP protocol will automatically connect to a server and download programs from that server. These programs could include a full TCP/IP protocol stack for other operations. Examples of these are shown in Figure 13.10(b).

Boot protocol

BOOTP was originally created for loading diskless computers. It has been designed to obtain all the information required for a computer to become fully operational on a TCP/IP network.

A diskless node may not be able to store its IP address, or the programs which make up its sophisticated operating system, or the TCP/IP network code. BOOTP allows such a node to broadcast requests onto a network and obtain the information required from a BOOTP server. A BOOTP server is a computer that listens for incoming BOOTP requests and generates responses from a database of configurations for the BOOTP clients on that network.

The BOOTP header is shown in Figure 13.11. These headers are sent in UDP datagrams from port 68 on the client to port 67 on a server. Each has a number of fields that, in the request, can show what information the client already knows, but primarily they are filled in by a server based on information in its database. The database file is usually called bootptab (in UNIX systems).

Op	HTYPE	HLEN	Hops
Transaction id			
Seconds		Unused flags	
Client IP address			
Your IP address			
Server IP address			
Gateway IP address			
Client hardware address (16 octets)			
Server host name (64 octets)			
Boot file name (128 octets)			
Vendor specific (64 octets)			

Figure 13.11 Format of the BOOTP datagram.

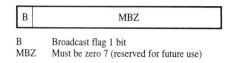

B   Broadcast flag 1 bit
MBZ   Must be zero 7 (reserved for future use)

Figure 13.12 Format of the 'flags' field.

On power up, the only information a diskless computer has regarding the network is often limited to the MAC address of its LAN card, as this is held in nonvolatile memory. As a BOOTP client, it will transmit a BOOTP message onto the network with the MAC address field filled in. It may also fill in generic information such as the type of operating system it is to load (UNIX, DOS or OS/2 for example), perhaps chosen by a user from a displayed menu.

A BOOTP server that receives such a request will check in its database looking for a match of the MAC address from the request datagram. It should find at least an IP address which will be returned to the client computer. As can be seen in Figure 13.11, there are other very useful fields that can be used in the BOOTP message to configure the client more fully.

The fields used in the BOOTP datagram are:

- *Operation – 1 octet*   message opcode / message type: 1 = BOOT REQUEST, 2 = BOOTREPLY.

- *HTYPE – 1 octet*   Used to identify the network type (1 = 10 Mbps Ethernet).

- *HLEN – 1 octet*   Length of hardware addresses (6 for 10 Mbps Ethernet).

- *HOPS – 1 octet*   Optionally used by gateways in cross-gateway booting.

- *Transaction ID – 4 octets*   Used to match this boot request with the responses it generates.

- *Seconds – 2 octets*   Filled in by the client; seconds elapsed since client started trying to boot.

- *Unused or flags – 2 octets*   The BOOTP 'unused' field was altered by RFC 1542 to become a 'flags' field with the format shown in Figure 13.12. Some clients cannot receive unicast IP datagrams until they have been configured with an IP address. Such clients should set the BROADCAST bit in the 'flags' field to 1 when they send a request. The BROADCAST bit will indicate to the server and BOOTP relay agent to broadcast replies to the client on the client's subnet.

- *Client IP address – 4 octets*   Filled in by client in bootrequest if known.

- *Your IP address – 4 octets*   Your (client) IP address; filled in by server if client does not know its own address (client address was 0).

- *Server IP address – 4 octets*   Returned in bootreply by server.

- *Gateway IP address – 4 octets*   Used in optional cross-gateway booting.

- *Client hardware address – 16 octets*   Filled in by client.

- *Server host name – 64 octets*   Optional server host name as a null terminated string.

- *Boot file name – 128 octets*   Boot file name as a null terminated string; in bootrequest, a 'generic' name such as UNIX or DOS to specify OS type for the reply (or null). Fully qualified directory-pathname on the server in bootreply.

- *Vendor-specific – 64 octets*   Optional vendor-specific area, for example could be hardware type/serial number on request, or 'capability'/remote file system handle on reply. This information may be set aside for use by a third-phase bootstrap or kernel.

The vendor-specific field, as one would expect, was intended for use for vendors' special requirements to enhance their own products, but it soon became evident that these fields could be used for more general information useful for any diskless client. A suggested use for these fields has now been standardized by RFC 1084.

The format of the vendor-specific field is that it starts with a 'magic cookie', which identifies the format of the fields following. If the format is to the standard defined in RFC 1084, the cookie is 99.130.83.99 (dotted decimal notation). Apart from any padding and end tags, this is followed by a number of fields that each have a one-octet tag field, a one-octet length field, and a many-octet value field. Table 13.8 shows the common fields available.

When a computer is initialized and needs to send a BOOTP datagram, it will have no idea of the IP address of BOOTP servers or the IP address of the network it is connected to, so it has no idea of the IP broadcast address on that network either. To get around this problem, a special address, 255.255.255.255, is used as the destination IP address. 0.0.0.0 is used as the source. In principle, this indicates that this datagram is destined for all hosts on all networks, but this address on TCP/IP systems has a special meaning: 'broadcast on the local cable (I do not know my network number)', so the BOOTP datagram is broadcast on the local cabling system by the LAN hardware.

This mechanism is fine provided the BOOTP server is located within that broadcast area. If it is in another area, across one or more routers,

Table 13.8 Common fields.

Name	Tag	Data	Description
Pad field	0	None	Used only for padding
Subnet mask field	1	4	Specifies the net and local subnet mask
Time offset field	2	4	Specifies the time offset of the local subnet in seconds from coordinated universal time (UTC); signed 32-bit integer
Gateway field	3	N octets	Specifies the IP addresses of $N/4$ gateways
Time server field	4	N octets	Specifies the IP addresses of $N/4$ time servers
IEN-116 name server field	5	N octets	Specifies the IP addresses of $N/4$ name servers
Domain name server field	6	N octets	Specifies the IP addresses of $N/4$ domain name servers
Log server field	7	N octets	Specifies the IP addresses of $N/4$ MIT-LCS UDP log server
Cookie/quote server field	8	N octets	Specifies the IP addresses of $N/4$ quote-of-the-day servers
LPR server field	9	N octets	Specifies the IP addresses of $N/4$ Berkeley 4BSD printer servers
Impress server field	10	N octets	Specifies the IP addresses of $N/4$ Impress servers
RLP server field	11	N octets	Specifies the IP addresses of $N/4$ resource location protocol servers
Hostname	12	N bytes of host name	Specifies the name of the client
Boot file size	13	2	A two-octet value (in network order) specifying the number of 512 octet blocks in the default boot file
Reserved fields	128–254	Undefined	Specifies additional site-specific information, to be interpreted on an implementation-specific basis
End field	255	None	Specifies end of usable data in the vendor information area. The rest of this field should be filled with PAD

these routers must recognize the broadcast IP address and choose whether or not to forward the BOOTP requests to all their connected networks. It is suggested in the BOOTP RFCs that routers which support the passing of BOOTP datagrams can be configured to define which individual networks they will forward them to, and that they should wait for a number of requests to be made before doing so. By waiting, they would then only relay these broadcasts if a local BOOTP server did not satisfy the request. The seconds field in the BOOTP header can assist with this decision as it indicates how long the client has been attempting to boot. One of the options when configuring a router port is whether IP broadcasts will be relayed on that port and what address is to be recognized as broadcast[†].

[†]Some early systems used 0.0.0.0 as the destination broadcast address. Continued use of this address is not encouraged.

Another dilemma with BOOTP is: how does a server respond to the client? The server cannot use the client's IP address as a destination for, in the most general case[†], the client does not yet know its IP address so the client will not respond to ARP requests. The server will already know the MAC address of the client as it is the MAC source address in the BOOTP request datagram, but not all systems allow programs to modify their ARP cache directly. To overcome these problems, it is common for the server response to be a broadcast back to the client if no IP address is given in the request, but if the client does know its IP address the response will be directly to that address, assuming that ARP will work. (The client must have enough software to run ARP.)

Since BOOTP uses UDP, BOOTP clients must add the reliability of getting the message to the BOOTP server. They will set a time-out and retransmit if that time-out matures.

Using BOOTP

These days, BOOTP is not used just for diskless workstations, but also for providing centralized control of IP addresses. It allows IP addresses to be managed from a single database and standard software configurations to be used even though the workstation may have disks.

System managers can define a standard software configuration that can be implemented on all systems without even having to configure an IP address on each workstation. The one key fact to obtain during installation is the physical (MAC) address of the LAN card for each installed system. This is the key to correct distribution of all other information. By this method, workstations can learn everything from their IP address to their default router, additional routers, domain name, host name, location of domain name servers and time servers.

Of course, the other use of BOOTP is for diskless workstations. In this case BOOTP is significant because it can allocate not just IP addresses for a node, but also the IP address of common hosts, routers and the name of program files to be downloaded. BOOTP does not download files; it will supply just the server IP address and the name of a file to be downloaded. TFTP is often used to download files indicated by BOOTP.

BOOTP can operate over routers if they support BOOTP relay or BOOTP assist. They will normally be configured with the server IP address that they should relay to and send requests only to that LAN and server.

DHCP

Dynamic Host Configuration Protocol (DHCP) is an enhancement to the BOOTP protocol. BOOTP requires manual configuration of the BOOTP

[†]It is possible for a computer to use BOOTP for information other than its IP address, in which case it could well already know its IP address.

table in a server. With BOOTP, a MAC address is allocated a fixed IP address; if the host with that MAC address moves to another network, the BOOTP table must be changed manually. If required, a DHCP server can allocate all IP internet parameters to a client workstation, without any preconfiguration specific to one device. This makes DHCP an excellent management tool for centralized configuration of TCP/IP systems. Also, DHCP has been designed to be backwards compatible with BOOTP systems so that it is possible for a BOOTP client to get a BOOTP response from a DHCP server, and for DHCP requests to be relayed by routers using BOOTP relay (BOOTP assist or BOOTP forwarding).

As DHCP is an enhancement to BOOTP, it uses the same port numbers as BOOTP; port 67 for the server and port 68 for the client.

The most significant facility provided by DHCP is its ability to *assign* individual IP addresses from a range. DHCP supports three mechanisms for IP address allocation, 'automatic allocation', 'dynamic allocation' and 'manual allocation'. Automatic allocation allows the DHCP server to permanently select an IP address from a predefined range when a new client requests configuration. With dynamic allocation the DHCP server allocates an address for a limited period, called a 'lease', and with manual allocation the network administrator assigns the IP address to be used for the client.

Dynamic allocation can be useful where a limited number of registered IP addresses are to be shared between a larger number of client computers. These computers can request, or lease, an address on a temporary basis when they need to use the Internet and return that address to the free pool once it is finished with.

The operation of DHCP is basically the same as BOOTP; a client broadcasts a DHCP datagram to all DHCP servers; servers reply with DHCP response datagrams containing an IP address and configuration parameters for the client. This basic process is enhanced by the DHCP functions which deal with negotiation of addresses and facilities. Multiple DHCP servers may be used for reliability; the client will first choose and 'bind' the IP address offered by one server, based on the configuration parameters offered and declining those IP addresses offered by other servers in the process. It then obtains other parameters from the server it has chosen.

One difference in the datagram formats is that the vendor-specific field of 64 octets becomes an enlarged options field with a minimum size of 312 octets. The options field begins with the same magic cookie – 99.130.83.99 – of the BOOTP vendor-specific information, specified originally in RFC 1084. The options field then contains tag (or code) length and data parameters as described in Table 13.8. But DHCP has a much larger table of acceptable tags. For example, each DHCP message parameter begins with the 'DHCP message type option', tag 53. The DHCP extensions use tags in the range 50–62.

Full details of all the BOOTP and DHCP options are described in RFC 1533. The protocol operation is described in RFC 1541.

Line printer services

As well as access to hosts for terminal services and file transfer, remote printing is a common requirement. This is especially true in the world of PC networking, where most users who have a PC will wish to print documents. In the past, it has been too expensive to supply them all with high-quality printers. Line Printer Services (LPS) allows these users to access printers controlled by a central resource, that is, a computer that has printers either directly or remotely connected to it, and that can handle the functions necessary to share printers or plotters.

LPS allows print output to be redirected from one computer to print queues on another. This enables print to be delivered where most appropriate, and makes best use of shared resources. LPS consists of two main processes: LPR, the client, and LPD, the server. LPD accepts print sent to it through LPR and places the output into a print queue, ready for printing on the machine running LPD.

The LPR/LPD protocol uses TCP as its transport. It has a basic format shown in Figure 13.13. The first byte defines the function of the command and the next field defines the target print queue with its name terminated by an ASCII line feed character, L_F. Some functions have extra fields where necessary.

The well-known port number for the LPD is 515 (0x0203). The LPR client must use source ports between 721 (0x02CF) and 731 (0x02DB).

Figure 13.13 (a) LPS command format with (b) example of print any waiting jobs command.

Using LPS

The biggest problem with LPS is configuring the relevant files correctly. LPS provides a number of useful standard utilities:

Table 13.9 Basic LPS commands.

Command code	Function
01	Print any waiting jobs
02	Receive a printer job
03	Send queue status (short)
04	Send queue status (long)
05	Remove jobs

Command	Action
Client	
lpr	Assign output to queue
lpq	Display a queue
lprm	Remove output from queue
Server	
lpc	Control queue

The LPD listens for incoming connections on port 515; once one is received, it analyses the request, then verifies that the host from which the user is connecting is acceptable and that the user has authority to print, and checks that the requested print queue exists.

LPR can be used in a number of ways, but the most common and the default is that the user just types

```
lpr filename
```

This causes filename to be printed on a remote default queue, but a queue can be explicitly defined, such as:

```
lpr -Pqueue1@oz memo.txt
```

This command would print the file memo.txt through a queue called queue1 on host oz.

The LPS protocol

As with most TCP/IP application layer services, LPS has a simple protocol that is used to control the necessary printing functions. The basic format of these commands is a one-octet command code followed by the queue name and terminated with the ASCII Line Feed character (^L_F) (see Figure 13.13).

Basic commands are listed in Table 13.9.

To print a file, the LPS client (LPR) sends a 'receive a printer job' command to the LPS server (LPD) and then uses one of the subcommands (Table 13.10) to indicate the operation to be handled.

If the 'receive control file' option is used, the details of a file that handles a set of special control commands are passed so that file is transferred to LPD. LPD will then perform those actions on the print file that

Table 13.10 LPS subcommands.

Sub-command code	Function
01	Abort job
02	Receive control file
03	Receive data file

follows. If the subcommand defines 'receive data file', the size and name of the print file are given. This name takes the form 'dfA' followed by a three-digit job number and then the host name of the originator, for example:

```
dfA003percy
```

Control filenames use the same format but start with cfA, for example

```
cfA005percy
```

Commands are acknowledged by a one-octet response from LPD. A value of zero indicates the command was accepted. Any other value indicates a failure of some kind.

A typical LPS print sequence is shown in Figure 13.14. A file called sometext.doc is to be printed from host gandalf on to host integv.

Using LPR

In simple configurations LPR is easy to use once it is set up. A user prints documents as normal, the software handles the rest. The print output is sent from the application across the network and put into a spool file for the relevant printer queue on the target host operating as the LPD server. Once the spool file is completed, that is, all the document to be printed has been received, the print manager on the target host will select the spool file and send it to the relevant print device. As with most spooling systems, nothing may come out on the printer until the whole print job has been completed. This can lead to inordinate delays for large print tasks.

Some systems allow control files that will manage the way data is printed on the remote printer to be sent to the host.

NetBIOS

Before describing the relationship between NetBIOS and TCP/IP, we will review how NetBIOS was developed and what it means for networks today. To assist with this explanation, we will consider the normal BIOS (Basic Input/Output System) that is used in IBM PCs and compatibles.

The BIOS in a PC is intended to provide a standard interface to hardware, such that the type of hardware supplied in the machine becomes irrelevant. The BIOS handles commands to send and receive

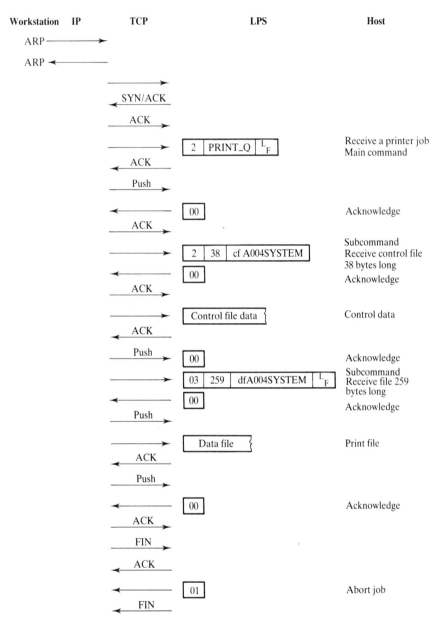

Figure 13.14 LPS transaction between hosts gandalf and integv.

information from the disks, keyboard, communication ports and screens. It provides a level of independence from their specific physical attributes and establishes a standard set of commands for programs and programmers (Figure 13.15).

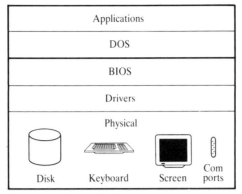

Com ports = Communication ports

Figure 13.15 PC architecture.

The BIOS has no concept of files – that is the function of the operating system that uses it – it just sends information to the relevant devices. This isolates programmers from the detail of the hardware – the screen, keyboard layout, and disk formats – of a particular machine implementation. It allows simple transportation of programs to different hardware platforms, compatibles and clones, without the need for exactly the same make and format of hardware. Applications become independent of (peripheral) hardware; they become BIOS dependent, but this has proved to be far more stable.

NetBIOS is an interface developed by IBM and Sytek Inc. (now part of Hughes LAN Systems) for the original IBM PC Network. It allows application programs to communicate with the underlying network protocols and hardware. NetBIOS is best thought of as an interface for naming and accessing resources in a LAN structure. It is equivalent to the BIOS in IBM's computer architecture.

When IBM and Sytek designed the network hardware for the IBM PC Network (circa 1984), they defined a similar interface to BIOS but to suit the networking environment. They called it the Network BIOS or NetBIOS (Figure 13.16). NetBIOS provided an interface to the Sytek network hardware and protocols, irrespective of their details. A major difference between the functions of BIOS and of NetBIOS is that before you can read and write information from network devices, you must connect to them first. NetBIOS supports the ability to open connections, read and write data, and close connections.

Above NetBIOS was a layer called the session layer. This equates to a Network Operating System (NOS), and manages access to resources on the network just as the local operating system, DOS for example, manages local resources.

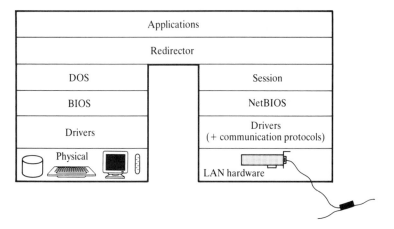

Figure 13.16 Architecture of a PC showing BIOS and NetBIOS.

Above the session layer and DOS is a layer called the redirector that chooses whether resources are local or across the network. It isolates applications from the network and local hardware and, in principle, the applications cannot tell the difference between data stored on a network and on local hardware. In machines which are also servers, it intercepts requests from remote clients and directs them to its local hardware without the local application being aware of it.

This allowed resource sharing of local area networking to become as transparent as it is today, introducing the concept of the **virtual drive**. A virtual drive appears no different to a local drive but is, in fact, on a remote machine and is potentially shared among many users.

The most common NetBIOS commands illustrate the functionality provided by this interface. The commands are in four groups:

(1) *General commands*

Reset	Reset the adapter: initializes the adapter to make it ready for use
Cancel	Allows a command that has been issued but not serviced to be cancelled
Adapter status	Provides a list of statistics and some configuration of the adapter card
Unlink	Used when performing remote program load to disconnect from the initial server

(2) *Name support*

Add name	Register a node's name on the network
Add group name	Register a group name on the network
Delete name	Remove a name from the network

(3) *Session support*

Call	Make a connection
Listen	Listen for a message
Hang up	Close a connection
Send	Send data
Chain send	Send multiple buffers of data
Receive	Data from a specific session
Receive any	Data
Session status	The status of a session

(4) *Datagram support*

Send datagram	Send a datagram
Send broadcast datagram	To all devices on a network
Receive datagram	Wait for a datagram
Receive broadcast datagram	Wait for a datagram from any device on the network

The commands are accessed through software interrupts in the same way as normal DOS and BIOS functions. It is these commands and naming conventions that remain standard across all implementations of NetBIOS. The details of the original Sytek and IBM implementation are today largely irrelevant. What a DOS application must see is the correct interface to the network through the DOS software interrupt structure, and the correct blocks of information in memory to generate each command and interpret the responses. How that information is carried across the network is not important to the application, another advantage of a layered architecture.

But NetBIOS is more than just an interface. To perform the commands does also require a protocol to carry the commands so that the remote node can understand what is intended. When this protocol was based on the Sytek network protocols, it was proprietary. Other manufacturers produced emulations of the NetBIOS interface on their own hardware but using their own protocols. This allowed applications which could interface to the IBM PC Network to run over any manufacturer's NetBIOS. Because the protocols that carried the NetBIOS commands were different, different vendors' NetBIOS products could not interoperate.

Now it should be clearer how NetBIOS and TCP/IP are related. NetBIOS is the standard interface, naming convention and command structure as seen by DOS applications. TCP/IP is one way of carrying that structure between participating workstations.

NetBIOS and TCP/IP

The commercial success of TCP/IP protocols has encouraged its use as a common single network protocol replacing proprietary protocols. The management advantages of one protocol are self-evident. As PC networks grew to such a significant market, there was a need to provide the NetBIOS interface over TCP/IP. The interested bodies cooperated to define how the NetBIOS interface should operate over TCP/IP. Because there is a defined standard, then every vendor's implementation of NetBIOS on a TCP/IP network has a strong possibility of being compatible.

There are two RFCs, 1001 and 1002, which define the implementation of NetBIOS over TCP/IP. The first describes how NetBIOS node names are handled and the second describes the protocol.

NetBIOS allows users to define names for their computers. To ensure that the name is unique, NetBIOS broadcasts it onto a network at start-up. If no other node indicates in a reply that it has registered that same name, then the originator can assume it is unique. When operating over TCP/IP, these names must be 'resolved' to IP addresses since all TCP/IP communication depends on the IP address; to make a connection to another NetBIOS node, a broadcast is sent out to discover the IP address of the remote node with the specified NetBIOS name.

This requirement to broadcast packets *throughout* a network, to check to see if your name is unique or to discover an IP address, is not practical in a large Internet. Potentially it could create a large number of broadcasts, so an alternative mechanism was required. The solution was to allow NetBIOS names to be associated with the domain name scheme (see Chapter 14) used with TCP/IP. The NetBIOS name is considered as a standard host name within one domain, so the test to see if a name is unique is then only relevant within a specific domain and not throughout the Internet.

If we have a NetBIOS server called 'lemming', this name would be concatenated with the domain name for our area. For example, in brewery.integralis.co.uk, the full name of the server would be:

```
lemming.brewery.integralis.co.uk
```

This domain name and NetBIOS name are often referred to as the **scope**. The test to see if a name is unique is now only performed with machines that are located in the same domain, brewery. integralis.co.uk.

NetBIOS servers

To complicate matters, when operating NetBIOS over TCP/IP, there are three different types of NetBIOS nodes. They are B nodes, P nodes and M nodes. B (or broadcast) nodes can only operate within a broadcast area, as they use broadcasts to discover other nodes and to register themselves to the network. P nodes communicate using directed datagrams and TCP; they need the services of a NetBIOS Name Server (NBNS) or a NetBIOS Datagram Distribution Server (NBDD). M nodes are a mix of B node and P node operation. They use NBNS and NBDD servers but can still function within a broadcast area if servers are not used or not available.

An NBNS is modelled as closely as possible on the standard domain name server, but, to support a NetBIOS service, a number of additional functions are necessary:

- Dynamic addition of entries
- Dynamic update of entries
- Support for group entities
- Support for entry time-to-live and messages to refresh its value
- New entry attributes

NetBIOS nodes normally register their names when they are first activated. This means a name server must be able to add entries to its tables dynamically. Standard TCP/IP domain name servers use fixed tables that are configured by network managers.

An NBDD operates in environments that do not support broadcasting and multicasting. It holds a list of all nodes within the same NetBIOS scope, together with their IP addresses. It has the ability to communicate with them all directly for name registration and look-up. A node will communicate directly with an NBDD to register its name rather than use broadcast. Thus only unicast messages are required with this type of server, but the end node must know the IP address of the NBDD. As reducing broadcast traffic is always a useful aim, using NBDD even in a broadcast environment could have performance advantages.

B nodes perform name registration and name discovery by broadcasting claim requests in the broadcast domain, P nodes by using an NBDD, and M nodes by first broadcasting and then using an NBNS. Names registered in an NBNS have a time-to-live value after which time they are flushed from the database or the NBNS will first perform a name challenge to see if the node is still using that name. If it is still active, the time-to-live timer will be reset.

NetBIOS name encoding

To map NetBIOS names into domain name server compatible form, two levels of encoding are performed. NetBIOS names are normally 16 octets long. Even if the name seen by the user is shorter, it is filled out with spaces[†] when passed across the network protocol. NetBIOS names are case sensitive so 'a' does not equal 'A'. Standard TCP/IP domain names are not case sensitive, so 'a'='A'. One of the reasons for encoding NetBIOS names is, therefore, to prevent clashes and ensure that they remain case sensitive. The encoding technique splits each octet into 4-bit quantities and adds them to ASCII character 'A', hexadecimal 0x41. This creates two uppercase ASCII characters from each character of the NetBIOS

[†]White space or ASCII character 0x20.

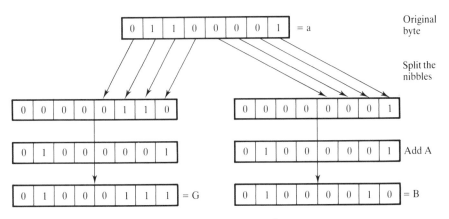

Figure 13.17 First level encoding for NetBIOS names.

name, so a NetBIOS name now becomes 32 octets long. Figure 13.17 gives an example of this encoding showing that lowercase 'a' becomes two uppercase characters 'G' and 'B'.

The name 'Server' in domain integralis.co.uk would be encoded as the string:

```
FDGFHCHGGFHCCACACACACACACACACACA.INTEGRALIS.CO.UK
```

Second-level encoding is exactly the same as for normal domain name system names and is explained in Chapter 14. In effect, the above name would then be encoded as:

```
32FDGFHCHGGFHCCACACACACACACACACACA10INTEGRALIS3CO2UK0
```

Keep-alive packets

Another feature of NetBIOS systems is their use of the **keep-alive packet**. This is a packet request-and-reply sequence to check that a connection is still functional when no data is flowing. Again, in an Internet, the background traffic this would generate is wasteful of capacity, so the standard allows keep-alive packets to be disabled.

RFC 1002 defines a well-known port for NetBIOS name services which is 137 for both TCP and UDP services. For TCP session services, NetBIOS uses port 139 and UDP datagrams services port 138. The maximum datagram length is 576 octets.

Using NetBIOS

NetBIOS provides a standard interface to LAN cards, allowing peer-to-peer connections to be established between machines. Although this interface was developed for the IBM PC, NetBIOS can now be found on mini- and mainframe computers as well. This allows mini- and mainframes to participate as file and print servers in what was originally a DOS PC domain. The term 'PC Network' has become obsolete. It is now a generic term for sharing data among any type of machine including PCs; it is more appropriate to talk today about Network Operating Systems (NOSs).

The NetBIOS interface is available with most NOSs. Microsoft LAN Manager and Microsoft Networks systems (MSNET) use NetBIOS. It is also available for Novell NetWare. NetBIOS can run over many networks, XNS, TCP/IP, IPX and X.25, so it has become a powerful tool for system integration. NetBIOS provides the 'interoperation' aspects of the internetworking equation. Two systems can, of course, only communicate if they are using the same interconnection methods, that is, the same network protocols to carry the NetBIOS commands.

A number of parameters can be set to improve operation. These are: session retry count (default 4), session time-out (30 seconds default) and keep-alive time-out (60 seconds default). In some systems keep-alive packets can be turned off altogether. With keep-alive packets enabled, the protocols detect network errors quicker than without, but the traffic they generate is not desirable over WAN connections.

Sockets library

When exploring TCP/IP literature one will often see reference to a **sockets library**. A sockets library is a set of programmer's tools for simplifying the development of applications over the TCP or UDP transport layer services. At a high level, it provides procedures or functions to create programs that will talk to application level services such as FTP, Telnet and TFTP; at the lower level, it provides access to the raw services of UDP or TCP which may just be used to develop a bespoke service. Some of the dangers of isolating programmers from the network quite so effectively were discussed in Chapter 7. Some faults and performance problems that occur in operational systems are due to programmers who did not appreciate the impact on the network of certain simple techniques available through the sockets interface.

The **socket** is the programmer's identifier for a communications path. In many programming environments, input/output devices are treated as generic objects that can be written to and/or read from. In UNIX systems the reference to such an object is a file descriptor, even though the object may be a printer or communications port; in the sockets environment this file descriptor equates to a socket.

The programmer uses sockets to refer to a remote application layer entity: if the program is not going to use existing servers, the developer must choose port numbers that have not been allocated to an existing application. The programmer can decide which transport service to use, TCP or UDP. With some implementations it is possible to generate and receive packets at any layer of the protocol stack[†], where an existing protocol would put too much restriction on the application.

The difference between reading and writing to a socket as compared with a local file descriptor is that the software has to establish a relationship with the remote node across the communications network. Once this relationship is established, reading and writing is identical to working with local objects.

WINSOCK

With the large increase in the use of PCs using Microsoft Windows as their environment for running TCP/IP applications, it became necessary to create a standard Application Program Interface (API) to enable Windows applications to access the TCP/IP protocol stack. This has allowed applications to be developed independent of the manufacturer of the communications environment. Traditionally TCP/IP applications have been developed through a sockets library. This gives programmers a standard access to UDP and TCP programming function calls. This is known as the BSD sockets interface. For Windows, the environment is different from DOS or UNIX. WINSOCK (WINdows SOCKets) was the solution, providing a sockets interface from within Windows. While WINSOCK has much in common with BSD sockets some additional function calls and techniques are required to ensure compatibility with the limited multitasking of Windows.

Extended WINSOCK interfaces are likely to appear in the future. One of these is WINISDN. This extends WINSOCK with commands to control the set-up of a remote connection over ISDN terminal equipment. Without this facility, ISDN can still be used, but a separate application has to set up a call before the TCP/IP application can operate.

WINSOCK allows any WINSOCK compliant application to operate over any WINSOCK compliant TCP/IP stack. This makes it practical to provide a TCP/IP stack with the WINSOCK interface as an integral part of an operating system. All newer operating systems for PCs are likely to support WINSOCK directly. This will change the commercial market from one where the TCP/IP stack was the deciding factor to one where the quality of application software becomes the key.

X protocol

With the recent demand for 'windows' applications – applications that operate through a Graphical User Interface (GUI) – a standard

---

[†]The Do-It-Yourself (DIY) interface.

programming interface that provides compatibility between different hardware systems is a useful addition to the application layer. To meet this requirement the X Window System is outlined in RFC 1013 and hence may be thought of as an 'open' standard, though it is developed by MIT (see Chapter 6). Full details of all the protocols are available from the X Window Consortium at MIT.

The operation of X Window System is not tied to any particular protocol but has so far been predominantly used with UNIX and hence on TCP/IP, so X Window has become associated with TCP/IP. The X Window System definition considers a program to consist of client and server modules that can be located on the same machine or on different machines across a network. The definition of how the client and server programs intercommunicate is defined by a protocol call the **X Protocol**.

X Window System goes a long way to providing computers with standards for accessing applications on different computing architectures. This is because it is much more involved in the representation of data to computer users than earlier techniques; it provides a standard interface between the true user interface and the remote software that drives that user interface. Using X Window System a user can access, in a standard way, any application that generates the X protocol as output, irrespective of what hardware or operating system that application is running on.

When discussing X Window, one must be careful with the terms 'server' and 'client'. Here the server is a program that controls the display of information to users; the client is an application that generates that information (Figure 13.18). X terminals are specific devices that are intelligent workstations dedicated to the task of being an X Window server. As the name suggests, X Window System is based on a windowed GUI environment where the mouse and menus are important additions to the keyboard in providing the user interface. These are all associated with the X server.

In a client/server architecture, the server normally only responds to client requests. Within the X Window environment, mouse movements and keystrokes are reported to the client through **event commands**.

X Window System is becoming an important vehicle for cross-platform compatibility. This is because any application that can operate as an X client can be used by an X server irrespective of what computers or operating system they may be using. What is required is a common network connection and protocol such as TCP/IP.

The X protocol is a complete definition of functions that support the mouse, keyboard input, drawing windows, boxes, lines, circles, in fact anything to do with displaying pictures and text in windows on a screen. The protocol uses TCP as a reliable stream transport. It opens a separate port for each window starting with port 6000 and adding 1 for each subsequent window. There are four different types of message used by the X protocol: requests, replies, errors and events.

In its basic form, every event is passed across the network between server and client. Moving a mouse on an X Window display can generate

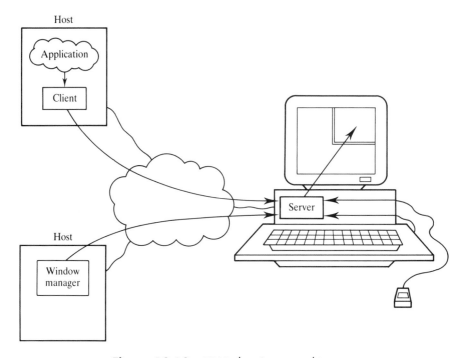

Figure 13.18 X Window System architecture.

a stream of network traffic. Such activity is only practical in a truly local environment, preferably on the same LAN cable. Recent changes to the X Window definition are aimed at changing the split between server and client activities; this will allocate more screen processing to the server and reduce the traffic between devices to levels acceptable over other types of link.

Implications of IPv6 for applications

For those accustomed to thinking about modern communications systems as independent layers, fully isolated from each other, mention of issues of a network layer protocol (IPv6) for applications may come as a surprise. After all, these layers are separated by another layer, either TCP or UDP; one might assume that isolation is complete. In the TCP/IP protocol stack this is not the case. Some applications have a built-in dependence on TCP and on IPv4 as the underlying network layer.

One example is the file transfer protocol. This uses a PORT command to advise its communicating partner of a free communications 'socket' to use for transferring a directory listing or file as described previously. An example of a port command is

PORT 158,152,24,121,13,128

The numbers are sent as ASCII characters exactly as shown. This means 'please prepare to open a connection to IP address 158.152.24.121 port 3456'. ($13 \times 256 + 128 = 3456$). In this one statement, FTP includes information from the current versions of both TCP and IP. There is therefore a dependence of FTP on both TCP and IPv4 which can only be removed by redefining FTP. It means redeveloping all implementations of FTP to work with a new network layer protocol, IPv6.

The Uniform Resource Locators (URLs) of the World Wide Web sometimes contain IP addresses and port numbers.

This interdependence also means that conversion from IPv4 to IPv6, referred to in Chapter 11, is not a simple network layer task for a router. It requires 'application gateway' functionality to examine the application context of every packet that is converted. This is not an insoluble problem; application level secure gateways for attachment of corporate networks to the Internet (Chapter 19), which convert between registered and unregistered IPv4 addresses, must solve similar problems.

There are a number of protocols, some in use and some under development, which pass a socket identification forward to another host to allow that host to establish a back connection. These will all fail to work if the network protocol is changed from IPv4 to IPv6. To correct the problem, new application versions will have to be created that can manage IPv6 addresses in addition to IPv4 addresses.

It should have become clear that the introduction of IPv6 is not a simple change of network layer protocol; considerable changes are needed in higher- and lower-level protocols before a fully working system can be given to end users. This work, explicitly on IPv6, has occupied the working committees of the IETF since mid-1994. At the time of going to print many draft RFCs and decisions relating to a complete and working implementation of IPv6 and all associated IP applications are yet to be finalized. Readers with the need for up-to-date information can follow these developments by obtaining the discussion documents from the IETF as described in Appendix B.

Miscellaneous services

TCP/IP normally provides a number of services at the application layer which can be very useful for node and network diagnostics. These services are selected through the well-known port numbers which differentiate them. The most common and useful are listed in Table 13.11.

Figure 13.19 shows the architecture of these services. As the services themselves are server software, they will reply to any incoming client requests on their respective ports.

A remote client that connects into the **echo** service will have data it sends returned or echoed back. This provides an excellent confidence test at a higher level than ping, the ICMP echo. Ping only indicates that

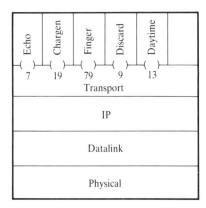

Figure 13.19 Architecture of the miscellaneous services.

a node exists and that its IP layer is operational. The application layer echo moves beyond the IP layer through TCP or UDP to the application layer, stopping just short of end-user applications, and therefore testing through all layers of the protocol stack. Use of ping and then this service can help differentiate between failure either of an application or at a particular point in the protocol stack; if the client is able to get a response from echo but cannot access the end-user application, the application is likely to be at fault; if the response comes only from ping, the transport and application layers are suspect.

Chargen is what is known as a 'barber-pole' test. When a connection is made to this service, it sends the ASCII printable character set continuously, sliding one character on each new line. This test was originally used to ensure that mechanical printers were working correctly, that they could print the complete ASCII set and support flow control. Today, this test can still be useful for checking a connection is functioning correctly by generating a continuous stream of traffic. With some hosts, a very high level of output traffic can be generated, so it can be a way of loading a system or network. It is not a test to run in a normal operational network unless the aim is to measure user tolerance! It can also still be used to check the integrity of flow control, to measure the throughput achieved on a particular route and to investigate the effects of altering the TCP/IP performance parameters of window and maximum segment sizes.

Table 13.11 Port numbers of miscellaneous services.

Service	Port number (decimal)
Echo	7
Chargen	19
Finger	79
Discard	9
Daytime	13

The **finger** service is intended to allow one person to determine the full details about another user from their user id. If someone is connected to a host remotely across a network, you can only see their user id, not their full name. User ids can be cryptic. The finger utility will request the full name and details of any user as furnished by the security access files in the user's own host. In most host security systems, a manager gives the full name and sometimes other details about a user against their user id; finger accesses this information. This is designed to allow a system manager, for example, to obtain the telephone number, room number and location of a remote user.

The **discard** utility is a bottomless pit for information, a 'null' destination. It allows information sent to a host to be completely ignored and discarded. This can be a useful way of checking the performance of networks and protocol stacks without producing significant load on a host's operating system. It can potentially differentiate between communications delays and host delays.

The **daytime** service returns the time and day in ASCII format so it can be read by programs or users. There are a number of other time-related services that provide the date and time in varying formats. These can be used to synchronize the time and date automatically on all computers in a network. This is a particularly useful function when mail systems are involved; mail sent by systems that have an incorrect date can cause administrative headaches in some operational environments.

Using debugging and measurement services

These services can be accessed by specially written programs (the sockets library) or connected to directly using Telnet. Telnet normally connects to server software by addressing its communications to port 23, but in many implementations of Telnet there is a command line option that allows the user to define the destination port number to be used. Any port number can be supplied and therefore Telnet can access any service. The possibility of a useful exchange with the server depends on the application layer protocol that server uses. Since many of the services just described send ASCII data streams, they can be usefully accessed for testing purposes via Telnet. There is an issue of performance and security. A network manager does not necessarily wish to encourage general computer users from using Telnet into well-known, but random, ports. There may be no general way of preventing this.

These tools might also be used through an application program. Some of these services require arguments to be passed to them. This is certainly easier from a specially constructed application. A service such as synchronizing the clocks on different computers is certainly better dealt with by an application.

How these miscellaneous services can be used is considered further in Chapter 18.

Relevant RFCs

General topics

1123   Requirements for Internet hosts – application and support
1173   Responsibilities of host and network managers: a summary of the 'oral tradition' of the Internet

Telnet and SUPDUP

698   Telnet extended ASCII option
726   Remote controlled transmission and echoing Telnet option
727   Telnet logout option
730   Extensible field addressing
732   Telnet data entry terminal option
735   Revised Telnet byte macro option
736   Telnet SUPDUP option
746   SUPDUP graphics extension
747   Recent extensions to the SUPDUP protocol
748   Telnet randomly-lose option
749   Telnet SUPDUP-output option
779   Telnet send-location option
854   Telnet protocol specification
855   Telnet option specifications
856   Telnet binary transmission
857   Telnet echo option
858   Telnet suppress go ahead option
859   Telnet status option
860   Telnet timing mark option
885   Telnet end of record option
927   TACACS user identification Telnet option
933   Output marking Telnet option
946   Telnet terminal location number option
1041   Telnet 3270 regime option
1043   Telnet data entry terminal option: DODIIS implementation
1073   Telnet window size option
1079   Telnet terminal speed option
1091   Telnet terminal-type option
1096   Telnet X display location option
1143   Q method of implementing Telnet option negotiation
1184   Telnet linemode option
1205   5250 Telnet interface
1372   Telnet remote flow control option
1576   TN3270 current practices
1646   TN3270 extensions for LUname and printer selection
1647   TN3270 enhancements

FTP and TFTP

737   FTP extension: XSEN
743   FTP extension: XRSQ/XRCP
775   Directory oriented FTP commands
959   File transfer protocol
1350 The TFTP protocol (revision 2) (updated by RFCs 1782, 1783, 1784, 1785)
1782 TFTP option extension (updates RFC 1350)
1783 TFTP blocksize option (updates RFC 1350)
1784 TFTP timeout interval and transfer size options (updates RFC 1350)
1785 TFTP option negotiation analysis (updates RFC 1350)

Mail

720   Address specification syntax for network mail
821   Simple mail transfer protocol
822   Standard for the format of ARPA Internet text messages (updated by RFC 1327)
974   Mail routing and the domain system
976   UUCP mail interchange format standard (updated by RFC 1137)
1026 Addendum to RFC 987: (mapping between X.400 and RFC-822) (updated by RFC 1138)
1056 PCMAIL: a distributed mail system for personal computers
1090 SMTP on X.25
1137 Mapping between full RFC 822 and RFC 822 with restricted encoding (updates RFC 976)
1138 Mapping between X.400(1988)/ISO 10021 and RFC 822 (updates RFC 822, RFC 1026)
1211 Problems with the maintenance of large mailing lists
1327 Mapping between X.400(1988)/ISO 10021 and RFC 822 (updates RFC 822; updated by RFC 1495)
1328 X.400 1988 to1984 downgrading
1421 Privacy enhancement for Internet electronic mail: Part I: Message encryption and authentication procedures
1422 Privacy enhancement for Internet electronic mail: Part II: Certificate-based key management
1423 Privacy enhancement for Internet electronic mail: Part III: Algorithms, modes and identifiers
1424 Privacy enhancement for Internet electronic mail: Part IV: Key certification and related services
1494 Equivalences between 1988 X.400 and RFC 822 message bodies
1495 Mapping between X.400 and RFC 822 message bodies (updates RFC 1327)
1496 Rules for downgrading messages from X.400/88 to X.400/84 when MIME content-types are present in the messages

1521   MIME (Multipurpose Internet mail extensions) Part One: Mechanisms for specifying and describing the format of Internet message bodies (updated by RFC 1590)

1522   MIME (Multipurpose Internet mail extensions) Part Two: Message header extensions for non-ASCII text

1590   Media type registration procedure (updates RFC 1521)

1652   SMTP service extension for 8-bit-MIME transport

1725   Post Office protocol – version 3

1734   POP3 AUTHentication command

1740   MIME encapsulation of Macintosh files – MacMIME

1741   MIME content type for BinHex encoded files

1767   MIME encapsulation of EDI objects

1847   Security multiparts for MIME: Multipart/signed and multipart/encrypted

1848   MIME object security services

1854   SMTP service extension for command pipelining

1864   The content-MD5 header field

1869   SMTP service extensions

1870   SMTP service extension for message size declaration

Bootstrapping and address management (DHCP)

906   Bootstrap loading using TFTP

951   Bootstrap protocol

1533   DHCP options and BOOTP vendor extensions

1534   Interoperation between DHCP and BOOTP

1541   Dynamic host configuration protocol

1542   Clarifications and extensions for the Bootstrap protocol

NetBIOS

1001   Protocol standard for a NetBIOS service on a TCP/UDP transport: concepts and methods

1002   Protocol standard for a NetBIOS service on a TCP/UDP transport: detailed specifications

X Window System

1013   X Window System protocol, version 11: alpha update April 1987

1198   FYI on the X Window System

World Wide Web

1630   Universal resource identifiers in WWW: A unifying syntax for the expression of names and addresses of objects on the network as used in the World Wide Web

1736   Functional requirements for Internet resource locators

Miscellaneous services

Summary

In this chapter we have considered all the most common services provided by a TCP/IP system at the application layer other than NFS (ONC) – see Chapter 15.

First we considered the architecture of these services. The key fact is that client and server software is required for all of them; client must talk to server. Two clients cannot communicate. In the PC environment, it is sometimes not sensible to provide server software as a DOS PC is not a multitasking system; it can only deal with one application at a time.

There are other application services available for TCP/IP systems, but their operation is most likely to be similar to one of those described in this chapter.

14

Working with names

People prefer to use names instead of numbering schemes to refer to computers. This becomes even more marked on systems that are large and complex. A well-defined name structure, which is easy for users to understand, will help them remember and formulate names as necessary, thus helping the non-technician feel more at ease with the technology. There are two ways this can be done with TCP/IP systems: through a personal file on each computer or through centrally managed services.

This chapter considers the operation of such systems. It introduces:

- The hosts file
- Domain name servers
- Domain name structure
- The domain name protocol
- Network information services

So far we have considered connecting to remote computers using their IP addresses. This is fine for computers as they can handle numbers far more efficiently than names, but those of us who have difficulty remembering complex numbering schemes find it easier to use simple names, for example SUN, VAX, IBM. These days we tend to find more adventurous names for our systems, such as Gandalf, Oz, Pooh, Eyore, Tiga – amusing names that are not only easy to remember, but make complex technology more approachable by the use of humour. In some situations, we may choose a more formal reference relating to the function of the computer.

However you may wish to approach naming and the management of names, as discussed in previous chapters, properly administered they can be extremely beneficial for the management and acceptability of computing systems.

TCP/IP uses a number of mechanisms to convert names to IP addresses. The most basic is the hosts file; another is the Domain Name System. NFS systems can use the Network Information Services (NIS). We will look at each of these in turn.

The hosts file

TCP/IP systems normally have a file called hosts that can be used to allow application services to request connections by using names instead of IP addresses. As shown in Figure 14.1, this file contains a simple list of IP addresses and the names that relate to them. Each address can have several names, usually a formal name and a number of less formal nicknames or aliases.

The problem with this type of system is that it can be difficult to control in a large network, where naming decisions cannot be left to individual users. In large networks, decentralized or distributed control of such facilities can be beneficial, but with an individual hosts file on each

```
; hosts file
;
;IP address      name            alias
;
127.0.0.0        Loopback        me       thisone
128.128.32.1     oz              zo
128.128.32.2     Gandalf         gandy    wizard
128.128.32.4     Pinball         pin
128.128.32.5     PC1             pc1
192.1.5.70       Extra.long.com  extra
```

Figure 14.1 Example of a hosts file.

and every computer, it becomes impossible to maintain a consistent set of names on all machines. Users will configure different names for the same hosts making it awkward for somebody else to use that computer system; or if IP addresses are added or changed on the network, every hosts file must be updated. Often the only way to do this is to visit each machine unless provision is made for automation of such processes.

With some systems the use of hosts files can be slow as their software is not particularly good at searching through a file to obtain the required mapping.

It is possible to manage hosts files by ensuring that a master version is kept on a central computer and that all other computers download that file at regular intervals. This mechanism is practical in small to medium systems, but for large systems, where responsibility needs to be devolved, it becomes difficult.

Figure 14.1 shows the layout of a hosts file giving IP addresses, names and a number of aliases used to refer to hosts. Any line starting with ';' is for comment only, to make the file more readable. Each machine is described on a separate line beginning with its IP address and followed by a list of names which all refer to that one IP address. This name list normally begins with a formal name and is followed by less formal aliases. Anywhere users would normally type an IP address to establish connection with a host, they can type an alias or a name. For example:

```
telnet 128.128.32.2<enter>
telnet Gandalf<enter>
telnet wizard<enter>
telnet gandy<enter>
```

are all requests to use Telnet to access the same computer.

When connected to a large internet it is likely that more complex names are in use, so aliases can be convenient in allowing a short or preferred name to be used locally instead. Figure 14.1 gives an example with IP address 192.1.5.70. Instead of typing the full name a user can type 'extra' to refer to the host.

The domain name system

So important is this central control of names in a general computing service that the IAB has produced a standard for the Domain Name System, DNS. A domain name allows a computer that is registered to the Internet to be uniquely identified by that name wherever it may be in the world. The second major function of the domain name system is to translate those names into the corresponding unique IP address, since all TCP/IP communications depends on knowing the IP address. The reverse translation is also possible.

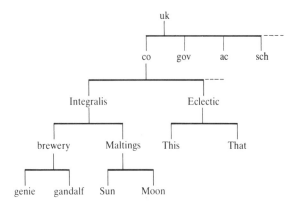

Host domain names:

1. genie   . brewery . Integralis . co . uk
2. gandalf . brewery . Integralis . co . uk
3. Sun   . Maltings . Integralis . co . uk
4. Moon   . Maltings . Integralis . co . uk
5.   This   . Eclectic   . co . uk
6.   That   . Eclectic   . co . uk

Figure 14.2   The domain name structure.

While these are the main functions of the DNS, it has a more general use. The standard allows the DNS to identify the types of applications that are available on a particular machine (well-known services), to identify gateways to networks and to show which machines are capable of mail relay and to which network. These are some of the functions required from a more general directory service.

To work with names, a general structure has to be defined. Any system where responsibility is devolved to successively lower levels of the structure is 'hierarchical'. The domain name system is hierarchical and uses separate components in a complete name to identify the different levels of management. Like other hierarchical systems, this one can be drawn as an inverted tree, with the trunk (or root as it is more often called) identifying the top level of management, and then spanning out into branches, twigs and leaves that point finally to an individual computer by name (see Figure 14.2).

The existing accepted structure of domain names is based upon that first produced by the Internet community. The system is a flexible and comprehensive scheme that allows two basic structures to be used; one is organizational, the other geographic. Multinational organizations tend to use the organizational approach while those organizations limited to operations within a single country tend to use geographical references.

Domain name	Explanation
COM	Commercial organizations
EDU	Educational organizations
GOV	Government organizations
MIL	Military groups
NET	Major network support centres
ORG	Other organizations
INT	International organizations

Figure 14.3   Internet top-level domain references.

Under the root level of the organizational approach are seven references as shown in Figure 14.3. The geographic approach uses country codes at the top level, with other local references beneath. Generally this second domain level refers to similar entities as the top-level organizational domains, that is, co – commercial, sch – school, ac – academic. Originally, countries were supposed to use their international telephone dialling code as an identifier but this has not happened. Instead, a two-letter abbreviation of the country name is used, as defined in ISO 3166. Some of these are listed in Figure 14.4. Many non-US connections to the Internet have adopted a second tier of domains that closely matches the organization classification used at the top level of the Internet.

Notice that there is a top-level domain for international organizations (INT) that do not fall into the other classifications. The only entry under this at present is NATO, which one would expect to be more suited to the MIL domain.

Choosing a domain name scheme

A large company that does not wish to connect to the Internet[†] can design its own naming structure to match its organization. It need not follow these Internet conventions. The technology of the DNS is independent of the actual names used at each level, as long as a consistent hierarchy is defined. There is the usual dilemma as to whether the domain name system should be purely geographic or purely organizational. Since the IP addressing scheme has a tendency to become geographic for efficient routing, making the DNS purely organizational might give additional flexibility. It is important that the scheme matches the organization as closely as possible, so that the names are easily recognizable; if the existing labels or abbreviations for company sites and divisions are adopted, employees will already be familiar with them.

[†]The authors recommend that the issue as to whether a network will attach to the Internet or not be considered very carefully before addressing and name schemes are put into effect. Changing them at a later date can be very costly.

Country code	Country name	Additional information
au	Australia	Sometimes oz.au or just oz
be	Belgium	
ca	Canada	Some Canadian systems use US conventions
ch	Switzerland	
de	Germany	
dk	Denmark	
es	Spain	
fi	Finland	
fr	France	
gr	Greece	
it	Italy	
jp	Japan	
kw	Kuwait	
nl	The Netherlands	
no	Norway	
nz	New Zealand	
se	Sweden	
us	United States of America	A second tier was defined which specified the state the host was in, e.g. ca.us for a host in California

Figure 14.4   Some domain name system country codes.

When written down, a fully qualified host name or fully qualified domain name consists of the host or node name followed by all the domain components in ascending order of authority as shown in the example below. The name ends with the root of the system. Each component is separated by dots, or periods. A naming scheme designed for an international company might be:

node.site.department.division.company.org.country

for example:

gandalf.theale.development.integralis.co.uk

which translates to the machine called Gandalf at the Theale site of the development division of the company called Integralis which is a commercial company, co[†], in the UK. Names are often all in lower case.

[†]For some countries, including the UK, the abbreviation 'co' is used for commercial and 'ac' is used for the academic community rather than the US equivalents of 'com' and 'edu'. The definition of domain names is further confused by the existence of an earlier scheme for the UK Joint Academic NETwork (JANET), where the most significant component is on the left – uk.ac.umist.cs.

Reverse address mapping

In certain circumstances it is beneficial to be able to perform inverse mappings, that is, find the domain name of a host from its IP address. This type of mechanism can be used to discover the IP address of gateways to a particular network. As IP addresses are not strictly geographic in their structure this can be difficult. To help manage this problem a special domain has been defined, IN-ADDR, standing for inverse (IN) address (ADDR). This domain is treated as the root of names that are based upon the IP address of hosts and networks so that a name can be formulated to discover hosts on a particular network. Examples of such names could be:

        52.0.2.10.IN_ADDR.ARPA
        10.IN_ADDR.ARPA
        2.3.194.IN_ADDR.ARPA

The addresses in these names are shown in reverse. 52.0.2.10.IN. ADDR.ARPA refers to IP address 10.2.0.52, host 2.0.52 on network 10, the ARPANET. 10.IN-ADDR.ARPA refers to the ARPANET itself. 2.3.194. IN-ADDR.ARPA refers to network 194.3.2.

An IN_ADDR.ARPA database would look something like the following:

10.IN_ADDR.ARPA	PTR	IN	MILNET-GW-.ISI.ARPA
10.IN_ADDR.ARPA	PTR	IN	GW.MIT.ARPA
18.IN_ADDR.ARPA	PTR	IN	GW.MIT.ARPA
26.IN_ADDR.ARPA	PTR	IN	MILNET-GW-.ISI.ARPA
22.0.2.10.IN_ADDR.ARPA	PTR	IN	MILNET-GW-.ISI.ARPA
103.0.0.26.IN_ADDR.ARPA	PTR	IN	MILNET-GW-.ISI.ARPA
77.0.0.10.IN_ADDR.ARPA	PTR	IN	GW.MIT.ARPA
4.0.10.18.IN_ADDR.ARPA	PTR	IN	GW.MIT.ARPA

Through use of this system it is possible to determine the names of gateways that connect to a particular network, first from their network reference to get their full domain names and then from these domain names to get the corresponding IP address.

The gateway MILNET-GW.ISI.ARPA appears in the table a number of times. As 10.IN_ADDR.ARPA and 26.IN_ADDR.ARPA it appears as a gateway connecting networks 10 and 26 together. It then appears with its full address on each network.

This structure allows a computer to request all devices that connect to the domain name 10.IN_ADDR.ARPA; the response will show the devices that connect to network 10:

10.IN_ADDR.ARPA	PTR	IN	MILNET-GW-.ISI.ARPA
10.IN_ADDR.ARPA	PTR	IN	GW.MIT.ARPA

It is also possible to find a machine's domain name from a test for its IP address, e.g. what is the domain name of IP address 10.0.0.77, or 77.0.0.10.IN-ADDR.ARPA?

Domain name servers

A domain name system is implemented through the interaction of two components, the name resolver and the name server. The resolver is client software on a user's computer that queries domain name servers, normally to translate domain names into IP addresses. The domain name server is a program that accesses a database of domain and host names and their associated IP addresses from which it answers queries from resolvers. The database must be defined by the manager of the domain.

It is normal to have two operational servers – a primary, and a secondary as a backup for the first. Those who connect to, and provide services on, the Internet must undertake to run two servers to ensure that one can always be available to answer name queries. Workstations and hosts should have the IP addresses of primary and secondary name servers configured at installation, so their resolver software knows where to call.

One factor which will influence the design of a naming structure is that there must be a server with authority for each subdomain in the name hierarchy. These could be handled by a single name server running on one machine.

The set of domains that a domain name server controls is referred to as a **zone**. A zone is a group of connected domain names within the hierarchy. It is possible for a zone to contain only a single domain. Whether a zone contains a single or multiple domain is dependent on the management requirements for each domain.

If a server is unable to answer a name query (because the name is controlled by a higher authority or is in a different branch of the name tree), either it will answer the query with the name and IP address of a server which is better able to provide the true answer or it will attempt to obtain the full answer on behalf of the requester. This latter process is known as **recursion**.

It is more common to use recursion than to provide the originator with an alternative name server. Assuming a system is correctly configured and working, a properly formatted request will always receive a response. The two most likely reasons that a request is not answered successfully are either that the domain name of a host was typed incorrectly or that the host is not registered in the appropriate domain name server's database.

Root servers are located at the top of the domain name structure and are used to tie together the organizational and geographic name servers. Domain name servers use root servers as the starting place to discover name-to-address mappings outside their own domain. Root servers can work their way down the domain name tree in order to resolve a name completely. If a name server cannot answer a query from a resolver it will pass the query to a root server if recursion is allowed.

Domain name server authority

A primary domain name server is given authority over a domain. Having authority over a domain requires it to hold the master database which has the names and IP addresses of nodes in that domain. Domain name servers normally keep a copy of answers they receive from other domains so repeat queries can be avoided. This speeds up responses and reduces network traffic.

To improve their performance, on start-up some host systems will query their domain name server to build their own mapping of IP addresses to names. A concern with this procedure is that this local database could become outdated as remote systems change. Any such system that caches domain names must also purge that information and reload it at intervals defined by the domain name server. This also applies to remote responses which are cached by the nonauthoritative servers discussed above. The time limit is set in seconds and can be up to three years, but values of a day (86 400 seconds) or a week (604 800 seconds) are more common.

Domain name protocol

The domain name message format is complex. It is divided into five sections which consist of the header, question, answer, authority and additional information sections, see Figure 14.5. The header includes a 16-bit parameter field, each bit of which is used as a flag, see Figure 14.6.

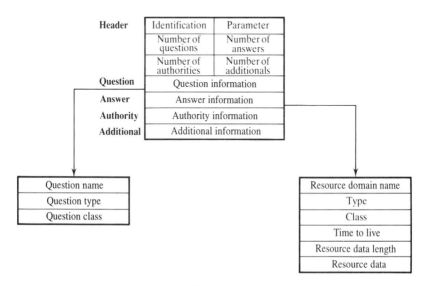

Figure 14.5 Format of the domain name server message.

Bit	Meaning
0	Operation: 0 = Query 1 = Response
1-4	Query type: 0 = Standard 1 = Inverse 2 = Obsolete 3 = Obsolete
5	1 = Answer authoritative
6	1 = Message is truncated
7	1 = Recursion is desired
8	1 = Recursion is available
9–11	Reserved
12–15	Response type 0 = No error 1 = Format error in query 2 = Server failure 3 = Name does not exist

Figure 14.6   The parameter field of the domain name server message.

The same format is used for requests as responses, but in some situations sections may be empty.

The best way of describing the operation of this system is to go through an example. We will start with a query for a host with a domain name of:

        oz.integralis.co.uk

from a host called genie in the domain eclectic.co.uk with an IP address of 128.128.1.77:

        genie.eclectic.co.uk

For this example, a request that cannot be answered immediately goes to genie's local DNS and is referred up the tree to the root server, which in this case is:

        co.uk

The flow of messages exchanged is shown in Figure 14.7. The initial request from the resolver in host genie is shown in Figure 14.8.

The initial request was sent to domain name server 128.128.0.100 (chelford.eclectic.co.uk) from host 128.128.1.77 (Figure 14.8). In this case, the domain name server did not have any reference to the

Figure 14.7 Flow of messages in domain name request.

host requested. As the host indicated that recursion was allowed, the domain name server of domain `eclectic.co.uk` repeated the request to the root server for the domain `co.uk` (128.1.0.100), shown in Figure 14.9. As host `oz` is known to that server, due to earlier requests, `co.uk` is able to provide the address mapping.

When domain name server 128.1.0.100 (root for `co.uk`) receives the request from 128.128.0.100 (`chelford.eclectic.co.uk`), it checks through its database and finds the answer, so it formulates and sends its reply, shown in Figure 14.10.

Mac header >		
IP header >		
IP addresses	Destination = 128.128.0.100	Source = 128.128.1.77
DNS header >	Identification = 4	Parameter = Query + Recursion
	Number of questions = 1	Number of answers = 0
	Number of authorities = 0	Number of additionals = 0
	Name = oz.integralis.co.uk Type = HOST Class = IN	

Figure 14.8 Initial DNS request.

Mac header >		
IP header >		
IP addresses	Destination = 128.128.128.100	Destination = 128.1.0.100
DNS header >	Identification = 2	Parameter = Query
	Number of questions = 1	Number of answers = 0
	Number of authorities = 0	Number of additionals = 0
Question	Name = oz.integralis.co.uk Type = HOST Class = IN	

Figure 14.9   DNS message from 128.128.0.100 to its root
DNS 128.1.0.100.

In its reply to `chelford.eclectic.co.uk` (Figure 14.11), `integralis.co.uk` indicates that the answer field is used (number of answers=1) and puts the result in the answer field. It also gives the length of time this answer can be cached for (20 864 seconds or approximately 5 hours 48 minutes). Also notice that it does not put the name of the resource in the answer field but sets a pointer to the name in the question field to save space.

To help reduce the size of DNS datagrams, domain names are encoded. The encoding is fairly simple – a length field followed by each domain reference or host name. In fact space is only saved if multiple domain names are used in the same datagram. The complete domain name is terminated by a zero length field or null (Figure 14.12). To conserve space when multiple answers that have common name areas are

Mac header >		
IP header >		
IP addresses	Destination = 128.128.0.100	Source = 128.1.0.100
DNS header >	Identification = 2	Parameter = Response authoritative Recursion available
	Number of questions = 1	Number of answers = 0
	Number of authorities = 0	Number of additionals = 0
Question	Name = oz.integralis.co.uk Type = HOST Class = IN	
Answer	name = (Pointer to name in Question section) type = HOST class = IN TTL = (20 864 seconds) Length = 4 Answer = 130.1.0.7	

Figure 14.10   DNS reply from `co.uk` to
`chelford.eclectic.co.uk`.

Mac header >		
IP header >		
IP addresses	Destination = 128.128.1.77	Source = 128.128.0.100
DNS header >	Identification = 4	Parameter = Response authoritative Recursion desired
	Number of questions = 1	Number of answers = 1
	Number of authorities = 0	Number of additionals = 0
Question	Name = oz.integralis.co.uk Type = HOST Class = IN	
Answer	name = (Pointer to name in Question section) type = HOST class = IN TTL = (20 864 seconds) Length = 4 Answer = 130.1.0.7	

Figure 14.11   DNS reply from `chelford.eclectic.co.uk` to the host `genie.eclectic.co.uk`.

returned, pointers that point back to the common point of the domain name are allowed.

In Figure 14.12, the name `oz.integralis.co.uk` is the first domain name in the field, but the name `brewery.integralis.co.uk` is sent as well. The lengths are shown in hexadecimal and the offset within the datagram is shown at the side to help with the example. Octet 40 is null or zero indicating the end of the name. The next name starts at octet 41 with the length of that name. The octet at offset 49 has both of its top bits set (0xC0). This indicates that the rest of the bits in that octet and the following octet, a total of 14 bits, should be used as a pointer. That is, that the first part of the domain name (`brewery`) should be concatenated with the domain name pointed to by the pointer. In this case the pointer is 0x17 which equates to decimal 23. So the complete domain name is `brewery.integralis.co.uk`.

Unlike most instances in the TCP/IP protocol suite, the name fields do not have to be padded out to a 32-bit boundary, because the length fields passed with these names measure name lengths in octets, not 32-bit words. As in this example, names are not always going to end on a 32-bit boundary.

Offset:

20	0x02	o	z	0x0A	i	n	t	e
28	g	r	a	l	i	s	0x02	c
36	o	0x02	u	k	0x00	0x07	b	r
44	e	w	e	r	y	0xC0	0x17	

Figure 14.12   Encoding of domain names.

Using domain name services

A domain name server is an application program on a computer running TCP/IP network software. DNS does not have to run on a dedicated machine. Only in the largest systems will there be a lot of requests to the domain name server, so the processing overheads of this application are not normally high; a domain name server program can operate as a background task on a multitasking operating system such as UNIX. UNIX is usually supplied with DNS software called the name daemon, named.

Reducing the dependence on individual hosts files is a good reason to use DNS. Applications such as mail and World Wide Web rely on DNS, thus DNS has become critical to services used by business. It is therefore important that there is at least one other domain name server acting as backup. If the domain name server is not available for any reason, workstations and hosts will not be able to resolve IP addresses and connect to services. This is especially important to machines that do not store name-to-address mappings.

Most TCP/IP implementations allow the IP addresses of two name servers, the primary and secondary, to be configured.

Types of name server

There are four types of name server: primary, secondary, caching and slave.

The **primary server** has the master database of names and IP addresses for its domain. It has authority over the mappings in its database. It enables this database when it first starts up.

A **secondary server** has the same database as its associated primary server and acts as a backup for the primary server. It will copy the database from the primary server at regular intervals and respond to requests from hosts in the same way as the primary server. As hosts are added or moved, it should only be necessary to make changes to the primary server in a domain. If the primary server fails, it will be the clients that switch to the secondary server based on their configuration for primary and secondary name servers.

A **caching server** does not have a database of mappings between IP addresses and names at start-up, but knows of primary and secondary servers that can supply such information if required. In large installations, this server is used to take some of the processing overhead away from primary and secondary servers.

A **slave server** operates in a similar way to a caching server. The slave server stores the addresses of primary and secondary servers. It is not as sophisticated as any of the other servers and can only be used with recursive operation – it cannot communicate with any servers other than those defined in its list. If a server was nonrecursive and returned a response telling of another server that should be contacted to resolve a name, the slave server would fail.

Configuring domain name systems

The main objective of this section is to give some aid to understanding the configuration of a practical domain name server. The detail for a specific product may differ and the manufacturer's documentation should always be consulted.

The decisions to be made when setting up this service are more organizational than technical. The most important decisions in setting up a domain name service are the appropriate organizational structure and the names to be used for hosts. It is important that the hierarchy is easily understood by the system users and that the names and their meanings are easily remembered. Once the scheme has been planned, it has to be configured into the machines that will operate as name servers.

The basic steps necessary are:

- Gather the mappings between names and IP addresses you wish to control from this server.
- Determine how many servers you will use and whether you wish to use primary, secondary, caching or slave servers. In most situations a primary and secondary should be sufficient.
- If in a subdomain, the IP addresses of the root servers are required.
- If not connected to the Internet you may have to configure your own root servers.
- Configure the database file.
- Configure the end-user hosts and workstations to have the addresses of primary and secondary domain name servers, either directly or using BOOTP extensions.

When working with domain name server files, the period or full stop character ('.') should be observed and used with great care. Firstly, a period on its own is used to indicate the root or top-level domain. More seriously, if there is no '.' on the end of a domain name, the existing domain is appended to that name and it is possible to unintentionally create a name that is incorrect. When a domain name server is first set up, it is advisable to run the software with the debug option set, to check that names and addresses have been entered as intended and are being resolved correctly.

Different implementations of TCP/IP domain name services use different files for configuration but most are similar to those used with Berkeley Internet Name Domain Server, commonly known as BIND. BIND is distributed with 4.3BSD UNIX and the examples in this section are based around the BIND configuration. Consistent configuration of all database files is difficult; some versions of UNIX provide scripts which convert a simple hosts file into consistent database files.

```
;
;      boot file
;
;type          domain                  Source file or host
domain      integralis.co.uk.
primary     integralis.co.uk.              named.db
primary     23.128.IN-ADDR.ARPA.           named.rev
primary     0.0.0.127.IN-ADDR.ARPA.        named.local
cache       .                              named.ca
```

Figure 14.13 Example boot file.

Generally, there are five files that should be configured:

(1) Boot file
(2) Hosts database file
(3) Cache file
(4) Reverse database file
(5) Loopback file

The significance and configuration of each of these is as follows.

Boot file

The boot file is the first to consider. This tells the server where to find, and what to do with, the different database files that it needs for its operation. There are normally four different database files that a server can use. Figure 14.13 shows an example boot file. As with some other examples of TCP/IP control files, any line starting with ';' is for comment only, to make the file more readable.

In Figure 14.13, the domain is defined as integralis.co.uk which the server will add to names it receives that do not have a period '.' in them, assuming them to be part of this domain. The main database file for integralis.co.uk. is in the file named.db. This is the primary server for the domain 23.128.IN-ADDR.ARPA which uses file named.rev to list the reverse look-up database. The loopback file, named.local, is also present. Here a cache file is also defined called named.ca.

Database file

The main database file is the database of the hosts in the domain over which this server has authority. This is the name-to-IP-address mapping of nodes within the domain of this server.

At first sight, the syntax of the database file may not be self-evident. Figure 14.14 shows the definition for a domain. When a name-to-IP-address mapping is requested within a particular authority, the

```
;
;         Database File
;
;
;              addr- entry-
;name     ttl   class type  server
;
@                   IN    SOA    integv.integralis.co.uk. root.integv (
                                       1       ; serial
                                       3600    ; Refresh
                                       600     ; Retry
                                       3600000 ; Expire
                                       86400 ) ; Minimum
                    IN    NS     integv.integralis.co.uk.
localhost           IN    A      127.0.0.1
integv              IN    A      128.128.16.99
issws               IN    A      128.128.16.98
gandalf             IN    A      128.128.16.100
merlin              IN    A      128.128.16.200
mac       360000    IN    A      128.128.16.112
```

Figure 14.14 Example database file.

domain name server software will look in this database for the name and, if found, return the matching IP address.

The file begins with comment lines starting with ';'. One of these lines gives the headings of the five fields that may occur on each line in the main body of the file:

```
;              addr- entry-
;name    ttl   class type   server
```

In this file, only four of the fields are used except for the entry for mac.
The meanings of these fields are as follows:

- *name*   The machine name to be described by this record. If this field is '@', it is a shorthand for the current domain for this domain name server.
- *ttl (time to live)*   The time, in seconds, after which information must be refreshed for this record if the record was copied to another DNS. Not used by this DNS, as it is authoritative and is the master record.

  The ttl is always a number and since no number is present after the domain field, it is clear that the ttl for this record is the default value.
- *address class*   The address class of this entry, IN. A record for a machine which is Internet-compatible.
- *entry type*   Possible values are: A, NS, SOA, MX, HINFO, WKS, CNAME.

In this first record, the entry type is SOA, start of authority, which indicates that there follows a complete description and set of DNS records for the domain name server which is the authority for the domain in the domain field of this record. (The database could contain the records for more than one domain managed by this machine, within the same zone.)

- *server*   The content depends on the entry type. It may be an IP address or a domain name.

The start of authority record   The start of authority record contains additional fields that describe the validity of this DNS information. Some of this information is used by secondary and caching servers to ensure that their information is current.

`integv.integralis.co.uk.` is the full domain name to which this SOA record refers. Note that it ends in a period '.' to indicate this is a full name.

`root.integv` is the name of the mailbox to which DNS related messages should be sent. This is the person responsible for this system. Normally, as with other SMTP mailboxes, this would be `root@integv` but the DNS specification says that in this position the @ should be replaced by a period '.'

Since `root.integv` does not end in a period '.' it is considered as part of the local domain and expanded to `root.integv.integralis.co.uk`.

Inside parentheses are values describing the validity of this DNS information. In this file, their use is indicated by comments (;).

- *seria*   A 16-bit serial number which starts at 1 and indicates the version of the database information. It may wrap through 65 535 to 0.

  This must be changed by the system manager manually each time a modified DNS database is put on-line. It indicates to secondary servers copying this database that their information is out of date.

- *refresh*   A 32-bit number, which is the time interval in seconds at which those servers copying this database should refresh their copy. In this example the value is 3600 or one hour.

- *retry*   A 32-bit number, which is the time interval in seconds at which those servers failing to refresh this database should retry the refresh (10 minutes).

- *expire*   A 32-bit number, which is the upper limit on time (in seconds) at which the zone is no longer authoritative (1000 hours).

- *minimum*   The minimum ttl field which should be exported with any resource record sent in response to an enquiry to this DNS (unless one is defined specifically with the record) (24 hours).

While these figures are chosen for use on the Internet, it is unusual to change these values in most operational systems.

The next part of the file is the detail of the database, showing the names and IP addresses within the authority. IN indicates the address is an Internet IP address.

The following are some valid values for the entry-type field:

- *A*   A host IP address record. What follows is the IP address of the host named in the name field.

- *NS*   An entry for a name server. In an SOA record this is a repetition of the domain name immediately after SOA.

- *MX*   A mail exchange record. Indicates that the host acts as a mail forwarder. When an SMTP mailer tries to deliver mail to a host, it will request the MX records to determine which mail routes there are to that host. It then attempts to deliver the mail to the mail forwarders in the order of preference for the destination host.

- *HINFO*   A host info record. Contains useful information about the host such as machine type, operating system and serial number.

- *WKS*   Well-known service record. Gives the address, protocol and service provided by a machine, for example:

  128.128.32.5   Telnet   FTP
- *CNAME*   A canonical name. A nickname for a host.

These fields allow extra useful management information to be stored in the DNS database: aliases, mail exchange information, details of services provided and of host hardware and operating system. All these details can be obtained from the domain name server by a remote host. Detailed information on these fields and how to configure them should be obtained from manufacturer's documentation.

Cache file

The cache file is loaded into domain name server memory when the server starts. It contains information which must be immediately available to the server and normally identifies the servers which have authority over this server's domain. It may also indicate the addresses of root domain name servers.

The cache file shown in Figure 14.15 shows the domain name server for this domain and the address of a root server which will be loaded into the database cache so the domain name server can call them directly without having to search for them. Note that some of these entries have their own ttl. The domain name server should contact the root server to determine that the root server information is current and then ignore what it initially loaded into the cache.

```
;
;          cache file
;
;                          addr-   entry-
;name                 ttl   class  type   server
integralis.co.uk.     999999 IN    NS     oz.brewery.
                                          integralis.co.uk.
                      999999 IN    NS     as.isi.edu.
                      999999 IN    NS     ns.us.co.uk.
;
;
oz.brewery.integralis.co.uk 999999 IN    A      128.128.16.100
as.isi.edu.uk.        999999 IN    A      26.3.0.103
ns.us.co.uk.          999999 IN    A      194.3.5.2
```

Figure 14.15   Example cache file.

Reverse mapping

The second database file is for reverse mappings. Like the main database file, this file contains names and IP addresses, but it is intended to allow domain names to be found from IP addresses (Figure 14.16).

Loopback file

The last file is a loopback file which holds the loopback address used by the host (Figure 14.17).

```
;
;                      named.rev file
;
;                      Reverse Mappings for network 128.128
;
128.128.IN_ADDR.ARPA.   IN   SOA  integv.integralis.
                                  root.integv.integralis.co.uk. (
                                  1  ; serial
                                  3600        ; Refresh
                                  600 ; Retry
                                  3600000     ; Expire
                                  86400 )     ; Minimum
                        IN   NS   integv.integralis.co.uk.
;
;
99.16                   IN   PTR  integv.integralis.co.uk.
98.16                   IN   PTR  issws.integralis.co.uk.
100.16                  IN   PTR  gandalf.integralis.co.uk.
200.16                  IN   PTR  merlin.integralis.co.uk.
112.16                  IN   PTR  mac.integralis.co.uk.
```

Figure 14.16   Example reverse mappings file.

```
;
;      named.local file
;
;      Local Mappings for loopback 127
;
@      IN      SOA       integv.integralis.uk.com. root.integv(
                                   1       ; serial
                                   3600    ; Refresh
                                   600     ; Retry
                                   3600000; Expire
                                   86400 ); Minimum
               IN      NS        integv.integralis.co.uk.
127.0.0.0      IN      PTR       localhost
```

Figure 14.17   Example loopback file.

DNS and IPv6

An upgraded domain name system is an important component in the transition from IPv4 to IPv6. It allows managers to upgrade a server node transparently to the nodes which communicate with it. The upgraded DNS returns the machine's IPv6 address only to those nodes that are also using IPv6.

DNS for IPv6 uses a record entry type 'AAAA' in the DNS database file. This complements the IPv4 record type 'A'. It stores a single host IPv6 address in the colon-separated hexadecimal text format of IPv6, described in Chapter 11.

For reverse look-up – given an IPv6 address what is the domain name – a record type of .IP6.INT. is used in the reverse mappings file (named.rev). This complements the IPv4 record type IN_ADDR.ARPA. An IPv6 address in inverse format is represented as individual hexadecimal numbers (nibbles) separated by dots or periods. An example in RFC 1886 shows that the reverse entry for 4321:0:1:2:3:4:567:89ab would become

```
b.a.9.8.7.6.5.0.4.0.0.0.3.0.0.0.2.0.0.0.1.0.0.0.0.
0.0.0.1.2.3.4.IP6.INT.
```

in the reverse mappings file.

A request for all DNS records from an IPv6 host will receive all type AAAA and type A records for that name.

Hosts files and the DNS

The hosts file can still exist alongside DNS. When a workstation is asked to connect to something that has the wrong format for an IP address, it assumes this to be a name. There is no agreed standard for using DNS and a hosts file at the same time. Some systems try the hosts file first and others try DNS first if a server address is configured. With some systems the order of search is a configuration option. These differences can cause problems if the DNS server is slow or fails.

The message 'Unable to resolve host name' could be the result of a mistyped IP address, a missing or invalid hosts file, no domain name server entry in the workstation configuration or a failed DNS or DNS search. Hopefully, systems will give more clues, but alas it is not always so.

The use of the period '.' is important in the significance of a name. If a name string typed on a command line does not end in a period '.', the host will append a predefined string to that name. There is normally a file that allows a string to be defined which is appended to names that do not end with a period '.'. Thus, from `genie.eclectic.co.uk.` one would expect the string configured to be that of the domain this machine is in which would be '`eclectic.co.uk.`'.

Typing the request:

```
telnet wizard
```

would most probably cause a resolver to attempt to connect to `wizard.eclectic.co.uk.` If the intention was to access `wizard.integralis.co.uk`, the command should be

```
telnet wizard.integralis.co.uk.
```

with a period on the end. If the period is omitted then the command will expand to:

```
telnet wizard.integralis.co.uk.eclectic.co.uk
```

which is not the intention. Some systems may allow the minimum statement:

```
telnet wizard.integralis.
```

NIS

Open Network Computing (ONC) systems (more commonly known as the Network File System (NFS)) can use a service known as Network Information Services (NIS) to allow name-to-IP-address resolution. This system is described in more detail in Chapter 15.

Relevant RFCs

881   Domain names plan and schedule
882   Domain names: concepts and facilities
883   Domain names: implementation specification
1034   Domain names – concepts and facilities (updated by RFC 1101)
1035   Domain names – implementation and specification (updated by RFC 1348)

Summary

A good naming scheme will make it easier for users to remember the names of the hosts they select. Use of the domain name system can simplify life for users, particularly in a large network, by making host addressing easier than having to rely on IP addresses. DNS provides for central control over names and IP addresses and removes the need for individual hosts files. It allows control to be applied in a distributed way, and where it can be most effective in local sites and divisions.

The domain name protocol is quite complex syntactically but its operation is straightforward. A host, given a name, asks the server for a name-to-address translation. If a name server does not have that translation, it asks a server with higher authority than itself. This request will eventually be honoured, providing the name is correctly formed.

The configuration for the basic operation of domain name server can be quite awkward in all but the simplest of configurations, but once the core of information is in place, adding extra nodes into the databases is easy.

For participation in the Internet it is essential that you use domain name servers so that you can advertise your services to others and you can access Internet services.

15

The network file system

The Network File System (NFS) is a network operating system that provides transparent connections between networked computers, allowing files and directories on remote computers to appear local. Of all TCP/IP applications, this transparent interface makes NFS easiest to use once configured correctly.

NFS facilities and services are often not well understood or appreciated. If used correctly, they can provide a sophisticated and effective network system that hides the complexity of networking in a heterogeneous environment from the users. In this chapter we discuss some of those facilities with the intent of overcoming some of this unfamiliarity, covering:

- NFS
- XDR
- RPC
- Portmapper
- mountd
- Lockd
- Network information services
- Automounter
- PC-NFS
- Showmount
- Rpcinfo

As with TCP/IP, the term 'NFS' refers to a complete family of products, although Sun Microsystems Inc., the developers of NFS, prefer to call it **Open Network Computing** (ONC). Sun Microsystems released the specifications of some of the components of NFS into the public domain as RFCs and it has become an integral part of the TCP/IP protocol suite.

A number of manufacturers have produced versions of NFS which operate on their systems, so it is now available on most computers, from PCs to large mainframes, in some form. NFS provides an excellent way of transparently connecting PCs, mini- and mainframe computer systems together; it allows files to be stored centrally, shared among communities of mixed computers and supports remote printing. In essence, NFS provides virtual disk drive connections between computers. A remote file system can appear as an extension to your own local file system. Many people can access the same file systems and share data.

Sun Microsystems Inc. extended this UNIX service to allow PCs to access their computers using NFS through a product called PC-NFS, since when NFS and PC-NFS have become available on most computing platforms. Unlike other TCP/IP applications, NFS users need no specific training in using this system. When NFS is properly configured, users merely believe they have acquired additional disk capacity and printers.

So NFS provides a resource-sharing network system with similar features to Novell NetWare or LAN Manager from Microsoft. The major difference is that NFS bases the major part of its functionality on the native operating system available on the server hosts. As it need not add its own security and disk access mechanisms, it may appear less functional than these proprietary systems; in fact it has many of the same features but uses the security and multiuser facilities of UNIX or DEC's VMS or IBM's VM or MVS. This is just as powerful, if not more so, as a PC network operating system.

NFS architecture

NFS is usually implemented over the TCP/IP protocol suite but is not exclusive to it. The architecture is shown in Figure 15.1.

There are three layers: RPC, which defines the format of messages used by Remote Procedure Calls; XDR, the eXternal Data Representation is a consistent representation of data between different machine architectures; and NFS, the Network File System, is an application layer interface for file transfer, access and management. This adds another three upper layers to the transport layer of the TCP/IP model, making a seven-layer model similar to the OSI reference model. In fact, the functionality of the layers maps quite closely to the OSI functionality available in the equivalent layers.

Sun Microsystems also produced a number of utilities that work with NFS to provide a seamless network system. These are also discussed in this chapter.

Figure 15.1 NFS architecture.

The operation of NFS is based on a **stateless relationship** between a client and a server. A stateless system never declares that there is any kind of fixed relationship between the two communicating computers; they pass transactions between each other. A datagram protocol is appropriate for such a system, so NFS uses UDP rather than TCP. Other components within the NFS family can use either TCP or UDP.

Being stateless allows clients to manage server failure easily. Only the client need have knowledge of what it is trying to do and where in the sequence of events it has reached. Because there are no connections to close, the client merely retries requests while waiting for a response. Once the server is operational again, clients can carry on where they left off. In a state-oriented system, if a server fails, connections to it fail and have to be re-established when the server recovers. If both machines are aware of the state, they must resynchronize, so that the client starts again from the relevant position.

As NFS often uses UDP and fixed retransmission time-outs, it performs best over LANs with a low and consistent delay and where the number of datagrams lost is small. Depending on the network characteristics and application requirements, NFS may not operate satisfactorily over all WAN paths. Some suppliers have adapted the NFS standards to use TCP transport, which is intended to provide reliable, high-performance connections over wide area links. While filling an important role, these products are not yet widely available.

Remote procedure calls

Remote procedure call (or client/server) technology is becoming increasingly popular as a way of realizing distributed computing. Distributed computing is, in turn, popular as it allows the processing power of all computers on a network to be harnessed to the greatest effect. Until distributed applications became available, resource-sharing networks primarily allowed disks and peripherals to be shared; distributed computing also allows the processing power of a computer to be shared with other machines on the network. The computers on a network can then be viewed as a single powerful computer with a network-wide operating system.

The best programming practice normally requires that a 'good' program is structured in self-contained procedures or functions; each procedure handles a specific task, such as 'display this message', 'get some data' or 'calculate this equation'. Often such procedures are common to many programs; if shared on a network, they could be useful to many different applications. Also, the local machine may not be the most appropriate place to perform a certain procedure. There may be other machines on the network optimized for that task. Distributed computing systems allow the best processor for the task to be identified and used.

Another strength of distributed computing is its ability to reduce the amount of data transferred across a network, especially where databases are concerned. Instead of transferring the entire database to each user's computer where some database sort or extraction would take place, the tasks are performed on the computer that holds the database. Only the requests (database queries) and their results are transmitted across the network. This changes the processing power required in different machines. The server is no longer just acting as a file server; like a traditional mainframe or minicomputer, it is an 'application server' and performs a significant proportion of the user's processing activities. The client machine becomes a sophisticated display station. The advantage is that the network is not saturated with unnecessary data traffic.

An example RPC

Figure 15.2 represents a program which gets two values (A and B), adds them together and displays the results on a screen. There is a 'main' routine that calls the individual procedures: first get the data, then perform the calculation and then display the results.

If we look at the operation of our program in a little more detail, we realize that the data required in the calculations is obtained by another computer, 128.1.0.22. Our program running on our PC, 128.1.0.1, has to make connections to 128.1.0.22 to retrieve the data each time it is required. Many other users on the network require the same data and the same calculations to be performed. Also, there is a computer on the network that would be far more efficient at calculating this result[†].

[†]In this example, we are only considering the trivial case of the addition of two numbers. It is assumed that in reality the calculation to be performed is a more complex operation.

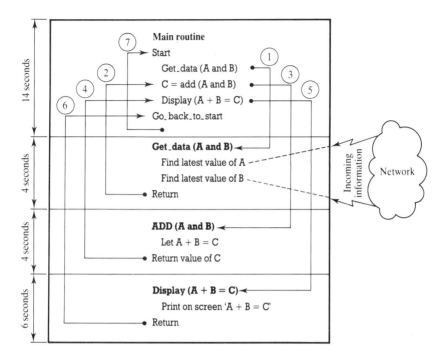

Figure 15.2 Diagrammatic form of simple program to add values.

As many users have the same needs, it makes sense to provide this calculation service as a utility, open to all computers on the network. It should run on a computer that can best perform it, from both a time and a cost perspective. The alternative is that the program runs on every PC. This is very costly due to the inordinate amounts of time it can take; while the computing time of a PC may be thought of as 'free', any unnecessary waste of users' time has an identifiable cost.

Traditional resource-sharing systems send large portions of data files in response to a simple request. It would also be beneficial to reduce the quantity of data passed to these many users, and allow programs to request specific items when necessary with a simple datagram call.

In our example (Figure 15.3), the data is on machine 128.1.0.22 and 128.1.0.5 is to be used for the calculations. So the whole program is to be distributed across the network with the procedure get_data on computer 128.1.0.22 and procedure add on computer 128.1.0.5. The main routine which coordinates the operation and displays the information is on PC 128.1.0.1.

The program on PC 128.1.0.1 will first send a request to 128.1.0.22 to get the numbers, then send them to 128.1.0.5 for adding and then display the result to the user on the PC's screen. By reducing the data volume and sharing a very powerful computer for the calculation, the

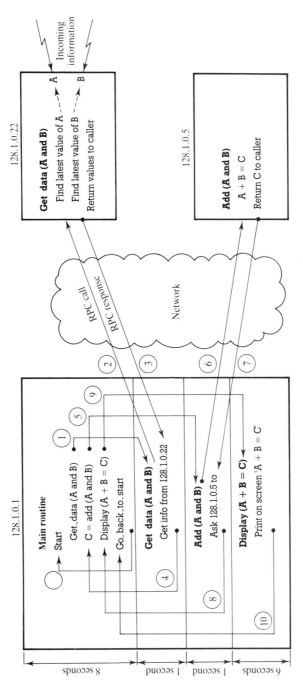

Figure 15.3 A simple distributed application.

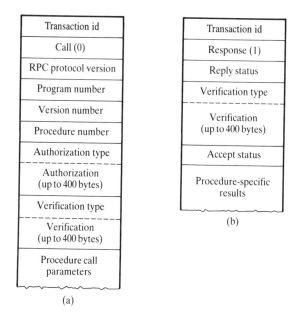

Figure 15.4   (a) RPC request and (b) RPC response headers.

time taken to execute the whole task may be reduced. In the example it has been reduced from 14 to 8 seconds (but then this example is hypothetical only).

The needs of a transparent networking system can be viewed in the same way. Many procedures are best performed by servers on the network, rather than performing all the work on the client. The principle is: distribute the functions to where they can be performed most efficiently and effectively. By using RPC technology, the operation of the system overall can be rationalized; rather than passing large amounts of data around the network, just pass the results required.

The RPC specification

The RPC request protocol header is shown in Figure 15.4. The RPC definition describes how remote procedures are accessed and how they should respond. It defines the structure of the protocol headers.

- *Transaction id*   This is used to identify requests uniquely and prevent them from being processed more than once. This is especially important, as RPC normally operates over UDP, so reliability is not assured. RPC must employ its own time-out, retry and check for duplicate requests.

A client does not know if a request has been performed unless it receives an appropriate response. If a request does not receive a response, the client assumes that the function was not performed on the server and it resends the request. Equally, it may be that the request arrived and the function was performed but the response did not reach the client. This uncertainty could cause any function to be requested twice which would cause difficulty with certain actions, such as deleting a file; the response to the second request would come back as 'file not found' since the file was already deleted by the original request. To prevent this confusion the server uses the transaction id. A server normally keeps a transaction cache (actually a transaction history file) to check for duplicate transaction ids. It will ignore the request from a client if it has already seen a particular transaction id. A client uses the transaction id to match responses with its request.

- *Call/response* This field indicates whether the header is a call, value 0, or a response, value 1.

- *RPC protocol version number* This allows multiple versions of RPC programs to be supported on a network. A server is able to respond to a request based upon the version of the request. For the NFS program, version 2 should currently be used.

- *Program number* This number identifies the particular RPC program to be accessed on a server. For example:

Program	Number
Portmapper	100000
rstatd	100001
ruserd	100002
NFS	100003
NIS	100004
mountd	100005
walld	100008
sprayd	100012
rexd	100017
lockd	100021

- *Program version* This number allows multiple versions of RPC programs to be supported on a network. A server is able to deal with a request based upon the version of the request. This simplifies upgrades and maintaining backwards compatibility.

- *Procedure number* Programs are normally composed of a number of different procedures. The procedure number defines which procedure within the program is required. For example, two of the NFS procedures are: 9 – create a file, and 10 – delete a file. A fuller list is given later.

- *Authorization information* This consists of two fields, the **credentials** and the **verification**. The credentials are used for authorizing the client to perform the action requested. RPC does not specify exactly how authentication should be performed, but version 2 suggests four types: none, UNIX, short and DES-encrypted.

  With UNIX authentication, the credentials field may contain:

  UNIX machine name
  user id (UID)
  group id (GID)
  an array of groups to which that user belongs

- *Authorization verification* In UNIX authentication, verification is not used. With DES-encrypted authentication, the verification field can contain a DES conversation key, encrypted using a Diffie–Hellman 192-bit public key encryption process.

- *Procedure call parameters* Any parameters required for the procedure call.

RPC defines the format of the header used to perform procedures on a server computer and is itself defined in XDR format.

External data representation

One of the problems with attempting to provide transparent networking in a heterogeneous computing environment is dealing with the representation of data, or, as it is called in OSI, presentation. Different computer operating systems and hardware have different ways of expressing information. How are values such as integers and negative numbers represented, and which bit is most significant, the first or the last?[†] A negative number can be represented with a **sign bit** or in **twos complement**. A computer that uses twos complement would misinterpret a value sent from another computer using sign-bit representation. Every type of numeric value or text character needs to be defined in a common way, to ensure that when they reach a remote machine, they arrive at an application in a form that retains the original meaning.

In OSI, the presentation layer protocols are explicit; each value exchanged has fields which define its type and size[‡]. In XDR the meaning is implicit; the format is predefined and there is no variation from the definition. A program communicating with a remote procedure using XDR must know what type of data to expect and so make provision for that. In an OSI system, each value is labelled with its type and size. While this is

---

[†]The different bit significance definitions used on computers are often referred to as 'little endian', least significant bit first, and 'big endian', most significant bit first.

[‡]The format for presentation is defined by ASN.1 and BER, described in Chapter 17.

more flexible, it also has potentially far more overhead, but the type of data exchanged can be understood unambiguously by any node receiving it.

XDR defines data in multiples of four bytes (32 bits). If the value to be represented does not fit exactly into a multiple of four bytes, the value is padded out with zeros. Some of the types of data defined are:

Type	Description
Integer	A value between −2 147 483 648 and 2 147 483 647
Unsigned integer	A value between 0 and 4 294 967 295
Enumeration	Similar to integer but for constants
Boolean	True or false
Floating point	A 'real' or floating-point value, for example 2.496
String	A string of characters
Arrays	Combinations of various types

XDR is a definition of how data should be formed before being transmitted over a network. An NFS client formats data based on XDR so an NFS server will translate data into the form understood by the local computer's operating system.

The services of NFS

NFS defines the top layer of the ONC architecture, which is an application layer interface. It maps remote file resources across the network so they appear as a file system to the local host computer. The network and networking issues are completely hidden from any application on that computer.

The services provided by this application layer are file system access and management (Table 15.1). Those familiar with the operations normally available on any file system may notice the absence of any open or close functions in this table. This is a consequence of a stateless system. NFS does not open files; it merely uses read and write to access areas of a file.

The NFS procedures shown in Table 15.1 are all accessed through program number 100003 and the procedure numbers used in the RPC header identify the specific procedure required of NFS.

Portmapper

Every program on a server needs to have a different UDP (or TCP) port number. ONC comprises a number of separate programs and requires several different ports. To reserve fixed well-known ports for the whole ONC family would be difficult to manage. Some of the numbers selected might already be used by other applications in some environments. This would complicate management as manual changes would have to be

Table 15.1 NFS procedures and procedure numbers.

NFS procedure	Procedure number	Description
null	0	Do no work, just return a response
getattr	1	Get file attributes
setattr	2	Set file attributes
getroot	3	Obsolete
lookup	4	Get file handle and attributes
readlink	5	Read from symbolic link
read	6	Read a defined number of bytes from a named file
cache	7	Write to cache
write	8	Write a defined number of bytes from a named file
create	9	Create a file
delete	10	Delete a file
rename	11	Rename a file
link	12	Link to a file
symlink	13	Create a symbolic link to a file
mkdir	14	Make a directory
rmdir	15	Remove a directory
readdir	16	Get a directory listing
statfsres	17	Get file system attributes

made for some machines at installation time and a consistent set of port numbers would not be available across all machines.

ONC programs use a process known as the **portmapper**. When an RPC process starts up, it obtains a free port number by some local means and then it registers itself and its port number with the portmapper process. When a program wishes to access a procedure on another computer, it uses the portmapper procedure on that machine. Portmapper is an RPC process that is always on well-known port 111. Using the portmapper procedure call, an application can find the port on which a particular program number has registered itself. The portmapper replies to the originator, giving the port number, so the originator is then able to send direct to the relevant port. This could be compared with the ARP process[†] or domain name server, but it is dealing with port numbers instead of IP addresses, MAC addresses or domain names.

In Figure 15.5, the NFS client wishes to communicate with NIS to make a request, but first it must discover the port number NIS is using on host 128.1.0.9. When NIS started on the host, it registered its port number with the portmapper. When 128.1.0.1 sends its request to the portmapper for the port number of NIS, the response indicates mountd is on port 2020. 128.1.0.1 can then make its call direct through port 2020.

[†]Analogies should not be taken too far. This request is not broadcast, it is to a specific server and it is a request about another process. Domain name server is a closer analogy.

Figure 15.5 Portmapper process.

mountd

As with other UNIX programs ending in 'd', **mountd** is the mount daemon in UNIX systems, although other operating systems will tend to use
the same name. mount is the command used on UNIX systems to make a
file system available, very much like typing a: or c: under DOS. mountd
is the server program for remote mount requests. As NFS is supposed to
provide a transparent service to the user, the same mount command is
used to establish connections with a remote system. The mount command is
modified slightly to cater for NFS; there is a command line option for this.

As NFS is a stateless system, it does not create a connection
between the client and server when mounting a file system. To establish
a relationship between the client and a particular area of disk on the
server, mount must have a reference to the appropriate directory; this
directory reference is usually provided by a numerical value known as a
file handle. When a remote file system is mounted through the mount
command, the mount client uses an RPC request to access the particular
file system to which the mount server (mountd) returns an appropriate
file handle.

Although it is stateless, mountd logs which clients have requested
a mount of the file system. This helps with network management when
there is some need to close the system or make other changes. But the

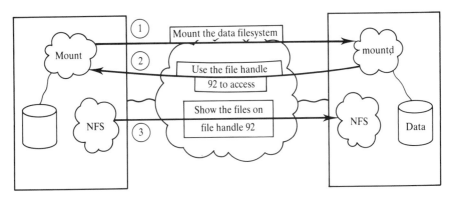

Figure 15.6 Mount.

record of clients is complicated by the stateless nature of the system. In the situation where a client using mountd fails, it will still remain logged in the mountd list. If a client does fail, when it restarts, it sends an 'unmount' message to all servers to ensure that outstanding requests are no longer valid.

In Figure 15.6, the client uses the mount command to access the file system on the remote host. mountd returns the file handle (92) for the appropriate file system, so NFS can now use that reference to access that disk or directory.

PC-NFS

Using PCs in the NFS environment has a particular problem, that of user validation. The user of a PC is rarely authenticated in any administrative way; anybody using a PC has access to all programs on it. If the PC programs in turn give access to services on networked hosts, it can compromise the security of those hosts unless the possibility has been considered and suitable security measures added.

Users on mini- and mainframe computers are usually validated for access to that computer. They are given individual user identification, passwords and perhaps account numbers that establish their rights to access certain areas of a system. The rights are often handled through a User IDentification number (UID) and Group IDentification number (GID). When users attempt to use a directory system or file, their UIDs and GIDs are checked for the relevant access rights. If such users attempt to access a remote system using NFS, their credentials on the original system, that is UID and GID, can be vetted for access on the other.

To allow PC users to access files on minis and mainframes, some method of authentication is required. For PC users of NFS, this is provided by a program called pcnfsd, which is a host-based RPC service. This

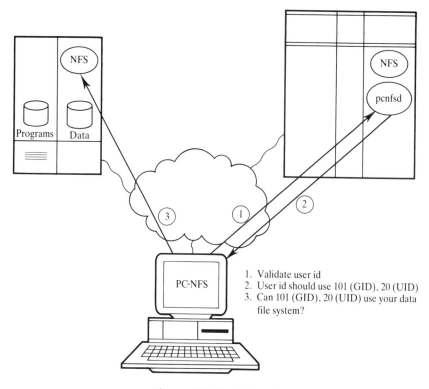

Figure 15.7 PC-NFS.

process runs on a mini- or mainframe and allows a system manager to define access rights for users of PCs. It asks for user identification and passwords from PC users before they are allowed to access any computers on a network. When a PC makes a request for connection, pcnfsd returns a UID and GID for that user to use when making a request to access remote file systems. This causes a PC user to be validated by a host like any other user. Of course for PC users to use pcnfsd they need to be managed by a host or NIS as with any other user.

Thus the pcnfsd is critical to the operation of PCs using NFS. It validates a user on that PC and controls their access to all other server computers within a network.

Figure 15.7 depicts the relationship between a PC using PC-NFS and pcnfsd. The address of the pcnfsd has to be programmed into the PC at installation. The PC first requests from the pcnfsd that the user id and password given at the login prompt be validated. If that user id is known to the computer operating pcnfsd and a valid password is given, pcnfsd will return a UID and GID. The PC can then use the UID and GID to access services on other hosts. In effect, the PC user is considered as a user of the computer that runs pcnfsd and has to be registered by the system manager as a user of that computer.

PC-NFS security

Security can be an issue with PC-NFS systems where there could be an attempted break-in across the network. The user id and password have to be transmitted across the network to the pcnfsd to be validated. As there is only rudimentary encoding[†] of this information, it is possible, given access to the encoding details, to decipher the user id and password from a network analyser trace. To combat this problem, there is a modified system based upon DES encryption, but this is not yet widely available.

The source code for the pcnfsd is widely available. Combined with other lax security, this could present an opportunity to those with ill intentions.

Network information services

When many computers are connected together using NFS, access rights to the files on those computers must be carefully managed. In a large network this will be complex. To simplify this, Sun Microsystems developed a system called Yellow Pages. This has since been renamed **Network Information Services** (NIS). Unlike RPC, XDR and NFS, the NIS specification is not published as an RFC. It is not a communications specification.

NIS is another RPC-based program service which is often available with NFS implementations. For file management purposes, NIS effectively treats the whole group of computers and network as a single logical computer. Access to all file services on all computers can be determined through a common access control database. The NIS database can be managed from any point in the network. This allows for a single point of control; instead of having to set up each user in every access control database on every computer that they wish to access, they can be configured just once in one central database.

NIS consists of a master database with slaves that can come into operation should the master fail. The slave servers are updated by the master to ensure concurrency throughout the system. Most of the files used by NIS are the standard access files used in a UNIX system, such as /etc/passwd, the password file and /etc/hosts, the hosts file. Because of this, NIS can be used in place of domain name servers, if all hosts use NIS to provide a common hosts file. This is an application that takes advantage of operating within a distributed computing environment.

When used on non-UNIX computers, suitable translation has to be performed to map the access control operation into the new computing system. This is a particular problem with PCs since they have no file access control.

[†]To put this into perspective, this is many times better than Telnet and FTP where user ids and passwords are transmitted in a readable 'clear text' format over a network.

NFS in operation

The biggest problem we have found with NFS is that some people have difficulty in understanding the mechanism for setting access rights to relevant directories and files on a server's disk. Once the access rights are established, NFS operation is largely trouble-free and transparent to users.

One of the major limitations of NFS relates to file formats. When moving data from one operating system to another, NFS does not translate files to suit the operating system of the destination machine. The files remain in the format of the operating system that generated them. When files are sent to a computer with a different operating system, it is possible that text files will not be in revisable format on the destination machine. Word processors on that machine will not be able to manipulate the file reliably. For example, the DOS text file format terminates each line with carriage return, line feed (0x0d0a). UNIX terminates a line with line feed only (0x0a). If the same file was examined with a DOS utility and then with a UNIX command, the output would appear in a different way. To overcome this problem, it is normal for NFS implementations to supply conversion programs to translate files from one form to another before they are revised. These are named to show the conversion performed, for example:

Action	Command name
UNIX to DOS	`unix2dos`
DOS to UNIX	`dos2unix`
VMS to UNIX	`vms2unix`
UNIX to VMS	`unix2vms`

Apart from the file format, file attributes are likely to differ as well. The DOS attributes define whether a file can be written to or only read from. If a file can be immediately read in DOS (it is not 'hidden' or 'system'), it can be executed, if it is an executable file. In UNIX, a file has more complex attributes that define three separate levels of access, and files that are executable are explicitly defined that way. Another difference is that, in a UNIX system, files have owners, but in DOS there is expected to be only one user at a time, so there is no concept of an owner. DEC VMS has four categories for file protection: system, owner, group and world. Each category may have a combination of read, write, execute and delete authority for the file. An access control list can disable access by individuals within a group.

A third issue is that of **name mapping**. It is common for different systems to have different limitations in the formation of file names. For example, DOS allows a name to be up to eight characters in length with an optional extension of three characters after a period (.). With many UNIX NFS servers, there can be up to 255 characters with any number of periods in the name. Names are case sensitive in some systems but not in others. Some NFS DOS client implementations will automatically convert long file names in a consistent way, but file names can, in any event, cause some difficulty on a network with mixed operating systems. The safe, but laborious, approach to preventing difficulty in accessing files is to define a common file-naming scheme which is acceptable across all hosts.

NFS datagrams

NFS always tries to send a UDP datagram of 8192 octets. This is of little consequence if the total transaction has less than 8192 octets of data. What happens at the datalink frame level depends on the LAN used, but most LANs support a maximum data unit of less than 8192. On Ethernet, with its maximum size of 1500 octets, this will cause six IP fragments or frames to be transmitted. Where the network is reliable, this provides very efficient transfer. But, if frames are lost or corrupted, the complete 8192-byte datagram will be retransmitted by the higher level protocol, as the loss of a single fragment causes all fragments to be retransmitted. In this case it may be desirable to modify NFS to use a lower NFS MTU.

General issues

Lock manager

Early versions of NFS, prior to SUN OS 3.0[†], did not provide file sharing of any kind, so users accessing the same file would potentially suffer the problem of multiple and inconsistent updates. The multiple update problem has existed since the beginning of multiuser systems. The basic problem is that if more than one user accesses the same file at the same time, they are all working on different copies of the original file. Programs normally load working copies of files from disk into RAM, so whichever file is saved last, back from RAM to disk, becomes the updated copy on disk. Changes made by the user who first saved the file will be over-written by the second and subsequent file saves; any changes made by the intermediate users who save early on will also be lost.

To manage the problem of multiuser access, file systems use file and record locking. **File locking** prevents more than one user from writing to a file at the same time[‡]. **Record locking** allows more than one user to write to the same file at the same time but restricts their updates to individual records within that file; this is commonly used with databases where access is to records rather than to the complete database.

[†]The early versions of file sharing were faulty. The problem is solved in SUN OS 3.2.

[‡]Ideally, it allows only one user to open a file with 'write access'. Any number may open it for read access provided they can tolerate the possibility that it is already out of date as someone is updating it. This assumes a file system which has the concept of opening for read and write. NFS does not.

An RPC program called the **lock daemon** or **lockd** manages record and file locking for an NFS system on a host. lockd allows files and areas of files to be locked on an NFS server to help prevent multiple updates. A major problem with lockd is that on some systems, it only provides advisory locking, that is, it does not prevent the file or areas of a file from being changed, but advises which files or areas are currently locked. For a networked system to function correctly with advisory locking, all devices using one host must consult the lockd and reliably check the lock status of files or records before writing to them. In advisory locking, if a procedure chooses to ignore the lockd and write anyway, the file could be corrupted. The alternative to advisory locking is mandatory locking, where only the procedure which locked the file or file area can perform a write. Whether lockd gives advisory or mandatory locking depends on the operating system which is supporting it.

With PC-NFS the requirement to use lockd is optional. If any single PC on a network is not configured to use lockd, that PC will not check for locks and hence can access files that others may be using, potentially corrupting the information in the file.

Another concern with lockd is what happens if the server or the client fails. This is a stateless system, but once a client locks an area or all of a file, it constitutes a 'state'. If a client fails when using a server with lockd, lockd will keep the relevant areas of files locked for the client even after it has failed. When the client becomes operational again it should send calls to ensure that all files, or files areas it had locked, are freed. If the server with lockd fails, it will not normally restore the locks on recovery, so computers using it will have difficulty with their applications when the server returns.

Printing

NFS allows PCs to redirect their print output to the NFS server. This allows centralized printers to be shared among many users as with any other network operating system. However, like any other network operating system, shared printing raises certain issues that need to be considered before it will operate reliably or satisfactorily.

For shared printing, print output is sent to a print queue as a spool file. The spool file holds the print until the printer is free, after which it can be sent to the printer and removed from the queue. It is the handling of these spool files that causes some difficulty. In spooled systems, to ensure that the printer can be used continuously, the print queue is processed in the order in which spool files are closed, not in the order in which they are opened. Short print tasks will emerge before long tasks which were started earlier.

One of the major problems with printing on a PC network is the result of the way certain older applications for DOS were written. When sending print to a printer, these applications assumed that the printer was physically connected to the port on the machine. In these circumstances any character sent to the printer would be printed immediately.

Some of the older PC applications do not send an end-of-file or perform any other action that signals to the operating system that printing is complete. This end-of-file is needed to close the print spool file output so that printing can commence. The end-of-file does not matter if a printer is directly connected, for when these applications were written they were the only applications on the PC. Now that the output is going to a spool file, if the file is not explicitly closed, it will not be printed. This problem is often easy to detect. When the application is closed and the DOS prompt reappears, suddenly files are printed. On closure of the application, the print redirector recognizes that the application must have finished printing and it automatically closes the output port. This in turn closes the spool file so it is printed.

Most network printing systems provide a number of ways to handle this. One possibility is a **hot key**. PC-NFS provides a hot key; when the user thinks the printing is finished they use the **hot key sequence** which causes the spool file to be closed and hence the file to be printed. This could cause a problem if the user misjudges the situation, so a more automatic method is preferable.

Such a method is the **inactivity timer**. This timer tests for inactivity on a spool file; if no data has been written to it for a specified amount of time, usually of the order of 20 to 60 seconds, the spooler program assumes that the print job is completed, and so closes the spool file. This works well in some circumstances but not all. As applications have become more complex, and printing has changed from just text to include bit-mapped graphics, the processing time to generate such print has become longer. If the spooler time-out is not long enough and there is a pause in output, the spool file will be closed and printed. The rest of the output becomes a new document and may well be delayed by other documents in the queue. Graphics and desktop-publishing packages that print text and complex drawings are particularly problematic. It can take considerable time to generate a 300 dpi A4 laser print of a drawing, so with a time-out that is too short, pictures or pictures and text intended for a single page may end up split across several sheets of paper.

One answer is to set long time-out values (60 seconds). This causes its own problems as a long time-out causes the spool file always to wait that time before printing. Even short files, single pages for example, take a long time to print, waiting for the time-out to mature. The safest solution is to dispose of mid-1980s applications and upgrade to newer versions that are network aware.

Another area of difficulty with NFS print comes from applications that allow users to escape to DOS without closing the application. If they use the EXIT command to return to the applications from DOS, this can cause the print port to be closed, hence closing the spool file and possibly delivering print before it is completed.

Sometimes there is difficulty with the standard print commands as well, so replacement commands such as `netprint` are provided as an alternative. It is usually recommended that the network print commands are used in place of standard print commands, as they will be more reliable and make more efficient use of the system.

Spooling is designed to allow many users to share one peripheral. When peripherals were slow and the time to produce the spool file (the time to create the print) was short, it could free the user's application for other activities even though the print had not been completed. In a networked environment, it is important to consider whether spooling is occurring more than once. When printing complex graphics output or the software-based fonts of Windows 3.1, the spool file may be many megabytes; the requirement to complete the spool file before anything is sent to the printer could delay any output for periods of minutes or hours if the application is wrongly configured. This was discussed in Chapter 7.

Automounter

Another server provided with later versions of SUN OS is the **automounter**. This system allows communications to be established with servers dynamically as and when required. The client does not have to mount many file systems permanently. When a utility or application attempts to use an area of a file system controlled by the automounter, it then attempts to make the necessary mount at that time; after a period of inactivity it will unmount the file system.

NFS testing

nfsping

NFS provides its own version of ping for testing that a server is available. **nfsping** is a client RPC command that attempts to get a response from the NFS server program on a host specified on the command line. If it does, it returns a message that tells the user that NFS is available.

nfsping is an RPC request to the 'null routine' of the normal NFS program. The NFS program returns the data sent, and the response can be timed by the client.

rpcinfo

The utility `rpcinfo` shows the program number and versions of RPC programs running on a host. This is a useful way to determine that all ONC services are available and working on a particular host.

```
rpcinfo    -u (over UDP)
           -t (over TCP)
           -p (by program number)
```

```
c:>rpcinfo -p integv
[program,        version,        protocol,    port ]:
100003,          2,      17,          2049
100004,          2,      17,          1027
100004,          2,      6,           1029
100004,          1,      17,          1027
100004,          1,      6,           1029
100012,          1,      17,          1050
100005,          1,      17,          1051
```

Figure 15.8   rpcinfo command.

The command:

```
rpcinfo   -u integv mountd
```

tells if the mountd program is operational on integv.

The example shown in Figure 15.8 shows the RPC services available on host integv. Program 100003 is NFS, version 2 running over UDP (protocol 17) on port 2049. Also shown is NIS, program number 100004 that has both version 1 and 2 running both on UDP (protocol 17) and TCP (protocol 6). 100012 is sprayd and 10005 is mountd.

showmount

As shown in Figure 15.9, the showmount command, run on the client, lists those parts of the file system that are available for mounting and the user ids at the server machine that are allowed to mount those directories.

nfsstat

This is the NFS equivalent to the netstat utility used with IP. It provides breakdown statistics of the number and type of RPC calls to NFS for server and client (Figure 15.10).

Calls shows the total number of RPC calls made to the server or from the client as appropriate, badcalls the number of errors, nullrecv an empty call, badlen a wrong length call and xdrcall a

```
c:>showmount gandalf
Export list for gandalf
/usr/user1    user1
/usr/guest    everyone
/usr/test     everyone
/             root
```

Figure 15.9   Example of showmount.

Client RPC						
calls	badcalls	retrans	badxid	timeout	wait	newcred
63	0	0	N/A	N/A	N/A	N/A

Client NFS						
calls	badcalls	ndget	ndsleep			
63						
null	getattn	setattn	root	lookup	readlink	read
0 0%	3 4%	0 0%	0 0%	15 24%	0 0%	0 0%
wrcache	write	create	remove	rename	link	symlink
0 0%	40 63%	0 0%	0 0%	0 0%	0 0%	0 0%
mkdir	rmdir	readdir	fsstat			
0 0%	0 0%	0 0%	5 8%			

Figure 15.10   Example of nfsstat.

problem in comprehending the content of the call. The rest of the values break the calls down into specific types.

spray

This is a test that can be used to check the integrity of an NFS system. The destination host must have an operational sprayd, the **spray daemon**. As its name might suggest, spray sends consecutive RPC spray requests without waiting for responses. It can be used to determine if a server can support the maximum data rate the client can achieve.

   This test can generate very high numbers of datagrams on a network, particularly from a high-performance workstation or server. It is important not to leave this test running on an operational network for more than a few seconds, especially if network loading is already high. It can interfere with the correct operation of other services.

Configuring NFS security

Newcomers to NFS are frequently confused by the configuration of the databases NFS uses to control access. There are normally two database files: one file, usually called 'export', defines which parts of the server's directory system are available for access; the other file is for security and defines which users and machines are allowed access.

   User access control is straightforward if the host systems use the same operating system. When they have different operating systems, there can be some difficulty in how to cross-map user ids from one host to the other. To access files on an NFS server, a valid user id is required on that server. A user connecting through NFS client software will have logged in to their local machine, but their login there will not relate to the user id required on the NFS server computer. To manage the mapping of user ids between the computers, a proxy database is used which relates the incoming user id to one that exists on the server. It is the mapping through this proxy database that often causes confusion and problems. One source of confusion is that there are two different items which are both loosely called 'user id'.

A computer user is allocated a unique alphanumeric user id which they type in reply to the logon prompt 'enter user id'. But a user on a VMS or UNIX operating system, for example, would also be referenced by the system through their UIC [group, member] or user id (UID)/group id (GID) pair of values. These are both *numerical* values. The VMS UIC member or UNIX UID is a number unique to each user and VMS UIC group or UNIX GID is used to collate users into groups. When you are assigned an alphanumeric user id on a UNIX host, the system manager also defines a UID and probably a GID, for example:

Claire   UID = 201   GID = 10
Katie   UID = 202   GID = 10

The two users, Katie and Claire, are both in the same group but have different user ids. NFS uses those numeric values of UID and GID to refer to a user rather than the alphanumeric user id or name.

A VMS host performs user id handling in a different way, so connecting between VMS and UNIX would require some conversion of the two security systems. Some systems map these names and group ids in very complex ways. Here we will use a more straightforward example. If Katie and Claire both need to access a VMS host using NFS, they require an account on the VMS host. The proxy database would define the mappings. Assume the two women are registered on the VMS host as Claire_unix and Katie_unix. The proxy database would be something like:

Claire_unix   UID = 201   GID = 10   host = unix
Katie_unix   UID = 202   GID = 10   host = *

This database structure is interpreted as defining that if a file access request is received on this host with a UID of 201 and GID 10, it would be assumed to be from Claire_unix and hence would have the access right of account Claire_unix on this host, but only if the requests came from a host called unix. A request with UID 202 and GID 10, on the other hand, would be checked against the access rights defined for Katie_unix and would be allowed from any host on the network. (Host = * is treated as a wildcard.)

The above explanation is not specific to any particular implementation; it is merely intended to highlight one of the major issues that has to be addressed when configuring an NFS system to operate effectively and securely across mixed vendor platforms.

This mapping problem becomes more acute for the **superuser** on a host. If the superuser (or **root** on UNIX) were to request remote access, in theory they could gain unrestricted access to the server host. This is likely to be unacceptable! It is common for a special setting to be defined for an incoming superuser which gives either restricted rights or no rights at all. If it was intended that superuser should have complete rights on a server, a suitable mapping could be devised, but fortunately this is not normally the default configuration.

The 'export' database defines which areas of a host will be made available to NFS clients. It lists the **export name** by which a file area will be known remotely and the hosts that are allowed access to that area. For example:

> net_chess   /usr/games/chess   pawn, queen, king

This configuration allows the files in the directory /usr/games/chess to be made available to NFS clients as a file area called net_chess. The NFS client would mount with a command something like:

```
mount -t /games gandalf:net_chess
```

Whenever the client is working in the directory games, it would be connected to the host gandalf accessing the exported name net_chess which would be known to the server as directory /usr/games/chess. The NFS client would see /games as the root of the directory, not as a subdirectory.

Configuration issues

Most NFS implementations provide a number of adjustable parameters. How these parameters are set depends upon the implementation, but they cover the following factors. NFS version 4 dynamically alters some of the parameters to achieve better performance over wide area links.

Soft mount

A NFS connection normally is considered as a **hard mount**; if the connection to the server fails, the client continues to retry until it gets a response when the server becomes operational again. Setting the option to operate as a **soft mount** causes the connection to fail if a server fails. The NFS client software will return an error message to the application software if NFS has retransmitted a request a specified number of times without obtaining a response.

While most applications use the hard mount option, some may benefit from soft mount so that they can quickly revert to fallback servers if there is a server failure. The use of this option is service dependent.

Read maximum transfer size

This sets the maximum size of data that can be read from the server in one request. This prevents the client from requesting a datagram that is too large for some hardware or software component in the network, but decreases efficiency if set smaller than necessary. This value should be in increments of 1024 but less than 8192.

Some implementations of UDP allow the Maximum Datagram Size (MDS) that UDP will send to IP to be restricted. The MDS must be greater than the read maximum transfer size to allow for the headers of UDP and RPC.

Reducing the size of this parameter reduces the amount of memory required but also decreases performance.

Write maximum transfer size

The same as the read maximum transfer size but for write operations.

Time-out

This sets the time-out value for RPC retransmissions. It is often set to a value of about 700 ms. Too low a value will cause unnecessary retransmissions on a system that may already be overloaded as it is failing to respond. Balanced against this is the need for quick recovery after an occasional network error.

Time-out can only be chosen once the performance of a particular installation is understood. If soft mount is used, it should be set in conjunction with retransmissions (see below). A system manager should never consider changing time-out without careful consideration. A good maxim is that it should only ever be increased, not decreased. It would be appropriate to increase it if regular time-outs were occurring over a 'slow' wide area link. The temptation is to use a low value (down to perhaps 150–200 ms) if the client/server path involves no wide area connections, a fast response is essential and there is an unexpectedly high error rate on the LAN – but this is the wrong technical solution. The proper action is to reduce the error rate so that the time-out never operates! The problem is that if it is server (or bridge) loading that is causing time-outs, repeating the request just adds to network and server load and will potentially cause network traffic to go unstable. The network fills up with retransmissions and the amount of useful work reduces to near zero. This is one cause of LAN 'meltdown' or the 'black hole' effect.

Retransmissions

This sets the number of successive retransmissions after a no response time-out on a soft mount connection. This value should be set along with time-out to suit the local conditions. The client will wait the time-out times the number of retransmissions before giving up and reporting a failure. Thus, one option is to keep the number of retransmissions small so the problem is reported as soon as possible. If the network is apt to lose datagrams, the retransmission count may be increased, but once again it would be far better to treat the disease (lost datagrams) and not the symptoms (error reports).

In most operational circumstances, retransmission counts range from 5 minimum to 25 maximum. The lower value reflects the fact that 5 successive retransmissions on a LAN should be quite exceptional, but 25 with a time-out of 700 ms gives a maximum of 15 seconds of network disruption. This could be due to the temporary failure or reinitialization of WAN equipment, or more likely some network operator changing a network cable. There should never be a need to set a higher retransmission value as this will tend to hide the underlying problem and is likely to exacerbate it. Instead, the real cause of the datagram loss should be solved.

Port

The default port number for NFS is 2049. It can be altered if necessary with the port option. Changing this value could allow different NFS server processes to operate on the same host identified by different port numbers. One could perhaps be for systems development staff, the other for the normal business production system.

If problems are experienced with PC-NFS that appear to relate to datagram sizes, it is possible that trailer encapsulation is being used. Trailer encapsulation can cause PC-NFS to fail if large frames are required.

Relevant RFCs

1014   XDR: External Data Representation standard
1057   RPC: Remote Procedure Call protocol specification (also covers portmapper)
1094   NFS: Network File System protocol specification (also covers mountd)
1790   An agreement between the Internet Society and Sun Microsystems, Inc. in the matter of ONC RPC and XDR protocols
1813   NFS version 3 protocol specification
1831   RPC: Remote procedure call protocol specification version 2
1832   XDR: External data representation standard
1833   Binding protocols for ONC RPC version 2

Summary

NFS provides a mechanism for connection between different computing systems which allows the remote disk and filing systems of a server to appear as extensions to the local filing system of the client. Access to a remote computer can be transparent to applications on a client computer.

To provide transparency, the NFS architecture uses XDR to define the representation of information and RPC operation to carry the requests and responses of the NFS.

NFS can provide a resource-sharing networking system just like Novell NetWare or LAN Manager from Microsoft. The major difference is that NFS bases the major part of its functionality on the operating systems available on the hosts.

NFS is now available on most computers from PCs to large mainframes, so, combined with its transparent interface, it is currently the best vehicle for integrating different computing systems and architectures over TCP/IP.

Consideration must be given to file and record locking, the configuration of access rights, and the conversion of (text) file types between different systems.

16

Routing IP

As networks grow larger and more complex, it becomes more important to use routers to divide the network into manageable areas. As well as providing better control of traffic, routers often act as the political boundary between systems. Many companies are therefore interested in the management issues of routers and the technical issues of how they work. In this section, we will consider the technical principles of routing and how they are implemented in TCP/IP networks. Some of the managerial issues were covered in Chapter 5.

Here we will cover:

- Principles of routing
- Router protocols
- Routing Information Protocol (RIP)
- The hello protocol
- The exterior gateway protocol
- Gated
- Open Shortest Path First (OSPF)
- IS–IS routing
- Border gateway protocol
- Using multiple routing protocols

Principles of routing

End systems and routers cooperate to make routing work. To consider the routing of TCP/IP, we must examine how routing works both in the end station and in the routers themselves.

Some of the design considerations and problems of routing TCP/IP have been further complicated by the confusion in terminology and in technology between bridges, routers, brouters and gateways. We have attempted to explain what these terms mean, how we use them and to use them consistently. Some authorities may disagree with our choice of terminology so be aware that these terms are still used differently by other bodies.

First of all, we will look at routing from the perspective of the end node and then move on to look at the network relays and the issues with routing and bridging. There are three major processes performed in a routing system:

(1) The end node needs to know how and when to communicate with a router.

(2) The router needs to know how to determine a suitable path to a remote network.

(3) The router on the destination network needs to know how to connect to the end node.

Routing is performed at layer 3 of the TCP/IP model, that is, at the network or IP layer. So, routing is transparent to the TCP and UDP layer. These layers have no concept of routing; they communicate end to end (Figure 16.1).

To allow routing to work, we have to apply the concept of networks having their own address or, in TCP/IP, a **network number**, sometimes referred to as a **network id**. Routing operates by recognizing that a particular network number relates to a specific area, like addressing of mail defines areas such as the United States of America, the United Kingdom or Germany. These countries are defined areas that a message could be routed to. The same technique is necessary for networks[†].

It is at this point that the differences between class A, B and C addressing schemes become significant. The significance is which of the 32 bits are dedicated to network number definition. It is this network number that end nodes and routers use to determine when and how to route datagrams to their destination. The basic routing rule of TCP/IP is:

[†]As discussed more fully in Chapter 5, the standard addressing scheme in TCP/IP is not hierarchical or geographic. IP network numbers really only identify organizations that are in control of a network rather than full geographic areas.

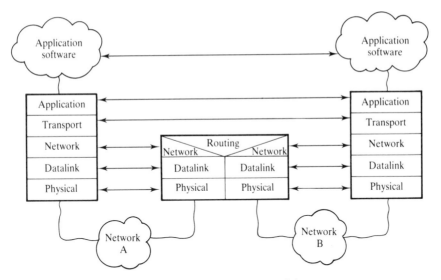

Figure 16.1   Routing model.

Systems on different ports of a router must have different network numbers (or subnetwork numbers).

When discussing technology, it is always difficult to agree on standard definitions. Throughout this book we have used the terms 'network' and 'local area network' without giving strict definitions. It is now possible to give an answer to the question 'what is a LAN?'. If systems at either side of a router require different network numbers (Figure 16.2), we have just defined a dividing line between one LAN and another. Therefore, we could suggest that a single LAN consists of all the components that create a system up to a router, which includes cable, repeaters, bridges and software up to the network layer. Joining these LANs together becomes internetworking, for which TCP/IP was designed.

One of the confusing areas of TCP/IP is that what the industry now calls *routers*, systems which relay information at the network layer, have been referred to as *gateways* for many years. Today's terminology uses the term 'gateway' to mean a device that provides conversion between two incompatible systems at a high level (protocol conversion). Gateways in TCP/IP converted between dissimilar network technologies, so the term was not inappropriate. TCP/IP books and manufacturers' product literature still use the term 'gateway'. Today, when TCP/IP literature refers to a gateway, it is likely that a router is being discussed. We have chosen to use the term 'router' throughout, except when talking about the devices and protocols in the Internet.

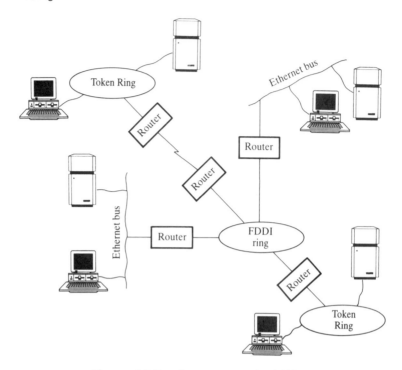

Figure 16.2 Routers connecting LANs.

Routing at the end node

For routing to work, an end node has to play its part. An end node has to decide whether a datagram it wishes to send is intended for the same network it is connected to, or for another. This, in principle, is quite a simple task. When asked to transmit an IP datagram, the IP layer first compares the network number portions of the source and destination IP addresses. If the network numbers are the same, the destination node must be on the same network. IP merely uses the ARP protocol, if it has not previously done so, to get the MAC address of the destination node. It then can send datagrams directly to that node. If the network numbers are different, then it is clear that the destination node is on a different network and the services of a router are required to relay this datagram. The end node now has to know how to transfer the datagram to a router. In most TCP/IP systems, the IP address of one router is configured into the software when it is set up, usually in a field referred to as the **default gateway**. (It would now be more appropriate for it to be called the default router, but that's all history!)

Having read the IP address of the default router from its configuration details, the end node sends the datagram to the router in the same way it would to any other IP device, by placing the MAC address of the router in the datalink frame. So the end node needs the MAC address of that router. It gets the MAC address, in the standard way, by broadcasting using the ARP protocol, if the address is not already in the ARP cache.

Three points emerge:

(1) Each router port has its own unique IP address on the IP network number to which that port connects.

(2) One router will be known by more than one IP address.

(3) One major function of this router IP address is that end systems can obtain the MAC address of the router by including the router's IP address in a standard ARP request.

It is also important to emphasize that the source and destination IP addresses in the datagram always refer to the two *end nodes* which are communicating. Only the MAC address of the router is used in the datagram; its IP address is only used to find that MAC address. To express this another way, MAC addresses are used in one-hop communication on the same LAN. IP addresses always describe the end-node-to-end-node communication, the original source and ultimate destination.

Once the end node sends the datagram with the router MAC address, it will be picked up by the MAC hardware of the router and passed up to its router IP layer. (Routers operate at the IP layer and hence run a full IP process.) The IP layer will realize that the destination address is not its own[†] and pass the datagram to the routing software, ready to be directed towards the relevant network.

Figure 16.3 summarizes the complete sequence of events for an end node wishing to send a datagram to a node located on a different network. It details the MAC and IP addressing of communication through a router. Note that, as stated above, the MAC addresses relate to the physical transportation between the *end node* and the *router*, and between the *router* and the *end node*, one-hop communication, whereas IP addressing relates to the end-to-end connection.

Node A (142.1.0.9) is about to make a connection with node B (30.0.0.1). First of all, the IP layer receives a datagram for node B. It compares the network address with its own, along with a subnet mask if necessary, and decides a router is required. It then decides to send the datagram to the router, but not knowing the MAC address of the router it has to perform ARP (frame 1) and gets an ARP response (frame 2). Node A now has the MAC address of the router so it sends the first frame, using the MAC address of the router with the IP address of node B.

When the router receives this datagram, it passes it to the IP layer on network 30.0.0.0 and realizes that it does not have the MAC address of node B, so it performs an ARP to get the MAC address (frame 4). It gets a response (frame 5) so it can then forward the datagram (frame 6) which

---

[†]Routers can act as end nodes for configuration and diagnostic messages.

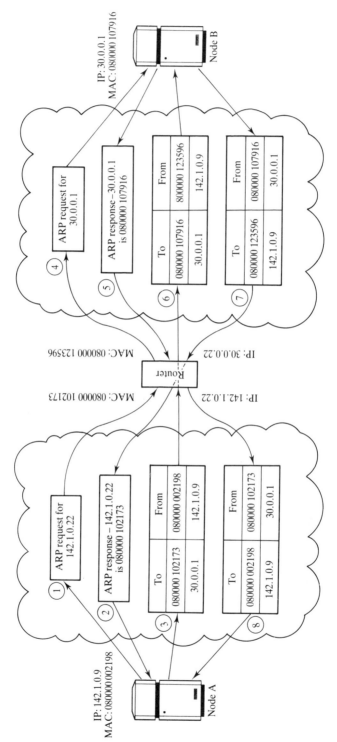

Figure 16.3 Routing at the end nodes.

is frame 3 with the MAC address changed to suit network 30.0.0.0. The response from node B is passed direct to the router (frame 7), as all of the MAC addresses have been learnt and the router passes the frame direct to node A (frame 8). From now on datagrams flow without the need for further ARP requests as the relevant addresses will be in the ARP caches.

In this simple example, there is only one router in the chain. In any chain of routers, the last router must direct the datagram to the destination end node. The process is the same: if it does not already know the mapping between the end node IP address and the MAC address (ARP cache), it uses the ARP protocol to obtain it. This is a standard procedure for the IP layer.

Note that ARP broadcasts do not travel through routers directly. In practice, one of the advantages of routers is their ability to block ARP broadcast traffic. In this example, ARP was required on both networks, so the broadcast was required at each end of the connection, giving the impression that the ARP request passed through the router. This is only the case if the end nodes have never communicated with the router. It is quite likely that a router will have discovered the address of a number of end nodes. Commonly used end nodes will be in many ARP caches, as they are operational for long periods of time. Routers will not have to keep relearning these MAC addresses.

The default gateway pitfall

A potential pitfall in routed networks is that routing must be considered separately for each direction of transmission. It is possible for datagrams to arrive at a host from a remote network and the recipient makes no attempt to reply. This is usually because the recipient has no return route configured. Even though information about a router is available from the incoming datagram, hosts will not reply unless they themselves are configured with a default gateway or otherwise know about a router for the return path.

Routing with more than one router

Our previous example was a relatively simple routing scenario. We now consider more complex configurations.

If we extend our example network of Figure 16.3, this creates two further issues (Figure 16.4):

(1) How do the routers know how to route between two end networks?

(2) How does the end node choose between multiple routers?

To solve the first problem, routers must learn about each other and the networks that are available. This can be done in two ways:

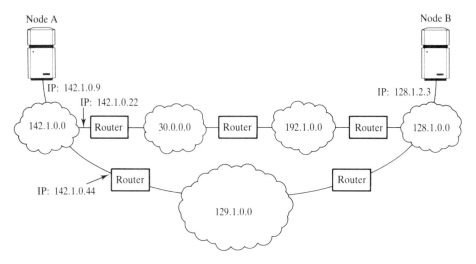

Figure 16.4 Routing between routers.

(1) By manually creating configuration tables in the router (routing tables). These tables list networks which exist, identified by network number and the IP address of the router that represents the next hop in the best route to that network.

(2) By using a protocol that allows the routers to discover each other and the networks they support.

Routers with both of the options are readily available, but it is more common for the routers to communicate with each other using a routing protocol rather than using fixed tables[†]. We will consider these protocols later.

A router sends an IP datagram towards the destination IP address by looking up the next hop router for the network number of that destination address in its routing tables; it sends the IP datagram to the MAC address of the port on that router, just as the final router will send it to the MAC address of the host.

How does an end node make use of more than one router if it can only be configured with the address of one default router? It only knows of that router, not of others that may be on the same network.

In many TCP/IP implementations, the default router is always the starting point. On trying to send datagrams to a new network, the end node will first send them to its default router. Standards state that if this router is aware that it does not hold the best route to the destination network, it will use the ICMP route-change request message to advise the end node to redirect the datagrams to a more appropriate router. On sending this

---

[†]Some organizations prefer to use manually configured tables as a security measure to control how networks can be accessed from each other. The most modern routing protocols address some of the security concerns that created this need.

message, the default router also forwards the first datagram that caused the redirect to the second router, which it suggested as a better route.

If the host does not obey the redirect, the default router must continue to forward any datagrams received. The purpose of the ICMP route change requests is to build a list in the host of the first routers it should use for current destinations – a routing table.

Secondary default routers

This dependence on a default router can affect system reliability. A workstation or host which can only identify one router is dependent on the availability of that router. This is fairly common with PC-based products. Even if multiple routers exist, when a default router fails it is possible that nodes configured for that router will not be able to send to other networks. The default router is configured in the software of each end node and cannot easily be changed. Some PC systems get around this by allowing a **secondary default router** to be defined.

ICMP router discovery

The preferred method for hosts to determine all the routers that are available on their LAN is by using ICMP router discovery protocol (Chapter 11). Of course, the routers must also have that protocol enabled. Most routers now support it. It is important to check that host implementations also support ICMP router discovery, particularly PC implementations. PC software developers were slow to adopt it.

Eavesdropping

Another method for determining the first router is for a host to listen to the routing information passing between routers. Known as eavesdropping, it is a common technique with more powerful computers such as UNIX machines. The host can then build its own internal routing table and immediately choose the best first hop router for a particular destination network. The disadvantage is that the host is dependent on a particular routing protocol (usually RIP, described below). As communications managers change to other more sophisticated routing protocols, they may need to continue to run RIP just to keep the eavesdropping hosts informed. This is *the* reason for the introduction of ICMP router discovery – it specifies exactly how hosts should discover their first router and removes host dependency on a particular routing protocol. Eavesdropping is now discouraged by IETF documents.

Routing architectures

There are a number of architectures that can be employed for routing. One is for all routers to know about all networks; another is for routers to know only about networks that are directly attached; yet another is for routing to be handled by a central controller. Different network architectures require different approaches.

The technique of all routers learning about all networks is fine in a small network, where the routing tables in each router would only be relatively small. In a large network, the size of tables and the amount of processing required become unacceptable and make for powerful and expensive routers.

In the second approach, where routers only know about locally attached networks, a datagram addressed to an unrecognized network number will be passed to all other routers in the hope that one of them can forward it successfully. This long-winded process can be extremely inefficient.

For a small commercial system with only tens of networks and belonging to a single company, routers that know about all networks would perform adequately and not be unduly expensive. Commercial networks have a way of growing. It is possible for such a system to require access to a large internet system, maybe a corporate backbone network. An architecture based on knowing all networks cannot grow indefinitely, so we need to deal with a mix of architectures. One possibility is a 'backbone' network that knows of all networks, combined with local systems that only need to know of local networks most of the time, but sometimes know of others in the corporate system. This type of structure can be handled by IP routing.

The routing architecture defined for the Internet deals with this problem by having two classes of routing, backbone routing and local, or autonomous system, routing. On the backbone system, all routers know about all networks. They can be dedicated to the task of backbone routing. Routers in individual autonomous system networks are configured to send datagrams to the backbone if the destination address is recognized as not being in the local system. This means that local routers only need to know of local networks and the default route to the backbone. This default route is usually known by the address 0.0.0.0. Through their routing protocol, routers will announce the route 0.0.0.0 as leading to the backbone connection. Any router receiving a datagram for a network they do not recognize will send it to the router which advertised the route to 0.0.0.0. As the backbone router knows all networks, when this datagram arrives it can decide whether it is for a valid network or merely has an incorrect destination IP address. In the latter case, it can be discarded immediately without having to travel through the network until its time to live reaches zero.

The research environment for which TCP/IP was designed was one in which many networks interconnected across large distances, so routing was important. However, many different 'standards' for routing have evolved over time, which has made the problem rather unruly.

Routing protocols

Having raised the subject of routing protocols, we now consider their function and the facilities of the most important ones.

So that routers can make sensible routing decisions, they need tables that indicate the addresses of networks that exist, how to get to them, and the 'cost' of each path. The basic function of a routing protocol is to 'advertise accessibility'[†] to networks so that each router in a network is able to determine the 'best' route from one network to another. We will consider the different ways that each routing protocol does this.

The important features of routing protocols were outlined in Chapter 5. A routing protocol should be designed to:

- Describe the cost of the best route in a number of different ways – the routing metrics.

- Allow multiple active routes between two networks.

- Propagate routing information accurately and avoid creating incorrect routes.

- Minimize the network traffic due to the routing protocol itself.

- Minimize the load on machines which are not performing routing.

- Avoid sudden peaks in network load after a route change.

- Scale well to large networks.

- Converge quickly on a single agreed topology throughout the network after a routing change.

- Avoid propagating routing faults over long distances.

- Have security features to prevent false advertisements.

Originally the Internet had a relatively simple structure (Figure 16.5a) closely controlled by one operations centre. A routing protocol, Gateway-to-Gateway Protocol (GGP), was defined for use solely in the core network. Organizations connecting to the Internet ('stub networks') used a different routing protocol, Exterior Gateway Protocol (EGP), to advertise their presence to the core Internet routers. Those organizations or autonomous systems also required their own routing protocols for describing networks and subnetworks inside the organization. These protocols were collectively referred to as Interior Gateway Protocols (IGPs), as their internal routing detail was not available from the exterior Internet.

That simple Internet core has now disappeared and has been replaced by hundreds of Internet service providers interconnected in a mesh 'network of networks'. Each service provider has its own agreements or 'policies' as to who provides service to which destinations

---

[†]Sometimes referred to in routing protocol literature as 'reachability'.

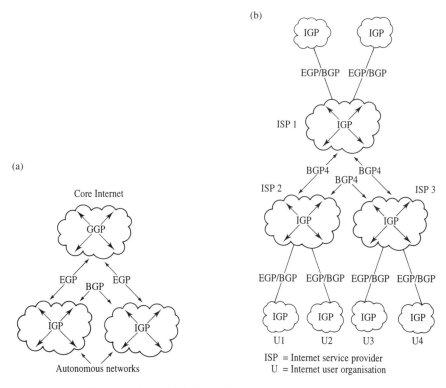

Figure 16.5 (a) Original core – stub Internet routing.
(b) Current mesh Internet routing.

(Figure 16.5b). This 'policy-based routing' requires a more sophisticated routing protocol for inter-autonomous system, or inter-domain, routing. It must identify routing paths based on the commercial agreements between Internet service providers and not merely on the existence of a path. The Border Gateway Protocol (BGP) was developed to meet this need and is currently used by those Internet service providers. BGP could also be used to interconnect corporate networks directly.

The IGP never appears on the Internet so IGP describes a need and not the name of a defined protocol. Since most corporate networks operate like autonomous systems, though they may not be connected to the Internet, IGPs are the most interesting area for us. Unfortunately, it is in this area that, until recently, there has been a lack of adequate standardization.

The most common IGPs are Routing Information Protocol (RIP) and the more recent Open Shortest Path First (OSPF). While EGP was not designed as an IGP, it can be used internally as well as talking to the 'exterior'.

We will now consider these routing protocols in more detail.

Routing information protocol

The major advantage of routing information protocol is its universal availability. RIP was supplied with BSD4.2 and hence has gained an undeserved reputation in TCP/IP circles as being *the* protocol to use. RIP is, however, only useful in small networks with a few routers.

RIP originates from the Xerox Network Systems protocol, XNS. In the TCP/IP world, RIP is more commonly known by the program name that implements the protocol which is **routed**, or **route daemon**.[†] routed is very much based upon the original RIP definition, but has a more general network address format than is required just for routing IP.

By the requirements of today's larger corporate networks, RIP is very limited. Its only measure of performance of a route (metric) is **hop count**, the number of routers between that point and the destination network. For performance reasons, it limits the maximum number of hops to 15. It has no explicit support for subnetworking so it cannot support variable length subnet masks (see Chapter 4). It cannot utilize multiple active routes between two networks; a single route with the smallest number of hops is chosen even if a route with more hops uses higher speed circuits and has a lower delay. RIP does not respond quickly to network failures; it does not scale well and it can consume considerable circuit capacity when table updates occur. It uses Ethernet broadcasts for table updates. These are received by and interrupt every processor attached to the LAN even if they have no interest in routing. Long-lasting routing loops were a feature of the original implementation. Later changes to the code have ensured that routing loops are more quickly resolved but at the expense of the volume of RIP traffic.

This catalogue of disadvantages should have deterred most implementors of larger networks from taking RIP seriously; certainly network operators anticipating more than two to three hops between end systems and more than five to ten routers should consider more modern alternatives. To be more positive, because of the general availability of RIP, many hosts eavesdrop to learn about the presence of routers on their LAN and are not dependent on one default gateway. Upgrades have been carried out in different ways to overcome these limitations and RIP is available in all UNIX machines. In small networks with limited traffic, RIP will be perfectly satisfactory.

When using equipment from different vendors, it is possible that they may use different versions of RIP which may not be compatible. They may not function as expected.

[†]The 'd' on the end of a program in UNIX systems usually refers to that program being a daemon, a program that uses little processing power until required for action.

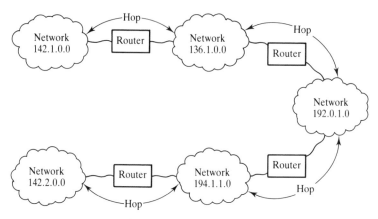

Figure 16.6 Hop count.

How RIP works

RIP is simple in its approach, which is probably one reason why it is so popular. When a RIP router starts, it knows from configuration files which networks it has connected directly to it. It collects this information into a routing table and uses broadcast frames to send it out on each of those networks as advertisements of the networks it can reach. RIP uses UDP on well-known port 520 (0x208). Other routers on a network listen for RIP advertisements and add the network addresses found in the advert to their routing tables. When a router next advertises its table of connections, it will include the new networks found in adverts from other routers. In this way all of the network addresses in a system become known to all routers.

The table in a routed router will have the following fields for each network address:

Address	IP address of a network
Gateway	The neighbouring router with a path to that network
Interface	The physical interface to use to access the router
Metric	The number of hops to that network
Timer	Time since this entry was last updated

In their advertisements, routers indicate the cost of getting to networks in **hops**. A hop is defined as a passage through one router. So a path that goes through three routers is three hops away. As a network advertisement is passed from one interface to another, the cost of reaching each network is incremented by one. In this way, a router that finds multiple paths to a network can decide which is the best, based upon the number of hops; the path with the smallest hop count is considered the best. In Figure 16.6, network 142.2.0.0 is four hops away from network 142.1.0.0.

Early versions of RIP used a very simple advertising structure which sent a complete copy of the connectivity table it had assembled from adverts received on its network connections. This simple mechanism caused a phenomenon known as **slow convergence**. Slow convergence results in a significant delay in the discovery that a route or router to a network has failed. As changes can only be detected when adverts are made, which in TCP/IP is usually at 30-second intervals, it can take many minutes for all routers in a system to realize that the connection to a network has been lost. As mentioned earlier, the maximum hop count allowed for by RIP is 15. A hop count of 16 is considered an unreachable network. This limit is set to reduce the time it takes for a system to converge, that is, to reduce the time it takes all routers to agree a common view of the new network structure after they discover and adjust to network failures.

This limitation of 15 hops also reduces the amount of traffic generated by certain datagrams looping around in a system continuously if there are redundant paths. Each time an IP datagram passes through a router its Time-To-Live (TTL) field is decremented, supposedly by the amount of time in seconds that the router delays it. By today's standards if a router was delaying datagrams by even one second it would be considered extremely slow, but the standard says that TTL must be reduced by at least one at each router. Consequently TTL has effectively become a 'hop count'. If a router receives an IP datagram that has a TTL of 0, it will not pass it on, so a datagram that does loop around will only continue until its TTL field is decremented to 0.

RIP in operation

In Figure 16.7(a), there are two routers, A and B, connecting three networks 1, 2 and 3. After a short period of time all routers will have seen each other's adverts and therefore be in a stable state advertising all these networks. Consider what will happen if network 3 fails. Figure 16.7(b) shows the adverts that would be generated. Router B will realize that network 3 has failed. The next advert on network 2 could be from router A, indicating that it has a connection to network 3 that is 2 hops away, as shown in Figure 16.7(b). Router B accepts this advert and considers that a new path exists between router A and network 3, for A is advertising a route of 2 hops, less cost than a failed network. B sets the cost to network 3 as 3 hops and the direction as through router A. In router B's next advert (Figure 16.7c) it advertises this fact back to router A. In Figure 16.7(d), router A has just seen the only advert for network 3 from router B. This was greater than its own, so it has to increment its hop count to cater for the new cost, so it advertises network 3 as 4 hops away. This to-and-fro advertising of network 3 continues until the hop count reaches 15. At this time, it is recognized that all connections to network 3 have failed.

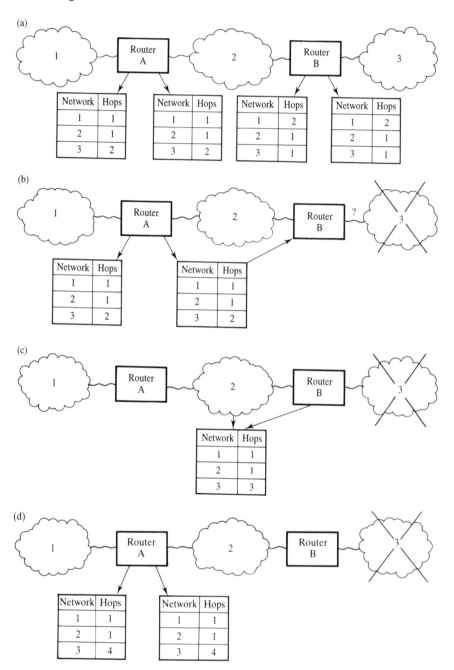

Figure 16.7 RIP in operation. (a) Stable. (b) Network 3 down. (c) Router B's next advert. (d) Router A sees router B's advert.

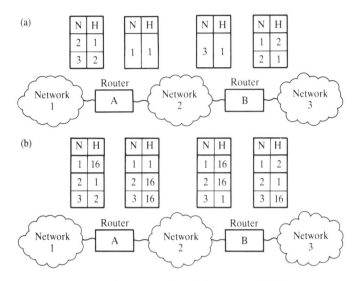

Figure 16.8 RIP advertising: (a) split horizon and (b) reverse poison.

RIP adverts are usually transmitted at 30-second intervals, so the steps shown in Figure 16.7 are in 30-second increments. To reach step 15, when the routers agree what the true situation is, could take around seven minutes. This is the convergence time for RIP.

In an attempt to improve on the convergence time a number of amendments have been made to RIP. These are called **split horizon**, **reverse poison** and **triggered updates**. Split horizon reduces the number of advertised networks and hence the volume of routing traffic and reduces convergence times by stopping routers from advertising networks back in the direction they learnt about them. In Figure 16.8, with split horizon, network 2 only carries adverts for networks 1 and 3, none for itself. In this case, a failure on network 3 will mean that router B will not see an advert from router A suggesting another path to network 3. However, it would still take some time for router A to realize that it is no longer receiving adverts for network 3, discard the information for this network and consider the path to network 3 as failed. This reduces the possibility of routing loops but the convergence is still slow.

Reverse poison improves RIP performance by still advertising all networks back along the path from which the advert came, but always with the hop count set to the value 16, indicating the path is not usable. In the event of a network failure, router B will *still* see network 3 advertised by router A, but at a cost of 16, so it would ignore it. Again, this reduces the possibility of routing loops but the convergence is still slow.

Triggered updates significantly improve RIP's speed of convergence. With triggered updates, routers are allowed to send out an advert indicating that the cost of reaching a network has reached infinity (16!) as soon as it detects the problem, rather than having to wait for the next normal

Command	Version	Reserved
Family of net 1		Net 1 address, octets 1–2
Net 1 address, octets 3–6		
Net 1 address, octets 7–10		
Net 1 address, octets 11–14		
Distance of network 1		
Family of net 2		Net 2 address, octets 1–2
Net 2 address, octets 3–6		
Net 2 address, octets 7–10		
Net 2 address, octets 11–14		
Distance of network 2		

⋮

Figure 16.9 RIP datagram format.

advertisement time. If all routers do this, convergence is fast, but at the expense of broadcast network traffic when any failure is detected. In a large RIP network, this traffic can become a serious concern with triggered updates.

There is a limitation on the size of RIP datagrams of 512 bytes (not including the IP and frame headers). If an advert cannot fit in a datagram of this size the router will generate more adverts to carry the remainder.

Reverse poison is the normal method of operation of recent RIP implementations.

RIP format

Figure 16.9 shows the format of the RIP datagram. The fields are as follows:

- *Command – 8 bits*   A value of 1 denotes a request for routing information, 2 denotes a response. Usually a router will broadcast unsolicited response datagrams at 30-second intervals.

- *Version – 8 bits*   The protocol version number. The format shown has a version number of 1.

- *Family of net 1 – 16 bits*   This field is supposed to be used to indicate the network protocol used on the networks being advertised, as RIP is not limited to any specific protocol. The address family for IP is 2.

- *Net 1 address – 112 bits*   This field is intended to be able to hold the network address of various different types of network and hence is much larger than the 32 bits needed for an IP address. It will normally be padded out with 0s. On TCP systems, the first 16 bits are left as 0 and then the IP address is inserted to be between 32-bit boundaries; the last 8 octets are also set to be 0.

- *Distance of net 1 – 32 bits* The number of hops to reach the network listed in net 1 address.

Configuring RIP systems

Computers using RIP can usually be configured as active RIP routers or as RIP listeners. An active RIP router is a node that has two or more network interfaces and routes datagrams between them. A RIP listener is a device that listens for RIP information so that it can perform RIP routing for itself. This ensures that it can reach the most appropriate router when sending datagrams to other networks. This type of operation causes some processing overhead on the computer and its impact is dependent on the amount of RIP traffic on the network.

It is often possible to prevent RIP from using broadcast datagrams, by setting an option and defining the specific IP addresses of neighbouring routers it should communicate with directly. It then uses MAC-level unicasts. This requires manual intervention, but it can be worthwhile in reducing the number of broadcast datagrams on a network, always a useful achievement in larger networks.

Most systems have a command for the manual configuration of routing tables that allows router addresses and the cost of taking that route to be defined by the network manager. Where not all routers are using RIP, there is a need to be able to predefine in the RIP tables specific routes (default routes) for networks available through non-RIP routers and of which RIP routers would be unaware. When the RIP-based router realizes it must send datagrams to one of those networks, it will then send direct to the appropriate router. Such static manually configured routes cannot recover from link or router failure.

Another option with RIP systems is the definition of the default route. The default route is advertised as 0.0.0.0. It is used to define the path on which datagrams should be sent if their destination network address is unknown to the router. This option allows the default route to be defined for this router, with a specified hop count, and overrides messages about the default route advertised by other routers.

Some RIP implementations can be configured so that they will only accept routing information from known routers (defined by their IP address). This is a security feature. It prevents false adverts from unauthorized routers from diverting data through other equipment and phantom networks that claim to have the shortest route. If false paths are advertised, connectivity with a network can be lost as datagrams are sent the wrong path.

RIP version 2

With RIP's advantages of simplicity, ease of management and low processing overheads in mind, RIP V2 has been defined to deal with some of the limitations found in the RIP V1 protocol.

Command	Version	Unused
Address family identifier		Route tag
IP address		
Subnet mask		
Next hop		
Metric		

Figure 16.10 RIP V2 datagram format.

New features in RIP V2 are: subnet masks, route tags, next hop addresses, authentication and multicasting. Figure 16.10 shows the format of the RIP V2 message. The command, version, unused, address family identifier, IP address and metric maintain the same functionality as RIP V1. The command will be 2 (a response), version is 2, unused must be 0, and AFI will normally be 2.

The inclusion of *subnet masks* in RIP was the major reason for updating the protocol. This was necessary to deal with multiple subnet masks and CIDR.

Route tags – 16 bits can propagate information such as autonomous systems numbers, acquired from an exterior gateway protocol.

The *next hop address – 32 bits* is used on networks with multiple interior gateway protocols. It allows a router running multiple IGPs to advertise the best route on behalf of another router which is not running RIP. It will have learnt that route from one of the other routing protocols.

In RIP V2, the *metric – 32 bits* is still limited to a hop count with a maximum value of 15 hops. This allows routes learnt from RIP V2 to be re-advertised and used by RIP V1 routers. It maximizes backwards compatibility.

Authentication has been added to protect against unauthorized route advertisements which could compromise network security. The initial specification only allows for a clear-text password, but other more sophisticated mechanisms could be adopted in the future. As there is little room in the header for authentication, a complete RIP entry is used for authentication fields, if present. An authentication entry is indicated by an AFI field of 0xFFFF. This denotes that the fields of that RIP entry contain 'authentication type' and 'authentication' information, Figure 16.11.

Authentication type field – 16 bits. At present, the only defined value for authentication type field is 2 which indicates authentication with a clear-text password. The password is carried in the 16-octet *authentication field.*

One criticism of RIP V1 is the number of broadcast messages it generates, and their detrimental effect on a network. RIP V2 can optionally use multicasts for table updates, which removes the load from non-RIP devices. It also allows RIP V2 routers to send updates which RIP V1

Command	Version	Unused
0xFFFF		Authentication type
Authentication		

Figure 16.11   RIP V2 authentication fields.

routers will not detect, but RIP V2 routers would normally use broadcast if RIP V1 routers were present.

The standard for RIP V1 requires that a router should ignore *fields* which it cannot interpret. Thus, a RIP V2 datagram can in theory contain both V1 and V2 fields; V2 fields should be ignored but V1 fields should be accepted by V1 routers. In practice, it was found that in using RIP V1 and RIP V2 routers on the same network, certain RIP V1 routers discard RIP V2 datagrams rather than ignoring the V2 fields.

RIPng

RIPng is the next generation version of the RIP protocol to exchange routing information in IPv6. It is based on the previous versions of RIP with no significant changes other than address format. IPv6 provides mechanisms for hosts to discover routers through use of the ICMPv6 router solicitation/router advertisement protocol. IPv6 hosts should not eavesdrop RIPng, therefore RIPng need only be implemented in routers.

RIPng is expected to use split horizon and triggered updates. More control will be provided on triggered update as it can cause excessive loading on wide area networks with limited resource particularly if there are large numbers of routers. The draft document discusses not sending complete routing tables on an event and suppressing the sending of updates to prevent them becoming too frequent.

No authentication/security mechanism is defined for RIPng; IPv6 itself provides enough security to protect RIPng datagrams. RIPng suggested format is shown in Figure 16.12.

Command	Version	Must be zero
IPv6 prefix		
Must be zero	Prefix len	Metric

Figure 16.12   RIPng suggested format.

The portion of the datagram from the beginning of the IPv6 prefix to the end of the metric is referred to as the Routing Entry (RTE). This may be repeated for each network being advertised. A single RIPng message is limited only by the MTU of the network interface.

The command field is 1 (Request) or 2 (Response) and the version field is version 1. The IPv6 prefix (128 bits) is the IPv6 address prefix from the 128 network address.

The prefix length field is the number of 1-bits, starting from the left, in the prefix.

The metric field contains the appropriate routing metric (hop count) for the specified network. As with previous versions of RIP this is limited to 15 hops and the value 16 means 'not reachable'.

Hello

Hello is a protocol used in the Distributed Computer Network (DCN) which was based on an implementation of PDP 11-based software called the fuzzball. Hello, unlike RIP, was designed to measure the delay to a network (a delay metric) instead of the number of hops (a distance metric), when considering the path cost. This is eminently more sensible because it allows the best path to be chosen based on a most important factor to end users – response time. Hello will always attempt to use the path with best response. However, hello has a number of other limitations which make it unsuitable for use in a modern network. We have included it as it is supported by the gated (see 'Gated' section p. 425).

Exterior gateway protocol

The Exterior Gateway Protocol (EGP) was designed as the mechanism for an autonomous system to tell the core gateways of the Internet about networks it wanted to advertise. EGP can be used as an IGP. EGP is now obsolescent for connecting to the Internet and is being replaced by BGP. RFC 1812 states that routers which implement EGP must also implement BGP.

In its time EGP was a reasonably sophisticated protocol. It has 10 message types that are used to establish connections with other EGP gateways and then pass network reachability information between them. EGP operates directly over IP using the IP protocol number of 8. The commands are:

Type	Function
Request	Request connection with a neighbouring router
Confirm	Confirm connection with a neighbouring router
Refuse	Refuse connection with a neighbouring router
Cease	Request disconnection from a neighbouring router
Cease-ack	Acknowledge disconnection from a neighbouring router
Hello	Check neighbouring router is still active

Version	Type	Code	Status
Checksum		Autonomous system number	
Sequence number			

Figure 16.13   Basic format of EGP.

I-H-U	Acknowledge to hello (I-Heard-You)
Poll	Request a routing table update
Update	A network routing table update
Error	An error report

The basic format of these messages is the same, as shown in Figure 16.13. Some messages have additional fields where necessary.

When a router using EGP is initialized, it first starts by requesting a connection with a known neighbouring EGP router, using the request command. It could get three possible responses to this, plus a possibility of no response at all. The replies could be:

Command (type-code)	*Possible responses (type-code)*
Request (3-0)	Confirm (3-1)
	Refuse (3-2)
	Error (8-0)

In the connection request the router indicates the frequency at which it would like to receive hello and poll commands. Typical values would be hello every 30 seconds and a poll for update every 2 minutes. Once the connection has been confirmed, the router clears all its tables and starts to receive and/or transmit hello and poll commands. The message sent then would be:

Command (type-code)	*Possible responses (type-code)*
Hello (5-0)	I-H-U (5-1)
	Error (8-0)
Poll (2-0)	Update (1-0)
	Error (8-0)

Lastly is the cease command, which is used to break the connection between two routers. This command is:

Command (type-code)	*Possible responses (type-code)*
Cease (3-3)	Cease-Ack(3-4)
	Error (8-0)

As can be seen from the set of commands, EGP is an active protocol (as opposed to the more passive approach of RIP) in which routers positively check that their neighbours are still accessible and request updates to their routing tables. Figure 16.14 shows the routing information

Version	Type (1)	Code (0)	Status
Checksum		Autonomous system number	
Sequence number		Internal gateways	Exterior gateways
IP source network			
Gateway A IP address (without net portion)			
Num. distances			
Distance A_1	Nets at A_1		
Network 1 at distance A_1			
Network 2 at distance A_1			

$\vdots$

Distance A_n	Nets at A_n
Network 1 at distance A_n	
Network 2 at distance A_n	

$\vdots$

Gateway N IP address (without net portion)
Num. distances

Distance N_1	Nets at N_1
Network 1 at distance N_1	
Network 2 at distance N_1	

$\vdots$

Last network at last distance for gateway N

Figure 16.14   EGP routing information datagram.

datagram of EGP. The type field is 1, for routing update, and the code field should always be 0. The status field can have one of the following values:

Status	Meaning
0	Intermediate
1	Up
2	Down
128	Unsolicited message bit

The remaining fields are described below. The terminology can seem quite complex but, in general, the format is a table of entries, where each entry consists of a counter or number that describes the number of sub-entries that follow. While not very readable to people, it is easy to write software to decode such a table.

- *Autonomous system number*   This is an assigned number to identify the autonomous system to which this datagram refers. If a registered autonomous system number has been obtained from the Internet Registry (see Chapter 3), it should be used here.

- *Sequence number*   To synchronize requests with responses.

- *Internal gateways*   The number of gateways within the autonomous system to which this datagram (advert) refers.

- *External gateways* The number of external gateways to which this datagram (advert) refers.

- *Gateway IP address* The address of the gateway which can route datagrams to the list of networks following

- *Num. distances* The number of distances: this refers to the number of groups of networks at different hop counts which will be described in this advert. Each group will have a different hop count from the gateway in the gateway IP address field (but each network address in the group will have the same hop count).

- *Distance* The number of hops required to reach each of the network addresses in this group.

- *Networks at distance* The number of networks in this particular group which are at a distance given by the previous distance field.

- *Network addresses* A list of IP addresses of the networks that are the number of hops away given in the distance field and hence can be reached by the gateway in the gateway IP address.

This will be followed by entries referring to other gateways by starting again with another gateway IP address and repeating the structure until the total number of gateways in the internal gateways and external gateways fields has been described.

Configuring EGP systems

EGP systems can be more complex to configure than RIP and hello because it is a more complex protocol. EGP expects to have an autonomous system number, a value that must be obtained from the Network Information Center if you connect to the Internet. If you never intend to connect to the Internet, you can put your own value in this field.

EGP must know the addresses of peer gateways. It has to have at least one other gateway to exchange EGP information with.

Gated

In recent years, a router has become a dedicated device, a specific product that connects networks. With TCP/IP systems, ordinary application hosts (minicomputers) have been able to do routing for many years. The hosts that perform routing have multiple communication interfaces connected to several physical networks. They run routing protocols to route between these networks as necessary.

Over time, a program was developed to run these routing protocols. Called **gated** (standing for gate daemon), it supports all three common routing protocols – RIP, hello and EGP – and allows them to be configured for each interface port individually. It also provides extra functions

Figure 16.15 Controlling data flows in domains.

for the management of traffic through a network. The system manager can control traffic flow and secure nodes or networks from outside access.

To control traffic flow with gated, costs are allocated to certain routes to coerce traffic to remain within a defined management domain. Figure 16.15 explains this more clearly. It shows six different management domains:

A^1	Company A site 1
A^2	Company A site 2
A^g	The whole company A
B^1	Company B site 1
B^2	Company B site 2
B^g	The whole company B

Within a site, domain A^1 for example, a number of routers may exist, probably controlling different subnetworks. For redundancy, there may be alternative paths between sites. In the figure, two separate paths are shown between hosts Z and Y, one having a hop count of 2, the other a hop count of 3. If we consider the hop count method for determining the best route, the lowest cost path goes outside the domain A^1. This causes traffic to leave domain A^1 on an external router just to get back to a host within the same site. This is a management nightmare; internal traffic could well be taking a lower performance path and tying up expensive resources intended for intersite traffic.

Gated brings this traffic back under management control by biasing the cost of crossing a domain boundary. For example, we can define the cross-boundary connection as having a cost equivalent to 100 hops. Now path 2 will have a cost of 202 (100 + 100 + 1 + 1), whereas path 1 will still have a cost of 3, and will now be the preferred path.

The same applies to the intercompany connections, but, if we only treated them the same as a cross-domain link and allocated them a cost of 100, paths could be chosen that traversed company B's network between two devices in company A. In some countries, these traffic flows could infringe local telecommunications regulations. Again, to prevent this, we can define the cost of going across a company domain as being 200, for example. This high minimum cost of going across a boundary between two organizations would make it always less expensive to remain within the company private network or to use the company's own external lines, and not someone else's lines.

In the complete system, all networks will be available to all others, but the management of path costs will keep the traffic within the required domains. This mechanism can, of course, be extended to have more domains, if necessary. With eight bits we can define a cost of up to 256. The minimum cost allocated to crossing a domain boundary must always be greater than the sum of the costs for staying within the domain.

Configuring gated systems

Because gated supports RIP, hello and EGP, it should be able to set the options that you would find with each of these protocols. It also has a number of facilities to decide which protocols are used on which interfaces.

As described above, gated normally allows interface metrics to be set to bias the cost of using a certain interface when crossing domains. In some implementations, it is possible to modify the hop count contained in incoming RIP datagrams. This allows the network manager to bias the cost of RIP routes rather than use a true hop count.

Gated usually allows the network manager to choose which networks or hosts are advertised or not advertised, which provides a degree of security within a system. Gated systems, as they handle multiple routing protocols, tend to store their metrics internally in milliseconds. This allows the granularity of hello to be preserved. RIP hop count metrics will be mapped onto this mechanism.

Open shortest path first

Open Shortest Path First (OSPF) was developed in 1989–90 in the classic TCP/IP manner, by a specialist engineering group set up to produce a specification for a scalable IGP that would fully satisfy the routing protocol requirements for large private networks (an IGP for large ASs). The design aims for OSPF recognized the limitations of existing protocols.

A requirement of the IAB is that new Internet standards must be specified so completely and rigorously, and written so clearly, that different designers can implement the standard successfully with no other source of information. To prove the standard, at least two totally independent implementations must be tested together, any anomalies resolved and necessary clarifications added to the standard. OSPF has completed this testing phase successfully.

In OSPF, 'open' is used to mean 'openly published and not controlled by a single manufacturer'. Shortest path first, also called the Dijkstra Algorithm, refers to the calculation which determines the best path. OSPF is what is known as a **link state vector protocol**, as opposed to RIP and EGP which are **distance vector protocols**. A link state vector protocol is one which considers the status of connections to a network, taking into account performance aspects other than hop count (the distance), when making routing decisions.

OSPF uses IP. It has been defined as protocol number 89. It is important, though not essential, that routing information is not discarded. OSPF uses small datagrams that do not need fragmentation, for in using fragmentation, any single lost fragment would result in the loss of the whole fragmented datagram. OSPF is designed to minimize routing traffic.

OSPF terminology

OSPF is a routing protocol for use within an autonomous system, a network under one overall management control. In OSPF parlance, an **area** is part of that autonomous system which is considered a self-contained routing domain. This could be one or more IP network addresses and could cover a few or many subnetwork addresses. Administration of routing within an area could be devolved to a particular body, so an area is firstly a management definition of a region within which an identifiable authority has control. But because an area is self-contained, it also has technical advantages as routing detail need not pass outside the area.

OSPF divides routing into three levels: **intra-area**, within area, **inter-area**, between areas, and **autonomous system external routes**. Areas communicate with each other through inter-area routers which themselves attach to a single backbone network that carries all inter-area traffic. There can only be one backbone and it must be contiguous. OSPF can 'import' external routes from other routing protocols, convert them to OSPF representations and re-advertise them within the autonomous system.

To assist the system manager with configuring the backbone, **virtual links** can also be defined. These are treated as a direct point-to-point path between two routers though physically there may be other routers in between. A fixed relationship is defined for traffic between the routers at either end of the virtual link.

Each intra-area router keeps its own topological database of the networks and other routers within the area it resides in. An inter-area router, connected to more than one area, will have separate topology databases for each area. Information regarding routing outside an area is considered as being only summary information and is not used to change routing within an area, so routing problems are contained in the area in which they occur and should not impact the routing databases elsewhere.

As with other router protocols, OSPF advertises reachability, but as it is a link state protocol, it does more than just indicate the hop count to different networks; it considers objects. An object can be a network or a router. In OSPF, the route adverts are called **Link State Advertisements** (LSAs). They contain information about known network addresses and the subnet mask that is used with each address. OSPF works with subnets and variable length subnet masks.

OSPF is designed to operate with point-to-point networks, broadcast networks and non-broadcast networks:

- A **point-to-point network** is one that joins a single pair of routers, for example a single point-to-point circuit.

- A **broadcast network** is one that can support many attached routers and can send a single message simultaneously to all attached devices. Examples are Ethernet or Token Ring LANs.

- A **non-broadcast network** is one in which there can be multiple destinations from a single interface but which does not allow broadcast, for example an X.25 packet switched data network.

The last two are examples of multi-access networks.

How OSPF works

When an OSPF router is initialized, it first uses its hello[†] protocol to establish connection with its neighbours. On point-to-point and non-broadcast networks, the addresses of these neighbour devices must be configured into the OSPF router. On a broadcast network, the router uses a well-known multicast IP address (224.0.0.5) as the destination in its hellos. All OSPF routers will recognize this address. It is one of those class D addresses which are reserved for multicast and experimental use and are not available for general IP comunications. This IP multicast is mapped in a standard way into IEEE 802.1 LAN multicast addresses.

On multi-access networks, broadcast and non-broadcast, the OSPF hello protocol is used to 'elect' a **Designated Router** (DR), which will be responsible for route advertising on behalf of all other routers on that

---

[†]Hello has become a general term. This 'hello' is just one message the OSPF protocol can send and is not to be confused with the complete protocol, DCN hello, described previously in this chapter.

network. Having a DR reduces the amount of traffic required to pass information back and forth between routers. A backup DR, which will take over should the DR fail, is also elected. We shall describe later how to control the priority with which routers take on these roles. Another class D multicast address, 224.0.0.6, is reserved as a destination address for DRs and backup DRs. Other routers use this multicast address to send messages to the master and backup DRs. Using multicast addresses allows multiple devices to receive the datagrams but without the problems of using broadcast frames.

Once the DRs are agreed, **adjacencies** are defined, that is, it is agreed which routers will communicate directly with each other. The path between two routers, be it logical or physical, is called an adjacency. This is fairly straightforward on point-to-point and virtual links, but it is more difficult on multi-access networks where all routers can hear each other. In this situation, the DR becomes the node that establishes adjacencies. In other words, the line of communication is restricted to being between the two DRs and the other routers. Non-DR routers do not communicate directly with each other. This allows information to be passed back and forth using unicast datagrams on non-broadcast networks and reserved multicast addresses on broadcast networks (such as IEEE LANs). This reduces the overall volume of routing traffic and its impact on other nodes on the network.

Figure 16.16 shows two multi-access networks, a LAN and an X.25 PDN. It is possible for all routers to communicate with each other, but to reduce traffic and simplify control of the system, in each case RT5 becomes the DR and RT6 the backup DR.

The adjacencies are then used to pass routing database information to all routers. In OSPF, these LSAs, generated by each router, indicate the state and cost of its interfaces and the adjacencies. LSAs always flow to and from the DRs, never directly between other routers. Each router in an area will therefore build its routing database from information provided by the DRs. All routers in an area receive the LSAs and from this they build a topological database of the interconnections throughout the area. From this database, and with itself as the 'root', each router builds a branching tree indicating connectivity to other networks. From the interface costs contained in the LSAs, it computes the cost of travelling each branch. Where two branches provide a connection to the same network, the higher cost path will not be used to carry traffic, unless the primary route fails. It will use the shortest path first, hence (O)SPF.

The cost of crossing each interface (for each TOS) must be decided and set up in the routers by the system manager. This gives the manager control of routing decisions within the network and hence allows traffic flow management.

Consider the more detailed example of Figure 16.17(a). The 10 networks in this system, N1–N10, use various cabling systems with

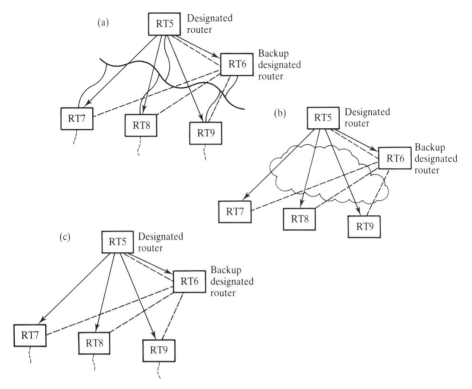

Figure 16.16 OSPF designated routers: (a) LAN, (b) X.25 PDN and (c) logical diagram.

different topologies and there are seven routers, RT1–RT7. A host, H1, is directly connected to RT6 using the Serial Line Internet Protocol (SLIP). The route to this directly connected host is advertised in OSPF as a host-specific route using the host's full IP address as a network address with a subnet mask of all 1s, or 0xFFFFFFFF. When a mask of all 1s is used, only one IP address, the host itself, can match that route. In OSPF, a default route can be advertised as any network address with a subnet mask of all 0s. Any IP address masked with all 0s will produce a match.

Now we will look at the cost of paths connecting the different routers and networks. This is normally shown as a **directed graph**. Figure 16.17(b) shows the paths between each entity and the cost of going down that path. Note that the cost of going from a network to a router is always zero.

Next, we split the network shown in Figure 16.17(a) into two areas with some external networks from another autonomous system connected through RT7. As shown in Figure 16.18(a), RT4 now becomes an inter-area router and RT7 a backbone router, part of a backbone network.

(a)

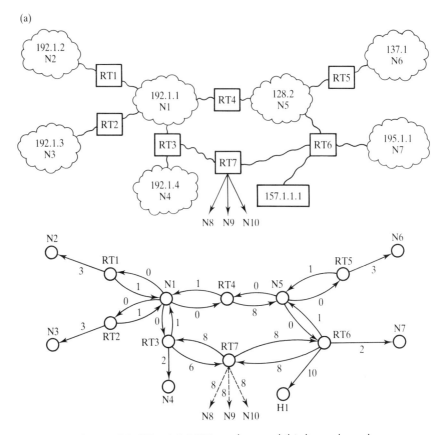

Figure 16.17 (a) OSPF topology and (b) directed graph.

If we now look at the area database for area 1, shown in Figure 16.18(b), we can see the cost of reaching every network. In this case we can see dual paths to certain objects, but they have different costs. If there were multiple paths with the same cost, OSPF would share datagrams among them (a useful improvement on other routing protocols). Note that RT7 is shown as a separate part of the database as it is not part of area 1. RT4 has two databases, one for area 1 and another for area 2.

Using OSPF

The definition of OSPF is thorough and it describes those parameters that need to be configured when installing an OSPF system. As with any node connection in an IP system, each network connection will need configuring with IP address and network mask and buffers.

The other important features required are:

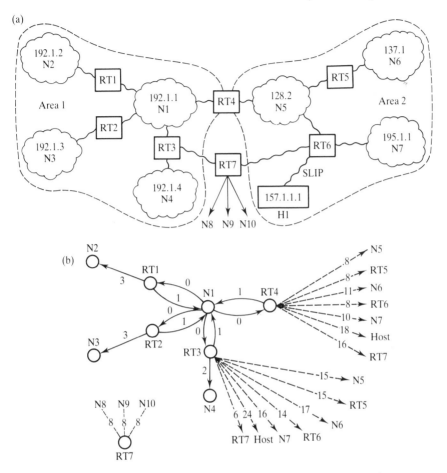

Figure 16.18   OSPF router network with two areas. (a) Topology.
(b) Area 1 database.

- *Interface cost*   This defines the cost of sending a datagram out across an interface of the router and is defined for each port. The cost units are arbitrarily chosen by the system manager with a range of 1 to 65 535. Router software will choose satisfactory defaults for interface cost inversely proportional to interface speed. There can be a different cost for each TOS considered by the router, determining the route based on high throughput, low relay, high reliability and true cost (the DTRC bits of the TOS flags in the IP datagram). Most commercial router implementations do not support TOS routing.

- *Advertisement interval*   Defined in seconds, this is the frequency at which LSAs are transmitted over an interface. Its value should be greater than the round trip delay across the interface concerned. A typical value for a local area network would be five seconds.

- *Transfer delay*   This is supposed to be the estimated number of seconds it takes to send a link state update message across this interface. This would typically be one second for a LAN.

- *Router priority*   This value is used to set which router becomes the DR on multi-access networks; the higher the value, the higher the likelihood of this router becoming the DR.

- *Hello interval*   The length of time in seconds between router hello datagrams. The value for this should be the same for all routers attached to the same multi-access network. The smaller this value is set, the quicker network failures will be detected, but using a very low value will cause more traffic on the network. A recommended value for LANs is around 10 seconds but nearer 30 seconds for an X.25 PDN.

- *Router dead interval*   The number of seconds from last seeing a router's hellos before declaring it has failed. This value should be the same for all routers on a multi-access network and should be a multiple of the hello interval, probably of the order of four. This would give a time of 40 seconds on a LAN or 2 minutes on an X.25 PDN. Since hellos are carried in IP datagrams and may occasionally be legitimately lost, this allows for up to three hellos to be missed.

- *Authentication key*   This is the authentication value used to validate link state updates. Today's implementations provide at best a simple clear-text password.

OSPF routers also need a unique **router identification** value. As each router already has at least two IP addresses, which themselves are unique in the network, it is suggested that the router identification is obtained by taking the smallest value IP address assigned to the router.

Routers within an area require an **area id**. This is a 32-bit number that must be greater than zero, as zero is reserved for the backbone area. Each router will require a list of all networks, and their subnet masks, used within its area.

While OSPF responds to complete failures of network links, it need not dynamically change the path costs entered by the system manager. These path costs must be carefully chosen during the network design phase and matched to the capacity and number of routes available so that the correct overall performance requirements for throughput, delay and resilience to failure are achieved.

The status of OSPF

OSPF has been implemented by a number of different manufacturers with 3Com, Cisco, Proteon, Wellfleet and ACC participating in early interworking trials. Reports of these initial trials are enthusiastic about performance. Rerouting around link failures occurs in a few seconds in situations where RIP fails to repair paths at all. The routing traffic is a few per cent of that of RIP. Routing traffic grows at a much slower rate as the network expands.

The IAB has accepted that its design aims for an IGP (some of which we outlined above) and its requirements for acceptance of OSPF as an Internet standard have been met. In September 1991, it endorsed OSPF as *the* recommended IGP for future use in autonomous systems connected to the Internet. To comply with the requirements for Internet routers (RFC 1812), a router must implement OSPF and the OSPF SNMP management functions. OSPF is now stable and mature. There are operational OSPF networks with many hundreds of routers benefiting from the improved convergence time and reduced routing traffic.

OSPF gives a network manager unprecedented control over TCP/IP routing functions in an organization. All the issues concerning RIP are removed if OSPF is used:

- OSPF works with subnets and variable length subnet masks although the management complexity of variable length subnet masks remains.

- In principle, different metrics can be allocated to particular links so that OSPF can make routing decisions on the TOS bits of the IP datagram. These bits can select a path based on delay, or throughput, or the underlying probability of transmission errors (reliability) or monetary cost. In practice, many router manufacturers have not implemented TOS routing with OSPF.

- Wide area point-to-point links between routers need not be identified with their own network number thus conserving valuable address space.

- OSPF divides a large network into different management areas.

- Details of routing within an area are not passed outside an area, which constrains the size and number of update messages, router processing power and memory requirements as networks grow.

- On IEEE LANs and Ethernet, updates are carried in multicast addressed frames rather than broadcast frames; the OSPF protocol is rejected by the network interface cards in application hosts, so unnecessary interrupts do not consume host processing power.

- OSPF has security features not present in previous TCP/IP routing protocols.

The TOS features and authentication schemes are optional. When choosing a router supplier, it is important to verify that your required options are implemented in the way you expect.

In view of OSPF's range of features and the IAB endorsement, it would appear that it is a good choice for any organization intending to implement a TCP/IP router network.

Type of service routing (TOS)

One purpose of TOS routing is to minimize fluctuations in delay for interactive traffic and maximize the throughput for file transfers. IAB standards for hosts and routers say that host applications *must* set the correct values for TOS; OSPF router developers are encouraged to implement TOS routing to optimize application performance over congested routes.

In practice, this does not happen. Host software often does not set the TOS bits correctly. One manufacturer fully implemented OSPF routing with TOS and later removed the TOS functions; they were an overhead on memory, processing power, software support and training, all for no benefit. The reasons for this failure are political, technical and economic but in any event, complex. Here are some pointers:

- Application developers find that their development tools either provide no interface to control these bits or the interface is obscure and difficult to use. They cannot set the TOS bits or never find out how to set them.

- Some application developers do not understand the need for TOS and may believe that network performance is not their problem. They see that the simple solution is faster circuits, and ignore technical and cost constraints.

- Hard-pressed corporate network managers need simplicity – 'plug and play'. TOS routing does not fit this requirement. It is more appropriate to service providers and facilities management companies.

- TOS routing will either prioritize low delay traffic on a single route (giving a small improvement), or reserve some routes for low delay traffic and others for bulk file transfer and printing. But ignoring redundancy, one circuit of 128 kbps will carry the same traffic with better performance than two parallel 64 kbps circuits. One circuit at high speed is usually cheaper and easier to manage than two lower-speed circuits.

- TOS routing can only prioritize the applications running over IP. Many corporate networks carry other network protocols too which are not prioritized. This would reduce the effectiveness of IP TOS routing.

- TOS routing takes memory and processing power in the routers, which can be devoted to routing packets if the bandwidth is available.

The option that is left is to provide faster network and circuits. These unit costs have reduced dramatically, but the overall spending of a company may not have reduced.

IPv4 TOS is a failure, a missed opportunity. IPv6 also supports traffic priority. The lesson is that priority in IPv6 will only be useful if all IPv6 development tools set the correct value for standard applications. As part of the software development cycle these tools must encourage the developer to choose an application priority class. Implementation of route priority in IPv6 routing protocols should be mandatory, though network managers will be able to turn it off.

Other routing protocols

The names of other routing protocols frequently appear in connection with TCP/IP routing. For completeness, the following paragraphs describe the main features of each without the technical detail required to manage them.

Integrated IS–IS

IS means 'intermediate system'. In OSI terms, an IS is a network layer relay component in the communication path between two end systems (or application hosts). In this context an IS is a router and IS–IS is the intermediate-system-to-intermediate-system routing protocol, standardized by the ISO OSI committees as IS10589, for use between routers[†] with the OSI Connectionless Network Protocol (OSI CLNP).

IS–IS routing protocol was developed in the late 1980s in parallel with OSPF, and it shares most of the desirable features of a 'good' routing protocol. ISO OSI potentially has to solve the routing problems of one global internet, based on OSI. The routing framework on which IS–IS is based divides into a four-level routing hierarchy of which IS–IS forms the lowest layer, equivalent to an IGP within IP. The Digital Equipment Corporation (DEC) adopted OSI CLNP, along with IP, as one of the main protocols for its phase V implementation of DECnet. DEC has had a significant influence in the development and promotion of IS–IS protocols. In 1990, RFC 1195, which describes **integrated IS–IS**, was issued by the IS–IS working group of the IETF, a development arm of the IAB. The principal author of RFC 1195 is from DEC.

Integrated IS–IS is a modification of pure OSI IS–IS to allow a router to interpret and route either OSI CLNP datagrams or IP datagrams or both simultaneously. A router that uses such an integrated approach should be more efficient and require less memory, processing and network capacity for routing tables and routing table updates than a traditional multiprotocol router which regards each network protocol and its corresponding routing protocol as separate entities.

[†]Another OSI routing protocol, End-System-to-Intermediate-System (ES–IS), allows an end system to discover all routers available to it.

Integrated IS–IS supports IP subnetting, variable length subnet masks, TOS routing by mapping to the equivalent OSI quality-of-service routing and external routing. It also supports routing authentication (routing security). As in OSPF, networks may be divided into two levels with the detail of each level hidden from the other. Level 2 routers form a backbone supporting many level 1 areas; level 1 routers support collections of networks or subnetworks and route to an IP network or subnetwork.

Though many of the features are similar to OSPF, integrated IS–IS has not received the same support from other manufacturers. The IAB's endorsement of OSPF and its development of IPv6 (rather than adopting CLNP – the IPv7 proposal) means that integrated IS–IS can no longer be considered as a major routing protocol for IP.

Border gateway protocol

The **Border Gateway Protocol** (BGP) is another 1990–91 addition to TCP/IP standards. As its name suggests, the BGP is not an IGP. The BGP is designed as a more efficient and flexible alternative to the earlier EGP for routing between organizations – inter-autonomous system routing. BGP places no restrictions on the interconnections that can exist between autonomous systems. It allows a router to identify multiple routes between systems, to detect and avoid routing loops and to choose between multiple available routes.

BGP meets a need for **policy-based routing** for Internet service providers and user organizations. They will have limits on the types of traffic and the organizations for which they are prepared to transport data.

Controlling the type of traffic carried by considering origin and destination is one of the functions of this new type of routing. Policy-based routing is about enforcing routing decisions based on the use, or avoidance, of selected autonomous systems or network numbers as transit networks, or on acting as a transit network on behalf of other autonomous systems. With registration, these numbers indicate the nature of the communicating organization – educational, commercial, governmental, military, external to the USA, or another unclassified type.

RFCs for the BGP were first published in June 1989; the current version is 4, known as BGP4. The BGP allows routers to exchange details of routes between autonomous systems. The paths are described as a list of network and autonomous system numbers; since subnetworks describe a level of detail internal to an autonomous system, BGP does not describe subnetworks. Two communicating autonomous systems can make a 'policy' decision on whether to use and advertise a route incorporating particular network numbers. An autonomous system must only advertise routes which it is prepared to use. It must decide whether it is prepared to be a transit network (a carrier). BGP only specifies how path details are exchanged; how autonomous system managers derive a routing policy and how they configure that policy in routing software is outside the specification.

As with OSPF, there are several independent implementations of BGP in use on the Internet. Later versions of gated support BGP and this code is public domain.

A feature of BGP is its ability to detect and suppress routing loops. EGP, used previously to describe routes external to the autonomous system, could only have one connection to the core. BGP is more efficient than EGP in its use of bandwidth and processing power for, after an initial exchange of a complete routing table, only changes to that table and keep-alive messages are sent. EGP does not perform well in congested networks where packet loss occurs. BGP is more tolerant as routing information is retransmitted over a reliable TCP connection.

BGP would seem to have a role to play in the larger commercial network, for example in a multinational company where there are a number of centres of equivalent status each with their own TCP/IP systems. BGP could provide the right degree of autonomy for each 'autonomous system'.

Interior gateway routing protocol

The **Interior Gateway Routing Protocol** (IGRP) is a proprietary protocol developed by Cisco Systems for their multiprotocol routers. It is used with TCP/IP and other protocols that Cisco routers support. IGRP predates both OSPF and integrated IS–IS. It was designed to overcome the limitations of RIP in a multiprotocol environment and can use multiple paths simultaneously.

Using multiple routing protocols

A complex network is unlikely to use just a single routing protocol, though once a modern sophisticated protocol like OSPF is mastered, there are few technical reasons to introduce another IGP. Routers can operate more than one routing protocol, each performing updates on a single routing table simultaneously. They may use OSPF and RIP to communicate inside the autonomous system, and BGP and EGP to communicate outside the organization. Most combinations should operate correctly. Occasionally, the detail learnt about the same routes by two different methods may conflict and cause a routing 'black hole': IP datagrams reach a router which does not know of the destination network; its only option is to discard the data and inform the originator using the error protocol, ICMP. Black holes are more likely where manual routing tables are used to supplement dynamic routing.

Managing routing errors and network congestion

Even in a quite simple TCP/IP network, network implementors must set up procedures to detect and manage link, network, and equipment

Figure 16.19   ICMP and multiple management domains.

failures and performance problems. Because of the way a TCP/IP installation is structured, successful management will require technical
cooperation across different management functions and organizations.
The indication that some remedial action is required is the presence of
certain types of ICMP error datagrams on a network.

When links and equipment fail, routes will change. During the
time taken for the whole network to agree a new stable configuration,
routers are likely to discard IP datagrams. When a router cannot forward
a datagram, it should generate an ICMP destination-unreachable error
message back to the source IP address of the discarded datagram.

In a complex network, this raises some organizational issues, for
this error message will travel across several management responsibilities. It could originate from a router under one communications
management control, addressed to a host system in another organization
and level of management; it might well be caused by a failure in a
network which is under yet another management control. The main
problem is that the management function which has the physical network problem probably receives no notification because the failure
is reported back along the route away from the source of the problem.
It is the originating host that will receive an error message (Figure
16.19).

When a system receives an ICMP message, it records the fact in a
set of counters for each ICMP message type. These counters can be read

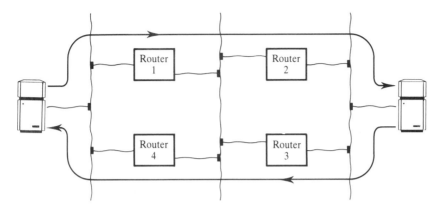

Figure 16.20 Asymmetric datagram transmission.

from the system console; in UNIX systems the command `netstat -s` will list network statistics which include the ICMP messages. In recent implementations, the counters from network equipment can be read across the network with an SNMP management system; summary information can be collected and collated centrally. If a logging system is turned on, the detail also may be recorded in a circular log file. Another way to see the detail is to trap ICMP error datagrams with a LAN analyser or remote monitor as they pass through the network.

Asymmetric and one-way transmission

A consequence of the flexibility of IP routing is that the path between two end systems need not be symmetric. In an internetwork with multiple paths between end systems and the routing protocols to take advantage of them, if a datagram travels between A and B through routers 1 and 2, in one direction, the response datagram may well travel back from B to A through routers 3 and 4 (Figure 16.20).

Even where there is only one available path, it is possible for datagrams to pass from A to B successfully but not from B to A. This could occur if B has no default router, if it has an incorrect subnet mask, or if the subnet masks are incorrect on some of the router ports. Subnet masks are only used on outbound datagrams so it is possible for them to be correct in one direction of transmission and incorrect in the other. When the router compares the destination network number, it may decide it has no route to that network. It should generate an ICMP destination unreachable or route change request message.

To determine where the fault lies requires a combination of good test equipment and methodical test techniques as discussed in Chapter 18.

Relevant RFCs

827	Exterior Gateway Protocol (EGP)
1058	Routing Information Protocol (updated by RFC 1723)
1102	Policy routing in Internet protocols
1104	Models of policy-based routing
1124	Policy issues in interconnecting networks
1125	Policy requirements for inter-administrative domain routing
1126	Goals and functional requirements for inter-autonomous system routing
1136	Administrative domains and routing domains: a model for routing in the Internet
1195	Use of OSI IS–IS for routing in TCP/IP and dual environments
1245	OSPF protocol analysis
1246	Experience with the OSPF protocol
1256	ICMP router discovery messages
1264	Internet routing protocol standardization criteria
1265	BGP protocol analysis
1266	Experience with the BGP protocol
1370	Applicability statement for OSPF
1397	Default route advertisement in BGP2 and BGP3 versions of the border gateway protocol
1403	BGP OSPF interaction
1467	Status of CIDR deployment in the Internet
1478	An architecture for inter-domain policy routing
1479	Inter-domain policy routing protocol specification: version 1
1517	Applicability statement for the implementation of classless inter-domain routing (CIDR)
1518	An architecture for IP address allocation with CIDR
1519	Classless inter-domain routing (CIDR): an address assignment and aggregation strategy
1581	Protocol analysis for extensions to RIP to support demand circuits
1582	Extensions to RIP to support demand circuits
1583	OSPF version 2
1584	Multicast extensions to OSPF
1585	MOSPF: analysis and experience
1586	Guidelines for running OSPF over frame relay networks
1587	The OSPF NSSA option
1721	RIP version 2 protocol analysis
1722	RIP version 2 protocol applicability statement
1723	RIP version 2 carrying additional information (updates RFC 1058)
1745	BGP4/IDRP for IP – OSPF interaction
1765	OSPF database overflow
1771	A border gateway protocol 4 (BGP4)
1772	Application of the border gateway protocol in the Internet

Summary

In this section we have considered the principles of routing and the major protocols used on most commercial TCP/IP networks. Where a company is intending to work with anything but the smallest network, it is important to understand the mechanics of the routing protocols so that they can be selected and tuned to provide the best level of service.

The principles behind routing protocols are basically the same but protocols continue to be enhanced to handle more complex architectures efficiently and to be more responsive to network changes. Many of the earlier less sophisticated routing protocols are still in use today; it is important to appreciate their limitations.

The latest and most sophisticated routing protocol for use with TCP/IP systems is OSPF. This should be considered when purchasing new equipment. Not all the features of the protocol (TOS routing) are available in commercial equipment, but with the right market pressure this will change. OSPF requires careful network planning and implementation. Configuration of a large OSPF network will be quite complex due to the need to determine the appropriate costs for each port on the network so that available paths are used with optimum effectiveness.

Mixing multiple routing protocols on a network should be approached with caution as their interoperation may cause routing loops.

17

Simple network management protocol

In recent years, the Simple Network Management Protocol (SNMP) has become increasingly important. It has become the dominant mechanism for the distributed management of network equipment.

The most significant aspect of implementations of SNMP is the power they provide to monitor and control networks. SNMP's simplicity and effectiveness have positioned it as the vehicle for the development of increasingly sophisticated mechanisms for controlling network systems.

Topics covered in this chapter are:

- SNMP
- MIBs
- ASN.1/BER
- Use of SNMP

The term 'SNMP' is commonly used to refer to the complete set of components that are required to manage a network. To be correct, SNMP is only the protocol used to communicate management information between devices on a network; its definition does not cover all aspects of the system. In this chapter we will look at the other components that are used with SNMP, such as the Management Information Bases (MIBs). Although defined for use with TCP/IP, SNMP was based on the OSI definitions for network management.

The need for management systems

During the 1980s, networks changed from being terminal access networks to resource-sharing networks consisting of PCs, minicomputers and mainframes all connected by cables and a network operating system. This is nothing less than a distributed computing system, with the internal communications paths of each computer replaced by the network. The overall function of this system is the basic tool of information technology and the network is the core of the whole system. Failure of the network can have a serious impact on a company. As networks become larger and more crucial to business success, the ability to keep that resource functioning becomes critical.

Before the advent of SNMP, network management was proprietary and developed by each manufacturer. For a heterogeneous network, a network operations centre would be filled with terminal screens, each providing management information on one manufacturer's network subsystem. With these techniques, network management was expensive. The production of an overall picture of network performance involved gathering large volumes of information manually and further manual processing to produce statistics and graphs.

While each item of equipment must contain network management software, the market for network management *systems* is small; an organization wants only one network management system for all types of equipment. Developing network management tools is also expensive. With the growth in popularity of TCP/IP, the IETF was able to solve this dilemma; there was a large enough single market for management software and systems; with TCP/IP, developers had traditionally cooperated to develop common standards. It was not until a number of organizations worked together to agree a common standard that the total market for a single set of tools became large enough to warrant development and reduced the costs to where sophisticated management systems became attractive even to smaller network operators.

Network management is a classic information technology problem. Large amounts of detailed information are required to understand what is happening within the system so that necessary decisions can be made on how to control, adapt and grow the service. This requires large amounts of disk space to retain the information over long periods so that short- and long-term trends can be discerned; it requires large amounts of memory and processing power to run complex analysis tools; it needs graphics workstations to display maps of the network and equipment diagrams on which alarms and faults can be overlaid. A potential issue is that a system may generate so much network traffic and information in managing itself, it becomes both a significant load on the network and self-perpetuating.

The development of management for TCP/IP

If a network management standard is to be successful then it must lead to simple, low-cost software for the many small items of network equipment. High-cost software must be confined to one, or a few, central management systems that collect and process management information. Developers must be able to produce a range of centralized management systems that are economic for different sized networks. One can trace SNMP's origins to the OSI network management initiatives (CMIS/CMIP) of the mid-1980s. While the two developments were initially closely aligned, it became clear that standards based on OSI developments could not meet these needs for simplicity and low cost. SNMP standards still show this early common work. The structure of management information is simplified from the OSI developments; SNMP has a presentation layer and the standards are defined using an OSI language, ASN.1.

At one time there were two proposals for TCP/IP management. One proposal was SNMP, the other Common Management Information Services and Protocol Over TCP/IP (RFC 1095), CMOT. CMOT uses the OSI standards Common Management Information Protocol (CMIP) and Common Management Information Services (CMIS), operating over TCP/IP communications protocols rather than OSI protocols. As a result, SNMP is a connectionless management system designed to operate over the UDP transport layer of TCP/IP. CMIP and CMIS (and hence CMOT) are based on connection-oriented systems. CMOT is now only of historic interest.

SNMP was first issued in April 1989 but the main implementation standards date from May 1990. SNMP Version 2 (SNMPv2, May 1993) improves upon those facilities: it provides additional commands to reduce network management traffic, particularly for large networks; it offers improved error reporting; and introduces new object definitions, larger event counters and better distributed management tools. It has stronger statements on conformance and compliance which should lead to assured interoperability between different manufacturers' equipments. SNMPv2 also includes better access control and rigorous authentication and security, but the security architecture is regarded by some as over-complex. The SNMPv2 core standards were updated in January 1996.

SNMP is regarded as an integral and essential component of TCP/IP systems. All the TCP/IP protocols below the application layer have their SNMP components; to claim compliance with the relevant protocol standards, manufacturers must also implement the corresponding network management standards. SNMP has been extended to cover non-TCP/IP equipment and some proprietary protocols, making it the most widely used standard for collecting network management information.

Gathering management information

In the past, statistics on network performance have often only been collected from an analyser connected to a single point on the network. This localized information does not represent an accurate view of the activity on the entire network unless in-depth studies of the protocols are made. This is technically complex, and rarely done, so the results can be misleading.

One of the benefits of local area networks is that every node connects to a common logical bus, so they all can be accessed, either for data or for management reasons, from any point on that LAN. If performance statistics are collected from every node, this distributes network measurement right to the periphery of the network. The picture of network performance developed from this information will be far more accurate.

The main problem then is that there is so much information generated, that it requires significant computing power and software sophistication to analyse the data and report appropriate exceptions or problems in a form network managers can easily recognize. With a common protocol for delivering the statistics, manufacturers can concentrate on differentiating their products by the power of their analysis and display tools.

Most network management systems today are effective at displaying alarms and collecting statistics; there is still not enough assistance with analysing and interpreting the meaning of those statistics.

SNMP architecture

The basic architecture of SNMP is shown in Figure 17.1. As previously described, the architecture of SNMP includes more than just the protocols. It consists of the Management Information Base (MIB) for each component of the protocol stack and the simple network management protocol.

Information encoding

When information is passed between different computer architectures, the computers must agree on the representation of that information. Management systems have to agree on the meaning of management

Figure 17.1 Simple network management architecture.

information as it is passed from computer to management system to prevent different computer architectures from misinterpreting it. SNMP has based the way it represents its data on two OSI standards: Abstract Syntax Notation 1 (ASN.1) and the Basic Encoding Rules (BER).

ASN.1 can be thought of as a strictly defined and 'highly typed' high-level computer language. Quantities to be described are defined in terms of primitive types like `integer` and `string`. Like any other high-level computer language, the results can be read and interpreted by both people and machines. The ASN.1 language can be compiled into a sequence of octets (bits) using the BER. SNMP uses only a subset of ASN.1, normally the types `integer`, `octet string`, `object identifier`, `sequence` and `null`. It is possible for other application-wide types to be defined, but these must resolve into the primitive types.

BER deals with the same problem as XDR does for NFS (ONC), but BER is an explicit and unambiguous system – each value is clearly and explicitly defined. This makes it quite easy for a LAN analyser to decipher any information on the network that is encoded in BER. To do this with XDR would require knowledge of the structure of the information used by the application that generated it. In both cases, it is necessary to understand the context of the information to understand its meaning completely. But whereas XDR assumes that the device receiving the information understands what to expect, BER includes a label with the information indicating exactly what it is.

Most of the other TCP/IP application layers we discussed used ASCII strings to pass their commands across the network. The meaning of the information could be seen on any LAN analyser that shows ASCII

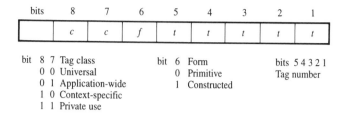

Figure 17.2 BER tag definition.

data. As SNMP uses BER, it is more difficult to analyse than these other TCP/IP protocols; data passing across a network is encoded as apparently meaningless octets. To give a clearer understanding of SNMP messages[†] we must look a little deeper into BER.

The underlying form of BER is shown in Figure 17.2. All data encoded by BER has a type and length field preceding it. The type field indicates the construction of data being carried and the length field its size. This allows many different types of information to be carried and deciphered by the remote computer.

To give additional flexibility for other structures that may be required in the future, the type field has three subfields; bits 8 and 7 are used to denote the **tag class** (*cc*), bit 6 the **form** (*f*) and bits 5 to 1 the **tag number**. Tags can be extended beyond a single octet but this does not change the concept and it is not necessary to describe the detail here. Some additional detail is given in Appendix J.

The length field is normally 1 octet long, but to describe long structures more than eight bits are needed. So, if bit 8 of the length field is 1, it denotes that the length field is more than one octet and that the remaining seven bits in the first octet actually denote the length of the length field, that is, these seven bits are a count of the number of following octets which are themselves the length field. A single octet length field can define data that has 127 octets, which will cover most cases for SNMP (Figure 17.3). For a detailed list of possible tags, see Appendix J.

Management information base

The Management Information Base (MIB) is a definition of the objects (quantities or fields) that should be provided on each managed node by the SNMP 'agent'. The management agent is the piece of software that responds to SNMP management requests from the central management station.

The objects of the MIB are arranged in groups. Some groups relate to each layer or protocol in the protocol stack and some relate to the

---

[†]Sometimes referred to as Protocol Data Units (PDUs), an OSI term.

Data to 127 octets

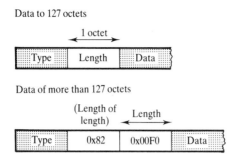

Figure 17.3 Length and extended length in BER.

system as a whole. Many of the quantities are counters of events and are therefore an accumulation of the number of events seen since the counter was last zeroed – the number of frames sent and received categorized as unicast, multicast and broadcast would be one set of counters at the MAC layer. The details of 'when' and 'who' are not available after the event. Another MIB definition, RMON (Remote MONitor), describes how to access a remote device that will gather packets from a remote network to which it is attached, and return them to the management station for analysis. The remote monitor should retain the detail of the events, but the quantity of information available will be correspondingly larger.

These common definitions of the variables on each type of node in a network make gathering information on any device quite simple and independent of the manufacturer. Many manufacturers have created their own extensions to the standard MIBs to provide better functionality with their own products. The protocol remains standard but the proprietary extensions make the management a little more complex. MIBs have been or are being defined for all (electronic) components of a network, from a repeater, through bridges and routers to hosts. They all contain elements of the protocol stack.

Because all of these systems follow the same MIB and protocol conventions, it is easy for management systems to use the standard and to provide cross-management of other vendors' products. Groups of manufacturers are now cooperating to exchange details of their proprietary MIB extensions which will allow complete management of each others' products.

Figure 17.4 shows the beginning of the Internet MIB II definition represented in ASN.1 syntax. This figure shows the basic object definitions that reference the individual groups of information that must be supported within managed equipment. These are: `system`, which identifies the product in use; `interfaces`, which details the network connections; and `at`, address translation. The rest detail facets of a particular protocol: `ip`, `icmp`, `tcp`, `udp` and `egp`.

Each of these groups has a varying number of further objects or fields defined within them. They describe a parameter relevant to that group. For example, within the `system` group is an object called the

```
mib               OBJECT IDENTIFIER ::= { mgmt 1 }

system            OBJECT IDENTIFIER ::= { mib 1 }
interfaces        OBJECT IDENTIFIER ::= { mib 2 }
at                OBJECT IDENTIFIER ::= { mib 3 }
ip                OBJECT IDENTIFIER ::= { mib 4 }
icmp              OBJECT IDENTIFIER ::= { mib 5 }
tcp               OBJECT IDENTIFIER ::= { mib 6 }
udp               OBJECT IDENTIFIER ::= { mib 7 }
egp               OBJECT IDENTIFIER ::= { mib 8 }
transmission      OBJECT IDENTIFIER ::= { mib 9 }
snmp              OBJECT IDENTIFIER ::= { mib 10}
```

Figure 17.4 MIB groups.

sysDescr or **system descriptor**. Figure 17.5 shows this definition in ASN.1 format. The system descriptor is a string object which identifies the name, hardware type, software operating system and network software. So retrieving this object from a node gives you a complete description of what type of system it is. From the ASN.1 definition, you can tell it is defined as an octet string – a string of 8-bit quantities. It is read only, so cannot be changed remotely and it is mandatory, so it must be provided on all implementations.

The third field is the sysUpTime, which indicates how long in hundredths of a second since this device was last reset in some way – (initialized or powered on).

The sysObjectID holds a vendor's authoritative identification. This is a definition of a registered identifier which is shown in dotted decimal notation and uniquely identifies a vendor's object groups and objects in their products.

The rules for the definition of the MIB descriptors are called the Structure of Management Information (SMI). This is based on OSI work for OSI management. Originally the MIB definitions were to be common between SNMP and CMIP, but they have now diverged.

Structure of a MIB

One function of these MIB definitions is to produce a sequence of numbers which will uniquely identify any management object in any management community, in this case the OSI or TCP/IP communities. These system object identifiers are derived from a hierarchical or tree structure starting at a root, which is unlabelled. Below that root are three 'main trunks' identifying the controlling organizations:

0   ITU-T
1   ISO
2   Joint-ISO-ITU-T

```
            -- the System group

    sysDescr OBJECT-TYPE
             SYNTAX   OCTET STRING
             ACCESS   read-only
             STATUS   mandatory
             ::= { system 1 }

    sysObjectID OBJECT-TYPE
             SYNTAX   OBJECT IDENTIFIER
             ACCESS   read-only
             STATUS   mandatory
             ::= { system 2 }

    sysUpTime OBJECT-TYPE
             SYNTAX   TimeTicks
             ACCESS   read-only
             STATUS   mandatory
             ::= { system 3 }
```

Figure 17.5 The 'system' group of the Internet MIB II.

There are further 'branches' beneath each of these. ISO has defined 'other international organizations' as being under a subtree number 3; one of these organizations is the US Department of Defense (DOD) as subtree number 6 off subtree 3 which is itself off the ISO trunk, 1. It is assumed that the DOD will define a further subtree of 1 for the Internet community. This generates a generic identifier for all TCP/IP management information of:

1   . 3   . 6 . 1
(ISO . Int org . dod . internet)

The next level of the definition is split in six ways as:

1 Directory
2 Management
3 Experimental
4 Private
5 Security
6 SNMPv2

'Directory' is reserved for future use. 'Management' (mgmt) contains the SNMPv1 MIB II tree that identifies all the objects that are managed under SNMPv1. SNMPv2 uses three different MIBs – snmpMIB, snmpM2M, partyMIB – defined separately under the snmpModules node of node 6. 'Experimental' is for temporary use with experimental systems and 'private'† is used to identify objects defined unilaterally for internal or private use. There is a subtree to 'private' defined for private extensions to the MIB system as:

> 1   enterprises

The result of this numbered tree is a sequence of numbers separated by periods (.) which define the path taken to a particular node on the management tree. Thus the object id:

> 1.3.6.1.4.1.42

could be used to refer to an individual manufacturer's extensions to the MIB of which:

> 1.3.6.1.4.1.42.1.1

could refer to a specific product as having a special MIB value.

A generic descriptor of 1.3.6.1.2.1.1.1 would refer specifically to the system descriptor (`sysDescr`); the numbers trace the values in the curly braces, { }, of the ASN.1 definition (see Figures 17.4 and 17.5).

BER encoding of MIB fields

When SNMP uses MIB fields, it refers to them through the object ids. In an SNMP datagram, the reference to the `sysDescr` would be 1.3.6.1.2.1.1.1. This would be expressed as a sequence of ASN.1 primitives and encoded using BER as:

> 0608 2B06 0102 0101 0100

The first octet defines the value as an **object identifier** (06), the second value is the length of the data (08) which is eight octets. With object identifiers, the first two octets can be combined in one octet. This will normally happen with SNMP values; they become 2B which translates back to 1 and 3. The following octets give the rest of the descriptor: 6.1.2.1.1.1. The 00 at the end is an octet to define which interface (referred to as an **instance**) on the computer this request relates to, if appropriate. If a computer has multiple interfaces, the instance used refers SNMP actions to the appropriate interface. On MIB fields where an instance is not appropriate, its value is set to 00. There can only be one `sysDescr` in a system, so the value of the 'instance octet' is always set to 00 with this object.

The object identifier shown would be followed by the value of the field in a response to an SNMP request or a null in the request itself. The BER type for null is 05, so an SNMP request is followed by 0500.

Consider another example of the use of the instance octet:

---

† If a system moves from experimental or private to a fully accepted and generally available technique, it should move its definitions to one of the permanent branches of the MIB.

```
ifType OBJECT-TYPE
        SYNTAX  INTEGER {
                other(1).-- none of the
                following
                regular1822(2),
                hdh1822(3),
                ddn-x25(4),
                rfc877-x25(5),
                ethernet-csmacd(6),
                iso88023-csmacd(7),
                iso88024-tokenBus(8),
                iso88025-tokenRing(9),
                iso88026-man(10),
                starLan(11),
                proteon-10MBit(12),
                proteon-80MBit(13),
                hyperchannel(14),
                fddi(15),
                lapb(16),
                sdlc(17),
                t1-carrier(18),
                cept(19),
                basicIsdn(20),
                primaryIsdn(21),
                    -- proprietary serial
                    propPointToPointSerial(22)
                }
        ACCESS  read-only
        STATUS  mandatory
        ::= { ifEntry 3 }
```

Figure 17.6 The ifType definition.

0608 2B06 0102 0102 0302

Tracing the tree, this refers to an object identifier (06) of length 8 on the tree 1.3.6.1.2 (the 'management' group of the DOD Internet). The next branch is mib (1) and the interfaces object (2) within that group. The next selector (3) refers to the interface type (ifType) field of which there could be more than one. So for a specific host, this identifier refers to iftype.2 on the computer specified. This should be its second interface and will be one of the standard interface types of Figure 17.6. A common type in TCP/IP would be 6, ethernet-csmacd. More detailed examples are shown later in this chapter.

Figure 17.6 shows a portion of the MIB entries for the interface group showing possible interface types. The numbers against the specific types of interface would be returned in a response to indicate the interface type.

```
-- the IP group

ipForwarding OBJECT-TYPE
  SYNTAX  INTEGER {
    gateway(1), -- entity forwards datagrams
    host(2) -- entity does NOT forward datagrams

          ACCESS  read-only
          STATUS  mandatory
          ::= { ip 1 }

  ipDefaultTTL OBJECT-TYPE
          SYNTAX  INTEGER
          ACCESS  read-write
          STATUS  mandatory
          ::= { ip 2 }

ipInReceives OBJECT-TYPE
          SYNTAX  Counter
          ACCESS  read-only
          STATUS  mandatory
          ::= { ip 3 }

ipInHdrErrors OBJECT-TYPE
          SYNTAX  Counter
          ACCESS  read-only
          STATUS  mandatory
          ::= { ip 4 }
```

Figure 17.7 Part of the IP group from MIB II.

Figure 17.7 shows the beginning of the IP group from the Internet MIB II. The first field is the `ipForwarding` field which identifies whether this host acts as an IP router or just as a host. Notice the field `ipDefault-TTL`. This field is `read-write`, so a management system (with suitable access rights) can modify the TTL for the IP stack in this host. This therefore allows configuration changes to be performed remotely.

The protocol

The simple network management protocol provides a mechanism to access MIB objects so that they can be read and changed. It also allows a device to send unsolicited messages to an SNMP management station to indicate that some predefined condition has been met. The message types used to perform these functions are:

```
get-request
get-next-request
```

```
get-bulk-request   (V2)
response
set-request
inform-request     (V2)
trap               (V1)
snmpV2-trap        (V2)
report             (V2)
```

V1 or V2 indicates message types available only in V1 or V2 protocol.

The message types are referred to as Protocol Data Units (PDUs), as in OSI standards. The `get-request` PDU is used by an SNMP network management station to obtain the value of a specific MIB variable from the SNMP management agent in a remote node. The `get-next-request` is similar to the `get-request`, except it allows MIB values to be received without defining them specifically. `get-next-request` is used where a table of variables, such as a routing table, exists. The client would not know the number of values in the table. The `get-bulk-request` is intended to reduce network traffic. It is used for requesting large amounts of data from a client, especially for the retrieval of large tables. It saves sending multiple `get-requests` or `get-next-requests` to retrieve multiple MIB values. Using `get-bulk-request` they will all be returned in a small number of large `response` PDUs.

The `response` PDU is the answer from the management agent to `get-request`, `get-next-request`, `get-bulk-request`, `set-request` and `inform-request`. The `set-request` is used by the management station to change MIB variables that can be altered in the management agent. One possibility is to set a trap for a defined event or condition detected by the management agent. When that condition occurs on the node, the agent sends an `snmpV2-trap` PDU to the management station. This message can be generated at any time, so a management station has to be listening for these continuously. The `inform-request` is used with the manager-to-manager MIB, snmpM2M, to allow management stations to notify each other of events and alarms. (The usual SNMP exchange is between a management station and a management agent.) This provides for distributed management with multiple management stations cooperating to manage a large network.

The `snmpV2-trap` messages use UDP well-known port number 162; other PDUs use port number 161. This allows `snmpV2-trap` messages to be handled independently of `get` and `set`.

The basic format of SNMP messages is shown in Figure 17.8. They all start with a version, which is 0 for version 1, followed by a **community** string. The community string defines a level of authentication which pertains to this message and hence determines whether it will have sufficient rights on a host to make changes or even read the information in the MIB.

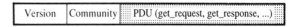

Figure 17.8 SNMP message format.

The community string is followed by one or more PDUs which define the overall message encapsulated in this datagram. In SNMPv1, all but the `trap` PDU are of the format shown in Figure 17.9(a), the `trap` PDU is shown in Figure 17.9(b). In SNMPv2 all but the `get-bulk-request` PDUs are of the format shown in Figure 17.9(a) and the `get-bulk-request` PDU is shown in Figure 17.9(c). The request id is used to relate requests to responses; these messages are likely to use UDP and hence there is no reliability. The request id field is followed by an error status field that is 0 if there is no error or by one of the following error messages:

1   The PDU is too big
2   No such name, that value does not exist
3   Bad value, that value is not suitable
4   Read only, the field cannot be altered
5   General error
6   No access   (V2)
7   Wrong type   (V2)
8   Wrong length   (V2)
9   Wrong encoding   (V2)
10 Wrong value   (V2)
11 No creation   (V2)
12 Inconsistent value   (V2)
13 Resource unavailable (V2)
14 Commit failed   (V2)
15 Undo failed   (V2)
16 Authorization error   (V2)
17 Not writable   (V2)
18 Inconsistent name   (V2)

V2 indicates error status values added in V2 protocol.

(a)

	Request id	Error status	Error index
MIB variable descriptor MIB variable data			

(b)

	Type of object	Address of object	Generic trap type
MIB variable descriptor MIB variable data			

(c)

	Non repeaters	Max repetitions	
MIB variable descriptor MIB variable data			

Figure 17.9 SNMP PDUs: (a) V1 & V2 normal; (b) V1 trap; (c) V2 bulk.

The error index field can provide extra information relating to the error message. Last is the variable binding, which is an object identifier and a suitable field that can contain the value of that object variable. The variable field is provided in requests as well as responses but in a request it is set to a null value.

Figure 17.10 is an example of an SNMP `get-request` and its response. The exchange is represented in hexadecimal and then each of the fields is decoded and explained. The request is for the system-up-time on a node (objectdescr 1.3.6.1.2.1.1.3.0) and the resulting reply. The octets of the SNMP PDU have been split into their respective fields, although the order of transmission has been retained. The first octet of BER encoding is type, so the left-hand column contains the type, length and then value of the field. Notice the description starts by indicating that the whole structure is a sequence. Most of the constructs from then on are simple, apart from the PDU type, which is a context-specific construction, and the object identifier, which is an object id. As mentioned previously, an object identifier can be compressed; the first two bytes of the descriptor, which are 1 and 3, are encoded to become the value 2B. The remaining values are all in hexadecimal – 6.1.2.1.1.3.0 – indicating the system-up-time. This is then followed by a null field.

The response SNMP PDU is almost identical to the request; only the PDU type and the response value change. The PDU type changes to 2, encoded as A2, a context-specific construction, and the field following the descriptor that was null is now filled with the actual up-time, in one hundredths of a second since the device was re-initialized.

Using SNMP

SNMP has brought the potential of cost-effective network management even to small LANs. It has provided a generic mechanism by which different manufacturers' equipment can be monitored and controlled from a common management device. An SNMP management agent can now be added to most components on a LAN so that they can now be monitored and controlled by SNMP. Even a piece of cable can have a device connected to it which will report its status, the status of the physical layer, to a management station. SNMP opens the door to higher level management of the network system, as both LAN and WAN components can be monitored and manipulated to increase effectiveness, reliability and security.

With the ability to instruct devices to report events (trap) and the ability to start processes on a node, the network can be manipulated to suit changing conditions within a system. In fact, a management system can be configured to perform any task on any identifiable condition being met. For example, imagine a network on which the manager is unable to sit watching the management screen all day just waiting for failures since some tasks require the manager's presence outside the office. It is

(a)

Washburn Fig 17.10(a)

(b)

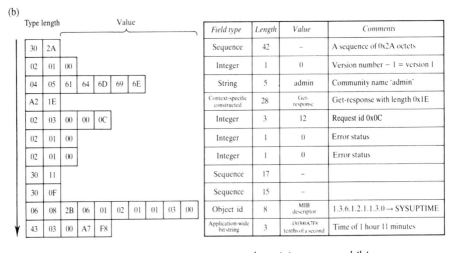

Figure 17.10 SNMP PDUs in BER encoding: (a) request and (b) response.

feasible to link a network management system with a paging network and configure the system such that a failure of any kind will trigger the management station, through traps, to communicate with the paging system and warn the manager of the condition, so that appropriate action can be taken. The management system could also react to the traps and take remedial action before paging the network manager. It would then warn that a particular system had been switched into a fallback mode. There are no practical limits to this, provided an event can be trapped unambiguously and the reaction can be programmed into a computer to be initiated on a particular event.

One possible approach is the dynamic allocation of circuit capacity on remote connections between LANs. Routers or bridges can be programmed to report that their high-speed lines have reached, or are close to reaching, saturation. On this condition, they can send a trap message to the management station. The management station can send SNMP set-requests to set flags in the router or bridge so that it will take action to establish another channel, using ISDN, dial-up modems, X.25, or any other WAN system that will allow dynamic setup of connections. This is particularly useful with WAN connections that are charged on usage as well as connect time, as they are only used when required.

This management system can also be programmed to remove the connections when load decreases, as the router or bridges can also be configured to send a trap when their load falls below a predefined level for a certain period. This type of system can easily be configured to invoke fallback after the failure of a WAN link. Some bridges and routers can perform dynamic connections on predefined conditions, but the ability to perform this from a central point, in a standard way, provides better control of the system as a whole and allows more sophisticated decisions to be made.

Network management platforms

Most management stations that use SNMP operate on a multitasking operating system within a windowed environment, often the UNIX operating systems and the X Window System GUI. This allows multiple tasks to be dealt with and the graphical interfaces make a complex system easier to understand.

The three most well-known management platforms are (in alphabetical order) HP OpenView, IBM NetView 6000 and SunNet Manager. Each of these systems provides software development tools for manufacturers to integrate their equipment, and any proprietary MIB extensions, into the management software. Graphics tools allow manufacturers to draw an exact replica of their equipment and its indicator lights; at the management station, an operator can observe the equipment as if they were adjacent to it. The status of individual cards and ports within the equipment can be examined.

For network managers, the platforms also provide diagrammatic interfaces and icons of all network components together with maps with which to represent the entire corporate network. These can be zoomed to pick out countries, towns, sites, buildings and the network segments and equipment within a building. By using X Window as the display standard, several operations centres can independently display different views of the management information collected centrally by one management platform. The management systems commonly represent errors as a red object on the display. To look at that object in more detail, the manager selects the object with a mouse pointer. The display zooms to the next level of the network hierarchy giving a more detailed view of the fault.

In any system of alarms, filtering out the most significant information is always an interesting design task. A problem with graphical management systems is how they react in the event of failure of a shared resource. This will cause numerous error messages to be reported and can make it impossible for the manager to discern which component has failed due to the multitude of error reports presented on the screen. This problem is often handled by some type of artificial intelligence. The outcome is usually that the management system will best guess which device is causing the problem, show it as red, and show other failed components as some other less significant colour. The manager is drawn towards the element which is most likely to have failed; the problem is most likely to be identified quicker provided the diagnosis is not erroneous!

The processing demands on a management station at a time of serious failure are likely to be very high. These stations require a significant amount of processing power and not just to display colour graphics; a system that fails due to the high level of failure messages from the network will be no use at all when it is most required. Equally, a management system that is configured to generate a high level of unsolicited messages advising that the network is overloaded is perhaps not using its management systems to the best advantage.

While the features described are all based on the information provided by SNMP, such user functions are beyond the standardization process. Another feature which has eluded standardization is the database structure that is used to store management information. This means that despite the unquestionable success of SNMP, it is still difficult to process statistics from more than one type of management platform into a cohesive report, unless the statistics are passed from one management system to another using SNMP itself. SNMPv2 adds functions which allow exchange of information between management systems.

It is up to the purchasers to decide what facilities are required in their management environment and to evaluate the competitive offerings. In view of the proprietary MIB extensions, it would be wise to check that all equipment that is to be managed is fully supported by the chosen management platform.

Relevant RFCs

Note: this RFC list *excludes* the many RFCs which are the MIB definitions for individual protocols and interfaces.

Summary

The requirements for network management are sure to expand significantly over the next few years, allowing networks, and even buildings, to be managed by standard management stations using the SNMP.

SNMP has paved the way for completely integrated management of networks. As the protocol itself is simple in its operation, the major activity has been agreeing the objects to be managed and their representation as the managed objects of a MIB. With many of these definitions in place, SNMP has been easy to include in products and already it is widely supported.

Most vendors of networking components are incorporating SNMP agents into products from repeaters to hosts. Some vendors have produced their own MIBs or extensions, but as these are defined in a standard fashion, it is technically easy to add support for all MIBs on any management station; copyright and royalty issues of proprietary MIB extensions might be more difficult to resolve.

MIBs will undoubtedly continue to grow and become more diverse as new products are introduced. As long as the existing definitions of ASN.1 are used and extended, a high level of compatibility is likely. Any device that has a defined MIB can be controlled by SNMP, so a natural extension is that standard machines will control building services such as air conditioning and any other building services that can benefit from centralized control. Once the standards are in place the technical problems are easily overcome. Organizational and managerial issues are more difficult to resolve as they involve the least standardized components – people.

18

Configuration and testing

This chapter brings together some of the configuration and testing issues covered in earlier chapters, with the aim of assisting with fault diagnosis. It also considers some of the standard tools that are available to ensure that TCP/IP systems are operating correctly.

In this chapter you will learn:

- A generic approach to testing TCP/IP systems
- Configuration issues
- More about debugging and measurement tools
- Common problems

In working with many different implementations of TCP/IP, we have found that product installation manuals rarely provide enough detail to understand fully how to configure all but the most rudimentary aspects of a system. This book is intended to provide the level of detail required to understand fully the ramifications of modifying parameters in a configuration setup, although we cannot expect to account for all the issues that may occur due to a particular vendor's implementation of TCP/IP.

Configuration

Configuration of a system can be easy or complex, depending on the way the product has been developed and which features the installer wishes to use. The more features and services that are used, the more complex the problem becomes. Often, systems are simply left at their default settings. This is usually of no consequence in small networks but it becomes important when a network grows. For example, many UNIX implementations of TCP/IP by default enable some services that are not necessary for most commercial installations. The effect of disabling such services varies from reducing the numbers of broadcast frames to preventing unauthorized access to a host.

With DOS-based PCs, the problem is simplified by the fact that they normally only run client services, and so the problem of other computers on the network gaining access is not usually a concern. On a computer using a multitasking operating system, it is worth while checking which features are enabled, before some TCP or host operating system expert on the network finds them first.

Minimum requirements

IP address

To get a workstation, host or router to function at a basic level is reasonably simple. The fundamental requirement for a node to work is that it has an IP address. It is important to ensure that the selected IP address matches the network address plan as described fully in Chapters 3 and 4.

Default gateway

If routing is to be used, a computer must be able to find a router. Either it should run the ICMP router discover protocol, or be configured with the IP address of a default gateway or it must run a program that listens to the routing protocols on the network, to learn about routers for itself (eavesdropping). More than one of these options may be used at the same time. Some systems allow more than one 'default' gateway to be defined so that a backup is available. Of course, an eavesdropping host must listen to an operational routing protocol; there is no point in the host listening for RIP if the routers are only speaking OSPF.

On PCs, the default gateway is a parameter in the configuration setup when the software is installed. On more complex hosts routing tables may have to be configured manually if they are not eavesdropping. Commonly, the command `route add` allows routes to be added or removed and the costs of using those routes, expressed in hops, to be adjusted. Unless default gateways are defined, it is possible that, as well as not being able to make calls to other networks, a host will not accept incoming requests or calls from a node on another network. This is so unexpected that it can easily be overlooked.

Subnetwork mask

If subnetworks are used, it is important to set the correct mask everywhere in the network. Variable masks are possible but must be used with care and with an understanding of how they are processed by routers. Initially, one value of mask should be used with one IP network number. In networks where the configuration is changed frequently, incorrect subnet masks are a source of obscure routing problems and can in some instances cause broadcast storms.

Domain name server

If name servers are to be used, the node has to be configured with the IP address of the domain name server and secondary server for fallback purposes.

User id and host name

With some of the application services such as the r commands, a PC has to be configured with a host name and user id. The r protocol uses these fields to tell the destination host these user details so that the user does not need to enter them each time the command is used. Any user operating the PC will be validated with the values stored in the PC. (Most hosts other than PCs will already know the user id and password as part of their configuration and user logon details anyway.)

More complex configuration

Configuration of TCP/IP systems to the level just described is straightforward. Most products explain these items fairly well in their supporting literature. The difficulty comes when a slightly more sophisticated configuration is required. Then, a manager's understanding of TCP/IP becomes important.

On many TCP/IP systems, whatever the computing platform, the files used to configure the system have standard names based upon those

```
#   @(#)netd.cf      1.4-88/11/15
#
#   This is a configuration file for host-based
#   TCP/IP using the el ethernet interface
#


#   open control streams for transport protocols
tcp = "/dev/tcp"
udp = "/dev/udp"

#   open an IP stream for each transport protocol
ip_tcp = "/dev/ip" nsap 6      #   bind stream to TCP protocol id
ip_udp = "/dev/ip" nsap 17     #   bind stream to UDP protocol id

#   open ARP for ethernet use
arp    = "/dev/arp" lsap 0x800

#   open link level devices
el_arp  = "/dev/el" lsap 0x806  #   stream for ARP messages
el_ip   = "/dev/el" lsap 0x800  #   stream for IP messages
loop    = "/dev/lo" lsap 0x800  #   stream for loopback driver

#   put it together
link ip_tcp under tcp
link ip_udp under udp

#   names must not assume a unit number so use as part of name
link loop under ip_tcp name "lo0"
link arp under ip_tcp name "el0"
link el_arp under arp type 0x101
link el_ip under arp type 0x1

#   initial configuration of interfaces
ifconfig "el0" gandalf up
ifconfig "lo0" localhost up
```

Figure 18.1   Format of netd.cf.

used in UNIX implementations. Where the names are different, it is usually easy to discern which aspects of configuration they relate to. The same
file structures as UNIX are used, as the same configuration parameters
have to be provided, determined by the RFCs that the software implements.

On UNIX systems important files for the basic operation of the
TCP/IP protocols are:

/etc/netd.cf
/etc/inetd.conf
/etc/services

netd.cf

This file (Figure 18.1) enables all but the application layer services of the
protocol stack. It is used to build (or bind) the components of the protocol
stack together, and here the IP addresses, subnet masks and broadcast
addresses used by the network hardware are stored. A program, usually
called ifconfig, performs the final binding of the parameters to the hardware. It is sometimes necessary to modify the netd.cf file when multiple
network interfaces are used.

```
#
#     Internet server configuration database
#         @(#)inetd.conf   1.2-88/11/11
#
ftp        stream   tcp    nowait   root   /etc/ftpd         ftpd
telnet     stream   tcp    nowait   root   /etc/telnetd      telnetd
shell      stream   tcp    nowait   root   /etc/rshd         rshd
login      stream   tcp    nowait   root   /etc/rlogind      rlogind
exec       stream   tcp    nowait   root   /etc/rexecd       rexecd
#    Run as user "uucp" if you don't want uucpd's wtmp entries.
uucp       stream   tcp    nowait   root   /etc/uucpd        uucpd
finger     stream   tcp    nowait   bin    /etc/fingerd      fingerd
tftp       dgram    udp    wait     root   /etc/tftpd        tftpd
#comsat    dgram    udp    wait     root   /etc/comsat       comsat
#talk      dgram    udp    wait     root   /etc/talkd        talkd
ntalk      dgram    udp    wait     root   /etc/ntalkd       ntalkd
echo       stream   tcp    nowait   root   internal
discard    stream   tcp    nowait   root   internal
chargen    stream   tcp    nowait   root   internal
daytime    stream   tcp    nowait   root   internal
time       stream   tcp    nowait   root   internal
#echo      dgram    udp    wait     root   internal
#discard            dgram  udp      wait   root    internal
#chargen            dgram  udp      wait   root    internal
#daytime            dgram  udp      wait   root    internal
#time      dgram    udp    wait     root   internal
```

Figure 18.2 Format of inetd.conf.

inetd.conf

The file inetd.conf (Figure 18.2) is used to enable the application layer services. It shows the common name of the services and relates them to the executable programs that are activated to implement that service. This file should be modified to prevent services that are not required from being started. In case this service is required in future, it is normal to disable the service by adding a comment character (#) in front of the line which would start it, rather than delete the line completely and lose the correct format.

services

The services file (Figure 18.3) lists the well-known ports used by this host. This should include any in-house or specialist programs used on the host.

Domain name server

There are a number of files required for the operation of a domain name server. These are normally explained in sufficient detail in manufacturer literature as their syntax is so awkward, and causes so many problems in all but the simplest of configurations. There are usually four configuration files used by domain name systems:

```
#
#       Network services, Internet style
#
echo            7/udp           ping
echo            7/tcp           ping
discard         9/udp           sink null
discard         9/tcp           sink null
systat          11/udp          users
systat          11/tcp          users
daytim          13/udp
daytime         13/tcp
netstat         15/tcp
quote           17/udp          text
quote           17/tcp          text
send            18/udp
send            18/tcp
chargen         19/udp          ttytst
chargen         19/tcp          ttytst
ftp-data        20/tcp
ftp             21/tcp
telnet          23/tcp
smtp            25/tcp          mail
time            37/udp          timeserver
time            37/tcp          timeserver
name4           2/tcp           nameserver
whois           43/tcp          nicname
domain          53/tcp          nameserver       #   name-domain server
domain          53/udp          nameserver
mtp             57/tcp                           #   deprecated
bootp           67/udp                           #   boot program server
tftp            69/udp
finger          79/tcp
hostnames       101/tcp         hostname         #   usually from nic
pop  2          109/tcp                          #   Post Office Protocol V2
pop  3          110/tcp                          #   Post Office Protocol V3
sunrpc          111/tcp
sunrpc          111/udp
nntp            119/tcp         readnews untp    #   UNSENET News Transfer Protoc
snmp1           61/udp
snmp-trap       162/udp         snmptrap
#
#     Host specific functions
#
tftp            69/udp
rje             77/tcp
finger          79/tcp
link            87/tcp          ttylink
supdup          95/tcp
ingreslock      1524/tcp
#
#     UNIX specific services
#
exec            512/tcp
login           513/tcp
shell           514/tcp         cmd              #   no passwords used
printer         515/tcp         spooler          #   experimental
efs             520/tcp                          #   for LucasFilm
courier         530/tcp         rpc              #   experimental
biff            512/udp         comsat
who             513/udp         whod
syslog          514/udp
talk            517/udp
route 520/udp   router routed   #                521 also
new-rwho        550/udp         new-who          #   experimental
rmonitor        560/udp         rmonitord        #   experimental
monitor         561/udp                          #   experimental
elcsd           704/udp                          #   errlog copy/server daemon
```

Figure 18.3   Format of services.

named.boot	Indicates which files should be loaded on start-up
named.db	This server's list of names (its authority)
named.rev	Used for reverse name look-up (IP to name)
named.ca	A list of names and IP addresses to be put into a cache

Further details on the use of these files were given in Chapter 14.

Debugging and measurement tools

Ping

Ping is the command that implements the ICMP echo functions. It is a useful confidence test if you can successfully 'ping' IP equipment. Most network connections that are identified with an IP address should reply to ping. The time to reply is usually given in milliseconds although the resolution may be limited to units of 10 or 20 ms.

In some implementations, ping gives access to the other features of the IP datagram header such as record route, time stamp, loose and strict source routing. Ping can then be used to gather statistics about network operation and test out the integrity and composition of a path to a remote node. It is usually possible to send different size datagrams to see if there is any limitation in the intervening network hardware. Ping normally reports on the response to each of its requests. Setting ping to operate continuously can be very useful for debugging a node that is failing to connect, as it provides a regular identifiable datagram which can be trapped on a protocol analyser.

But we must remember that ping only tests as far as the IP layer in the remote host, which may not be high enough in the TCP/IP stack to detect the fault. If ping works, it implies that all IP layers involved in the communication path are operational (Figure 18.4).

Most TCP/IP nodes have an address called 'local' or 'localhost' or 'me' or 'loopback' that is reserved for loopback testing. This can be used to check your own node with ping; executing 'ping loopback' or 'ping local' will test some of the local protocol stack and perhaps the network hardware. What 'pinging' your own node achieves is sometimes questionable, as the way it works varies from implementation to implementation. The best versions ping your machine all the way to the network hardware interface so the network card and the IP stack are tested. The poorer implementations of ping loopback, which unfortunately are most of them, only test down to the IP layer and back to the ICMP software. Yet other implementations allow the depth of testing to be specified, which is most useful. The problem for a network maintainer is that a negative result to 'ping loopback' indicates a fault but is rarely seen; a successful test is common but may not be of much value.

More detailed testing with ping is discussed later.

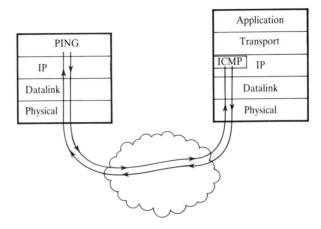

Figure 18.4   ICMP echo test (ping).

Standard services

There are many application layer services defined for use over the TCP/IP protocol stack. A number are of interest in this chapter as they are intended for use as diagnostic tools. These services are used to perform tests from other nodes on a network and are not particularly useful to the system where they reside. The most common application layer services are shown in Table 18.1.

Echo is a service normally provided in the application layer that will return characters received from a remote TCP connection or in a UDP datagram. This may not seem very exciting, but it provides an excellent confidence test and checks more than ping can. Ping is capable of detecting that a node exists and its IP layer is operational; the application layer echo moves beyond the IP layer through TCP or UDP to the application layer, but stops short of an application. You may fail to connect to the application but get to echo; this indicates a fault with the application.

Figure 18.5 indicates the aspects of a protocol stack tested by the various echo mechanisms. ping checks the bottom three layers, applica-

Table 18.1   Standard services.

Service	Port number (decimal)	Function
Echo	7	Echoes character back to caller
Chargen	19	Sends the complete ASCII character set continuously
Finger	79	Discovers the real name of a user from their user identification
Discard	9	Receives information but does no work
Daytime	13	Gives the time and date

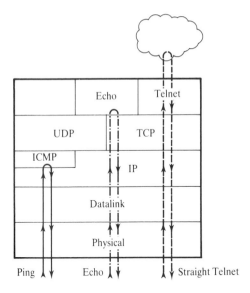

Figure 18.5   Ping, echo and O/S echo.

tion layer echo checks to the application layer and connection through Telnet to the operating system checks all but UDP.

These services can be accessed through special use of Telnet client software. By default, Telnet normally connects to its server software using port 23, but most implementations allow a command line option that lets the user specify an alternative port number. This allows you to connect directly to the port number of one of the services shown in Table 18.1 for testing. Another way these application layer services might be used is through an application. It would be fairly simple to write an application that would use the echo service at regular intervals to check a number of nodes to see they were available. Echo and chargen are the most useful programs for this type of testing. Chargen can be used to generate a load on a system and network, whereas echo tests that a connection is possible.

Netstat

Netstat, or a program of similar functionality to it, is provided on most TCP/IP products. The nearest equivalent commands on PC-based systems, which will only provide a subset of the information, may be called **status** or sometimes **inet**. To access these on a PC running DOS while a TCP/IP application is running, it will be necessary to leave the TCP/IP environment temporarily and run a copy of the DOS command processor, COMMAND.COM. This is called **shelling out to DOS** and usually involves typing the '!' character at the TCP/IP application command line. Different TCP/IP implementations will require slightly different actions. Having run the DOS command (`status` or `inet`) use EXIT to return from the DOS shell to TCP/IP.

On UNIX systems the usage or options available with a particular command can be determined by typing the command with `-?` as the option or sometimes without options altogether. For example

```
netstat -?<enter>
```

Whatever the name, this utility is the means of examining various aspects of the protocol stack to see how they are functioning. Netstat has some very useful diagnostic options for a TCP/IP stack on a host.

netstat -i

This option shows if the network drivers and interface cards are operational and how many good or errored frames they have seen. This is a useful confidence test. If the frames received value produced by netstat -i is increasing, it is likely that the drivers themselves are functioning. If, at the same time, the transmit counters are not increasing, the stack in that machine is having difficulty communicating with the drivers. If there are large numbers of errors then clearly there are problems either at the datalink level on the medium or with the drivers themselves.

netstat -r

This is usually the option for displaying the router tables. From this you can determine if the node is learning about routers on the internetwork and if it has a default gateway configured correctly.

netstat -a

Another netstat option allows the active server processes be viewed, showing that a server program is waiting for incoming connections. This option also shows connections established, indicating the IP address and port of the remote node. This option makes it clear what application level services are active on the host. If they are not in the netstat -a output, they are not active so users cannot connect to them. Of course the inverse is also true; if they are in the list, they are available to the network and this may show applications listening for connections that you would rather disable in the /etc/inetd.conf file.

Often, some of the utilities are shown by the port number they use, so a table of port numbers may be required to know what each utility is. There is a full list of port numbers in Appendix G but if there are locally developed applications, it is necessary to know their port numbers. Normally they will all be found in the /etc/services configuration file on the host computer.

Other netstat options

Two other useful options might be netstat -s, which gives the statistics of network operation and errors, similar to those reported by an SNMP management agent in a host, and netstat -m which lists buffer memory utilization. This will show whether a machine is correctly configured for the network tasks which have been processed, for it will indicate the number of buffers available and the average and maximum in use. It may also show any failure to provide a buffer when required.

There can be many more facilities than described here for netstat. The appropriate vendor's manuals should be consulted to ascertain the full functionality.

Traceroute

Traceroute, provided on many UNIX implementations and on Windows NT, determines the active route to a destination address. Rather than use record route options, which until recently was not universally implemented, it sends datagrams with low values of hop count, increasing from one. This forces each router in the chain to return an ICMP time exceeded message indicating which router was reached at that number of hops. Traceroute usually probes each hop three times, indicates the delay and any failure to receive a response. It may convert router IP addresses into domain names.

Traceroute is particularly useful for isolating Internet performance bottlenecks. It can indicate how many router hops there are to a destination, which Internet providers are involved (deduced from the domain name) and which part of the path has a high delay or high error rate. Once the router addresses are known, ping can provide additional delay and packet loss statistics.

NSlookup

NSlookup (name server look-up) is also provided on UNIX systems; there are shareware and public domain implementations for the PC and Windows/WINSOCK. It generates DNS requests to a chosen domain name server for a particular type of record and displays the reply. One use for NSlookup is to check the external appearance of a corporate LAN from the Internet, for example, checking that MX records return the right priorities.

LAN analysers

For anybody who regularly deals with the installation of TCP/IP systems, it is almost mandatory to have open access to some kind of LAN analyser. Even for the most basic problems, a LAN analyser immediately allows you to detect whether there are any frames on the LAN and if a particular node is active. This does not always mean that a specialized expensive piece of test equipment must be purchased. Software such as etherfind or tcpdump, available on many UNIX implementations of TCP/IP, will monitor frames on the network and is adequate for a basic test. It is certainly better than no analyser at all.

There are also a number of low-cost analysers based on standard LAN interface cards and PCs. These may have limited performance and may not reliably record all traffic in a normal operational environment, only in simpler test installations. But a fast 386/486 PC with good video performance and a 16- or 32-bit interface card should be fast enough for the more lightly loaded system. In the busiest of networks, a specialist analyser with many megabytes of storage and the ability to capture frames for extended periods at high network loading is essential. The issue is that when looking for complex faults you must be able to trust the test equipment. If it is producing misleading results, you may waste a considerable amount of time chasing false leads.

If one of the more complex problems exists, an analyser is essential, along with the knowledge of how the protocol operates to the level covered in this book. With this book in hand and a properly functioning analyser, you should be able to solve most problems! For intractable problems, hiring a high-performance analyser for a week should be considered.

An analyser will show each phase of a connection as it is established, so failure at a certain point in the conversation between the computers can identify at what layer of the model difficulties start.

A significant benefit of using an analyser is that it can display ICMP datagrams. Even though ICMP datagrams are sent back to a specific computer to indicate some type of transmission problem, it is very rare for these events to be reported to the operator. As indicated in Chapters 11 and 16, the likely result is the incrementing of some ICMP statistics counter available to netstat or its equivalent. The detail is lost. The analyser can see all. The cause of many problems can be quickly identified from ICMP datagrams. Other than ICMP echo, which should only be generated by those testing for faults, most ICMP datagrams should occur infrequently. A useful starting point on a network in difficulty is to look for any ICMP datagrams and explain why they are occurring.

Debug

Many TCP/IP services can operate in a **debug** mode through a command option. This mode will provide a list of the steps the protocol goes through, either to the user's screen or to a file. The debug feature is only useful if the observer understands the function and detail of the protocol. It is rare for the output of a debug listing to be explained thoroughly by a manufacturer's documentation.

Most of the operations described by a debug utility are detailed in this book, so having got this far you are in a perfect position to understand a debug listing! Where the problem seems to occur within computer software and not on the network, knowing about system configuration and the relation to the protocol model will help track down the more difficult problems.

Finding faults

Fault-finding is costly in users' and maintainers' time. The best approach is to design the network and its management and installation procedures so that operational faults are rare.

A big mistake when starting to solve network problems is to rush around changing configuration values and pulling cables. This is inappropriate. For success, it is essential to approach the problem methodically and to take detailed notes of what was changed at every stage. Otherwise the situation becomes confused or the problem disappears and nobody is any wiser as to why.

One problem is the conflict in commerce between fault resolution and service restoration. The pressure is to restore service to a user so that business may continue, not to record the detailed symptoms of some system failure. If service restoration is the driving force, true fault resolution may never happen, and nothing is learnt from each event that would help prevent the problem in the future. When looking for faults, first think about the environment and any aspects about the problem that point clearly to the relevant area.

In recent years, some organizations have adopted a policy of remote fault diagnosis where, as far as is possible, faults are determined without visiting the equipment. Remote network management systems and tools may depend for their operation on the very network they are trying to diagnose. Where faults are intermittent and may be related to performance and system loading, it is prudent to remember that remote test systems may be affected by the fault conditions themselves. In some cases, the management traffic may itself be the extra loading that is causing the fault.

Approach

The initial approach to a problem with TCP/IP will be significantly different depending on whether the system has worked and then failed or if it has never worked at all. Here we will consider the 'never worked at all' scenario, as fault-finding on a system which has worked is a subset of the more general case. As there must be an infinite number of possibilities for system failure, we can only consider basic methods. The approach described is a mixture of remote and local testing. It can be adapted for remote testing as long as the previous caution about remote testing systems is observed.

The first step in fault-finding undoubtedly starts with 'it does not work'. If the local host is switched on, the operating system is running and the user can access the client program, the normal error message seen is something similar to 'host not found'. This message can be caused by anything from typing the wrong IP address to a major component of the network being faulty. The error messages given from most products are at best a rough indication of some problem. Rarely do they provide useful information for maintainers to guide them in the process of isolating the fault to a particular component.

The flowcharts in Figure 18.6 give a guide to steps that can be taken to track down a problem in an IP system using netstat and ping. If these steps fail, it is time to get the analyser out and start tracing the problem based on the operation of the protocol.

The first part of the flowchart checks that the correct addresses are being used and that the node can talk to other machines on the network, thus proving its software and network connection is operational. If this proves to be the case, the other possibility is that there is a fault with the routing mechanism; either the default router (default gateway)

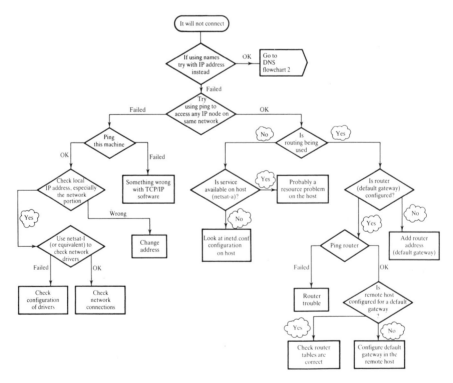

Figure 18.6 (a) Fault-finding flowchart 1.

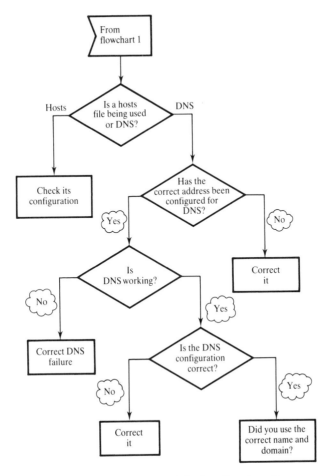

Figure 18.6 (b) Fault-finding flowchart 2.

has not been configured or there is something wrong with the routers themselves.

Flowchart 3 looks at the approach to using an analyser should use of flowcharts 1 and 2 fail. First it considers the basic operation of a TCP/IP connection (Figure 18.7). This sequence is the same even if routing is used. The only difference is that the ARP request will be for the MAC address of the router instead of the end node. If DNS is in use the ARP will be to find the DNS server. If the DNS server is on the same network it will ARP directly for it; if it is on another network the ARP will again be for the router.

Check the destination IP address is correct The best way to approach this test is to consider the steps the protocol goes through to establish a connection. Check if the address being used for the remote node is the correct IP address and that the IP address of this node is also correct.

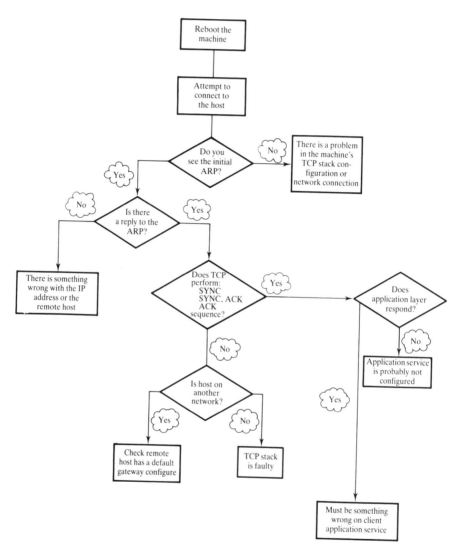

Figure 18.6 (c) Fault-finding flowchart 3.

Test local stack with Telnet or ping If a system fails to respond, start testing first with a service that is simple to use, such as Telnet or FTP, to establish what components in the network do operate. Telnet can be very useful for this on multitasking operating systems, as it is possible to Telnet to one's own IP address as a simple loopback test. This will not generate any network traffic. (This is not possible with a PC running DOS, as it is a 'client-only' implementation.)

Frame	Direction	IP layer	Transport layer	Application layer
1	→	ARP request		
2	←	ARP response		
3	→		TCP sync	
4	←		TCP sync, ack	
5	→		TCP ack	
6	↔			Application layer protocol
n	↔		. . .	. . .
$n + m$	↔			Application layer protocol
$l-2$	←		TCP fin	
$l-1$	→		TCP fin, ack	
l	←		TCP ack	

Figure 18.7 Basic operation of a TCP connection.

Use netstat to check the datalink drivers are working If a local test works with Telnet or ping, you can be reasonably sure that the TCP/IP stack is all right. The next area to test is that the network drivers for the datalink are functioning. Problems often occur with network drivers, but there is very little diagnostic help in this area. The best mechanism available is netstat -i (status of the network interface) or its equivalent. With this command, you obtain information about the status of the interface; whether it is up (operational) or down (non-operational) or not available, that is, it does not appear in the netstat -i list of interfaces. In this case the software build is wrong or, due to a faulty configuration, the operating system has removed the driver. We discuss later how you might check the configuration.

Check that the IP address and subnet mask of the local host is correct If netstat reports that the drivers are operational and local test worked, it is probable that the local computer and its network software is functional. Check then that the IP address and the network masks are correct[†]. If using names, instead temporarily use the IP address of the destination to verify that there is a path or whether there is a problem with the name-to-IP-address resolution in local tables or through a domain name server.

If routing is being used check that the host knows of a gateway First, try to connect to a local host to determine that communication is possible if no router is needed. Then make sure the node is configured with the correct IP address of the default gateway. If the destination

---

[†]Today most TCP/IP software uses subnet masks, even if subnetworking is not being used, by defining a default mask that matches the class of address being used.

network is on a different network number and no default gateway is configured, few products will give an explicit diagnostic message, even though the software must know exactly why it could not connect. It may report 'network unreachable' rather than 'host unreachable'. The former message normally indicates a problem with routing rather than a problem with the host, but the routing problem could be 'no default gateway'.

If routing is being used check that the distant node has a gateway configured Even though your node may be able to send datagrams to a remote computer through routers, many implementations of TCP/IP will not respond if they themselves do not have a default gateway configured. (This problem is explained in more detail below.)

By now you should have a good idea where the problem lies if not exactly why it is happening. Keep reviewing the facts that you have collected to narrow your search.

Testing with ping

Since each port with an IP address should respond to ping, and that includes routers, ping can be used to test successively more remote points in a chain between two systems. By methodically working away from the source station, it is possible to determine the exact point at which communications fail. Each side of a router should be tested as it has a separate address. For this to be possible, maintainers must have a network diagram with all routers and their IP addresses marked on it.

While all TCP/IP equipment is *supposed* to implement ICMP and respond to ICMP echo, some hosts will refuse to respond to an unknown IP address, that is, an address which is not in the hosts file or some other security file. Equally, some cut-down versions used by management systems may not respond even though the equipment has an IP address. Knowing which of the equipment in your network will respond is part of the learning process of a network maintainer.

Ping can also be used to test a bridged network by pinging hosts at successively more remote points across the chain of bridges. Those bridges that are managed by SNMP or Telnet will have their own IP addresses for management. Some SNMP implementations and most Telnet implementations may respond to ping.

Some ping implementations by default send only one request and then exit; others send repeatedly without a further option being specified. Also, because they must first generate an ARP, some implementations of ping will fail the first time they send an echo request to a particular host. If you just type

```
ping 128.128.10.100
```

it may fail because only one request is generated; run it a second time and it will pass! Most ping implementations have options to specify how many times the host should be pinged, at what intervals, how long to wait for a reply and how much data to send.

A continuous ping test can produce four different results:

(1) *There is no response to ping at all*   First, is there an entry for the destination IP address in the ARP cache if the host had the same network number, or an entry for a router if it did not? This shows at least that ARP got a reply. If not, are there any entries in the ARP cache which would show the basic host hardware and drivers can transmit and receive frames? If not, either the IP address does not exist (some entries) or there is a cable or driver fault (no entries).

Can anything else which is known to be operational ping this host? Can the host ping anything? Can it ping itself?

The problem is that the gap between being able to ping loopback and being able to ping another machine is quite large. If the machine is being tested then reduce the test network to the simplest possible implementation with two machines directly connected. If it is on an operational network use an analyser to check whether it is transmitting any datagrams. Check the ARP cache to see whether the ARP, which works directly over the LAN interface, is working.

(2) *Ping works but replies are lost*   A small number of lost replies is possible on any datagram-based network, perhaps more so when wide area connections are involved, but if these losses are more than 2–3%, then there is a 'lost datagram' problem to be investigated, particularly if this only occurs when the network is busy.

The fault will be:

(a) transmission errors on WAN or LAN cables,

(b) overloaded bridges or routers.

(3) *Every request is acknowledged and the echo time varies*   This is normal due to variations in host and network loading. If the variations in response time are wide and if they are regularly longer than 100 ms then the cause should be investigated, as such delays will make Telnet less acceptable to users and will have an impact on the performance of other applications, particularly those that use UDP. Likely causes are:

(a) overloaded wide area links which are too slow for the traffic offered,

(b) an overloaded host which is being pinged,

(c) overloaded bridges or routers,

(d) overloaded backbone LANs.

In the latter two cases, the problem is more likely to result in datagram loss as well as delay.

(4) *Every request is acknowledged and the echo time is reasonably constant* Congratulations, this is the best possible result and ping can tell you nothing more. Move on to more advanced tests.

Remember that ping is an ICMP message. ICMP error messages are never generated about problems with other ICMP messages. At some point in testing if routing errors are thought to be involved, application layer echo, port 7, should be used rather than ping, to see if an ICMP message results which can better pinpoint the problem.

Some common problems

Subnet masks

Check that your TCP/IP implementation automatically selects a suitable default subnet mask, even though subnetworking is not being used. If the implementation does not select a suitable subnet mask, it may not be possible to connect to all hosts dependent on the bits used in their IP address. We have seen systems that always select a 24-bit mask as default irrespective of their own IP address. This causes problems with class A and B addressing schemes, as part of the node address is considered as subnetwork bits.

IP addresses

A common fault is the incorrect use of IP addresses, which usually happens due to lack of understanding of the address structure[†]. It is common to see installations of minicomputers using the default class of address and network number that comes with the unit, usually the manufacturer's registered address. This could well be unsuitable for the network the host is operating on.

Routing

If the default gateway (router) has not been configured, it is common for software to 'hang' or return with a 'host not available' message, or sometimes a more helpful but not explicit 'network unreachable'.

A second problem is with hosts that eavesdrop on RIP. Using RIP is appropriate if routers on the system are also using RIP. If not, it is redundant and the host must have a default gateway configured so that it can find the router.

[†]This is explained in great detail in Chapters 3 and 4.

A third problem is if the destination computer does not have a default gateway configured. Some systems work because they can obtain the IP address of a router from the incoming datagram. But many systems cannot make use of this information and will not reply if they receive a request to start a TCP connection which comes from a network number different from their own and they do not have a default gateway configured. We have found missing default gateways and missing *return* static routes to be the most common routing fault, particularly in organizations where the network design is split across two management authorities or where manually-configured routes are employed.

Yet another problem occurs when the default gateway known to a node fails. It is likely that the node then cannot make connections to other networks even though there may be redundant paths. This is because the node relies on that one gateway being available. Some software only allows a single default gateway (router) to be defined.

Drivers

Many problems are related to software drivers for network hardware (LAN and WAN interface cards). Driver software rarely provides any assistance for fault diagnosis; there is no good indication whether it is operating or not, a particular problem with PCs.

The problem may manifest itself when the driver is loading, or the TCP/IP protocol may load, but the computer cannot send frames to the network; local ping works but remote ping does not. In this case a LAN analyser may show that datagrams are being sent on the network and responses are returning, but the protocol stack does not recognize the responses. This problem is usually caused by settings on the network hardware or in the drivers. Hardware settings may conflict with other settings in the computer, or with other cards, or the driver software may not have settings which match the hardware. Detection of this type of problem almost certainly needs a LAN analyser to be confident that this is what is happening.

On systems that have the netstat utility, netstat -i is useful. It shows that the drivers are active and the number of datagrams they receive and send. No change in the values of the counters provided by this utility on an active network, or no drivers being shown, gives a hint as to the problem. In UNIX systems check netd.cf to determine that ifconfig is binding the driver to the interface and if appropriate, use sysadm, the UNIX management utility, to check the match between hardware and driver software settings for interrupts, shared memory, DMA and I/O address. In the latter case be careful that you do not destroy the UNIX kernel!

If there are problems with the interrupt settings between software or hardware, the network software will have difficulty interrupting the main processor and so incoming information will be lost. If the input/output or DMA settings are incorrect, it will be output that is affected.

Buffers

Lack of buffers on a system will cause throughput to be slow for TCP connections or cause datagrams to be missed if UDP is used. While netstat -m is sometimes available to show buffer utilization, the only clear way of seeing this problem is through an analyser showing that the window sizes in the TCP segments frequently reduce to a low value or zero. Many systems provide a management function to increase the number of buffers available. This allows an improvement in performance, but at the expense of more memory for the protocol stack.

A common setting found on PCs is the low window threshold. This value can be set to limit the minimum size of buffer that will be announced after the buffers have been filled. This is done to prevent the 'silly window syndrome' which occurs when a node has filled its buffers, empties a few bytes, advertises a few bytes free, which become filled, empties a few bytes, advertises a few free and so on .... There is a very high overhead from TCP and IP headers in sending these few bytes each time. The minimum window threshold sets the point at which the window is re-advertised, so that a reasonable, significant size of frame can be sent.

Domain names

Problems with domain name systems are normally with the configuration of the databases in the domain name servers and the use of domain names themselves. One of the most common problems is with use of the dot (.) on a domain name. Leaving the dot off a name in the configuration files usually indicates that the default domain should be added to this name, which can result in a request for incorrect long domain names.

The second problem area is through not specifying enough of the domain name of a system for the address to be resolved, mainly when connecting between different domains.

Hosts file

The main problems with hosts files are errors in configuring them, incorrect IP addresses or names typed incorrectly. Another area to be aware of is the difference between the name of a node and its aliases. Some software does not look for aliases when searching through the hosts file. Requesting a connection to the alias instead of the main name results in a 'host not known', or a similar message, perhaps a more helpful 'unable to resolve host name'.

Some PC software indicates the name and location of the file for 'hosts' in a configuration parameter, for example:

```
C:\TCPIP\hosts
```

If this path and file name are set wrongly, the software may be 'unable to resolve host name' rather than 'hosts file not found'.

Summary

In this chapter we have presented a few ideas on how fault-finding in TCP/IP systems should be approached and some of the unexpected and slightly obscure situations we have discovered in the field. Using this information as a basis, each system maintainer will quickly build upon this foundation and gradually determine what are the important diagnostic tools in his or her particular environment. Maintainers are also likely to end up with a list of surprises where particular implementations are 'rich in features' that the standards developers did not intend.

19

The Internet

While the Internet has been important to US organizations since the early 1990s, it is now of considerable interest to all commerce, worldwide. Internet communications is challenging the traditional methods of international communications for data and mail based on FAX dial-up, leased lines, X.25, X.400. There are experiments at using it for international voice communications, which when acceptable quality is achieved will challenge the existing telephone and radio services. While there are many specialist works on the Internet available, a description of the TCP/IP protocol suite is not complete without some discussion of the protocols and applications of the Internet which are influencing commerce at the end of this century. We discuss:

- Structure of the Internet
- Using the Internet commercially
- Internet applications and their protocols
  - Web servers, CGI, HTTP, WAIS
  - Network news and NNTP
  - Gopher
  - Archie and anonymous FTP
- Security and firewalls

The Internet is a collection of physical and logical relationships between many millions of computers distributed around the world. Nobody knows how many, but 5.5 million are easily identified at present. The growth has followed an exponential curve since the first machines were interconnected in the early 1970s.

When discussing the Internet, we have used the following convention. When you see internet, with a small 'i', we are referring to small networks or components of the large all-compassing Internet, with a big 'I'. Internet 'services providers' give you connectivity to the Internet through their smaller internets.

Physically, the Internet is based around networks built by the service providers. These internets are usually based on physical connections made available from local PTTs or telecommunications companies with the routing and connection management made available by the service provider who acts as a hub connecting together all of their customers. These networks, or internets, are star-based systems which are in turn connected together. A user on one provider's internet can access a computer on another because the TCP/IP protocol discovers a path between the two, routing over a number of intermediate internets. This collection of 'small' internets logically forms what is known as the Internet. This structure is illustrated in Figure 19.1. Routing through the Internet is invisible to the user, although programs such as *traceroute* can be used to determine the intermediate hops. The Internet provides transparent service unless low performance is encountered.

One enabling force in the growth of the Internet has been its charging regime. Most service providers charge a flat fee for a particular speed of connection. Unlike many of the public networks, there are no additional charges for the duration of time on-line, for the volume of data transferred or for the distance over which it is transferred. The other driving forces are its almost global coverage, the universal coverage of SMTP electronic mail and the quantity and quality of technical information, software updates and services available from computer and network system providers and commercial organizations. People are now using the Internet for commercial purposes. It was estimated that in 1995, 2.5 million purchases were made across the Internet.

The service which has caused the greatest increase in commercial use of the Internet is the World Wide Web often referred to as WWW, or W[3], or sometimes 3W. WWW allows logical relationships to be defined between information stored on host computers anywhere on the Internet; a document on one host can refer an application to documents on other hosts. When a user of WWW selects a particular directory or button on their computer screen, that may cause a document or file to be retrieved from another host computer anywhere in the worldwide Internet. This reduces the need for duplication of information; just configure a document to point to the original source of information, so requests for that information are made directly to the one computer holding it, Figure 19.2.

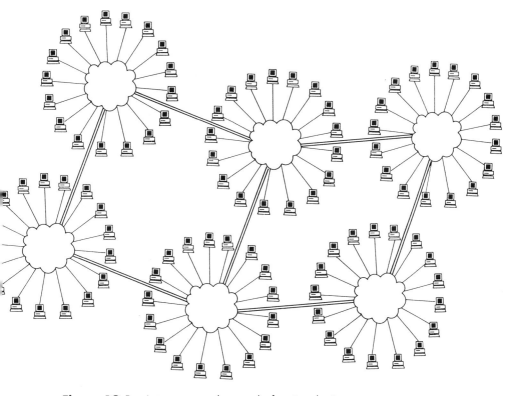

Figure 19.1 Interconnected networks forming the Internet.

Under some circumstances it may still be appropriate to have duplication of information. One reason is the performance of international network links, and the second is the performance of host computers. If a service is used heavily, that information should be replicated on several computers in strategic places around the Internet. This will reduce the processing overhead on any single computer and spread the network traffic. Sites providing this type of duplication are often referred to as 'mirror sites'.

Using the Internet commercially

From a commercial view, the main issues with the Internet are security and service levels.

Security

Any connection of a corporate network to the Internet raises concerns about 'hacking' or the retrieval of a virus into the corporate environment; commercial use of the Internet may require exchange of confidential or financial information. It is essential to formulate a security policy and to

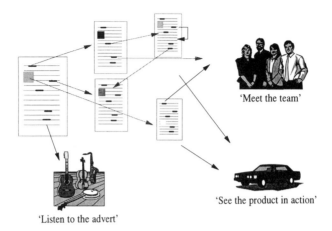

'Meet the team'

'See the product in action'

'Listen to the advert'

Figure 19.2 The World Wide Web.

place a 'firewall' between the corporate network and the Internet[†]. It is highly advisable to virus-check all incoming executable files before use, particularly those from untrusted hosts. It is also advisable to encrypt all transfers of commercial, confidential and financial information. Commercial firewall products and virus-checking mail gateways are both now available.

There is an enormous amount of development which addresses these security concerns of commercial businesses. Two extensions to WWW provide for encryption of traffic between client and server. Also, there are a number of pilot systems testing out financial transfers over the Internet, both for business-to-business and home use. Some of these financial mechanisms are designed for very low value transactions. This will allow information providers to make a small charge for data they provide for application use, or, in the entertainment business, to apply a charge for each move in a game.

Service levels

A service provider normally makes some statement about the availability of the link between a customer's premises and their first router but any connection between two machines may use many other internets outside the control of that one service provider. There are therefore no guarantees of the end-to-end service between two Internet-connected computers; there are no statements of reliability, error rate or performance. It may be unwise to commit business and time critical applications, particularly international applications, to this transport medium without having an alternative means of communication which bypasses the Internet. One

---

[†]See *Firewalls and Internet Security* by William R Cheswick and Steven M Bellovin, Addison-Wesley (1994), ISBN 0-201-63357-4.

reason for this concern is the number of routing hops (10–20) and the number of service providers that a typical international connection passes through. In practice, this may not be very different from the international telephone network, but as the Internet becomes more commercial it must prove that it can deliver the required availability, reliability and response times.

The Internet standards continue to develop towards higher performance and more demanding applications. The basic technology for video conferencing over IP is already available for LAN based systems. Also systems are now available which allow audio to be directed to an individual's computer, allowing music and radio broadcasts to be received. The major delaying factors in deploying these technologies on the Internet are capacity and performance. However, as commercial use grows, network performance will also grow to release the full potential of this system. It remains to be seen whether this level of growth can be funded by the same flat rate charging mechanisms that have supported the expansion of lower performance Internet services.

Web services – an 'intranet'

Some organizations are beginning to see the benefit of using internet technology internally, irrespective of whether they are connected to the public Internet or not. Web and news servers are excellent mechanisms for distributing information to large numbers of people. The cost of distributing internal documentation, whether for personnel, facilities or financial information, can be considerable. Many documents could be distributed in a far more cost effective manner using web technology.

Where Internet access is also required, the web is an excellent way of simplifying and reducing the number of interfaces a user has to deal with, for a web client can act as a common front end for databases, ftp, mail, news, gopher and telnet. This reduces the overall cost of providing services as less software is required, less training and less technical expertise, compared with multiple application environments.

A web browser can provide access to database systems through technology such as Wide Area Information Servers (WAIS). WAIS is a system for high-speed data searches. These systems can also integrate into existing database systems. A WAIS server can connect to many different types of database or text flat-file system and index that information. Gateways convert output from the WAIS search engines into HTML templates so that it is suitable for display by a web browser. This capability allows organizations to integrate their existing information systems and databases into the web for internal or external use, without modification.

Another powerful aspect of the World Wide Web is Common Gateway Interface (CGI). This interface allows a web server to initiate a program or script on that server. This significantly increases the power of web servers as they can be programmed to process forms input or start other programs as a user selects services from a web page.

Internet applications and their protocols

Web servers

Web servers form the foundation of the World Wide Web. They manage the access to information and the presentation of it. Information presented by web servers can include graphics, text or sound. Web information is organized in pages (disk files). Each page contains hypertext 'links' which refer to other pages or to other places on the same page. Referenced information can be on any web server connected to the same internet. A link can refer to one original source of information which is maintained at the most convenient point in the Internet. The fact that information is distributed on multiple web servers across a wide geographic area is transparent to users.

Communications between web client software and a web server are through the HyperText Transfer Protocol (HTTP). HTTP generally operates over TCP connections on well-known port number 80 (decimal).

The HyperText Mark-up Language (HTML) defines the formatting of a document for use on a web server, Figure 19.3. It is a simple text-based mark-up language, based on the ISO Standardized General Mark-up Language (SGML). As a text-based mark-up language, HTML fields can be added to any text document with a simple text editor, though more sophisticated editors have appeared as add-ons to the common word processors. Figure 19.4 shows the output represented by the HTML of Figure 19.3.

An important concept used in HTML is the Uniform Resource Locator (URL). A URL points to a document or to a reference point in a document on any specific computer. A URL is divided into the following fields:

```
HTTP://www.integralis.co.uk/public/homepage.html
```

Protocol:	`HTTP://`
Host domain name:	`www.integralis.co.uk`
Directory on computer:	`/public`
File in directory:	`/homepage.html`

The web server is identified by its host domain name (or indeed IP address) and the file path follows normal UNIX conventions.

One may also see the term URI (Universal Resource Identifier). A URI is a generic form of defining a resource across an internet. A URL is a TCP-specific URI, because the domain name reference used in a URL is normally only used by TCP/IP systems.

```
<!DOCTYPE HTML PUBLIC "-//IETF//DTD HTML//EN">
<HTML VERSION="2.0">
<HEAD>
<TITLE>Whats New</TITLE>
</HEAD>
<BODY>
<P><IMG SRC="products.gif" width=600 height=40>
<h2>Purveyor from Process</h2><IMG SRC=" new.gif"
width=50 height=50 HREF="process/white-paper/purveyor/
index.html"></A>
Purveyor is a World Wide Web server solution for Windows
NT and future Win32 platforms such as Windows 95. With
the ease-of-use of Windows, Purveyor enables organiza-
tions to publish public and confidential multimedia infor-
mation on the Internet as well as their corporate LANs.
<HR>
<I>Integralis Ltd, Brewery Court, High St, Theale,
Reading, Berks </I><BR>
<I>Tel +44 1734 306060, Fax +44 1734 302143, BBS +44 1734
303321 </I><BR>
<I>Email support@integralis.co.uk,
sales@integralis.co.uk, info@integralis.co.uk </I><BR>
<H3>Copyright &#169; 1996 Integralis Ltd.
<P><I>Integralis Ltd, Brewery Court, High St, Theale,
Reading</I> </BODY>
</HTML>
```

Figure 19.3   Example of HTML.

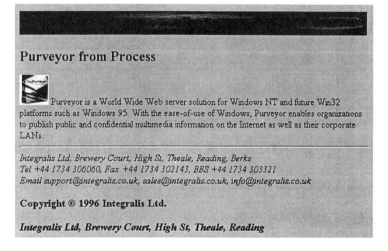

Figure 19.4   How the HTML document would appear on a browser.

Common Gateway Interface (CGI)

Common gateway interface and its associated scripts form the server language which allows data sent by the user of a web client to be repackaged for processing by an application and data returned by the application to be repackaged as HTML for returning to the user. HTML can describe a GUI form with all the text boxes, drop-down boxes, check boxes, radio buttons and other features of the X Window System or Microsoft Windows. The combination of CGI and HTML means that a web client can be a platform-independent front end to any type of application running on the web server or indeed an application running on another host to which the web server has access.

No development is necessary at the client to support a particular application; all application development takes place at the server. In a commercial environment of many different machines and operating systems, or in an environment where the systems manager does not control the types of machines available to his data users, such independence is invaluable.

While web technology quickly gained an enthusiastic audience amongst academics and hobbyists on the Internet, corporate IT managers have been slower to appreciate its potential. Because of its flexibility, we anticipate that HTML, HTTP and web server technology will become commonplace in many corporate internets.

HyperText Transfer Protocol (HTTP)

HTTP is the application layer protocol used on World Wide Web servers for the distribution of 'hypermedia', text, image, sound and animation. It is a stateless protocol in that it establishes connections only when retrieving information. It does not maintain connections when not actively transferring information. On demand, connections are opened, data transferred and then closed.

The addition of new features and of new implementations of HTTP has far outpaced the process of IETF standardization. There were a few implementations of HTTP running to the proposed version 3.0, and version 2 was common while version 1 was not formally accepted. This makes it impossible to present an accurate description of HTTP, so the following describes the proposed standard at present, HTTP/1.0. This will give an appreciation of how the protocols operate.

HTTP is based upon requests and responses. Requests are commands, known as methods. It is expected that the number of methods used will expand with new protocol versions. In version 1 there are three common 'methods': GET, HEAD and POST.

The HTTP request format is shown in Figure 19.5:

Method   the command to be sent.

Uniform resource identifier   the reference to the information.

Method	URI	Version	CrLf
Header:	Value	CrLf	
CrLf			

Figure 19.5 HTTP request format.

Version for example 'HTTP/1.0' as a text string including the quotes.

CrLf Carriage Return Line Feed, which is used as the line terminator. If CrLf is used alone on a line it defines the end of the message.

The *Header* and associated *Value* are optional. The most common header commands are 'Accept' and 'User-Agent'. Accept indicates to the server what object types the client is able to display or process; User-Agent tells the server what browser software the client is using.

Any number of commands can be used between the *method* and the ending *CrLf*, but each command must be on its own line (see Figure 19.6). On transmission this would appear as:

Get /index.html 'HTTP/1.0'
Accept: text/plain
Accept: text/html
Accept: */*
User-Agent: *Name of agent*

GET is used by a client to retrieve information from a server. The information returned should be that referred to by the URI, shown as 'index.html' in the example above.

The HEAD method is the same as GET except that no data should be returned, just header information. A description of the header information returned in a response, as shown later, will make the purpose of the header clearer.

The POST command is used to send information to the server, either for mail, news, bulletin boards or submitting information from a form.

GET	/index.html	'HTTP/1.0'	CrLf
Accept:	text/plain	CrLf	
Accept:	text/html	CrLf	
Accept:	*/*	CrLf	
User-Agent:	*Name of agent*	CrLf	
CrLf			

Figure 19.6

Version	result-code	message	CrLf
Header	value	CrLf	
CrLf			

Figure 19.7

Responses have a similar format to the *requests,* as shown in Figure 19.7.

Version   for example 'HTTP/1.0'.

Result-code   this is described below.

Message   optional and usually text-based, relating to the result code; the message is similar to those used in FTP and SMTP.

Examples of the *header* and *value* fields are shown below. An example response would be as shown in Figure 19.8:

Result codes fall into several classes:

1xx   Informational
2xx   Successful
      200 OK
      201 Created
      202 Accepted
      204 No content
3xx   Redirection
      301 Moved permanently
      302 Moved temporarily
      304 Not modified

'HTTP/1.0'	200	OK	CrLf
Server:	Purveyor/1.1	CrLf	
MIME-version:	1.0	CrLf	
Content-type:	text/html	CrLf	
Last-modified:	*Thu Nov 17 15:42:32 1995*	CrLf	
Content-length:	*2000*	CrLf	
CrLf			
HTML document			
CrLf			

Figure 19.8

4xx   Client errors
      400 Bad request
      401 Unauthorized
      403 Forbidden
      404 Not found
5xx   Server error
      500 Internal server error
      501 Not implemented
      502 Bad gateway
      503 Service unavailable

Header field definitions are shown in Table 19.1.

Wide Area Information Server (WAIS)

The major function of the Internet is to allow access to large amounts of information. One of the problems of having large amounts of information is finding what you actually need! This means that the Internet must provide search mechanisms. One such mechanism is a Wide Area Information Server (WAIS). Developed for cataloguing library contents and document abstracts, WAIS uses a standard protocol, Z39.50, for indexing and enabling searches through large amounts of information. With a WAIS server to a corporate database and gateways between that WAIS server and the Internet, it is possible to make corporate information easily searchable from the Internet.

News clients and servers

The name News disguises the functionality and usefulness of this system. News is in reality a system of bulletin board discussion group servers. On the Internet, News supports a truly international distributed bulletin board system, and allows people from all around the world to participate in discussions on any topic. At present there are around 14 000 Internet news discussion groups, a small number of which have commercial value.

Another system, Usenet news, is often discussed along with NNTP news. Usenet was a forerunner to News, but being mostly UNIX-based, it used UNIX-to-UNIX CoPy (UUCP) for communications. Usenet was designed for the UNIX host environment rather than the more complex heterogeneous network systems of the Internet.

News client software allows people to choose which Newsgroups they wish to subscribe to, that is, which discussions they wish to follow. The client software will then retrieve all new messages or 'articles' from the subscribed groups and the user can send messages or 'post articles' to all other members of a subscribed group. Subscribing merely tells the client software which group messages it should retrieve.

The News system is operated through Network News Transfer Protocol (NNTP). This protocol deals with the distribution of News

Table 19.1 Header field definitions.

Header	Example	Description
Allow	Allow: GET, HEAD	This field indicates allowable methods supported by the resource referred to in URI
Authorization	Authorization: credentials	Used by a client to provide authorization details (for example a user id and password) to a server after receiving a 401 result code
Content-encoding	Content-encoding: x-gip	Indicates what encoding has been applied to the resource
Content-type	Content-type: text/html	Indicates the media type of the body
Date	Date: Sun, 5 Nov 1995 09:01:10 GMT	The date and time the resource was originated
Expires	Expires: Sun, 5 Nov 1995 09:01:10 GMT	The date and time at which the resource should be considered out of date
From	From: webmaster@eclectic.co.uk	The email address of the user controlling the client agent
If-modified-since	If-modified-since: Sun, 5 Nov 1995 09:01:10 GMT	If the requested resource has been modified since the date given, then retrieve a new copy. Otherwise leave it
Last-modified	Last-modified: Sun, 5 Nov 1995 09:01:10 GMT	Indicates when the sender believes the resource was last modified
Location	Location: http://www.integralis.co.uk	Indicates the exact location of the resource identified by a Request-URI
MIME-version	MIME-Version: 1.0	Indicates the MIME version used to construct a message
Pragma	Pragma: 'no-cache'	Used to send implementation-specific directives along a request/response chain
Referrer	Referrer: http:/www.eclectic.co.uk /data/Overview.htm	To indicate to a server the source of a Request-URI
Server	Server: 'Purveyor 1.0'	Information about the software used by the server responding to the request
User-Agent	User-Agent: NetManage 4.1	Information about the software generating the request
WWW-authenticate	WWW-authenticate: basic realm='hereandnow'	Must be included in 401 Response messages
Auth-scheme	auth-scheme: token	Used for authentication. See standards for a full description of how this field is used
Auth-param	auth-param: token '=' quoted scheme	Used for authentication. See standards for a full description of how this field is used

Figure 19.9 An example of a NEWS client showing threads.

updates to all servers in the News system. News distributes articles through the Internet by a process known as flooding, that is, each News server sends all its new News articles to all the servers it feeds. In turn, these News servers forward the articles on to the servers they feed. With flooding, it is possible that some duplication occurs because a server may receive an article from two sources. In this case, for simplicity, it is recommended that the server merely ignores the later message copy.

The NNTP command set deals with two paradigms – communication between server and server and between client and server. In essence the protocol is similar to that of SMTP. It uses the same command/ response mechanism, but a different set of commands. News uses port 119 for its server, and TCP for reliable transfer.

The major object of the protocol is to enable a client to list newsgroups, retrieve articles from them and post responses to those articles. The client will provide the interface for these activities and retain its own lists of all available and subscribed newsgroups. It is now common practice to display a discussion as a *thread* through the messages in a group. It is likely that articles will be delivered to a client in a random order from a number of separate discussion topics, or threads. A thread shows a specific set of messages on a particular topic of discussion in a way which follows the sequence in which articles were written. Separating them into their threads simplifies the problem of following the discussion. It is now common for client software to display a thread as a tree structure (Figure 19.9), similar to Windows File Manager, the file and directory browser for the PC.

The following is a brief overview of the commands and responses used in the NNTP protocol. For more detail the appropriate RFCs should be consulted.

Command	Description
ARTICLE (selector)	This requests a specific article from a server as referenced by the selector. The selector can be a message id or a message number. This will set the 'current article pointer' to the article referenced.
BODY (selector)	This command is the same as ARTICLE except that only the body of the article is requested.
GROUP (news.group)	Selects a specific newsgroup.
HEAD (selector)	This command is the same as ARTICLE except that only the header of the article is requested.
HELP	Returns a list of commands supported by the server.
IHAVE (message id)	Informs the server that the client has an article (message id). The server can instruct the client to send the article if it so desires.
LAST	Sets the 'current article pointer' of the server to the previous article in the current newsgroup.
LIST	Returns a list of newsgroups, a single line for each in the following form: *group_name last_article first_article posting_allowed* This indicates the name, the number of the first and last articles and whether posting is allowed Y or N.
NEWS GROUPS *date time distribution*	Returns a list of newsgroups created since *date* and *time*. Distribution identifies specific distribution groups, if used.
NEWNEWS *news groups date time distribution*	Returns a list of message ids of articles received since *date* and *time*. *Newsgroups* references specific groups and *distribution* can be used to narrow the scope of the request to specific distribution parameters.
NEXT	This moves the 'current article pointer' to the next article.
POST	Allows the client to post an article to the server. The command is followed by the article headers and body and terminated by a full stop '.' at the beginning of a blank line.
QUIT	Tells the server to close the connection.

SLAVE   Tells the server the requests are coming from a
                          slave server not a client.

STAT (selector)   This command is the same as ARTICLE except
                          that no text is returned. The server should set the
                          'current article pointer'.

The table below gives a list of typical responses to the commands above.

Response	Textual explanation
100	Help text follows
199	Debug output follows
200	Server ready – posting allowed
201	Server ready – no posting allowed
202	Slave status noted
205	Closing connection – goodbye
211	n f l s group selected (n = estimated number of articles in group; f = first article number in the group; l = last article number in the group; s = name of the group).
215	List of newsgroups follows
220	n <a> article retrieved – head and body follows[†]
221	n <a> article retrieved – head follows[†]
222	n <a> article retrieved – body follows[†]
223	n <a> article retrieved – request text separately[†]
230	List of new articles by message id follows
231	List of new newsgroups follows
235	Article transferred OK
240	Article posted OK
335	Send article to be transferred. End with <CrLf>.<CrLf>
340	Send article to be posted. End with <CrLf>.<CrLf>
400	Service discontinued
411	No such newsgroup
412	No newsgroup has been selected
420	No current article has been selected
421	No next article in this group
422	No previous article in this group
423	No such article number in this group
430	No such article found
435	Article not wanted – do not send it
436	Transfer failed – try again later
437	Article rejected – do not try again
440	Posting not allowed
441	Posting failed
500	Command not recognized
501	Command syntax error
502	Access restriction or permission denied
503	Program fault – command not performed

[†]n = article number, <a> = message-id

As with other TCP/IP application services the application layer protocol is relatively simple and uses plain text commands. Viewing this protocol with an analyser would show the commands and responses given above. Some systems provide debugging facilities which will also show the commands and responses, useful when tracing problems.

Gopher

Gopher is one of the early Internet application services. It was designed to be a file system browser, a system for document search and retrieval in a distributed computing environment. In fact, implementations of gopher under Microsoft Windows look very much like the File Manager; they show the directory structure on the left half of the screen and on the right show the directory that you have selected. By using a mouse to select directories, you are able to navigate through information without being aware of the computer it is located on.

Through use of search servers such as VERONICA (Very Easy Rodent Oriented Network Information Computer Archive), it is possible to search, based on keywords, through the file systems of supporting computers.

As with most other TCP/IP application layer services gopher conforms to a client server model and is fairly simple in its operation. It uses port 70 over TCP. The gopher protocol consists of simple interactions between client and server. The client sends a server selector (a line of text) to which a server responds with a block of text terminated by a '.' on a blank line.

A gopher session is started by the client making a connection to a particular server. The server should accept the connection but will not send any information. The client then sends an empty line, terminated by CrLf, to which the server will return a block of information listing its top level directory. The lines which are sent by the server are of the following format:

Selector	T	Display string	T	File reference	T	Host domain name	T	Port number

The 'T's are TAB characters, which are used to separate each field.

The selector identifies the type of reference, these are:

Selector	Type of item
0	File
1	Directory
2	CSO phone book server
3	Error
4	BinHexed Macintosh file
5	DOS binary archive
6	UNIX UUENCODED file
7	Index-search server

8	Points to a text-based telnet session
9	Binary file
+	A redundant server
T	Point to a text based tn3270 session
g	a GIF formatted graphics file
I	an image file

The *display string* is intended to be displayed to the user as the reference to the item of concern. The *file reference* is the string which the client must send to the server to retrieve that item. The *host domain name* and *port number* define the location *the file reference* should be sent to.

The following is an example gopher interaction between client and server:

```
Client:(Opens connection to gopher.integralis.co.uk
on port 70)
Server:(Accepts the connection, no data returned)
Client:<cr><lf>{An empty line terminated by carriage
return/line feed characters}
Server:
0About  Integralis<tab>about.us<tab>gopher.integra-
lis.co.uk<tab>70<tab><cr><lf>
0About Eclectic Systems<tab>about.ecl<tab>sun.eclec-
tic.co.uk<tab>70<tab><cr><lf>
1Seminar  dates<tab>seminar.txt<tab>sunny.integra-
lis.co.uk<tab>70<tab><cr><lf>
1Phone  Numbers<tab>phone.doc<tab>ibm.eclectic.co.
uk<tab>70<tab><cr><lf>
gMap  to  find  us<tab>map.gif  <tab>sunny.integralis.
co.uk<tab>70<tab><cr><lf>.<cr><lf>
```

This should display to the user as:

```
About  Integralis
About  Eclectic  Systems
Seminar Dates
Phone Numbers
Map to find us
```

For example, selecting Seminar Dates should cause the client to send:

Client: seminar.txt

This will be sent to sunny.integralis.co.uk on port 70. For further protocol details, refer to the RFCs.

The simplicity of this protocol is seen as key. Most of the sophistication of the gopher system is provided in the implementation of the client interface. Current software uses icons to differentiate the types of data item. As with File Manager or news threads the relationship of items can be represented in a tree structure tracing the directory structure.

As gopher servers are gradually being replaced by WWW servers and WWW browsers give access to the remaining gopher resources, gopher is less important in the Internet than it once was.

Archie and anonymous FTP

Archie was one of the earliest systems for searching for information on the Internet. It is a mechanism for searching the file names and directory names in directory listings of those Internet servers that support 'anonymous FTP'. It is therefore only of interest to those looking for a file which is already known approximately and is located on an unknown FTP server.

Anonymous FTP servers accept a login from anyone on the basis of the user id 'anonymous' and a password of a valid mail address, normally that user's mail address. Some servers will check that the domain name of the mail address corresponds to the domain of the IP address of the connecting machine. The user is then allowed limited access to the public directories on that machine.

Initially archie was available on remote host computers via telnet. More recently archie client software has become available for PCs. Archie can also be accessed from web client software; separate archie software is unlikely to be required by the commercial user as archie is mainly of interest to those who make extensive use of anonymous FTP and public domain software.

Security

Connecting any corporate network to the Internet understandably raises the question of network security. The concerns are around the opportunity, intent, curiosity and possible malice of the members of the Internet community. In a worldwide network of an estimated 40 million users, not all members of that community can be expected to exhibit the highest standards of behaviour.

The Internet was originally created as an open network of trusted users; doors could be, and were, left open for the good of all – members of the community were trusted to explore but do no damage. Unfortunately, as with most modern societies, such trust has been exploited by the unscrupulous and a different ethos is now required even amongst the original users of the Internet.

Corporate network managers must consider that:

- Global connectivity gives opportunity to millions to at least 'knock on the door';

- The community contains some of the most knowledgeable and able technical brains in the computing world;

- Some individuals have a strong but misplaced desire to explore your system, the known technical limitations of network protocols and system security, and *your understanding* of those limitations;

- A small percentage of individuals will attempt to break system security with mischievous or malicious intent;

- One possible attack on a system is to prevent it from providing services to its genuine users, rather than to gain information from it. Such 'denial of service' attacks may be simpler to achieve than retrieving unauthorized information.

Those who attempt to break system security are commonly referred to as 'hackers', an illustration of the apparently random attempts to break system security at potentially weak points. It is difficult to present in a few paragraphs a balanced view of the risks involved, but certainly corporate networks cannot afford to connect directly to the Internet. They must have technology that restricts and monitors attempted incoming accesses – firewall technology.

Security procedures and policy

The most important aspects of network security are the security procedures and policy – *procedures* to ensure that all necessary steps are being taken to prevent breaches and that monitoring is performed to check for attempted access; *policy* to indicate what actions should be taken when an attack is identified.

Procedures will consider physical aspects of work in an office, through password allocation, protection and changes to the process of adding new devices to a network.

Encryption

One of the best ways of securing information is to use encryption. This is scrambling data to a set of given rules based upon keys known only to the owner of the data and those allowed access to it. A significant amount of development work has been undertaken into the production of secure transmission mechanisms for use on the Internet. Probably the most significant is the Secure Sockets Layer (SSL). SSL provides encrypted transfers between client and server. It operates over the TCP protocol, encrypting the data sent by any application that uses it. These systems make it almost impossible to decrypt the information sent between two systems, or at least too costly to achieve in a suitable amount of time.

SSL uses a bulk encryption mechanism, that is, it encrypts information in real time or on the fly as it is to be transmitted. Bulk encryption mechanisms are designed to allow this real-time encryption and are to be compared with public key mechanisms, such as Pretty Good Privacy (PGP), which only allow information to be encrypted in advance of transmission. With PGP a data file has to be encrypted by the PGP application and then transmitted. It can then be decrypted at the receiving device.

Public key encryption systems use a publicized or 'public' key, which is made widely available by someone wishing to receive secure data. Data encrypted with this key can for most practical purposes only be decrypted by the originator of the public key. It is now quite common to see people advertising a PGP public key so you can send them credit card transactions or other secured information.

Similar mechanisms are used for digital signatures to authenticate the originator of a message. This must be distinguished from the encryption of message data. The export and use of data encryption technology is subject to government control; digital signature and authentication is generally less controversial.

Physical network layout

A full network audit of security must consider the network layout. Many complex security systems are put in place only to discover that some employee has installed a modem for dial-in behind the security wall. This may be for a legitimate purpose such as maintenance. However, it can open a back door to the network and be a serious breach of security.

To be economic, security mechanisms must be developed around the concept of 'who can be trusted'. If the level of trust is low, the costs are increased. It follows that good security is difficult to achieve where network management and development is distributed rather than centrally controlled; in such circumstances, it may be necessary to assume that anyone you do not directly control cannot be trusted even if they are part of the same organization! Security is a political as well as a technological problem.

If a commercial network is to allow access to systems from the Internet, it is important to separate the computers that allow external access from any internal networks, and install strong protection between the external host services and the internal network. The assumption is that any traffic from the Internet cannot be trusted. This is done by providing an intermediate network between the Internet connection and the internal network.

This allows a system manager to clearly separate incoming and outgoing traffic, physically and logically. The hosts on the intermediate network are assumed vulnerable to attack and must be checked regularly for changes. Complete images of all applications on these machines should be kept on the internal network and downloaded into the vulnerable machines at regular intervals.

It is much more difficult to protect a corporate network from attack if there is more than one path to insecure networks such as the Internet, or to trading partners who may in turn be connected to the Internet by insecure mechanisms. Ideally every external connection should be through a single access point where all activity is monitored and secured. That security is provided by a firewall.

Firewalls

Use of firewalls

Firewalls are used as a security tool designed to prevent unauthorized access to network resources. They can be used for the following types of control:

- Primarily, to prevent unauthorized access from the external Internet to an internal private network.

- To control what external Internet resources can be accessed from the internal private network.

- To control access from private dedicated connections to trading partners.

- To control access from one internal division or network segment to another.

- As a network management tool for recording all attempts at unauthorized access.

Each of these types of control indicates a different level of trust. Some organizations use firewalls internally to control what their own users do, particularly in a corporate network with different divisions where multiple connections to external organizations are thought to place the network at risk.

Firewalls may operate at the network level (IP packet or datagram) or at the application level (connection level). Application level security systems are often referred to as application gateways.

Static packet filtering

Static packet filtering is available on most dedicated router systems and is part of the modern router requirements of the IETF. It allows certain datagrams to be filtered, based on IP address and/or the port numbers in a datagram. These systems are inadequate where a protocol such as FTP is used. During one user session, FTP uses many different port numbers for communication between client and server. Virtually every transaction requires different port numbers through a single connection. A static packet filter system cannot track such activity and hence has to allow all datagrams with port numbers above 1024 to pass through. This protects most, but not all applications, as their port numbers are less than this value.

Dynamic packet filtering

An alternative is a dynamic packet filter which can be totally transparent to users and provide a low to medium level of security for a limited number of applications.

Dynamic packet filtering is an important extension to static packet filtering; the difference is that the firewall has the ability to track the port numbers used by a protocol such as FTP. The firewall dynamically adjusts its security filters to allow the protocol to use certain IP address and port number combinations for a single session. It does this by eavesdropping the FTP application protocol PORT commands and anticipating the immediate requirements of the protocol. When the transfer is completed those ports are again inhibited. A dynamic packet filter can be totally transparent to users, independent of the applications and provide a high level of security.

Application gateway

An application gateway is a system which acts as a 'proxy server' for authorized external or internal users. It consists of modified client and server software. The server software accepts connections, validates the user and then triggers its client to communicate with the destination server on behalf of the user. It relays all application level messages it receives between the real client and ultimate server. These systems are not always transparent to users. Apart from requiring double login, they also severely limit the applications a user can access through them, as the client and server software must be built for each application individually.

An application level gateway can provide a very high level of security for a single application.

Address translation gateways

A significant problem with the present Internet based on IPv4 is the lack of IP address space. This problem is compounded in that a number of organizations do not use registered addresses but now wish to connect to the Internet without having to change all the addresses on their networks. Address translation gateways solve this problem. There are two forms of translation – static and dynamic.

To use a translation gateway, a registered address range is required for the Internet connected side of the gateway. With a static translation gateway, a translation table maintains a fixed one-to-one relationship between internal IP addresses and external Internet IP addresses. Therefore, to the Internet a specific internal IP address appears as one of the registered addresses. As a datagram passes through the gateway, the addresses are substituted as necessary.

If IP were rigid in its use of protocol layering, it would be simple to do address translation. However, certain application layer protocols, such as FTP, are aware of IP addresses. When FTP sends a 'PORT' command, it indicates the IP address and port it wishes to receive data on; that message also needs to be intercepted and the address in the PORT command must be translated. Therefore, a translation gateway has to decode a packet to the application layer, not just the network layer.

The dynamic address translation gateway does not have a fixed table, but allocates addresses as required from a pool of available registered addresses. The dynamic translation gateway must build its translation table through interaction with domain name servers. As a request is made to connect to a host on the Internet, the translation gateway intercepts DNS requests and responses, modifying them as necessary to perform the required translation and using them to update the translation table. Indeed, the corporate domain name space seen from the Internet will be totally different from that seen internally and the address translator must be an integral part of this process.

Two major benefits of the dynamic translator are that the translation table requires less maintenance and the registered addresses are not fixed to individual corporate machines. A small number of registered addresses can then be shared amongst a much larger number of corporate users, provided there are enough addresses for all those devices that are active simultaneously.

The most flexible translation gateways allow the system manager to choose a mix of dynamic and fixed use according to local needs. It is likely that these devices will be upgraded to provide conversion between IPv4 and IPv6 and will form a key component in the migration between the two systems.

Summary

In March 1993, when the first edition of this book was published, it was not an anomaly to ignore the Internet as a corporate technology. At that time, corporate interest in the Internet was limited to North America. But such is the rate of progress, to leave out the Internet and WWW now would be unthinkable.

For many, the Internet is still a matter of experimentation; for others it is already *the* way of exchanging files and mail and a feature of corporate advertising. For the adventurous, it is a way of trading domestically and more importantly, internationally. It is an 'enabling technology' for virtual corporations, home working and electronic villages.

The key application is WWW with its ability to reproduce multimedia information on any platform without changing the server data. For the corporate application developer, this important feature has a role to play both internally for corporate users and externally to customers and suppliers on the Internet.

Epilogue

So what of the future of TCP/IP and of the Internet?

In January 1996, some of the key standards for IPv6 were finally issued as full RFCs. While this process has been slower than many expected or hoped, these standards represent the formal 'laying of the foundation stone' for the next phase of TCP/IP development and expansion. They are particularly important for the development of the Internet which is itself becoming a significant tool for communications in business and leisure.

The Internet and Internet service providers desperately need IPv6; particularly they need its hierarchical geographic routing to limit the growth of routing tables between Internet service providers and they need the larger address space that IPv6 provides. Without these, Internet addressing and routing will fail – registered addresses are becoming a scarce commodity and therefore, in a commercial market, have a high commercial value, something that would have been unthinkable under the original ethos of the Internet. The router tables are overflowing because CIDR, designed to reduce that very possibility, is difficult to manage and only a short-term solution.

There is little doubt that IPv6 will be a success in the core of the Internet. How quickly corporate network managers will adopt it for internal corporate use, is less clear. TCP/IP version 4 is now a low-cost commodity item; the software is packaged along with applications and operating systems. There is an IPv4 installed base working satisfactorily for internal corporate communications; since a firewall is required for Internet security, the firewall is an obvious place to do address translation to IPv6. Coexistence and translation between IPv4 and IPv6 is a key design aim of IPv6. All these reasons will delay the deployment of IPv6.

However, IPv6 offers the network manager a large address space without the cumbersome network mask; it offers automatic configuration of workstations and hence lower support overheads (but those who use DHCP/BOOTP may already have these features within IPv4). It offers automatic configuration of mobile or roaming portable workstations. These features will only become important as new applications are introduced which require the features of IPv6, and will only be adopted if the transition to IPv6 is low cost and cost effective. The cost of the software and its ease of installation in a large environment will be key, for ultimately these are overheads on the core purpose of a business; communications is rarely an end in itself.

As for the future of the Internet, for those whose existence depends on selling, distributing or processing information that can be represented digitally, the Internet presents a major opportunity, or a threat or both. To us, that seems to encompass a large portion of modern industry and commerce; for example publishing in all its forms, arts, entertainment, TV, film, radio, music, software production and distribution, banking, finance, insurance and catalogue shopping, to name just a few. The older industries – the utilities, food production, engineering and transportation – are less directly affected. But they will still be touched by the internal use of Internet technology and for them it is more likely to be an opportunity than a threat.

With the existence of a very high performance Internet (for example, based on ATM), a corporate future in these information industries depends on the skill value it adds, its ability to find customers for that value and to successfully charge for it, and perhaps on the ability to identify and protect its intellectual property rights under international laws.

As an example, access to the Internet aided the writing of this book. It gave us free and rapid access to information in the form of draft and final RFCs provided by the open philosophy of the IETF. It allowed facts to be verified and other people's views of techniques which are under evaluation to be considered. This allowed us to give a more balanced view of what we expect to happen over the next few years.

The Internet is growing at a dramatic rate; that we can embrace it and move forward at the pace it has attained is a marvel in itself. But it needs to go through a transformation from the system it is today, to a reliable, fully available, fully connected communication system, like the telephone system. This may not happen, but, with the momentum and wide support it has today, it is more likely that it will succeed than fail.

PART III

Appendices

A

Contacting the Network Information Centres

The first edition of this book gave details of how to contact the Network Information Center (NIC) for information services for the Internet, such as IP address and domain name registration as well as access to RFCs. Since that time, dramatic changes have taken place. The NIC still exists but caters specifically for the American Department of Defense (DOD). The interNIC has taken its place to cater for other organizations in the USA. Two other centres have been formed, one to deal with Europe, RIPE (Réseaux IP Européens) and one for the Asian Pacific region, APNIC.

User organizations no longer obtain domain names and IP address blocks from these NICs; they now obtain them from a local Internet service provider These centres provide information and registration only for Internet service providers while users are expected to obtain registered names and addresses from such a service provider. However, in the absence of any other point of contact, the NIC should be able to provide a list of registered service providers in a particular country.

The NICs still act as documentation stores. The simplest way to connect to any of the NICs at the following locations is using a World Wide Web browser, but if you can do that, you may already know of these URLs.

```
www.internic.net    The US InterNIC
www.ripe.net        The European NIC
www.apnic.net       The Asian Pacific NIC
```

However, NICs can be accessed by other mechanisms such as FTP, Telnet, gopher, by replacing the 'www' with the appropriate service or perhaps 'info' for telnet access. Electronic mail, normal mail or telephone contact are all possible, if so desired, at the following addresses.

US InterNIC Registration Service:
Network Solutions Inc.
AttN: InterNIC Registration Services
505 Huntmar Park Drive
Herndon,
VA 22070
USA

Phone: 1-703-742-4777.
Email: hostmaster@internic.net

If electronic mail only is available, try the following for more information: send a mail message to `mailserv@rs.internic.net`. In the SUBJECT field, put the word 'Index'. The main part of the message can be left blank. This will return a master index of all documents available from the InterNIC registration service.

RIPE Network Coordination Centre:
Kruislaan 409
NL-1098 SJ Amsterdam
The Netherlands

Phone: +31 20 592 5065
Fax: +31 20 592 5090
Email: ncc@ripe.net

Asian Pacific Network Information Center:
c/o The United Nations University
53-70 Jingumae 5-Chome
Shibuya-ku
Tokyo, 150 Japan

Phone: +81-3-5467-7014
Fax: +81-3-5467-7015
Email: hostmaster@apnic.net

B

Obtaining RFCs

The first edition of this book gave details of how mail systems, electronic and post, could be used to obtain indexes of all RFCs and the RFCs themselves. As the Internet has developed and become widely available to most engineers and network managers, those who would wish to read RFCs most probably have access to it. Therefore, it now makes more sense to show how they can be accessed using the Internet itself.

The IETF and associated organizations have set up World Wide Web and FTP sites which allow RFCs to be copied. (The associated organizations are 'mirror' sites of the IETF.) These sites hold 'draft', 'proposed' and 'standard' RFCs. Using WWW you can search by topic or RFC number. The Internet Drafts provide early knowledge of new developments.

The main sites for these documents are:

USA

World Wide Web	http://www.ietf.cnri.reston.va.us
FTP	ftp.ietf.cnri.reston.va.us

Asian Pacific

This includes: Australia, China, Guam, Hong Kong, India, Japan, Republic of Korea, Malaysia, Philippines, Singapore and Thailand.

World Wide Web	http://www.apnic.net
FTP	ftp.apnic.net

Europe

World Wide Web	http://www.ripe.net
FTP	ftp.ripe.net

Rest of world

World Wide Web	http://www.internic.net
FTP	ds.internic.net

For those who cannot access via ftp, the mailserver at `mailserv@ds.internic.net` will return documents by mail. To obtain a full help file, send a message to `mailserv@ds.internic.net` with any subject and the single word `help` as a message.

To find other mirror sites, retrieve the document rfc-retrieval.txt from the directory /rfc (/ietf/rfc at apnic). For an index to all RFCs, retrieve the file rfc-index.txt from the /rfc directory.

C

The Internet STD protocols and their RFCs

The following is a list of Internet official standard protocols with their standard numbers and the RFCs that describe them. It is summarized from RFC 1800, INTERNET OFFICIAL PROTOCOL STANDARDS, July 1995, by J Postel, Internet Architecture Board.

Standard protocols

STD	Protocol	Name	Status	RFC
1	–	Internet official protocol standards	Req	1800
2	–	Assigned numbers	Req	1700
3	–	Host requirements – communications	Req	1122
3	–	Host requirements – applications	Req	1123
5	IP	Internet protocol as amended by:	Req	791
5	–	IP subnet extension	Req	950
5	–	IP broadcast datagrams	Req	919
5	–	IP broadcast datagrams with subnets	Req	922
5	ICMP	Internet control message protocol	Req	792
5	IGMP	Internet group multicast protocol	Rec	1112
6	UDP	User datagram protocol	Rec	768
7	TCP	Transmission control protocol	Rec	793
8	TELNET	Telnet protocol	Rec	854,855
9	FTP	File transfer protocol	Rec	959
10	SMTP	Simple Mail Transfer Protocol	Rec	821
11	MAIL	Format of electronic mail messages	Rec	822
12	NTPV2	Network time protocol (version 2)	Rec	1119
13	DOMAIN	Domain name system	Rec	1034,1035
14	DNS-MX	Mail routing and the domain system	Rec	974
15	SNMP	Simple network management protocol	Rec	1157
16	SMI	Structure of management information	Rec	1155
16	Concise-MIB	Concise MIB definitions	Rec	1212
17	MIB-II	Management information base-II	Rec	1213
19	NETBIOS	NetBIOS service protocols	Ele	1001,1002
20	ECHO	Echo protocol	Rec	862
21	DISCARD	Discard protocol	Ele	863
22	CHARGEN	Character generator protocol	Ele	864

23	QUOTE	Quote of the day protocol	Ele	865
24	USERS	Active users protocol	Ele	866
25	DAYTIME	Daytime protocol	Ele	867
26	TIME	Time server protocol	Ele	868
33	TFTP	Trivial file transfer protocol	Ele	1350
34	RIP	Routing information protocol	Ele	1058
35	TP-TCP	ISO transport service on top of the TCP	Ele	1006
50	ETHER-MIB	Ethernet MIB	Ele	1643
51	PPP	Point-to-point protocol (PPP)	Ele	1661
51	PPP-HDLC	PPP in HDLC framing	Ele	1662

Telnet options

The Telnet options have their own standards and status:

STD	Protocol	Name	Option	Status	RFC
27	TOPT-BIN	Binary transmission	0	Rec	856
28	TOPT-ECHO	Echo	1	Rec	857
	TOPT-RECN	Reconnection	2	Ele	
29	TOPT-SUPP	Suppress go ahead	3	Rec	858
	TOPT-APRX	Approx message size negotiation	4	Ele	
30	TOPT-STAT	Status	5	Rec	859
31	TOPT-TIM	Timing mark	6	Rec	860
	TOPT-REM	Remote controlled trans and echo	7	Ele	726
	TOPT-OLW	Output line width	8	Ele	
	TOPT-OPS	Output page size	9	Ele	
	TOPT-OCRD	Output carriage-return disposition	10	Ele	652
	TOPT-OHT	Output horizontal tabstops	11	Ele	653
	TOPT-OHTD	Output horizontal tab disposition	12	Ele	654
	TOPT-OFD	Output formfeed disposition	13	Ele	655
	TOPT-OVT	Output vertical tabstops	14	Ele	656
	TOPT-OVTD	Output vertical tab disposition	15	Ele	657
	TOPT-OLD	Output linefeed disposition	16	Ele	658
	TOPT-EXT	Extended ASCII	17	Ele	659
	TOPT-LOGO	Logout	18	Ele	727
	TOPT-BYTE	Byte micro	19	Ele	735
	TOPT-DATA	Data entry terminal	20	Ele	1043
	TOPT-SUP	SUPDUP	21	Ele	736
	TOPT-SUPO	SUPDUP output	22	Ele	749
	TOPT-SNDL	Send location	23	Ele	779
	TOPT-Term	Terminal type	24	Ele	1091
	TOPT-EOR	End of record	25	Ele	885
	TOPT-TACACS	TACACS user identification	26	Ele	927
	TOPT-OM	Output marking	27	Ele	933
	TOPT-TLN	Terminal location number	28	Ele	946
	TOPT-3270	Telnet 3207 regime	29	Ele	1041
	TOPT-X.3	X.3 PAD	30	Ele	1053
	TOPT-NAWS	Negotiate about window size	31	Ele	1073
	TOPT-TS	Terminal speed	32	Ele	1079
	TOPT-RFC	Remote flow control	33	Ele	1372
	TOPT-LINE	Linemode	34	Ele	1184
	TOPT-XDL	X display location	35	Ele	1096
	TOPT-ENVIR	Telnet environment option	36	Not	1408
	TOPT-AUTH	Telnet authentication option	37	Ele	1416

	TOPT-ENVIR	Telnet environment option	39	Ele	1572
32	TOPT-EXTOP	Extended-options-list	255	Rec	861

Network-specific standards protocols

All network-specific standards have elective status:

STD*	Protocol	Name	Status	RFC
	IP-ATM	Classical IP and ARP over ATM	Prop	1577
	IP-FR	Multiprotocol over frame relay	Draft	1490
	ATM-ENCAP	Multiprotocol encapsulation over ATM	Prop	1483
	IP-TR-MC	IP multicast over token-ring LANs	Prop	1469
36	IP-FDDI	Transmission of IP and ARP over FDDI net	Std	1390
	IP-HIPPI	IP and ARP on HIPPI	Prop	1374
	IP-X.25	X.25 and ISDN in the packet mode	Draft	1356
	IP-FDDI	Internet protocol on FDDI networks	Draft	1188
37	ARP	Address resolution protocol	Std	826
38	RARP	A reverse address resolution protocol	Std	903
39	IP-ARPA	Internet protocol on ARPANET	Std	BBN1822
40	IP-WB	Internet protocol on wideband network	Std	907
41	IP-E	Internet protocol on Ethernet networks	Std	894
42	IP-EE	Internet protocol on exp. Ethernet nets	Std	895
43	IP-IEEE	Internet protocol on IEEE 802	Std	1042
44	IP-DC	Internet protocol on DC networks	Std	891
45	IP-HC	Internet protocol Hyperchannel	Std	1044
46	IP-ARC	Transmitting IP traffic over ARCNET nets	Std	1201
47	IP-SLIP	Transmission of IP over serial lines	Std	1055
48	IP-NETBIOS	Transmission of IP over NetBIOS	Std	1088
49	IP-IPX	Transmission of 802.2 over IPX networks	Std	1132
52*	IP-SMDS	IP datagrams over the SMDS service	Std	1209

Historic protocols

Many protocols previously used, perhaps widely, have been replaced by later versions or by other protocols that achieve the same aims more efficiently. These protocols have been named Historic. All Historic protocols have 'Not Recommended' status. They should not be used.

STD	Protocol	Name	Status	RFC
*	BGP3	Border gateway protocol 3 (BGO-3)		1267,1268
4		Gateway requirements	Rec	1009
18	EGP	Exterior gateway protocol	Rec	904
	NMP-MUX	SNMP MUX protocol and MIB		1227
	OIM-MIB-II	OSI Internet management: MIB-II		1214
	IMAP3	Interactive mail access protocol v3		1203
	SUN-RPC	Remote procedure call protocol version 1		1050
	802.4-MIP	IEEE 802.4 token bus Mib		1230
	CMOT	Common management information services		1189
		Mail privacy: procedures		1113
		Mail privacy: key management		1114
		Mail privacy: algorithms		1115
	NFILE	A file access protocol		1037
	HOSTNAME	HOSTNAME protocol		953
	SFTP	Simple file transfer protocol		913
	SUPDUP	SUPDUP protocol		734
	BGP	Border gateway protocol		1163,1164

MIB-I	MIB-I	1156
SGMP	Simple gateway monitoring protocol	1028
HEMS	High level entity management protocol	1021
STATSRV	Statistics server	996
POP2	Post office protocol, version 2	937
RATP	Reliable asynchronous transfer protocol	916
HFEP	Host – front end protocol	929
THINWIRE	Thinwire protocol	914
HMP	Host monitoring protocol	869
GGP	Gateway gateway protocol	823
RTELNET	Remote Telnet service	818
CLOCK	DCNET time server protocol	778
MPM	Internet message protocol	759
NETRJS	Remote job service	740
NETED	Network standard text editor	569
RJE	Remote job entry	407
XNET	Cross net debugger	IEN-158
NAMESERVER	Host name server protocol	IEN-116
MUX	Multiplexing protocol	IEN-90
GRAPHICS	Graphics protocol	NIC-24308

The status field indicates whether the protocol is

Req   Required
Rec   Recommended
Ele   Elective

These describe the importance of the particular protocol or technique to implementations which connect to the Internet.

Subnetting a class B address

With the introduction of Classless Interdomain Routing (CIDR) the concept of classes is obsolescent; the network number, or network prefix, is indicated by the number of 1s in the network mask. Once this concept is incorporated into host software, it will be possible to use any mask with any range of addresses. It will also be possible to use the first and last network numbers. However, there is still a large amount of historic software that recognizes address classes and restricts the mask that can be used. This software may also restrict the number of usable subnetworks. The following table shows, in a summarized form, all possible subnets for a single class B address to the point where there are 254 hosts per subnetwork. This is equivalent to subnetting the address to the same as a class C address. The table headings are as follows:

- *Subnet bits* The number of additional bits which are added to the default class B subnet mask of 255.255.0.0.

- *Subnet mask* The subnet mask which is the result of adding subnet bits to the default mask.

- *No. of networks* The number of usable networks that will result. With software that is not designed for CIDR, this is two fewer than might be expected because of 'this network' reservation and the broadcast network.

- *No. of hosts* The maximum number of hosts on each subnetwork.

- *Net no.* A designator to indicate the position in the sequence of networks (from 1 up to number of networks). This is purely for convenience in this table; it has no significance in TCP/IP conventions.

- *Net step* The value in the third and fourth octets of the IP address which must be added to distinguish the successive networks.

- *Net id* The IP address which identifies the network – a host id of all 0s.

continued on page 528

Subnet bits	Subnet mask	No. of networks	No. of hosts	Net no.	Net step	Net id	First host	Last host	Local broadcast
0	255.255.0.0	1	65 534	0	0.0	XXX.YYY.0.0	XXX.YYY.0.1	XXX.YYY.255.254	XXX.YYY.255.255
1	255.255.128.0	0	32 766	0*	128.0				
				1*					
2	255.255.192.0	2	16 382	0*	64.0				
				1		XXX.YYY.64.0	XXX.YYY.64.1	XXX.YYY.127.254	XXX.YYY.127.255
				2		XXX.YYY.128.0	XXX.YYY.128.1	XXX.YYY.191.254	XXX.YYY.191.255
				3*					
3	255.255.224.0	6	8190	0*	32.0	XXX.YYY.32.0	XXX.YYY.32.1	XXX.YYY.63.254	XXX.YYY.63.255
				1		XXX.YYY.64.0			
				2		XXX.YYY.96.0			
				3					
				4		XXX.YYY.128.0	+32.0	+32.0	+32.0
				5		XXX.YYY.140.0			
				6		XXX.YYY.192.0	XXX.YYY.192.1	XXX.YYY.223.254	XXX.YYY.223.255
				7*					
4	255.255.240.0	14	4094	0*	16.0	XXX.YYY.16.0	XXX.YYY.16.1	XXX.YYY.31.254	XXX.YYY.31.255
				1		XXX.YYY.32.0	XXX.YYY.32.1	XXX.YYY.47.254	XXX.YYY.47.255
				2					
				.					
				.		+16.0	+16.0	+16.0	+16.0
				.					
				13		XXX.YYY.208.0	XXX.YYY.208.1	XXX.YYY.223.254	XXX.YYY.223.255
				14		XXX.YYY.224.0	XXX.YYY.224.1	XXX.YYY.239.254	XXX.YYY.239.255
				15*					

Subnet bits	Subnet mask	No. of networks	No. of hosts	Net no.	Net step	Net id	First host	Last host	Local broadcast
5	255.255.248.0	30	2046	0*	8.0	XXX.YYY.8.0	XXX.YYY.8.1	XXX.YYY.15.254	XXX.YYY.15.255
				1		+8.0	+8.0	+8.0	+8.0
				·					
				·					
				29		XXX.YYY.240.0	XXX.YYY.240.1	XXX.YYY.247.254	XXX.YYY.247.255
				30		XXX.YYY.248.0	XXX.YYY.248.1	XXX.YYY.255.254	XXX.YYY.255.255
				31*					
6	255.255.252.0	62	1022	0*	4.0	XXX.YYY.4.0	XXX.YYY.4.1	XXX.YYY.7.254	XXX.YYY.7.255
				1		+4.0	+4.0	+4.0	+4.0
				·					
				62		XXX.YYY.248.0	XXX.YYY.248.1	XXX.YYY.251.254	XXX.YYY.251.255
				63*					
7	255.255.254.0	126	510	0*	2.0	XXX.YYY.2.0	XXX.YYY.2.1	XXX.YYY.3.254	XXX.YYY.3.255
				1		+2.0	+2.0	+2.0	+2.0
				·					
				126		XXX.YYY.252.0	XXX.YYY.252.1	XXX.YYY.253.254	XXX.YYY.253.255
				127*					
8	255.255.255.0	254	254	0*	1.0	XXX.YYY.1.0	XXX.YYY.1.1	XXX.YYY.1.254	XXX.YYY.1.255
				1		+1.0	+1.0	+1.0	+1.0
				·					
				254		XXX.YYY.254.0	XXX.YYY.254.1	XXX.YYY.254.254	XXX.YYY.254.255
				255*					

Note: the first and last network numbers shown with * should be used with caution. With the introduction of CIDR, these subnets *should* be available, but older software regards the last subnet as unusable and some older software may prevent use of the first subnet also.

- *First host*   The first usable host id on this network.

- *Last host*   The last usable host id on this network.

- *Local broadcast*   The address used to indicate (at the IP layer) a directed broadcast to this network.

E

Subnetting a class C address

With the introduction of Classless InterDomain Routing (CIDR) the concept of classes is obsolescent; the network number, or network prefix, is indicated by the number of 1s in the network mask. Once this concept is incorporated into host software, it will be possible to use any mask with any range of addresses. It will also be possible to use the first and last network numbers without restriction. However, there is still a large amount of historic software that recognizes address classes and restricts the mask and the subnetwork numbers that can be used.

A single Class C network can support 254 hosts. As with class A or B addresses, a class C network may be divided into subnetworks with an appropriate subnetwork mask, and with a loss in the total hosts supported. Because of the small number of hosts, not all subdivisions produce useful results.

Total mask bits	Added mask bits	Mask	No. of nets	Hosts per net	Total hosts, all subnets
25	1	255.255.255.128	0 (2)	126	0 (252)
26	2	255.255.255.192	2 (4)	62	124 (248)
27	3	255.255.255.224	6 (8)	30	180 (240)
28	4	255.255.255.240	14 (16)	14	196 (224)
29	5	255.255.255.240	30 (32)	6	180 (192)

Note: Numbers in parentheses show the 'number of nets' and 'total hosts' available if the first (0) and last (all 1s) subnets are available using software to CIDR standards. The first and last network numbers should be used with caution. With the introduction of CIDR, these subnets *should* be available, but older software regards the last subnet as unusable and some older software may prevent use of the first subnet also.

F

Protocol traces

This appendix describes more fully the format of the examples of protocol traces shown in the main chapters and appendices. These are examples of the TCP/IP protocol in action. Each network frame is shown in two formats:

(1) The complete frame in hexadecimal with ASCII representation (a hexadecimal dump) but without preamble or cyclic redundancy check.

(2) A breakdown of each layer of the protocol showing the fields and their values.

Here are a few examples to explain the format of these traces.

The first frame (frame 1) is the bit stream of the frame exactly as taken from an Ethernet network but shown in hexadecimal. All that is missing is the preamble and the CRC. In this example, the Ethernet header is shown shaded.

First is the destination address of the frame (FFFF FFFF FFFF), which is a broadcast, then the source address (02608C0AC49D) then the type field (0806). The type field value is that for ARP, so we know the Ethernet frame is carrying an ARP datagram, therefore the following information is an ARP header.

The dots and characters at the end of each line are an ASCII representation of the hexadecimal values. Dots are used when the ASCII representation of the hexadecimal value is not a printable character. If it is printable, it will be printed so we see some recognizable characters. When a frame is carrying user data, this data can be read in this part of the trace.

Frame 1

```
FFFF  FFFF  FFFF  0260  8C0A  C49D  0806  0001      ........`..D.....
0800  0604  0001  0260  8C0A  C49D  1E00  0001      ........`..D.....
0000  0000  0000  1E00  0063  0000  0000  0000      .........C......
0000  0000  0000  0000  0000  0000                  ............
```

The following is a further breakdown of frame 1, decoding the hexadecimal values into the elements of the protocol. It deciphers the fields of frame 1 into something comprehensible. In this case, the datalink frame can clearly be identified, followed by the ARP header and the information encoded in it.

Datalink:	Dest MAC:	FFFFFFFFFFFF	Source MAC:	02608C 0AC49D	Type(Length):	0806
ARP:	Hardware:	0001	Protocol:	0800	HLEN:	06
	PLEN:	04	Operation:	01		
	Source IP:	30.0.0.1	Source MAC:	02608C 0AC49D		
	Dest IP:	30.0.0.99	Dest MAC:	000000000000		

Frame 2 is another example. This is an Ethernet frame (the first shaded part), carrying an IP datagram (unshaded), carrying a TCP segment (shaded), with FTP control messages (unshaded), between an FTP client and server. The message sent by the server can be seen to the right of the hexadecimal listing represented in ASCII (226 Closing data connection <cr,lf>).

Frame 2

```
0260  8C0A  C49D  AA00  0400  0104  0800  4500    .`..D.*.......E.
0046  0B6D  0000  3C06  36E2  1E00  0063  1E00    .F.m...6b...c..
0001  0015  1A57  1245  BC13  0000  17BA  5018    .....W.E....:P.
07DA  601B  0000  3232  3620  436C  6F73  696E    .Z`...226 Closin
6720  6461  7461  2063  6F6E  6E65  6374  696F    g data connectio
6E2E  0D0A                                        n...
```

The above frame is decoded in the following table to describe the functions and options being used:

Datalink:	Dest MAC:	02608C 0AC49D	Source MAC:	AA0004 000104	Type(Length):	0800
IP:	Version:	4	IHL:	5	Type of service:	00
	Length:	0046	ID:	0B6D	FLAGS:	0
	Offset:	0	Time to live:	3C60	Protocol:	06
	Checksum:	36E2	Source IP:	30.0.0.99	Dest IP:	30.0.0.1
TCP:	Source port:	FTP-Control	Dest port:	1A57	Sequence:	1245BC13
	Acknowledge:	000017BA	Offset:	5	Code:	18(psh,ack)
	Window:	07DA	Checksum:	601B		
Data:	226 Closing data connection...					

The frames used in normal examples will not be shaded. Shading is used here to identify the different levels of the protocol in the respective headers in the frame.

Sometimes a frame will be less than the minimum 64 octets required by Ethernet. Some characters will be left in the end fields of the frame and are in fact only fill characters. Where this occurs the fill information will not be translated.

For those who must diagnose more difficult faults on internetworked systems, having the equipment to display and decode information at this level is essential. Once the test equipment is acquired, the skills to use it effectively are just as important.

G

Well-known ports

The following is an edited list of well-known port numbers (below 1024) from the Assigned Numbers RFC, RFC 1700, used by privileged processes on a UNIX system. There are many other protocol ports in common use with higher numbers. These are listed in RFC 1700 as Registered Port Numbers. Port numbers that are potentially used by local software are listed in the /etc/protocols file of a UNIX system or the equivalent protocols file on other systems.

Most port numbers are listed for the same application under TCP or UDP, even where such use does not occur in practice; for example Telnet and FTP always use TCP though they are listed with UDP as well.

Keyword	Decimal	Description
—	0/tcp/udp	Reserved
tcpmux	1/tcp/udp	TCP Port Service Multiplexer
compressnet	2/tcp/udp	Management Utility
compressnet	3/tcp/udp	Compression Process
rje	5/tcp/udp	Remote Job Entry
echo	7/tcp/udp	Echo
discard	9/tcp/udp	Discard
systat	11/tcp/udp	Active Users
daytime	13/tcp/udp	Daytime
qotd	17/tcp/udp	Quote of the Day
msp	18/tcp/udp	Message Send Protocol
chargen	19/tcp/udp	Character Generator
ftp-data	20/tcp/udp	File Transfer [Default Data]
ftp	21/tcp/udp	File Transfer [Control]
telnet	23/tcp/udp	Telnet
—	24/tcp/udp	Any private mail system
smtp	25/tcp/udp	Simple Mail Transfer
nsw-fe	27/tcp/udp	NSW User System FE
msg-icp	29/tcp/udp	MSG ICP
msg-auth	31/tcp/udp	MSG Authentication
dsp	33/tcp/udp	Display Support Protocol
—	35/tcp/udp	Any private printer server
time	37/tcp/udp	Time

Keyword	Decimal	Description
rap	38/tcp/udp	Route Access Protocol
rlp	39/tcp/udp	Resource Location Protocol
graphics	41/tcp/udp	Graphics
nameserver	42/tcp/udp	Host Name Server
nicname	43/tcp/udp	Who Is
mpm-flags	44/tcp/udp	MPM FLAGS Protocol
mpm	45/tcp/udp	Message Processing Module [recv]
mpm-snd	46/tcp/udp	MPM [default send]
ni-ftp	47/tcp/udp	NI FTP
auditd	48/tcp/udp	Digital Audit Daemon
login	49/tcp/udp	Login Host Protocol
re-mail-ck	50/tcp/udp	Remote Mail Checking Protocol
la-maint	51/tcp/udp	IMP Logical Address Maintenance
xns-time	52/tcp/udp	XNS Time Protocol
domain	53/tcp/udp	Domain Name Server
xns-ch	54/tcp/udp	XNS Clearinghouse
isi-gl	55/tcp/udp	ISI Graphics Language
xns-auth	56/tcp/udp	XNS Authentication
—	57/tcp/udp	Any private terminal access
xns-mail	58/tcp/udp	XNS Mail
—	59/tcp/udp	Any private file service
—	60/tcp/udp	Unassigned
ni-mail	61/tcp/udp	NI MAIL
acas	62/tcp/udp	ACA Services
covia	64/tcp/udp	Communications Integrator (CI)
covia	64/udp/udp	Communications Integrator (CI)
tacacs-ds	65/tcp/udp	TACACS-Database Service
sql*net	66/tcp/udp	Oracle SQL*NET
bootps	67/tcp/udp	Bootstrap Protocol Server
bootpc	68/tcp/udp	Bootstrap Protocol Client
tftp	69/tcp/udp	Trivial File Transfer
gopher	70/tcp/udp	Gopher
netrjs-1	71/tcp/udp	Remote Job Service
netrjs-2	72/tcp/udp	Remote Job Service
netrjs-3	73/tcp/udp	Remote Job Service
netrjs-4	74/tcp/udp	Remote Job Service
—	75/tcp	Any private dial out service
deos	76/tcp/udp	Distributed External Object Store
—	77/tcp/udp	Any private RJE service
vettcp	78/tcp/udp	vettcp
finger	79/tcp/udp	Finger
www-http	80/tcp/udp	World Wide Web HTTP
hosts2-ns	81/tcp/udp	HOSTS2 Name Server
xfer	82/tcp/udp	XFER Utility
mit-ml-dev	83/tcp/udp	MIT ML Device
ctf	84/tcp/udp	Common Trace Facility
mit-ml-dev	85/tcp/udp	MIT ML Device
mfcobol	86/tcp/udp	Micro Focus Cobol
—	87/tcp/udp	Any private terminal link
kerberos	88/tcp/udp	Kerberos
su-mit-tg	89/tcp/udp	SU/MIT Telnet Gateway
dnsix	90/tcp/udp	DNSIX Securit Attribute Token Map
mit-dov	91/tcp/udp	MIT Dover Spooler

Keyword	Decimal	Description
npp	92/tcp/udp	Network Printing Protocol
dcp	93/tcp/udp	Device Control Protocol
objcall	94/tcp/udp	Tivoli Object Dispatcher
supdup	95/tcp/udp	SUPDUP
dixie	96/tcp/udp	DIXIE Protocol Specification
swift-rvf	97/tcp/udp	Swift Remote Vitural File Protocol
tacnews	98/tcp/udp	TAC News
metagram	99/tcp/udp	Metagram Relay
newacct	100/tcp	[unauthorized use]
hostname	101/tcp/udp	NIC Host Name Server
iso-tsap	102/tcp/udp	ISO-TSAP
gppitnp	103/tcp/udp	Genesis Point-to-Point Trans Net
acr-nema	104/tcp/udp	ACR-NEMA Digital Imag. & Comm. 300
csnet-ns	105/tcp/udp	Mailbox Name Nameserver
3com-tsmux	106/tcp/udp	3COM-TSMUX
rtelnet	107/tcp/udp	Remote Telnet Service
snagas	108/tcp/udp	SNA Gateway Access Server
pop2	109/tcp/udp	Post Office Protocol - Version 2
pop3	110/tcp/udp	Post Office Protocol - Version 3
sunrpc	111/tcp/udp	SUN Remote Procedure Call
mcidas	112/tcp/udp	McIDAS Data Transmission Protocol
auth	113/tcp/udp	Authentication Service
audionews	114/tcp/udp	Audio News Multicast
sftp	115/tcp/udp	Simple File Transfer Protocol
ansanotify	116/tcp/udp	ANSA REX Notify
uucp-path	117/tcp/udp	UUCP Path Service
sqlserv	118/tcp/udp	SQL Services
nntp	119/tcp/udp	Network News Transfer Protocol
cfdptkt	120/tcp/udp	CFDPTKT
erpc	121/tcp/udp	Encore Expedited Remote Pro.Call
smakynet	122/tcp/udp	SMAKYNET
ntp	123/tcp/udp	Network Time Protocol
ansatrader	124/tcp/udp	ANSA REX Trader
locus-map	125/tcp/udp	Locus PC-Interface Net Map Ser
unitary	126/tcp/udp	Unisys Unitary Login
locus-con	127/tcp/udp	Locus PC-Interface Conn Server
gss-xlicen	128/tcp/udp	GSS X License Verification
pwdgen	129/tcp/udp	Password Generator Protocol
cisco-fna	130/tcp/udp	cisco FNATIVE
cisco-tna	131/tcp/udp	cisco TNATIVE
cisco-sys	132/tcp/udp	cisco SYSMAINT
statsrv	133/tcp/udp	Statistics Service
ingres-net	134/tcp/udp	INGRES-NET Service
loc-srv	135/tcp/udp	Location Service
profile	136/tcp/udp	PROFILE Naming System
netbios-ns	137/tcp/udp	NETBIOS Name Service
netbios-dgm	138/tcp/udp	NETBIOS Datagram Service
netbios-ssn	139/tcp/udp	NETBIOS Session Service
emfis-data	140/tcp/udp	EMFIS Data Service
emfis-cntl	141/tcp/udp	EMFIS Control Service
bl-idm	142/tcp/udp	Britton-Lee IDM
imap2	143/tcp/udp	Interim Mail Access Protocol v2
news	144/tcp/udp	NewS

Keyword	Decimal	Description
uaac	145/tcp/udp	UAAC Protocol
iso-tp0	146/tcp/udp	ISO-IP0
iso-ip	147/tcp/udp	ISO-IP
cronus	148/tcp/udp	CRONUS-SUPPORT
aed-512	149/tcp/udp	AED 512 Emulation Service
sql-net	150/tcp/udp	SQL-NET
hems	151/tcp/udp	HEMS
bftp	152/tcp/udp	Background File Transfer Program
sgmp	153/tcp/udp	SGMP
netsc-prod	154/tcp/udp	NETSC
netsc-dev	155/tcp/udp	NETSC
sqlsrv	156/tcp/udp	SQL Service
knet-cmp	157/tcp/udp	KNET/VM Command/Message Protocol
pcmail-srv	158/tcp/udp	PCMail Server
nss-routing	159/tcp/udp	NSS-Routing
sgmp-traps	160/tcp/udp	SGMP-TRAPS
snmp	161/tcp/udp	SNMP
snmptrap	162/tcp/udp	SNMPTRAP
cmip-man	163/tcp/udp	CMIP/TCP Manager
cmip-agent	164/tcp/udp	CMIP/TCP Agent
xns-courier	165/tcp/udp	Xerox
s-net	166/tcp/udp	Sirius Systems
namp	167/tcp/udp	NAMP
rsvd	168/tcp/udp	RSVD
send	169/tcp/udp	SEND
print-srv	170/tcp/udp	Network PostScript
multiplex	171/tcp/udp	Network Innovations Multiplex
cl/1	172/tcp/udp	Network Innovations CL/1
xyplex-mux	173/tcp/udp	Xyplex
mailq	174/tcp/udp	MAILQ
vmnet	175/tcp/udp	VMNET
genrad-mux	176/tcp/udp	GENRAD-MUX
xdmcp	177/tcp/udp	X Display Manager Control Protocol
nextstep	178/tcp/udp	NextStep Window Server
bgp	179/tcp/udp	Border Gateway Protocol
ris	180/tcp/udp	Intergraph
unify	181/tcp/udp	Unify
audit	182/tcp/udp	Unisys Audit SITP
ocbinder	183/tcp/udp	OCBinder
ocserver	184/tcp/udp	OCServer
remote-kis	185/tcp/udp	Remote-KIS
kis	186/tcp/udp	KIS Protocol
aci	187/tcp/udp	Application Communication Interface
mumps	188/tcp/udp	Plus Five's MUMPS
qft	189/tcp/udp	Queued File Transport
gacp	190/tcp/udp	Gateway Access Control Protocol
prospero	191/tcp/udp	Prospero Directory Service
osu-nms	192/tcp/udp	OSU Network Monitoring System
srmp	193/tcp/udp	Spider Remote Monitoring Protocol
irc	194/tcp/udp	Internet Relay Chat Protocol
dn6-nlm-aud	195/tcp/udp	DNSIX Network Level Module Audit
dn6-smm-red	196/tcp/udp	DNSIX Session Mgt Module Audit Redir
dls	197/tcp/udp	Directory Location Service

Keyword	Decimal	Description
dls-mon	198/tcp/udp	Directory Location Service Monitor
smux	199/tcp/udp	SMUX
src	200/tcp/udp	IBM System Resource Controller
at-rtmp	201/tcp/udp	AppleTalk Routing Maintenance
at-nbp	202/tcp/udp	AppleTalk Name Binding
at-3	203/tcp/udp	AppleTalk Unused
at-echo	204/tcp/udp	AppleTalk Echo
at-5	205/tcp/udp	AppleTalk Unused
at-zis	206/tcp/udp	AppleTalk Zone Information
at-7	207/tcp/udp	AppleTalk Unused
at-8	208/tcp/udp	AppleTalk Unused
tam	209/tcp/udp	Trivial Authenticated Mail Protocol
z39.50	210/tcp/udp	ANSI Z39.50
914c/g	211/tcp/udp	Texas Instruments 914C/G Terminal
anet	212/tcp/udp	ATEXSSTR
ipx	213/tcp/udp	IPX
vmpwscs	214/tcp/udp	VM PWSCS
softpc	215/tcp/udp	Insignia Solutions
atls	216/tcp/udp	Access Technology License Server
dbase	217/tcp/udp	dBASE Unix
mpp	218/tcp/udp	Netix Message Posting Protocol
uarps	219/tcp/udp	Unisys ARPs
imap3	220/tcp/udp	Interactive Mail Access Protocol v3
fln-spx	221/tcp/udp	Berkeley rlogind with SPX auth
rsh-spx	222/tcp/udp	Berkeley rshd with SPX auth
cdc	223/tcp/udp	Certificate Distribution Center
sur-meas	243/tcp/udp	Survey Measurement
link	245/tcp/udp	LINK
dsp3270	246/tcp/udp	Display Systems Protocol
pdap	344/tcp/udp	Prospero Data Access Protocol
pawserv	345/tcp/udp	Perf Analysis Workbench
zserv	346/tcp/udp	Zebra server
fatserv	347/tcp/udp	Fatmen Server
csi-sgwp	348/tcp/udp	Cabletron Management Protocol
clearcase	371/tcp/udp	Clearcase
ulistserv	372/tcp/udp	Unix Listserv
legent-1	373/tcp/udp	Legent Corporation
legent-2	374/tcp/udp	Legent Corporation
hassle	375/tcp/udp	Hassle
nip	376/tcp/udp	Amiga Envoy Network Inquiry Proto
tnETOS	377/tcp/udp	NEC Corporation
dsETOS	378/tcp/udp	NEC Corporation
is99c	379/tcp/udp	TIA/EIA/IS-99 modem client
is99s	380/tcp/udp	TIA/EIA/IS-99 modem server
hp-collector	381/tcp/udp	hp performance data collector
hp-managed-node	382/tcp/udp	hp performance data managed node
hp-alarm-mgr	383/tcp/udp	hp performance data alarm manager
arns	384/tcp/udp	A Remote Network Server System
ibm-app	385/tcp/udp	IBM Application
asa	386/tcp/udp	ASA Message Router Object Def.
aurp	387/tcp/udp	Appletalk Update-Based Routing Pro.
unidata-ldm	388/tcp/udp	Unidata LDM Version 4
ldap	389/tcp/udp	Lightweight Directory Access Protocol

Keyword	Decimal	Description
uis	390/tcp/udp	UIS
synotics-relay	391/tcp/udp	SynOptics SNMP Relay Port
synotics-broker	392/tcp/udp	SynOptics Port Broker Port
dis	393/tcp/udp	Data Interpretation System
embl-ndt	394/tcp/udp	EMBL Nucleic Data Transfer
netcp	395/tcp/udp	NETscout Control Protocol
netware-ip	396/tcp/udp	Novell Netware over IP
mptn	397/tcp/udp	Multi Protocol Trans. Net.
kryptolan	398/tcp/udp	Kryptolan
work-sol	400/tcp/udp	Workstation Solutions
ups	401/tcp/udp	Uninterruptible Power Supply
genie	402/tcp/udp	Genie Protocol
decap	403/tcp/udp	decap
nced	404/tcp/udp	nced
ncld	405/tcp/udp	ncld
imsp	406/tcp/udp	Interactive Mail Support Protocol
timbuktu	407/tcp/udp	Timbuktu
prm-sm	408/tcp/udp	Prospero Resource Manager Sys. Man.
prm-nm	409/tcp/udp	Prospero Resource Manager Node Man.
decladebug	410/tcp/udp	DECLadebug Remote Debug Protocol
rmt	411/tcp/udp	Remote MT Protocol
synoptics-trap	412/tcp/udp	Trap Convention Port
smsp	413/tcp/udp	SMSP
infoseek	414/tcp/udp	InfoSeek
bnet	415/tcp/udp	BNet
silverplatter	416/tcp/udp	Silverplatter
onmux	417/tcp/udp	Onmux
hyper-g	418/tcp/udp	Hyper-G
ariel1	419/tcp/udp	Ariel
smpte	420/tcp/udp	SMPTE
ariel2	421/tcp/udp	Ariel
ariel3	422/tcp/udp	Ariel
opc-job-start	423/tcp/udp	IBM Operations Planning and Control Start
opc-job-track	424/tcp/udp	IBM Operations Planning and Control Track
icad-el	425/tcp/udp	ICAD
smartsdp	426/tcp/udp	smartsdp
svrloc	427/tcp/udp	Server Location
ocs_cmu	428/tcp/udp	OCS_CMU
ocs_amu	429/tcp/udp	OCS_AMU
utmpsd	430/tcp/udp	UTMPSD
utmpcd	431/tcp/udp	UTMPCD
iasd	432/tcp/udp	IASD
nnsp	433/tcp/udp	NNSP
mobileip-agent	434/tcp/udp	MobileIP-Agent
mobilip-mn	435/tcp/udp	MobilIP-MN
dna-cml	436/tcp/udp	DNA-CML
comscm	437/tcp/udp	comscm
dsfgw	438/tcp/udp	dsfgw
dasp	439/tcp/udp	dasp
sgcp	440/tcp/udp	sgcp
decvms-sysmgt	441/tcp/udp	decvms-sysmgt
cvc_hostd	442/tcp/udp	cvc_hostd
https	443/tcp/udp	https MCom

Keyword	Decimal	Description
snpp	444/tcp/udp	Simple Network Paging Protocol
microsoft-ds	445/tcp/udp	Microsoft-DS
ddm-rdb	446/tcp/udp	DDM-RDB
ddm-dfm	447/tcp/udp	DDM-RFM
ddm-byte	448/tcp/udp	DDM-BYTE
as-servermap	449/tcp/udp	AS Server Mapper
tserver	450/tcp/udp	TServer
exec	512/tcp	Remote process execution
biff	512/udp	Used by mail system to notify users
login	513/tcp	Remote login a la telnet
who	513/udp	Maintains databases showing who's
cmd	514/tcp	Like exec, but automatic
syslog	514/udp	
printer	515/tcp/udp	Spooler
talk	517/tcp/udp	Like tenex link, but across tcp connection is established)
ntalk	518/tcp/udp	
utime	519/tcp/udp	unixtime
efs	520/tcp	Extended file name server
router	520/udp	Local routing process (on site)
timed	525/tcp/udp	Timeserver
tempo	526/tcp/udp	Newdate
courier	530/tcp/udp	rpc
conference	531/tcp/udp	chat
netnews	532/tcp/udp	readnews
netwall	533/tcp/udp	For emergency broadcasts
apertus-ldp	539/tcp/udp	Apertus Technologies Load Determination
uucp	540/tcp/udp	uucpd
uucp-rlogin	541/tcp/udp	uucp-rlogin
klogin	543/tcp/udp	
kshell	544/tcp/udp	krcmd
new-rwho	550/tcp/udp	new-who
dsf	555/tcp/udp	
remotefs	556/tcp/udp	rfs server
rmonitor	560/tcp/udp	rmonitord
monitor	561/tcp/udp	
chshell	562/tcp/udp	chcmd
9pfs	564/tcp/udp	Plan 9 file service
whoami	565/tcp/udp	whoami
meter	570/tcp/udp	demon
meter	571/tcp/udp	udemon
ipcserver	600/tcp/udp	Sun IPC server
urm	606/tcp/udp	Cray Unified Resource Manager
nqs	607/tcp/udp	nqs
sift-uft	608/tcp/udp	Sender-Initiated/Unsolicited File Transfer
npmp-trap	609/tcp/udp	npmp-trap
npmp-local	610/tcp/udp	npmp-local
npmp-gui	611/tcp/udp	npmp-gui
ginad	634/tcp/udp	ginad
mdqs	666/tcp/udp	
doom	666/tcp/udp	doom Id Software
elcsd	704/tcp/udp	errlog copy/server daemon
entrustmanager	709/tcp/udp	EntrustManager

Keyword	Decimal	Description
netviewdm1	729/tcp/udp	IBM NetView DM/6000 Server/Client
netviewdm2	730/tcp/udp	IBM NetView DM/6000 send/tcp
netviewdm3	731/tcp/udp	IBM NetView DM/6000 receive/tcp
netgw	741/tcp/udp	netGW
netrcs	742/tcp/udp	Network based Rev. Cont. Sys.
flexlm	744/tcp/udp	Flexible License Manager
fujitsu-dev	747/tcp/udp	Fujitsu Device Control
ris-cm	748/tcp/udp	Russell Info Sci Calendar Manager
kerberos-adm	749/tcp/udp	kerberos administration
rfile	750/tcp	
loadav	750/udp	
pump	751/tcp/udp	
qrh	752/tcp/udp	
rrh	753/tcp/udp	
tell	754/tcp/udp	Send
nlogin	758/tcp/udp	
con	759/tcp/udp	
ns	760/tcp/udp	
rxe	761/tcp/udp	
quotad	762/tcp/udp	
cycleserv	763/tcp/udp	
omserv	764/tcp/udp	
webster	765/tcp/udp	
phonebook	767/tcp/udp	Phone
vid	769/tcp/udp	
cadlock	770/tcp/udp	
rtip	771/tcp/udp	
cycleserv2	772/tcp/udp	
submit	773/tcp	
notify	773/udp	
rpasswd	774/tcp	
acmaint_dbd	774/udp	
entomb	775/tcp	
acmaint_transd	775/udp	
wpages	776/tcp/udp	
wpgs	780/tcp/udp	
concert	786/tcp/udp	Concert
mdbs_daemon	800/tcp/udp	
device	801/tcp/udp	
xtreelic	996/tcp/udp	Central Point Software
maitrd	997/tcp/udp	
busboy	998/tcp	
puparp	998/udp	
garcon	999/tcp	
applix	999/udp	Applix ac
puprouter	999/tcp/udp	
cadlock	1000/tcp	
ock	1000/udp	
	1023/tcp	Reserved
	1024/udp	Reserved

Telnet protocol traces

This appendix shows actual traces taken from an operational network using the Telnet protocol. In this example, we show Ethernet frames in hexadecimal without the preamble or the cyclic redundancy check. The table beneath the frame gives a breakdown of the fields in the frame and their values. For a further explanation of the format of these examples, see Appendix F.

This example shows a user 'system' logging in to a host. The frames show the user typing the user id, and the replies and acknowledgements to this. Notice the Telnet negotiation in certain frames and messages coming back from the host.

Frame 1 (host welfare banner)

```
0260  8C0A  C49D  AA00  0400  0104  0800  4500    .`..D.*.......E.
004D  0B0E  0000  3C06  373A  1E00  0063  1E00    .M.....7:...c...
0001  0017  19CB  11E7  39BE  0000  3E39  5018    .....K.g9..9P...
0400  514F  0000  0A20  2020  2020  2020  2057    ..QO...        W
656C  636F  6D65  2074  6F20  5641  582F  564D    elcome to VAX/VM
5320  5635  2E33  2020  2020  0D                  S V5.3     .
```

Datalink:	Dest MAC:	02608C 0AC49D	Source MAC:	AA0004 000104	Type(Length):	0800
IP:	Version:	4	IHL:	5	Type of service:	00
	Length:	004D	ID:	0B0E	Flags:	0
	Offset:	0	Time to live:	60	Protocol:	06
	Checksum:	373A	Source IP:	30.0.0.99	Dest IP:	30.0.0.1
TCP:	Source port:	Telnet(0017)	Dest port:	19CB	Sequence:	11E739BE
	Acknowledge:	00003E39	Offset:	5	Code:	18(Ack,Push)
	Window:	0400	Checksum:	514F		
Data:	Welcome to VAX/VMS V5.3 <sp> <sp><sp><sp><cr>					

Frame 2 (<lf> <cr> from host)

```
0260  8C0A  C49D  AA00  0400  0104  0800  4500    .`..D.*.......E.
002A  0B0F  0000  3C06  375C  1E00  0063  1E00    .*.....7\...c...
0001  0017  19CB  11E7  39E3  0000  3E39  5018    .....K.g9c..9P..
0400  C174  0000  0A0D  0000  0000              ..At........
```

Datalink:	Dest MAC:	02608C 0AC49D	Source MAC:	AA0004 000104	Type(Length):	0800
IP:	Version:	4	IHL:	5	Type of service:	00
	Length:	002A	ID:	0B0E	Flags:	0
	Offset:	0	Time to live:	3C(60)	Protocol:	06
	Checksum:	375C	Source IP:	30.0.0.99	Dest IP:	30.0.0.1
TCP:	Source port:	Telnet(0017)	Dest port:	19CB	Sequence:	11E739E3
	Acknowledge:	00003E39	Offset:	5	Code:	18(Ack,Push)
	Window:	0400	Checksum:	C174		
Data:	<lf><cr>					

Frame 3 (acknowledge)

```
AA00  0400  0104  0260  8C0A  C49D  0800  4500    *......`..D...E.
0028  0004  0000  FF06  7F68  1E00  0001  1E00    .(.......h......
0063  19CB  0017  0000  3E39  11E7  39BB  5010    .c.K....9.g9;P..
0400  CBB3  0000  0000  0000  0000              ..K3........
```

Datalink:	Dest MAC:	AA0004 000104	Source MAC:	02608C 0AC49D	Type(Length):	0800
IP:	Version:	4	IHL:	5	Type of service:	00
	Length:	0028	ID:	0004	Flags:	0
	Offset:	0	Time to live:	FF(255)	Protocol:	06
	Checksum:	7F68	Source IP:	30.0.0.1	Dest IP:	30.0.0.99
TCP:	Source port:	Telnet(0017)	Dest port:	19CB	Sequence:	00003E39
	Acknowledge:	11E739BB	Offset:	5	Code:	10(Ack)
	Window:	0400	Checksum:	CBB3		
Data:						

Frame 4 (use name prompt)

```
0260  8C0A  C49D  AA00  0400  0104  0800  4500    .`..D.*.......E.
0035  0B10  0000  3C06  3750  1E00  0063  1E00    .5.....7P...c..
0001  0017  19CB  11E7  39E5  0000  3E39  5018    .....K.g9e..9P.
0400  F496  0000  0A0D  0055  7365  726E  616D    ..t......Usernam
653A  20                                          e:
```

Datalink:	Dest MAC:	02608C 0AC49D	Source MAC:	AA0004 000104	Type(Length):	0800
IP:	Version:	4	IHL:	5	Type of service:	00
	Length:	0035	ID:	0B10	Flags:	0
	Offset:	0	Time to live:	3C(60)	Protocol:	06
	Checksum:	3750	Source IP:	30.0.0.99	Dest IP:	30.0.0.1
TCP:	Source port:	Telnet(0017)	Dest port:	19CB	Sequence:	11E739E5
	Acknowledge:	00003E39	Offset:	5	Code:	18(Ack,Push)
	Window:	0400	Checksum:	F496		
Data:	<lf><cr>Username:<sp>					

Frame 5 (acknowledge)

```
AA00   0400   0104   0260   8C0A   C49D   0800   4500      *......`..D...E.
0028   0008   0000   FF06   7F64   1E00   0001   1E00      .(........d......
0063   19CB   0017   0000   3E39   11E7   39F2   5010      .c.K....9.g9rP.
0400   CB7C   0000                                         ..K|..
```

Datalink:	Dest MAC:	AA0004 000104	Source MAC:	02608C 0AC49D	Type(Length):	0800
IP:	Version:	4	IHL:	5	Type of service:	00
	Length:	0028	ID:	0004	Flags:	0
	Offset:	0	Time to live:	FF(255)	Protocol:	06
	Checksum:	7F64	Source IP:	30.0.0.1	Dest IP:	30.0.0.99
TCP:	Source port:	Telnet(0017)	Dest port:	19CB	Sequence:	00003E39
	Acknowledge:	11E739F2	Offset:	5	Code:	10(Ack)
	Window:	0400	Checksum:	CB7C		
Data:						

Frame 6 (Telnet negotiation)

```
AA00   0400   0104   0260   8C0A   C49D   0800   4500      *......`..D...E.
0031   0009   0000   FF06   7F5A   1E00   0001   1E00      .1.......Z......
0063   19CB   0017   0000   3E39   11E7   39F2   5018      .c.K....9.g9rP.
0400   B36D   0000   FFFD   03FF   FC03   FFFC   18        ..3m...}..|..|.
```

Datalink:	Dest MAC:	AA0004 000104	Source MAC:	02608C 0AC49D	Type(Length):	0800
IP:	Version:	4	IHL:	5	Type of service:	00
	Length:	0031	ID:	0009	Flags:	0
	Offset:	0	Time to live:	FF(255)	Protocol:	06
	Checksum:	7F5A	Source IP:	30.0.0.1	Dest IP:	30.0.0.99
TCP:	Source port:	Telnet(0017)	Dest port:	19CB	Sequence:	00003E39
	Acknowledge:	11E739F2	Offset:	5	Code:	18(Ack,Push)
	Window:	0400	Checksum:	B36D		
Data:	[Do Suppress-go-ahead(FFFD03)][Won't Go-ahead(FFFC03)][Won't terminal type(FFFC18)]					

Frame 7 (acknowledge)

```
0260   8C0A   C49D   AA00   0400   0104   0800   4500      .`..D.*.......E.
0028   0B11   0000   3C06   375C   1E00   0063   1E00      .(.....7\...c..
0001   0017   19CB   11E7   39F2   0000   3E42   5010      .....K.g9r..BP.
0400   CB73   0000   0000   0000   0000                    ..Ks........
```

Datalink:	Dest MAC:	02608C 0AC49D	Source MAC:	AA0004 000104	Type(Length):	0800
IP:	Version:	4	IHL:	5	Type of service:	00
	Length:	0028	ID:	0B11	Flags:	0
	Offset:	0	Time to live:	3C(60)	Protocol:	06
	Checksum:	375C	Source IP:	30.0.0.99	Dest IP:	30.0.0.1
TCP:	Source port:	Telnet(0017)	Dest port:	19CB	Sequence:	11E739F2
	Acknowledge:	00003E42	Offset:	5	Code:	10(Ack)
	Window:	0400	Checksum:	CB73		
Data:						

Frame 8 (acknowledge)

```
AA00  0400  0104  0260  8C0A  C49D  0800  4500      *......`..D...E.
0028  000B  0000  FF06  7F61  1E00  0001  1E00      .(.........a......
0063  19CB  0017  0000  3E42  11E7  39F2  5010      .c.K....B.g9rP.
0400  CB73  0000                                    ..Ks..
```

Datalink:	Dest MAC:	AA0004 000104	Source MAC:	02608C 0AC49D	Type(Length):	0800
IP:	Version:	4	IHL:	5	Type of service:	00
	Length:	0028	ID:	000B	Flags:	0
	Offset:	0	Time to live:	FF(255)	Protocol:	06
	Checksum:	7F61	Source IP:	30.0.0.1	Dest IP:	30.0.0.99
TCP:	Source port:	Telnet(0017)	Dest port:	19CB	Sequence:	00003E42
	Acknowledge:	11E739F2	Offset:	5	Code:	10(Ack)
	Window:	0400	Checksum:	CB73		
Data:	ahead					

Frame 9 ("s")

```
AA00  0400  0104  0260  8C0A  C49D  0800  4500      *......`..D...E.
0029  000C  0000  FF06  7F5F  1E00  0001  1E00      .).......__......
0063  19CB  0017  0000  3E42  11E7  39F2  5018      .c.K....B.g9rP.
0400  586A  0000  73                                ..Xj..s
```

Datalink:	Dest MAC:	AA0004 000104	Source MAC:	02608C 0AC49D	Type(Length):	0800
IP:	Version:	4	IHL:	5	Type of service:	00
	Length:	0029	ID:	000C	Flags:	0
	Offset:	0	Time to live:	FF(255)	Protocol:	06
	Checksum:	7F5F	Source IP:	30.0.0.1	Dest IP:	30.0.0.99
TCP:	Source port:	Telnet(0017)	Dest port:	19CB	Sequence:	00003E42
	Acknowledge:	11E739F2	Offset:	5	Code:	18(Ack,Psh)
	Window:	0400	Checksum:	586A		
Data:	s					

Frame 10 (acknowledge, negotiation and echo "S")

```
0260  8C0A  C49D  AA00  0400  0104  0800  4500      .`..D.*.......E.
002C  0B12  0000  3C06  3757  1E00  0063  1E00      .,.....7W...c..
0001  0017  19CB  11E7  39F2  0000  3E43  5018      .....K.g9r..CP.
0400  C814  0000  FFFE  0353  0000                  ..H....~.S..
```

Datalink:	Dest MAC:	02608C 0AC49D	Source MAC:	AA0004 000104	Type(Length):	0800
IP:	Version:	4	IHL:	5	Type of service:	00
	Length:	002C	ID:	0B12	Flags:	0
	Offset:	0	Time to live:	3C(60)	Protocol:	06
	Checksum:	375C	Source IP:	30.0.0.99	Dest IP:	30.0.0.1
TCP:	Source port:	Telnet(0017)	Dest port:	19CB	Sequence:	11E739F2
	Acknowledge:	00003E43	Offset:	5	Code:	18(Ack,Push)
	Window:	0400	Checksum:	C814		
Data:	[Don't Suppress-go-ahead(FFFE03)] S					

Frame 11 (acknowledge)

```
AA00   0400   0104   0260   8C0A   C49D   0800   4500      *......`..D...E.
0028   000D   0000   FF06   7F5F   1E00   0001   1E00      .(........_......
0063   19CB   0017   0000   3E43   11E7   39F6   5010      .c.K....C.g9vP.
0400   CB6E   0000                                         ..Kn..
```

Datalink:	Dest MAC:	AA0004 000104	Source MAC:	02608C 0AC49D	Type(Length):	0800
IP:	Version:	4	IHL:	5	Type of service:	00
	Length:	0028	ID:	000D	Flags:	0
	Offset:	0	Time to live:	255	Protocol:	06
	Checksum:	7F5F	Source IP:	30.0.0.1	Dest IP:	30.0.0.99
TCP:	Source port:	Telnet(0017)	Dest port:	19CB	Sequence:	00003E43
	Acknowledge:	11E739F6	Offset:	5	Code:	18(Ack,Psh)
	Window:	0400	Checksum:	CB6E		
Data:						

Frame 12 ("y")

```
AA00   0400   0104   0260   8C0A   C49D   0800   4500      *......`..D...E.
0029   000E   0000   FF06   7F5D   1E00   0001   1E00      .)........].....
0063   19CB   0017   0000   3E43   11E7   39F6   5018      .c.K....C.g9vP.
0400   5265   0000   79                                    ..Re..y
```

Datalink:	Dest MAC:	AA0004 000104	Source MAC:	02608C 0AC49D	Type(Length):	0800
IP:	Version:	4	IHL:	5	Type of service:	00
	Length:	0029	ID:	000E	Flags:	0
	Offset:	0	Time to live:	FF(255)	Protocol:	06
	Checksum:	7F5D	Source IP:	30.0.0.1	Dest IP:	30.0.0.99
TCP:	Source port:	Telnet(0017)	Dest port:	19CB	Sequence:	00003E43
	Acknowledge:	11E739F6	Offset:	5	Code:	18(Ack,Psh)
	Window:	0400	Checksum:	5265		
Data:	y					

Frame 13 (acknowledge and echo "Y")

```
0260   8C0A   C49D   AA00   0400   0104   0800   4500      .`..D.*.......E.
0029   0B13   0000   3C06   3759   1E00   0063   1E00      .).....7Y...c..
0001   0017   19CB   11E7   39F6   0000   3E44   5018      .....K.g9v..DP.
0400   7264   0000   5900   0000   0000                    ..rd..Y.....
```

Datalink:	Dest MAC:	02608C 0AC49D	Source MAC:	AA0004 000104	Type(Length):	0800
IP:	Version:	4	IHL:	5	Type of service:	00
	Length:	002C	ID:	0B13	Flags:	0
	Offset:	0	Time to live:	60	Protocol:	06
	Checksum:	3759	Source IP:	30.0.0.99	Dest IP:	30.0.0.1
TCP:	Source port:	Telnet(0017)	Dest port:	19CB	Sequence:	11E739F6
	Acknowledge:	00003E44	Offset:	5	Code:	18(Ack,Push)
	Window:	0400	Checksum:	7264		
Data:	Y					

Frame 14 (acknowledge)

```
AA00  0400  0104  0260  8C0A  C49D  0800  4500    *......`..D...E.
0028  000F  0000  FF06  7F5D  1E00  0001  1E00    .(.......]......
0063  19CB  0017  0000  3E44  11E7  39F7  5010    .c.K....D.g9wP.
0400  CB6C  0000                                  ..Kl.
```

Datalink:	Dest MAC:	AA0004 000104	Source MAC:	02608C 0AC49D	Type(Length):	0800
IP:	Version:	4	IHL:	5	Type of service:	00
	Length:	0028	ID:	000F	Flags:	0
	Offset:	0	Time to live:	FF(255)	Protocol:	06
	Checksum:	7F5D	Source IP:	30.0.0.1	Dest IP:	30.0.0.99
TCP:	Source port:	Telnet(0017)	Dest port:	19CB	Sequence:	00003E44
	Acknowledge:	11E739F7	Offset:	5	Code:	10(Ack)
	Window:	0400	Checksum:	CB6C		
Data:						

Frame 15 ("s")

```
AA00  0400  0104  0260  8C0A  C49D  0800  4500    *......`..D...E.
0029  0010  0000  FF06  7F5B  1E00  0001  1E00    .).......[......
0063  19CB  0017  0000  3E44  11E7  39F7  5018    .c.K....D.g9wP.
0400  5863  0000  7300                            ..Xc..s
```

Datalink:	Dest MAC:	AA0004 000104	Source MAC:	02608C 0AC49D	Type(Length):	0800
IP:	Version:	4	IHL:	5	Type of service:	00
	Length:	0029	ID:	0010	Flags:	0
	Offset:	0	Time to live:	FF(255)	Protocol:	06
	Checksum:	7F5B	Source IP:	30.0.0.1	Dest IP:	30.0.0.99
TCP:	Source port:	Telnet(0017)	Dest port:	19CB	Sequence:	00003E44
	Acknowledge:	11E739F7	Offset:	5	Code:	18(Ack,Psh)
	Window:	0400	Checksum:	5863		
Data:	s					

Frame 16

```
0260  8C0A  C49D  AA00  0400  0104  0800  4500    .`..D.*.......E.
0029  0B14  0000  3C06  3758  1E00  0063  1E00    .).....7X...c..
0001  0017  19CB  11E7  39F7  0000  3E45  5018    .....K.g9w..EP.
0400  7862  0000  53                              ..xb..S.....
```

Datalink:	Dest MAC:	02608C 0AC49D	Source MAC:	AA0004 000104	Type(Length):	0800
IP:	Version:	4	IHL:	5	Type of service:	00
	Length:	0029	ID:	0B14	Flags:	0
	Offset:	0	Time to live:	3C(60)	Protocol:	06
	Checksum:	3758	Source IP:	30.0.0.99	Dest IP:	30.0.0.1
TCP:	Source port:	Telnet((0017)	Dest port:	19CB	Sequence:	11E739F7
	Acknowledge:	00003E45	Offset:	5	Code:	18(Ack,Push)
	Window:	0400	Checksum:	7862		
Data:	S					

Frame 17 (acknowledge)

```
AA00  0400  0104  0260  8C0A  C49D  0800  4500    *......`..D...E.
0028  0011  0000  FF06  7F5B  1E00  0001  1E00    .(.......[......
0063  19CB  0017  0000  3E45  11E7  39F8  5010    .c.K....E.g9xP.
0400  CB6A  0000                                  ..Kj..
```

Datalink:	Dest MAC:	AA0004 000104	Source MAC:	02608C 0AC49D	Type(Length):	0800
IP:	Version:	4	IHL:	5	Type of service:	00
	Length:	0028	ID:	0011	Flags:	0
	Offset:	0	Time to live:	255	Protocol:	06
	Checksum:	7F5B	Source IP:	30.0.0.1	Dest IP:	30.0.0.99
TCP:	Source port:	Telnet(0017)	Dest port:	19CB	Sequence:	00003E45
	Acknowledge:	11E739F8	Offset:	5	Code:	10(Ack)
	Window:	0400	Checksum:	CB6A		
Data:						

Frame 18("t")

```
AA00  0400  0104  0260  8C0A  C49D  0800  4500    *......`..D...E.
0029  0012  0000  FF06  7F59  1E00  0001  1E00    .).......Y......
0063  19CB  0017  0000  3E45  11E7  39F8  5018    .c.K....E.g9xP.
0400  5761  0000  74                              ..Wa..t
```

Datalink:	Dest MAC:	AA0004 000104	Source MAC:	02608C 0AC49D	Type(Length):	0800
IP:	Version:	4	IHL:	5	Type of service:	00
	Length:	0029	ID:	0012	Flags:	0
	Offset:	0	Time to live:	255	Protocol:	06
	Checksum:	7F59	Source IP:	30.0.0.1	Dest IP:	30.0.0.99
TCP:	Source port:	Telnet(0017)	Dest port:	19CB	Sequence:	00003E45
	Acknowledge:	11E739F8	Offset:	5	Code:	18(Ack,Psh)
	Window:	0400	Checksum:	5761		
Data:	t					

Frame 19 (acknowledge and echo "T")

```
0260  8C0A  C49D  AA00  0400  0104  0800  4500    .`..D.*.......E.
0029  0B15  0000  3C06  3757  1E00  0063  1E00    .).....7W...c..
0001  0017  19CB  11E7  39F8  0000  3E46  5018    .....K.g9x..FP.
0400  7760  0000  54                              ..w`..T
```

Datalink:	Dest MAC:	02608C 0AC49D	Source MAC:	AA0004 000104	Type(Length):	0800
IP:	Version:	4	IHL:	5	Type of service:	00
	Length:	0029	ID:	0B15	Flags:	0
	Offset:	0	Time to live:	60	Protocol:	06
	Checksum:	3757	Source IP:	30.0.0.99	Dest IP:	30.0.0.1
TCP:	Source port:	Telnet(0017)	Dest port:	19CB	Sequence:	11E739F8
	Acknowledge:	00003E46	Offset:	5	Code:	18(Ack,Push)
	Window:	0400	Checksum:	7760		
Data:	T					

Frame 20 (acknowledge)

```
AA00   0400   0104   0260   8C0A   C49D   0800   4500     *......`..D...E.
0028   0013   0000   FF06   7F59   1E00   0001   1E00     .(.......Y......
0063   19CB   0017   0000   3E46   11E7   39F9   5010     .c.K....F.g9yP.
0400   CB68   0000                                        ..Kh..
```

Datalink:	Dest MAC:	AA0004 000104	Source MAC:	02608C 0AC49D	Type(Length):	0800
IP:	Version:	4	IHL:	5	Type of service:	00
	Length:	0028	ID:	0013	Flags:	0
	Offset:	0	Time to live:	FF(255)	Protocol:	06
	Checksum:	7F59	Source IP:	30.0.0.1	Dest IP:	30.0.0.99
TCP:	Source port:	Telnet((0017)	Dest port:	19CB	Sequence:	00003E46
	Acknowledge:	11E739F9	Offset:	5	Code:	18(Ack,Psh)
	Window:	0400	Checksum:	CB68		
Data:						

Frame 21 ("e")

```
AA00   0400   0104   0260   8C0A   C49D   0800   4500     *......`..D...E.
0029   0014   0000   FF06   7F57   1E00   0001   1E00     .).......W......
0063   19CB   0017   0000   3E46   11E7   39F9   5018     .c.K....F.g9yP.
0400   665F   0000   65                                   ..f_..e
```

Datalink:	Dest MAC:	AA0004 000104	Source MAC:	02608C 0AC49D	Type(Length):	0800
IP:	Version:	4	IHL:	5	Type of service:	00
	Length:	0029	ID:	0014	Flags:	0
	Offset:	0	Time to live:	FF(255)	Protocol:	06
	Checksum:	7F57	Source IP:	30.0.0.1	Dest IP:	30.0.0.99
TCP:	Source port:	Telnet(0017)	Dest port:	19CB	Sequence:	00003E46
	Acknowledge:	11E739F9	Offset:	5	Code:	18(Ack,Psh)
	Window:	0400	Checksum:	665F		
Data:	e					

Frame 22 (acknowledge and echo "E")

```
0260   8C0A   C49D   AA00   0400   0104   0800   4500     .`..D.*.......E.
0029   0B16   0000   3C06   3756   1E00   0063   1E00     .).....7V...c..
0001   0017   19CB   11E7   39F9   0000   3E47   5018     .....K.g9y..GP.
0400   865E   0000   45                                   ...^..E
```

Datalink:	Dest MAC:	02608C 0AC49D	Source MAC:	AA0004 000104	Type(Length):	0800
IP:	Version:	4	IHL:	5	Type of service:	00
	Length:	0029	ID:	0B16	Flags:	0
	Offset:	0	Time to live:	60	Protocol:	06
	Checksum:	3756	Source IP:	30.0.0.99	Dest IP:	30.0.0.1
TCP:	Source port:	Telnet(0017)	Dest port:	19CB	Sequence:	11E739F9
	Acknowledge:	00003E47	Offset:	5	Code:	18(Ack,Push)
	Window:	0400	Checksum:	865E		
Data:	E					

Frame 23 (acknowledge)

```
AA00  0400  0104  0260  8C0A  C49D  0800  4500    *......`..D...E.
0028  0015  0000  FF06  7F57  1E00  0001  1E00    .(.......W......
0063  19CB  0017  0000  3E47  11E7  39FA  5010    .c.K....G.g9zP.
0400  CB66  0000                                  ..Kf..
```

Datalink:	Dest MAC:	AA0004 000104	Source MAC:	02608C 0AC49D	Type(Length):	0800
IP:	Version:	4	IHL:	5	Type of service:	00
	Length:	0028	ID:	0015	Flags:	0
	Offset:	0	Time to live:	255	Protocol:	06
	Checksum:	7F57	Source IP:	30.0.0.1	Dest IP:	30.0.0.99
TCP:	Source port:	Telnet(0017)	Dest port:	19CB	Sequence:	00003E47
	Acknowledge:	11E739FA	Offset:	5	Code:	10(Ack)
	Window:	0400	Checksum:	CB66		
Data:						

Frame 24 (acknowledge)

```
0260  8C0A  C49D  AA00  0400  0104  0800  4500    .`..D.*.......E.
0028  0B17  0000  3C06  3756  1E00  0063  1E00    .(.....7V...c..
0001  0017  19CB  11E7  39FA  0000  3E47  5010    .....K.g9z..GP.
0800  C766  0000                                  ..Gf..
```

Datalink:	Dest MAC	02608C 0AC49D	Source MAC:	AA0004 000104	Type(Length):	0800
IP:	Version:	4	IHL:	5	Type of service:	00
	Length:	0028	ID:	0B17	Flags:	0
	Offset:	0	Time to live:	60	Protocol:	06
	Checksum:	3756	Source IP:	30.0.0.99	Dest IP:	30.0.0.1
TCP:	Source port:	Telnet(0017)	Dest port:	19CB	Sequence:	11E739FA
	Acknowledge:	00003E47	Offset:	5	Code:	10(Ack)
	Window:	0400	Checksum:	C766		
Data:						

Frame 25 ("m")

```
AA00  0400  0104  0260  8C0A  C49D  0800  4500    *......`..D...E.
0029  0016  0000  FF06  7F55  1E00  0001  1E00    .).......U......
0063  19CB  0017  0000  3E47  11E7  39FA  5018    .c.K....G.g9zP.
0400  5E5D  0000  6D                              ..^]..m
```

Datalink:	Dest MAC:	AA0004 000104	Source MAC:	02608C 0AC49D	Type(Length):	0800
IP:	Version:	4	IHL:	5	Type of service:	00
	Length:	0029	ID:	0016	Flags:	0
	Offset:	0	Time to live:	255	Protocol:	06
	Checksum:	7F55	Source IP:	30.0.0.1	Dest IP:	30.0.0.99
TCP:	Source port:	Telnet(0017)	Dest port:	19CB	Sequence:	00003E47
	Acknowledge:	11E739FA	Offset:	5	Code:	18(Ack,Psh)
	Window:	0400	Checksum:	5E5D		
Data:	m					

Frame 26 (acknowledge and echo "M")

```
0260  8C0A  C49D  AA00  0400  0104  0800  4500    .`..D.*.......E.
0029  0B18  0000  3C06  3754  1E00  0063  1E00    .)......7T...c..
0001  0017  19CB  11E7  39FA  0000  3E48  5018    .....K.g9z..HP.
0800  7A5C  0000  4D                              ..z\..M
```

Datalink:	Dest MAC:	02608C 0AC49D	Source MAC:	AA0004 000104	Type(Length):	0800
IP:	Version:	4	IHL:	5	Type of service:	00
	Length:	0029	ID:	0B18	Flags:	0
	Offset:	0	Time to live:	3C(60)	Protocol:	06
	Checksum:	3754	Source IP:	30.0.0.99	Dest IP:	30.0.0.1
TCP:	Source port:	Telnet(0017)	Dest port:	19CB	Sequence:	11E739FA
	Acknowledge:	00003E48	Offset:	5	Code:	18(Ack,Psh)
	Window:	0400	Checksum:	7A5C		
Data:	M					

Frame 27 (acknowledge)

```
AA00  0400  0104  0260  8C0A  C49D  0800  4500    *......`..D....E.
0028  0017  0000  FF06  7F55  1E00  0001  1E00    .(.......U.....
0063  19CB  0017  0000  3E48  11E7  39FB  5010    .c.K....H.g9{P.
0400  CB64  0000                                  ..Kd..
```

Datalink:	Dest MAC:	AA0004 000104	Source MAC:	02608C 0AC49D	Type(Length):	0800
IP:	Version:	4	IHL:	5	Type of service:	00
	Length:	0028	ID:	0017	Flags:	0
	Offset:	0	Time to live:	FF(255)	Protocol:	06
	Checksum:	7F55	Source IP:	30.0.0.1	Dest IP:	30.0.0.99
TCP:	Source port:	Telnet(0017)	Dest port:	19CB	Sequence:	00003E42
	Acknowledge:	11E739F2	Offset:	5	Code:	10(Ack)
	Window:	0400	Checksum:	CB64		
Data:						

Frame 28 (password prompt)

```
0260  8C0A  C49D  AA00  0400  0104  0800  4500    .`..D.*.......E.
0034  0B1B  0000  3C06  3746  1E00  0063  1E00    .4.....7F...c..
0001  0017  19CB  11E7  39FD  0000  3E4A  5018    .....K.g9}..JP.
0800  D283  0000  0D00  5061  7373  776F  7264    ..R.....Password
3A20                                              :
```

Datalink:	Dest MAC:	02608C 0AC49D	Source MAC:	AA0004 000104	Type(Length):	0800
IP:	Version:	4	IHL:	5	Type of service:	00
	Length:	0034	ID:	0B1B	Flags:	0
	Offset:	0	Time to live:	3C(60)	Protocol:	06
	Checksum:	3746	Source IP:	30.0.0.99	Dest IP:	30.0.0.1
TCP:	Source port:	Telnet(0017)	Dest port:	19CB	Sequence:	11E739FD
	Acknowledge:	00003E4A	Offset:	5	Code:	18(Ack,Psh)
	Window:	0400	Checksum:	D283		
Data:	<cr>Password<sp>					

Frame 29 (acknowledge)

```
AA00  0400  0104  0260  8C0A  C49D  0800  4500    *......`..D...E.
0028  001D  0000  FF06  7F4F  1E00  0001  1E00    .(........O......
0063  19CB  0017  0000  3E4A  11E7  3A09  5010    .c.K....J.g:.P.
0400  CB54  0000                                  ..KT..
```

Datalink:	Dest MAC:	AA0004 000104	Source MAC:	02608C 0AC49D	Type(Length):	0800
IP:	Version:	4	IHL:	5	Type of service:	00
	Length:	0028	ID:	001D	Flags:	0
	Offset:	0	Time to live:	FF(255)	Protocol:	06
	Checksum:	7F4F	Source IP:	30.0.0.1	Dest IP:	30.0.0.99
TCP:	Source port:	Telnet(0017)	Dest port:	19CB	Sequence:	00003E4A
	Acknowledge:	11E73A09	Offset:	5	Code:	18(Ack,Psh)
	Window:	0400	Checksum:	CB54		
Data:						

FTP traces

This trace shows part of an FTP session, showing the user login and a directory listing. Parts of the trace have been left out as they did not add any new information about the protocol interaction, which is of interest to us here (in the missing frames usually the two nodes were exchanging acknowledgements).

Note particularly the use of the ASCII commands and responses, the FTP control port used for those commands and the new data port opened for a transfer. Note also that this version of FTP requests an IP type of service of 'throughput' (THRPT) for data transfer.

All acknowledgement Ethernet frames are padded out with six octets to make the minimum Ethernet size frame of 64 octets. The four octets of frame check sequence (cyclic redundancy check) are not shown. This padding can first be seen clearly in frame 8.

Frame 1 (TCP "syn" and mss negotiation of 1024)

```
AA00  0400  0104  0260  8C0A  C49D  0800  4500      *......`..D...E.
002C  0075  0000  FF06  7EF3  1E00  0001  1E00      .,.u....~s......
0063  1A57  0015  0000  1732  11E7  4257  6002      .c.W.....2.gBW`.
0400  D39A  0000  0204  0400  0000                  ..S.........
```

Datalink:	Dest MAC:	AA0004 000104	Source MAC:	02608C 0AC49D	Type(Length):	0800
IP:	Version:	4	IHL:	5	Type of service:	00
	Length:	0044	ID:	0075	Flags:	0
	Offset:	0	Time to live:	FF(255)	Protocol:	06
	Checksum:	7EF3	Source IP:	30.0.0.1	Dest IP:	30.0.0.99
TCP:	Source port:	1A57	Dest port:	FTP-Control	Sequence:	00001732
	Acknowledge:	NONE	Offset:	6	Code:	02(syn)
	Window:	0400	Checksum:	D39A	Options:	MSS 1024
Data:						

Frame 2 (TCP "syn" and "ack" and mss negotiation of 1024)

```
0260  8C0A  C49D  AA00  0400  0104  0800  4500    .`..D.*.......E.
002C  0B56  0000  3C06  3713  1E00  0063  1E00    .,.V...7....c..
0001  0015  1A57  1245  B9C0  0000  1733  6012    .....W.E9@...3`.
0400  5BC2  0000  0204  0400  0000                 ..[B......
```

Datalink:	Dest MAC:	02608C 0AC49D	Source MAC:	AA0004 000104	Type(Length):	0800
IP:	Version:	4	IHL:	5	Type of service:	00
	Length:	002C	ID:	0B56	Flags:	0
	Offset:	0	Time to live:	3C(60)	Protocol:	06
	Checksum:	3713	Source IP:	30.0.0.99	Dest IP:	30.0.0.1
TCP:	Source port:	FTP-Control	Dest port:	1A57	Sequence:	1245B9??
	Acknowledge:	000017??	Offset:	6	Code:	12(SYN,ACK)
	Window:	0400	Checksum:		Options:	mss1024
Data:						

Frame 3 (acknowledge)

```
AA00  0400  0104  0260  8C0A  C49D  0800  4500    *.......`..D...E.
0028  0076  0000  FF06  7EF6  1E00  0001  1E00    .(.v....~v.....
0063  1A57  0015  0000  1733  1245  B9C1  5018    .c.W.....3.E9AP.
0400  71C3  0000  0001  0800  0604                 ..qC.......
```

Datalink:	Dest MAC:	AA0004 000104	Source MAC:	02608C 0AC49D	Type(Length):	0800
IP:	Version:	4	IHL:	5	Type of service:	00
	Length:	0028	ID:	0076	Flags:	0
	Offset:	0	Time to live:	FF(255)	Protocol:	06
	Checksum:	7EF6	Source IP:	30.0.0.1	Dest IP:	30.0.0.99
TCP:	Source port:	1A57	Dest port:	FTP-Control	Sequence:	00001733
	Acknowledge:	1245B9C1	Offset:	5	Code:	18(psh,ack)
	Window:	0400	Checksum:	71C3		
Data:						

Frame 4 (FTP welcome banner)

```
0260  8C0A  C49D  AA00  0400  0104  0800  4500    .`..D.*.......E.
0099  0B57  0000  3C06  36A5  1E00  0063  1E00    ...W...6%...c..
0001  0015  1A57  1245  B9C1  0000  1733  5018    .....W.E9A...3P.
0400  82C8  0000  3232  302D  436F  6E6E  6563    ...H..220-Connec
7465  6420  746F  2046  5553  494F  4E20  4E65    ted to FUSION Ne
7477  6F72  6B20  536F  6674  7761  7265  2046    twork Software F
5450  2073  6572  7665  720D  0A32  3230  2040    TP server..220 @
2823  2920  5072  6F67  7261  6D20  5665  7273    (#) Program Vers
696F  6E3A  2039  2F31  2F38  3920  4020  3134    ion: 9/1/89 @ 14
3A34  303A  3030  202D  2D2D  2033  2E33  2E37    :40:00 --- 3.3.7
2040  2823  290D  0A                               @(#)..
```

Datalink:	Dest MAC:	02608C 0AC49D	Source MAC:	AA0004 000104	Type(Length):	0800
IP:	Version:	4	IHL:	5	Type of service:	00
	Length:	99	ID:	0B57	Flags:	0
	Offset:	0	Time to live:	3C(60)	Protocol:	06
	Checksum:	36A5	Source IP:	30.0.0.99	Dest IP:	30.0.0.1
TCP:	Source port:	FTP-Control	Dest port:	1A57	Sequence:	1245B9C1
	Acknowledge:	00001733	Offset:	5	Code:	
	Window:	0400	Checksum:	82C8		
Data:	220-Connected to FUSION Network Software FTP server..220 @(#)					
	Program Version: 9/1/89 @ 14:40:00 ---3.3.7@(#)<cr><lf>					

Connection established to FTP server

Frame 5 (acknowledge)

```
AA00  0400  0104  0260  8C0A  C49D  0800  4500    *......`..D...E.
0028  0077  0000  FF06  7EF5  1E00  0001  1E00    .(.w....~u......
0063  1A57  0015  0000  1733  1245  BA32  5010    .c.W.....3.E:2P.
0400  715A  0000  0001  0800  0604                ..qZ........
```

Datalink:	Dest MAC:	AA0004 000104	Source MAC:	02608C 0AC49D	Type(Length):	0800
IP:	Version:	4	IHL:	5	Type of service:	00
	Length:		ID:		Flags:	0
	Offset:	0	Time to live:	FF(255)	Protocol:	06
	Checksum:		Source IP:	30.0.0.1	Dest IP:	30.0.0.99
TCP:	Source port:	1A57	Dest port:	FTP-Control	Sequence:	000017??
	Acknowledge:		Offset:	5	Code:	18(psh,ack)
	Window:	0400	Checksum:			
Data:						

Frame 6 (FTP user login command for user "system")

```
AA00  0400  0104  0260  8C0A  C49D  0800  4500    *......`..D...E.
0035  0078  0000  FF06  7EE7  1E00  0001  1E00    .5.x....~g......
0063  1A57  0015  0000  1733  1245  BA32  5018    .c.W.....3.E:2P.
0400  5146  0000  5553  4552  2073  7973  7465    ..QF..USER syste
6D0D  0A                                          m..
```

Datalink:	Dest MAC:	AA0004 000104	Source MAC:	02608C 0AC49D	Type(Length):	0800
IP:	Version:	4	IHL:	5	Type of service:	00
	Length:	35	ID:	0078	Flags:	0
	Offset:	0	Time to live:	FF(255)	Protocol:	06
	Checksum:	7EE7	Source IP:	30.0.0.1	Dest IP:	30.0.0.99
TCP:	Source port:	1A57	Dest port:	FTP-Control	Sequence:	00001733
	Acknowledge:	1245BA32	Offset:	5	Code:	18(psh,ack)
	Window:	0400	Checksum:	5146		
Data:	USER system <cr><lf>					

Frame 7 (response from the FTP server)

```
0260  8C0A  C49D  AA00  0400  0104  0800  4500    .`..D.*.......E.
004C  0B58  0000  3C06  36F1  1E00  0063  1E00    .L.X...6q...c..
0001  0015  1A57  1245  BA32  0000  1740  5018    .....W.E:2...@P.
0400  C417  0000  3333  3120  5573  6572  206E    ..D...331 User n
616D  6520  6F6B  6179  2C20  6E65  6564  2070    ame okay, need p
6173  7377  6F72  642E  0D0A                      assword...
```

Datalink:	Dest MAC:	02608C 0AC49D	Source MAC:	AA0004 000104	Type(Length):	0800
IP:	Version:	4	IHL:	5	Type of service:	00
	Length:	004C	ID:	0B58	Flags:	0
	Offset:	0	Time to live:	3C(60)	Protocol:	06
	Checksum:	36F1	Source IP:	30.0.0.99	Dest IP:	30.0.0.1
TCP:	Source port:	FTP-Control	Dest port:	1A57	Sequence:	1245BA32
	Acknowledge:	00001740	Offset:	5	Code:	12(syn,psh)
	Window:	0400	Checksum:	C417		
Data:	331 User name okay, need password <cr><lf>					

Frame 8 (acknowledgement)

```
AA00   0400   0104   0260   8C0A   C49D   0800   4500      *......`..D...E.
0028   0079   0000   FF06   7EF3   1E00   0001   1E00      .(.y....~s......
0063   1A57   0015   0000   1740   1245   BA56   5010      .c.W.....@.E:VP.
0400   7129   0000   5553   4552   2073                    ..q)..USER s
```

Datalink:	Dest MAC:	AA0004 000104	Source MAC:	02608C 0AC49D	Type(Length):	0800
IP:	Version:	4	IHL:	5	Type of service:	00
	Length:	28	ID:	0079	Flags:	0
	Offset:	0	Time to live:	FF(255)	Protocol:	06
	Checksum:	7EF3	Source IP:	30.0.0.1	Dest IP:	30.0.0.99
TCP:	Source port:	1A57	Dest port:	FTP-Control	Sequence:	00001740
	Acknowledge:	1245BA56	Offset:	5	Code:	10(ack)
	Window:	0400	Checksum:	7129		
Data:						

Note the padding 'USER s' in this acknowledgement frame. This is formed from random characters in the buffer from the last data frame sent by this machine.

Frame 9 (acknowledgement)

```
0260   8C0A   C49D   AA00   0400   0104   0800   4500      .`..D.*.......E.
0028   0B59   0000   3C06   3714   1E00   0063   1E00      .(.Y...7....c..
0001   0015   1A57   1245   BA56   0000   174D   5010      .....W.E:V...MP.
0400   711C   0000   0000   0000   0000                    ..q.........
```

Datalink:	Dest MAC:	02608C 0AC49D	Source MAC:	AA0004 000104	Type(Length):	0800
IP:	Version:	4	IHL:	5	Type of service:	00
	Length:	0028	ID:	0B59	Flags:	0
	Offset:	0	Time to live:	3C(60)	Protocol:	06
	Checksum:	3714	Source IP:	30.0.0.99	Dest IP:	30.0.0.1
TCP:	Source port:	FTP-Control	Dest port:	1A57	Sequence:	1245BA56
	Acknowledge:	0000174D	Offset:	5	Code:	10(ACK)
	Window:	0400	Checksum:	711C		
Data:						

The password transmission has been omitted.

Frame 10 (acknowledgement)

```
AA00   0400   0104   0260   8C0A   C49D   0800   4500      *......`..D...E.
0028   007C   0000   FF06   7EF0   1E00   0001   1E00      .(.|....~p......
0063   1A57   0015   0000   174D   1245   BA56   5010      .c.W.....M.E:VP.
0400   711C   0000   5041   5353   2069                    ..q...PASS i
```

Datalink:	Dest MAC:	AA0004 000104	Source MAC:	02608C 0AC49D	Type(Length):	0800
IP:	Version:	4	IHL:	5	Type of service:	00
	Length:	0028	ID:	007C	Flags:	0
	Offset:	0	Time to live:	FF(255)	Protocol:	06
	Checksum:	7EF0	Source IP:	30.0.0.1	Dest IP:	30.0.0.99
TCP:	Source port:	1A57	Dest port:	FTP-Control	Sequence:	0000174D
	Acknowledge:	1245BA56	Offset:	5	Code:	19(ack)
	Window:	0400	Checksum:	711C		
Data:						

Frame 11 (user logged in message to FTP client)

```
0260  8C0A  C49D  AA00  0400  0104  0800  4500    .`..D.*.......E.
0046  0B5A  0000  3C06  36F5  1E00  0063  1E00    .F.Z...6u...c..
0001  0015  1A57  1245  BA56  0000  174D  5018    .....W.E:V...MP.
0400  AC61  0000  3233  3020  5573  6572  206C    ..,a..230 User l
6F67  6765  6420  696E  2C20  7072  6F63  6565    ogged in, procee
642E  0D0A                                        d...
```

Datalink:	Dest MAC:	02608C 0AC49D	Source MAC:	AA0004 000104	Type(Length):	0800
IP:	Version:	4	IHL:	5	Type of service:	00
	Length:	0046	ID:	0B5A	Flags:	0
	Offset:	0	Time to live:	3C(60)	Protocol:	06
	Checksum:	36F5	Source IP:	30.0.0.99	Dest IP:	30.0.0.1
TCP:	Source port:	FTP-Control	Dest port:	1A57	Sequence:	1245BA56
	Acknowledge:	0000174D	Offset:	5	Code:	18(psh,ack)
	Window:	0400	Checksum:	AC61		
Data:	230 User logged in, proceed <cr><lf>					

Frame 12 (acknowledge)

```
AA00  0400  0104  0260  8C0A  C49D  0800  4500    *......`..D...E.
0028  007D  0000  FF06  7EEF  1E00  0001  1E00    .(.}....~o......
0063  1A57  0015  0000  174D  1245  BA74  5010    .c.W.....M.E:tP.
0400  70FE  0000  5041  5353  2069                 ..p~..PASS i
```

Datalink:	Dest MAC:	AA0004 000104	Source MAC:	02608C 0AC49D	Type(Length):	0800
IP:	Version:	4	IHL:	5	Type of service:	00
	Length:	28	ID:	007D	Flags:	0
	Offset:	0	Time to live:	FF(255)	Protocol:	06
	Checksum:	7EEF	Source IP:	30.0.0.1	Dest IP:	30.0.0.99
TCP:	Source port:	1A57	Dest port:	FTP-Control	Sequence:	0000174D
	Acknowledge:	1245BA74	Offset:	5	Code:	10(ack)
	Window:	0400	Checksum:	70FE		
Data:						

Frame 13 (FTP command CWD changes working directory on the server to 'user1')

```
AA00  0400  0104  0260  8C0A  C49D  0800  4500    *......`..D...E.
0033  008C  0000  FF06  7ED5  1E00  0001  1E00    .3......~U......
0063  1A57  0015  0000  1794  1245  BB8D  5018    .c.W.......E;.P.
0400  D220  0000  4357  4420  7573  6572  310D    ..R ..CWD user1.
0A                                                 .
```

Datalink:	Dest MAC:	AA0004 000104	Source MAC:	02608C 0AC49D	Type(Length):	0800
IP:	Version:	4	IHL:	5	Type of service:	00
	Length:	33	ID:	008C	Flags:	0
	Offset:	0	Time to live:	FF(255)	Protocol:	06
	Checksum:	7ED5	Source IP:	30.0.0.1	Dest IP:	30.0.0.99
TCP:	Source port:	1A57	Dest port:	FTP-Control	Sequence:	00001794
	Acknowledge:	1245BB8D	Offset:	5	Code:	18(psh,ack)
	Window:	0400	Checksum:	D220		
Data:	CWD user1 <cr><lf>					

Frame 14 (response from FTP server)

```
0260  8C0A  C49D  AA00  0400  0104  0800  4500    .`..D.*.......E.
0061  0B66  0000  3C06  36CE  1E00  0063  1E00    .a.f...6N...c..
0001  0015  1A57  1245  BB8D  0000  179F  5018    .....W.E;.....P.
07F5  1FCD  0000  3235  3020  4469  7265  6374    .u.M..250 Direct
6F72  7920  6368  616E  6765  6420  746F  2022    ory changed to "
444B  4233  3030  3A5B  3030  3030  3030  2E47    DKB300:[000000.G
5545  5354  2E55  5345  5231  5D22  2E0D  0A      UEST.USER1]"...
```

Datalink:	Dest MAC:	02608C 0AC49D	Source MAC:	AA0004 000104	Type(Length):	0800
IP:	Version:	4	IHL:	5	Type of service:	00
	Length:	0061	ID:	0B66	Flags:	0
	Offset:	0	Time to live:	3C(60)	Protocol:	06
	Checksum:	36CE	Source IP:	30.0.0.99	Dest IP:	30.0.0.1
TCP:	Source port:	FTP-Control	Dest port:	1A57	Sequence:	1245BB8D
	Acknowledge:	0000179F	Offset:	5	Code:	18(psh,ack)
	Window:	07F5	Checksum:	1FCD		
Data:	250 Directory changed to "DKB300:[000000.GUEST.USER1]"<cr><lf>					

Frame 15

```
AA00  0400  0104  0260  8C0A  C49D  0800  4500    *......`..D...E.
0028  008D  0000  FF06  7EDF  1E00  0001  1E00    .(......~_.....
0063  1A57  0015  0000  179F  1245  BBC6  5010    .c.W.......E;FP.
0400  6F5A  0000  4357  4420  7573              ..oZ..CWD us
```

Datalink:	Dest MAC:	AA0004 000104	Source MAC:	02608C 0AC49D	Type(Length):	0800
IP:	Version:	4	IHL:	5	Type of service:	00
	Length:	28	ID:	008D	Flags:	0
	Offset:	0	Time to live:	FF(255)	Protocol:	06
	Checksum:	7EDF	Source IP:	30.0.0.1	Dest IP:	30.0.0.99
TCP:	Source port:	1A57	Dest port:	FTP-Control	Sequence:	0000179F
	Acknowledge:	1245BBC6	Offset:	5	Code:	10(ack)
	Window:	0400	Checksum:	6F5A		
Data:						

Frame 16 (FTP client indicates the socket [ip address and port] the server should use to return the results of the following command)

```
AA00  0400  0104  0260  8C0A  C49D  0800  4500    *......`..D...E.
003D  008E  0000  FF06  7EC9  1E00  0001  1E00    .=......~I......
0063  1A57  0015  0000  179F  1245  BBC6  5018    .c.W.......E;FP.
0400  5044  0000  504F  5254  2033  302C  302C    ..PD..PORT 30,0,
302C  312C  3132  2C32  330D  0A               0,1,12,23..
```

Datalink:	Dest MAC:	AA0004 000104	Source MAC:	02608C 0AC49D	Type(Length):	0800
IP:	Version:	4	IHL:	5	Type of service:	00
	Length:	003D	ID:	008E	Flags:	0
	Offset:	0	Time to live:	FF(255)	Protocol:	06
	Checksum:	7EC9	Source IP:	30.0.0.1	Dest IP:	30.0.0.99
TCP:	Source port:	1A57	Dest port:	FTP-Control	Sequence:	0000179F
	Acknowledge:	1245BBC6	Offset:	5	Code:	18(psh,ack)
	Window:	0400	Checksum:	5044		
Data:	PORT 30,0,0,1,12,23<cr><lf>					

Frame 17 (FTP server response)

```
0260   8C0A   C49D   AA00   0400   0104   0800   4500      .`..D.*.......E.
003B   0B67   0000   3C06   36F3   1E00   0063   1E00      .;.g...6s...c..
0001   0015   1A57   1245   BBC6   0000   17B4   5018      .....W.E;F...4P.
07E0   899C   0000   3230   3020   436F   6D6D   616E      .`....200 Comman
6420   6F6B   6179   2E0D   0A                             d okay...
```

Datalink:	Dest MAC:	02608C 0AC49D	Source MAC:	AA0004 000104	Type(Length):	0800
IP:	Version:	4	IHL:	5	Type of service:	00
	Length:	003B	ID:	0B67	Flags:	0
	Offset:	0	Time to live:	3C(60)	Protocol:	06
	Checksum:	36F3	Source IP:	30.0.0.99	Dest IP:	30.0.0.1
TCP:	Source port:	FTP-Control	Dest port:	1A57	Sequence:	1245BBC6
	Acknowledge:	000017B4	Offset:	5	Code:	18(psh,ack)
	Window:	07E0	Checksum:	899C		
Data:	200 Command okay <cr><lf>					

Frame 18 (acknowledgement)

```
AA00   0400   0104   0260   8C0A   C49D   0800   4500      *......`..D...E.
0028   008F   0000   FF06   7EDD   1E00   0001   1E00      .(.......~]......
0063   1A57   0015   0000   17B4   1245   BBD9   5010      .c.W.....4.E;YP.
0400   6F32   0000   504F   5254   2033                    ..o2..PORT 3
```

Datalink:	Dest MAC:	AA0004 000104	Source MAC:	02608C 0AC49D	Type(Length):	0800
IP:	Version:	4	IHL:	5	Type of service:	00
	Length:	0028	ID:	008F	Flags:	0
	Offset:	0	Time to live:	FF(255)	Protocol:	06
	Checksum:	7EDD	Source IP:	30.0.0.1	Dest IP:	30.0.0.99
TCP:	Source port:	1A57	Dest port:	FTP-Control	Sequence:	000017B4
	Acknowledge:	1245BBD9	Offset:	5	Code:	10(ack)
	Window:	0400	Checksum:	6F32		
Data:						

Frame 19 (FTP client sends directory listing command LIST to FTP server)

```
AA00   0400   0104   0260   8C0A   C49D   0800   4500      *......`..D...E.
002E   0090   0000   FF06   7ED6   1E00   0001   1E00      .........~V......
0063   1A57   0015   0000   17B4   1245   BBD9   5018      .c.W.....4.E;YP.
0400   C27C   0000   4C49   5354   0D0A                    ..B|..LIST..
```

Datalink:	Dest MAC:	AA0004 000104	Source MAC:	02608C 0AC49D	Type(Length):	0800
IP:	Version:	4	IHL:	5	Type of service:	00
	Length:	002E	ID:	0090	Flags:	0
	Offset:	0	Time to live:	FF(255)	Protocol:	06
	Checksum:	7ED6	Source IP:	30.0.0.1	Dest IP:	30.0.0.99
TCP:	Source port:	1A57	Dest port:	FTP-Control	Sequence:	000017B4
	Acknowledge:	1245BBD9	Offset:	5	Code:	18(psh,ack)
	Window:	0400	Checksum:	C2C7		
Data:	LIST <cr><lf>					

Frame 20 (FTP server acknowledging the request to perform a LIST command and return the output to socket 30.0.0.1.12.23 [12.13 represents the port (12*256 + 13) 3095 in decimal, 0C17 in hexadecimal])

```
0260  8C0A  C49D  AA00  0400  0104  0800  4500    .`..D.*.......E.
0062  0B68  0000  3C06  36CB  1E00  0063  1E00    .b.h...6K...c..
0001  0015  1A57  1245  BBD9  0000  17BA  5018    .....W.E;Y...:P.
07DA  1E58  0000  3135  3020  4F70  656E  696E    .Z.X..150 Openin
6720  6461  7461  2063  6F6E  6E65  6374  696F    g data connectio
6E20  666F  7220  284C  4953  5420  2920  2833    n for (LIST ) (3
302E  302E  302E  312C  3330  3935  292E  0D0A    0.0.0.1,3095)...
```

Datalink:	Dest MAC:	02608C 0AC49D	Source MAC:	AA0004 000104	Type(Length):	0800
IP:	Version:	4	IHL:	5	Type of service:	00
	Length:	0062	ID:	0B68	Flags:	0
	Offset:	0	Time to live:	3C(60)	Protocol:	06
	Checksum:	36CB	Source IP:	30.0.0.99	Dest IP:	30.0.0.1
TCP:	Source port:	FTP-Control	Dest port:	1A57	Sequence:	1245B9D9
	Acknowledge:	000017BA	Offset:	5	Code:	18(psh,ack)
	Window:	0400	Checksum:			
Data:	:	150 Opening data connection for (LIST) (30.0.0.1,3095) <cr><lf>				

Insignificant frames left out

Frame 21 (FTP server starting a new connection to port 30.0.0.1.12.23 ready to transfer the data from the LIST command)

```
0260  8C0A  C49D  AA00  0400  0104  0800  4500    .`..D.*.......E.
002C  0B69  0000  3C06  3700  1E00  0063  1E00    .,.i...7....c..
0001  0014  0C17  180C  CAF6  0000  0000  6002    ........Jv....`.
0000  6CC1  0000  0204  0588  0000              ..lA........
```

Datalink:	Dest MAC:	02608C 0AC49D	Source MAC:	AA0004 000104	Type(Length):	0800
IP:	Version:	4	IHL:	5	Type of service:	00
	Length:	002C	ID:	0B69	Flags:	0
	Offset:	0	Time to live:	3C(60)	Protocol:	06
	Checksum:	3700	Source IP:	30.0.0.99	Dest IP:	30.0.0.1
TCP:	Source port:	FTP-DATA	Dest port:	0C17	Sequence:	180CCAF6
	Acknowledge:	NONE	Offset:	6	Code:	02(SYN)
	Window:	0	Checksum:		options:	MSS 1416
Data:	:					

Frame 22 (acknowledge to 20)

```
AA00  0400  0104  0260  8C0A  C49D  0800  4500    *......`..D...E.
0028  0091  0000  FF06  7EDB  1E00  0001  1E00    .(.......~[......
0063  1A57  0015  0000  17BA  1245  BC13  5010    .c.W.....:.E.P.
0400  6EF2  0000  0D00  0000  0000              ..nr........
```

Datalink:	Dest MAC:	AA0004 000104	Source MAC:	02608C 0AC49D	Type(Length):	0800
IP:	Version:	4	IHL:	5	Type of service:	00
	Length:	0028	ID:	0091	Flags:	0
	Offset:	0	Time to live:	FF(255)	Protocol:	06
	Checksum:	7EDB	Source IP:	30.0.0.1	Dest IP:	30.0.0.99
TCP:	Source port:	1A57	Dest port:	FTP-Control	Sequence:	000017BA
	Acknowledge:	1245BC13	Offset:	5	Code:	10(ack)
	Window:	0400	Checksum:	6EF2		
Data:						

Frame 23 ("syn" and "ack" for new connection plus mss negotiation)

```
AA00  0400  0104  0260  8C0A  C49D  0800  4500      *......`..D...E.
002C  0092  0000  FF06  7ED6  1E00  0001  1E00      .,......~V......
0063  0C17  0014  0000  0A9E  180C  CAF7  6012      .c...........Jw`.
0400  5F9A  0000  0204  0400  4F70                  .._.......Op
```

Datalink:	Dest MAC:	AA0004 000104	Source MAC:	02608C 0AC49D	Type(Length):	0800
IP:	Version:	4	IHL:	5	Type of service:	00
	Length:	002C	ID:	0092	Flags:	0
	Offset:	0	Time to live:	255	Protocol:	06
	Checksum:	7ED6	Source IP:	30.0.0.1	Dest IP:	30.0.0.99
TCP:	Source port:	0C17	Dest port:	FTP-DATA	Sequence:	000017??
	Acknowledge:		Offset:	5	Code:	12(syn,ack)
	Window:	0400	Checksum:	5F9A	options:	MSS 1024
Data:						

Frame 24 (acknowledge)

```
0260  8C0A  C49D  AA00  0400  0104  0800  4500      .`..D.*.......E.
0028  0B6A  0000  3C06  3703  1E00  0063  1E00      .(.j...7....c..
0001  0014  0C17  180C  CAF7  0000  0A9F  5010      ........Jw....P.
0400  75A3  0000  0000  0000  0000                  ..u#........
```

Datalink:	Dest MAC:	02608C 0AC49D	Source MAC:	AA0004 000104	Type(Length):	0800
IP:	Version:	4	IHL:	5	Type of service:	00
	Length:	0028	ID:	0B6A	Flags:	0
	Offset:	0	Time to live:	60	Protocol:	06
	Checksum:	3703	Source IP:	30.0.0.99	Dest IP:	30.0.0.1
TCP:	Source port:	FTP-DATA	Dest port:	0C17	Sequence:	180CCAF7
	Acknowledge:	00000A9F	Offset:	5	Code:	12(ACK)
	Window:	0400	Checksum:	75A3		
Data:						

Frame 25 (directory listing being transferred)

```
0260  8C0A  C49D  AA00  0400  0104  0800  4508      .`..D.*.......E.
0278  0B6B  0000  3C06  34AA  1E00  0063  1E00      .x.k...4*...c..
0001  0014  0C17  180C  CAF7  0000  0A9F  5018      ........Jw....P.
0400  8B59  0000  4654  5044  2E4C  4F47  3B32      ...Y..FTPD.LOG;2
2020  2020  2020  2020  2020  205B  5553  4552            [USER
315D  2020  2020  352F  3620  2020  2032  362D      1]    5/6    26-
```

Frame 25 continued on page 562

4155	472D	3139	3930	2031	353A	3534	2020	AUG-1990 15:54
2852	5745	442C	5257	4544	2C52	452C	290D	(RWED,RWED,RE,).
0A46	5450	442E	4C4F	473B	3120	2020	2020	.FTPD.LOG;1
2020	2020	2020	5B55	5345	5231	5D20	2020	[USER1]
2035	2F36	2020	2020	3236	2D41	5547	2D31	5/6 26-AUG-1
3939	3020	3135	3A35	3420	2028	5257	4544	990 15:54 (RWED
2C52	5745	442C	5245	2C29	0D0A	4753	532E	,RWED,RE,)..GSS.
3B31	2020	2020	2020	2020	2020	2020	2020	;1
205B	4755	4553	545D	2020	2020	302F	3133	[GUEST] 0/13
3737	2020	312D	4A55	4E2D	3139	3930	2031	77 1-JUN-1990 1
303A	3337	2020	2852	5744	2C52	5744	2C52	0:37 (RWD,RWD,R
5744	2C52	5744	290D	0A48	454C	4C4F	2E4D	WD,RWD)..HELLO.M
5347	3B31	2020	2020	2020	2020	2020	5B55	SG;1 [U
5345	5231	5D20	2020	2031	2F33	2020	2020	SER1] 1/3
3234	2D4A	554C	2D31	3939	3020	3039	3A31	24-JUL-1990 09:1
3120	2028	5257	4544	2C52	5745	442C	5245	1 (RWED,RWED,RE
2C29	0D0A	4D41	494C	2E4D	4149	3B31	2020	,)..MAIL.MAI;1
2020	2020	2020	2020	205B	5553	4552	315D	[USER1]
2020	2033	302F	3330	2020	2032	342D	4A55	30/30 24-JU
4C2D	3139	3930	2031	343A	3334	2020	2852	L-1990 14:34 (R
572C	5257	2C2C	290D	0A4D	452E	3B31	2020	W,RW,,)..ME.;1
2020	2020	2020	2020	2020	2020	2020	5B55	[U
5345	5231	5D20	2020	2031	2F33	2020	2020	SER1] 1/3
3234	2D4A	554C	2D31	3939	3020	3134	3A33	24-JUL-1990 14:3
3920	2028	5257	4544	2C52	5745	442C	5245	9 (RWED,RWED,RE
2C29	0D0A	5354	432E	3B31	2020	2020	2020	,)..STC.;1
2020	2020	2020	2020	205B	4755	4553	545D	[GUEST]
2020	2033	382F	3435	2020	2033	312D	4D41	38/45 31-MA
592D	3139	3930	2031	393A	3334	2020	2852	Y-1990 19:34 (R
5744	2C52	5744	2C52	5744	2C52	5744	290D	WD,RWD,RWD,RWD).
0A54	454D	502E	434F	4D3B	3120	2020	2020	.TEMP.COM;1
2020	2020	2020	5B47	5545	5354	5D20	2020	[GUEST]
3137	2F31	3820	2020	2031	2D4A	554E	2D31	17/18 1-JUN-1
3939	3020	3130	3A33	3120	2028	522C	522C	990 10:31 (R,R,
522C	5229	0D0A						R,R)..

Datalink:	Dest MAC:	02608C 0AC49D	Source MAC:	AA0004 000104	Type(Length):	0800
IP:	Version:	4	IHL:	5	Type of service:	08(THRPT)
	Length:	0278	ID:	0B6B	Flags:	0
	Offset:	0	Time to live:	60	Protocol:	06
	Checksum:	34AA	Source IP:	30.0.0.99	Dest IP:	30.0.0.1
TCP:	Source port:	FTP-DATA	Dest port:	0C17	Sequence:	180CCAF7
	Acknowledge:	00000A9F	Offset:	5	Code:	18(psh,ack)
	Window:	0400	Checksum:	8B59		

Data:				
	FTPD.LOG;2		[USER1]	5/6 26-AUG-1990
	15:54 (RWED,RWED,RE,)..FTPD.LOG;1			[USER1]
	5/6 26-AUG-1990 15:54 (RWED,RWED,RE,)..GSS.;1
	[GUEST]		0/1377	1-JUN-1990 10:37
	(RWD,RWD,RWD,RWD)..HELLO.MSG;1			[USER1]
	1/3			24-JUL-1990 09:11
	(RWED,RWED,RE,)..MAIL.MAI;1			[USER1]
	30/30		24-JUL-1990 14:34
	[USER1]		1/3	(RW,RW,,)..ME.;1
				24-JUL-1990 14:39
	(RWED,RWED,RE,)..STC.;1			[GUEST]
	38/45		31-MAY-1990	19:34
	(RWD,RWD,RWD,RWD)..TEMP.COM;1			[GUEST]
	17/18 1-JUN-1990 10:31 (R,R,R,R). <cr><lf>

Frame 26 (acknowledgement)

```
AA00  0400  0104  0260  8C0A  C49D  0800  4500        *.......`..D...E.
0028  0093  0000  FF06  7ED9  1E00  0001  1E00        .(.......~Y......
0063  0C17  0014  0000  0A9F  180C  CD47  5010        .c..........MGP.
0400  7353  0000  4F70  656E  696E                    ..sS..Openin
```

Datalink:	Dest MAC:	AA0004 000104	Source MAC:	02608C 0AC49D	Type(Length):	0800
IP:	Version:	4	IHL:	5	Type of service:	00
	Length:	0028	ID:	0093	Flags:	0
	Offset:	0	Time to live:	FF(255)	Protocol:	06
	Checksum:	7ED9	Source IP:	30.0.0.1	Dest IP:	30.0.0.99
TCP:	Source port:	1A57	Dest port:	FTP-DATA	Sequence:	00000A9F
	Acknowledge:	180CCD47	Offset:	5	Code:	10(ack)
	Window:	0400	Checksum:	7353		
Data:						

Frame 27 (more of the directory listing)

```
0260  8C0A  C49D  AA00  0400  0104  0800  4508        .`..D.*.......E.
0075  0B6C  0000  3C06  36AC  1E00  0063  1E00        .u.l...6,...c..
0001  0014  0C17  180C  CD47  0000  0A9F  5019        ........MG....P.
0001  1E46  0000  544F  5543  484F  5349  2E43        ...F..TOUCHOSI.C
4647  3B31  2020  2020  2020  205B  4755  4553        FG;1        [GUES
545D  2020  2020  362F  3920  2020  2020  312D        T]      6/9       1-
4A55  4E2D  3139  3930  2031  303A  3032  2020        JUN-1990 10:02
2852  5744  2C52  5744  2C52  5744  2C52  5744        (RWD,RWD,RWD,RWD
290D  0A                                              )..
```

Datalink:	Dest MAC:	02608C 0AC49D	Source MAC:	AA0004 000104	Type(Length):	0800
IP:	Version:	4	IHL:	5	Type of service:	08(THRPT)
	Length:	0075	ID:	0B6C	Flags:	0
	Offset:	0	Time to live:	3C(60)	Protocol:	06
	Checksum:	36AC	Source IP:	30.0.0.99	Dest IP:	30.0.0.1
TCP:	Source port:	FTP-DATA	Dest port:	0C17	Sequence:	180CCD47
	Acknowledge:	00000A9F	Offset:	5	Code:	19(psh,fin,ack)
	Window:	0001	Checksum:	1E46		
Data:	TOUCHOSI.CFG;1		[GUEST]	6/9	1-JUN-1990	
	10:02 (RWD,RWD,RWD,RWD) <cr><lf>					

Frame 28 (the data connection is finished with)

```
0260  8C0A  C49D  AA00  0400  0104  0800  4500        .`..D.*.......E.
0046  0B6D  0000  3C06  36E2  1E00  0063  1E00        .F.m...6b...c..
0001  0015  1A57  1245  BC13  0000  17BA  5018        .....W.E....:P.
07DA  601B  0000  3232  3620  436C  6F73  696E        .Z`...226 Closin
6720  6461  7461  2063  6F6E  6E65  6374  696F        g data connectio
6E2E  0D0A                                            n...
```

Datalink:	Dest MAC:	02608C 0AC49D	Source MAC:	AA0004 000104	Type(Length):	0800
IP:	Version:	4	IHL:	5	Type of service:	00
	Length:	0046	ID:	0B6D	Flags:	0
	Offset:	0	Time to live:	3C(60)	Protocol:	06
	Checksum:	36E2	Source IP:	30.0.0.99	Dest IP:	30.0.0.1
TCP:	Source port:	FTP-Control	Dest port:	1A57	Sequence:	1245BC13
	Acknowledge:	000017BA	Offset:	5	Code:	18(psh,ack)
	Window:	07DA	Checksum:	601B		
Data:	226 Closing data connection <cr><lf>					

Frame 29 (acknowledge, data connection)

```
AA00   0400   0104   0260   8C0A   C49D   0800   4500      *......`..D...E.
0028   0094   0000   FF06   7ED8   1E00   0001   1E00      .(......~X......
0063   0C17   0014   0000   0A9F   180C   CD95   5010      .c..........M.P.
0400   7305   0000   0D00   0000   0000                    ..s.........
```

Datalink:	Dest MAC:	AA0004 000104	Source MAC:	02608C 0AC49D	Type(Length):	0800
IP:	Version:	4	IHL:	5	Type of service:	00
	Length:	0028	ID:	0094	Flags:	0
	Offset:	0	Time to live:	FF(255)	Protocol:	06
	Checksum:	7ED8	Source IP:	30.0.0.1	Dest IP:	30.0.0.99
TCP:	Source port:	0C17	Dest port:	FTP-DATA	Sequence:	00000A9F
	Acknowledge:	180CCD95	Offset:	5	Code:	10(ack)
	Window:	0400	Checksum:	7305		
Data:	:					

Frame 30 (acknowledge control connection)

```
AA00   0400   0104   0260   8C0A   C49D   0800   4500      *......`..D...E.
0028   0095   0000   FF06   7ED7   1E00   0001   1E00      .(......~W......
0063   1A57   0015   0000   17BA   1245   BC31   5010      .c.W.....:.EP.
0400   6ED4   0000   484F   5349   2E43                    ..nT..HOSI.C
```

Datalink:	Dest MAC:	AA0004 000104	Source MAC:	02608C 0AC49D	Type(Length):	0800
IP:	Version:	4	IHL:	5	Type of service:	00
	Length:	0028	ID:	0095	Flags:	0
	Offset:	0	Time to live:	FF(255)	Protocol:	06
	Checksum:	7ED7	Source IP:	30.0.0.1	Dest IP:	30.0.0.99
TCP:	Source port:	1A57	Dest port:	FTP-Control	Sequence:	000017BA
	Acknowledge:	1245BC31	Offset:	5	Code:	10(ack)
	Window:	0400	Checksum:	6ED4		
Data:	:					

Frame 31 (data connection closing)

```
AA00   0400   0104   0260   8C0A   C49D   0800   4500      *......`..D...E.
0028   0096   0000   FF06   7ED6   1E00   0001   1E00      .(......~V......
0063   0C17   0014   0000   0A9F   180C   CD95   5019      .c..........M.P.
0400   72FC   0000   436C   6F73   696E                    ..r|..Closin
```

Datalink:	Dest MAC:	AA0004 000104	Source MAC:	02608C 0AC49D	Type(Length):	0800
IP:	Version:	4	IHL:	5	Type of service:	00
	Length:	0028	ID:	0096	Flags:	0
	Offset:	0	Time to live:	FF(255)	Protocol:	06
	Checksum:	7ED6	Source IP:	30.0.0.1	Dest IP:	30.0.0.99
TCP:	Source port:	0C17	Dest port:	FTP-DATA	Sequence:	00000A9F
	Acknowledge:	180CCD95	Offset:	5	Code:	19(psh,ack,fin)
	Window:	0400	Checksum:	72FC		
Data:	:					

J

ASN.1 and BER tag types

ASN.1 (Abstract Syntax Notation Number 1) is an international high-level language used with software which allows 'objects' to be defined and described in a standard way, based on a few fundamental types and values such as object identifiers, integers, Boolean, real numbers, strings, characters, sequences, sets and enumerated values. In network management these objects are used to refer to aspects of a communication system, such as a serial number or software type and version, an interface card and its frame counts, collisions and error conditions it sees.

The Basic Encoding Rules (BER) describe how the ASN.1 language 'compiles' to a sequence of octets that unambiguously represents the description of the object and is what can be seen in protocol traces of SNMP. There are four classes of identifiers: universal, application, context specific and private. Of these, 'universal' is the class which will ensure that objects can be understood by everyone.

The first octet of any description contains the tag which classifies the object. The second (and perhaps later) octets give the length of the whole description. As discussed in Chapter 17, a tag consists of three components: the class, the form (a primitive/constructed flag) and the tag number within the class (Table J.1).

Table J.1 Tag components.

Name	Bits	Values	Meaning
Tag class	8,7	00	Universal
		01	Application wide
		10	Context specific
		11	Private use
Form	6	0	Primitive
		1	Constructed
Tag value	5,4,3,2,1	0–30	The value indicates the characteristics of the item

Table J.2 SNMP tags.

ASN.1 identifier	Class	P/C*	Number
Integer	Universal	P	2
Octet string	Universal	P	4
Object identifier	Universal	P	6
Sequence	Universal	C	16
Null	Universal	P	5

* P/C is primitive/constructed

The universal class of tags defines up to 30 basic types of items for which a single octet can act as a header. These basic types are predefined or reserved by ISO/CCITT. Further and indefinite extension beyond 30 types is possible as the tag with the value 31 is used to indicate that the following octets indicate a tag value bigger than 31. But this extension is not required for SNMP which uses only five simple types. One of these is **sequence**. By using sequence, more complex constructed types can be built.

The ASN.1 identifiers used by SNMP and their tags are listed in Table J.2. When these are encoded using the BER, the octet identifiers which result are those given in Table J.3.

An octet of Table J.3 will be the first octet of a sequence which describes one item and it will be followed by a single- or multiple-octet length field which indicates how many octets follow in this item. A single-octet length, which can indicate a length up to 127, is normally all that is required for SNMP.

When SNMP is used to manage Internet equipment, the tag object identifier defines the item or object from the management information base (MIB) which is to be described. An MIB is a tree structure in which the branches and leaves identify objects and the parameters which are to be managed. The start of the tree for Internet MIB II is shown in Figure J.1. Each object can be described as a sequence of numbers. For human use these are written down in dotted notation, reading from the top of the tree. If we wish to refer to the ICMP protocol, the sequence would be:

1.3.6.1.2.1.5

Table J.3 Encoding SNMP basic identifiers.

ASN.1 identifier	Binary	Hex
Integer	00000010	2
Octet string	00000100	4
Object identifier	00000110	6
Sequence	00110000	30
Null	00000101	5

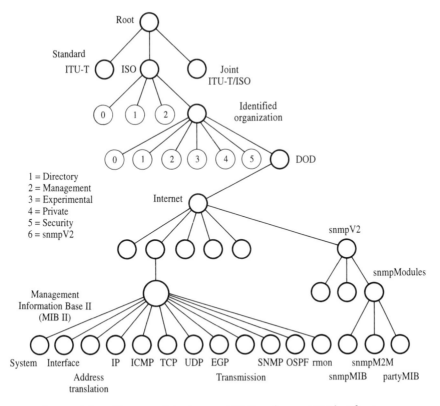

Figure J.1   The start of the Internet MIB II and snmp V2 identifier trees.

We cannot give the whole MIB, but we find the ICMP group contains items to access counters for all the major types of ICMP messages received, for example destination unreachable (3), time exceeded (4), source quench (6) and redirect requests (7). So each of these would be referred to as:

      1.3.6.1.2.1.5.3
      1.3.6.1.2.1.5.4
      1.3.6.1.2.1.5.6
      1.3.6.1.2.1.5.7

SNMPv2 uses a new set of MIBs as branch 6 from the Internet identifier – an item in the snmpV2MIB is identified by

      1.3.6.1.6.3.1

Basic encoding rules

The Basic Encoding Rules (BER) describe how the identifiers of ASN.1 are carried on a network. When the numeric sequences produced above are transmitted across a network in SNMP, they are preceded by the tag for object identifier. The sequence of numbers

0607 2B06 0102 0105 07

can then be decoded as follows: From Table J.3, the value 06 is an object identifier. The next octet 07 indicates that seven further octets describe this object. Since the item 'object identifier' comes from the set of identifiers controlled by one of the international standards bodies, the next number identifies that body. But to save an octet, the next octet, 2B, is an encoded version of two numbers in the tree. As the root of the tree will always have few branches, this octet contains the first two numbers from the identifying dotted sequence. If these two numbers are X and Y then this octet has the value $(X * 40) + Y$. The hex value 2B is 43 decimal so in this case X is 1 and Y is 3 (giving $40 * 1 + 3 = 43$).

The complete decoded sequence is then expressed in dotted form as:

1.3.6.1.2.1.5.7

Looking at Figure J.1, this is object 7 in the ICMP group of Internet MIB II. As mentioned above, object 7 is the counter for received redirect requests (change route requests).

Index